MW01050451

From watching actual classroom video footage of teachers and students interacting to building standards-based lessons and web-based portfolios . . . from a robust resource library of the "What Every Teacher Should Know About" series to complete instruction on writing an effective research paper . . . **MyLabSchool** brings together an amazing collection of resources for future teachers. This website gives you a wealth of videos, print and simulated cases, career advice, and much more.

Use **MyLabSchool** with this Allyn and Bacon Education text, and you will have everything you need to succeed in your course. Assignment IDs have also been incorporated into many Allyn and Bacon Education texts to link to the online material in **MyLabSchool** . . . connecting the teachers of tomorrow to the information they need today.

VISIT www.mylabschool.com to learn more about this invaluable resource and Take a Tour!

Here's what you'll find in mylabschool

Where the classroom comes to life!

VideoLab ►

Access hundreds of video clips of actual classroom situations from a variety of grade levels and school settings. These 3- to 5-minute closed-captioned video clips illustrate real teacher–student interaction, and are organized both topically *and* by discipline. Students can test their knowledge of classroom concepts with integrated observation questions.

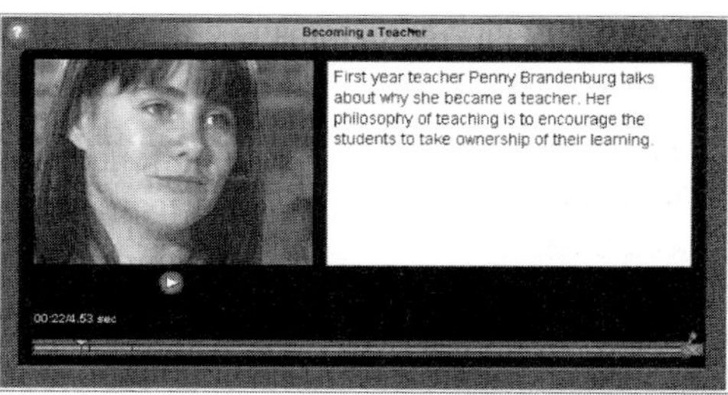

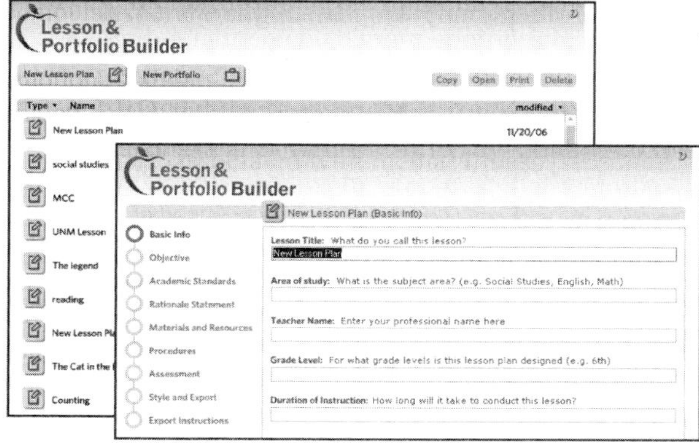

◄ Lesson & Portfolio Builder

This feature enables students to create, maintain, update, and share online portfolios and standards-based lesson plans. The Lesson Planner walks students, step-by-step, through the process of creating a complete lesson plan, including verifiable objectives, assessments, and related state standards. Upon completion, the lesson plan can be printed, saved, e-mailed, or uploaded to a website.

Here's what you'll find in mylabschool™

Where the classroom comes to life!

Simulations ▶

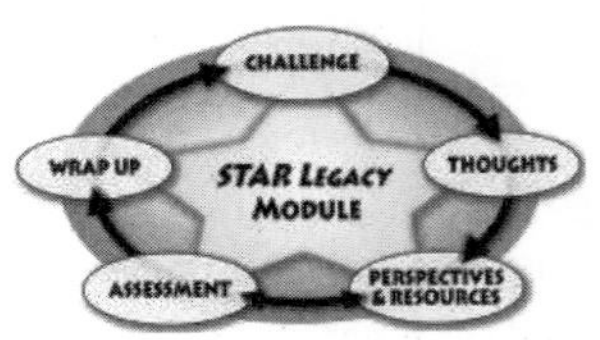

This area of MyLabSchool contains interactive tools designed to better prepare future teachers to provide an appropriate education to students with special needs. To achieve this goal, the IRIS (IDEA and Research for Inclusive Settings) Center at Vanderbilt University has created course enhancement materials. These resources include online interactive modules, case study units, information briefs, student activities, an online dictionary, and a searchable directory of disability-related web sites.

◀ Resource Library

MyLabSchool includes a collection of PDF files on crucial and timely topics within education. Each topic is applicable to any education class, and these documents are ideal resources to prepare students for the challenges they will face in the classroom. This resource can be used to reinforce a central topic of the course, or to enhance coverage of a topic you need to explore in more depth.

Research Navigator ▶

This comprehensive research tool gives users access to four exclusive databases of authoritative and reliable source material. It offers a comprehensive, step-by-step walk-through of the research process. In addition, students can view sample research papers and consult guidelines on how to prepare endnotes and bibliographies. The latest release also features a new bibliography-maker program—AutoCite.

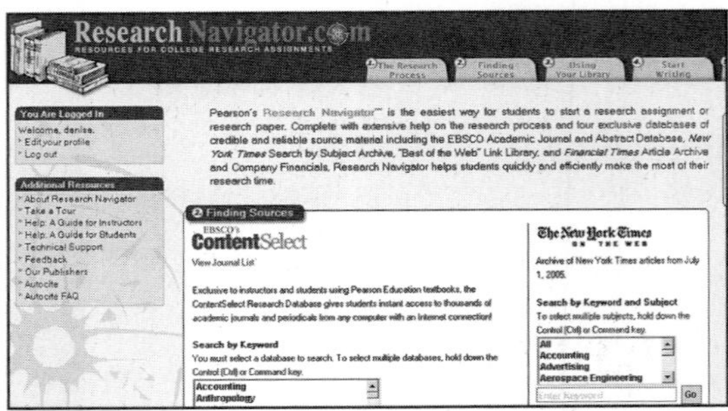

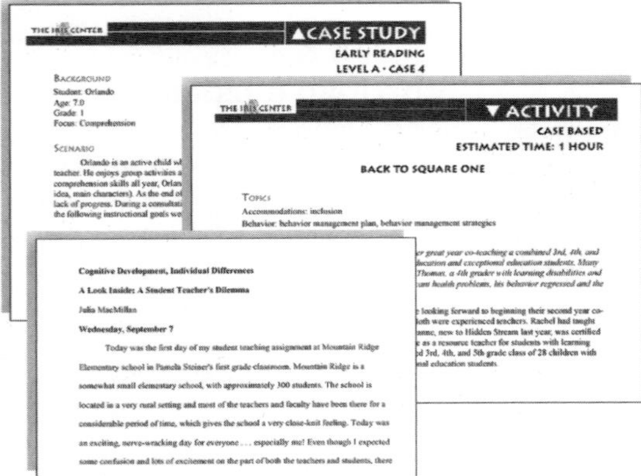

◀ Case Archive

This collection of print and simulated cases can be easily accessed by topic and subject area, and can be integrated into your course. The cases are drawn from Allyn & Bacon's best-selling books, and represent the complete range of disciplines and student ages. It's an ideal way to consider and react to real classroom scenarios. The possibilities for using these high-quality cases within the course are endless.

FIFTH EDITION

Emotional and Behavioral Disorders

Theory and Practice

Jo Webber
Texas State University

Cynthia A. Plotts
Texas State University

Boston New York San Francisco
Mexico City Montreal Toronto London Madrid Munich Paris
Hong Kong Singapore Tokyo Cape Town Sydney

Executive Editor: Virginia Lanigan
Editorial Assistant: Matthew Buchholz
Production Supervisor: Joe Sweeney
Editorial-Production Service: Pine Tree Composition, Inc.
Composition and Prepress Buyer: Linda Cox
Manufacturing Buyer: Linda Morris
Cover Administrator: Joel Gendron
Composition: Pine Tree Composition, Inc.

For related titles and support materials, visit our online catalog at www.ablongman.com.

ISBN-10: 0-205-41066-9
ISBN-13: 978-0-205-41066-8

Library of Congress Cataloging-in-Publication Data

Webber, Jo.
Emotional and behavioral disorders : theory and practice / Jo Webber, Cynthia A. Plotts.— 5th ed.
p. cm.
Rev. ed. of: Emotional and behavioral disorders / Margaret Cecil Coleman. 3rd ed.. 1996.
Includes bibliographical references and index.
ISBN-13: 978-0-205-41066-8
ISBN-10: 0-205-41066-9
1. Problem children—Education. 2. Behavior disorders in children. 3. Special education. 4. Teaching. I. Plotts, Cynthia A. II. Coleman, Margaret Cecil. Emotional and behavioral disorders. III. Title.
LC4801.W43 2008
371.94—dc22

2007011484

Printed in the United States of America

10 9 8 7 6 5 4 3 2 1 11 10 09 08 07

CONTENTS

PREFACE

The most obvious change to this fifth edition of *Emotional and Behavioral Disorders: Theory and Practice* is the replacement of former senior author, Margaret (Maggie) Coleman, with a new second author, Cindy Plotts. After single-handedly conceptualizing and developing this text through three revisions, Maggie decided to fully retire from such work. We will miss her informed perspective about the field and her conceptual and literary skills. Cindy, a colleague in School Psychology at Texas State University, brings a fresh view and a wealth of knowledge about psychological conditions of children and youth, and related assessment and treatment practices. Her work on this edition is notable.

Also obvious is the increased length of the book. An abundance of new material has been added and the number of chapters increased from 11 to 12. Less obvious until you open the book are the substantial changes at the beginning and end and the addition of multiple student-oriented cognitive organizers. A new first chapter, "Definition and Characteristics," was added to better describe students with emotional and behavioral disorders (EBD) before giving more detailed information about their education and treatment. Chapter 2, "A Historical Perspective," was updated to include information about the No Child Left Behind (NCLB) Act and the Individuals with Disabilities Act (IDEA) 2004 and their impact on programming for students with EBD; also included are reviews of recent mental health and special education (SPED) reports and studies. Chapter 3 was extensively revised to singularly focus on identification and assessment issues, instruments, and current practices.

Chapters 4–8, as in the previous edition, describe five primary theoretical models of disturbance (biophysical, psychodynamic, cognitive, behavioral, ecological/systems) with information about applications of these theories in schools. These chapters have been updated. Revised Chapters 9 and 10 address internalizing (anxiety and depression) and externalizing (attention-deficit hyperactivity disorder and conduct disorders) disorders in depth. An updated Chapter 11 presents special issues and information about adolescents and includes topics such as social rejection, drug abuse, gangs, self-destructive behavior, and troubled girls. The last chapter, "Special Issues in the Schools," has been appreciably revised to address four major topics thought to be of interest to school personnel and pertinent to educational programming for students with EBD: (1) youth violence, (2) positive behavioral interventions and supports (PBIS), (3) academic interventions for students with EBD, and (4) inclusion issues and practices.

For this edition, we have also added a wealth of material to assist with instruction and content comprehension. Each chapter begins with a list of questions as advanced organizers to engage readers and prepare them for the subsequent content. Each chapter now contains additional boxes and case studies; key points, homework assignments, and recommended readings and resources appear after each chapter's conclusion. Students are encouraged to access pertinent information, reports, and other resources from the Internet links provided. Also available to aid with teaching and learning the content are an ***Instructor's Manual*** and ***Test Bank*** for instructors and a ***Companion Website*** for students described below:

- ***Instructor's Manual and Test Bank:*** The Instructor's Manual includes instructional materials and interesting ideas designed to help instructors teach the course. Each chapter includes learning objectives, key terms, power point lecture slides, websites, and recommended supplementary resources. There is also a test bank for each chapter. (Please request this item from your local Allyn & Bacon sales representative; also available for download from the Instructor's Resource Center at www.ablongman.com/irc.
- ***Companion Website.*** Created to accompany *Emotional and Behavioral Disorders: Theory and Practice,* this online site offers tools and activities to help students understand and extend the text discussion and study more effectively. It includes, for each text chapter, learning objectives, web links, homework activities, flash cards for terms, and study guides. Visit www.ablongman.com/webber5e.

What has not changed in this edition are the main purposes of the book: (1) to present the primary theoretical models of disturbance with corresponding applications, (2) to describe characteristics of various types of students who manifest EBD and the various environmental forces affecting them, and (3) to review special education issues and practices that pertain to students with EBD and their teachers. Additionally, the theme of an ecological or systems perspective for explaining and treating emotional and behavioral disorders remains the primary one.

Since the last edition, many extraordinary worldwide events, political reactions, and legal mandates have occurred that directly impact the well-being of children and youth with EBD and their families. Now, more than ever, general and special educators need to work together and collaborate with other agencies, which also target the well-being of children and youth, to provide multifaceted, comprehensive educational programs and community and family supports. As attention moves away from social programs in this country, and away from flexible educational curriculum and structures, toward the mass production of technologically competent college graduates, students with EBD may easily be "left behind." Special educators must continue to advocate for these special students and their families in an informed, thoughtful way to ensure effective instruction and treatment. We hope that this textbook will assist with that endeavor.

Finally, we thank the reviewers of the fifth edition: Corina Frankland, Western New Mexico University; Joni Baldwin, Minnesota State University; and Sarup R. Mathur, Arizona State University.

J. Webber
C. Plotts

CONTRIBUTORS

Barbara Yonan, Ph.D., School Psychologist, Dallas, Texas

Diana Rogers-Adkinson, Associate Professor and Chair, Department of Special Education, University of Wisconsin-Whitewater

Dona Stallworth, Ph.D., Assistant Principal, Round Rock, Texas

Erika Garza, former graduate student, Texas State University

Glenna Billingsley, high school special education teacher, Austin, Texas

Kevin Stark, Professor of Educational Psychology, The University of Texas at Austin

Kirstyn Jorgenson, School Psychology Intern, Texas State University

Krystol Clark, John Davis, Tiffany Kuchar, and Rebekah Canu, former graduate students, Texas State University

Michael Kirby, Ph.D., School Psychologist, Mapleton Public Schools, Denver, Colorado

Rebecca Brown, M.A., Therapist, and Beth Dennis, MSSW-CSW, Therapist and Grant Coordinator, Austin Child Guidance Center, Austin, Texas

Samira Munir, M.A., School Psychologist, Central Texas

Sarah Sims, M.Ed., Psychological Associate, The Devereux Foundation, Victoria, Texas

Sue N. Baugh, M.Ed., Coordinator of Rehabilitation Services, The Devereux Foundation, Victoria, Texas

Theresa Lopez, Special Education Teacher, San Antonio, TX

CHAPTER

1 Definition and Characteristics

Defining Emotional and Behavioral Disorders
Concepts, Problems, and a Definition

Characteristics of Students with Emotional and Behavioral Disorders
Framework, Dimensions, Demographics. Characteristics, Prevalence

QUESTIONS TO CONSIDER

- What constitutes abnormal or deviant behavior and who decides what is abnormal?
- What are the main factors affecting how we define deviance and emotional disturbance?
- How are emotional/behavioral disorders defined and how does an imperfect definition impact students and educators?
- What are the most common characteristics of students labeled emotionally and/or behaviorally disordered and how will those characteristics impact educational decisions?
- Should teachers of students with emotional and/or behavioral disorders concentrate more on academic instruction or managing problem behaviors?
- Are the public schools doing an adequate job of identifying and serving students with emotional and/or behavioral disorders?
- Are the public school teachers assigned to teach students with emotional and/or behavioral disorders well suited for the job?

Orientation

This is a book about children and youth who have been determined to deviate from the norm to such a degree to warrant special services. In the case of emotional and behavioral disorders (EBD), the differences might be manifested in behavior, thinking, feelings, interactions, and/or biophysical structure. These are children who others may find disturbing because of their differences. Usually we celebrate and promote individual differences, but how do we know when someone differs to such a degree that he or she needs to be labeled "disturbed," "deviant," or "disordered"? Who determines what is normal and, more importantly, what is abnormal? How can we be sure that we are correct in our judgments? In 1982, Eli Bower wrote about the attempt to define emotional and behavioral disorders that

"Along with the hazards of street crime, drunk driving, and Christmas shopping is that of defining what is meant by 'emotional disturbance.' . . . Emotion is non-rational, nonlinear, and so far has been pretty elusive to being pinned down by precise prose" (pp. 55–56). Eli Bower used humor to describe what is in reality a very complex and frustrating problem for all professionals who work with students with EBD.

Overview

Difficulties in defining a disability leads to difficulties in describing the population, determining prevalence rates, providing appropriate services, obtaining resources, choosing best practices, and reliably measuring outcomes. Unfortunately, the definition of EBD continues to be the most elusive one in special education (Forness, 2005). In this chapter we explore a number of issues related to the effort to define EBD and we delineate general characteristics of those who have been so defined. Knowledge of characteristics sets the foundation for effective instructional decisions.

Defining Emotional and Behavioral Disorders

Since its appearance more than 50 years ago, emotional disturbance has been an umbrella term for such varied conditions as schizophrenia, autism, psychosomatic disorders, phobias, withdrawal, depression, anxiety, elective mutism, aggression, antisocial behavior, and a host of other pathologies. The term *emotional disturbance* is one of many terms used to classify abnormal, atypical, or deviant behaviors. Other terms sometimes used interchangeably include *emotional maladjustment, impairment,* or *handicap, mental disorder, psychological disorder, psychopathology,* and *mental illness.* This variation in terminology reflects concepts that are unique to particular professions or theoretical positions and those positions are often opposed in regard to assessment and treatment recommendations. Added to the definitional problem is a general reluctance by agency personnel to define large numbers of individuals as EBD, thus needing expensive treatments. Educators have made great strides in other areas, however, the field continues to be plagued by a lack of consensus on definition and terminology.

Factors Influencing Concepts of Deviance

Deviance is most often defined by differences in behavior, with subsequent assumptions about cognitive and emotional differences. However, several related factors influence personal and professional decisions about the acceptability of behaviors and the concept of deviance. Among these factors are the following:

- Variation in individuals' tolerance ranges for behavior
- Differences in the theoretical models from which professionals operate
- Differences in terminology associated with emotional and behavioral problems
- Sociological parameters of behavior
- Concomitant disorders

Tolerance Ranges. Referrals for special education services as EBD may be subjectively based on teachers' tolerance of student behaviors. Everyone has preferences for certain types of behavior and aversions to other types. Teachers also differ radically in their opinions of what is acceptable in the classroom, and it is not unusual for teachers to prefer teaching certain types of students. Although the literature consistently reports teacher preference for passive or conforming students and unfavorable teacher attitudes toward aggressive students, individual teachers' tolerance ranges as well as their reactions to specific individuals vary widely. For example, dependent behavior may elicit sympathy and concern from one teacher, no reaction from another, and a negative attitude from a teacher who places a premium on independence and self-initiation.

Teachers' potential for interaction with students has been found to be a function of their tolerance levels for behaviors exhibited by those students (Algozzine & Curran, 1979). Hewett and Taylor (1980) hypothesized that teachers have two general ranges of tolerance, one for academic differences and one for behavioral differences. They further proposed that the tolerance for academic differences is much broader: If a student falls within the expected range for behavior, then she is more likely to be maintained in the general education classroom despite serious academic problems. Other researchers have found that behavioral and academic expectations are interactive: If a teacher has low behavioral expectations for a student, then cognitive or academic expectations will also be lowered (Brophy & Good, 1986; Good & Brophy, 2002; Good & Grouws, 1972). While the exact relationship between academic and behavioral expectations remains unspecified, it is clear that teachers do react differently to various types of behavior exhibited in the classroom. This state of affairs led Algozzine (1977) to question whether students with EBD are not better described as "disturbing" rather than "disturbed."

Theoretical Models. A second factor influencing concepts of deviance is the number of conflicting theories of how emotional and behavioral problems develop. Each theory has unique terminology, identification procedures, and a preferred mode of treatment. Although many classification schemes for theories of disordered behavior have been developed, Rhodes and Tracy (1974) grouped the numerous theories of emotional/behavioral disorders under five major conceptual models: behavioral, biophysical, psychodynamic, ecological, and sociological. While there are some common elements, each model promotes a different view of definition, etiology, identification procedures, and intervention methods. A variation of these models will be discussed in detail in Chapters 4 through 8.

All professionals, whether they articulate it or not, operate from beliefs that are based on one or more of these models. Personal perceptions of deviance and subsequent decisions about definition and identification are heavily influenced by such theoretical beliefs. These beliefs depend, in part, on the theoretical and philosophical persuasion of the training program from which an individual graduates. Physicians, psychologists, social workers, and educators emerge from a wide variety of training programs that emphasize different theoretical views, diagnostic tools, and treatment procedures. These theoretical orientations are further reinforced in the work setting. A multidisciplinary team charged with making decisions about an individual student may represent several theoretical stances and thus may view the student in very different ways. The team may fail to agree on whether the student has a disorder or what diagnostic instruments and procedures should be used in the evaluation. They may even use entirely different terms to describe the same symptoms and problems. According to Hobbs (1975a), a particular child "may be regarded as mentally ill by a psychiatrist, as emotionally disturbed by a psychologist, and as behavior disordered by a special educator" (p. 57).

Terminology. A third factor influencing personal perceptions of deviance is the terminology associated with EBD. There is little agreement among professionals on the basic term that most aptly describes deviant behavior in children and youth, perhaps because of limited perspectives. Educators are interested in managing students, parents in living peacefully with their children, psychologists in inner feelings, psychiatrists in effective medications, and social workers in interactions and family systems. Teachers need to become familiar with psychiatric and educational terminology while staying cognizant of various professional orientations. The psychiatric terminology encountered in psychological evaluations and records of students with EBD is usually based on a classification system developed by the American Psychiatric Association. The sourcebook, the *Diagnostic and Statistical Manual of Mental Disorders,* the Revised Fourth Edition (DSM-IV-TR; American Psychiatric Association, 2000), is a comprehensive classification scheme that allows assignment of a diagnostic label based on symptomology.

Although the DSM-IV-TR differs from the classification system used in the public schools, the manual provides guidelines for assessing behavioral and emotional problems that are relevant to the school setting. The emergence of school-based health clinics has created the need for mental health school practitioners who are familiar with psychiatric classification systems and who can develop expertise in the use of the DSM (Adelman, 1996; Power, DuPaul, Shapiro, & Parrish, 1995; Woodruff et al., 1998).

The DSM-IV-TR sourcebook contains 10 major headings under "Disorders of Infancy, Childhood or Adolescence." Listed below are these headings and some examples of subclassifications.

1. Mental Retardation
2. Learning Disorders
   - Reading Disorder
   - Arithmetic Disorder
   - Disorder of Written Expression
   - Learning Disorder NOS (not otherwise specified)
3. Motor Skills Disorder
   - Developmental Coordination Disorder
4. Communication Disorders
   - Expressive Language Disorder
   - Expressive/Receptive Language Disorder
   - Phonological Disorder
   - Stuttering
   - Communication Disorder NOS
5. Pervasive Developmental Disorders
   - Autistic Disorder
   - Rett's Disorder

Childhood Disintegration Disorder
Asperger's Disorder
Pervasive Developmental Disorder NOS (not otherwise specified)

6. Attention-Deficit and Disruptive Emotional and Behavioral Disorders
Attention-Deficit Hyperactivity Disorder
Oppositional Defiant Disorder
Conduct Disorder
Disruptive Behavior Disorder

7. Feeding and Eating Disorders of Infancy or Early Childhood
Pica
Rumination
Feeding Disorder of Infancy or Early Childhood

8. Tic Disorders
Transient Tic
Chronic Motor or Vocal Tic
Tourette's Disorder

9. Elimination Disorders
Enuresis
Encopresis

10. Other Disorders of Infancy, Childhood, or Adolescence
Separation Anxiety Disorder
Selective Mutism
Reactive Attachment Disorder of Infancy or Early Childhood
Stereotypic Movement Disorder (American Psychiatric Association, 2000)

The DSM-IV-TR classification system was devised to facilitate communication among the medical, psychological, and psychiatric professions and to codify recommendations for medication and therapy. In order to foster communication between the education and mental health communities and to ensure systematic classification of EBD, some states have adopted the DSM-IV-TR system for identification of students with emotional and/or behavioral disorders for special education purposes in the schools.

Unfortunately, educators use different terminology than the psychiatric community to denote disorders doing little to clarify the concept or to promote understanding among professionals. Although the educational concept of EBD has undergone an evolution of labels in the past 50 years, *emotionally disturbed* is the term promoted for special education services by federal regulations stemming from Public Law 94-142 (now referred to as the Individuals with Disabilities Education Act, or IDEA). Some states adopted this term or a similar one, such as *emotionally impaired,* while other states have adopted the term *behavior disordered* to describe this category within special education. Both the term and the definition outlined in federal regulations are advisory; states may therefore adopt their own, provided that neither varies significantly from those provided in the federal regulations (Wood et al., 1991).

The term *behavior disordered* is often seen as less stigmatizing, less severe, more socially acceptable, and more practical than the term *emotionally disturbed.* The term *behavior disordered* grew out of the behavioral model, which posits that teachers can see and describe disordered behavior but cannot easily describe disturbed emotions. Many educators seem to prefer *behavior disordered* because it seems more plausible, as a teacher, to deal directly with disordered behavior than with disturbed emotions.

In the early 1990s, the Council for Children with Behavioral Disorders (CCBD), a division of The Council for Exceptional Children (CEC), and the National Mental Health and Special Education Coalition, representing 30 different education, mental health, advocacy, and parent associations, lobbied to have the federal terminology changed to reflect both positions by using the term *emotional/behavioral disorders* (EBD) (Forness & Kavale, 2000). The change in terminology was proposed as an amendment to pending legislation in the summer of 1992, and because various stakeholders had been involved, it was expected to pass quickly. However, at the last minute the National School Boards Association objected, fearing that too many children would be eligible for expensive special education services and be protected by the IDEA. Subsequently, the amendment was not passed and a "notice of inquiry" was published by the Department of Education in the Federal Register (Invitation to comment, 1993). Although 66 percent of the 1,200 comments were in favor of the new terminology, the results were never submitted to Congress for action (Forness & Kavale, 2000). In this text, the terms *emotionally disturbed* and *behaviorally disordered* are used interchangeably in keeping with the models and popular usage, but emotional/behavioral disorders (EBD) is the term of choice.

Sociological Parameters of Behavior. Sociological parameters constitute a fourth factor that influences personal views of deviance. Behavior that causes a child to be labeled as disordered rarely occurs in isolation; rather, it arises from interactions that are influenced by subcultural and social role factors.

The U.S. society comprises strata of subcultures: racial and ethnic groups, socioeconomic levels, religious denominations, and geographic regions are examples of various subculture boundaries. Whether explicit or implicit, each subculture has its own provisions for membership, standards of behavior, and moral codes. For example, fighting and stealing may be adaptive behaviors for streetwise, inner-city adolescents and may be condoned by their community. The same behaviors would probably be viewed as totally unacceptable by the community at large or by another subculture with different standards. Thus, subcultural expectations are one factor in setting parameters for how behavior is viewed.

Social-role expectations are another sociological parameter of behavior. Sociologists believe that a large portion of an individual's behavior can be predicted and explained on the basis of the individual's status in society and the social roles associated with this status (Brophy, 1977). Behavior that fails to conform to these expectations may be considered deviant. Age and sex roles are major factors: certain behaviors are acceptable for a certain age level or gender, but may be considered highly inappropriate for an older age or the opposite sex. For example, consider the age or gender expectations attached to the following behaviors: thumb sucking, temper tantrums, enuresis, tattling, fist fighting, and use of explicit sexual language. Each of these behaviors is generally considered normal for a certain developmental period but may alarm parents and other adults if displayed in excess outside that period. In addition, many of the behaviors are considered more acceptable for one gender than for the other.

The deviance perspective implies that a state of emotional disturbance is determined by the extent that an individual's behavior deviates from the norm. However, behavior considered deviant and inappropriate in one circumstance may be judged as appropriate in another context. No matter how unusual or extreme a behavior may appear, that behavior does not necessarily signify a state of emotional disturbance or a behavioral disorder.

From the deviance perspective, EBD might best be described as based on one's culturally or socially relevant point of view (Newcomer, 1993); in other words, deviance is a social construct (Kavale & Mosert, 2003). According to Kauffman (2005), student behavior and deviance is defined by adeptness at regulating behavior in common environments, avoiding censure, and obtaining others' approval. Society defines behavioral norms that include a range of deviant behaviors that are often acceptable. When the deviant behaviors fall outside this acceptable range, disturbance or disorder is identified. This does not necessarily mean that EBD is synonymous with mental illness or psychopathology, but only that behaviors fall outside the acceptable range in terms of frequency, consistency, and appropriateness. For example, think about how our societal norms changed from the 1950s "teeny bopper" and the 1960s hippies to the current teenage image. How would typical adolescents today have been judged in the 1950s? Freddie, the case example in Box 1.1, represents a typical referral to special education as a student with emotional/behavioral disorders for five reasons: (1) he is male, (2) he is from a lower socioeconomic family, (3) he exhibits aggressive and disruptive behaviors, (4) he is academically behind, and (5) he has not responded positively to the general education teacher's attempts to work with him. Social class is a factor because more aggressive and acting-out behaviors have been found in families of lower socioeconomic status (Graubard, 1973), and these types of behaviors are more likely to become classified as disordered. Think about Freddie as you read the remainder of this chapter. Does your opinion about whether or not he might have emotional and/or behavioral disorders change?

Concomitant Disorders. A final factor affecting definition is the fact that emotional and behavioral disorders often occur together (Forness, 2005) or with other disabilities such as learning disabilities and mental retardation. About 25–35% of students with EBD also show defining characteristics of learning disabilities (U.S. Department of Education, 2000). One study revealed that of a sample of 124 students admitted to a psychiatric hospital for behavioral/emotional problems, 38 percent had a concomitant learning disability and 18 percent had a significant learning problem (Fessler, Rosenberg, & Rosenberg, 1991). Having both of these disorders may promote symptoms in both academic and social/emotional functioning, be serious enough to warrant either diagnosis alone, impair functioning not only in school but also at home or in the community, and may predispose the student to other disorders (Rock, Fessler, & Church, 1997). So, students with both EBD and LD not only present with severe social and behavioral problems but also with severe academic and learning problems (Handwerk & Marshall, 1998).

Students with mental retardation may also have emotional and behavioral disorders that prevent them from adapting, learning appropriate social behaviors, and becoming independent (Reder & Borcherding, 1997). Children with mental retardation may also suffer from mood disorders (5–15%), anxiety disorders (25%), psychosis, posttraumatic stress disorder, and obsessive–compulsive disorder (Reder, 2001). Likewise, students with traumatic brain injury and sensory impairments may display EBD and require such a diagnosis (Algozzine, Serna, & Patton, 2001). EBD has also been found to occur in tandem with communication disorders (Getty & Summy, 2006; Hyter, 2003; Hyter, Rogers-Adkinson, Self,

BOX 1.1
Freddie

Freddie is a 10-year-old third grader from a lower socioeconomic status minority family. He failed second grade and is perilously close to repeating the third grade because he doesn't turn in assignments or complete work in class. He struggles with academics even when he is attentive and has been a constant source of frustration to the teachers at Willough Elementary since transferring from across town last year. His reputation as a difficult and disruptive student preceded him to his new school and appears to be well earned.

Although Ms. Perkins, his current teacher, tries to handle most discipline problems herself, she has been so exasperated by Freddie that she has sent him to the principal's office for disciplinary measures an average of three times a week since the beginning of school. Freddie has been involved in several fights in school and on the bus; one was serious enough to get him suspended because the other student had to receive medical attention. On many occasions he has told Ms. Perkins to "get off his back" and to "go to hell."

Although Ms. Perkins says these occurrences bothered her at the time, it is Freddie's emotional state that upsets her most; she describes him as often "sullen and hostile," and when he gets in these moods, he talks out in class, refuses to work, and becomes disruptive in any number of ingenious ways. Ms. Perkins has tried reasoning, punishment by revoking privileges, and ignoring his outbursts whenever possible. She has talked to his mother, who was nice but not very supportive of the disciplinary methods suggested and, she suspects, not very capable of carrying them out. The school psychologist recommended a positive reinforcement system for nondisruptive behavior, but Ms. Perkins doesn't have the time necessary to institute it and she doesn't really feel that Freddie should be rewarded for "something he should be doing anyway." She believes that Freddie can best be served by someone who is trained to deal with emotional and behavioral problems, such as the special education teacher. She has been keeping notes on his behavior and talking to Freddie's previous teacher as well as the principal because she wants to be able to defend her referral.

Contributed by Theresa Lopez, Special Education Teacher in San Antonio, Texas.

Simmons, & Jantz, 2001; Rogers-Adkinson & Griffith, 1999). Not only is it difficult to define EBD in a way that distinguishes it while allowing for coexistence with these other disorders, but it is also difficult to decide which disorder should receive the primary diagnosis.

Co-occurrence of types of emotional and behavioral disorders is common. For example, students with ADHD may also have anxiety disorders and students with conduct disorders may also be depressed and/or have ADHD or schizophrenia (Tankersley & Landrum, 1997). Cullinan and Epstein (2001) found that many students with EBD show more than one of the five characteristics listed in the IDEA definition of ED (discussed later in this chapter and again in Chapter 3) and that the combinations varied by age. Thus, a singular definition, as in the IDEA, of the various forms and combinations of EBD may lead to underidentification or misidentification of serious disorders.

To summarize, five factors influencing individuals' concepts of deviance are (1) differences in personal tolerance ranges, (2) differing theoretical models, (3) terminology, (4) sociological parameters of behavior, and (5) concomitant disorders. These factors influence personal and professional definitions of normalcy versus deviance and, subsequently, perceptions of problem behavior and the individuals who display them.

Defining and Classifying Emotional/Behavioral Disorders

While recognizing that numerous factors influence social, personal, and professional concepts of deviance, professionals still must establish a common ground for working with students with EBD. Although difficult, defining the population to be served is the first step in reaching a workable consensus and providing students with necessary services. This section explores the need for defining EBD and analyzes the definition promoted by federal law.

Utility of Definitions and Classification Systems. Defining EBD is useful for the purposes of determining prevalence, providing services, conducting and communicating research, and for determining treatment outcomes. However, definitions, due to lack of specificity, do not identify individuals; rather, they describe a population. Therefore, state and local education agencies must create regulations that outline specific criteria for identification purposes. Definitions allow description of students in broad, general terms, but are much too obscure to be used as criteria for selecting individual students (Hammill, 1976).

Classification is the key to understanding large groups of events, objects, or phenomena. The main purpose of classification systems is to provide a means of communication among professionals by defining the rules by which psychological constructs such as emotional disturbance are defined (Quay, 1986a). Classification systems and rules are necessary for the development of operational definitions that, in turn, affect services. While the use of classification systems in the behavioral sciences has been controversial, such systems facilitate the understanding, treatment, and possibly the prevention of some emotional and behavioral disorders.

As you will learn in Chapter 3, when a diagnostic staff person conducts a formal assessment of children or adolescents to determine the nature and severity of a behavioral or emotional problem, one of the primary purposes of the assessment is to determine an appropriate diagnosis or classification. Diagnosis means to distinguish or differentiate (Kendall, 1975) in order "to reduce uncertainty" (Achenbach, 1974, p. 568). The term *diagnosis* has historically been linked with the medical model of psychological disorders, whereas the term *classification* is used more in education professions.

The uses of classification systems have been controversial because of the imperfections inherent in the existing systems and the lack of empirical precision in developing these systems (Kaufman, 2005; Taylor, 1997). However, good classification systems can help to identify the probable outcome or prognosis of a disorder and whether a person with an identified disorder is likely to respond to certain types of treatments. Although making predictions of outcomes is important, all predictions have error and inherent dangers. Persons with specific diagnoses do not fall neatly into clear-cut categories, thus information can be lost by attempting to fit individuals into arbitrary classifications (Forness, 2005; Rosenberg, Wilson, Maheady, & Sindelar, 1997). People within the same diagnostic category may share certain characteristics, but may also demonstrate many differences in behavior and temperament. Perhaps one of the most controversial dangers of classification is in the stigmatization associated with psychological labels (Forness & Kavale, 2000; Taylor, Smiley, & Ziegler, 1983). It is obvious that labels may affect how others interact with individuals identified with specific diagnoses. Consequently, classification systems should be used with caution, and only by individuals with expertise in assessment and diagnosis (Salvia & Ysseldyke, 1995).

Public Law Definition. The definition of emotional disturbance specified in Public Law 94–142 and later in the reauthorizations of IDEA was first proposed by Eli Bower in 1957 and lists his five defining characteristics. Additional phrases were added (see italics) by the federal bureaucrats, which triggered much criticism due to their exclusionary nature. This definition, originally defining serious emotional disturbance (SED), changed to emotional disturbance (ED) in the 1997 IDEA reauthorization, has been adopted in some form by many state departments of education:

> Emotional disturbance is defined as follows: (i) the term means a condition exhibiting one or more of the following characteristics over a long period of time and to a marked degree, *that adversely affects a child's educational performance:* (a) an inability to learn that cannot be explained by intellectual, sensory, or health factors; (b) an inability to build or maintain satisfactory interpersonal relationships with peers and teachers; (c) inappropriate types of behavior or feelings under normal circumstances; (d) a general pervasive mood of unhappiness or depression; or (e) a tendency to develop physical symptoms or fears associated with personal or school problems. (ii) *The term includes schizophrenia. The term does not apply to children who are socially maladjusted, unless it is determined that they have an emotional disturbance.* [Code of Federal Regulation, title 34, Section 300.7(b)(9)]

Bower (1982) points out that one or more of the noted characteristics could be observed in almost all so-called normal children to some extent at some point; therefore, the crucial difference in his research was that children with EBD exhibited such characteristics to a marked degree over a period of time. Bower made this observation regarding 207 students designated as emotionally disturbed:

> The emotionally disturbed children were poor learners, although potentially able to learn; they had few if any satisfactory interpersonal relationships; they behaved oddly or inappropriately; they were depressed or unhappy and developed illnesses or phobias. It was also noted that one or more of these characteristics were true of almost all non-designated students to some extent at different times. The crucial differentiation was based on the observation and assessment that in the emotionally disturbed child the characteristics existed to a marked degree over a period of time. (p. 57)

Bower believed that this definition was practical in educational settings because it avoids presumptions about the child's "intrapsychic condition" or "clinical designation"; it stays within an observable setting and within the conceptual range of school personnel; and it assumes that behavior may vary from setting to setting.

Despite Bower's attempt to stay within a practical, school-oriented framework, the definition has been the focus of considerable discussion. Bower himself (1982) took issue with the modification of his original wording by the addition of the word *seriously* and *disturbed* to the term *emotionally handicapped* and the exclusion of children deemed socially maladjusted. Bower contended that if only seriously emotionally disturbed students are to be served, the implications would be that mildly or moderately emotionally disturbed students would be excluded and, furthermore, that educators would be able to distinguish degrees of disturbance on a continuum of severity. Fortunately, this one criticism has been addressed with the change to the term *emotional disturbance.* However, many more questions and criticisms of the IDEA definition have been raised (Cullinan, 2004; Epstein, Cullinan, Ryser, & Pearson, 2002).

Problems with the Federal Definition. The lack of direction provided to states by the federal definition was addressed by the executive committee of the Council for Children with Behavioral Disorders (CCBD) in a 1987 position paper. Among the problems identified were:

1. A variety of state definitions exist, resulting in diverse identification procedures. Such diversity in procedures causes a discrepancy between states in the number of children who are identified. Therefore, it is conceivable that many children and adolescents who would be identified and served in one state would not qualify for services in another state.
2. Since it is difficult to operationalize the current federal definition, professionals continue to rely on subjective clinical judgment rather than replicable objective data. Subjectivity in the identification process leads to disagreement, confusion, and lack of consensus about whom we are supposed to be serving.
3. The third and most controversial point of contention with the federal definition is its exclusion of the term *socially maladjusted* from the definition of *seriously emotionally disturbed.* Social maladjustment is often equated to conduct disorders. The supposed exclusion of students with conduct disorders from special education classrooms is in direct contradiction to practice, as the majority of students referred for and served in special education classrooms for emotional/behavioral disorders score high on measures of conduct disorders (Forness & Kavale, 2000).

The social maladjustment exclusion clause in the definition seems to be based on several assumptions. First, it assumes that a population exists whose antisocial behavior does not represent a disabling condition. Second is the assumption that these students can be differentiated from students with emotional/behavioral disorders who have a disability. Third is the assumption that it is not appropriate for special education to serve groups of youth who have been tagged by other systems such as the juvenile justice system.

The second assumption is especially suspect because "there appears to be a consistent body of professional literature illustrating the interrelated nature of those behaviors described as 'disturbed' or 'disordered' with the behavior commonly thought to constitute 'social maladjustment'" (Council for Children with Behavioral Disorders, 1987, p. 12). It therefore may not be defensible to attempt to differentiate between an emotional/behavioral disorder with social maladjustment and an emotional/behavioral disorder without social maladjustment. Additional opposition to this exclusionary practice was voiced by the General Assembly of the American Psychological Association (APA) in 1989; their resolution specifically opposed efforts by states to exclude children and youth with conduct disorders from special education services.

The CCBD Committee concluded its position paper by recommending that the federal definition be revised to "a functional educational definition of this handicapping condition" that does not eliminate the socially maladjusted (p. 16). In 1988, the National Mental Health and Special Education Coalition addressed the educational definition of, at that time, serious emotional disturbance (SED). The work of CCBD was expanded by this committee to include a proposed new term of EBD and a revised definition. This proposal was put forth by this group as an amendment in order to change the IDEA definition (Forness & Kavale, 2000). Unfortunately, as mentioned previously, the National School Board Association (NSBA) blocked its passage (NSBA 1992). The proposed EBD definition was as follows:

1. The term "emotional or behavioral disorder" means a disability that is characterized by behavioral or emotional responses in school programs so different from appropriate age, cultural, or ethnic norms that the responses adversely affect educational performance, including academic, social, vocational, or personal skills; more than a temporary, expected response to stressful events in the environment; consistently exhibited in two different settings, at least one of which is school-related; and unresponsive to direct intervention applied in general education, or the condition of a child is such that general education interventions would be insufficient.
2. The term includes such a disability that co-exists with other disabilities. The term includes a schizophrenic disorder, affective disorder, anxiety disorder, or other sustained disorder of conduct or adjustment, affecting a child if the disorder affects educational performance as described in paragraph (1). (Federal Register, February 10, 1993, p. 7938)

There were several advantages to this proposed definition and many professionals were and still are dismayed by the fact that it was not included in subsequent IDEA reauthorizations. Some of the advantages of this definition included: (1) children's responses would be considered in the context of school and ethnic and cultural norms; (2) it included four qualifying statements that would raise the probability that only children who qualify appropriately would be eligible for special education services; (3) it emphasized a two-step diagnostic process and stressed the need for multiple sources of case data; (4) it enhanced the possibility of early identification; (5) it would facilitate referrals to and from the mental health community; and (6) it eliminated the futile effort of distinguishing between social and emotional maladjustment (Kavale & Forness, 2000).

One last significant criticism of the current definition is directed toward the portion of the definition indicating that, to qualify under the emotional disturbance classification, one's behavior and emotions should adversely affect educational performance. "Adverse educational performance" has been interpreted at times as "adverse academic performance," as opposed to problems in social and/or behavioral performance (Forness & Knitzer, 1992). By including this clause, students who may be suffering from mood disorders or anxiety, but able to keep up their schoolwork, will remain unidentified and excluded from special education services, perhaps at great risk to them. The most recent reauthorization (2004) of the IDEA once again failed to alter the 1997 definition of emotional disturbance (stated previously). Clearly, the controversies surrounding the problems with the federal definition of emotional disturbance have yet to be resolved.

Characteristics of Students with Emotional and Behavioral Disorders

In this section we describe the general characteristics of students with EBD and highlight research pertaining to these characteristics. Included are a conceptual framework for EBD characteristics, dimensions of abnormal behavior that distinguish it from normal behavior, demographics of the population, social and academic characteristics, a comparison of student and teacher characteristics, post-school outcomes for students with EBD, and prevalence of this disability for children and youth. We also provide brief case studies that illustrate several common characteristics.

A Conceptual Framework

In order to discuss specific characteristics of students with EBD, it will be necessary to move from a general definition to a universally accepted model. One useful framework for conceptualizing deviant behavior is the notion of internalizing versus externalizing behaviors. Although these terms were popularized by Achenbach and Edelbrock (1978, 1983), the basic dichotomy is an old one. Peterson (1961) used the terms *personality problem* versus *conduct problem,* and Miller (1967) used the terms *inhibition* versus *aggression* to describe the same concepts.

Internalizing and Externalizing. The internalizing profile of EBD represents problems of an introverted nature, that is, problems with self that include worries, fears, somatic complaints, and social withdrawal. This profile also has been called overcontrolled, overinhibited, shy–anxious, and personality disorder (Achenbach & Edelbrock, 1978). The externalizing profile represents extroversive behaviors including aggression, overactivity, disobedience, temper tantrums, and delinquency. Externalizing also has been referred to as undercontrolled, aggressive, acting out, and conduct disordered (Achenbach & Edelbrock, 1978). It has been suggested that internalizers tend to be more reflective and externalizers more impulsive.

These two basic styles of behaving are shaped by environmental as well as biological factors; they represent pervasive differences in children's reactions to stress. Some evidence indicates that among both normal and disordered populations, males tend to be externalizers and females tend to be internalizers (Achenbach & Edelbrock, 1981). It also has been established that externalizers have a poorer prognosis for treatment than internalizers and internalizers are less problematic for teachers (Ysseldyke, Algozzine, & Thurlow, 1992). However, Achenbach and Edelbrock (1983) warned that these are not distinctly separate factors; rather, they represent "contrasting styles of behavior that are not mutually exclusive" (p. 33). In fact, these researchers have found a clear, positive association between the two profiles and therefore suggested that perhaps a general underlying factor exists among individuals with behavioral difficulties, much the same as a general (*g*) factor is thought to exist for intelligence tests. Nonetheless *internalizing* and *externalizing* can be useful terms in understanding deviant behavior.

A number of well-designed behavior checklists follow the internalizing–externalizing paradigm. The *Child Behavior Checklist (CBCL)* (Achenbach & Rescorla, 2001) has long been considered one of the best checklists for measuring emotional and behavioral problems in children and adolescents. The *Behavior Assessment System for Children (BASC-2)* (Reynolds & Kamphaus, 2004), a frequently used behavior instrument, follows the internalizing–externalizing framework in its format for teacher report and parent report.

Among children and adolescents with EBD, three basic behavioral profiles have been consistently identified over the past 35 years. The classic study of Quay, Morse, and Cutler (1966) established this model, which subsequently has been supported (Conners, 1970; Kaufman, Swan, & Wood, 1979; Quay, 1966). Quay and his colleagues analyzed teacher ratings of the behavior of 441 children in public school classes for EBD and found students exhibiting three major profiles:

1. Conduct disorder, characterized by "aggressive, hostile and contentious behavior" (p. 297)
2. Personality problem, characterized by "anxious, withdrawn, introvertive behavior" (p. 29)
3. Inadequacy–immaturity, a less distinct profile involving "pre-occupation, lack of interest, sluggishness, laziness, daydreaming and passivity" (p. 298). This profile has also been linked to lack of interest in or awareness of the environment and other autistic-like behaviors.

A fourth profile of deviant behavior that closely approximates social maladjustment was also found. Quay (1972, 1975) identified this cluster of behaviors, called "socialized delinquency." Most of these behaviors relate to participation in subgroups or gangs who break rules or laws such as those against truancy, stealing, and curfew violation. Thus, students characterized as socialized delinquents behave in ways that their peer group condones but society rejects.

These basic profiles of EBD students can easily be classified into the internalizing–externalizing framework: personality problem and inadequacy–immaturity clearly represent internalizing behaviors; conduct disorder and socialized delinquency clearly represent externalizing behaviors. Some of the specific behaviors identified in the studies by Quay and Kaufman are presented in Table 1.1.

Research also supports the notion that students in classrooms for emotional/behavioral disorders tend to be externalizers (Cullinan & Sabornie, 2004; Smith, Wood, & Grimes, 1988; Tobin & Sugai, 1999). The internalizing–externalizing dichotomy will be used as a framework to present characteristics in Chapters 9 and 10. Anxiety and depression will be presented as internalizing behaviors. Conduct disorders and hyperactivity will be presented as externalizing behaviors.

Dimensions of Emotional/Behavioral Disorders

The dimensions of *chronicity, frequency,* and *severity* are also essential elements in describing normal and abnormal behavior. Severity or extremeness of behavior is usually readily apparent because of its negative impact or shock value; a behavior such as masturbation in the classroom will immediately receive a great deal of negative attention. However, chronicity and frequency of behavior are not so apparent and may require some record keeping on the part of school personnel.

TABLE 1.1 Variables of Disordered Behavior Identified by Quay et al. (1966) and Kaufman et al. (1979)[a]

Internalizing Behaviors	Externalizing Behaviors
Shy, withdrawn	Defiant, disobedient
Inferiority	Aggression toward property, rules, and other children
Self-conscious, overly sensitive	Demands excessive attention
Fearful, anxious	Swears
Avoids participating in groups	Distrusts, blames others
Sad, moody, irritable	Destructive
Apathetic	Hyperactive
Preoccupied, inattentive	Temper tantrums
	Jealous

[a]The current author labeled these variables as internalizing or externalizing; Quay and Kaufman each found three factors of disordered behavior.

As we have mentioned, the federal definition of emotional disturbance stipulates that the student's condition be present "over a long period of time" (chronicity) and "to a marked degree" (severity and/or frequency). The goal of such stipulation is to exclude temporary or moderate behavior problems that may be reactions to situational stress or normal developmental difficulties. Indeed, it has been established that, at some point in their lives, the vast majority of children exhibit behaviors that could be classified as disturbed or pathological (Bower, 1982; Kanner, 1957; Kessler, 1966). As Kessler (1966) asserts, "There is no abnormal behavior which cannot be found in normal individuals at certain ages and under certain conditions" (p. 69). Although no objective criteria have been established for determining what constitutes "a long period of time" or "a marked degree," there are some obvious implications.

Chronicity refers to a pattern of behavior that has been relatively stable over time; it may even disappear for short periods of time but reappear at intervals to interfere with normal or adaptive functioning. Frequency and severity are related in that the more severe the behavior, the less often it has to occur before being construed as indicative of disturbance. Consider the following examples: A junior high student loses his temper and verbally threatens the teacher. If this behavior had occurred only once during the student's otherwise clean school record, it would likely be treated as an isolated incident and dismissed with a disciplinary action. If, however, it occurred two or three times a week, the student would likely be referred for some type of psychological services as well as school disciplinary measures. Another junior high student makes a bomb threat; in this instance, the single occurrence will probably be considered serious enough to warrant instant disciplinary action, and perhaps referrals to juvenile authorities and to psychological services.

The classroom teacher should use an objective measure to help determine the chronicity, severity, and frequency of problem behaviors. It often proves very difficult for the teacher to distinguish disturbed from disturbing behavior, especially when the behaviors are particularly obnoxious, disruptive, or personally displeasing. In those instances, the teacher's discomfort may result in unintentional exaggeration of the severity of a problem or in overestimation of the number of times the behavior occurs. Behavior recording or the use of checklists or rating scales may be necessary to provide an objective estimate of how often the behavior actually occurs or how abnormal it is in comparison to other students' behavior. Classroom observations by a third party can also help the teacher distinguish disturbed from disturbing behavior.

Demographics

What do we know about the population of students who have been classified as EBD and are receiving special education services? We know that they are predominantly male, likely to be African American, and to be between the ages of 8 and 17 years old (U.S. Department of Education, 2001). These students are often over age 13 when they are identified for services and usually come from a family with an annual income under $12,000 (Woodruff et al., 1998). About 44 percent come from single-parent homes (Friedman, Kutash, & Duchnowski, 1996). While the exact gender ratio of pupils receiving services for emotional/behavioral disorders has not been established, it has been determined that boys are decidedly more at risk than girls (Cullinan, Osborne, & Epstein, 2004; Rosenberg et al., 1997; Werry & Quay, 1971). It is estimated that only 15–25 percent of EBD students are female (U.S. Department of Education, 1998; Wagner, 1995). Researchers have proposed an explanation for this disparity: behaviors that are more typical of boys are more likely to be labeled as disordered. However, Cullinan et al. (2004) found that girls labeled EBD also displayed high levels of defiant, aggressive, and disruptive behavior, and, as a group, manifested all five characteristics of the IDEA definition. Furthermore, nearly 33 percent of the 218 girls with EBD in their study experienced two or more characteristics of the federal definition of ED to an extreme extent. Rhonda in Box 1.2 represents the typical female student with EBD because (1) she is aggressive, (2) has learning disabilities, (3) has few if any friends, and (4) may be depressed. Why do you think that Rhonda acts the way she does?

It should be noted that students with EBD are also disproportionally African American (27%) with about 62 percent white, 9 percent Hispanic and 2 percent other ethnic groups (U.S. Department of Education, 2000). From the Special Education Elementary Longitudinal Study (SEELS) and the National Longitudinal Transition Study–2 (NLTS2) supported by the Office of Special Education Programs (OSEP) in 2003, Bradley and Monfore (2004) reported that for elementary and middle school students with EBD, 56.9 percent were white, 27 percent were African American, 12.8 percent were Hispanic, and 1.7 percent were other ethnic populations. For secondary students with EBD, 61.4 percent were white, 24 percent were African American, 10.2 percent were Hispanic, and 3% were other ethnic populations. The U.S. Department of Education (2006) reports that Black students were 2.25 times more likely to receive special education and related services for serious emotional disturbance than all other racial/ethnic groups combined. The disproportionate number of African American students labeled EBD raises questions about whether behavior judged to be deviant is in fact a function of a child's cultural heritage (Cartledge, Kea, & Ida, 2000; Osher et al., 2004). It is important to remember that "cultural differences that do not put the youngster at risk in the larger society should be accepted; only values and be-

BOX 1.2
Rhonda

Rhonda is a middle school student who receives special education services as a student with emotional disturbance and a learning disability in reading and written expression. She self-reports that she is a member of a juvenile neighborhood gang. Rhonda's mother and school authorities doubt this is true, because she seemingly has no true friends in or out of school. After being served in a resource setting, she failed all classes in sixth grade and was "placed" in a self-contained program for seventh and eighth graders.

By October of her seventh grade year, Rhonda had been in four physical altercations with other students in the classroom, cafeteria, and recess grounds and suspended the maximum number of days. She is described as having a "short fuse," angering easily if someone "looks at her wrong" or "crosses her." One fight resulted because a student accidentally bumped into her desk. Rhonda's classroom language is often profane and her attitude toward school and anyone in authority is poor. She even spit at the assistant principal as he walked past her class as they were filing into the library. Rhonda seldom smiles, calls her classmates names, and laughs at their academic mistakes. However, if Rhonda is taunted, she flies into a rage and usually assaults the offending party.

Rhonda refuses to even attempt academic tasks, referring to them as stupid. The only assignment she completed for the first grading period was a beautifully pencil-colored map of the fifty states. However, she would not write the name and capital of each state, a requirement for the assignment. Nonetheless, the teacher displayed it with the others; Rhonda tore it down and threw it away.

Contributed by Glenna Billingsley, Special Education Teacher, Austin, Texas.

---

haviors that are incompatible with achieving the larger goals of education (self-actualization, independence, and responsibility) should be modified" (Kaufman, 2005, p. 238).

Students with EBD, about 48 percent of them, are more likely than other mild disability populations to be educated in restrictive settings such as self-contained classrooms, separate schools, residential facilities, and hospital environments (U.S. Department of Education, 26th Annual Report to Congress 2006). During the 2001–2002 school year 18 percent of students with EBD were educated in a separate facility such as a special school or hospital. The thinking is that students with the most severe academic and behavioral deficits receive more appropriate education and more therapeutic treatments in more restrictive settings. There is speculation, however, that this is not true for students with EBD and that, too often, restrictive placements are for disciplinary rather than therapeutic reasons (Lane, Wehby, Little, & Cooley, 2005).

Although parents report initial identification of a problem by age 6 or 7, services for students with EBD typically begin at about age 8 or 9 (Danino, Costello, & Angold, 1999). This delay in treatment, common across most cases of mental illness, does not bode well for students. "Researchers supported by the National Institute of Mental Health (NIMH) have found that half of all lifetime cases of mental illness begin by age 14, and that despite effective treatments, there are long delays—sometimes decades—between the first onset of symptoms and when people seek and receive treatment. The study also reveals that an untreated mental disorder can lead to a more severe, more difficult to treat illness, and to the development of co-occurring mental illnesses" (Egan & Asher, 2005, paragraph 1). It appears that mental disorders are a "chronic disease of the young" (paragraph 6). In the NIMH study of 9,282 responders, researchers found that females have higher rates of mood and anxiety disorders and males have higher rates of substance use and impulse disorders.

Social and Behavioral Characteristics

Given that schools are required to use the five characteristics presented in the federal IDEA definition and adhere to the ideas of chronicity, severity, and frequency imbedded in that definition, it is not surprising that students labeled EBD exhibit learning and relationship problems, misbehaviors, depression, and physical symptoms and fears to an elevated extent (Cullinan & Sabornie, 2004). These students usually fail to get along with their peers, adults, or family members. Their externalizing behaviors such as bullying, threatening, and disrupting others and their internalizing behaviors such as an unwillingness to communicate put them at great risk for rejection and isolation (Bullis, Bull, Johnson, & Johnson, 1994; Epstein & Cullinan, 1998).

The rejection and isolation, in turn, may trigger further aggression and/or withdrawal. Students with EBD typically exhibit elevated levels of defiance, aggression, and destructiveness (Cullinan, Epstein, & Kaufman, 1984; Epstein, Cullinan, & Rosemier, 1983; Tobin & Sugai, 1999) and are more often depressed and anxious (Newcomer, Barenbaum, & Pearson, 1995). Thus, they are likely to be taking medication such as antipsychotics, stimulants, antidepressants, and anti-anxiety drugs for their disability (Bradley & Monfore, 2004).

Students with EBD are also at risk for antisocial behavior and delinquency. Those with ADHD seem particularly at risk, especially if they use drugs or alcohol, are aggressive at a young age, and are an African American male (Zabel & Nigro, 1999). In a sample of 91 adolescents confined to a Kansas juvenile detention facility who had a disability, these authors found that 61 percent had been labeled EBD, many also with learning disabilities, in school. The 91 students with disabilities made up 37 percent of the total number of those incarcerated. It is estimated that, nationwide, 20–50 percent of incarcerated juvenile offenders have a mental disorder (Cocozza & Skowyra, 2000). Unfortunately, research shows that youth with EBD typically have a long history of emotional problems resulting in multiple diagnoses and problem behaviors that affect social, academic, and community functioning for much of their lives (Friedman et al., 1996).

Intellectual and Academic Functioning

Research also indicates that the majority of students with EBD (excluding those with psychosis) fall within the low-average range on intelligence measures. In a review of 25 studies assessing the academic and intellectual characteristics of a variety of populations with emotional/behavioral disorders, Mastropieri, Jenkins, and Scruggs (1985) reported average IQs ranging from 89.5 in a public school EBD sample to 96.5 in an outpatient psychiatric sample. More recently, Trout, Nordness, Pierce, and Epstein (2003) reviewed 57 studies of students with EBD conducted between 1961 and 2000 where IQ scores were reported, and noted an average IQ of 94. This average was validated in a review of 25 studies of students with EBD (Reid et al., 2004). The 25 data sets from Trout's study between the years 1991 and 2000 reflected an average IQ of 96 (Trout et al., 2003). Research over the past 25 years is consistent in that no investigators have found average IQ scores for students with EBD that were 100 or higher. Although no causal links between emotional problems and intelligence have been established, it appears that, as a group, students with EBD do score lower on intelligence measures and therefore would be expected to experience some degree of academic difficulty.

Indeed, failure to achieve in school is one of the major characteristics of students with EBD (Bower, 1961; Foley & Epstein, 1992; Reid et al., 2004; Rosenblatt & Rosenblatt, 1999; Wagner, 1995) Even when compared to expected achievement based on intellectual functioning (i.e., IQ), the majority of students with EBD show academic deficits, usually a year or more below grade level (Bower, 1969; Forness, Bennett, & Tose, 1983; Kauffman, 2005). Ruhl and Berlinghoff (1992), in their review of the literature, estimated that between 33–81 percent of students with EBD have academic difficulties. Furthermore students with EBD, compared to students in other moderate disability categories, are retained more often and receive lower and more failing grades (Locke & Fuchs, 1995).

Investigators have sought to determine whether students with EBD experience more difficulty in one academic area than another. Some have found more extreme deficits in math (e.g., Epstein, Kinder, & Bursuck, 1989; Greenbaum et al., 1996) and spelling, with less underachievement in reading (without coexistence of LD) as compared to peers with LD (Reid et al., 2004). In their meta-analysis of the academic status of students with EBD, Reid and his colleagues conclude that "there is a moderate to large overall difference in the academic performance of students with EBD compared to students without disabilities" (2004, p. 138), which is consistent with previous research that noted persistent problems with low achievement. Others have found that adolescents with EBD fall significantly below grade level in reading, math, and written language (Nelson, Benner, Lane, & Smith, 2004).

Students with both EBD and LD are particularly at risk for academic (e.g., reading) deficits (Fessler et al., 1991). As you have learned, learning disabilities often coexist with emotional/behavioral disorders, perhaps in a reciprocal relationship (Walker, Ramsey, & Gresham, 2004). Academic failure is a good predictor of problem behavior and social failure (Morrison & D'Incau, 1997); conversely, problem behavior and social deficits predispose students to academic failure (Bower, 1961; Kauffman, 2005). This "chicken or egg" determination regarding primary causal factors continues to elude us. However, it is important to examine the learning–behavior relationship from an instructional point of view; for example, do instructional programs for students with EBD emphasize behavior management to the exclusion of academic instruction when academic success might very well improve behavior?

Given that most students with EBD display academic deficits, we would assume that a great deal of programmatic emphasis would be placed on academic instruction. However, Bradley and Monfore (2004) report that teacher surveys revealed about 17 percent of students with EBD had little or no academic curriculum available to them; about 33 percent of students with EBD were given general education curriculum without modification and 50 percent received this curriculum with only some modification (e.g., more time to complete work). Furthermore, relatively few well-designed research studies addressing academic instruction of students with EBD have been conducted to date (Coleman & Vaughn, 2000; Gunter, Hummel, & Venn, 1998; Mooney, Epstein, Reid, & Nelson, 2003). These authors and others (e.g., Knitzer, Steinberg, & Fleisch, 1990) have also questioned whether academic instruction for students with EBD takes a backseat to behavior management. In any case, it appears that effective instructional practices have not been implemented with students with EBD to such a degree to allow effective evaluation of the results (Gunter et al., 1998). Current mandates for higher academic achievement and the dismal academic record of students with EBD seem to indicate more attention and time to effective academic instruction. This issue will be discussed further in Chapter 12.

In summary, although wide variation exists among individuals, students with EBD as a group consistently have scored lower than average on both IQ and achievement measures. Some investigators have found math and spelling achievement to be lower than reading, but this finding is not consistent across investigations. While the specific relationship between emotional, behavioral, and intellectual functioning remains unclear, teachers of these students should expect them to be experiencing academic difficulties as well as socioemotional problems, and should prepare to address academic achievement in a comprehensive manner. Unfortunately, it has also been found that these students' social, behavioral, and academic deficits become more resistant to intervention efforts over time (O'Shaughnessy, Lane, Gresham, & Beebe-Frankenberger, 2002). Aggression appears to remain stable over time while academic performance may actually worsen (Nelson et al., 2004). Earl, in Box 1.3 represents a typical adolescent with EBD. Notice the toxic combination of his characteristics. He (1) is male, (2) is in trouble with the law, (3) is failing and not engaged academically, (4) has received mental health treatment, (5) has learning disabilities, and (6) is aggressive and anti-social. What do you think school personnel could do at this point to provide an appropriate education for Earl?

Language Characteristics

Since the early 1980s extensive research has explored the interaction of language ability and emotional behavioral disorders. These co-occurring delays are believed to be an artifact of the simultaneous neurocognitive development of behavioral self-regulation and language skills at about 3 years of age. These two skill areas are symbiotic in that internal self-talk and verbal expression aid in developing self-control and conflict negotiation with others. For example, in one study of preschool children with a diagnosed emotional disorder or language impairment, the children with either disorder scored similarly in measures of language performance and behavioral competence (Rogers-Adkinson & Rinaldi, in review). This pattern of comorbidity appears to continue developmentally with language performance noted to actually decrease with time in children with EBD (Nelson, Brenner, & Rogers-Adkinson, 2003).

Currently, language performance measures are not an integrated part of the comprehensive assessment process for children with EBD, so the exact nature of the language problems in this population are not known (Getty & Summy, 2006). In 2002 the American Institute of Research suggested that over 50 percent of all children with EBD have a coexisting language disorder and that assessment should occur in the areas of language processing and pragmatics (American Institute of Research, 2002).

BOX 1.3
Earl

Earl is a ninth-grade student attending Spring Creek High School. He qualifies for special education services as a student with an emotional disability and a learning disability in the areas of reading and written expression. Review of testing indicates Earl is currently functioning in the borderline range of intelligence, with strengths in mathematics and performance tasks. He has a history of inpatient hospitalizations for emotional difficulties since he was 9 years old. During the past year he has been hospitalized approximately four times with lengths of stay up to 2 months. Earl has attempted suicide and threatened to kill his mother. His emotional outbursts at school have resulted in law enforcement intervention due to truancy, assaulting another student, and assaulting a police officer. Each incident resulted in placement at the County Mental Health Center. The most current hospitalization began 3 weeks ago.

Earl is currently on probation and his mother reports that he violated his conditions of probation last month by bringing a knife into the probation department. His probation officer did not file charges for this incident; however, he called the school administration, due to the possibility that Earl had previously had the knife at school. Later, Earl's mother learned that the knife was stolen out of his grandfather's collection. Mr. Smith, the school counselor, wrote a letter last month requesting that Earl's current academic placement change to avoid ongoing behavior problems. He is currently attending all classes except for one elective in the special education self-contained classroom.

A recent observation in the self-contained classroom revealed Earl walking around the room. The teacher asked if he had finished his assignment and he said yes. She informed him that he had earned his reinforcement time. Earl continued to walk around the room for about 20 minutes. He did not appear upset, but did not interact with the other students. When asked how he earned his reinforcement time and what he was allowed to do during this time, he responded by shrugging his shoulders. Upon further questioning he reported that he earned reinforcement time by "behaving." Earl appeared nervous about the presence of an observer in the classroom. During the observations Earl did not complete any academic assignments or get involved in classroom discussions.

Contributed by Theresa Lopez, Special Education Teacher, San Antonio, Texas.

The impact of language deficits on behavior can be great. Deficits in receptive language ability might adversely affect a student's ability to comply with directions and requests (Fujiki, Brinton, Moran, & Hart, 1999), resulting in more negative interactions with adults. Actually, low language ability is thought to make behavior problems worse over time. Language deficits often correlate with increases in problem behavior and antisocial behavior (Gallagher, 1999; Ruhl, Hughes, & Camarata, 1992) because individuals are forced to "act out" what they want to say or what they feel, rather than using verbal expression for such purposes. Additionally, expressive language deficits may undermine verbally mediated crisis deescalation techniques and social skills interventions, which are commonly used in the field of EBD. Finally, co-occurring EBD and language deficits correlate with written language, reading, and math problems (Nelson et al., 2003). This is not surprising since most academics are language based. Given that language deficits are so prevalent in this population, teachers will need to learn about language assessment and curriculum and work with speech-language pathologists (SLPs) to develop appropriate language goals for their students.

Post-School Outcomes

Unfortunately, due to the combination of social, behavioral, intellectual, language, and learning problems, post-school outcomes for students with EBD are not often positive. Compared to other students with mild disabilities, students with EBD graduate from high school less often, and are less likely to attend postsecondary schools (Kauffman, 2005; Wagner, 1995). In 2001–2002 almost 61.2 percent of students with EBD dropped out of school (U.S. Department of Education, 2006) and it was estimated that about 70 percent of these students would be arrested within 3 years of leaving school (U.S. Department of Health and Human Services, 1999). Furthermore, Wagner, Newman, et al. (2003) reported that about 72 percent of students with EBD had been suspended or expelled from school compared to 22 percent for students without disabilities and almost 35 percent had been arrested (compared to 13% of students without disabilities). Three years after leaving high school, it is reported that most former students with EBD are unemployed, have been arrested, and do not live independently (Cullinan, 2002), and 15 percent live in correctional or mental health facilities (Wagner, 1995).

Many studies have documented the relationship among academic achievement, intellectual functioning, dropping out, disability, and delinquency (Archwamety & Katsiyannis, 2000; Beebe & Mueller, 1993; Doren, Bullis, & Benz, 1996; Wagner, D'Amico, Marder, Newman, & Blackorby, 1992). Given the propensity of students with EBD to such negative outcomes, it becomes evident that teaching them requires skill and commitment. Students with EBD who are not effectively educated pose personal, social, and financial costs not only to themselves but also to their families and society in general. "There should be little doubt that effective teaching for students with ED has the power not only to help the young people but to reduce tragic, alarming, and expensive problems for the school and the society" (Cullinan, 2002, p. 24).

Teacher Characteristics

What do we know about the teachers who are assigned to teach students with EBD? In a recent national study of 859 teachers of students with EBD compared to 3,687 other special education teachers, Billingsley, Fall, and Williams (2006) found that teachers of students with EBD are among the least qualified special educators. This survey found that a high percentage of new teachers for this population were uncertified in their assigned teaching area, many were teaching with emergency permits or had no teaching certificate at all, and a higher percentage entered teaching through alternative certification routes. Of the teachers surveyed, 33 percent of the EBD group respondents claimed that their preparation did not match the first-year realities of teaching such students. Special education teacher preparation programs may be remiss in their preparation of teachers for students with EBD because most states now offer generic, not specialist, teaching certificates (Maag & Katsiyannis, 1999) and, subsequent to the No Child Left Behind Act (2001), emphasize academic preparation for teachers to the exclusion of pedagogy and specialized skills.

In any case, lack of preparation is a major reason for teachers leaving the profession (Miller, Brownell, & Smith, 1999). Additionally, high teacher turnover is a function of work-related stress and burnout (Seery, 1990). Cross and Billingsley (1994) found that teachers of students with EBD reported greater stress than other special education teachers. Not only may this exacerbate teacher attrition (Center & Callaway, 1999; Zabel & Zabel, 2001), but may also decrease the number of teachers entering the EBD field. The American Association for Employment in Education (AAEE; 1999) found that teachers of students with EBD are among the highest ranked needs areas across the United States. High teacher turnover and reliance on temporary or out-of-field teachers perpetuates a scenario of multiple, untrained teachers marching through classrooms of students who most need consistent relationships and instructional competence. Some have speculated that students with EBD will suffer, not only from the handicapping nature of their disability but also from under-prepared teachers (Sutherland, Denny, & Gunter, 2005). It might be that the dismal and disappointing school outcomes for these students are actually due to a generally unqualified and/or unavailable teacher workforce (Billingsley et al., 2006).

Demographically, the study found that teachers of students with EBD are disproportionally male, and are of greater racial diversity than other special education teacher groups, significantly younger, and less experienced. However, teachers entering the field of EBD are, like all special education teacher groups, predominantly female and Caucasian (Billingsley, 2005). These demographics digress from EBD student characteristics (i.e., majority male, disproportionately African American). There is a danger that the disparity between student and teacher gender and cultural backgrounds may serve to confound and prevent teacher understanding of student behavior and feelings (Chamberlain, 2005). Table 1.2 summarizes student and teacher characteristics. Consider the ramifications of the various differences in characteristics in terms of appropriate educational opportunities for these students.

Prevalence

Accurate estimation of the prevalence of children and youth with EBD is hampered by differences in data gathering methods and definition. Bower (1969), in his definitive work with students with emotional disturbance in California, estimated that about 10 percent of the school-age population needed intervention for behavioral or emotional problems. However, more recent studies indicate that between 9 and 20 percent of the child and adolescent population in this country suffer from a diagnosable mental/emotional problem requiring intervention (Costello, Gordon, Keeler, & Angold, 2001; Friedman et al., 1996; U.S. Department of Health and Human Services [USDHHS], 1999). The Surgeon General's 1999 report (USDHHS, 1999) also suggested that school is the primary setting for the identification of mental disorders in children and youth. Unfortunately, the Center for Mental Health Services estimated that about 57 percent of the children seeking community mental health services were not receiving special education services at the time of intake (Woodruff et al., 1998).

Perhaps a more reasonable estimate of children and youth needing special education services for emotional/behavioral problems is between 3 and 6 percent (Kauffman, 2005; U.S. Department of Health and Human Services, 2001). However, in sharp contrast to these needs, the U.S. Department of Education (DOE) has historically established a prevalence

TABLE 1.2 Common Characteristics of Students with EBD and Their Teachers

Type of Characteristic	Students with EBD	Teachers of Students with EBD
Demographics	75–85% male 62% Caucasian 27% African American 8–17 years old	72% female, higher male percentage than other teacher groups 82% Caucasian, 15% African American As a group, more diverse and younger than other SPED teacher groups
Affective	Anxious Depressed Noncompliant Aggressive/defiant Often victims of rejection and isolation	As a group, feel least prepared and have fewer years of teaching than other SPED teacher groups 3% attrition rate per year, higher than other teacher groups Report greater stress than other SPED teacher groups
Academic preparation	Up to 81% have academic difficulties and learning problems Compared to other SPED students, receive lower and more failing grades Retained most often 72% have been suspended or expelled 51% drop out of school 70% will be arrested within 3 years	Only 40% of first-year teachers were fully certified (higher percentage uncertified than other teacher groups) 12% are prepared through alternative certification routes, higher than other teacher groups Only a small percentage in grades 6–12 are certified in core academic subject Among least qualified special educators

level of 2 percent of the school-age population to be served in special education under the category of EBD. In the 2001–2002 school year, a mere .72 percent of the public school population was served under the category of emotional disturbance (ED) (U.S. Department of Education, 2003), indicating that this population is greatly underserved even when compared to the extremely conservative cap of 2 percent. In 2001–2002, 477,627 students, ages 6–21, were served as ED under IDEA (U.S. Department of Education, 2006). This was about 8.1 percent of the special education population. Reluctance of school personnel to identify students as EBD appears to be based on a fear that aggressive and defiant students would be protected under the IDEA preventing school administrators from unilaterally expelling or suspending these students, both widely used discipline techniques.

Even with the underidentification of students as EBD for special education services, it is now accepted that schools are a major component of a continuum of mental health services to children and youth and that school mental health services are in need of support and improvement (Foster, Rollefson, Doksum, Noonan, & Robinson, 2005). The Surgeon General's report (USDHHS, 1999) found that 3–5 percent of school-age children are diagnosed with attention-deficit/hyperactivity disorder in a 6-month period; 5 percent of children age 9–17 are diagnosed with major depression; and the combined prevalence of various anxiety disorders for children age 9–17 is 13 percent. Foster et al. (2005) further found that the most common school mental health providers were school counselors, nurses, school psychologists, and social workers. Two-thirds of the 83,000 schools surveyed reported that the need for mental health services had increased while available funds for such services decreased and that the main funding sources continue to be through the federal IDEA and state special education funds. Funding, school staff training, and service effectiveness issues still plague the schools, preventing early intervention for what seems to be ever-increasing numbers of children in need.

Conclusions

Defining and identifying individuals with emotional and behavioral disorders continues to challenge school personnel. This is partly due to confusing terminology, a defective educational definition, the confounding effects of cultural and socioeconomic influences, comorbidity, and the nature of the disability itself. Students with EBD manifest social, intellectual, academic, language, and behavioral difficulties to such a degree that they require intensive and effective strategies to avoid very negative outcomes. These students are predominantly male, aggressive, and disproportionally African American. Their teachers, on the other hand, tend to be young, female, Caucasian, inexperienced, and often underprepared for dealing with such a challenging population. Furthermore, students with EBD appear to be increasingly more difficult to educate. Walker, Zeller, Close, Webber, and Gresham (1999) state that "Today, students who receive the EBD label in school seem qualitatively different. The student population . . . seems more violent, its problems more intensely pathological, and its negative outcomes more destructive" (p. 297). These challenging characteristics, the apparently chronic pathology of mental illness, and the high cost of mental health and special education services combine to make school-based services necessary yet lacking. Thus, the majority of students needing mental health services are not currently receiving them. As you can see, the challenges of teaching students with EBD are many.

KEY POINTS

1. Personal and social concepts of deviance determine who is perceived as EBD.
2. Terminology used by educators usually differs from that used by mental health professionals, adding to the confusion of the labeling process. New terminology has been proposed.
3. The federal definition of emotional disturbance has been adopted by most states but has been roundly criticized as inadequate. Many states may consider adopting alternate definitions.
4. Whether to include or exclude students considered socially maladjusted from special education is controversial, with many advocates for including them.
5. The characteristics of students with EBD can be conceptualized as either internalizing (e.g., anxiety, depression) or externalizing (e.g., conduct disorders, ADHD). Most students served as EBD exhibit externalizing characteristics.

6. The dimensions of chronicity, frequency, and severity should always be considered when determining whether behavior is disordered.
7. Students with EBD are likely to be male and between the ages of 8 and 17 years old. African American students are disproportionally represented in the EBD population. Students with EBD will typically exhibit relationship and social problems, perform below grade level academically, have a below-average IQ, and make failing grades.
8. Students with EBD are also likely to drop out of school, get in trouble with the law, and be unemployed after leaving high school.
9. Teachers of students with EBD are likely to be female, Caucasian, young, new to teaching, lacking appropriate certification, stressed, and feeling unprepared.
10. The prevalence of students served in special education as EBD falls significantly below professional estimates of the number of students who need mental health services.

HOMEWORK QUESTIONS

1. Discuss one of the cases (Freddie, Earl, or Rhonda) using the dimensions of chronicity, frequency, and severity.
2. Decide if you think that Freddie (Box 1.1) will qualify for special education services as EBD and explain your answer.
3. In one paragraph, describe what role you think Earl's learning disabilities play in his behavior.
4. Describe what you think Rhonda (Box 1.2) feels when she walks into school each day.
5. After reviewing Table 1.2 of characteristics of students with EBD and their teachers, briefly discuss the reciprocal influences of these characteristics.
6. Consider whether you think students with EBD are likely to receive an appropriate public education, given what you have learned in this chapter.

ADDITIONAL READINGS AND RESOURCES

Cultural biases in the identification of students with behavior disorders, by Park, E. K., Pullis, M., Reilly, T., & Towsend, B. L., in R. Peterson and S. Ishii-Jordan (eds.), *Multicultural issues in the education of students with behavioral disorders,* 1994, Cambridge, MA: Brookline, for a treatise on how understanding or lack of understanding of different cultures can influence perceptions of what is deviant.

Emotional or behavioral disorders: Background and current status of the EBD terminology and definition, by Forness, S., & Kavale, K., *Behavioral Disorders, 25*(3), 2000, for a historical view of the move to change the IDEA definition and terminology pertaining to students with EBD.

Handbook of Research in Emotional and Behavioral Disorders edited by R. B. Rutherford, M. M. Quinn, and S. R. Mathur (2004), New York: The Gulford Press for a series of chapters, several addressing definitions and characteristics, that review current research pertaining to relevant topics in EBD.

The emotionally disturbed child: Disturbing or disturbed?, by Bob Algozzine, *Journal of Abnormal Child Psychology, 5,* 1977, for an article on the notion that children's behavior may be more bothersome than pathological.

Who's crazy? II, by C. M. Nelson, in S. Braaten, R. B. Rutherford, Jr., & C. A. Kardash (eds.), *Programming for adolescents with behavior disorders,* Reston, VA: Council for Children with Behavior Disorders, 1984, for a treatise on "craziness," which requires the reader to assess self and to question the education process.

Disability profiles of elementary and middle school students with disabilities, by Wagner, M., & Blackorby, J. 2002, Menlo Park, CA: SRI International. For a description of student characteristics (*http://www.sri.com/policy/cehs/dispolicy/*)

A meta-analysis of the academic status of students with emotional/behavioral disturbance, by Reid, R., et al., *Journal of Special Education, 38*(3), 2004, 130–143, for a review of studies pertaining to academic characteristics of students with EBD.

Outcomes for children and youth with emotional and behavioral disorders and their families: Programs and evaluation best practices (2nd ed.), by M. Epstein, K. Kutash, & A. Duchnowski, Austin, TX: Pro-Ed, 2005, for a review of empirical evidence supporting effective mental health services delivered to children and their families.

Behavioral Disorders 29(1), November 2003, for an entire special journal issue edited by Diana Rogers-Adkinson and Stephen Hooper regarding the relationship of language and behavior for students with EBD.

Office of Special Education and Rehabilitation Services (OSERS), U.S. Department of Education: *http://www.ed.gov/about/offices/list/osers/osep/index.html*, for information from the Office of Special Education Programs (OSEP) about students with disabilities.

OSERS publications *http://www.ed.gov/about/offices/list/osers/osep/products.html*, for OSEP's annual reports to Congress on the Implementation of the IDEA.

CEC publications: *http://www.cec.sped.org/AM/Template.cfm?Section=Publications1,* for information about teaching students with disabilities.

SRI International reports: *http://www.sri.com/policy/cehs/dispolicy/*, for studies regarding education and human services such as the National Early Intervention Longitudinal Study (NEILS), Special Education Elementary Longitudinal Study (SEELS), National Longitudinal Transition Study—2 (NLTS2), and National Behavior Research Coordination Center (NBRCC).

U.S. Department of Health and Human Services, Substance Abuse and Mental Health Services Administration (SAMHSA): *http://store.mentalhealth.org/publications/browse.asp*, for publications and reports pertaining to children's mental health issues in the schools (e.g., *School Mental Health Services in the US, 2002–2003* and various fact sheets).

Report of the Surgeon General's Conference on Children's Mental Health: A National Action Agenda (1999), U.S. Department of Health and Human Services (http://www.surgeongeneral.gov/library/mentalhealth/home.html), for recommendations for a mental health agenda to promote overall health and well-being in children and youth.

National Comorbidity Survey Replication (NCS-R) (2005), National Institute of Mental Health: *http://www.nimh.nih.gov/healthinformation/ncs-r.cfm*, for information about trends in mental health prevalence, impairment, and service use throughout the 1990s.

CHAPTER

2 A Historical Perspective

QUESTIONS TO CONSIDER

- What factors seem to influence how we have historically treated individuals with emotional or behavioral disorders?
- How have attitudes toward deviance changed throughout history?
- What can we learn from historical descriptions in terms of our own dispositions toward deviance?
- What role does superstition play in concepts of deviance? Do you think superstition plays a role today?
- What are the major political and social factors impacting how we treat individuals with EBD today?

Orientation

Throughout history, humans have sought to explain and to treat behavior that was considered deviant. For those of you who are preparing to work with students labeled as EBD, knowledge of the historical development of services for this population can provide perspective about your own niche—where you and your efforts fit into the overall chronology of events. However, more important than knowledge of specific people and events is the realization that deviance has always been a political and social issue, and that services for this population are a reflection of the political and social climate of the times.

Overview

Human fascination with the concept of insanity or mental disturbance can be traced to prehistoric cultures. Survival was difficult during these times, as humans were learning to cope with the natural elements. Mere physical survival was the major goal for thousands of years, and survival of the fittest was paramount to the perpetuation of the human race. Humans who were physically fit and most likely to adapt and survive were valued; the physically unfit were often shunned, left to die, or even put to death. In those early years of human existence, survival of the fittest also applied to the behaviorally deviant. A form of social Darwinism prevailed, in which survival of the group or the culture was valued above the life of the individual. Deviants, whether physically or behaviorally different, were considered a detriment to group survival and were not valued.

During the era when humans were essentially helpless and exerted little control over their environment, they invented superstitious beliefs in an effort to explain and control the ills that plagued them. Supernatural causes were evoked to explain illness, disease, and various disasters of nature such as floods, famines, earthquakes, and volcanic eruptions. Routine natural phenomena such as lightning, thunder, and fire were also attributed to supernatural causes.

Demonology, or belief in possession by demons, was common in ancient times and is prevalent in the early writings of many cultures. A logical extension of superstitious beliefs, demonology was an explanation for aberrant behavior. Both good and evil spirits were believed capable of entering the human person. Possessed individuals were accorded varying treatments. Some were beaten, ostracized, or put to death, whereas others were elevated to the priesthood. Individuals whose demeanor suggested possession by good spirits were accorded respect and preferential treatment. If the spirits were judged to be evil, however, rites of exorcism ranging from prayer and exhortation to cruel and barbaric measures were performed to drive the evil spirits out of the body.

By creating explanations for natural phenomena and aberrant behavior, humans were able to establish some systematic attempt to manipulate the environment, thereby instilling a meager sense of control. Historians have noted that superstitious beliefs prevail in times and societies in which humans are unable to explain scientifically the environment or to exert a degree of control over the environment because of social or political constraints. Conversely, superstition is minimal in cultures in which scientific thought, political freedom, and the rights of individuals are championed. The following historical perspective demonstrates this inverse relationship, as superstitious beliefs about aberrant behavior are shown to wax and wane over the centuries. The Greeks and Romans give us the first written accounts attributing deviant behavior to purely natural causes; however, during the Middle Ages, when most scientific inquiry was effectively repressed and the church imposed tight social control, superstition again prevailed.

Historically, treatment of deviant individuals falls into three very broad phases:

1. *Segregation phase (Early Middle Ages to the 1600s):* The primary concern was to isolate deviants from the rest of society; hospitals and asylums were established to care for physical needs but psychological needs were essentially ignored.
2. *Transition phase (1700s to 1800s):* A number of vocal advocates were successful in implementing humane treatment and establishing training schools.
3. *Service phase (1900s to the present):* Attempts are made to help individuals become functional members of society.

Ancient Views: Greeks and Romans

Although pre-Hellenic civilizations had attempted scientific thought, most historians agree that "their science was indistinguishable from theology" (Durant, 1961, p. 51). It is the ancient Greeks who are credited with enlightening their contemporaries about natural causes of mental and behavioral disorders. Chief among the early Greek contributors were the physician Hippocrates and the philosophers Plato and Aristotle. Hippocrates became a clinical observer of human behavior and was responsible for the first medical writings that systematically classified mental problems and attributed them to natural causes. He attacked the commonly accepted notion that human ailments were caused by gods and insisted that philosophical theories have no place in medicine. His most widely known theory of mental disorders concerned the four "bodily humors": Hippocrates stated that mental imbalance was the result of a disturbance in one or more of the humors—black bile, yellow bile, blood, or phlegm. Hippocrates further proposed that the cure for mental disturbance was to restore the imbalance among the humors, a precursor to modern endocrinology, or the study of endocrine secretions.

Plato hypothesized three main sources of human behavior: desire (instinct), which is primarily sexual in nature and is seated in the loins; emotions, located in the heart; and knowledge (reason), located in the head. According to Plato, humans have varying degrees of these qualities, which partially account for differences in personality and styles of behavior. Plato also anticipated modern psychoanalysis by almost 2,000 years in insisting that dream interpretation was a key to personality. "In all of us, even in good men, there is such a latent wild beast nature, which peers out in sleep" (cited in Durant, 1961, p. 23).

Aristotle also ventured his opinion about the causes of mental distress; he believed that very hot bile caused both amorous and suicidal impulses. Although such theories represent advanced thinking for the age in which they appeared, they hardly constituted a basis for effective treatment. As Durant summarized the scientific contributions of the Greeks:

> Greek science went as far as could be expected without instruments of observation and precision, and without experimental methods. It would have done better had it not been harassed by religion and discouraged by philosophy. (Durant, 1939, p. 348)

The Greeks did influence the thinking of several physicians who advanced naturalistic theories in later centuries. Notable among these is Aretaeus of Cappadocia, who claimed that many mental disorders were merely extreme manifestations of normal mental processes or personality dispositions. He also devoted attention to differential diagnosis of illnesses with similar clinical symptoms. Galen, another Greek physician who lived in Rome, is best known for his principle that a physical symptom could occur in a part of the body separate from the actual diseased area, which led to treatment of the illness rather than the symptom. Galen also proposed that the major causes of mental illness could be divided into either mental or physical categories.

Early Middle Ages to the 1600s (Segregation Phase)

The science of mental health took a giant step backward during the Middle Ages, as demonology and other superstitious beliefs once again prevailed. Scientific explanations of the Greeks and Romans were rejected; popular thought reverted to demonology and again attributed abnormal behavior to unnatural and unscientific causes. An increase in abnormal behavior also occurred toward the latter part of the Middle Ages. One notable manifestation was group hysteria, which occurred in the form of dance manias. Historians believe that mass hysteria occurred as early as the 10th century, and descriptive accounts of dance manias were recorded in the 13th century. These accounts indicate that during Saint Vitus's dance, as it was commonly called, large groups of people jumped about excitedly and danced themselves into frenzies. These frenzies reached epidemic proportions in the 15th and 16th centuries but apparently faded during the 17th century.

In early medieval times, monasteries were havens for people afflicted with mental disorders. The clergy generally were kind to afflicted individuals, providing shelter and protection, and treating them with prayer or other rites. However, as theologians began to promote the doctrine of inherent evil and possession by demons, methods of treatment became progressively more severe. A reversion to the unpleasant methods of the ancients occurred. Coleman describes it thus: "Flogging, starving, chains, immersion in hot water, and other tortuous methods were devised in order to make the body such an unpleasant place of residence that no self-respecting devil would remain in it" (1964, p. 32).

During the latter part of the Middle Ages, most forms of mental illness were considered to be signs of consorting with the devil, and elaborate torture devices were devised to extract confessions from persons accused of practicing witchcraft. With the full support of the church and the state, hundreds of thousands of heretics and witches were beheaded or burned at the stake. Even those who dared question the existence of witches or the methods used during trials were in danger of being declared heretics and meeting the same fate. Although these trials were primarily instruments of religious and political persecution and were not aimed at the insane populace, they did provide an avenue for accusation and punishment of those exhibiting abnormal behaviors. Witch hunting peaked during the 16th and 17th centuries in Europe and spread to some American colonies. In Salem, Massachusetts, where the most notorious colonial witch trials were held, a mood of paranoia prevailed as neighbor turned against neighbor, and the slightest aberration in behavior was cause for accusation and trial.

Despite the risk of being labeled a heretic, many writers and scientists in the 16th century began to question openly the concepts of witchcraft and demonology. With the establishment of mental hospitals, the mentally ill were viewed as wretched creatures and victims of fate but were no longer accused of perpetrating evil through witchcraft. These early hospitals or asylums were attempts to segregate the mentally ill and were little more than penal institutions with deplorable conditions.

The first and most famous of these asylums, the Hospital of St. Mary of Bethlehem, was established in 1547 in London. Due to colloquial pronunciation it became popularly known as Bedlam, the modern meaning of which stems from the noise emanating from the

London asylum. Asylums such as Bedlam were viewed by the public with great curiosity; Shakespeare even referred to the "lunatics of Bedlam" in one of his plays. The gradual shift in the view of mental illness that was occurring during this period is captured by Despert:

> Another questionable form of entertainment was the accepted custom of taking the children to visit the mentally ill at Bedlam and other asylums. . . . As is well known, the mentally ill were chained, starved, beaten and kept in filth and darkness. The visit was a routine holiday program akin to a visit to the zoo in our days. The difference is that strict rules apply to the teasing and tormenting of animals, whereas of the period we speak, teasing was not only legitimate, but considered more or less a duty since the insane were thought to be more or less possessed. (1965, p. 89)

The 1700s to 1800s (Transition Phase)

During the 1700s in Europe, a number of changes were occurring that eventually led to humanistic reforms in both child care and treatment of persons with mental illness. Until the latter part of the century, children were treated more as commodities than individuals. Infant and child mortality rates were extremely high. At the age of 7, and oftentimes younger, children were expected to carry the workloads of adults; they had no rights and paternal authority was absolute (Despert, 1965).

During the middle of the 18th century, European writers and philosophers began to champion the rights of children and adults as individuals in society, and the French and American revolutions gave new impetus to the concepts of freedom and individual rights. Soon after the end of the French Revolution, the French physician Philippe Pinel undertook a daring experiment: he removed the chains from some of the patients at La Bicetre, a hospital for persons with mental illness in Paris. Pinel wanted to test his hypothesis that these patients would respond when treated with kindness and respect rather than cruelty and imprisonment. Fortunately for Pinel, the experiment was dramatically successful and some patients showed nearly miraculous improvement. This humane treatment was called moral therapy or moral treatment and was widely adopted both in Europe and America during the early part of the 19th century.

Beginning in the mid-1700s, anecdotal writings describing aberrant behavior in children began to appear. These writings were usually case studies or diaries. The most notable case study was written by Jean Itard, a student of Pinel's, who described his efforts to educate Victor, the "wild boy of Averyon." Victor had been found roaming the forests of southern France; it was believed that he had been abandoned at an early age and had managed to survive without human contact. He exhibited many bizarre behaviors and was labeled an idiot, but Itard believed that Victor was capable of learning many skills, including speech. Although Victor never learned more than a few words, Itard was successful at teaching him some social and practical skills. Itard's work was emulated by his contemporaries and is heralded today as one of the first systematic attempts to teach an individual who had mental and behavioral disorders.

Another individual who furthered the cause of humanistic treatment of children was Dr. Benjamin Rush of Philadelphia. Known as the father of U.S. psychiatry, Rush was a supporter of public education for all children and an advocate of kind and humane disciplinary methods. His writings furthered the implementation of moral therapy in U.S. asylums in the early 19th century and established him as an important writer in the transition between two eras.

Despite the efforts of a few advocates of humane treatment for children, few practical advances were made prior to 1800. In the mid-1800s, reforms emerged in the treatment of individuals with mental illness and mental retardation, largely due to the efforts of a few crusaders. Chief among these reformers were Dorothea Dix and Samuel Gridley Howe. Dix, a vocal proponent of the rights of the incarcerated, waged a 40-year campaign during which she appealed not only to the general public but also to legislatures in over 20 states. Her reforms reached Canada, Scotland, and other countries. Before her career ended, Dix was responsible for the establishment of 32 mental hospitals (Coleman, 1964). Howe was renowned as a pioneer in education for deaf-blind children and served as director of the Perkins Institution for the Blind before he convinced Massachusetts to establish a public school for "feebleminded children." His influence was felt throughout New England, as he was instrumental in establishing other training schools that were based on a model developed in France and brought to the United States by Edouard Seguin at around 1850.

By the mid-19th century, many training schools and educational programs in asylums for the insane (mental illness) and the idiotic (mental retardation) were being established. The majority of programs were based on the concept of moral treatment, of which education was an integral part. In public schools, the passage of legislation was eventually to have an enormous impact on services for this population. Toward the end of the century, compulsory school attendance laws were enacted in a number of states. Beginning with Rhode Island in 1840, many states followed suit with compulsory attendance laws, and by the turn of the century nearly all states had enacted compulsory education legislation (Aiello, 1976). Although originally intended as a means of socializing thousands of children immigrating to the United States during this period, compulsory attendance laws had the effect of encouraging educators in public schools to deal with all categories of less able children. The subsequent planning for these children may be viewed as the beginning of the field of special education; many cities established ungraded classes for children who did not flow easily into the mainstream of public education.

Writings of this period began to focus on etiology or causes of disturbance or disorders in children. In Europe, textbooks on the concepts of childhood mental disorders offered many diverse etiologies, ranging from degeneracy and masturbation to religious preoccupation (Kanner, 1962). Although the causes proposed in such writings seem amusing today, these textbooks represent the earliest attempts to collect and solidify a body of literature focusing specifically on childhood mental disorders.

In summary, sociological changes beginning in the 18th century finally culminated in the late 1800s in a new awareness of children as individuals with rights and of children with emotional and behavioral disorders as deserving recipients of humane treatment and special schooling. However, the picture at the beginning of the 20th century was still rather bleak. Although attitudes about these children were beginning to change, in practice the majority were receiving little more than custodial services and cursory attempts at education.

The Early 1900s (Service Phase)

The first three decades of the 20th century hosted a number of significant events as well as the establishment of national organizations dedicated to the welfare of individuals with mental disorders. One of the most significant of these was the establishment of the National Committee for Mental Hygiene, founded primarily by Clifford Beers and the psychologist William James. In 1908, Beers, a young Yale University graduate, published his autobiography, *A Mind That Found Itself,* which was a personal account of his mental breakdown and subsequent poor treatment in three institutions before his eventual recovery in the home of a sympathetic attendant. Beers mounted a campaign to enlighten the general public about poor conditions and the need for improved treatment for persons with mental illness. Largely as a result of his personal campaign, the National Committee for Mental Hygiene was created in 1909. Establishment of this organization is often viewed as the beginning of the mental health movement in the United States, which had a widespread influence on public awareness of mental health problems and led to the establishment of clinics and mental health programs for children in the public schools. By 1930, many such programs had been instituted across the country, and in 1931, the first children's psychiatric hospital was founded in Rhode Island.

During this period, other national organizations that focused on the study and education of children with disabilities were founded. The Council for Exceptional Children (CEC), a lobbying organization composed primarily of educators and parents of children with disabilities, was created in 1922. Members of CEC have crusaded for the rights of children and youth with disabilities, and, particularly since World War II, have been instrumental in the passage of favorable legislation. In 1924, the American Orthopsychiatric Association was formed. As the name *orthopsychiatric* implies, this organization is dedicated to research and procurement of information on childhood behavioral disorders.

In 1930, an event occurred that demonstrated that both the general public and the federal government were showing increased interest in the welfare of children with disabilities. This event was the White House Conference on Child Health and Protection, a milestone in the field of special education because it marked the first time that special education was nationally recognized as a legitimate part of education (Aiello, 1976). In addition to the national publicity afforded by the conference, the participants' recommendation that the Office of Education include a department of special education was enacted in the early 1930s.

The Mid-1900s

Research and Emergence of Model Programs

It was also in the 1930s that systematic attempts to delineate etiology, therapy, and prognosis for children with severe disorders were set in motion. However, these attempts focused on the condition of childhood schizophrenia and were plagued by philosophical differences over the feasibility and utility of classification systems (Kanner, 1962). Notable among these early attempts at definition were Kanner's (1943) description of early infantile autism, Mahler's (1952) description of symbiotic infantile psychosis, and Bender's (1954) attempt to classify childhood schizophrenia into three distinct clinical types.

While some researchers emphasized classification schemes of youngsters with severe disorders, others were turning their attention to descriptions of milder emotional/behavioral disorders. A classic monograph entitled *Children's Behavior and Teachers' Attitudes* was published by Wickman in 1928. This study contrasted the attitudes of public school teachers and mental health clinicians toward 50 problem behaviors. Wickman's results suggested that, whereas clinicians were more interested in withdrawing and other nonsocial forms of behavior, teachers were more concerned with classroom management and authority problems. The Wickman report touched off a controversy that raged for the next 30 years, mainly due to his view that teachers should adopt a hierarchy of attitudes toward behavior more consonant with that of clinicians (Beilin, 1959). This controversy was fueled by widespread misinterpretation of the results; for example, many descriptions of the study failed to report that teachers and clinicians were responding to two different sets of instructions. Nonetheless, the study was cited as justification for adding coursework in mental health to teacher education programs across the country.

Beginning in the 1930s and continuing through the 1950s, model education programs for children with severe emotional disorders were established. Lauretta Bender, a distinguished psychiatrist at Bellevue Hospital in New York, was responsible for setting up classrooms for children with emotional/behavioral disorders at Bellevue in 1935. A decade later in Chicago, Bruno Bettelheim established the Orthogenic School for youth with emotional/behavioral disorders and pioneered the concept of a therapeutic milieu, a contrived environment conducive to treatment. In 1946, New York City opened the "600" schools, which were programs for this population. Around the same time, Fritz Redl and David Wineman opened Pioneer House in Detroit. This residential treatment center was for delinquent and aggressive boys, later dubbed "the children nobody wants" by Redl and Wineman (1957). Treatment at Pioneer House centered around the therapeutic milieu; Redl and Wineman chose to forego psychiatric treatment in favor of group therapy and a structured, psychologically sound environment. Pioneer House operated less than 2 years due to lack of financial support, but it became a model for numerous programs throughout the country, and its treatment principles continued to influence services for these children.

Another model program, the League School, was founded by Carl Fenichel in New York City in 1953. Based on his conviction that residential placement is not the ideal solution for youngsters with emotional and behavioral disorders, Fenichel opened a day school "to work exclusively with children who had been turned down by every school and agency except mental institutions" (Fenichel, 1974, p. 55). From a modest beginning in a Brooklyn brownstone with one teacher and two children, the League School soon expanded to capacity and by the mid-1970s was serving over 120 youngsters (Fenichel, 1974). The program at the League School incorporated the basics of most current model programs: individually tailored educational plans, a multidisciplinary team approach, and an underlying philosophy aimed at the ultimate goal of teaching students self-control.

National Trends

The postwar era gave new impetus to the general special education movement, as thousands of disabled veterans returned to the United States to be integrated into society. As the federal government sought to provide financial aid and rehabilitation services to the veterans, parents of children with disabilities became more visible and more willing to seek help. Consequently, a number of parent organizations were founded in the late 1940s and early 1950s. The National Association for Retarded Citizens was formed in 1950, and partially due to its lobbying power, all states had passed laws pertaining to education of individuals with mental disabilities by 1956. However, services for students with emotional and behavioral disabilities lagged behind other special populations. Among the reasons proposed for this lack of development were the reluctance of parents to become advocates because of meager economic resources and feelings of guilt (Hoffman, 1974), and a lack of direction among educators due to confusion over definition, etiology, and intervention methods. It was not until the mid-1960s that national organizations for parents and educators of children with behavioral disorders were established. In 1964, the Council for Children with Behavioral Disorders, a division of CEC, was founded, and in 1965, the National Society for Autistic Children, now the Autism Society of America (ASA) was organized as a parent advocacy group.

1960 to 1980

Model Programs and Research

Beginning in the early 1960s, the scattered information on educating students with emotional/behavioral disorders was molded into a cohesive body of literature. Although much of the groundwork had been laid prior to that time, it was only after 1960 that the literature began to outline specific classroom practices. The following section is an overview of model programs and works of major contributors to the field, but it is by no means an exhaustive review of the accomplishments of this era.

A highly specific description of classroom procedures for children with behavior problems was published by William M. Cruickshank and colleagues in *A Teaching Method for Brain-Injured and Hyperactive Children* (Cruickshank, Bentzen, Ratzeburg, & Tannhauser, 1961). Although the children in the experimental classroom were labeled "hyperactive" or "brain damaged," terms that Cruickshank linked to learning disabilities, many of the youngsters experienced severe emotional problems. As Cruickshank and colleagues observed:

> If a child has a healthy body, but one that will not do what he wants it to—if he has eyes that see, but that do not see things the way other eyes see them—if he has ears that hear, but they have not learned to hear the way other ears do—he cannot tell anyone what his difficulty is:

> it just seems to him that he is always wrong. No one can see that he is not like everyone else, so he is expected to act like everyone else. These are the things that happen to such children. This is the kind of behavior in a learning situation which the teacher will have to understand if she is to help the child. (p. 131)

Drawing heavily from the landmark work of Strauss and Lehtinen (1947) with children with brain injuries, Cruickshank set up a pilot demonstration project housed in three elementary schools in Montgomery County, Maryland. The initial success of the program was attributed to a high degree of structure and an absence of excessive auditory and visual stimuli in the learning environment. The study specified physiologically based symptoms that interfere with learning (e.g., distractibility and perseveration) and gave concomitant instructional strategies that inspired a new confidence in teaching children with such problems. However, subsequent data were not as encouraging; the overall strategy for classroom organization was questioned after the third year (Bentzen & Petersen, 1962).

In 1962, Norris Haring and Lakin Phillips published a book describing their efforts to establish successful experimental classrooms for children with emotional/behavioral disorders in the public schools of Arlington, Virginia. In *Educating Emotionally Disturbed Children,* Haring and Phillips provided explicit instructions for replication of their program. Classrooms were organized according to behavioral principles and Cruickshank's concept of a structured environment, and the total program stressed the child's interactions both at home and in school.

Pearl Berkowitz and Esther Rothman coauthored *The Disturbed Child* in 1960 and thus formed a professional liaison that produced numerous publications over the next two decades. Having received training at the Bellevue school founded by Bender, Berkowitz and Rothman initially favored a heavily psychoanalytic approach. However, their later writings reflected a more moderate approach as they moved toward a model in which both therapy and positive educational experiences were viewed as equally important to the child's developing ego and self-concept (Berkowitz, 1974). Due to their extensive research and continued involvement in several treatment settings in the New York City area, Rothman and Berkowitz are considered pioneers in the development of services for children and youth with emotional and behavioral disorders.

One of the first instruments designed to screen children with emotional problems in the schools was published in 1962. *A Process for In-School Screening of Children with Emotional Handicaps* (Bower & Lambert, 1962) is based on teacher, peer, and self-ratings. The authors cautioned that it is to be used for screening only and not for identification or classification purposes. The instrument was based on several years' research by Bower and his colleagues in California and, for quite some time, was the only instrument available for such purposes. Ironically, the aspect of Bower's work with the most pervasive effect was not the screening instrument but the definition of emotional disturbance that accompanied the research. This definition was adopted in the federal regulations of Public Law 94-142, now the IDEA, in 1977 and today constitutes the basis for most state definitions.

Nicholas Hobbs is the name most often associated with the development of Project Re-ED. Funded by the National Institute of Mental Health and the states of Tennessee and North Carolina in 1961 as a demonstration project, pilot residential schools were established by Hobbs in Nashville and Durham. The Re-ED programs operate from an ecological philosophy, which posits that all social systems of the child must be taken into account if treatment is to be effective. In accordance with this strategy, interventions in the home, school, and community are carried out by liaison teachers. Intervention in the residential program is carried out by teacher-counselors who focus on two major goals: (1) helping the child develop competence and experience success in academic areas, and (2) helping the child learn adaptive behaviors that will aid transition back into the home environment. As Hobbs states: "teacher-counselors work in a coordinated effort, not to cure the child, which we believe is a meaningless concept, but to make the ecological system . . . work" (1974, pp. 155–156). Today there are 16 agencies nationwide that base their treatment programs on the Re-ED model (e.g., Fields, Farmer, Aperson, Mustillo, & Simmers, 2006).

In the mid-1960s, another model program emerged. Originally known as the Santa Monica Project, Frank Hewett's engineered classroom epitomizes the behavioral approach. Although a clinical psychologist by training, Hewett developed his model out of a need for pragmatism during his teaching experiences. The engineered classroom emerged from his beliefs that:

- You have to have structure (avoid failure by engineering the environment).
- You have to have motivation (use reinforcers).
- You have to have something to say (set up specific educational goals). (1974, pp. 117–127)

Translated to classroom practice, structure involves use of activity centers and specific times for specific subjects; motivation involves an elaborate check system as reinforcement; and something to say involves establishing a hierarchy of educational tasks. Hewett's model and Project Re-ED represent two distinctly different but highly successful approaches to educating students with emotional or behavioral disorders.

In 1965, the classic book, *Conflict in the Classroom,* was published by Nicholas Long, William Morse, and Ruth Newman. Consisting of a collection of writings from the most prominent educators of the time, this book was one of the first attempts to put together under one cover the widely divergent views of psychoanalytic, psychodynamic, and behavioral theory. Moreover, topics included identification and assessment, modes of therapy, model programs, and management techniques relevant to educational planning; consequently, *Conflict in the Classroom* was widely adopted as a textbook in teacher-training institutions and retains its status as a classic and bestseller in the field. In 1969, what is now the Office of Special Education Programs (OSEP) in the U.S. Department of Education funded the Regional Intervention Program (RIP) in Nashville, Tennessee, to provide early intervention services to children with challenging behavior through a parent-training intervention model. Outcomes such as school completion and entrance into higher education for these participants have been impressive (Bradley, Henderson, & Monfore, 2004). Today RIP programs have expanded across Tennessee and to other states (go to www.ripnetwork.org for more information).

The 1970s saw much progress in educating children with severe disorders, including those with autism and schizophrenia. Research on etiology yielded no clear-cut answers, but research on instructional methodology became definitive. With the use of operant conditioning techniques, students with severe disorders were taught speech and language

(Hewett, 1965; Lovaas, 1966, 1977); eye contact and elimination of self-stimulation behaviors (Foxx, 1977; Foxx & Azrin, 1973); and attention to instruction in large groups (Koegel & Rincover, 1974). Successful classroom programs were reported by Kozloff (1975) and Donnellan-Walsh, Gossage, LaVigna, Schuler, and Traphagen (1976). Parenting programs specifically for parents of children with autism were also established (Kozloff, 1973).

Legislation and Litigation

Another trend of the 1960s and 1970s was the demand for rights of the individual by most any group that perceived itself a minority: women, African Americans, Mexican Americans, gays, and numerous other activist groups literally stormed the streets in protest. This period of unrest and activism was unprecedented in our history and undoubtedly influenced individuals with disabilities to press for rights sanctioned by law. Although numerous court cases were decided and several federal laws were enacted that have affected the education of individuals with disabilities, only the three most significant of these are reviewed below.

1. *Mills v. Board of Education of District of Columbia (1971).* This court case expanded the right to education to all children with disabilities and ordered that school systems develop due process procedures for parents and comprehensive plans for identification, assessment, and placement of students with disabilities. This case laid the groundwork for Public Law 94-142, passed in 1975.
2. *Public Law 93-112 (Rehabilitation Act of 1973).* This piece of legislation focused on three key issues: provision of services for persons with severe disabilities, an emphasis on research and training, and delineation of special responsibilities of the federal government. The most significant parts of this law are contained in Sections 503 and 504, which require affirmative action toward persons with disabilities by employers and administrators of any programs receiving federal funds. The latter phrase pertains to colleges and universities receiving federal funds, thereby extending certain rights to college students with disabilities.
3. *Public Law 94-142 (Education for All Handicapped Children Act, 1975).* This law has guided the direction of special education since its passage in 1975. Its most basic provision was that all children with disabilities between the ages of 5 and 18 inclusive must be provided a free, appropriate public education. An important requirement of the law was a multidisciplinary planning process culminating in the individual education plan, the IEP, which is a blueprint for each student's educational goals and services.

In summary, the period beginning in 1960 was most productive for educators of children with emotional and behavioral disorders. Research became more definitive, and instructional and management methods were better defined. These advances were reflected in highly successful model programs and more sophisticated literature. In the 1970s, litigation and legislation designed to procure and protect the rights of individuals with disabilities became powerful enough to direct the course of special education through the following decades. A summary of the milestones in the development of services for students with emotional and behavioral disorders during the 20th century is shown in Table 2.1.

TABLE 2.1 20th-Century Milestones in the Development of Services for Students with Behavioral Disorders

	Events		Model Programs		Publications	
Early 1900s	1909	National Committee for Mental Hygiene	1931	Children's psychiatric hospital established in Rhode Island	1908	Beers publishes *A Mind That Found Itself*
	1922	Council for Exceptional Children			1928	Wickman surveys teachers' attitudes toward problem behaviors
	1924	American Orthopsychiatric Association				
	1930	White House Conference on Child Health and Protection				
Mid-1900s			1945	Bettelheim's Orthogenic School (Chicago)	1943–1954	Kanner, Mahler, and Bender attempt to define and classify severe emotional disorders
			1946	New York City's "600" Schools		
			1946	Redl and Wineman's Pioneer House (Detroit, MI)		
			1953	Fenichel's League School (New York City)		
1960s to 1999	1964	Council for Children with Behavioral Disorders	1960	Hobbs's Re-ED schools (Nashville, TN, and Durham, NC)	1961	Cruickshank and colleagues publish *A Teaching Method for Brain-Injured and Hyperactive Children*
	1965	National Society for Autistic Children	1962	Haring and Phillips's public school ED classrooms (Arlington, VA)	1962	Bower and Lambert publish *A Process for In-School Screening of Children with Emotional Handicaps*
	1971	*Mills v. Board of Education of D.C.*	1964	Hewett's Engineered Classroom (Santa Monica, CA)	1965	Long, Morse, and Newman publish *Conflict in the Classroom*
	1973	P.L. 93-112 *(Rehabilitation Act of 1973)*	1969	OSEP funded Regional Intervention Programs (RIP) to target young children with challenging behaviors	1970s	Successful instructional techniques reported with autistic children by Foxx, Kozloff, Lovaas, and others
	1975	P.L. 94-142 *(Education for All Handicapped Children Act)*	1984	NIMH offers CASSP grants to states to develop service delivery models	1989	Knitzer et al. publish *At the Schoolhouse Door*
	1983	P.L. 98-199 (EHA Amendments)	1997	OSEP funded Center for Effective Collaboration and Practice (CECP)	1993	NMHA publishes *All Systems Failure*
	1987	P.L. 99-457 (EHA Amendments)				
	1990	P.L. 101-476 *(Individuals with Disabilities Education Act, IDEA)*				
	1990	*Americans with Disabilities Act* (ADA)				

	1997 P.L. 105-17 *(IDEA Amendments of 1997)* 1999 Surgeon General's Conference on Children's Mental Health		1994 OSEP publishes *National Agenda for Achieving Better Results for Children and Youth with E/BD* 1995 HRSA develops Mental Health in schools program and funds two national training and technical assistance centers 1997 OSEP funds the *Special Education Elementary Longitudinal Study (SEELS)* 1998 CECP publishes *Early Warning, Timely Response: a Guide to Safe Schools*
2000 to present	2001 P.L. 107-110 (No Child Left Behind Act [NCLB]) 2001 President's Commission on Excellence in Special Education 2004 P.L. 108-446 (IDEA Amendments of 2004)	2000 OSEP funded the Center on Evidence-Based Practices: Young Children with Challenging Behavior (University of South Florida) 2000 OSEP funded the Center for Positive Behavioral Interventions (University of Oregon) 2003 OSEP funded the Centers for Implementing K–3 Behavior and Reading Intervention (Nebraska, Texas, Oregon, North Carolina, Kansas) 2001 OSEP funded the National Center for Students with Intensive Social, Emotional and Behavioral Needs (REACH) 2002 Center on Education, Disability and Juvenile Justice (EDJJ) partnership is formed	2001 U.S. Public Health Service publishes *Mental Health: A Report of the Surgeon General* 2001 *National Longitudinal Transition Sudy—2 (NLTS2)* is initiated 2001 NIH Blueprint for Change: Research on Child and Adolescent Mental Health is published 2002 President's Commission's Report: *A New Era: Revitalizing Special Education for Children and Their Families* is published

The 1980s and 1990s

Political Climate and Legislation

Periodically, P.L. 94-142 undergoes amendment and reauthorization. The first of these processes, in 1983, resulted in P.L. 98-199, which left the original law essentially intact and added services for the transition of secondary students from school to work. The second amendment process (P.L. 99-457), in 1987, expanded provision of special education services to infants and toddlers and mandated services to preschool-age children with disabilities. In 1990, P.L. 101-476 extended the idea of a participatory planning process to the system level. Subsequently, the Office of Special Education Programs was mandated to develop a national agenda to focus attention on achieving better outcomes for children and youth with emotional and behavioral disorders (Osher, Osher, & Smith, 1994). Additionally, two new disability categories were added, autism and traumatic brain injury, and regulations pertaining to newly mandated transition services were specified.

The most significant, and contentious, amendments to Public Law 94-142 to date were passed in June 1997 as Public Law 105-17 (the Individuals with Disabilities Education Act [IDEA] Amendments of 1997). The deliberations for these amendments were in response to a general backlash against special education and general concerns about cost and protections offered students with behavior problems. Special education advocacy efforts sought more funding for special education, increased research, inclusive practices, parent involvement, earlier intervention efforts, and more inclusive state assessment practices. Generally, Congressional lawmakers supported this legislation but the area of most contention pertained to discipline procedures. School administrators and lawmakers concerned about school violence resulting from several tragic school shootings wanted to be able to exclude students who were disruptive (a distinguishing characteristic of the EBD population). Special education advocates were concerned that students with emotional and behavioral disorders would be denied a free appropriate public education by virtue of their disability.

Fortunately, the 1997 law resulted in a stronger role for parents, greater access to a general education curriculum, reduced paperwork requirements, increased attention to disproportionate student populations, and cooperative teams (Yell & Shriner, 1997). However, the provisions most affecting students with emotional and behavioral disorders were those regarding discipline for students who threaten safe and orderly school environments (Conroy, Clark, Gable, & Fox, 1999; Johns, Guetzloe, & Yell, 1999). The discipline provisions mandated significant changes and continued to be debated even after the amendments were signed into law. Table 2.2 lists the discipline procedures added in the 1997 amendments. Note that the law specified instances when a special education student could be removed from school for disciplinary reasons and/or placed in an interim alternative educational placement. At the same time, the student's guarantee to a free, appropriate education was preserved. Another interesting aspect of the law was the addition of a requirement for behavioral assessment (specifically functional behavioral assessment [FBA]) and for behavior intervention plans (BIPs). Both FBAs and behavior planning will be discussed further in Chapter 7.

Although these controversial amendments were passed in June 1997, not until March 1999 were the final regulations published. The 2-year delay was primarily a result of contin-

Table 2.2 Summary of Discipline Procedures from P.L. 105-17, the Individuals with Disabilities Education Act Amendments of 1997

I. Removal from School:

A. Special education students may be removed from school for misconduct for up to ten school days for each episode as long as it does not constitute a pattern.

B. Special education students who are removed for more than ten school days in a year must continue to receive a free, appropriate public education.

C. A special education student may be removed from school for disciplinary reasons without continuation of services if (1) the exclusion does not exceed ten consecutive days or constitute a change in placement and (2) a non-disabled child who engaged in that behavior would receive the same consequence.

D. A special education student involved with drugs, possessing a weapon in school, or engaging in behavior that could harm self or others may be disciplined as non-disabled students are disciplined except that s/he must continue to receive educational services (usually in an Interim Alternative Education Setting, IAES).

E. If, however, *the behavior is a manifestation of the disability,* then for drugs, weapons, and injury to self or others, the student may be removed to an IAES for up to 45 school days. The IEP must be reviewed, a functional behavioral assessment conducted, and a behavioral intervention plan implemented. After 45 days, the student returns to his home school unless the parents and school personnel agree otherwise.

II. Manifestation Determination

The IEP team determines if a behavior is related to the disability by reviewing the appropriateness of the IEP, determining if the student can understand the impact of behavior and be able to control the behavior, and determining if the IEP had been implemented.

III. Parental Appeal

Parents may appeal removal decisions. During the appeal process, the student remains in the current placement if no drugs or weapons were involved unless the hearing officer rules that injury is likely.

ued attempts by some lawmakers to make it easier for school personnel to exclude and segregate students with behavior problems and to reduce the ever-increasing paperwork load (e.g., Sack, 1999). There was also an attempt to eliminate educational benefits to students with disabilities who were in prison. The contention surrounding the fourth amendments to IDEA caused great concern for those in the field of emotional and behavioral disorders. The apparent mood of intolerance toward children and youth displaying disruptive behavior highlighted the need for continual advocacy and legal protection.

Another significant piece of legislation, the Americans with Disabilities Act (ADA), was passed in 1990 and took effect in 1992. The ADA prohibits private employers and state and local governments from discriminating against qualified individuals with disabilities in hiring, firing, advancement, and other conditions related to employment. The ADA's four main goals—equality of opportunity, full participation, independent living, and economic self-sufficiency—have resulted in a raised awareness of disability issues in general. In 2006, 50 million Americans were thought to have disabilities (ED Review, 2006). ADA has implications for all of these individuals with disabilities, including those with EBD, as they seek independent living and employment in a competitive job market. In addition to landmark legislation, the 1980s and 1990s were marked by continuing efforts to document our nationwide status in educating students with EBD and the emergence of interagency collaboration as a service delivery model for these students.

2000 to the Present

Political Climate and Legislation

With the emergence of a new millennium and the election of a new President came a renewed effort to reform public education by raising academic standards and ushering in the age of accountability. One of the most sweeping educational reform efforts in a generation was based on the premise that *all* children in the United States, including those with disabilities, can and should demonstrate proficiency in ever higher academic standards, this in response to international test scores showing American children lagging behind other nations, particularly in literacy, math, and science (National Center for Educational Statistics, 1999). The most contentious component of this reform effort mandated that individual schools, school districts, and states be held accountable for ensuring that *all* students meet grade level core academic standards and if standards were not met, negative consequences would follow.

No Child Left Behind Act The 2001 reauthorization of the Elementary and Secondary Education Act, known as the *No Child Left Behind Act* (NCLB Act; P.L. 107-110), has had a major influence on the way that schools in the United States do business and, subsequently, on the major tenets of the IDEA. The NCLB Act is based on several major principles:

1. Increased accountability of states, local school districts, and individual schools through a grading system based on annual student performance progress and other indicators.
2. Increased choices for parents and students from disadvantaged backgrounds regarding where they can attend school and what supplemental assistance is available for ensuring high academic performance.
3. Flexible federal funding to states and local districts allowing combinations of federal grant funds.
4. The Reading First Initiative supported by federal investment in scientifically based reading instruction programs in early grades.
5. The combination of existing federal programs to support NCLB.
6. Strengthened teacher qualifications through a mandate to place a highly qualified teacher in every classroom by school year 2006–2007.
7. Confirmation of adequate yearly progress (AYP) for each student, including SPED students, through regularly administered standardized tests developed by each state and validated by sample student performance on the National Assessment of Educational Progress (NAEP).

8. Promotion of English proficiency for growing numbers of limited English proficient (LEP) students.

The main goal of the NCLB Act was to have all students in the United States demonstrate proficiency in academic core subjects no later than the 2013–2014 school year. This mandate included students with disabilities who most often are initially referred to special education because they are failing in the core academic curriculum. States, under NCLB, must assess 95 percent of students with disabilities on the same grade level assessments as those given to students without disabilities. One percent of SPED students, presumably those with severe cognitive delays, could be exempted from this testing, but must be assessed with alternative assessment procedures. The thinking was that students with disabilities had the same right to be included in state-mandated standards, assessments, and accountability systems as other students so that we would know how well they were performing and whether or not public schools were serving their needs (Olson, 2004).

Not only must students with disabilities be regularly assessed in grade level core academic subjects, but schools, school districts, and states are graded as to how well the students perform annually (i.e., AYP). State standardized test data were required to be disaggregated for the following groups: SPED students, African American students, Hispanic students, white students, economically disadvantaged students, and LEP, students. Schools not meeting standards for each group were to be punished through low ratings, and possible closure (e.g., Bush & Bloomberg, 2006; Hollingsworth, 2006; Riley & Paine, 2006). Attendance, graduation, and participation rates were also AYP indicators.

"The contentious 'No Child' law" (Cuban, 2004) has been severely criticized by school personnel, parents, politicians, governors, policymakers, and professional organizations due to the federal intrusiveness, lack of funding, unreasonable and costly testing mandates, and punitive nature (CEC, 2005). Special Education, in particular, has been cause for concern. Although most agreed with the law's goals and wanted to improve SPED student performance and school accountability, testing students with disabilities who must have demonstrated *inadequate* educational progress in order to receive SPED services in the first place, at grade levels instead of instructional levels, seemed, to many, unreasonable and often inappropriate. In response, some states filed lawsuits against the U.S. Department of Education, and some states discussed dropping federal funds so as not to have to comply with NCLB mandates (Cavanagh, 2004; CEC, 2005; Green, 2006). Other states were fined large sums for exempting more than the desired number of SPED students from grade-level standardized tests, instead using alternative assessments that matched their instructional levels (e.g., Gest, 2005; Hollingsworth, 2006). Furthermore, a recent Gallup Poll (Green, 2006) found that 58 percent of Americans believe that the NCLB Act has had no effect on schools or has actually harmed schools, most disagreeing with the unreasonable methods for compliance. Similarly, a National Education Association Survey found that 48 percent of its members believe the act has hurt schools (30% thought it has helped) (Green, 2006).

The NCLB mandates have resulted in many changes in programming for SPED students, including those with EBD. SPED students now are typically prescribed, as a matter of policy instead of individualized deliberations, a rigorous academic educational plan with the same standards as students without disabilities (Samuels, 2006). Concern focuses on the fact that standardizing curricular requirements, rather than individually determining what students need to learn, may result in SPED students learning fewer functional skills related to what they need for coping with environmental demands. Additionally, the effect of NCLB has been that more SPED students are spending more of their time in general education classrooms in order to receive academic instruction. Unfortunately, many general education teachers feel unprepared for this task (Samuels, 2006), and it is felt that placing students where they initially failed may not be good practice unless proper supports are also put into place (Kauffman, Mantz, & McCullough, 2002; Schumaker et al., 2002). In any case, the NCLB Act had a powerful impact on the 2004 reauthorization of IDEA.

President's Commission on Excellence in Special Education. In October 2001, President George W. Bush, as part of his education reform agenda appointed a commission to evaluate SPED programming in light of the NCLB goals. Its report, *A New Era: Revitalizing Special Education for Children and Their Families,* was issued in July 2002 (Devore & Zionts, 2003). This report essentially supported the notion that special education needed radical reform and must be moved to a culture of higher academic standards and accountability for results. It further recommended closing the achievement gap between special education students and their peers, improving general education, removing bureaucracy and regulations that prevent closing the gap, embracing a model of prevention of academic problems rather than failure, improving referral and identification practices, addressing disproportional representation of minorities in special education, and promoting more placement in general education classrooms. Some took issue with this report seen as devaluing special education and presenting the current system as outmoded, biased, and ineffective (Kauffman, 2003). Kauffman (2003) laments that recommendations in this report, not founded in logic and reality, did not appear to be in the best interest of students with disabilities, particularly those with EBD.

2004 IDEA Reauthorization. Within the context of this massive educational reform and criticism of special education by the President's Commission, the goal for the reauthorization of the IDEA was primarily to align it with the NCLB Act. This was not an easy task since the two federal laws seemed to conflict, one mandating standard academic curriculum-driven programming and the other mandating child-driven individualized programming. After 3 years of negotiations, the IDEA reauthorization was passed by Congress on November 19, 2004, and signed into law on December 3, 2004. Called IDEA 2004, the result is a mandate to set high academic standards for all students with disabilities and to ensure a quality education (No Child Left Behind, 2006). The notion of determining standards for individual students based on individualized assessment appears to have been compromised by the NCLB agenda.

Unlike the 1997 reauthorization process where advocates were afraid that students would be excluded from educational services for disciplinary reasons, the fear during the 2004 reauthorization was that special education students would be forced to be included in, perhaps, inappropriate programming for the sake of standardized test scores. The main provisions of IDEA 2004 pertained to:

1. Teacher quality
2. Flexibility in methods of diagnosing students with learning disabilities

3. Allowance for SPED funds to be used in general education to prevent SPED referrals
4. Demonstration programs for multiyear IEPs
5. Paperwork reduction and revised IEPs
6. Ambiguous changes to the 1997 discipline provisions. (CEC, 2004)

Because several of these components were cause for debate, the Office of Special Education and Rehabilitation Services (OSERS) invited public comment before drawing up the final regulations for the law. In spring 2005, OSERS conducted public meetings across the country. In June 2005 a draft of the new regulations was published. A second series of public meetings were held and the final regulations were published on August 3, 2006, with few substantive changes (CEC pleased. . . , 2006).

The mandates from both NCLB and IDEA 2004 that will most likely impact students with EBD have to do with (1) the regulations regarding "highly qualified" teachers, (2) the push to include SPED students in the general education curriculum, (3) the grade-level testing required to document AYP, and (4) the revised discipline provisions (CEC, 2004; Mooney & Gunter, 2004). The highly qualified (HQ) regulations essentially require SPED teachers to demonstrate proficiency in each core academic subject (math, English, computer literacy, history, reading, civics, government, geography, etc.) that they teach. Proficiency is measured primarily with certification exams for each content area administered by states. The idea that teachers should be qualified to teach the curriculum is well accepted, however, for teachers who teach multiple subjects, such as many teachers of students with EBD, obtaining multiple certifications does not seem feasible. Furthermore, there is a severe shortage of SPED teachers in general, many are prepared through alternative certification programs, and SPED teacher retention, especially for those teaching students with EBD, is poor (George, George, Gersten, & Grosenick, 1995). Teacher recruitment, under the circumstances, may suffer (Mooney & Gunter, 2004).

Another ramification of the highly qualified teacher issue pertains to the schools' reaction when qualified teachers cannot be found. Many students with EBD are being placed into general education classrooms with little support, particularly at the secondary level where teachers are qualified to teach the core subject, not based on what the students need but based on the effort to meet the HQ provision (Shumaker et al., 2002). We can only speculate about what effect that will have on students who presumably were referred to special education by those very teachers. Inclusion models are being promoted in order to bypass the HQ requirements for SPED teachers by making general education teachers the teacher of record. Unfortunately, in a profession already suffering from high turnover (George et al., 1995), it is feared that many SPED teachers might simply become glorified tutors and want to leave the profession.

The push to have all students master high academic standards regardless of disability has resulted in an effort to better instruct SPED students in academics and to find scientifically based practices that improve instructional outcomes (Mooney & Gunter, 2004). However, there are questions about whether accessing the general education curriculum is indeed "appropriate education" in all instances and whether we have compromised the individualized basis of IDEA (Kauffman et al., 2002). The NCLB requirement that all students, SPED students included, must be tested with grade-level academic tests is particularly troublesome. The impact of forcing students who might be several grade levels behind in school to take tests they have no hope of passing is yet to be determined and may actually be harmful (e.g., Mills-Faraudo, 2006; Wagner et al., 2006). The impact of grading schools based on these students' performance has also not been established; but might we speculate that students with EBD who are behind academically and forced back into general education classes may not find favor with teachers and administrators alike (e.g., "Don't Blame . . . , 2006; Kauffman et al., 2002)?

Finally, the discipline provisions in IDEA allow school personnel on a "case-by-case basis" to consider unique circumstances when determining a change of placement for a student who violates the code of student conduct (CEC, 2004). "Unique circumstances" have not been defined and could open the door for students to be more easily placed in interim alternative placements. Additionally, school officials can now place students in interim alternative placement for up to 45 school days, rather than 45 days. Fortunately, the discipline provisions were not greatly modified to exclude students, which had been the fear in 1997.

One interesting component of the NCLB Act and the IDEA 2004 is a distinct preference for "education programs grounded in scientifically based research" (U.S. Department of Education, 2003, p. 29) in order to promote high standards for program validation and adoption. Related funding has been restricted to such validated programs. As a result, Mooney and Gunter (2004) challenge those in the field of EBD to develop a repertoire of scientifically based treatments for students with EBD, to emphasize reading, math, and science instruction, and to consider long-term interventions to impact student progress over time. At the time of this writing, effects of general education reform on SPED students, particularly those with EBD, has not been fully established. As Brigham, Gustashaw, Wiley, and Brigham (2004) write, "If the data suggest that the NCLB (and IDEA) changes make general education a more productive and supportive place for students with EBD, special educators should certainly play in the orchestra. If not, it may be time to reconsider 'solo projects' and resurrect the dedicated service delivery models that have faded in recent years. In either case, we should let the data, rather than our biases, guide our actions" (p. 308).

Status of Services for Students with EBD

Since the 1980s several publications have been produced to survey and summarize the status of services for students with EBD. A classic study by Knitzer, Steinberg, and Fleisch (1989) *At the Schoolhouse Door: An Examination of Programs and Policies for Children with Behavioral and Emotional Problems,* was based on the assumption that it is difficult to know what to change until we know what's wrong; this study was a comprehensive attempt to collect national data on the current status of services and gaps in services to these children. Data were collected through national surveys to special education and mental health agencies, site visits to programs in several states, phone surveys to staff of programs, and a survey of parents of children with emotional and behavioral disorders. The report became a seminal work for beginning systems changes in services delivery. Knitzer and colleagues concluded their report with 10 major recommendations that require local, state, and federal involvement in policy changes. Chief among these recommendations were the following:

1. A federal mandate (similar to IDEA) for mental health agencies to provide services.
2. Designation, in each student's individual education plan, of a lead agency responsible for coordinating services.
3. Development of a full continuum of educational and mental health services.

Some states and regions to date have incorporated partnerships between mental health agencies and schools to enhance services to students with EBD (Robbins & Armstrong, 2005; Wagner et al., 2006), but there still exists a general lack of mental health services delivered directly to students with EBD. The good news is that research supports school-based mental health models (Atkins, Frazier, & Abdul-Adil, 2003; Weiss, Harris, & Catron, 2003) and innovative funding strategies for sustainability of such programs are being developed (Huang et al., 2005).

Continuing the effort to gather data, in 1993 the National Mental Health Association, in conjunction with the Federation of Families for Children's Mental Health, published a two-volume report, *All Systems Failure: An Examination of the Results of Neglecting the Needs of Children with Serious Emotional Disturbance* (Koyanagi & Gaines, 1993). The purpose of this report was to draw attention to "the abysmal record of failure" (p. 1) by mental health and educational agencies to meet the needs of children and youth with serious emotional disturbance. Soon thereafter, a document was published reiterating the previously published issues and recommending comprehensive, coordinated, school-linked services for students with EBD as the preferred treatment model (McLaughlin, Leone, Warren, & Schofield, 1994). This document presented a "new vision for a system of coordinated, flexible services to meet the needs of students and families" (p. 1).

As a function of research advances in neurosciences, genetics, behavioral sciences, and social sciences, the U.S. Department of Health and Human Services in 1999 published a landmark document, *Mental Health: A Report of the Surgeon General,* that greatly raised public awareness of mental health issues (National Institutes of Health, 2001). This report was quickly followed by a *Report of the Surgeon General's Conference on Children's Mental Health: A National Action Agenda* in 2000. The 2000 report was a collaborative effort of the departments of Education, Justice, and Health and Human Services and listed several areas of concern including the need for more training for doctors, teachers, and school counselors in early warning signs; better information on effective treatments; more emphasis on prevention; better coordination between programs; and a sustained public effort to dispel the stigma that prevents families from seeking treatment. The report outlined several goals reiterating those put forth by Knitzer et al. in 1989:

1. To promote public awareness of children's mental health issues and reduce the stigma associated with mental illness.
2. To continue to develop, disseminate, and implement scientifically proven prevention and treatment services.
3. To improve the assessment and recognition of mental health needs in children.
4. To eliminate racial/ethnic and socioeconomic disparities in access to healthcare.
5. To improve the infrastructure for children's mental health services.
6. To increase access to and coordination of quality mental healthcare services.
7. To train providers to recognize and manage mental health issues.
8. To monitor the access to and coordination of quality mental healthcare services.

Building on these reports, the National Institutes of Health published *Blueprint for Change: Research on Child and Adolescent Mental Health* in 2001, citing that one in 10 children suffered from mental illness severe enough to result in significant functional impairment. The issues addressed in this report concerned the fact that children and their families were still not receiving adequate treatment and that research regarding the efficacy of various treatments was lacking. The report outlines current research regarding biophysical etiologies, psychopharmacological treatments, and treatment efficacy studies. The recommendations from this report fell into three broad areas: (1) interdisciplinary research *development* in child and adolescent mental health; (2) interdisciplinary research *training* in child and adolescent mental health; and (3) program development in neuroscience, behavioral science, prevention, psychosocial interventions, psychopharmacology, and combined treatment approaches.

More recently, two longitudinal studies, available on the World Wide Web, provide information regarding the status of students with EBD. As part of the 1997 IDEA, the Office of Special Education Programs funded the *Special Education Elementary Longitudinal Study (SEELS)* to examine the status of school-age SPED students (Wagner, Kutash, Duchnowski, & Epstein, 2005). The SEELS study is, at the time of publication, documenting the school experiences of a national sample of students as they move from elementary to middle school and from middle to high school from 2000–2006. Designed to assess student changes over time, data are not analyzed for any single point in time. Data were collected through school staff and parent interviews, direct assessment, and through direct observation.

A second study, the *National Longitudinal Transition Study—2 (NLTS2)*, is being funded by the U.S. Department of Education for the purpose of documenting information about a national sample of students who were 13 to 16 years of age in 2000 as they move from secondary school into adult roles (Wagner, Kutash, et al., 2005). The focus of the NLTS2 is to obtain information about high school coursework, extracurricular activities, academic performance, postsecondary education and training, employment, independent living, and community participation of SPED students (*www.nlts2.org*). In this study about 6,000 parents (70% of respondents) completed phone interviews and 3,000 youth were interviewed. The data from both of these studies pertaining to students with EBD are described in several journal articles (Wagner, Kutush, Ducknowski, and Epstein, 2005; Wagner, Kutush, Ducknowski, Epstein, and Sumi, 2005; Wagner et al., 2006).

Conclusions from these studies for students with EBD reflect what was written in the 1980s and 1990s while incorporating the impact of the NCLB Act and IDEA 2004. The studies confirmed that students with EBD manifest both emotional and academic characteristics that impede their learning and that ineffective school programs can and do create formidable barriers for these students (Wagner et al., 2006). Large schools, particularly high schools, with large numbers of students with disabilities may adversely affect school attendance; untrained general and special education teachers who do not use research-based practices undermine access to and mastery of the general education curriculum, a lack of mental health services for students with EBD and their families perpetuate problems across settings and time, and overly punitive and exclusionary discipline systems, as opposed to positive behavior management techniques, result in more intensive behavior challenges. Wagner, Kutash, Duchnowski, Epstein & Sumi (2005) recommend a much closer partnership between school and mental health systems and professionals in all schools building on earlier reports' recommendations.

Model Programs

During the past 15 years, the Office of Special Education Programs (OSEP) has continued to fund several model programs and centers addressing the needs of children at risk for or with emotional and behavioral disorders (Bradley, Henderson, & Monfore, 2004). Building on the RIP programs, the Center for Evidenced-Based Practice: Young Children with Challenging Behaviors at the University of South Florida (*http://challengingbehavior.fmhi .usf.edu*) completed a series of research syntheses focused on very young children. Their purpose is to raise awareness, to implement positive evidenced-based practices, and to create a database of such practices for dissemination purposes. Similarly, the Center for Positive Behavioral Interventions and Supports (PBIS) at the University of Oregon (*www .pbis.org*) provides technical assistance to states, school districts, and schools pertaining to school- and classwide support systems that prevent problem behaviors throughout the school. A data-driven system, PBIS presumes that behavior is a function of the context in which it happens and therefore will change when the context is altered. Further discussion of PBIS and its ramifications for students with EBD will be discussed in Chapters 7 and 12.

Combining reading and behavior supports, OSEP funded six Centers for Implementing K–3 Behavior and Reading Interventions. The centers consist of two early behavior research centers, two early reading centers, and two combination centers in Oregon, Kansas, North Carolina, Texas, and Nebraska. The reading and behavior models are based on a three-tiered concept of schoolwide systems, initiated by the Center on PBIS, that provide ever more intensive interventions to the most needy students. The National Center for Students with Intensive Social, Emotional and Behavioral Needs (REACH) (*http://www .state.ky.us/agencies/behave/bi/intensive.html*) in Kentucky primarily focuses on educating students with the most intensive problem behaviors. Finally, OSEP has also supported the Center on Education, Disability and Juvenile Justice (EDJJ) (*http://www.edjj.org/*) to address growing numbers of children with disabilities who might be involved with the juvenile justice system. This Center provides research and technical assistance to schools and community agencies.

Interagency Collaboration

Beginning in the 1990s subsequent to the Knitzer et al. (1989) and Koyanagi & Gaines (1993) reports, special educators witnessed a move toward interagency collaboration. A technical assistance program, CASSP (Child and Adolescent Service System Program), was instrumental in the adoption of interagency collaboration models. Sponsored by the National Institute of Mental Health in 1984, CASSP grants were available to states interested in developing models for effective services delivery to these children and their families. CASSP promoted itself as a philosophy because its specifics varied from locale to locale, depending on resources. The core values of the philosophy were that services should be child centered and community based, meaning that the needs of the child should dictate the mix of services to be delivered, and that services should be provided at the community level. A multiagency approach was required to provide the recommended range of services. To assist with the development and implementation of CASSP programs, the National Technical Assistance Center at Georgetown University and two Research and Training

Centers at The University of South Florida and Portland State University were formed and funded. CASSP is described more fully and an example of a CASSP model is given in Chapter 8 under "Systems Changes."

Additionally, as mentioned in Chapter 1, in 1991, an interagency coalition of professionals met for the purpose of developing a new definition under IDEA for students with emotional and behavioral disorders (Forness & Knitzer, 1992). Although the Mental Health and Special Education Coalition was not successful in revising the definition, the effort promoted advocacy and scholarly discussions. In 1994, the Office of Special Education Programs (OSEP) published the *National Agenda for Achieving Better Results for Children and Youth with Serious Emotional Disturbance* (Osher, Osher, & Smith, 1994). This agenda, promoting a collaborative model, consisted of the following seven connected strategic targets that would promote successful outcomes for children and youth with serious emotional disturbance.

1. Expand positive learning opportunities and results: To provide engaging, useful, and positive learning opportunities that are results driven based on a child's needs.
2. Strengthen school and community capacity: To assist schools and communities to serve students with EBD in the least restrictive environment.
3. Value and address diversity: To encourage culturally sensitive exchanges among families, professionals, students, and communities.
4. Collaborate with families: To include families in a collaborative process of implementing family-focused educational services.
5. Promote appropriate assessment: To ensure assessment as an integral component of identification, design, and service delivery to students with EBD.
6. Provide ongoing skill development and support: To promote the attainment of knowledge, understanding, and sensitivity among service providers.
7. Create comprehensive and collaborative systems, known as systems of care: To promote systems change for the purpose of developing coherent child-centered services.

An update of outcomes and programs based on the CASSP model, or Systems of Care, was published in 2005 (Epstein, Kutash, & Duchnowski, 2005). These authors report that more than 60 communities across the country have received funding to establish Systems of Care, affecting more than 60,000 children and their families. They also write that program emphasis is now on evidenced-based practices and rigorous program evaluations.

In 1995 the U.S. Health Resources and Services Administration (HRSA) (Maternal and Child Health Bureau) established the Mental Health in Schools Program to increase the capacity of policy makers, administrators, school personnel, primary care health providers, mental health specialists, agency staff, consumers and other stakeholders for addressing psychosocial and mental health concerns of children and youth. Two national training and technical assistance centers were funded at UCLA and the University of Maryland. The guiding goals for these centers included (1) creating an accurate perception of mental health, (2) enhancing the roles of schools, communities and homes, (3) confronting equity issues in terms of services, (4) addressing the fragmentation of policies, organizations, and practices, and (5) addressing the challenges of evidence-based strategies. At UCLA, the Center for Mental Health in Schools has initiated a process to establish initiative networks in every state through summits, networks, and core advisors (Center for Mental Health in Schools, 2006).

Finally, building on the notion of collaboration, OSEP funded the Center for Effective Collaboration and Practice (CECP) in 1997. The purpose of the CECP was to address the gap between issues and the actual practice of serving children and youth with EBD. CECP, utilizing the national agenda, developed four objectives: (1) to facilitate and expand effective interagency collaboration, (2) to identify and develop useful and usable information, (3) to foster the exchange of such information, and (4) to evaluate the Center's activities. The CECP has become a major influence in obtaining, consolidating, and disseminating important information to a large constituency on behalf of children and youth with EBD.

One example of CECP's influence was a collaborative effort with the U.S. Departments of Education and Justice to prepare an early warning guide for schools to address school violence. This guide, *Early Warning, Timely Response: A Guide to Safe Schools* (Dwyer, Osher, & Warger, 1998), was nationally distributed free of charge. The guide emphasized that students with severe behavior problems would benefit from coordinated service systems that are family- and child-driven and that provide a wide array of instructional and treatment approaches. The guide further emphasized that punitive techniques, as a singular approach to school violence, had not been found to be effective for violence prevention nor for treating students with EBD. More details about the contents of this guide can be found in Chapter 12 under "Youth Violence." If nothing else, efforts that began in the 1990s and continue today have resulted in more stakeholders working together for the treatment of children and youth at risk for and manifesting emotional and behavioral disorders. At the same time, goals for the widespread provision of mental health services to students with EBD in the schools have yet to be realized.

Conclusions

Historically, deviance has always been defined by its societal context. The routine treatment of persons who were socially or behaviorally deviant in previous centuries is appalling to us today. However, a historical perspective of such treatment gives us an appreciation not only of the reformers who have helped shape humane treatment of individuals with emotional and behavioral disorders, but also of the strides that have been made in services for this population over the past 50 years. Although changes of this magnitude may occur slowly—perhaps imperceptibly—it is important to remember that progress continues in working with students with emotional and behavioral disorders and that advocacy will most likely always be necessary.

KEY POINTS

1. Superstitious beliefs about deviant behavior have been created by humans throughout history to give themselves a sense of control over the environment.
2. Not until the 1700s were children recognized as individuals with rights, and prior to 1800, few services for children with emotional disorders existed.

3. The philosophy of humane treatment for persons with mental illness was promoted by Pinel in Europe and by Rush in America in the early 1800s.

4. Reformers such as Dorothea Dix and Samuel Gridley Howe were instrumental in attaining rights and better treatment for individuals with mental retardation and mental illness in the 1800s.

5. The enactment by states of compulsory school attendance laws by the turn of the century forced educators to deal with all categories of less able children.

6. In the early part of the 20th century, the autobiography of Clifford Beers and the founding of the National Committee for Mental Hygiene had a profound influence on public awareness of mental health.

7. Although services for children with emotional/behavioral disorders lagged behind services for other categories of exceptionality, by the middle of the 20th century a number of model programs were being established.

8. In the 1970s, legislation and litigation established the right to education for all children with disabilities, ushering in a new era of special programming backed by federal mandates and funding.

9. In the 1980s and 1990s, much attention was directed toward (a) determining the current gaps in services nationwide, and (b) establishing working interagency partnerships to fill these gaps.

10. At the turn of the century, attention turned to school accountability for ensuring that *all* children master ever higher academic standards and that their teachers are highly qualified to teach all subject matter.

HOMEWORK QUESTIONS

1. In no more than four paragraphs, discuss how the current political climate has affected children with emotional and behavioral disorders in the United States.

2. After browsing the NCLB website provided in the Additional Readings and Resources section, debate both sides of the Highly Qualified Teacher mandate as it pertains to students with EBD using a 1-page single-spaced dialog. For example:

   HENRY: "I think it's a good thing that teachers know what they are supposed to be teaching."

   EVE: "But some teachers are required to teach many subjects. How can they be highly qualified in all of them?"

3. Briefly compare and contrast treatment of students with EBD 30 years ago and today in terms of economic, political, and social influences.

4. Briefly discuss the challenges that might impede collaborative efforts between mental health and education agencies in services to children with mental illness.

5. Find several definitions of "evidenced-based" or "research-based" practices. What do you think would make a practice "evidenced-based"?

6. With several current special education journal articles as references, list as many evidenced-based educational practices as you can on one single-spaced page. Cite a reference next to each one. Does each meet the criteria you found in #5?

7. Describe your own disposition toward deviance. Where would you draw the line between deviance and normalcy? Is it a thin or thick line? Explain.

ADDITIONAL READINGS AND RESOURCES

A mind that found itself: by Clifford Beers, New York: Longmans, Green, 1908, for an autobiographical account of experiences with mental institutions in the early part of this century.

All systems failure: An examination of the results of neglecting the needs of children with serious emotional disturbance, by Chris Koyanagi and Sam Gaines, Alexandria, VA: National Mental Health Association, 1993, for a report to parents, advocates, and policymakers regarding the failure of mental health and educational agencies to adequately serve children and youth with serious emotional disturbance.

Conflict in the classroom (5th ed.), edited by Nicholas Long, William Morse, and Ruth Newman, Austin, TX: Pro-Ed, 1965, for a marvelous collection of readings on emotional disturbance that served as the only textbook for educators for several years.

Doing things differently; Issues and options for creating comprehensive school-linked services for children and youth with emotional or behavioral disorders, by Margaret McLaughlin, Peter Leone, Sandra Warren, and Patricia Schofield, College Park, MD: University of Maryland, in affiliation with Westat, Inc., 1994, for a review of issues related to serving students with emotional and behavioral disorders and preventing serious behavior problems in the schools.

Early warning, timely response: A guide to safe schools, by Kevin Dwyer, David Osher, and Cynthia Warger, Washington DC: U.S. Department of Education, 1998, for an example of a collaborative effort addressing school violence and recommending a systems approach to treatment.

Personal perspectives on emotional disturbance/emotional disorders, edited by Benjamin Brooks and David Sabatino, Austin, TX: Pro-Ed, 1995, for a book of readings about the history and the current status of educating children with emotional/behavioral disorders according to leaders in the field today.

Behavioral Disorders, 29(3), 2004, a special issue on critical issues and trends in the education of students with EBD, edited by Antonis Katsiyannis and Mitchel Yell, for an overview of the impact of current legislation on educational programming for students with EBD.

Systems of Care: Promising Practices in Children's Mental Health: The Role of Education in a System of Care, by Darren Woodruff et al., Washington, DC: CECP, American Institutes for Research, 1998, for an overview of model mental health and educational collaborations.

SRI International reports: *http://www.sri.com/policy/cehs/dispolicy/*, for studies regarding education and human services such as the National Early Intervention Longitudinal Study (NEILS), Special Education Elementary Longitudinal Study (SEELS), National Longitudinal Transition Study—2 (NLTS2), and National Behavior Research Coordination Center (NBRCC).

National Technical Assistance Center for Children's Mental Health: for information regarding CASSP programs. *http://gucchd.georgetown.edu/programs/ta_center/index.html.*

School Mental Health Project-UCLA Center for Mental Health in Schools, (*http://smhp.psych.ucla.edu/*) for information regarding policy and program analysis for the purpose of enhancing education's role in improving the emotional well-being of children and youth.

U.S. Department of Education: for information regarding the NCLB Act. *http://www.ed.gov/nclb/landing.jhtml.*

Office of Special Education Programs (OSEP): for information regarding IDEA and programs funded by this agency. *http://www.ed.gov/about/offices/list/osers/osep/index.html.*

CHAPTER

3 Identification and Assessment

Identifying Emotional and Behavioral Disorders
Procedures, Comorbidity, Guidelines

Assessment Strategies
Preferred, Instruments, Teams

Planning
Linking assessment to instruction, Multicultural considerations

QUESTIONS TO CONSIDER

- What are the five possible manifestations described in IDEA for identification of EBD?
- What other qualifiers must be assessed and met for classification of EBD?
- What tests or techniques are typically used to assess for EBD? What are the strengths and limitations of each of these techniques?
- What is the role of the special education teacher in identification and assessment of EBD?
- How does the assessment for EBD interface with the development of the individualized education plan?

Orientation

In Chapter 1 you learned about the difficulties inherent in defining emotional and behavioral disorders. Disagreement about terminology, a defective federal definition, confounding cultural, socioeconomic, and comorbidity factors, along with the nature of the disability itself, makes it a challenge to reliably describe and subsequently identify when a student has an emotional or behavioral disorder. At what point do negative emotional states and the associated behaviors become emotional/behavioral disorders? And when do these characteristics qualify a student to receive special education services? These questions lie at the heart of EBD identification and assessment. Assessment personnel are charged with the task of ensuring that all students who have such disorders receive necessary services while also ensuring that students who do not have an identifiable disability are not inappropriately placed in special education. Given the difficulties in defining EBD, identification and assessment become challenging tasks. Additionally, as you learned in Chapter 1, many school administrators are reluctant to have students with very disturbing behavior protected by the IDEA. Thus, assessment personnel may be encouraged to find ways to keep such students from qualifying for special education services. It is imperative that assessment personnel and assessment team members understand and commit to meeting the IDEA requirements for assessment. In this way, assessment errors will be avoided and all students who need special education will receive it.

Overview

In this chapter, you will learn about the criteria and the assessment procedures, tests, and techniques used to identify children with EBD for special education purposes. Assessment personnel such as school psychologists will typically lead this effort, but special education teachers can often play an important role. Certainly, the assessment findings will directly relate to educational planning, which is the teacher's domain. Therefore, it is important for teachers to understand the issues associated with identification, typical assessment procedures and strategies, and the role of the special education teacher in the identification process. You will also be acquainted with the link between comprehensive assessment data used to identify EBD and the development of educational plans.

Identifying Emotional and Behavioral Disorders

Because emotional and behavioral problems can significantly interfere with the acquisition of academic, social, and vocational skills, early identification of these problems is imperative. Before effective educational interventions can be developed, professionals must reach consensus on which students should be served through special education under the classification of emotional disturbance, or whatever label has been adopted by individual state departments of education. In this book, the label *emotional and behavioral disorders (EBD)* is used to refer to all labels pertaining to emotional disturbance as defined by the IDEA. Although federal regulations have provided some direction for definition and evaluation, the identification procedures for these students are complex. As you learned in Chapter 1, many factors—including (1) tolerance for behavior problems, (2) differences in theoretical models, (3) differences in terminology, and (4) presence of coexisting disorders—contribute to inconsistencies in the identification of EBD. Furthermore, selection of tests and techniques for identification and determination of educational need complicate the assessment process. As teachers, you should be knowledgeable regarding the basic criteria, procedures, and guidelines for identification of children requiring special education services for EBD. Awareness of your own personal and professional biases and how they could affect your role in the team process is also essential.

In the following section, the definition of emotional disturbance (ED) included in the IDEA and the specific procedures required to identify children with EBD are reviewed. Additional professional guidelines for identification and intervention are also explored.

Federal Law Definition

The federal definition of emotional disturbance was first specified in Public Law 94-142 and later in the 1997 Individuals with Disabilities Education Act (IDEA) and the 2004 Individuals with Disabilities Education Improvement Act (IDEIA). The definition, as discussed in Chapter 1 and stated below, has not changed substantially with these reauthorizations and continues to provoke debate.

> I. The term means a condition exhibiting one or more of the following characteristics over a long period of time and to a marked degree that adversely affects educational performance:
>
> A. An inability to learn that cannot be explained by intellectual, sensory or health factors;
>
> B. An inability to build or maintain satisfactory interpersonal relationships with peers and teachers;
>
> C. Inappropriate types of behavior or feelings under normal circumstances;
>
> D. A general pervasive mood of unhappiness or depression; or
>
> E. A tendency to develop physical symptoms or fears associated with personal or school problems.
>
> II. The term includes schizophrenia. The term does not apply to children who are socially maladjusted, unless it is determined that they have an emotional disturbance. [Code of Federal Regulation, Title 34, Section 300.7(b)(9)]

The federal law definition includes five main characteristics of emotional disturbance, identified in sections (A) through (E). As noted in the statement preceding these characteristics, an identified student must exhibit at least one, but may exhibit more, of these characteristics in order to be identified as emotionally disturbed. Cullinan and Sabornie (2004), in a study of the five eligibility characteristics among 1,210 secondary students with or without EBD, found that adolescents with EBD exceed adolescents without this diagnosis on the five characteristics, thus providing some validation of their usefulness. However, as observed by Merrell (2003), this definition, while appearing superficially objective, is actually considerably subjective. Furthermore, results from the Cullinan and Sabornie study revealed differential patterns of age, gender, and ethnicity on these five characteristics, suggesting more research is needed regarding the developmental and multicultural influences on the expression of these features of EBD. For example, these authors found that when examining middle schoolers and high schoolers with EBD, only middle school students had higher scores than non-EBD students on the characteristics of unhappiness/depression and physical symptoms or fears. They also noted category-by-gender patterns specific to each racial or ethnic group (European Americans, African American, and Hispanics). Furthermore, they found specific racial/ethnic group-by-category interactions, including the finding that European Americans exhibited greater physical symptoms or fears than African Americans, whereas Hispanics did not differ from either of the other two groups on this characteristic.

Even if one or more of the five characteristics is met, there are other qualifiers, as you learned in Chapter 1, inherent in this definition, including "over a long period of time," "to a marked degree," and "adversely affects educational performance." These qualifiers must also be considered before identifying a student as eligible for special education under the classification of EBD. Because all individuals may exhibit characteristics of emotional distress at some time in their lives, it is necessary to distinguish emotional disturbance that requires special education intervention from more transient negative emotional states, and these qualifiers represent an effort to make this distinction. The severity of emotional and behavioral problems must be such that they are persistent over time, exceed the norm for peers in terms of severity, and, as a result, negatively affect performance in school.

Each of these three qualifiers has provoked debate with respect to their meaning. Operationalization of duration, severity, and negative educational impact is not provided in federal law; therefore, it is up to the states and the professionals who identify students as EBD to interpret these characteristics and qualifiers and how to assess them. Therefore, across states, and even across individual school districts, guidelines and practices for identification may vary. While some states mandate specific assessment procedures, such as rating scales or behavioral observations, other states may require that a psychiatrist or other medical doctor evaluate the child before allowing classification (Merrell, 2003).

Also as you learned in Chapter 1, the specification in this definition that "socially maladjusted" children are not included unless they also have an emotional disturbance has also created confusion and debate, particularly since individuals with socially maladjusted behaviors typically have impaired relationships with peers and other adults, including teachers (one of the IDEA qualifiers). Individuals determined to be socially maladjusted, a term that is not concretely defined in the law, are excluded from eligibility as EBD unless they also exhibit at least one of the five main characteristics over a long period of time, to a marked degree, and with adverse effects on educational performance (Epstein, Cullinan, Ryser, & Pearson, 2002). Traditionally, the term *social maladjustment* has been used to describe a pattern of behavioral problems that are thought to be goal oriented, volitional, and often reinforced by a student's peer reference group (Merrell, 2003). However, the distinction between EBD and social maladjustment has remained problematic. It is important to remember that students who appear socially maladjusted may also be eligible for special education under the classification of EBD if they otherwise meet the criteria set out in the IDEA.

Procedural Requirements under IDEA

The basic elements required for eligibility as EBD for special education services have been presented in the IDEA definition. However, it is also important for teachers to understand that the law mandates that specific procedures be followed to ensure accuracy and fairness in the evaluation process. Prior to the passage of P.L. 94-142 in 1975 (IDEA), it was not uncommon for students to be evaluated with a single test and recommended for special education services by a single evaluator. In order to ensure a more comprehensive evaluation procedure involving more decision makers, a number of mandates, in addition to the legal definition of EBD, were laid out in the law.

Parent consent provisions mandate that informed parent consent be obtained before the evaluation is conducted. School personnel may seek a due process hearing if parents refuse to consent to assessment for a child who is clearly in need of assistance to progress in school. Consent for special education placement, should the child be eligible, is a separate process.

Full individual evaluation by the IEP team means that eligibility must be determined by a *multidisciplinary team* based on information from a full individual evaluation in a number of areas such as language, cognitive-intellectual, academic, emotional-social, medical-physical, and behavioral, with specific areas of formal and informal assessment determined by the IEP team. When multidisciplinary teams were mandated by P.L. 94-142, the reasons were to ensure that different perspectives from diverse groups were considered, to limit the decision-making authority of any one individual, and to involve parents.

According to the 2004 reauthorization of IDEA, the multidisciplinary team must include the parents, not less than one general education teacher of the child (if the child is or may be participating in the general education environment), not less than one special education teacher, the person responsible for assessment who can interpret the instructional implications of evaluation results, an administrator (or other representative who has knowledge of instruction in special and regular education and the availability of resources of the school), any other persons with knowledge or special expertise as appropriate, and, whenever appropriate, the student. Surveys of practices in eligibility decision making indicate that the teams are multidisciplinary in composition and average from five to seven members; individuals most often participating are parents, school administrators, special education teachers, school psychologists, general education teachers, and special education administrators (Gilliam & Coleman, 1981; Thurlow & Ysseldyke, 1980; Ysseldyke & Algozzine, 1982).

In a survey, Grosenick, George, George, and Lewis (1991) identified not only the persons but also the factors reported by administrators to be involved in identifying students with emotional/behavioral disorders. In that study, persons most often involved in eligibility decisions were special education administrators, parents, and general education administrators; persons most often making placement decisions were EBD teachers, special education administrators, parents, and general education teachers. According to the survey, the most influential factors in determining both eligibility and placement decisions were (1) the severity of the student's overt behavior and (2) the degree to which that behavior violated normative standards.

Parental involvement on the IEP team ensures that parents have the right to participate in making decisions regarding the education of their child, including placement decisions and development of the individualized education plan (IEP). Over the past several decades since the passage of P.L. 94-142, the emphasis on family involvement in school decision making has increased in response to federal mandates, and also because of increased recognition that home–school collaboration yields positive results for children (Elizalde-Utnick, 2002; Hubbard & Adams, 2002). As members of the school team, parents should be included as equal and integral members, participating in the assessment plan, as well as in the implementation and evaluation of special education services. In a discussion of techniques to increase home–school collaboration, Esler, Godber, and Christenson (2002) observe that such positive partnerships are correlated with higher school achievement. Furthermore, parents must be provided with a copy of the evaluation report and the documentation of eligibility determination.

Nondiscriminatory testing means that state and local education agencies (LEAs) must establish guidelines to ensure that identification procedures are not culturally or racially biased. The child must be evaluated in the language and form most likely to yield accurate information on what the child knows and can do academically, developmentally, and functionally, unless it is not feasible to provide testing in such form or language.

Multitrait/multimethod assessment techniques are encouraged so that no single test or criterion shall be used in making placement decisions, and the IEP team shall be charged with making the final decision. This provision in the law is intended to ensure that no child is placed in special education without a comprehensive assessment to determine if a team can concur that criteria for eligibility are met. Toffalo and Pederson (2005) conducted an investigation of the identification of EBD among 215 school psychologists in Pennsylvania. The school psychologists reviewed hypothetical referral forms and vignettes for children who met federal eligibility criteria for EBD as well as for children who did not meet criteria. These investigators found that school psychologists in the study were just as likely to recommend children as eligible for classification when they carried a psychiatric diagnosis, but did not meet criteria, as when they met criteria but had no psychiatric diagnosis. The authors concluded that when a psychiatric diagnosis is available in the referral information, the child has a greater likelihood of being classified as EBD and in need of special education services. Of concern is that the school psychologists who are most often conducting the evaluation may be prone to view externally provided psychiatric diagnosis as acceptable confirmation for the presence of EBD criteria required by federal law. This power of one external diagnosis contradicts the IDEA, which clearly requires that the identification process include a full individual evaluation and that the IEP team must determine whether the child meets the eligbility criteria outlined in IDEA using multiple sources of information, whether or not there is a psychiatric diagnosis.

Appropriate test selection and administration is required so that tests are reliable and valid for the purposes for which they are used, and that they are administered by trained and knowledgeable personnel in accordance with the procedures provided by the test producers. The child must be assessed in all areas of suspected disability. Furthermore, any assessment tools and strategies employed must provide relevant information that directly assists the team in determining the educational needs of the child. In other words, the assessment techniques must be selected so that results are reliable, valid, and useful for designing practical interventions based on the child's educational needs.

Reevaluation provisions require that the child placed in special education must be reevaluated at least once every 3 years, although the evaluation does not have to involve formal assessment (may be limited to review of records and current behavior and performance) unless it is suspected that the child's disability condition has changed. The IEP team is responsible for determining the specific reevaluation techniques that are needed.

From these basic mandates, state agencies have adopted regulations and guidelines to assist local school districts in devising appropriate identification procedures. Although specific regulations vary from state to state, a few commonalities exist. In the case of a student to be considered for services under the category EBD, many states require that a licensed or certified mental health professional (e.g., psychologist or psychiatrist) be responsible for the evaluation. Illustrated in Box 3.1 are the identification procedures for Richard, a fourth grader referred for psychological evaluation by his teacher, who believed him to be emotionally/behaviorally disordered.

BOX 3.1
Richard[1]

Richard was referred by his fourth grade teacher because of her concerns about his lying, aggression toward peers, noncompliance with school authorities, disruptive classroom behavior, and low academic achievement. Upon questioning, the teacher expressed her belief that Richard was emotionally disturbed and that he should be removed from the regular classroom setting.

Data from classroom observations corroborated the teacher's referral. During instructional periods, Richard was off task 87 percent of the time. During unstructured recess time, he displayed aggressive behavior an average of every four minutes. Whenever an adult attempted to exercise authority, Richard responded by either denying responsibility or projecting blame. Compliance with adult requests was also charted, with Richard demonstrating compliance approximately 10 percent of the time.

Richard's parents were interviewed to obtain information about his behavior outside of school. They indicated that his behavior at home, in Cub Scouts, and in church was very similar to his behavior at school. However, the parents reported that Richard usually displayed far fewer problem behaviors during organized team sports. A phone call to Richard's soccer coach confirmed the parents' observations. Richard was very athletic and very successful at most sports he tried.

During individual testing, Richard's scores were above average on a standardized test of intelligence. Richard displayed relative strengths in general knowledge and vocabulary. He did very poorly on items involving attention and concentration. Results from an achievement battery were above average in all areas except reading and spelling, which were significantly lower.

Data from personality testing indicated an extremely strong achievement motivation, heightened emotional sensitivity and suspiciousness, low self-esteem, impulsiveness, and mild depression. Richard's test responses also indicated that his emotional security was closely tied to external indicators of success, such as awards and praise. No evidence of severe emotional problems such as sociopathy, thought disorder, or debilitating anxiety was found. Although aggressive themes were common in Richard's responses, they usually surfaced as a reaction to perceptions of frustration or harassment.

Observations, interview data, and test results consistently underscored problems with self-control in the absence of psychopathology; therefore, Richard's teacher and parents were asked to complete a behavior rating scale designed to assess problems associated with attention deficit hyperactivity disorder (ADHD). Richard's scores from both sources indicated extreme levels of hyperactivity, impulsiveness, and distractibility relative to other children his age. These three characteristics are considered the classic triad of symptoms associated with ADHD.

All data just described were presented at a multidisciplinary team meeting attended by Richard's parents and the involved educational personnel. In addition, pertinent information was presented by the school nurse, learning disabilities specialist, school social worker, and speech and language specialist. After discussing all data, the team members agreed upon diagnoses of attention deficit hyperactivity disorder and a learning disability in reading. The team members agreed that because Richard was capable of behaving well under conditions of success (i.e., during soccer) and because personality testing revealed a high achievement motivation coupled with need for external evidence of competence, many of Richard's behavioral and emotional symptoms were secondary to his lack of success in school.

Richard was subsequently placed in a resource room for help with reading. Four short-term interventions also were implemented in order to help Richard decrease impulsive behavior and interact more appropriately with peers: (1) family services consisting of consultation on behavior management issues in the home; (2) behavioral consultation with the regular classroom teacher; (3) individual, cognitive-based therapy to help Richard increase self-control; and (4) placement into a regular education social skills group. Although Richard will likely continue to struggle with problems attendant with ADHD, his school program is now more tailored to his needs, and his teachers and parents are now working together to ensure that he stays on track.

Contributed by Michael C. Kirby, Ph.D., Licensed Psychologist, Mapleton Public Schools, Denver, Colorado.

[1]Selected information in this case study has been altered to preserve confidentiality. The name "Richard" is fictitious.

Comorbidity of Other Disorders with Emotional/Behavioral Disorders

The issue of social maladjustment as distinct from emotional/behavioral disorders, as presented in the federal definition, leads to discussion of the larger issue of comorbidity of disorders. Cormorbidity refers to the coexistence of two or more diagnosable disorders in the same individual. As you learned in Chapter 1, emotional and behavioral disorders often occur in conjunction with other disabilities. EBD is very commonly associated with the diagnostic categories of oppositional defiant–conduct disorder, attention-deficit hyperactivity disorder (ADHD), autistic disorder, mental retardation, and depression and anxiety disorders (Mash & Dozois, 1996). Similarly, children with ADHD and learning disabilities frequently display emotional and behavioral problems (Fessler et al., 1991); it may be difficult or impossible to determine which disorder, if any, is primary and what symptoms have developed as complications of a preexisting disorder. Children with acute or chronic medical conditions, such as traumatic brain injury, diabetes, or seizure disorders, may also present with emotional/behavioral problems (McConaughy & Ritter, 2002). Unfortunately, children with more than one coexisting disorder are more likely to continue to have longer lasting and more severe problems than those with only one diagnosed disorder (Nottelmann & Jensen, 1995). The combination of ADHD and conduct disorder has been found to be particularly toxic in that such children, referred to as "fledging psychopaths," are extremely difficult to treat successfully (Gresham, Lane, & Lambros, 2000). However, as previously stated, the presence of a medical or psychiatric diagnosis in the context of emotional/behavioral problems does not necessarily indicate that a child should be identified as EBD for special education purposes.

While frequent comorbidity of disorders has been well established among children classified as EBD, it is not necessarily the case that a psychiatric diagnosis, typically from the *Diagnostic and Statistical Manual of Mental Disorders* (DSM-IV-TR; American Psychiatric Association, 2000) justifies identification as EBD and placement in special education. Often, children have been assessed by mental health professionals such as psychiatrists and psychologists outside the school setting. In these cases, assessment reports with psychiatric diagnoses are often submitted to school personnel when a child is referred for special education. Such assessment information should be considered by the IEP team, but the team is not required to base special education eligibility on the presence or absence of a psychiatric diagnosis. In some school settings, the school psychologist is expected to provide a DSM-IV diagnosis when identifying a student as EBD, even though this practice is discouraged in other school settings because of the overreliance on the medical model (internal causation for psychopathology) and the weak link from a medical model to educational intervention. Merrell (2003) cautions that pathologizing young children by assigning DSM-IV diagnoses should be avoided since many of the diagnostic categories are not appropriate for them.

Children and adolescents who have emotional and behavioral disorders are a heterogeneous group, and they have unique histories, temperaments, personality traits, cognitive skills, and social and adaptive skills. Consequently, the assessment process for identification of these children should involve an approach that views each child as a unique individual and not as a child who only represents a psychological disorder (Sattler, 2002). Furthermore, the need to evaluate a unique individual in every case necessitates the use of a comprehensive evaluation model, with tests and techniques selected to assess all relevant factors. Professionals may differ in their selection of tests and techniques, depending on the unique history and problem presentation of each child. Differences in professional training may also result in variations in selection of assessment techniques.

While consideration of the uniqueness of the individual can contribute to personalization of the assessment process, it may also lead to a frustrating lack of consistency in the approach to identification of EBD. Diagnostic guidelines have been proposed by various professional groups to address this need for consistency in the identification of children with EBD. The guidelines proposed by the National Association of School Psychologists are discussed below.

National Association of School Psychologists (NASP) Guidelines

Given the lack of clarity in the federal definition of EBD and complications of frequent comorbidity of disorders, the National Association of School Psychologists has provided a 2002 position statement on students with emotional and behavioral disorders. This position statement can be reviewed by accessing the online reference under "Additional Readings and Resources" at the end of this chapter. NASP has adopted the definition proposed by the National Mental Health and Special Education coalition. As you learned in Chapter 1, the major elements of this definition of EBD are:

1. EBD is a condition in which an individual's emotional or behavioral responses in school settings are markedly different from generally accepted, age-appropriate, ethnic or cultural norms and that they adversely affect performance in areas including self care, social relationships, personal adjustment, academic progress, classroom behavior, or work adjustment.
2. EBD is more than a transient and expected response to stressors and would persist even with individualized interventions.
3. Eligibility for special education must be based on multiple sources of data and the associated behaviors must be exhibited in at least two different settings, at least one of which is school related.
4. EBD can exist with other handicapping conditions.

5. EBD may include children with schizophrenia, affective disorders, anxiety disorders, or persistent disturbances of conduct, attention, or adjustment.

NASP's position statement also specifies that assessment identify both the strengths and weaknesses of the individual and of the systems (e.g., school, home) with which the student interacts. Results should describe the student's difficulties in a functional, objective, and observable fashion, with consideration of environmental and personal history variables that may relate to the student's school difficulties. The intensity, pervasiveness, and persistence of emotional and behavioral problems must be assessed, and the response to well-organized, empirically based, and individualized intervention efforts documented. Developmental and behavioral status with respect to expectations for children of the same age, culture, and ethnic background must also be addressed. Illustrated in Box 3.2 are the assessment procedures, findings, and recommendations for James, a kindergartener referred by his teacher for assessment for EBD. This case is of interest in that environmental and family variables appeared to be contributed to his emotional and behavioral difficulties.

BOX 3.2
James

James is a 6-year-old kindergarten student at Hilltop Elementary, where he enrolled in November after transferring from another school district. His aggressive behavior has been a concern to teachers and other school staff throughout the year, thus a referral for an assessment for emotional/behavioral disturbance was made. At the time of the referral in February, James was already receiving speech services from the speech-language pathologist and counseling services with the school counselor on a regular basis.

Over 1 year ago, James's parents became separated. Following the separation, he lived with his father, except for a period of time when his mother took him and his siblings out of school to live with her. A short time after James returned to live with his father, his mother passed away. Mrs. Ames is his current kindergarten teacher, although there has also been a student teacher in the classroom. Since moving to Hilltop, James has been suspended from school due to an incident in which he poked another student in the hand and mouth with a pencil. He has also been disciplined for his misbehavior on the school bus.

Throughout his time in Mrs. Ames's classroom, James has progressed academically, although his behavior at times may be described as aggressive and defiant. Mrs. Ames and his kindergarten teacher from his previous school both report that James may hit or threaten others, and call others names. Both teachers also indicate that James will not do something that he does not want to do; instead, he will "shut down" and refuse to do anything.

The assessment process revealed that James exhibited significant behavior problems, with concerns shared by his former and current kindergarten teacher, as well as his father. James's problem behaviors appear to be related to the adjustment to the major changes and stressors that he experienced over the past year, including his parents' separation, his mother's death, and numerous moves. He was determined by the IEP team to be currently not eligible for special education as a student with an emotional/behavioral disorder. This decision was based on several factors, including current lack of educational need since James's academic performance was adequate, the perception of the IEP team that his problem behaviors are linked to recent significant

(*continued*)

BOX 3.2 Continued

stressors, and the team's perception that he may need more time to adjust to his changed circumstances.

Recommendations for James included increased structure in the classroom, more immediate feedback regarding behavior, an increased level of positive reinforcement, and direct instruction in social skills. Temporarily reduced academic demands, as well as a stable and consistent environment at school and preparation for changes in daily routine, were also viewed as helpful interventions. The team felt that James would benefit from more regular and frequent individual sessions with the school counselor, utilizing supportive and expressive techniques such as play or sandtray therapy. Development of a behavior management strategy by the teacher and school psychologist was recommended to encourage James to more effectively communicate and appropriately gain attention in the classroom. Support from other school resources such as the school social worker, a school buddy, or a mentor were other interventions suggested from assessment data. Because James does have a speech impairment, he will continue to receive speech-language therapy. The team recommended that James's behavior continue to be monitored, with reevaluation considered at a later time, if needed.

Contributed by Erica Garza, former School Psychology Intern for a school district in central Texas.

These guidelines, along with federal definitions and mandates, provide a framework within which a child's unique needs can be considered with regard to assessment for EBD. It is up to the IEP team, with the guidance of assessment professionals, to ensure that an appropriate and thorough evaluation is completed with every child who is referred before a decision can be made regarding placement into special education. The identification of EBD can be conceptualized as occurring in three phases: (1) early identification of children at risk and provision of prereferral interventions, (2) formal assessment for EBD, and (3) placement decisions and provision of special education services. Kovaleski (2002) noted that determination of whether or not a child should be placed in special education should also depend in part on response to intervention (RTI) efforts implemented prior to assessment for special education. RTI interventions, discussed further in Chapter 12, are implemented by general educators so that it can be determined if the child's problems are due to teacher, curricular, and/or other classroom variables. If various effective instructional strategies are tried and the student still displays learning problems, then it might be assumed that the problems may be of a pathological nature. At this point, a referral to special education can be initiated and a full individual evaluation conducted. Although not required by federal law, in many states prereferral interventions (e.g., behavior management strategies, academic supports) are required as a precondition for referral for a comprehensive evaluation for special education eligibility and may be considered as part of the assessment process.

Assessment Procedures

Assessment procedures are used in the first two phases, early identification and prereferral, and formal assessment of emotional and behavioral disorders. For the last phase, assessment information is used to formulate educational plans and placement decisions.

Prereferral Interventions

Prereferral interventions serve an important role in the early identification of emotional/behavioral problems that, if not recognized and addressed, may result in a chronic emotional/behavioral disorder. Early identification and intervention is essential, whether or not a child is ultimately placed in special education, because emotional and behavioral problems interfere with academic, vocational, and social development. As observed by Lane, Gresham, and O'Shaughnessy (2002), intervention is more effective before maladaptive behavior has become firmly entrenched in a child's behavioral repertoire. While there are early identification and prevention programs available, educators are often uncertain about how to best intervene with children identified as at risk for EBD and may pursue referral to special education before alternative interventions have been tried.

During the 1980s, the popularity of school-based prereferral teams increased in response to an alarming increase in the numbers of students identified for special education. As educators sought techniques to reduce overidentification of students with disabilities, many school systems developed child study teams to provide consultation for teachers dealing with students having classroom difficulties (Kovaleski, 2002). By the late 1980s, many states required that a team consult with teachers regarding interventions as a precondition for referral and assessment for special education (Carter & Sugai, 1989).

Prereferral intervention systems are implemented by many school districts as the first step in the special education referral process. Prereferral interventions are based on the ecological or systems premise (see Chapter 8) that learning and behavior problems should be viewed within the larger context of the classroom, school, and home. The goals of prereferral intervention are to (1) provide general education classroom teachers with needed assistance and support, (2) reduce inappropriate referrals for testing, and (3) reduce inappropriate special education placements (Graden, Casey, & Bonstrom, 1985). A further goal is to reduce the emotional and behavioral interference that may lead to underachievement as early as possible.

One popular prereferral intervention model is based on a three-tiered approach to discipline and the prevention of problem behavior. Positive Behavioral Supports (PBS), mentioned in Chapter 2, is based on the premise that if students are taught specific behavioral expectations and reinforced for meeting those expectations, then problem behavior will be prevented. PBS is a systems model requiring school district leadership and data collection and analysis, schoolwide teams, expectations, and promotion strategies, classwide expectations and promotion activities, and individual supports for those relatively few students who, under such a system, still display problem behavior (Scott & Nelson, 1999; Sprague, Sugai, Horner, & Walker, 1999; Sugai & Horner, 1999). More detail about PBS will be given in Chapters 7 and 12.

Many prereferral interventions are based on consulting services to the general education classroom teacher in order to provide information, support, and/or materials that will aid in him or her working successfully with a student displaying problem behavior. Teacher interviews are an integral part of this process and allow for collaboration between the classroom teacher dealing with the problem behavior on a daily basis and other education professionals, such as school psychologists or special education teachers, who may provide support and insight. According to Zins and Erchul (2002), consultation procedures are intended to prevent problems from becoming more severe and to keep additional problems from developing. For further information on rationale and implementation of prereferral systems, refer to an article by Kovaleski listed under "Additional Readings and Resources" at the end of this chapter.

Tests and Techniques for Assessment of EBD

As noted previously, a full individual evaluation is required by IDEA for every child referred for special education services. While the specific tests to be given are typically left to the discretion of assessment personnel, most of whom are school psychologists trained at the masters, specialist, or doctoral level, the following elements should be formally assessed in the initial evaluation of children suspected of having EBD:

1. Developmental history to establish risk factors, duration, chronicity, and possible sources for emotional and behavioral problems
2. Emotional/behavioral functioning, including behavioral observations, behavior rating scales and checklists, student and teacher interviews, and projective techniques to explore the nature and severity of problems relative to peers in school settings
3. Academic achievement levels to establish educational competencies and determine educational need
4. Intellectual functioning level to gauge patterns of learning abilities and to identify potential factors in academic underachievement

Other areas that may require formal or informal assessment, depending on referral questions, include speech, language, vision, hearing, motor, and adaptive behavior skills. The IEP team will determine the specific areas requiring assessment to ensure that all areas of suspected disability are assessed and that results can be used to plan the education program. Various professionals, including speech-language pathologists, occupational or physical therapists, and other educational or medical specialists, may be involved in portions of the full evaluation; however, the school psychologist or other licensed or certified mental health professional will typically complete the personality and emotional portions of the test battery. Teachers, parents, the referred child, and others may complete various behavior checklists and rating scales, although their interpretation is usually made by the assessment professional.

Rationales for and brief descriptions of recommended techniques for identification of EBD, ranging from more structured, direct measures such as behavioral observations and rating scales, to more subjective and indirect measures such as projective techniques are presented below. A thorough discussion of standardized tests of intelligence and achievement, which are necessary elements for any comprehensive psychoeducational evaluation, can be found in other references, including Sattler (2002).

Developmental History. Given the comorbidity issues involved in identification of EBD, and the need to document duration, severity, chronicity, and effects on school progress, it is essential to gain a thorough understanding of developmental history as part of the assessment process. Since early medical, developmental, or family problems may contribute to later school difficulties, including learning and behavior problems, a careful history-taking is an integral component of assessment for EBD.

The developmental history is usually obtained from the parents or other caretakers in the context of a face-face interview. Schools often employ background information forms that can serve as a guide, but not as a substitute for the interview, since parents may inadvertently leave out important information if responses are not probed. Typically, the interview to obtain developmental history will be conducted by the school psychologist, psychological examiner, or other mental health professional who is trained in interview procedures.

Essential elements of the developmental history include gathering historical and current functioning information in the following general areas:

1. Medical (including gestation and birth history, pregnancy complications, maternal health, significant illnesses, head injuries, hospitalizations)
2. Developmental (motor and language milestones, emotional attachment, eating and sleeping habits, and toilet training)
3. School (attendance at daycare or preschool, any prior group or individual educational assessments, grades, tutoring or interventions, frequent moves)
4. Family history (psychiatric, genetic, or other disorder among family members, including extended family; separation, divorce, death, or other family stressors that may affect adjustment; behavior management techniques and their effectiveness)
5. Social (peer relationships, family relationships, interactions with teachers and other adults, extracurricular activities)

Another important component of background information is the collection of any relevant medical, psychological, psychiatric, or other evaluation or treatment reports that may relate to the referral problem. Unless parents or prior school districts are specifically asked to provide prior reports of assessment or intervention, they may not realize such records are pertinent to accurate diagnosis. A further complication is that if prior records are not gathered, testing may be unnecessarily duplicated that was completed in another school district or setting.

Examples of interview formats and forms that can be used to gather developmental history are available in commonly used behavior checklists such as the *Behavior Assessment System for Children—2* (BASC-2; Reynolds & Kamphaus, 2004) and the *Child Behavior Checklist* (CBCL; Achenbach & Rescorla, 2001), as well as in reference texts, such as Sattler (2002), listed under "Additional Readings and Resources" at the end of this chapter.

Behavioral Observations. Observation of serious problem behavior by parents and/or teachers is the typical reason for referral for EBD assessment. It follows that structured and deliberate observation of a referred child's behavior in various settings is a cornerstone tool for the assessment of emotional, social, and behavioral problems among children and adolescents. Direct behavioral observation involves procedures in which observers develop operational descriptions of behaviors of concern, observe the behaviors in everyday settings, and record their observations. These techniques stem from behavioral psychology theory (see Chapter 7) and have the advantage of identifying important antecedent stimuli and controlling consequences of behavior, which takes into account the system in which a child functions, rather than focusing on the internal pathology. Another advantage of behavioral observations is that they can be directly linked to the development of individualized interventions (Merrell, 2003).

Specific behavioral observation techniques are reviewed in Sattler (2002) and Merrell (2003). At this point, it is important to remember that behavioral observations are an essential element of comprehensive assessment designed to yield practical and effective educational programs. Teachers are particularly well positioned to complete formal behavioral observations in natural settings as part of the identification process; other professionals, such as school psychologists, educational diagnosticians, counselors, or administrators may also participate in the observation process.

Behavior Checklists and Rating Scales. Many behavior checklists and rating scales are available for completion by parents, teachers, and, in some cases, the referred child. These measures assume that emotional disorders can best be understood through a careful evaluation of current behavioral symptoms, their duration, and intensity from the perspective of individuals most closely involved with the child. Whereas some of the measures are broad and encompass a wide range of behavioral symptoms, others are more specific to certain disorders, such as anxiety, depression, or attention-deficit hyperactivity disorder. In this chapter, several major broad-spectrum checklists are discussed, followed by a listing of several disorder-specific techniques.

The use of rating scales to assist in determining behavioral pathology has increased in popularity since about the mid-1980s. Behavior rating scales provide a standardized format for judgments regarding behavioral characteristics by informants, including teachers or other school personnel and parents, who are familiar with the child. Items are usually rated on a continuum of frequency or severity, and the rater is asked to compare the student to average or typical students of the same age. Behavior rating scales are less direct than behavioral observations because they measure perceptions of behaviors rather than the behaviors themselves; however, they are fairly objective measures and thus may yield more reliable data than unstructured interviews or projective techniques. Another advantage of behavior rating scales is that they are cost-efficient with respect to amount of professional time involved and amount of training needed to use such techniques (Merrell, 2003).

However, there are some potential limitations to the validity and reliability of behavior rating scales. Sattler (2002) cautions that judgments about a child's functioning can be subject to informant bias and distortion. Informants may differ in their familiarity with a child and in their sensitivity to and tolerance for behavior problems, or in their opportunities to observe behaviors across settings. For example, a teacher who is angry at a student and therefore wants him out of the classroom may rate his behavior as more severe than it really manifests. Another potential problem is that rating scale items, no matter how clearly stated, may be misinterpreted. These potential problems can be controlled to some extent by the inclusion of validity scales that attempt to take into account respondents' tendencies to answer items in either a socially desirable manner or to rate the child in an overly critical manner.

Best practices in using behavior rating scales require seeking input from multiple informants across multiple settings and interpreting the findings with respect to information gathered from other techniques, including interviews, behavioral observations, and other tests. As with all tests, assessment personnel should consider the representativeness of the norm group and the reliability and validity of the measures. Norms are best when the test has been standardized on a large, nationally stratified sample that includes equal numbers of males and females. It is also preferable if gender and age norms, in addition to combined sample norms, are provided.

Teachers are often the best source of information regarding a child's behavior since they have the opportunity to observe students in situations under various circumstances and contexts. However, the usefulness of teacher information varies according to the age of the child. Elementary school children frequently have one teacher who makes observations across several class periods and frequently throughout the entire day. High school teachers often have students for one class during the day. Therefore, the amount of information that a teacher can provide regarding a child's behavior decreases at the secondary level (Taylor, 1997). Another factor that influences teacher ratings is the frame of reference, or standard, that teachers use to make behavioral ratings. Teachers often rate behaviors based on a comparison to other children in their classroom or in their previous experience. Consequently, teacher ratings may be related to the teacher's own worldview and therefore may not be an adequate representation of the sample population. Despite the limitations, behavior rating scales by teachers are a critical element of a comprehensive assessment of children's emotional and behavioral functioning.

Many behavior checklists and rating scales are available for assessing emotional/behavioral disorders in schools. Selected measures will be briefly reviewed, based on their relatively prominent use in the field and the availability of reviews in the relevant literature.

Rating Scales Based on IDEA Criteria. Three scales have been developed that are based specifically on the federal definition of emotional disturbance. *The Social-Emotional Dimension Scale* (SEDS-2), developed by Hutton and Roberts (2004), is a 74-item scale with six factors that relate directly to components of the federal definition (1) avoidance of peer interaction, (2) avoidance of teacher interaction, (3) aggressive interaction, (4) inappropriate behavior, (5) depressive reaction, and (6) physical-fear reaction. The SEDS-2 total score can be used to identify levels of risk for a student when compared to "typical" children his age. A 15-item screener and a structured interview for use in functional behavior assessments is also available in the SEDS-2.

The *Behavior Evaluation Scale—2* (BES-2; McCarney & Leigh, 1990) is another rating scale based on the federal definition. The BES-2 is composed of 76 items and five subscales: (1) learning problems, (2) interpersonal difficulties, (3) inappropriate behavior, (4) unhappiness–depression, and (5) physical fears–symptoms. Problem areas correlating to those outlined in the definition can be identified from the subscales.

The *Scale for Assessing Emotional Disturbance* (SAED; Epstein & Cullinan, 1998) contains 52 items comprising seven subscales: (1) inability to learn, (2) relationship problems, (3) inappropriate behavior, (4) unhappiness or depression, (5) physical symptoms or fears, and (6) social maladjustment. Interestingly, the SAED operationally defines social maladjustment as comprised of antisocial acts occurring outside of school, thus distinguishing it from inappropriate in-school behavior. Whether or not a child has a high socially maladjusted subscale score is irrelevant to the decision as to whether that student

TABLE 3.1 Federal Definition and Corresponding Subscales of Behavior Rating Scales

Federal Definition Components	SEDS-2 Subscale (Hutton & Roberts, 1996)	BES-2 Subscale (McCarney & Leigh, 1990)	SAED Subscale (Epstein & Cullinan, 1998)
"Inability to learn . . ."		Learning problems	Inability to learn
"Inability to build/maintain satisfactory relationships with teachers and peers"	Avoidance of peer interaction Avoidance of teacher interaction Aggressive interaction	Interpersonal difficulties	Relationship problems
"Inappropriate behavior or feelings under normal circumstances"	Inappropriate behavior	Inappropriate behavior	Inappropriate behavior
"General pervasive mood of unhappiness or depression"	Depressive reaction	Unhappiness–depression	Unhappiness or depression
"Tendency to develop physical symptoms or fears"	Physical–fear reaction	Physical fears–symptoms	Physical symptoms or fears

meets criteria to be classified as EBD. In addition to subscales matching the five federal criteria, there is a subscale for overall competence. One item is included that assesses whether identified problems adversely affect the student's educational performance. Components of the federal definition and corresponding subscales from the SEDS-2, the BES-2, and the SAED are listed in Table 3.1.

Scores from measures such as these are helpful to the team who must make eligibility decisions for several reasons. First, ratings on the same student from several teachers or school personnel may be obtained, thereby satisfying one requirement for multiple sources of information. Second, when discrepancies occur among these multiple ratings, then assessment personnel can observe and/or interview the individual whose rating was discrepant. Students who pose a problem for only one teacher or only in one class would not be considered EBD. Third, behavior rating scales focus primarily on observable behavior rather than inferred characteristics, thereby lending some degree of objectivity to the process, although ratings by individuals about other individuals always retain a degree of subjectivity.

General-Purpose Behavior Rating Scales. Currently a number of multidimensional behavior rating scales that assess a wide range of potential problems are available. Three widely available and frequently employed scales are reviewed here.

The *Behavior Assessment System for Children—2* (BASC-2; Reynolds & Kamphaus, 2004) is a comprehensive system for assessing child and adolescent behavior. This system includes parent and teacher rating scales for children ages 4–18. There are also comprehen-

with EBD are often involved in placement decisions after eligibility for placement has been determined. Ideally, the special education teacher should be involved in all the stages of the identification process: during screening and prereferral interventions, during assessment and placement, and certainly during instructional planning.

Prior to or upon initial referral, the special education teacher can be a valuable resource to the general education classroom teacher in helping to obtain as much objective data as possible. With their specialized training in behavior observation and instructional modification techniques, they can serve as consultants to general education classroom teachers regarding behavioral interventions. Other possible roles include aiding in the process of behavior observations and behavior recording during class time, helping the teacher develop his or her own unobtrusive recording system, and making available some of the numerous published checklists and behavior rating scales. Participation in other data-gathering activities may be requested by the evaluator if the student is eventually referred and evaluated for eligibility for special education.

It is also important for special education teachers to participate in placement decisions and instructional planning. Data have shown that they do participate in the vast majority of these meetings, and that they are ranked as the most important and influential members by other participants. If these data are a true reflection of practice, then the special education teacher has been assigned a leadership role in the identification process. First-hand knowledge of the various levels of placement and least restrictive environment option, as well as experience in instructional techniques and practices in special education, is invaluable to the multidisciplinary team, some of whom have never been in a teaching role.

A further opportunity for special education teachers exists in the legally mandated reevaluation process that must occur no less frequently than once every 3 years. The IEP team must recommend whether formal testing is needed for reevaluation, with the option of reviewing records and student progress without requiring formal testing. The special education teacher, with day-to-day knowledge of a student's progress and regularly updated IEP information, is particularly well placed to inform the committee about the need for further assessment.

There are a number of things one can do to prepare for this role. First, become thoroughly aware of one's own personal biases, theoretical orientations, and tolerance levels for certain types of behavior and people. Second, be familiar with the specific instruments and measures used for screening and identification. Third, have a working knowledge of federal, state, and local regulations governing identification procedures. And fourth, believe in one's right to voice an opinion among other professionals and have confidence in one's own judgment. Taking an active role in using assessment data to guide intervention is one example of a leadership role that can be assumed by special education teachers.

Linking Assessment to Intervention

If assessment is to be useful to children, parents, and teachers, then the findings must extend beyond identification and placement in special education. The link between assessment findings and interventions must be considered when the assessment plan is designed by the IEP team. Too often, a disconnect occurs between the results of the assessment and the initiation of special education services, so that the IEP is developed and implemented as a process distinct from the identification process. Lack of treatment validity of assessment data is addressed by Shinn (2002) in a discussion of curriculum-based measurement. The link between assessment and intervention can be strengthened through (1) selection of appropriate assessment tools that have strong ties to intervention strategies and (2) dissemination of results and recommendations in a manner that is understandable to teachers, parents, and others who will be implementing interventions.

The prereferral intervention models (e.g., RTI, PBS, consultation) serve as a blueprint for the design of effective assessment to intervention links. If assessment is done with ecological validity (consideration of the whole system in which the child functions), collaborative problem solving between teachers, parents, and assessment personnel, and regular monitoring and evaluation of the intervention, then the relationship between data gathering and intervention is strengthened. Even if a prereferral intervention is insufficient to ameliorate serious emotional and behavioral problems, the foundation will have been laid for collaborative problem solving, including teamwork in identification of intrapersonal, interpersonal, and environmental variables contributing to the child's difficulties in school. Numerous school consultation models exist, but most emphasize collaborative problem solving for effecting behavioral change (Allen & Graden, 2002); such techniques may focus on instructional needs or behavioral needs, depending on the teacher's perception and the outcome of observations and other assessment data.

Numerous examples of efforts to tie various forms of assessment to practical interventions are available in the literature. Naglieri (2002) provides a model for a cognitive approach to problem solving based on intelligence assessment results with the *Cognitive Assessment System* (CAS; Naglieri & Das, 1997), in which cognitive processing measures, such as planning and attention, are assessed, then instruction is designed to improve effectiveness of these processes. Shinn (2002) writes about curriculum-based measurement and its value in helping to align assessment and intervention by focusing on the effects of instructional programs on students. Curriculum-based measurement (CBM) is the assessment of a student's mastery of curricular objectives. Assessment instruments are often included with curricular materials. Unfortunately, Shinn also notes that all too frequently IEP goals and objectives are written without current student performance data and lack observable, measurable outcomes.

In the domain of externalizing disorders, characterized by acting-out, aggressive, disruptive, oppositional, defiant, and hyperactive behaviors, research suggests that direct behavioral techniques that take into account environmental variables and interpersonal interactions are most productive for generating effective intervention (Hoff, Doepke, & Landau, 2002; Lane et al., 2002). In other words, functional behavioral assessments (FBAs) (see Chapter 7) can be very effective with children who exhibit primarily externalizing problem behaviors.

In contrast, internalizing disorders are characterized by overcontrol of behavior and may be harder to detect. This domain includes symptoms such as depressed mood, social withdrawal, anxiety, and somatic complaints. Because the associated behaviors are less likely to be directly observable and noxious to the classroom teacher, it may be harder to identify antecedents and cues, or consequences that can be modified. Nevertheless, there are effective interventions available for internalizing disorders when a comprehensive, individualized assessment has been completed. Cognitive-behavioral interventions (see Chapter 6) receive the most support in the literature for internalizing disorders. Careful study of student responses to self-report checklists and interview questions can help guide the selection of intervention techniques that can be highly effective. Illustrated in Box 3.3 is the referral, assessment, and intervention process for Ethan, a boy referred for assessment of internalizing emotional/behavioral problems.

In summary, the development of the intervention plan, usually in the form of an IEP for children identified as having EBD, should represent a collaborative effort of the multidisciplinary team in which assessment findings are used to design practical and realistic interventions.

BOX 3.3

Ethan[1]

Ethan was referred by his third-grade teacher due to concerns about his academic progress in the areas of mathematical reasoning and written expression. He was also referred due to concerns regarding his emotional stability and levels of anxiety.

From information obtained during the teacher interview, Ethan's teacher reported that Ethan tends to "constantly worry and fret about details." He requires continual reassurance about exact procedures, instructions, and teacher expectations before settling down to perform any task. While completing the task, Ethan demonstrates a compulsive need to be certain of his progress and performance. In addition, inconsistencies and changes in the daily routine can often disturb him.

Data from classroom observations supported the teacher's concerns about Ethan's obsessive–compulsive tendencies (need for constant reassurance/feedback), dependency upon the teacher for emotional support and direction, and high levels of anxiety related to task performance.

According to information provided by Ethan's mother (a single parent) during the parent interview, Ethan exhibits heightened anxiety in multiple circumstances both at home and at school. She reported that he "worries often" about things like money and his future. For example, she explained that on his own initiative, Ethan has been saving money for law school. She indicated that he is often "needy and clingy" in his attachment to her, becomes jealous when his siblings receive attention, and becomes easily agitated when his mother arrives even a few minutes late from work. He "always wants affection" and can never seem to get enough. Emotionally, Ethan's mother stated that her son misses his father and harbors the hope that his parents might reconcile. Behaviorally, Ethan tends to be preoccupied with order and perfection within the home. His room is always tidy and organized, and he becomes easily upset when his belongings are touched or moved from their original positions. In addition, he demonstrates impatience and irritation with other family members for not keeping things orderly.

Testing results reveal scores in the average range on measures of both intelligence and achievement. Ethan demonstrated strength in the areas of verbal comprehension and spatial reasoning, while also performing well on academic tests in reading and math calculation. He demonstrated relative weakness in the areas of cognitive efficiency and working memory, as well as on tests of mathematical reasoning. No significant discrepancies between IQ and achievement scores were obtained. Therefore, Ethan did not qualify as a student with a learning disability.

Overall, results obtained from all measures of personality assessment (behavior checklists, parent/teacher interviews, self-report instruments, and projective tests) indicated that Ethan demonstrates

(*continued*)

BOX 3.3 Continued

high achievement motivation, heightened anxiety related to school success as well as in regards to obtaining peer acceptance, and obsessive–compulsive tendencies. Results also revealed that Ethan exhibits emotional insecurity in association with his continual need for parental attention/validation and with his need for a father figure in his life. The criterion for an emotional/behavioral disorder "tendency to develop physical symptoms or fears associated with personal or school problems" was met across settings, to a marked degree, and occurred over a period of 6 months. Therefore, Ethan did meet federal eligibility requirements as a student with an emotional/behavioral disorder.

Assessment results were discussed during a multidisciplinary team meeting attended by Ethan's parents and educational personnel (classroom teacher, special education teacher, school psychologist, school counselor, and administrator). Team members agreed with the recommendation for Ethan to be admitted into special education as a student classified with an emotional/behavioral disorder. All team members also agreed in implementing the following services/interventions: inclusion support for math, general education counseling, the development of behavioral IEP goals, and behavioral consultation with Ethan's classroom teacher. His counseling goals included: (1) developing coping skills and stress management; (2) learning relaxation techniques; (3) learning to form realistic expectations of self and others; and (4) developing appropriate social skills when interacting with peers. Behavioral IEP goals were developed and agreed upon in order to decrease Ethan's level of anxiety and obsessive–compulsive tendencies (i.e., allow opportunity to discuss fears/worries with a peer, mentor, or teacher; reduce emphasis on competition; increase positive feedback indicating that Ethan is successful and competent; provide Ethan with a schedule of daily events and expectations; assign a peer tutor to model task expectations/procedures, etc.).

After 2 months, the assessment specialist (school psychologist) consulted with the classroom teacher in order to assess Ethan's progress and to modify his previously developed behavioral IEP goals. Given his dependency upon the teacher to complete assignments, the following goals were added: (1) encourage Ethan to first attempt the task on his own prior to requesting assistance; (2) provide Ethan with a checklist for performing particular assignments independently; and (3) reinforce Ethan for performing tasks independently.

Although Ethan continued to require monitoring, his obsessive–compulsive behaviors and levels of anxiety decreased, while his ability to cope with academic stress appeared to increase as the school year progressed. He remained in special education as a student with EBD during the following year, but continued to show progress in reaching his IEP goals.

Contributed by Samira Munir, M.A., School Psychologist for a school district in central Texas.

[1]Selected information in this case study has been altered to preserve confidentiality. The name "Ethan" is fictitious.

Multicultural Considerations

According to Ortiz and Flanagan (2002), the foremost principle for using best practices in working with culturally diverse children and families is that "any individual's own culture greatly affects the way they view the world and others, including people from both within and outside the culture" (p. 337). This statement underscores the need for special education teachers to recognize their own biases and how they might affect assessment and intervention with children and families from cultures different from their own. Attention to cultural diversity within educational and psychological assessment has only fairly recently become a focus of professional preparation and practice. As noted by Baker, Kamphaus, Horne, and Winsor (2006), diversity in American schools is increasing, resulting in increasing variability in academic as well as inter- and intrapersonal behavior of children in classrooms.

The terms *test bias* and *assessment bias* refer to test instruments or methods that result in one group being systematically disadvantaged or yield group differences on characteristics other than those being measured by the test or technique. It is an ethical violation to use tests or methods that are not appropriate for the purpose of the assessment or that unfairly discriminate against any group (American Educational Research Association, American Psychological Association, National Council on Measurement in Education, 1999). Ortiz (2002) has observed that since complete elimination of every potential source of bias is unrealistic, the goal of nondiscriminatory assessment should be to reduce it to the maximum extent possible.

That the violation of normative behavioral standards influences referral and placement decisions is not surprising and is consistent with other research on behavioral deviance. However, it becomes a matter of concern when considering the relationship between cultural expectations and concepts of deviance. It has been shown that teachers apply different standards or perceptions of ideal behavior to different racial groups (Carlson & Stephens, 1986). Many African Americans and Hispanic Americans have been inappropriately placed in several categories of special education, including classes for students with EBD (Park, Pullis, Reilly, & Townsend, 1994). In fact, as you learned in Chapter 1, the disproportionality of African Americans served as EBD is of national concern (Cartledge, Key, & Ida, 2000). One contributor to inappropriate placement has been the use of culturally biased norm-referenced tests, often in isolation from other important sources of data. Nondiscriminatory assessment requires that other sources, including nonstandardized methods and information, be included. Furthermore, all information gathered in an assessment should be considered with respect to the individual's unique experience and background (Ortiz, 2002).

Other explanations for misdiagnosis of culturally different students have been cited by Park et al. (1994).

1. Lack of understanding by teachers of different learning styles and of the influence of students' cultural backgrounds (Osher et al., 2004; Sue, 1988)
2. The multiple effects of limited English proficiency on some culturally different students, leading to lower academic performance, lower teacher expectations, and possibly misinterpretation of students' classroom behavior (Argulewicz & Sanchez, 1983; Cartledge et al., 2000)
3. Unavailability of instruments needed to assess bilingual students (Ortiz & Maldonado, 1986; Rodriguez, 1988)
4. Lack of bilingual special education personnel and appropriate materials (Yee, 1988)
5. Development of problem behaviors by culturally different students from inappropriate and frustrating experiences in the classroom (Osher et al., 2004).

The influence of an individual's cultural background on his or her behavior and performance in school is pervasive and complex. Sugai (1992) has offered a six-component explanation suggesting that cultural beliefs are primarily transmitted to the child through family values and expectations, family interactions, and childrearing and management practices of the parents or family unit. He suggests a number of practical guidelines for assessing whether a culturally different student needs special education services for emotional/behavioral disorders. Included in these guidelines are (1) use of comprehensive prereferral intervention strategies; (2) a functional analysis of teacher behavior, student behavior, and the setting or context; and (3) examination of the communicative function of behavior, which recognizes that students from culturally different backgrounds may use different behavioral indicators than those expected by the dominant culture.

Merrell (2003) offers further recommendations for culturally competent assessment practice. Some of these recommendations are (1) obtaining sufficient cultural background information before planning and conducting assessment; (2) using a multimethod, multisource, multisetting approach to minimize culturally limiting factors of any one method; (3) being flexible in the design and implementation of the assessment; (4) striving for honesty and open communication regarding cultural issues with students and their families in both the assessment and feedback process; (5) developing awareness of individual as well as group cultural differences; and (6) examining one's own cultural background, values, beliefs, and assumptions. All of these suggestions underscore the need to view any student's behavior from within the student's own cultural context, and with recognition of one's own cultural perspective.

Conclusions

In summary, the identification procedures of students with emotional/behavioral disorders are complex and vary across school districts, states, and the nation, although federal law mandates the general procedures to be followed. Recommended techniques for assessment and identification include employment of screening techniques and prereferral interventions, developmental histories, interviews, behavior checklists and rating scales, and intellectual and achievement testing. Projective techniques continue to be used in school-based assessment for EBD, although problems exist with reliability and validity. The link between assessment and intervention is strengthened when there is collaborative problem solving among the multidisciplinary team, including the parents, and when assessment and associated interventions have ecological validity. All children's behavior should be viewed within each individual's own cultural context, so that assessment and placement bias is reduced.

The issue of how to distinguish socially maladjusted students from students with EBD remains controversial, as is the lack of specificity with regard to the concept of educational need. On the optimistic side, some positive changes have taken place in identification procedures: the institution of prereferral intervention systems in many districts, availability of multiple-gating procedures such as Walker and Severson's (1992, 2002) systematic screening, and greater reliance on observational data, interviews, and behavior rating scales from multiple sources that can be linked to targeted intervention. Table 3.2 provides a summary of the identification process for children who may have EBD.

TABLE 3.2 Summary of EBD Identification Process

Prereferral	Referral	Evaluation
Meet with prereferral team, including parents, teachers, staff, others as needed to review concerns, educational records, and prior interventions	Review effectiveness of prereferral intervention outcomes and determine need for referral	Conduct behavioral observations across settings and parent interview to obtain developmental history
Design general education interventions, including consultation with school psychologist, special education t eacher, behavior specialist, parents, etc.	Meet with IEP team, including parents, regular and special education teachers, appraisal staff, and administrator, others as needed	Conduct FIE, including behavior checklists and rating scales from parents and teachers, cognitive and achievement tests, and other personality tests as needed
Implement and evaluate interventions (e.g., RTI)	Complete referral paperwork, including parent consent for evaluation	Meet with IEP team to determine eligibility, placement, and IEP

KEY POINTS

1. The federal IDEA definition of emotional disturbance has been adopted by most states but has been roundly criticized as inadequate.
2. Students who are determined to be socially maladjusted may not be excluded from special education if they also meet other criteria set out in the federal definition of EBD.
3. A full individual evaluation is mandated by IDEA, and should include multiple methods and multiple informants across at least two settings, including at least home and school.
4. Assessment and placement decisions are likely to be more effective when parents are active and equal members of the IEP team.
5. Teachers can improve the identification process by offering observational data, curriculum-based measurement, and other information for instructional and behavioral planning.
6. Difficulties in identifying students for services for emotional/behavioral disorders may be compounded when students of culturally or racially different backgrounds are referred if potential sources of bias are not recognized.
7. The link between individualized assessment and practical, realistic interventions should be emphasized by the IEP team, by using a collaborative problem-solving model.

HOMEWORK QUESTIONS

1. In the case of Ethan, describe how educational need was documented in determining his eligibility for special education as emotionally disturbed.
2. Briefly explain how Richard's diagnosis of ADHD is related to the emotional and behavioral concerns described by his referring teacher. In another brief paragraph, describe

the instruments and techniques used in this case to aid in the diagnosis of ADHD.

3. Describe why James was not eligible for special education as emotionally disturbed, even though he had exhibited behaviors of concern for at least 1 year.

4. Why should a thorough developmental history be obtained when a child is referred for assessment for EDB? Explain your thoughts in no more than one paragraph.

ADDITIONAL READINGS AND RESOURCES

Position statement on students with emotional and behavioral disorders, by NASP, 2002, *http://www.nasponline.org/information/pospaper_sebd.html* for a discussion of recommended procedures for assessing and serving students with EBD.

Assessment of children: Behavioral and clinical applications (4th ed.), by Jerome M. Sattler, San Diego, CA: Author, 2002, for a review of and formats for interviews, observation procedures, and a discussion of behavior rating scales.

Behavioral, social, and emotional assessment of children and adolescents (2nd ed.), by Kenneth W. Merrell, Mahwah, NJ: Erlbaum, 2003, for a detailed discussion of various identification issues, including specific assessment techniques and multicultural issues.

Best Practices in Operating Pre-Referral Intervention Teams by Joseph S. Kovaleski, Bethesda, MD: NASP, 2002, for guidelines for developing effective pre-referral intervention teams involving parents.

Cultural biases in the identification of students with behavior disorders, by Park, E. K., Pullis, M., Reilly, T., and Townsend, B. L., in R. Peterson and S. Ishii-Jordan (Eds.), *Multicultural issues in the education of students with behavioral disorders,* 1994, Cambridge, MA: Brookline, for a treatise on how understanding or lack of understanding of different cultures can influence perceptions of what is deviant.

Racial inequality in special education, by the Harvard Civic Rights Project, 2002, Arlington, VA: Council for Exceptional Children, for an exposé of inequalities experienced by minority special education students.

Educational assessment of the culturally diverse and behavior disordered student, by George Sugai, in Alba Ortiz and Bruce Ramirez (eds.), *Schools and the culturally diverse exceptional student,* 1988, Reston, VA: Council for Exceptional Children, for a description of a framework that can be applied to help determine the impact of culture on perceptions of deviance and normalcy.

Reducing disproportionate representation of culturally diverse students in special education, 1997, Arlington, VA: Council for Exceptional Children, recommends alternate assessment strategies and a contextual view of behavior.

Standards-based instruction and assessment for English language learners, by Mary Ann Lachat, 2004, Arlington, VA: Council for Exceptional Children, helps administrators and teachers implement effective practices for English language learners.

Implementing a prereferral intervention system: Part I, The model, and Part II, The data, by J. L. Graden and colleagues, *Exceptional Children, 51,* 1985, for descriptions of how such a system was conceptualized and field-tested in six schools.

Systematic screening of pupils in the elementary age range at risk for behavior disorders: Development and trial testing of a multiple gating model, by Hill M. Walker and colleagues, *RASE, 9,* 1988. For a more detailed description of the SSBD screening procedure.

Replication of the Systematic Screening for Behavior Disorders (SSBD): Procedure for the identification of at-risk children, by Hill M. Walker and colleagues, *Journal of Emotional and Behavioral Disorders, 2*(2), 1994, for an article further describing the use of the SSBD.

A promising approach for expanding and sustaining school-wide positive behavior support, by Georg Sugai and Robert H. Horner, *School Psychology Review 2*(2), 2006, for a discussion of the use of positive behavioral supports as a means of systematic and sustained interventions for problem behaviors.

CHAPTER

4 Biophysical Model

Definition and Etiology
Genetic Factors, Biochemical/Neurological Factors, Temperament

Typical Evaluation Procedures
Developmental Histories, Neurological and Neuropsychological Assessment

Educational Application
Genetic Technologies, Psychopharmacology, Nutrition Therapy, Teacher's Role

QUESTIONS TO CONSIDER

- How do theoretical models affect assessment and intervention for EBD?
- What is the biophysical view of EBD? Is it applicable to all children with EBD?
- How do recent advances in the understanding of human genetics affect the future of assessment and interventions for EBD?
- Which disorders of emotion and behavior have received the most attention in the biophysical research literature?
- How common is medication treatment for EBD?
- What is the role of the special education teacher in assessment and intervention when medical or physical issues are involved?

Orientation

As a teacher, your personal view of disorders partially determines how you will attempt to instruct and manage students with emotional/behavioral disorders. Before aligning yourself with a particular theoretical model, you should be aware of the alternatives posed by other treatment models. In addition to expanding your range of information and expertise, knowledge of numerous models and techniques enables you to understand and communicate with colleagues and other professionals who are operating from different theoretical bases. The biophysical model presented in this chapter views disordered behavior as a function of physical or organic differences particular to an individual that may be treated primarily through medical means by physicians and psychiatrists.

Overview

Although numerous conceptual frameworks have been devised to explain disordered behavior, five major schools of thought seem to prevail: biophysical, psychodynamic, cognitive, behavioral, and ecological. This chapter and the next four provide a descriptive overview of the five models, tying theory to practice. The biophysical, psychodynamic, and cognitive explanations of disturbance assume that the primary cause for the malady is an internal state; thus, assessment and treatment focus on the individual in question. The behavioral and ecological models assume that disturbance is primarily a function of environmental interactions, implying that assessment and intervention strategies include contextual as well as individual factors. Four characteristics of each model are addressed:

1. Definition and basic view of disturbance
2. Etiology and development of disordered behavior
3. Typical evaluation procedures
4. Educational applications

Definition and Basic View[1]

> The disturbed child is one who because of organic and/or environmental influences, chronically displays: (a) inability to learn at a rate commensurate with his intellectual, sensory-motor and physical development, (b) inability to establish and maintain adequate social relationships, (c) inability to respond appropriately in day to day life situations, and (d) a variety of excessive behavior ranging from hyperactive, impulsive responses to depression and withdrawal. (Haring, 1963, p. 291)

This definition represents the biophysical view of disordered behavior in its attribution of causality to "organic and/or environmental influences." The biophysical model is basically a medical model that assumes that the problem or pathology lies within the individual. Many advocates of the biophysical viewpoint are from the medical, health, or psychiatric professions who are encouraged by research indicating that many so-called emotional disorders may stem from physiological abnormalities. Some biophysical theorists propose purely biological causes for certain disorders (e.g., autism), whereas other theorists consider the role of a stressful environment in activating dormant biological problems or genetic predispositions (e.g., schizophrenia). In other words, some believe that biological factors rarely operate as constants but depend on the circumstances under which an individual develops, while others believe that some combination of biological defects ultimately will be found for all mental disorders.

Pennington (2002) presents the idea of a "neuroscientific" framework that attempts to relate behavior and mind to the brain and asserts that the traditional clinical distinction between "functional" and "organic" psychopathology is fundamentally incorrect. In other words, for most disorders of emotion and behavior, multiple genetic and environmental factors affect outcome. For special education teachers, it appears to be particularly important to attend to the multiple variables that contribute to problem behaviors at home and school.

Etiology and Development of Disordered Behavior

Although the research on biological causes of emotional/behavioral disorders is varied and complex, it can be divided into three major categories: genetic, biochemical/neurological, and temperament factors. Research on the first two factors was originally undertaken with more severely impaired populations, primarily autistic and schizophrenic. In this research, children identified as autistic or schizophrenic exhibited many bizarre, repetitive behaviors and were characterized by impaired sensory perception and communication abilities. In fact, characteristics of the syndromes were so similar that much of the literature prior to the 1970s failed to clearly distinguish between the two. It was not until 1977 that a consensual definition of autism was established. Currently, autism is considered a developmental rather than an emotional disorder, and it constitutes a category of special education separate from emotionally/behaviorally disordered. Although the term *schizophrenia* is currently less often used as a diagnostic term for children, it is still used. Children diagnosed as having schizophrenia are included in the federal definition of emotional disturbance and possible biophysical causes will be reviewed here.

Genetic Factors

The genetic factor refers to the influence of genes and their variants (called alleles) on human behavior. A "genotype" has been described as the raw material and blueprints (genes and chromosomes) for growth and development provided through the merging of the parental genotypes (Goldstein & Reynolds, 1999). Charles Darwin's evolutionary theory helped establish the understanding that behavioral traits can be inherited. However, this idea became less influential because learning was seen as the major influence on behavior (Garrett, 2003).

Even though for over a century inherited traits were a suspected influence in mental illness, only relatively recently has the field of genetics experienced a revolution. This revolution has resulted in a major international research initiative (Human Genome Project) aimed at deciphering the chemical makeup of human genetic material (genome) and mapping 26,000 to 40,000 genes (earlier estimates were about 100,000 genes) (Collins, 2006; Goodman, 1998; Pennington, 2002). The goals of this research are (1) to develop an understanding of genetic disorders so that they can be prevented and treated; (2) to examine the ethical, legal, and social implications of genetic technologies; and (3) to educate the public about the findings (Berk, 1999). Three major research tools are being developed.

1. *Genetic mapping:* locating sequences of genes on chromosomes that might indicate traits or disorders.
2. *Physical mapping:* a complicated process of further identifying specific genes.
3. *Sequence mapping:* creating a sequence map of all 3 billion DNA bases of the human genome so that specific genes can be identified.

Analysis of the basic human physical construction will allow us to determine the specific factors that might predispose an individual to disorders. Not only will genetic indicators be identified for schizophrenia and bipolar disorder, which we already suspect to be genetically transmitted, but it may also be determined that clear genetic links exist for characteristics such as shyness, Type A personalities, other forms of depression, and antisocial personalities (Barondes, 1998; Berk, 1999; Plomin, 1994). According to Garrett (2003), most of the behavioral disorders, including alcoholism and other drug addiction, major mood disorders, anxiety, and schizophrenia, are partially hereditary. In their textbook, Goldstein and Reynolds (1999) describe learning disabilites, attention-deficit/hyperactivity disorder, Tourette syndrome, anxiety disorders, autism, and other pervasive developmental disorders as characterized by accepted, though not completely identified, genetic etiologies.

The National Institute of Mental Health has made the "genetics of mental illness" (Barondes, 1998, p. 5) a priority, as have government and industry, since there is such a high potential for positive results. It is speculated that, as a result of the "new genetics" (Hodapp & Fidler, 1999), psychiatric diagnosis will radically change in the future (Barondes, 1998). Disorders will probably be categorized by causes rather than by symptoms, and DNA testing will most likely become a regular component of all assessment. Additionally, many mental disorders may be divided into subtypes based on etiology. At present, it appears that prevention and intervention will most likely include drug treatment; thus, pharmaceutical companies will continue to be key stakeholders in this massive research effort. It might be surmised that connecting genetic disorders directly to specific behavioral traits may eventually preempt more traditional models of disturbance (e.g., psychodynamic and cognitive) and may indeed revolutionize the field of psychology and psychiatry (e.g., Barondes, 1998; Hodapp & Fidler, 1999).

Genes do not, however, provide the final script for behavior; rather, they control the production of proteins, which then affect the development of brain structures, neurotransmitters and their receptors, and the functioning of the endocrine system, all of which interact to produce behavior (Garrett, 2003; Pennington, 2002). As noted by Goldstein and Reynolds (1999), traits that are known to be genetically determined, such as height, can be altered in the course of development, or even later in life, by environmental determinants. According to these authors, few components of human behavior are too simple to be influenced by the environment and too complex to be related to the genotype. Genetic methods are essential for understanding the etiology of disturbed development and behavior because there are genetic influences on virtually all development psychopathologies (Pennington, 2002).

The more traditional approach to linking heritability and disorders has been through investigating prevalence rates among twins and other relatives of particular individuals. Research referred to as kinship studies compares the characteristics of family members. For example, researchers determine whether identical twins (who share all their genes) are more likely to possess similar traits than are fraternal twins (who only share some of their genes). Adoption studies also provide information about genetic influences. If adopted children show traits more similar to their biological parents (with whom they share genes) than to their adoptive parents (with whom they live), then it might be assumed that heritability is a potent factor. Such studies have shown that intelligence, sociability, emotional expressiveness, and activity level are moderately influenced by genetics (e.g., Goldsmith, Buss, & Lemery, 1997; Loehlin, 1992; Scarr, 1997). Another way to determine the relative influence of genetics on behavior is by determining a concordance rate. A concordance rate refers to the frequency that relatives are alike in a characteristic (Garrett, 2006). If the concordance rate for this trait is higher for identical twins than for fraternal twins, it can be assumed that the similarity in genes is cause for the concordance. High concordance rates for schizophrenia, autism, ADHD, and severe depression support the notion of heredity (Bailey et al., 1995; Plomin, 1994; Zametkin, 1995). With regard to conduct disorders in children, there appears to be a small genetic effect and a large environmental effect. Adult criminality, however, is characterized by a larger genetic effect (Pennington, 2002). Many genetic disorders have high degrees of variability in expression, often for unknown reasons; however, possible explanations include treatment-related variables and biological–environmental interactions (Goldstein & Reynolds, 1999).

A classic study was reported by Kallmann (1956) who followed the biological relatives of all persons with schizophrenia admitted to a hospital during a 10-year period. Follow-up nearly 30 years later indicated that while schizophrenia occurs in about 1 percent of the population, if one parent were schizophrenic, one-sixth of the offspring were also schizophrenic; if both parents were schizophrenic, more than two-thirds of the offspring were also affected. Similar results were found for siblings, with rates of 85 percent concordance among identical twins, 15 percent among fraternal twins and full siblings, and 7 percent among half-siblings.

Pennington (2002) summarizes general findings of over 40 family studies of schizophrenia, including both twin and adoption studies, and concludes that cumulative results clearly document the heritability of this disorder, with an average concordance of 48 percent for identical twins reared together, 17 percent for fraternal twins, and 9 percent for siblings. Because the concordance for identical twins is considerably less than 100 percent, it is believed that there must be nonshared environmental risk factors for schizophrenia. Furthermore, the discrepancy between the average sibling concordance (9%) and the fraternal twin discordance (17%), who have the same degree of genetic relationship, suggests that the difference in risk must be environmental and may implicate the prenatal environment as a shared risk factor. Most authorities currently agree that a predisposing factor may be inherited that renders an individual susceptible to environmental influences.

Biochemical/Neurological Factors

Most of the research in this area can be divided into three categories: (1) studies of neurotransmitters, which are chemicals in the brain that relay neural impulses from one neuron to the next; (2) organic causes, which include structural abnormalities in the brain and/or unspecified brain dysfunction; and (3) studies of metabolism, the body's use of chemicals to use and produce energy.

Neurotransmitter Studies. The search for neurotransmitter abnormalities in autism has gone on for about 40 years, with no firm conclusions (Pennington, 2002). The only consistent result across numerous neurotransmitter studies involving children with autism has been the finding of elevated serotonin levels in peripheral blood (not in the central nervous system) in about one-fourth of the individuals studied. Serotonin is a neurotransmitter, a chemical that facilitates transmission of nerve impulses; it is found in minute quantities in the bloodstream where it is carried by platelets. A biochemical cause for schizophrenia also has been suspected for over 100 years, but no single neurotransmitter has been identified. In fact, a single neurotransmitter hypothesis of schizophrenia has been rejected as evidence for the involvement of multiple neurotransmitters has increased (Byne, Kemether, Jones, Haroutunian, & Davis, 1999). The single neurotransmitter hypothesis focused on the role of excess dopamine in the brains of persons with schizophrenia due to their reactions to certain drugs known to affect dopamine activity (i.e., phenothiazines); however, the symptoms of schizophrenia are likely the result of alterations in multiple neurotransmitter systems (Pennington, 2002).

Abnormalities in the neurotransmitters norepinephrine, dopamine, and serotonin have been implicated in depression, but this finding does not indicate causality (Sinacola & Peters-Strickland, 2006). The genetic predisposition may affect the balance of neurotransmitters (Cicchetti & Toth, 1998; Pennington, 2002). Since depression is often alleviated by drugs that heighten serotonin levels (e.g., Prozac, Paxil, Zoloft), it might be assumed that low levels of this neurotransmitter affect mood. Serotonin deficiency has also been implicated in obesity, obsessive–compulsive disorder, eating disorders, social phobias, premenstrual syndrome, anxiety and panic, migraines, and even extreme violence (Lemonick, 1997). However, most brain functions appear to result from the multiple influences of several different neurotransmitters (Sinacola & Peters-Strickland, 2006).

Organic Causes. A variety of organic etiologies for autism, depression, and schizophrenia have been proposed. Organic causes for autism were posited by some of the earliest pioneers in studying this population of children (Asperger, 1944/1991; Bender, 1968; Kanner, 1943; Rimland, 1964; Rutter, 1965). With advanced neuroimaging technology, abnormalities in brain structure have been demonstrated, with macrocephaly (unusually large brain size) in about one-fourth of cases the best replicated finding (Pennington, 2002). Other, less consistent findings include abnormalities in the cerebellum, enlarged lateral ventricles, and reduced volume in the limbic system. Even though definitive neurological abnormalities have not been demonstrated, there is considerable evidence that the etiology of autism resides in the operation of a neurobiological factor or factors. Individuals with autism are more likely to demonstrate neurological "soft signs," persistent primitive reflexes, abnormalities on EEGs and brain scans, and an increased likelihood of seizures (Klin & Volkmar, 1999).

It should be noted that an organic cause of any disorder would not exclude the possibility of neurotransmitter abnormalities; the term *organic* is a more general term that could include a number of specific etiologies, including but not limited to structural abnormalities and neurotransmitter difficulties. Neurological dysfunction also has been found in patients suffering from depression, indicating a biophysical concomitant of depression that has yet to be specified. The main structural findings appear to be enlarged lateral ventricles and decreased volume in the frontal lobes and parts of the subcortical structures (Pennington, 2002). As one researcher summarized the state of neuropsychological research into depression, "It seems likely that depressive affect will be found not in one place in the brain, but many. Although this distribution of affective control mechanisms at multiple levels of brain organization causes difficulty for any simple notions of the biology of depression, it also causes the study of depressed affect to be more than the study of an isolated disease process" (Tucker, 1988, p. 125). More recent research supports this conclusion, and suggests that depression results from a complex interaction of brain structure, brain function, metabolic activity, and environmental factors (Pennington, 2002).

Metabolic Factors. Disorders such as phenylketonuria (PKU) highlight the importance of the metabolic system in the mediation of learning and behavior. PKU is a recessive genetic disorder that causes the body to be unable to metabolize the protein phenylalanine. When uncontrolled by diet, this disorder is characterized by severe mental retardation, convulsions, and behavioral problems, among other symptoms (Sattler & Hoge, 2006). There are a number of other specific disorders (e.g., insulin-dependent diabetes, congenital hypothyroidism) that affect metabolism and that when poorly controlled may negatively impact children's behavior and learning. However, the role of food allergies and severe vitamin deficiencies in disorders such as ADHD is less well supported by the research literature.

The concept of food allergies as a causative factor of ADHD was popularized by Feingold (1975b). Feingold, a pediatric allergist, initially became interested in allergies when treating adverse reactions to aspirin; eventually he and his associates began to suspect widespread allergic reactions to salicylates, a natural compound that is contained in many fruits and that has a structure very similar to aspirin. Combining this hypothesis with known reactions to food additives such as artificial flavors and colorings, Feingold developed a strict diet that he claimed should be successful in alleviating symptoms in "about 50 percent of hyperkinetic-learning disabled children" (1975a, p. 803). The efficacy of both megavitamin therapy and nutrition therapy depends on alleviation of symptoms. Currently, neither approach can claim undisputed positive results and these forms of intervention for ADHD receive only scant negative attention in recent research commentaries (Pennington, 2002; Sattler & Hoge, 2006). We will return to a discussion of nutrition therapy later in this chapter.

As with studies on genetic factors, the research on biochemical/neurological factors is promising but not conclusive in determining the etiology of emotional/behavioral disorders. We will return to a more detailed description of efficacy studies in the "Applications" section of biophysical research.

Temperament Factors

Temperament refers to a behavioral style that is an inborn tendency but also highly influenced by the environment. The temperament factor emerges primarily from a longitudinal study begun in 1956 by Thomas, Chess, and Birch. Following a sample of over 100 children from infancy to adulthood, Thomas and his colleagues (Thomas & Chess, 1977; Thomas, Chess, & Birch, 1969) identified the following nine characteristics of temperament that were stable and endured through maturity: activity level, regularity (of biological functions), adaptability, threshold of responsiveness, intensity of reaction, mood quality, distractibility, persistence, and attention span.

From these characteristics, three major patterns of temperament emerged that accounted for 65 percent of the children: (1) the easy child, accounting for 40 percent of the sample and characterized by regularity, adaptability, and a positive approach to new stimuli; (2) the difficult child, accounting for 10 percent of the sample and characterized by irregularity in biological functions, poor adaptability, and negative and intense moods; and (3) the slow-to-warm-up child, accounting for 15 percent of the sample and characterized by a slow but eventually positive adaptability both to change and to new situations. The remaining 35 percent of the sample showed no consistent temperament patterns. These three categories were not totally predictive of problem behavior. As might be anticipated, the difficult child was more likely to develop problem behaviors, but not all difficult children eventually did so. Thomas and his colleagues believed that with this type of child, interactions between the parent and child were most influential in the development of problem behavior. Parental consistency and pressure toward conformity were especially significant. Moreover, some children characterized as easy or slow-to-warm-up later manifested emotional/behavioral disorders. Overall, the study showed interesting and stable styles of temperament but no clear and indisputable relationship between temperament and eventual problem behavior. Instead, environmental influences such as social pressures and interpersonal relationships were shown to interact with temperament to produce varying results.

The Thomas, Chess, and Birch research was reevaluated by Buss and Plomin (1985) who concluded that the scales actually measured only two temperament characteristics rather than the nine proposed by the original authors. Buss and Plomin further questioned whether the easy–difficult classification at infancy was predictive of future adjustment, although conceding that temperament ratings at ages 4 and 5 do appear to be more reliable. As an alternative schema, Buss and Plomin propose three aspects of temperament: emotionality, activity, and sociability. Emotionality is the arousal threshold of the infant, especially under conditions of fear or anger. Activity may be loosely defined as the enthusiasm, or vigor and rate at which an infant performs behaviors. Sociability is the tendency to seek the company of others; low sociability connotes a low need to interact rather than shyness, which connotes discomfort or fear in social interactions.

A later model of temperament that combines dimensions of previous research was proposed by Rothbart and Mauro (1990). This model retained the dimensions of activity level, rhythmicity, fearful distress, and positive affect, but combined distractibility and attention span into one factor, called attention span/persistence. These researchers also added a dimension for irritable/distress (fussing, crying, and showing distress when frustrated).

In summary, although there is no agreement about which schema of temperament most accurately describes and predicts future behavior, most researchers do acknowledge that individuals are born with certain tendencies such as adaptability or intensity; these tendencies can be measured, are stable over time, and interact with the environment to produce general patterns of behavior that may be predictable. For example, infants and toddlers who score high on irritability, shyness, attention span, and sociability tend to display similar characteristics throughout childhood and often as adults (Kochanska & Radke-Yarrow, 1992; Pedlow, Sanson, Prior, & Oberklaid, 1993). However, the stability of temperament over time seems most strongly related to those children at the extreme ends of the continuum (Kerr, Lambert, Stattin, & Klackenberg-Larsson, 1994). Concordance rates indicate that about half of the temperament differences among us can be attributed to differences in our genetic makeup (Caspi, 1998).

Summary of Etiology

Under the biophysical model, disordered behavior is variously attributed to genetic factors, biochemical/neurological irregularities, or temperament. Each of these factors has its advocates backed by a body of research; however, none of the advocates can promote definitive conclusions until further research provides clearer answers. Let us now turn our attention to evaluation procedures stemming from the biophysical view.

Typical Evaluation Procedures

Identification of biophysical causes of disorders is usually the domain of medical personnel. Although pediatricians, psychiatrists, neuropsychologists, and neurologists occupy the central roles in making such diagnoses, teachers may be instrumental in detecting potential problems and initiating referrals to medical personnel. In this section, developmental histories and neurological assessment are described. Although DNA testing may become a common way of diagnosing mental disorders, the scope of this book does not lend itself to a review of such a complex technique.

Developmental Histories

Extensive developmental histories should be a part of evaluations of students manifesting problem behavior because genetic problems, physical trauma, or medical conditions that affect behavior may be revealed. Information on the following conditions that may have influenced the student's physical well-being or development is typically acquired. A discussion of the purpose and use of developmental histories can be reviewed in Chapter 3.

1. *Prenatal and perinatal conditions:* problems or unusual conditions associated with pregnancy or birth
2. *Developmental milestones:* ages at which the child walked, was toilet trained, talked, and so forth
3. *Physical development:* severe illnesses, diseases, or accidents; unusual eating habits, sleep patterns, or other behaviors; general activity level
4. *Social development:* relationships with peers; indications of emotional tension or stress; effective discipline methods and child's reaction to discipline
5. *General health:* overall physical condition; special health conditions requiring medication; asthma, allergies, diabetes, heart condition
6. *Family history:* number and age of siblings; divorce and remarriage issues; health or education; problems experienced by parents or siblings; mental health problems of relatives

Experiences that may have caused neurological impairment such as malnutrition, prolonged high fever, severe poisoning, head injuries, chronic seizure disorders, or diseases such as meningitis and encephalitis are particularly noteworthy. Since most developmental histories depend on interviews with parents or guardians, school psychologists or other assessment personnel are usually responsible for making this information a part of the student's educational file.

Neurological and Neuropsychological Assessment

Neurological assessment is an important aspect of biophysical evaluations of disorders because many unusual or bizarre behaviors have neurological bases. Examples are repetitive speech and mannerisms, abnormal motor function, and overreaction to sensory stimuli such as loud noises or flickering lights. However, neurological assessments are not a routine part of identifying emotional/behavioral disorders in children.

Disorders affecting brain function, brain damage, and sensorimotor problems are typically diagnosed through some form of neurological testing. Neurological screening is occasionally carried out by trained school assessment personnel, but a neurological evaluation is confined to a neurologist's office. A standard neurological evaluation assesses functioning in the areas of motor skills, coordination, reflexes, mental alertness, sensory discrimination, and integrity of cranial nerves. Except for reflexes, most of these areas are assessed by asking the subject to perform verbal or motor tasks that are quite simple for unimpaired individuals. For example, to check mental alertness, the subject may be asked to demonstrate adequate memory of facts or personal information; to check coordination, the subject may be asked to touch the end of the nose with the index finger; and to check sensory discrimination, the subject may be asked to identify a number being traced in the palm of the hand. If screening measures indicate problems with these or similar tasks, the neurologist may choose to do an electroencephalogram (EEG), or brain scan, such as computerized tomography (CT) or magnetic resonance imaging (MRI), which sometimes allows the site of dysfunction, if any, to be located (Bigler et. al., 1999).

Neuropsychology refers to the study of brain–behavior relationships (Reynolds & Mayfield, 1999). Many tests of neuropsychological functioning are available, but their use is typically restricted to trained neuropsychologists. Some test batteries are designed by the school psychologist or neuropsychologist to address specific referral questions; such batteries may consist of various cognitive, achievement, language, motor, sensory, memory, and personality tests.

The *Halstead-Reitan Neuropsychological Test Battery* (Reitan & Wolfson, 1985) is a comprehensive neuropsychological evaluation that assesses cognitive and perceptual–motor abilities. There are three versions of this battery for different age levels (5–8 years [Reitan-Indiana Battery], 9–14 years, and 15–adult), with some overlap in subtests. It is one of the most widely used batteries of its type and is useful as a screening procedure for identifying children with brain injuries. Among its subtests are measures of verbal and nonverbal intelligence, concept formation, expressive and receptive language, auditory perception, time perception, memory, perceptual motor speed, and spatial relations (Sattler & Hoge, 2006). Administration and interpretation of the battery is time-consuming and is limited to trained neuropsychologists.

Another comprehensive assessment in this area is the *Luria-Nebraska Neuropsychological Battery—Children's Revision* (Golden, 1986). Based on the work of A. R. Luria, a Russian neuropsychologist, this standardized assessment contains 149 items covering 11 major areas of neuropsychological functioning, many of which overlap with those of the Halstead-Reitan. In addition, responses are rated according to accuracy, speed, quality, time lapse, number of trials, or number of responses. Despite its popularity, the Luria has drawbacks in that Luria himself provided no guidelines for standardized administration or interpretation, resulting in few investigations into the reliability and validity of the instrument (C. J. Golden, 1981; Sattler, 2006).

Two other, more recent neuropsychological test batteries receiving attention in the educational arena are the *Dean-Woodcock Neuropsychological Assessment System* (Dean & Woodcock, 2003), which incorporates the *Woodcock-Johnson-III Tests of Cognitive Ability and Achievement,* and the *NEPSY—A Developmental Neuropsychological Assessment* (Korkman, Kirk, & Kemp, 1998). Both of these test batteries are standardized, comprehensive neuropsychological assessment batteries appropriate for use with school-age children.

Educational Applications

In the biophysical model, medical interventions are sought when a physiological cause for emotional/behavioral disorders is hypothesized or identified. Medical or health-related personnel are usually responsible for evaluation and treatment, and the teacher's primary role is observer and monitor of the student's in-school behavior. Two major interventions traditionally employed under the biophysical model are drug therapy and nutrition therapy. These methods were not developed for exclusive use with individuals with disorders, but each has strong ramifications for behavior change. Both biophysical therapies have been controversial since their introduction to the medical and educational communities. The interested reader is referred to a review article by Pescara-Kovach and Alexander (1994).

Genetic Technologies

Applications of knowledge gleaned from the Human Genome Project will likely lead to rapid advances in genetic counseling and prenatal diagnosis (Berk, 1999; Collins, 2006), thus preventing many disorders. Additionally, treatments such as psychopharmacology may be enhanced by such knowledge. Furthermore, the new molecular medicine will likely see advances in gene splicing whereby healthy genes are delivered to an individual's cells to combat the effects of an "abnormal" gene. To date, several children with inherited immune system deficiencies have benefited from gene splicing (Bodmer & McKie, 1997; Cavazzana-Calvo et al., 2000). Although the ability to successfully insert the right gene into a person's genome is a huge challenge, the implications of such treatment are invaluable. On the other hand, the discovery of genetic technologies is fraught with ethical, legal, and social concerns. As advancements in these treatments are made, it will be imperative that individuals who are diagnosed with certain disorders, but who do not yet show symptoms, be protected from discrimination and harm (Marshall, 1996).

The role of the special educator during treatments for genetic disorders will be to apply effective instruction given what is known about certain disorders. Hodapp and Fidler (1999) recommend four guiding principles for special educators relative to etiologically based approaches.

1. Environmental interventions can help to improve functioning for individuals, regardless of their genetic constitution.
2. Individual differences exist within any group of individuals with a specific genetic disorder.
3. All behaviors result from many factors, although a genetic disorder may alert professionals to potential maladaptive behaviors.
4. Children with genetic disorders change as they get older.

The key for special educators will be to link specific behavioral profiles with more effective intervention outcomes. Pennington (2002) cautions that "the etiology of a disorder does not necessarily dictate its treatment" (p. 323). Psychosocial interventions can be highly effective with highly heritable disorders such as autism, while medications may be very effective for disorders that are primarily environmental, such as posttraumatic stress disorder.

Psychopharmacology or Drug Therapy

Psychopharmacology or drug (psychotropic) therapy is the most widely used biophysical intervention (Sinacola & Peters-Strickland, 2006). In the past, drug therapy was somewhat simpler than today: Antipsychotics were used to treat schizophrenia and other severe disorders, antidepressants were used to treat major depression, and stimulants were used to treat attention-deficit hyperactivity disorder. However, major advances in drug therapy have been made, due to the nature of the newly developed drugs themselves and to the protocol of their use. In contrast to the "shotgun" approach of the past, newer medications better target specific neurological activity. Additionally, combinations of drugs of different classes are being used with treatment-resistant individuals and those with multiple diagnoses. Other advances include the availability of a wider range of medications for specific disorders, medications with fewer and less severe side effects, and medications with less potential lethality (Marsh & Fristad, 2002).

Prevalence of Psychopharmacology with Children and Youth. At the end of the 20th century, more children and adolescents than ever were taking prescription drugs. In 1994, for example, 200,000 prescriptions for Prozac were filled for children ages 5 to 10, and 150,000 prescriptions for both Prozac and Zoloft were filled for adolescents (Talan, 1997). These figures represent a half-million prescriptions for antidepressant drugs that were not even on the market several years ago. About this same time, 3 million Ritalin prescriptions were filled for school-age children diagnosed with attention-deficit hyperactivity disorder (ADHD) (Read, 1995). In 2003, about 13 million children in kindergarten through 12th grade were reported to have taken medication in any 2-week time period (Vail, 2005). Most common were ADHD medications. The many articles and discussions published in popular media sources attest to public concern about whether or not children are getting the right medication for the right purpose, and uncertainty about the safety of some prescribed medications.

In an article in the *Harvard Mental Health Letter* (Harvard Medical School, 2005) regarding the safety of antidepressant drugs, it was reported that the number of antidepressant prescriptions for children rose rapidly during the 1990s, but has begun a steep decline in recent years. This decline seems to have resulted from concerns regarding increased suicide risk for patients under the age of 18 who were taking a specific class of antidepressants (specific serotonin reuptake inhibitors, or SSRIs). Many studies have been done with varied results, but the overall conclusion is that there may be a doubling of risk, from 1 to 2 percent, to 2 to 4 percent in both children and adults taking antidepressants. In 2004 the Food and Drug Administration (FDA) issued a "Black Box Warning" regarding risk of suicidal thoughts, hostility, and agitation, which is placed in the package inserts for all commonly used antidepressants. Even so, a report from the National Institute of Mental Health

([NIMH], February 8, 2005) summarized recent findings by concluding that there are substantial benefits from medication therapy for adolescents with moderate to severe depression, including many with suicidal ideation.

How prevalent is drug therapy for children and youth with emotional and behavioral disorders? Hallfors, Fallon, and Watson (1998) attempted to answer this question for a sample of 488 students in two states who were identified as having serious emotional disturbance and who were being maintained in the community despite being at risk for residential placement. The most common diagnoses for the youth were ADHD, oppositional-defiant disorder, and conduct disorder. Among those children who were also identified by the public schools as EBD, 56 percent were on some type of psychotropic medication; in fact, children receiving special education services were nearly three times as likely to be on medication. Children and youth with ADHD were the most likely to be medicated (75–80 percent), followed by those with major psychopathology, such as bipolar disorder or schizophrenia. Children with conduct disorder but not ADHD were among the least likely to be prescribed medication. Data from the Centers for Disease Control (CDC; 2006) indicates that in 2003, approximately 4.4 million children ages 4–17 years had a history of diagnosis of ADHD. Of that group, about 2.5 million (56 percent) were reported to be taking medication for the disorder.

Another study retrieved from CDC (2006) was based on a survey of 4,668 children ages 4–17 years conducted by the National Center for Health Statistics (Simpson, Coren, Pastor, & Reuben, 2005). About 5 percent of these children had received medication treatment during the past 12 months; of that group about 88 percent were prescribed medications for ADHD. According to Zewekas, Vitiello, and Norquist (2006), the prevalence of stimulant use among U.S. children with ADHD has remained relatively constant from 1997 to 2002. The use of stimulant medication was highest in the 6- to 12-year age group (4.8 percent) and lowest in children under age 6 (.3 percent). These prevalence rates were found to be stable rather than escalating. Use was highest among white males, but an increase was noted in use of stimulant medication in African American males.

Another group of researchers (Runnheim, Frankenberger, & Hazelkorn, 1996) looked specifically at use of medications for ADHD with students with EBD. In a statewide survey, they found that the incidence of identification of ADHD and of medication dropped with age: 40 percent of elementary students, 32 percent of middle and junior high students, and 15 percent of high school students with EBD were diagnosed as ADHD and were being treated with medication. Ritalin was the drug of choice in two-thirds of the cases. Teachers were also surveyed about their opinions of the effectiveness of medications in their classrooms. Although they generally agreed that medication helped to reduce the incidences of inappropriate behavior in the classroom, they were less sure that it helped to improve academic performance.

Forness and Kavale (2001), in a discussion of the efficacy of pharmacological treatments for children with emotional or behavioral disorders, concluded that for a significant number of children with EBD, diagnoses that lead to effective pharmacological treatments are critical for successful outcomes. They further noted that despite widespread concern, considerable evidence exists for the efficacy safety of psychopharmacological treatment, particularly for ADHD, and advocate for a "new medical model" that includes consideration of diagnoses that warrant medication intervention. Forness and Kavale suggest that this model should be integrated with the behavioral model (see Chapter 7) currently prominent in special education. Their recommendations include (1) collaborating with teachers of LD students on detecting EBD, (2) assisting special education and related professionals in recognition of comorbid disorders, (3) collaborating with medical professionals regarding psychopharmacological treatment, and (4) helping parents and early childhood teachers to recognize early signs of psychopathology.

Drugs Commonly Prescribed for Students with EBD. Teachers of students with EBD will inevitably encounter many students taking medication in their classrooms. The most prescribed medication will be Ritalin for ADHD. However, it is important to be aware of other common medications because of the impact that they may have on children's behavior, cognition, and overall well-being. Sweeney, Forness, Kavale, and Levitt (1997) described the most commonly prescribed psychotropic medications for children and youth under four major categories: psychostimulants, antidepressants, antipsychotics, and anticonvulsants. Sweeney et al. provide a comprehensive review of research on these classes of drugs and present information on (1) when these medications are indicated by Food and Drug Administration (FDA) approval, (2) when these medications are contraindicated, and (3) their known side effects. A condensed version is presented in Table 4.1; for more complete information, the reader is referred to the original article. Wilens (1999) provides a thorough, readable review of the use of psychiatric medications in children. This resource is designed for parents and includes resources for monitoring medication effects that would be particularly useful for special education teachers (see "Additional Readings and Resources" at the end of the chapter).

Surprisingly, few large-scale studies have been conducted on the efficacy of psychotropic medications with children and youth. According to Sweeney et al. (1997), the FDA does not require pharmaceutical companies to research new medications in pediatric populations before putting the medication on the market, resulting in little funding for such research. This lack of research then contributes to the lack of FDA approval, which requires that safety and effectiveness be demonstrated. In fact, Sweeney and colleagues reported that "in virtually every article reviewed for this study, the researchers expressed concern over the lack of controlled, double-blind studies to determine the efficacy of these new drugs and their relative safety when used with children younger than 16 years of age" (p. 19). In a more recent commentary, Kavale and Forness (2001) reported the results of a multisite, multimodality treatment study of ADHD (MTA) in which 579 children with a primary diagnosis of ADHD received treatment across six different sites. Treatment conditions included stimulant or related medication only, intensive behavioral treatment only, combined behavioral and medication treatment, and community treatment (typically involving one or two physician consultations per year for medication/management). Findings indicated that for treatment of ADHD, medication treatment was statistically and clinically more effective than comprehensive behavioral or psychosocial interventions (MTA Cooperative Group, 1999).

Teachers and parents can play a key role in observing and offering feedback to physicians once a student has been placed on medication (Hoff, Doepke, & Landau, 2002; Glantz, 1996; Sweeney et al., 1997). Minimally, teachers need to be aware of which medications their students are taking and the potential side effects that may affect behavior and cognition in the classroom.

TABLE 4.1 Commonly Prescribed Drugs for Students with EBD

Type Brand Name	FDA-approved Indications	Absolute Contraindications	Known Side-Effects
Stimulants: Ritalin, Cylert, Dexedrine	ADHD Narcolepsy	Liver problems (for Cylert)	Insomnia, decreased appetite, GI pain, irritability, increased heart rate, worsening of symptoms
Antidepressants: *Tricyclic:* Imipramine, Elavil, Desipramine, Tofranil	Enuresis	Pregnancy, prior hypersensitivity reaction	Psychosis, cardiac complications, impulsivity, mania, seizures, confusion, high blood pressure, rash, tics, tremors, uncoordination, anxiety, insomnia and/or nightmares
SSRIs: Prozac, Zoloft, Paxil	None	Known hypersensitivity reactions pregnancy, liver disease, using other antidepressants	GI problems, decreased appetite, nervousness, weight loss (for Prozac), anxiety, sweating, insomnia, motor restlessness, dry mouth
Lithium	Bipolar disorder	Allergic drug reaction, pregnancy, kidney disease, thyroid disease, heart disease	GI problems, tremors, decreased white blood cells, malaise
Antipsychotics (neuroleptics, major tranquilizers) Thorazine, Mellaril, Prolixin, Serentil, Stelazine, Trilafon, Compazine	Psychosis, ADHD mania, aggressive behavior, nonpsychotic anxiety, Tourette's syndrome	Hypersensitivity to neuroleptics, other central nervous system depressants being used, pregnancy, low white cell count	Cardiac arrhythmia, sedation, affective blunting, cognitive dulling, social withdrawal, tardive dyskinesia, liver toxicity, death
Clozaril, Risperdal	Not currently FDA approved for use under age 12, but promising results		Minimal side effects
Anticonvulsants: Tegretol, Dilantin, Depakene	Epileptic seizures, bipolar disorder, alcohol withdrawal, chronic pain due to nerve injury	Known hypersensitivity, pregnancy, bone marrow depression, use of other antidepressants	Differs with specific drug, but common; problems with motor coordination, tremor, drowsiness, GI upset, skin rashes

Adapted from Sweeney, D. P., Forness, S. R., Kavale, K. A., & Levitt, J. G. (1997). An update on psychopharmacologic medication: What teachers, clinicians, and parents need to know. *Intervention in School and Clinic, 33*(1), 4–21. Used with permission of the publisher.

Nutrition Therapy

The concept of food allergies and the Feingold diet were alluded to in the section on etiology. The Feingold diet (Feingold, 1975a) initially eliminates all foods with the preservatives BHT and BHA, artificial colors and flavorings, and natural salicylates. Among the seemingly nutritious foods containing salicylates are apples, peaches, berries, tomatoes, oranges, grapes, and raisins. Other forbidden items are toothpaste, mouthwash, throat lozenges, cough drops, perfume, and most over-the-counter drugs such as aspirin. After a period of time, some of the foods containing salicylates are reintroduced one by one to check whether there is an adverse reaction. Many children can resume eating these foods, but the artificial additives are never reinstated in the diet. Although Feingold claimed success for only a moderate percentage of ADHD children, the diet received an inordinate amount of publicity because parents often reported dramatic behavior changes and established the Feingold Association, a national network of parents.

Pescara-Kovach and Alexander (1994) reviewed a number of controlled, double-blind studies and concluded thus:

> Though Feingold's research demonstrated his concern for the children's well-being, no absolute or concurrent evidence has emerged in favor of the link between food ingested and adverse behavior. In fact, much of the evidence suggests the contrary. Recent research continues to challenge the link between food additives and behavior. (p. 145)

Goldstein (1999) advised that while nontraditional treatments, such as dietary manipulation, are popular for ADHD, they have not stood the test of rigorous scientific research and should not be recommended as treatments of choice for ADHD. Nevertheless, a recent Internet search yielded 319,000 websites containing discussion of the Feingold diet, so it continues to attract attention as a treatment option. As with medication, use of the Feingold diet should be discussed with and supervised by competent medical personnel.

Teachers' Role

Biophysical interventions require the services of specialists: physicians, allergists, geneticists, neurologists, and others. The role of the teacher may initially appear to be restricted to making a referral and following up through contacts with the specialists. Although these tasks are important, it is also essential that the teacher help monitor the classroom behavior of a child on medication or on a specialized diet. In order to modify the intervention effectively, the specialist needs both anecdotal and systematic observations from the classroom. Medications are often started on a trial basis, with the dosage too high or too low because physicians cannot predict exactly how a dosage will affect any given child. Fluctuations in behavior as well as symptoms of side effects should be reported both to parents and to the specialist. If no specific information on side effects is offered to the teacher, he or she should request it so he or she will know what to look for. Often the concerned teacher must take the initiative to maintain contact with specialists such as physicians. There is no substitute for the information a teacher can glean from observing the child on a daily basis in the classroom!

The teacher also can help parents by providing materials on the pros and cons of some of the questionable therapies that may not be standard practice in the medical community. Golden (1980) offers guidelines to help parents and teachers identify and critique nonstandard therapies:

1. They are reportedly based on biochemical or neurophysiological theories that are incongruent with current concepts of the central nervous system.
2. They are said to be absolutely harmless.
3. The children with whom they are supposedly effective are a broad, ill-defined group.
4. The studies cited as supportive research are usually anecdotal and testimonial rather than well-controlled experimental studies.
5. The therapies have an emotional appeal, and their detractors are attacked defensively.

Parents and teachers would be wise to question any therapies designed to correct learning and behavior problems that exhibit several of these characteristics.

Summary

The biophysical model assumes that there are organic causes of emotional disturbance that can be treated medically or physically. Etiological theories, evaluation procedures, and intervention strategies are summarized in Table 4.2. Box 4.1 provides a case study of Sam, who suffered traumatic brain injury at the age of 7 and manifested emotional and behavioral problems much later. Read about Sam and discuss the ramifications of the interaction of his physical disorder and subsequent EBD.

The research on causative factors is advancing rapidly but remains inconclusive for many disorders that affect emotional and behavioral functioning. Such biophysical interventions as drug therapy and nutrition therapy remain controversial, while we are only on the frontier of genetic technologies. However, at least for ADHD, the efficacy of pharmacological interventions is well established.

The teacher's role is viewed as a liaison to specialists and a daily monitor of the intervention prescribed. Teachers may also provide information to parents regarding advantages and disadvantages of biophysical therapies.

TABLE 4.2 Summary of Biophysical Model

Etiological Factor	Evaluation Procedures	Applications
Genetic	Developmental histories Genetic testing	Genetic counseling/technologies
Biochemical/neurological	Neurological assessment Neuropsychological assessment	Psychopharmacology
Temperament	DNA testing Temperament assessment	Nutrition therapy Counseling/behavioral interventions

BOX 4.1
Sam

Children often exhibit changes in behavior or mood after traumatic brain injury (TBI). Since the child's behavior often appears similar to that observed in other disorders, particularly emotional disturbance, ADHD, oppositional-defiant disorder, and conduct disorder, the TBI may go unrecognized as the source of the emotional and behavioral problems. Numerous differences exist between children with TBI and those with emotional disturbance related to other etiologies. Children with TBI experience a sudden onset of disability, usually accompanied by cognitive impairment, physical challenges, emotional difficulties, and disrupted social functioning. Impairment in any of these areas may contribute to unpredictable behavioral problems. Disruptions in executive functioning (including organizing, problem-solving, planning, judgment, and abstract thinking abilities) are common consequences of TBI and may impact academics and behavior. While peer interactions are likely to be affected by behavioral difficulties in children with emotional disturbances, the interactions of a child with a brain injury are also affected by cognitive deficits. This case study illustrates the difficulty in differentiating the effects of a TBI from other disability categories and underscores the need for a thorough developmental and medical history as a prerequisite to appropriate classification and intervention.

Sam, an 18-year-old male, sustained a closed head injury at age 7 in a car accident. Afterward, he remained in a coma for 4 days. Computerized tomography (CT) scans revealed minimal right frontal lobe damage. During the initial hospitalization, the clinical examination found evidence of language loss (aphasia), memory deficits, and right-sided weakness. Sam was discharged from the hospital 1 week after the accident. He returned to public school after a period of several months and received speech and occupational therapy for 2 years. Sam was prescribed Ritalin prior to his return to school to modulate concentration and activity levels. In the fifth grade, Sam began to manifest significant social and behavioral problems. At puberty, he frequently became verbally aggressive with peers, made inappropriate sexual comments, and had several instances of "blowing up" in class where he threatened to harm himself and others. At this time, he also began to make suicidal and homicidal threats and gestures: he threatened to jump out of a window, to use a knife to kill himself and others, and to set fire to the family home. At age 13, he entered residential treatment with behaviors of concern including property destruction, disruptive behavior, verbal and physical aggression, stealing, and antisocial behavior. At age 15, he was admitted to a second residential treatment facility specializing in treatment of children with brain injuries, where he remained until he graduated from high school at age 18. While at this facility, Sam was mainstreamed into the local high school.

It is clear from Sam's history that many of his behavioral problems, including impulsivity, disinhibition, agitation, aggression, and inappropriate social behavior, were related to the effects of a brain injury sustained at age 7. However, despite extensive medical documentation, he was not officially classified as TBI in the public school special education system until 12th grade. With the resolution of problems with speech and organizational skills in elementary school, additional complications from the closed head injury were left unidentified. School personnel felt that the student's needs could be met in the general education setting, and special education services were discontinued after 2 years. No plan to monitor his progress was established.

When behavioral difficulties escalated 5 years later, they were attributed to an emotional disturbance rather than to brain injury. His psychological evaluation made note of the TBI, but made no connection between the brain injury and his behavioral problems. Additionally, later impulsivity, agitation, and aggression (which were likely related to the TBI) were attributed to a diagnosis of oppositional-defiant disorder. Thus, Sam was misdiagnosed with respect to eligibility for special education services throughout most of his school years, resulting in services that did not fully address specific needs associated with his brain injury. For example, while Sam was provided with social skills training in a classroom setting, his informal social interactions were unsupervised. Eventually, problems with impulsivity, agitation, low frustration tolerance, sexual inappropriateness, and overall poor social judgment led to aggressive incidents, social isolation and rejection, and expulsion from school. When the TBI classification was formalized in 12th grade, the student was assigned an aide to be his escort during non-class times. The occurrence of multiple aggressive outbursts each month decreased to one outburst every few months and Sam was able to graduate from high school.

As this case study illustrates, appropriate classification within the special education system for students with a traumatic brain injury can be uncertain and complex, given the overlap in symptoms with other emotional and behavioral disorders. However, appropriate classification is imperative as it dictates expectations, planning, interventions, and discipline procedures for students in special education.

Contributed by Krystol Clark, John Davis, Tiffany Kuchar, and Rebekah Canu, former graduate students at Texas State University–San Marcos.

Conclusions

Understanding disordered behavior from a biophysical perspective allows educators to appreciate medical interventions that might be helpful with children with well-researched disorders such as schizophrenia, mood disorders, and ADHD. Many researchers believe that some biologically based cause will eventually be found for many psychological disorders. Much of the current research points to a combination of genetic predispositions and environmental catalysts in the development of these disorders.

KEY POINTS

1. An understanding of theoretical models is crucial in dealing with students with EBD because our views, evaluation procedures, and interventions are based on assumptions of these models.
2. The biophysical model assumes that physical/brain-related factors cause or contribute to many emotional/behavioral disorders.
3. Much biophysical research has been conducted with neurotransmitters in populations with ADHD, autism, schizophrenia, and depression; much of this research is promising but inconclusive in determining either causes or cures.
4. Teachers are ideally involved in biophysical interventions such as medication therapy in their primary role as monitors of effectiveness and side effects.
5. Knowledge gleaned from the Human Genome Project appears to be leading toward effective genetic counseling, treatment, and ultimately prevention of many psychological disorders.
6. As many as half of students with emotional/behavioral disorders may be on some type of medication; ADHD is the most common diagnosis and Ritalin is the most common medication.
7. Although prescriptions for psychotropic medications increased dramatically in the 1990s for children younger than 16, prevalence of medication therapy appears to have stabilized in the past 5–10 years, at least for antidepressants and psychostimulants.

HOMEWORK QUESTIONS

1. What is your opinion of medication treatment for ADHD? On what information do you base your opinion? Address these questions in no more than one paragraph.
2. Briefly describe the importance of the developmental history in helping to understand intervention options for children with EBD.
3. How might the understanding of autism and/or schizophrenia as a biophysical disorder change the perception of teachers and other professionals who design and monitor interventions? Address this issue in no more than two paragraphs.
4. Conduct an Internet search of information regarding the Human Genome Project, then write a four-paragraph reaction paper. Include your thoughts regarding the changes in special education that will result from better prevention of behavioral and psychological disorders.
5. In one to three paragraphs explain how twin and adoption studies can make the case for genetic influences on manifested characteristics.

ADDITIONAL READINGS AND RESOURCES

What teachers, clinicians, and parents need to know, by D. Sweeney, S. Forness, K. Kavale, & J. Levitt, 1997, *Intervention in School and Clinic, 33*(1), 4–21, for an excellent synopsis of the major medications prescribed for children and youth with EBD.

Straight talk about psychiatric medications, by T. E. Wilens, 1999, New York: Guilford Press, for a very thorough and readable discussion of medications for each major diagnosis; includes tables for side effects, dosage, and monitoring.

The book of man: The Human Genome Project and the quest to discover our genetic heritage, by W. Bodmer, and R. McKie, 1997, New York: Oxford University Press, for an explanation of the intricacies of the Human Genome Project and its implications.

Centers for Disease Control and Prevention: *http://www.cdc.gov/,* for information about current studies regarding etiologies and treatment of diseases and disorders affecting children and youth, and for studies pertaining to factors negatively impacting childrens' health (e.g., school violence).

The Genome-Wide Association Studies (GWAS) by the National Institutes of Health (NIH): *http://grants.nih.gov/grants/gwas/index.htm,* for updates on genome studies to isolate etiologies of diseases and disorders.

ENDNOTE

1. For illustrative purposes, the present authors have selected definitions from the literature to represent the models. The authors of the definitions did not create them to represent these specific models, nor do the authors necessarily subscribe to the theoretical model to which their definitions have been attached in this text.

CHAPTER 5 Psychodynamic Model

Definition and Etiology
Genetic Factors, Biochemical/Neurological Factors, Temperament

Typical Evaluation Procedures
Developmental Histories, Neurological and Neuropsychological Assessment

Educational Applications
Genetic Technologies, Psychopharmacology, Nutrition Therapy, Teacher's Role

QUESTIONS TO CONSIDER

- According to the psychodynamic model, how are emotional and behavioral disorders caused?
- What are the major developmental stages in Freud's psychoanalytic theory?
- How does Erickson's developmental stage theory differ from Freud's conceptualization?
- What are some of the major projective evaluation techniques and how are they believed to elicit information about personality and emotional functioning?
- How do educational applications for school-age children that stem from the psychodynamic model differ from interventions based on the biophysical model?
- What does research tell us about the effectiveness of psychotherapy?

Orientation

Psychodynamic theory is the most traditional explanation of disordered behavior. Based on the assumption that internal psychological processes are dysfunctional, treatment according to this model involves methods for facilitating healthy emotional development. Some of these treatments are time-consuming and expensive, with little research to substantiate efficacy, whereas others have received at least adequate research support. Nevertheless, many aspects of the psychodynamic model are founded in developmental psychology, are in common use in schools and other settings, and will benefit students with emotional and behavioral disorders.

Overview

Developmental theories are most often stage theories explaining human thought and behavior, with a basic premise that humans, given adequate environmental supports, are internally motivated to mature through developmental milestones. If an individual does not successfully negotiate developmental milestones, then internal processes are examined and, ideally, modified through treatment. Psychodynamic theories are developmental in nature, which means that children with emotional and behavioral disorders are viewed as developmentally delayed in terms of emotional maturity. Consequently, treatment consists of efforts to facilitate healthy psychological functioning by confronting psychic barriers. This model, like the biophysical model, views disturbance as internal to the individual, although environmental triggers may contribute to the development of emotional and behavioral disorders.

Definition and Basic View

> The emotionally disturbed child . . . is so thwarted in satisfaction of his needs for safety, affection, acceptance, and self-esteem that he is unable intellectually to function efficiently, cannot adapt to reasonable requirements of social regulation and convention, or is so plagued with inner conflict, anxiety, and guilt that he is unable to perceive reality clearly or meet the ordinary demands of the environment in which he lives. (Blackham, 1967, p. 73)

The references to "thwarted . . . needs for safety, affection, acceptance, and self-esteem" and the terms "inner conflict, anxiety, and guilt" give this definition a psychodynamic orientation. Psychodynamic theorists are concerned with the needs of the individual. Conflict, anxiety, and guilt also are prime concerns of these theorists, especially psychoanalysts who believe that any of these states may serve as catalysts for personality development. In line with these concerns, evaluation techniques of the psychodynamic model focus on unconscious drives, needs, anxiety, guilt, and conflict. The psychodynamic model is a conglomerate of theories that attempts to explain motivation of human behavior. Falling under this model are the diverse theories of psychoanalysis, ego psychology, phenomenology, Gestalt psychology, individual psychology, and humanistic psychology. Freud's theory of psychoanalytic psychology is the seminal work from which the other branches of psychodynamic thought have emerged. Although arguments are often made for treatment of each of these views as separate and distinct, in this text psychodynamic is a broad descriptor that encompasses the other views. Psychodynamic theory is discussed as two major schools of thought: psychoanalytic thought as espoused by Freud and the neo-Freudians Horney and Erikson, and humanistic thought as espoused by Rogers and Maslow. A related theory by Adler, which contains elements of psychodynamic theory, is discussed as well.

Psychoanalytic thought is unique among psychodynamic theories in its emphasis on unconscious drives that may conflict with conscious desires, and thus cause disorders; in contrast, other theories emphasize conscious experiences such as the individual's perception of the environment. In addition, psychoanalytic thought stresses a "predetermined sequence of personality growth" (Rezmierski & Kotre, 1972); that is, there are specific stages through which an individual passes in normal progress to adulthood. Psychoanalysts believe that emotional health depends on the successful resolution of the conflicts arising during these developmental stages and that disordered emotions and behaviors arise when these conflicts are not resolved.

Some humanistic theorists do not share this concept of the importance of sequential developmental stages; rather, they emphasize the importance of self-perception, self-understanding, and a growth-facilitating environment at all stages. Although it is difficult to promote a singular view of psychodynamic theory, a few commonalities may be extracted. The most basic commonality is implied by the definition of the term *psychodynamic,* which literally means the "dynamics of mental activities and processes." All theorists ascribing to the psychodynamic view are concerned about the process of development and change. A second commonality is that anxiety and emotional crises are important motivators of personal growth and self-development. A third commonality is that significant individuals in one's early life play important roles as catalysts or deterrents of personality growth and healthy development. The fourth common concept is the emphasis on intrapsychic reckonings of the individual. Although many psychodynamic theorists recognize the role of the environment in personality development, it is nonetheless the individual's internal perceptions and feelings about that environment, whether conscious or unconscious, that are the focus of intervention.

Etiology and Development of Disordered Behavior

Psychoanalytic Theory: Freud

Sigmund Freud (1856–1939) was a physician whose fascination with the emotional problems of his patients led him to develop a new branch of psychological theory. In addition to being a physician, he was a psychologist, philosopher, scientist, critic, and psychoanalyst. Born in Freiberg in the former Czechoslovakia, Freud moved to Vienna when he was 3 years old and left when the Nazis entered the city in 1938.

According to Freud, the personality has three major systems of psychic energy: the id, the ego, and the superego; behavior is the result of an interaction among these three systems. The id is the original system that is present at birth and furnishes psychic energy for the other two systems. In other words, the ego is differentiated out of the id, and the superego is differentiated out of the ego. The id represents the inner world of subjective experience and has no knowledge of objective reality. It operates through instinctive drives to reduce tension in the organism, that is, to avoid pain and to obtain pleasure; it is said to operate by the pleasure principle. The ego develops out of a need to temper the subjective view of the id with the objective world of reality; it is the part of the id that has been modified by the external world. It obeys the reality principle, which is characterized by logical and rational thinking. The ego is called the executive of the personality because it controls action by mediating between the real environment and the demands of the id.

The superego represents the moral standards imposed upon a child by society, which are enforced by parents and other societal agents. The superego has two aspects: the positive (ego ideal), which rewards, and the negative (conscience), which punishes. The superego represents the ideal and strives toward perfection. Freud also developed the term *psychic energy* to connote mental activity. He believed that this psychic energy is fluid and is never lost or diminished, but that dynamics of personality are determined by its distribution among the three systems of the id, ego, and superego.

Defense mechanisms are a function of the ego employed to ward off threatening demands of the id and to relieve anxiety. Defense mechanisms are not inherently pathological; in fact, they are used by well-adjusted, mature adults. However, when used excessively, defense mechanisms become debilitating to the personality. They operate unconsciously and deny or distort reality so that the individual is unaware of internal conflict. The principle defense mechanisms are presented in Table 5.1.

Freud postulated five stages of psychosexual development through which a child passes from infancy through adolescence: (1) the oral stage, birth to 2 years of age; (2) the anal stage, 2–4 years; (3) the phallic stage, 4–6 years; (4) the latency period, 6 until puberty; and (5) the genital stage, occurring at puberty. The implications of these stages for disordered behavior are based on two of Freud's premises. The first is that the first few years of life determine the formation of personality. The second premise is that abnormal personality development is due to fixations or arrests at specific stages of psychosexual development. A person may become fixated at a stage for a number of reasons, including excessive gratification, excessive deprivation, fear of transition to the next stage, and physical and psychological factors. It is possible for the personality to be arrested in only one developmental area while progressing normally through the remainder of the stages. Examples of adjustment problems resulting from pathological fixations are outlined in Table 5.2.

In summary, Freud viewed abnormal behavior or disordered behavior as arising from the inability to resolve a conflict within a specific psychosexual stage. In his view, when an individual becomes fixated at a given stage, personal adjustment in that area becomes very difficult and the majority of the individual's interpersonal interactions become a replay of the difficulties encountered during that stage. In other words, psychopathology is a result of a *neurotic conflict,* meaning that there is unconscious conflict between impulses of the id and the ego's defense against the emergence of these impulses into consciousness or behavior (Merydith, 1999).

TABLE 5.1 Principle Defense Mechanisms of the Ego

I.	Repression	Forcing alarming thoughts or feelings from conscious awareness
II.	Projection	Attributing causes of negative impulses or feelings to the external world rather than to oneself
III.	Reaction–Formation	Adopting the behavior or attitude opposite to what one really feels
IV.	Fixation	Failing to pass into the next stage of psychosexual development
V.	Regression	Retreating to an earlier stage of psychosexual development or temporary flight from controlled and realistic thinking

Adapted from Hall (1954) and Hall and Lindzey (1970).

TABLE 5.2 Adjustment Problems Based on Fixations at Psychosexual Stages

Stage	Adjustment Problems
I. Oral stage (birth to 2 years)	Sarcasm, argumentativeness, greediness, acquisitiveness, overdependency
II. Anal stage (2–4 years)	Emotional outbursts such as rages and temper tantrums; compulsive orderliness and over controlled behavior
III. Phallic stage (4–6 years)	Problems with gender identification
IV. Genital stage (puberty to adulthood)	Narcissism or extreme self-love

Adapted from Hall (1954).

Neo-Freudian Theory: Horney and Erikson

Karen Horney (1885–1952) was a proponent of neo-Freudian social theory. Along with Harry Stack Sullivan and Erich Fromm, she downplayed Freud's biological orientation and emphasized social factors in the development of abnormal behavior. Central to Horney's theory is anxiety, which stems from a child's feelings of isolation and helplessness in a world that may be perceived by the child as hostile. A child has a basic need for security that must be supplied by significant others in the child's life through warmth, support, and affection.

According to Horney, as a child struggles with anxiety and the security issue, various behavioral strategies may be tried and eventually a character pattern will be adopted. Horney (1937) postulated three such character patterns: (1) moving toward people, characterized by compliance, submissive behavior, and a need for love; (2) moving against people, characterized by arrogance, hostility, and a need for power: and (3) moving away from people, characterized by social avoidance, withdrawal, and a need for independence. Emotional and behavioral disorders are viewed as the adoption of one of these rigid patterns to the exclusion of the others, which results in inflexible interpersonal interactions. A basic conflict is experienced by individuals who have adopted a rigid character pattern; such individuals experience severe anxiety when called upon to interact in a manner contrary to the adopted pattern. For example, the person characterized by arrogance and hostility may have a difficult time in giving and receiving affection and warmth. Although healthy people occasionally experience such conflicts, the neurotic person, due to lack of a supportive environment early in life, faces such conflicts on a daily basis. Horney believed that such conflict is avoidable and resolvable if a child is reared in an atmosphere of security, warmth, love, trust, and respect.

Erik Erikson (1902–1994) joined theorists such as Anna Freud and Heinz Hartmann in a new conceptualization of the role of the ego in personality development. These theorists view the ego not as an extension of the id, but as autonomous both in origin and function. In other words, the ego is not a passive mediator but an active force with its own energy source. The environment and societal values are central to this new view of the ego, a view that resulted in "the addition of an entire social and cultural dimension to the concept of personality growth" (Rezmierski & Kotre, 1974, p. 209).

Erikson's contribution to the understanding of disordered behavior centers around his concepts of crisis and the importance of crisis resolution during critical periods of development. Erikson proposes eight stages of psychosocial development that roughly parallel Freud's stages of psychosexual development; as implied by the different terminology, Erikson's stages focus on character traits that arise from interpersonal interactions, whereas Freud's stages emphasize character traits arising from experience of a biological or sexual nature. According to Erikson, if the crisis in each stage is not dealt with successfully, the individual will continue to demonstrate behaviors commensurate with that stage, which may be several years below the individual's mental and physical development. Thus, Erikson stresses the developmental nature of personality growth. He further cautions that the successful resolution of a crisis is not a permanent achievement; instead, healthy adults continue to struggle with the issues on a superficial level throughout life. Table 5.3 presents the five psychosocial stages most pertinent to school-age children along with adjustment problems stemming from inadequate resolution.

Humanistic Theory: Rogers and Maslow

Carl Rogers (1902–1987) and Abraham Maslow (1908–1970) share the basic view that human beings are inherently good and capable of actualizing their potential if they can somehow avoid the frustrating and detrimental experiences imposed by society. Rogers asserts that behavior may be understood only in terms of the individual's frame of reference, that is, one's personal experiences and perceptions of the world. In order to understand the development of conflict in an individual's world, Rogers (1959) proposes two concepts. The first is the organismic valuing process, which develops from infancy and refers to a regulatory system that tells the infant (organism) how well it is satisfying basic needs. This valu-

TABLE 5.3 Erikson's Psychosocial Stages

Developmental Phase	Psychosocial Stage	Related Adjustment Problems
I. Infancy	Trust vs. mistrust	Mistrust of others
II. Early childhood (ages 1–3)	Autonomy vs. shame and doubt	Doubt in oneself and mistrust in environment
III. Play age (ages 3–5)	Initiative vs. guilt	Overdeveloped conscience which prevents independent action; excessive guilt
IV. School age (ages 5–10)	Industry vs. inferiority	Doubt in one's ability to perform adequately for society; feelings of inferiority and inadequacy
V. Adolescence	Identity vs. identity diffusion	Doubt about one's sexual, ethnic, or occupational identity

Adapted from E. H. Erikson (1959).

ing process leads the infant to select, inasmuch as possible, those experiences that will be positive and enhance the organism, and to avoid experiences that will be negative and debilitating. Thus, there exists an innate wisdom for preservation and actualization.

As the infant grows, experiences become differentiated between environment and self, and the young child formulates a concept of the self. As the self-concept emerges, so does a need for positive regard, a universal need for acceptance and respect. The need for positive regard then motivates the developing person to judge personal actions in terms of societal values. Conflict arises when the innate criteria clash with societal values so that the person is torn between the organismic valuing process and the need for positive regard. As Rogers (1959) states, disturbance or maladjustment occurs when there is "an incongruence between self and experience." This incongruence is then usually dealt with either by distortion or denial of the experience. If these strategies fail, a serious breakdown of the self-concept may occur and the individual experiences disorganization characterized by irrational or psychotic behaviors. In other words, psychopathology develops from a child's reaction to conditional love (Moore, Presbury, Smith, & McKee, 1999).

Rogers proposes that incongruence can be avoided in an ideal course of development in which the infant receives only unconditional positive regard from the parents. When applying his theory to education, Rogers (1969) states that learning should be self-initiated and congruent with personal experience. The classroom should offer a climate for experiential learning, and the teacher should facilitate the learning process.

Maslow did not address emotional/behavioral disorders in depth, but his theory of human needs and motivation provides a model of health and creativity that has been widely accepted by both psychologists and educators. Similar to Rogers, his theory viewed people as rational and basically trustworthy, as having dignity and worth, and as striving to grow and enhance their potential in harmony with others in their world (Gelso, 1992). Maslow (1967) differentiates between basic needs, which are deficiency needs, and meta-needs, which are growth needs. The basic needs of safety, hunger, satiation, affection, security, and self-esteem are hierarchical: lower ones must be satisfied by the individual before the higher ones can be attained. Meta-needs such as justice, goodness, beauty, and unity are equally important and are not hierarchical. According to Maslow, only a very few select persons are able to realize and internalize the meta-needs; these self-actualized people are characterized by autonomy, spontaneity, democratic values, creativity, and a resistance to conformity. They are able to transcend rather than tolerate the environment, which is the final step in becoming fully human. Although his theory concentrates on the healthy, self-actualizing being, Maslow does eloquently address disordered behavior:

> [I]t is now seen clearly that psychopathology in general results from the denial or the frustration or the twisting of man's essential nature. By this conception what is good? Anything that conduces to this desirable development in the direction of actualization of the inner nature of man. What is pathological? Anything that disturbs or frustrates or twists the course of self-actualization. What is psychotherapy, or for that matter any therapy of any kind? Any means of any kind that helps to restore the person to the path of self-actualization and of development along the lines that his inner nature dictates. (1954, pp. 340–341)

A related theory of human behavior was developed by Adler in the early 20th century. He believed that humans are responsible, creative, and social beings characterized by purposive, goal-directed behavior (Kelly, 1999). Psychopathology, from this view, results from the discouragement that develops when children cannot effectively cope with feelings of inferiority. One of Adler's colleagues and students, Rudolph Dreikurs, continued Adler's work, particularly in the area of understanding children's misbehavior. The four goals of children's misbehavior (which may be progressive and build over time if not corrected) according to Dreikurs (1948) are:

1. *Attention seeking:* the child believes he or she is insignificant unless the center of attention.
2. *Power:* the child demonstrates an aversion to control by adults and other authority figures.
3. *Revenge:* the child wants to retaliate against adults or the society that is viewed as inflicting hurt or injury
4. *Assumed disability:* the child ceases to be an active behavior problem and becomes passive and withdrawn.

The behaviors reflecting these goals will typically be directed at the significant adults in the child's life (e.g., parents and teachers). In order to correct behavior problems and promote healthy emotional development, influential adults would focus on encouragement and re-education to correct distorted beliefs and self-defeating behaviors (Kelly, 1999).

The Psychodynamic Goal: Healthy Development

Although it is difficult to distinguish a singular psychodynamic view of the etiology of problem behavior, it is not difficult to perceive a singular psychodynamic goal of intervention, namely, healthy development. The process by which this goal is attained may be determined largely by variables inherent in the individual, but psychodynamic theorists agree that six basic characteristics are common in the development of a healthy personality:

1. *Attitude toward self:* a realistic view of self, including self-esteem
2. *Resistance to stress:* an ability to cope successfully with crises and stressful situations
3. *Autonomy and independence:* a sense of active participation in and partial control of one's life
4. *Interpersonal relations:* awareness and acceptance of others' needs and an ability to establish meaningful relationships with other people
5. *Curiosity, creativity, and expressiveness:* the most positive aspects of human potential that find expression when individuals are nurtured rather than frustrated
6. *Cognitive and language skills:* skills necessary for making sense of the world and for successful interaction in an educational environment. (Cheney & Morse, 1974)

These characteristics form the basis for psychodynamic interventions, which will be addressed after evaluation procedures are discussed.

Typical Evaluation Procedures

Psychodynamic theory is rich in evaluative instruments such as projective and self-concept measures. Historically, these techniques were liberally used in batteries to identify students with emotional or behavioral disorders, although now they are less commonly used than more objective measures such as direct observations and behavior rating scales. However, projectives may still be widely used as diagnostic tools for individuals in psychotherapy and may also be used in school settings (see Chapter 3 for a discussion of their use in comprehensive evaluations for identification of children with EBD).

Projectives

Projective techniques are based on the premise that, when given a neutral or ambiguous stimulus, a person will project unconscious as well as conscious feelings onto the stimulus.

> [Projectives] tend to solicit rich material, depicting the child's perceptions and interpretations of reality. As the child imposes his own cognitive scheme on stimulus materials, he tends to reveal inner thoughts, feelings and attitudes about various aspects of his world. Such tests enable the examiner to secure material which is unobtainable through other means . . . to get at data which the child might guard against revealing, were he asked directly. (Sigel, 1960, p. 360)

The psychoanalytic premise is that information obtained from projectives comes largely from the subconscious and is therefore inaccessible by more direct means. As projective techniques draw upon unconscious perceptions of reality, they are less susceptible to intentional distortion or faking. However, this necessary ambiguity and lack of structure also undermines their technical adequacy in that reliability and validity data are very difficult to establish.

Projective instruments are widely used with adults in clinical settings. In their use with children, a developmental factor emerges that adds to the complexity of interpretation. A diagnostic evaluation of abnormal child development depends on the concept of normal child development, a multidimensional and complex concept. A child may reveal perceptions of distorted reality due to limited exposure and experience, lack of knowledge, or limited language skills. Therefore, the clinician must distinguish between responses that are immature and those that are deviant. Characteristics of the child that must be considered are socioeconomic status, gender, intellectual ability, verbal facility, and fantasy skill (Sigel, 1960). Projective techniques may take the form of elicited drawings, verbal responses to inkblots and pictures, and written responses to sentence stems. Those techniques most widely used with children are described.

Rorschach Inkblot Test. The Rorschach (Exner & Weiner, 1982; Rorschach, 1921) consists of 10 cards, each containing a symmetrical inkblot; five are black and white and five contain color. The cards are presented one by one to the examinee who gives a spontaneous impression of what is seen; the examiner may then start over with the first card and ask which features were most important upon initial impression. Responses are scored according to several categories: which aspects of the blot determined the response (form, movement, color, shading); where the determinant was located; whether the response was human, animal, or inanimate; whether the response was common or original, and so forth. The number of responses in each category is analyzed to form one basis for conclusions. For example, a high number of color responses is thought to indicate emotionality, and a high number of movement responses is thought to indicate imagination. Analysis of responses for broad categories of information such as reality awareness, empathy, self-concept, emotionality, and coping mechanisms may be helpful in personality assessment of children (Halpern, 1960).

Children's Apperception Test (CAT). The CAT (Bellak & Bellak, 1949) is a series of 10 plates, each depicting animal characters. The examinee is shown the pictures one at a time and asked to orally relate a story about each. The CAT is designed for use with children ages 3–10 and is based on three propositions: (1) that projective techniques allow clinicians to make inferences about personality features; (2) that the animal scenes depicting activities of eating, sleeping, toileting, and punishment are especially relevant to children and thus will elicit accurate information about the way they handle such daily activities in their own lives; and (3) that children would more readily relate to and identify with animals than human figures (Bellak & Adelman, 1960). Children's responses are analyzed for thematic content or commonalities within 10 categories: (1) main theme, (2) main hero, (3) main needs of the hero, (4) conception of the environment, (5) view of other figures, (6) significant conflicts, (7) nature of anxieties, (8) main defenses, (9) severity of the superego, and (10) integration of the ego. Interpretation is obviously psychoanalytic in nature, as needs, conflict, anxiety, and guilt are heavily weighted.

Three similar measures are sometimes used with children: the *Thematic Apperception Test* (TAT; Murray, 1943), a technique using pictures of adults and designed for use with adolescents and adults; the *Education Apperception Test* (EAT; Thompson & Sones, 1973), which depicts only scenes related to school and achievement; and the *Roberts Apperception Test for Children* (RATC; McArthur & Roberts, 1982), which depicts interpersonal and family scenes.

Sentence Completions. An expanded version of the word association technique, sentence completions consist of sentence stems the examinee is asked to complete. They are commonly used in personality assessment because of the relative ease of administration and interpretation; they may supply the clinician with much information in a short time. Although commercially produced sentence-completion instruments are available, many psychologists develop their own informal measures. Item content is usually aimed at obtaining information about such issues as anxiety, coping skills, and attitudes toward authority figures, siblings, parents, teachers, peers, and school. Sentence completion measures are generally designed to tap the same areas covered by other projectives, but the clinical interpretation is even less structured and therefore more dependent upon the interpreter. Sample sentence stems are presented in Table 5.4.

Human Figure Drawings. The value of children's drawings in personality assessment lies in the assumption that spontaneous drawings may reveal information that is not distorted by difficulty with language or writing skills nor by deliberate falsification. Many psychologists believe that "drawings speak louder than words," especially in the early

TABLE 5.4 A Sampling of Sentence Completion Stems

1. When I can't do something in school, I ____________________
2. Most kids in my class think I am ____________________
3. I wish my father would ____________________
4. When I read out loud, I ____________________
5. My greatest fear is ____________________
6. My teacher makes me feel ____________________
7. I am good at ____________________
8. When I get worried, I ____________________
9. I wish my mother wouldn't ____________________
10. I am happiest when ____________________

developmental stages (Klepsch & Logie, 1982). In addition, drawings are readily obtained, as most children enjoy drawing and do not resist the task. Klepsch and Logie (1982) outline four major projective uses for children's human figure drawings: a measure of personality, a measure of self in relation to others (group drawings), a measure of group values (of racial, cultural, or ethnic groups), and a measure of attitude toward others (drawing teachers or parents, for example). Oster and Gould (1987) provide interpretive examples of features elicited in drawings. For example, depressed individuals might produce drawings characterized by decreased color, more empty space, constrictiveness, disorganization, incompletion, and minimal efforts. Drawings made by persons with schizophrenia may include themes of religious content and symbols of paranoia, such as prominent eyes and windows.

Empirical support for the reliability and validity of human figure drawings as measures of emotional or behavioral functioning has been mixed (Bruening, Wagner, & Johnson, 1997). Human figure drawings have also been used to assess a child's developmental status or intellectual ability. Scoring systems for estimating intelligence from figure drawings have been developed by Harris (1963) and Koppitz (1968).

Test administration consists of presenting the child with a white, unlined sheet of paper and the general directions to "Draw a person, a whole person, not a stick figure or cartoon." No additional directions other than encouragement are given. The drawing may then be scored by a system such as the one used by Koppitz (1968). The 30 emotional indicators in this system fall into one of three categories: (1) items relating to the quality of the drawing, such as size, integration, and symmetry; (2) unusual features such as teeth, crossed eyes, big hands, or monsterlike quality; or (3) omission of essential features such as eyes, mouth, nose, neck, arms, or legs (Klepsch & Logie, 1982). Presence of two or more indicators is considered suggestive of emotional/behavioral disorders. Koppitz also believes that the following three principles are useful in clinical interpretation of human figure drawings in children ages 5–12:

- Regardless of who is drawn, the drawing is a self-portrait and therefore indicative of self-concept.

- The person who is drawn is the person of greatest importance in the child's life at that time.
- Interpretation of the drawing may be twofold, for it may represent actual attitudes and conflicts or wishes.

Naglieri, McNeish, and Bardos (1991) developed a standardized scoring system for using human figure drawings as a screening procedure for emotional disturbance (*Draw a Person: Screening Procedure for Emotional Disturbance* [DAP:SPED]). This structured system involves using templates and specific scoring rules for various features of human figure drawings. The obtained scores are compared to a national sample of children and adolescents that were representative of the U.S. population. Naglieri and Pfeiffer (1992) found significantly higher DAP:SPED scores for a sample of 54 emotionally disturbed students in a day treatment program compared to matched controls. These findings were replicated in a 1993 study by McNeish and Naglieri, in which the DAP:SPED discriminated a sample of 81 emotionally disturbed children from 81 matched controls.

Most clinicians do not use drawings as a basis upon which to diagnose emotional/behavioral disorders; rather, they use drawings to formulate hypotheses about emotional issues or conflicts that the child may be unable to verbalize. Such hypotheses may then be confirmed or disconfirmed upon obtaining further information from the child, parents, and teachers. Box 5.1 illustrates how the drawings in Figures 5.1 and 5.2 were used.

Projective techniques are given a critical review by Anastasi (1988), who cites the following points:

1. As a group, projectives make a poor showing when evaluated for technical adequacy, yet they continue to be popular clinical instruments.
2. The majority of projectives have questionable theoretical rationale and do not meet test standards.
3. Standardization of administration and scoring procedures, adequacy of norms, reliability, and validity are all questionable.
4. The validity of the Rorschach Inkblot Test and Human Figure Drawing are particularly suspect.
5. The final interpretation of a projective test may reveal more about background, training, and personal orientation of the examiner than the personality of the examinee.

Anastasi concludes that projective techniques may best be viewed not as tests but as clinical tools that can provide supplemental information as an interviewing technique. The implications drawn from the drawings in Box 5.1 illustrate this process with Human Figure Drawings.

Self-Report Measures

How one views oneself in relation to others and the environment is a main concern of psychodynamic theorists; thus, the construct of self-concept has generated much interest. Although implicit indicators of self-concept may be obtained from projective measures, some instruments have been devised explicitly for this purpose. Two examples are the *Piers-Harris Children's Self-Concept Scale* (Piers & Harris, 1969) and the *Self-Perception*

FIGURE 5.1 Human Figure Drawing by a 7 Year-Old Boy

Profile for Children (Harter, 1985). The Piers-Harris consists of 80 descriptive items to be answered *Yes* or *No* and six factors: behavior, school status, physical appearance, anxiety, popularity, and happiness. Percentile ranks are available for each of these factors as well as overall self-concept. The Self-Perception Profile has 36 items to be rated on a 4-point scale that yields five domains plus general self-esteem: scholastic competence, athletic competence, social acceptance, physical appearance, and behavioral conduct. Harter also asks the respondent to rank the importance of each domain. She maintains that self-concept can vary according to different domains, and furthermore, that a person's poor performance in a domain will only affect self-concept if that domain is important to the person.

Other self-report techniques were discussed in Chapter 3, including depression and anxiety inventories. These measures are frequently used in schools by school psychologists and can contribute useful information regarding a child's internal experiences and self-perception in relation to others and to the demands of the environment, including school.

In summary, a psychologist using psychodynamic techniques might employ projective stimuli such as inkblots or picture cards, or may analyze the child's own drawings. Sentence completions and other self-report measures are also liberally used by psychodynamic psychologists to obtain the child's own perception of his or her world.

FIGURE 5.2 Human Figure Drawing by an 8-Year-Old

Educational Applications

Psychoanalytic theorists had an impact on education in the early part of the 20th century, as conformity in the classroom came to be viewed by some educators as detrimental to a child's natural development. Educational practices reflecting a more permissive philosophy resulted.

By midcentury, the psychodynamic view had moderated, but the basic tenets remained unchanged. Psychodynamic theorists generally agree that the educational process should be less repressive, more facilitative of emotional expression, and more sensitive to crises experienced by children (Brendtro, Brokenleg, & Van Brockern, 1990; Rezmierski & Kotre, 1974). In accordance, an educational environment should provide not only opportunities for expression and acceptance of conflicts but also active support in dealing with such conflicts as they arise. Nicholas Hobbs (1982), in his classic text on troubled and troubling children, describes the adult attributes necessary to work with students displaying emotional and behavioral disorders. His view clearly illustrates the importance of the teacher as a person rather than a technician—a key component of the psychodynamic model. Hobbs suggests that successful adults must "have the qualities of personality that make [each day] rewarding and . . . must have the resilience to keep at it week after week."

BOX 5.1

Interpretation of Human Figure Drawings

Figures 5.1 and 5.2 are the human figure drawings of two boys only 3 months apart in age. Both were referred for evaluations due to learning problems.

The artist of Figure 5.1 was 7 years, 10 months old and had been retained in first grade due to overall low achievement. He obtained an IQ score of 81 on the Wechsler Intelligence Scale for Children—Revised (WISC-R). He was described as a well-behaved child who always tried hard. His developmental score for the drawing was a little lower than his IQ, and there were three emotional indicators (according to Koppitz's system); poor integration of body parts, transparencies, and hands bigger than the face of the figure. Implications: obtain other drawings for comparison purposes; obtain other drawings in the future to gauge improvement, explore the child's feelings with him by talking with him and through self-report measures; and explore with teachers and parents their observations about possible emotional difficulties.

Figure 5.2 was drawn by a boy who was 8 years, 1 month old. His IQ as measured by the WISC-R was 111. Although average in math and considered bright by his parents and teachers, he experienced severe reading problems. He was sociable, likeable, and described by parents as the negotiator in the family. While his human figure drawing was much more sophisticated than Figure 5.1 and therefore did not reflect abnormal scores according to either the developmental system or the emotional indicators system, it did depict an aggressive incident. Themes of overt aggression were also evident in all three of the other drawings he was asked to complete. His answers to all self-report measures were very appropriate and well within normal ranges; however, the theme of aggression in all four pictures was cause for concern.

Implications: Talk with the child about what was happening in the pictures and why; share concerns with the parents; and refer for psychological testing to explore whether the pictures represent harmless fantasy or other issues that need attention.

This person must "be able to do things with competence and assurance" (p. 89) and must also be a person who is "able to give and receive affection, to live relaxed, and to be firm; a person with private resources for the nourishment and refreshment of his own life; . . . a person with a sense of the significance of time, of the usefulness of today and the promise of tomorrow; a person of hope, quiet confidence, and joy; one who has committed himself to children and to the proposition that children who are disturbed can be helped" (p. 82).

There are many applications of psychodynamic theory with students who are emotionally or behaviorally disordered. Seven specific educational applications are reviewed:

1. Humanistic education
2. The therapeutic milieu
3. Group process
4. The life space interview
5. Reality therapy
6. Psychotherapy
7. Affective education

Humanistic Education

Humanistic educators generally view schools as places where development of happy, well-adjusted individuals takes precedence over acquisition of academic skills. Humanistic educators are also vocal about the shortcomings of our current educational system, with the result that some of the more extreme theorists are labeled countertheoretical or radical. Rogers, in his book *Freedom to Learn* (1969), emphasized that he was interested only in facilitating the process of learning, not in teaching or instructing individuals, who were expected to set their own goals. Holt and Glasser are proponents of humanistic education who, over 25 years ago, proposed changes in the educational system aimed at reducing failure. In his book *How Children Learn,* Holt (1967) took issue with the sequential skills timetable imposed by the educational curriculum; he proposed instead that children decide for themselves both the pace and the content of their learning and that the teacher become a facilitator rather than a dictator of learning. In *Schools Without Failure,* Glasser (1969) described the atmosphere of failure propagated in our schools by such abuses as A-B-C-D grading systems, use of objective tests and the normal curve, and irrelevant homework. He further suggested that morality issues and social values should be dealt with openly in the classroom. Glasser and Holt shared the humanistic ideals that (1) children have an innate ability to learn independently and creatively and (2) schoolwork should be relevant to students' daily lives.

Applications of Maslow's (1967) hierarchy of needs are evident in many school programs. This theory, assuming that lower-order survival and esteem needs must be met before an individual can move to self-actualization, underlies most traditional public assistance programs and youth clubs. Free school breakfasts and lunches, school nurses and health care clinics, and the current emphasis on school safety are just a few examples of meeting children's basic needs in the areas of hunger, health, and safety so they can progress cognitively and emotionally. Self-esteem curricula, various school clubs and teams, honor societies, Boy and Girl Scouts and clubs, and cooperative learning groups (Johnson, Johnson, Holubec, & Roy, 1984) are all applications of the notion that children's needs for belongingness and esteem must be met prior to academic advancement.

One clear example of humanistic education, the Foxfire experiences (Wiggington, 1986), allowed students to participate fully in the creation of curriculum and learning. Students, operating within groups, set their own reading and writing goals. For example, one experience was to publish a book of folk tales. Each student was assigned a role; each was involved in planning, interviewing, compiling, writing, editing, and publishing. The Foxfire products are famous for their quality, but most of all for the lasting personal benefits for each student as a result of such an experience. In humanistic education, it is presumed that students will naturally be motivated to achieve when their basic needs are not a concern.

Brendtro and his colleagues (1990, 1994) suggested a humanistic model of education as a way to reach troubled and alienated students. Founded in Native American values, their humanistic features include the following:

1. Allowing students to belong to a supportive community, rather than remaining lost in a depersonalized bureaucracy
2. Facilitating students' mastery of important products, rather than having them endure inflexible systems

3. Allowing students to determine their own future, while simultaneously protecting others from harmful behavior
4. Expecting young people to be caregivers, rather than helpless dependents. Note that these features could easily fit into individual classrooms, provided that the teachers are able to give and receive affection and to see the world from the student's point of view.

Another application of humanistic theory resulted from the 1990 National and Community Service Act, which allocated federal funds for school-based service learning (Kielsmeier, 2000). Service learning is a method whereby students learn and develop through active participation, rather than teacher-directed lessons, in organized service. The service activities are structured such that they meet the needs of a community, are coordinated with various educational agencies in the community, help to foster civic responsibility, enhance core academic curriculum, and provide opportunities for students to reflect on their experience (Billig, 2000). Service learning should result in equal benefit to the learner and the community and should engage students in highly motivating experiential activities that are closely tied to the real world. In a variety of projects, students tackle community issues such as violence, illiteracy, HIV, school funding inequities, voter apathy, hunger, pollution, aging, and community history (Hornbeck, 2000).

Service-learning programs have spread widely across the country. Proponents claim that students who participate in these programs show increases in measures of personal and social responsibility, communication, a sense of educational and social competence, self-esteem, and self-efficacy. Furthermore, it is claimed that students participating in service-learning programs show fewer behavioral problems and reduced levels of alienation and are less likely to engage in behaviors that lead to pregnancy or arrest (Billig, 2000). It is thought that service learning teaches empathy, commitment, generosity, acceptance of diversity, and civic responsibility. However, there is a need for more and better quality research to substantiate specific benefits. "There is not enough research to date to know which types of students are most affected, which specific program designs are most powerful, what type of reciprocity with service recipients is needed, how connected to the community the service needs to be, what impacts occur on the school as an organization or on the community as an entity, and so on" (Billig, 2000, p. 663).

Muscott (2001) maintained that while there is much evidence for the effectiveness of service learning in regular public education and undergraduate college programs, it is still too early for programs for students with EBD to make similar claims, and cited four reasons: (1) most programs have been assessed qualitatively, using anecdotal evidence; (2) many programs provide little or no information about specific methodology; (3) few studies of effectiveness use comparison groups or pre–post designs; and (4) no studies cited use of curriculum-based assessment or single-subject designs to examine effects on individual students.

Despite these shortcomings in evaluation, service-learning approaches are receiving much attention in the literature for educators (Allen, 2003). An entire issue of *Beyond Behavior* (Spring 2001), a publication of the Council for Children with Behavioral Disorders, is devoted to discussion of service-learning programs. This resource is included under the *Additional Readings and Resources* section at the end of this chapter.

Regardless of the structure of a program, a positive teacher–student relationship is key to the success of humanistic education. A significant body of research and writing has been devoted to the results of such a relationship on academic achievement, student motivation, and student behavior (e.g., Brophy & Good, 1986; Deiro, 2003; Jones & Jones, 1995; Wehlage, Rutter, Smith, Lesko, & Fernandez, 1989). The necessary components for a positive relationship lie in the teachers' beliefs, values, and behavior. Teachers have been encouraged to accept personal responsibility for student success, extend their role to caring for students, develop persistence and a willingness to teach students even when they did not seem to want to learn, and express a belief that all students can learn (Wehlage et al., 1989). Gordon (1974), in his classic book *Teacher Effectiveness Training,* indicated that a teacher–student relationship is positive when it consists of the following:

1. Openness, so each is able to risk honesty with the other
2. Caring, when each feels valued
3. Interdependence, as opposed to competition or dependency
4. Separateness, so that each can grow and preserve individuality
5. Meeting each others' needs and no one's needs go unmet

Specific activities for developing positive relationships might include active listening; setting realistic expectations; using positive comments while avoiding criticism and judgment; letting students lead conversations; modeling appropriate behavior; using suggestion boxes; sending notes, cards, and letters to students; and participating in school events and student games. Teachers have many opportunities to create a humanistic environment, supportive of emotional development.

The Therapeutic Milieu

Long and colleagues (1980; 1996) articulate a number of principles of the psychoeducational approach introduced in Chapter 2, which is heavily steeped in psychodynamic theory. Basically, the psychoeducational approach promotes the view that emotional difficulties can best be resolved through a supportive educational environment and positive learning experiences. The following are condensed from their original list of 18 principles and beliefs.

1. Cognitive and affective processes are in continuous interaction.
2. A special environment must be created so that initially each pupil can function successfully at his or her level.
3. Teachers must be cognizant of the fact that pupils with EBD have a special vulnerability to normal developmental tasks such as competition, testing, learning to share, and so forth.
4. Pupils with EBD need to associate adult intervention with acceptance and protection, not hostility and rejection.
5. Teachers must listen to pupils and focus on their feelings if academic progress and behavioral change are to occur.
6. Crises are excellent times for teachers to teach and for pupils to learn.

These principles form the basis for the general environment or milieu that is needed by students with emotional and behavioral problems. The therapeutic milieu was applied to students in residential settings by Redl (1959b) and Hobbs (1966), and later extended to public school settings by Redl (1966) and Morse (Cheney & Morse, 1974). These educators sought to implement their beliefs that schools can greatly enhance a child's chance for success through careful selection of material, gradation of steps toward a goal, provision of therapeutic teaching, and by ending "demands for perfection" (Cheney & Morse, 1974, p. 341). This individualization process greatly reduces stress in the school environment, thereby providing a supportive atmosphere in which academic and behavioral gains are more easily attained. Appropriate adult role models also are important in milieu therapy.

In addition to individualizing instruction, milieu therapy may require manipulating daily schedules and activities, or involving the entire staff in an intervention plan so that consistent reactions from adults are ensured. Consideration is also given to the physical environment, including space, equipment, and props. Specific changes in the environment may be made on the basis of individual needs, with the result that the student's entire program may be tailored for maximum success. There is a definite emphasis on accommodating the environment to the student.

Group Process

In addition to a therapeutic milieu, psychoeducational classrooms promoted other applications of psychodynamic theory (e.g., Hobbs, 1982), such as group participation and processing. Group processing allows teachers and students to explore feelings and values, solve problems, discuss personal crises, communicate acceptance, and establish healthy interpersonal relationships. In classrooms for students with emotional disturbance, there may be a group process every morning, or twice a day, or whenever crises occur. The goals of such a process usually consist of conflict resolution and establishing self-control capabilities (Coleman & Webber, 1988).

The structure of such groups varies depending on the purpose of the group. However, most groups are conducted with students in a circle at prearranged times. The group process usually includes goal setting, rituals, adult participation, positive reinforcement, and self-evaluation (Coleman & Webber, 1988). An emphasis on effective communication skills is recommended (Gordon, 1974; Jones & Jones, 1995). It is believed that the power of a group lies in the cumulative effect of relationships within the group. Thus, students have a unique opportunity to learn about others and themselves through others' perceptions.

In addition to classroom groups, schools often provide small-group counseling facilitated by school counselors, school psychologists, and special education teachers. This modality is often preferred over individual counseling in school settings because of increased efficiency and greater opportunity to address common issues and interpersonal problem solving (Moore et al., 1999). Purposes for such counseling groups might include, for example, friendship, social skills training, anger management, coping with divorce, abuse issues, and alcohol and substance use and abuse issues. Clearly, appropriate group counseling training and consideration of issues of privacy and confidentiality are essential in forming such groups.

Sometimes crises are such that a group process is not feasible. In this case, individual counseling techniques might be indicated. Two of these techniques, illustrative of the psychodynamic model, are life space interviewing and reality therapy.

The Life Space Interview

The life space interview is a direct intervention technique that focuses on the student. The life space interview (LSI) was pioneered in residential settings as part of a therapeutic milieu for students with EBD. The interview is conducted by an adult "who is perceived by the child to be part of his 'natural habitat or life space,' with some pretty clear role and power-influence in his daily living" (Redl, 1965, p. 364). The adult's role is not to exercise authority but to gain an idea of the child's perceptions of a given event.

Redl (1959a) differentiates between two types of life space interviews: emotional first aid on the spot and clinical exploitation of life events. The primary difference between these two is the goal for the interview, a decision that is made in the initial stages but that, if necessary, may be changed in the middle of the interview. As its title implies, emotional first aid on the spot is a temporary support in which the teacher seeks to help the student overcome an immediate obstacle or work through a difficult situation. There is no long-range plan or treatment strategy other than provision of temporary relief and support. In contrast, the intention of clinical exploitation of life events is to exploit a momentary experience in order to facilitate long-range goals for a particular student. Consider the following example:

> The teacher realizes that Sue Ellen is having a particularly bad day, which began with an argument with her mother before she left home that morning. Sue Ellen has a long-standing habit of rationalizing or making elaborate excuses for her obnoxious behavior. When she begins to taunt a classmate, the classmate blows up and a near-scuffle ensues. Arriving at the scene, the teacher may choose simply to break up the argument and talk to Sue Ellen about her difficult day (emotional first aid) or may decide to use the event to illustrate to Sue Ellen her habit of taking out her frustration on others and then excusing it (clinical exploitation).

Selected subcategories of both types of interviews are briefly described in Table 5.5.

TABLE 5.5 Categories and Selected Subcategories of the Life Space Interview (Redl, 1959b)

Emotional first aid on the spot

Drain-off of frustration acidity: sympathizing with a student who is upset at an interruption in scheduling or during a pleasant activity

Support for management of panic, fury, and guilt: providing support during a tantrum or emotional outbursts, and afterward, helping the student gain perspective

Umpire services: helping a student make a decision or mediating in conflicts such as quarrels and fights

Clinical exploitation of life events

Reality rub-in: helping a student to interpret situations clearly and to see the relationship between behavior and its consequences

Massaging numb value areas: appealing to a student's personal value system (e.g., fairness, peer approval)

Use of the life space interview in school settings was promoted by Morse (1969b) and Wood and Long (1991), who recommend it as a problem-solving technique in less serious situations or with students who are experiencing adjustment problems.

Little systematic research on the effectiveness of the LSI has been conducted. Gardner (1990) has questioned the widespread acceptance and practice of the life space interview because of the lack of empirical evidence supporting its effectiveness. Other criticisms by Gardner were as follows:

- LSI potentially detracts from academic learning time.
- The emphasis on feelings may provide students with excuses for their behavior.
- Adult attention for inappropriate behavior may serve to increase the behavior rather than help to decrease it.

Gardner further suggested that LSI be used as a proactive intervention; that is, it should be used in a preventive way rather than a reaction to an episode of unacceptable behavior. These criticisms were addressed by Long (1990), who maintains that LSI is an effective way to deal with affect and improve behavior (Long, Wood, & Fecser, 2001). Regarding the academic time issue, Long indicated that LSI usually takes only minutes after the student has calmed down, and that the student in such an emotional state would not be academically engaged anyway. When implemented properly, as part of a continuum of behavioral interventions and as a reaction to emotional flare-ups, Long believes that LSI neither excuses instances of inappropriate behavior nor increases their frequency. One point of agreement between Long, Gardner, and other professionals interested in LSI is that more substantial data are needed about the effectiveness of LSI in a variety of educational settings. It also seems essential that practitioners of this technique receive formal training and supervision before attempting to use it with children with EBD.

Reality Therapy

For reality therapy, Glasser (1965) emphasized the three R's: responsibility, reality, and right-and-wrong. Responsibility is the keystone of reality therapy; Glasser holds the nontraditional view that people become "disordered" because they are irresponsible and therefore they can become "undisordered" by learning to become responsible. Responsible behavior is defined as the ability to meet one's needs without infringing upon the rights of others to meet their needs. Reality is an important concept because individuals who are disturbed deny the reality of the world around them; they do not understand or accept the rules and regulations of society; they deny connections between their behavior and its consequences, and they become adept at blaming other people or external events for their difficulties. Reality therapists do not accept rationalizations or excuses as valid justifications for behavior. The third R, right-and-wrong, sets reality therapy apart from most other therapies that avoid attaching value judgments to behavior. According to Glasser, disordered or deviant behavior is wrong because it is harmful to the individual or to others. Therefore, the individual must learn to view his maladaptive behavior as wrong and must learn to behave in more adaptive ways.

School interventions that have been developed from reality therapy approaches include classroom meetings, which can be open-ended (centered around thought-provoking questions that stimulate intellectual curiosity), education–diagnostic (related to alternative assessment of learning), or social–problem-solving (dealing with individual or group problems). Such meetings would typically be facilitated by the classroom teacher with the children seated in a circle (Fuller & Fuller, 1999). A 10-step, schoolwide, non-punitive discipline program has also been developed using principles of reality therapy (Fuller & Fuller, 1999). Glasser (1965) and Towns (1981) reported successful applications of reality therapy with adolescent populations. Newcomer (1993) recommended its use in settings where the adult has substantial control over the consequences of irresponsible behavior, such as residential settings.

Psychotherapy

The term *psychotherapy* has been used loosely to describe sessions during which someone with emotional stresses or problems talks with someone who is trained in the psychological processes of the human mind. Stricter interpretations would apply psychotherapy only to sessions in which psychodynamic or psychoanalytic principles are applied. For example, dynamic therapists emphasize emotional conflicts and the relationship with the therapist, and identify patterns in feelings and behavior, often by focusing on fantasies, dreams, and wishes (Harvard Health Publications, 2006). The terms *therapy* or *counseling* would be applied to other forms of therapy. In this discussion, psychotherapy is used in its more general sense, that is, borrowing from Smith and Glass (1977), "The informed and planful application of techniques derived from established psychological principles, by persons qualified through training and experience . . ." (p. 6). Many children with EBD receive psychotherapy from either the school counselor or a mental health practitioner outside the school setting.

The effectiveness of psychotherapy has been hotly debated over the years, with early researchers concluding that psychotherapy with both adults (Eysenck, 1965; Rachman, 1971) and children (Levitt, 1963, 1971) was not much better than no treatment. Research in the 1970s and 1980s with children and adolescents was somewhat more positive, but researchers also underscored the methodological problems with conducting this type of research (Barrett, Hampe, & Miller, 1978; Tramontana, 1980). Goals of psychotherapy typically have been difficult to precisely define and to measure. These researchers used the traditional approach of evaluating the literature from a critical, not statistical, perspective.

Other studies have used meta-analysis, a statistical technique that compares effect sizes of treatment and control groups in the studies. Casey and Berman (1985) reviewed 75 studies comparing psychotherapy with children and adolescents to a control group or to another treatment. They found an effect size of 0.71, indicating that the average outcome for treated children was 0.71 of a standard deviation better than that of untreated children. Prout and DeMartino (1986) included only studies of school-based psychotherapy. From 33 studies published between 1962 and 1982, the authors concluded that school-based psychotherapy is "at least moderately effective." Their findings also suggested that group therapy is more effective than individual therapy in the schools, and that behavioral theory (especially cognitive-behavioral) produced stronger effects than other theoretical approaches. Observable behavior and problem-solving skills were most amenable to treatment.

In a critical review of these and other meta-analyses, Kazdin (1993) stated, "The conclusion from each of these analyses has been that psychotherapy for children and adolescents produces effects that exceed changes associated with no treatment (i.e., child therapy is effective)" (p. 646). Kazdin goes on to point out that a number of recent methodological advances have contributed to the positive results. These advances include improved measures of childhood dysfunction and the establishment of normative levels of functioning at different age levels, such as was done by the authors of the *Child Behavior Checklist* (First Edition) (Achenbach & Edelbrock, 1983).

In a recent newsletter, Harvard Health Publications (2006) reported results from a meta-analysis by Leichsenring et al. (2004) of 17 studies of the efficacy of short-term psychodynamic psychotherapy completed over a period of 35 years. Short-term therapy was defined as an average of 7–40 sessions, compared to being placed on a waiting list or receiving another type of therapy (e.g., cognitive-behavioral therapy). Short-term dynamic therapy was found to be, on the average, superior to no therapy and as effective as other types of therapy in reducing symptoms of disorders and improving overall functioning.

Affective Education

Affective education is based on the psychodynamic and humanistic premise that teaching children involves more than cognitive development. Education also involves teaching about feelings, attitudes, values, and interpersonal relationships (i.e., developing social–emotional competence). In the 1960s and 1970s many general education teachers wove affective objectives together with cognitive objectives (Harmin, Kirschenbaum, & Simon, 1973). For example, students would not only learn about the discovery of America, but also how it must feel to be an explorer setting out to unknown dangers and destinations. Typical affective educational objectives might include the following:

1. Identifying characteristics of winners and losers
2. Identifying character traits needed for acceptance by others
3. Stating how positive characteristics make one feel good
4. Naming basic physical and emotional needs
5. Identifying differences in self and others
6. Identifying personal interests and abilities
7. Identifying own accomplishments and successes
8. Identifying expectations that others may have of you
9. Identifying emotions based on verbal and nonverbal information from others
10. Identifying feelings associated with certain situations

Usually, affective lessons are conducted with small groups of students by the school counselor or the teacher. The lessons may include drama, creative writing, discussion, art projects, group process, listening activities, voting exercises, or brainstorming. Teaching affective objectives rarely indicates a teacher-directed format. Rather, the teacher's role is that of a stimulus, facilitator, and listener (Abrams, 1992; Gordon, 1974; Jones & Jones, 1995; Leachman & Victor, 2003). Several affective curricula are available for classroom use, and many currently recommend similar activities as a method of preventing school violence (Johnson, Johnson, Stevahn, & Hodne, 1997; Naierman, 1997; Nunez & Collignon, 1997; Olweus, 2003; Weissberg, Resnik, Payton, & O'Brien, 2003).

Values clarification (Raths, Harmin, & Simon, 1978; Simon, Howe, & Kirschenbaum, 1972) is an affective curriculum based on the belief that behavior problems occur because children and youth are confused about their values. Values are believed to be the tools used to resolve conflicts, make choices, and make decisions (Abrams, 1992). Also, these authors assert that values give meaning and order to our lives and form the basis of self-identity. The major goals of values clarification are (1) to encourage students to examine their attitudes, beliefs, interests, and feelings, (2) to reflect on feelings and values, and (3) to allow others to do the same. The teacher's role is to conduct valuing activities (e.g., "List 10 things you love to do" or "Describe a personal hero") and the subsequent discussion. The teacher should not teach values, but should teach a values exploration process, which is an important distinction.

Curricula to enhance self-concept abound; however, one popular book, *100 Ways to Enhance Self-concept in the Classroom: A Handbook for Teachers and Parents* (Canfield & Wells, 1994), illustrates recommended activities. Students may be asked to write an autobiography answering questions such as "What major goals are you working on right now?" or "What does friendship mean to you?" (p. 25). Or students may be asked to create a coat of arms illustrating significant life events or goals. Many activities include art and voting exercises. Canfield has expanded his belief in the importance of healthy self-concepts to adult populations with his publication of books such as *Chicken Soup for the Soul: 101 Stories to Open the Heart and Rekindle the Spirit* (Canfield & Hansen, 1995).

More recently, affective education has been called character education (Berreth & Berman, 1997; Inlay, 2003). Character education promotes personality traits such as trustworthiness, respect, responsibility, justice, fairness, integrity, and caring, but usually refers to these traits, for political purposes, as empathy and self-discipline skills. Whether or not it is intended, teachers teach values; perhaps the most effective character education is for teachers to model the values they hope to impart to their students (Inlay, 2003). Berreth and Berman (1997) delineate the basic goals of character education as follows:

1. Teach basic decision-making and perspective-taking skills.
2. Teach persistence and delayed gratification.
3. Facilitate positive value development.
4. Teach responsible behavior.
5. Provide ample opportunities to practice empathy and self-discipline.

Inlay (2003) adds to these goals with a discussion of the goal of fostering both personal and social responsibility. The efficacy of affective programs is difficult to evaluate for a number of reasons. First and foremost is the difficulty in measuring affective concepts or constructs, such as "communication skills," "self-concept," and "understanding oneself." The majority of research studies utilize some measure of self-concept, which may be an established, commercially produced instrument or one developed by the authors of the affective program being evaluated. As Medway and Smith (1978) point out, the use of differing definitions and instruments to measure the same concept is not likely to produce consistent or comparable results. A second difficulty is that most of these measures are a form of self-report or self-evaluation. Problems with self-report measures in research include subjects' tendencies to give socially acceptable responses, and great differences across situations and across subjects in their willingness to self-disclose.

Carpenter and Apter (1988) studied several reviews of affective curricula and programs and added these criticisms:

- Differential age responses to a particular curriculum indicate the need to assess student-to-program match rather than applying a program wholesale to a class or group.
- The teacher is a confounding factor in efficacy research because affective issues are greatly influenced by personal variables such as personality.
- Methodological flaws in many studies make it difficult to draw conclusions about the research that has been conducted.

Weissbert and colleagues (2003) observe that the education marketplace is crowded with unsubstantiated programs purported to create caring schools. In the current climate of state and federal accountability in education, poor empirical support for interventions represents a high risk for the continuation of such programs. The Collaborative for Academic, Social, and Emotional Learning (CASEL), based at the University of Illinois at Chicago, was organized to provide a forum for high-quality research that will advance the practice and science of social and emotional learning. After a review of 80 out of 250 identified social and emotional learning programs, CASEL identified 22 "select" programs and three exemplary social and emotional learning programs (Weissbert et al., 2003). A description and discussion of these programs can be reviewed in *Evaluating Social and Emotional Learning Programs,* a reading included at the end of this chapter.

In summary, although special educators recognize the importance of integrating academic with affective concerns in the classroom, the effectiveness of much of the available commercial affective curricula remains unproven. However, this state of affairs may reflect inconsistencies in research methodology and program implementation rather than ineffectiveness of the curricula. Efforts to critically evaluate these programs, such as the review by CASEL described above, represent a much-needed effort to establish empirical support.

Summary

Although the psychodynamic model encompasses varied theories, two major schools of thought, psychoanalytic and humanistic, were delineated in this chapter. Psychoanalytic theorists such as Freud emphasize the role of unconscious drives and conflict in determining personality. Humanistic theorists such as Rogers, Maslow, and Adler stress the individual's need for accurate self-perception and self-understanding, as well as supportive or corrective environments, as prerequisites for healthy development. Healthy personality development is a common goal of psychodynamic theorists who are also concerned with the dynamics of self-growth toward that goal. Box 5.2 describes the use of a psychodynamic technique—sandtray therapy—with Andrea, a student with EBD. After reading about Andrea, discuss how this therapy and/or the results of the therapy might help her teachers better program for her. Why would such a therapy be difficult to provide in a school situation?

BOX 5.2
Sandtray Therapy with Andrea

Andrea, an 18-year-old female who resided in a residential treatment center, lost both parents in an automobile accident when she was 4 years old. Her two siblings were severely injured, as was Andrea. Andrea sustained a head injury that left residual speech and motor problems, along with subtle cognitive impairments. The children were adopted by family members with whom Andrea lived until her behavior became unmanageable in adolescence. At that time, she became suicidal, made homicidal threats, engaged in sexual acting-out, and ran away multiple times. Following several psychiatric placements, she eventually entered residential treatment where she remained for 5 years. Psychological evaluation revealed that she was of average or above-average intelligence, with severe emotional problems that required medication for depression and psychotic thinking. Her human figure drawing and family drawings indicated a desire to be independent and to begin a family, but also included features of aggression, poor self-concept, and impulsivity, making efforts toward autonomy a high-risk goal. During the time she was in residential treatment, Andrea received speech therapy, cognitive-behavioral psychotherapy, social skills training, and behavior-modification programming, in addition to individualized academic instruction. Despite these efforts, she remained emotionally and behaviorally volatile, often engaging in unpredictable and risky behaviors.

As part of her psychotherapy, sandtray therapy was incorporated for the last 2 years of her treatment. During the sandtray sessions, Andrea was presented with an open box of fine, clean sand and an array of miniature figures, such as animals, people, objects of nature such as trees and flowers, vehicles, and building materials (bridges, fences, houses, etc.), among others. This technique encouraged Andrea to select figures and create scenes that described her "world" as she perceived it. During some sessions, she elected to describe her current world, while in others she depicted the past or the future. The goals of these sessions were to encourage integration of the parts of her life that had become fragmented since the loss of her parents, the impairment of aspects of motor and cognitive functioning, and the multiple treatment settings she had experienced. Further goals included promoting communication that did not depend on language skills, fostering a safe, supportive, and trusting relationship, and facilitating emotional healing through unconditional acceptance of her expression of memories, feelings, and thoughts. Verbalization is not required for sandtray therapy and many clients profit from the opportunity to work with this multisensory technique without speaking. However, Andrea chose to narrate and interpret her sandtray scenes.

Andrea's expression in the sandtray was both poignant and symbolic. She created one scene in which the female figure was depicted as a baby, with numerous other babies added to the sandtray. Her description of this scene included "guards" who represented the treatment center and a magical figure that represented the legal system that would be determining her placement when she reached adulthood. The multiple babies represented her sense of helplessness and dependence upon others. One baby was injured when a stroller fell over, possibly symbolizing her injury in the automobile accident. There were no parents present in the scene, but rather caseworkers and systems, which accurately described her current life circumstances. Over the course of the 2 years of sandtray therapy, in the context of the other treatments she received, Andrea showed much improvement in her capacity to appropriately express feelings and control impulsive acting-out that had interfered with her desire for autonomy. The sandtray process served as a means of safe expression without the immediate need to explain or change behavior as was often required to receive reinforcement in her therapeutic setting. Although she continued to have problems in behavior and social relationships, this period of her psychotherapy was viewed as successful in that she developed a trusting relationship with the therapist and seemed able to better link her life experiences with her feelings and behavioral choices.

TABLE 5.6 Summary of the Psychodynamic Model

Etiological Factors	Evaluation Measures	Educational Applications
Conflict between unconscious drives and conscious desires Conflict between one's view of self and societal values Excessive use of defense mechanisms Failure to resolve normal developmental crises of a biological (psychosexual) or interpersonal (psychosocial) nature	Projectives: *Rorschach Inkblot Test* (Rorschach, 1921) *Children's Apperception Test* (Bellak & Bellak, 1949) *Roberts Apperception Test for Children* (McArthur & Roberts, 1982) Human figure drawings Sentence completions Self-report scales	Humanistic education Service learning programs The therapeutic milieu Group process Life space interview Reality therapy Psychotherapy Affective education

Evaluation procedures arising from the psychodynamic model include projective techniques and self-report measures, which are used widely by psychologists in evaluating emotional problems. In applying psychodynamic principles to education, theorists emphasize the importance of a supportive, therapeutic school environment that encourages students to express and to deal openly with their needs and conflicts. Cognitive and affective issues are given equal status in the classroom. Views of etiology, evaluation measures, and educational applications of the psychodynamic model are summarized in Table 5.6.

Conclusions

Viewing disordered behavior from a psychodynamic perspective allows educators to understand much of our history in evaluating and treating students with EBD. Freud and other psychodynamic theorists left an unmistakable mark in the treatment of emotional problems. While purely Freudian techniques do not lend themselves to application in educational settings, the majority of early interventions for students with EBD in the schools were based on psychodynamic principles. In addition, students may receive psychotherapy from counselors within the schools or from psychologists, psychiatrists, or social workers outside the school setting. Furthermore, many current programs aimed at building character and civic responsibility have roots in psychodynamic theories.

KEY POINTS

1. The psychodynamic model focuses on the internal mechanisms of personality development and emotional functioning in individuals.
2. Healthy personality development is a common goal of psychodynamic theorists.

3. Psychodynamic evaluation techniques include projective techniques and self-report measures that are used extensively in clinical settings to diagnose emotional problems.
4. Projective techniques currently are not used as primary tools to diagnose emotional/behavioral disorders for special education intervention.
5. Projective techniques are often included in comprehensive evaluations as clinical interview and hypotheses-generating tools.
6. Psychodynamic theorists promote humanistic and therapeutic school environments in which emotional and personal growth, and social responsibility, are as important as academic success.
7. In addition to humanistic and therapeutic environments, psychodynamic theory has spawned other educational approaches: service learning, group process, life space interview, reality therapy, psychotherapy, and affective education.

HOMEWORK QUESTIONS

1. Considering your own educational experience, describe in one or two paragraphs your opinion about the value of affective or character education in schools.
2. How does the psychosexual stage theory of development fit with the characteristics of children with EBD as described in Chapter 1 of this book? Provide a two-paragraph explanation.
3. Briefly describe how the school behavior of a child might look if he or she failed to resolve the industry versus inferiority stage in Erikson's theory.
4. With respect to the psychodynamic model, what information might you, as a classroom teacher, be able to contribute to an initial evaluation for EBD? In other words, what kind of information would you consider and collect for the school psychologist or other mental health professional to aid in the identification process?
5. Research and list various commercial affective curricula. What are the primary methods of delivering the curricula (e.g., discussion, video, drama)? What are the primary goals for the curricula?
6. Choose one of the curricula you found in your search in #5 above and attempt to find research or evidence of its effectiveness.
7. Given the mandates of the NCLB Act and IDEA 2004, discuss ways to incorporate psychodynamic strategies and affective curricula for students with EBD.

ADDITIONAL READINGS AND RESOURCES

A primer of Freudian psychology, by C. S. Hall, New York: World Publishing (Mentor Books), 1954, for a condensation of Freud's theories.

Comprehensive classroom management: Creating positive learning environments for all students, by Vernon Jones and Louise Jones, Boston: Allyn & Bacon, 2007, for practical applications of psychodynamic theory in the classroom.

Part I: Health and pathology, in *The farther reaches of human nature,* by A. H. Maslow, New York: Viking Compass, 1971, for the views of a well-known humanistic theorist.

Psychotherapy for children and adolescents: Current progress and future directions, by Alan Kazdin, in *American Psychologist,* June 1993, 644–648, for an overview of outcome studies and the issues that should be addressed in future research of the effectiveness of psychotherapy for children and youth.

Teacher–student relationships: Causes and consequences by J. Brophy and T. Good, New York:

Holt, Rinehart & Winston, 1974, for a classic book about the relationship between the teacher as a person and students' feelings and behaviors.

For more information about service learning, contact the National Youth Leadership Council (NYLC), St. Paul, MN: *www.nylc.org*, or Learning in Deed: Making a Difference through Service Learning, W. K. Kellogg Foundation, Battle Creek, MI: *www.LearningInDeed.org*. The reader is also referred to the May 2000 Kappan special section on service-learning, *Phi Delta Kappan, 81*(9), and to the Spring 2001 edition of *Beyond Behavior, 10*(3), from the Council for Children with Behavior Disorders.

For more information regarding character education, the issues surrounding affective education in the schools, and practical strategies, the reader is referred to the special section of the May 1995 *Phi Delta Kappan, 76*(9), on youth and caring, and the March 2003 issue of *Educational Leadership, 54*(8), on social and emotional learning. Several character education resources can be found through National Professional Resources, Inc. (1-800-453-7461; *www.nprinc.com*), Goodcharacter.com (*www.goodcharacter.com*), and University of Illinois Extension (*www.urbanext.uivc.edu*).

For further information about social and emotional learning, the Collaborative for Social, Emotional and Academic Learning (CASEL) at the University of Illinois at Chicago provides resources for evidence-based programs that have been successful in school settings (*http://www.casel.org*)

CHAPTER 6 Cognitive Model

QUESTIONS TO CONSIDER

- How are what and how you think related to your feelings and behavior?
- Can people change their thinking patterns?
- Which thinking patterns are likely to lead to mental health? Mental illness?
- How can we determine what and how someone is thinking?
- Can cognitive interventions help students with EBD?
- What is learned helplessness and how does it impact emotional well-being?
- Can counting or rating your behavior cause it to change?

Orientation

The cognitive model as a psychological therapy emerged in the 1960–1970s, proposing that disordered behavior and emotional disturbance arise from faulty cognitions or constructions of reality (Kelly, 1955). This theoretical model is based on the proposition that cognitions, or the way people think about and perceive the world, precipitate extreme emotions, which in turn affect behavior. Cognitive psychologists presume that cognitions are under the control of the individual; thus, "we can make ourselves crazy." Fortunately, by changing what and how we think, we can also make ourselves sane. It is important to become familiar with strategies for motivating people to change the way they think. Some of these techniques have been found to positively affect student feelings, behavior, interactions, and learning and are often recommended as treatment for students with emotional and behavioral disorders.

Overview

Cognitive psychologists believe that people can change their emotional and behavioral responses by changing their perceptions and beliefs, adjusting their self-instruction and self-talk, and adopting the capacity for self-regulation. By teaching people to more accurately think about their goals, behavior, and thoughts, and to guide their own behavior in healthy ways, their lives can be enhanced. Two basic ways that people are taught to think differently are (1) by restructuring their cognitions and view of the world and/or (2) by using new or different cognitive skills and strategies. The first method is typically implemented in clinical situations under the guidance of counselors, although we present some school-based approaches for restructuring cognitive distortions. The second method is very common in schools as we teach students to utilize step-by-step thinking aids to improve their memory, comprehension, and ability to solve problems and as we teach them various skills for tracking and changing their behavior. Because cognitive treatment generally results in self-management or self-regulation of emotions and behavior, many of the techniques can also be adopted by teachers for their own psychological well-being.

Definition and Basic View

> Emotions and behavior are primarily a function of how events are construed. Clinical improvement, in turn, depends critically on changes in thinking. (Haaga & Davison, 1991, p. 148)

> Cognitive psychologists contend that what a person thinks, believes, expects, attends to—in short, his or her mental life—influences how he or she behaves. . . . Disordered cognitive processes cause some psychological disorders and . . . by changing these cognitions, the disorder can be alleviated and perhaps even cured. (Rosenhan & Seligman, 1989, p. 118)

The cognitive explanation of disturbance is a fairly recent theoretical approach that developed primarily as a reaction to and outgrowth of the behavioral model (Mayer, Lochman, & Van Aker, 2005). The behavioral model, as you will see in Chapter 7, explains human behavior and disturbance solely as a function of external events. Cognitive and cognitive-behavioral psychologists believe that not only external events but also the way people construe the events influence human behavior. Furthermore, they believe in a reciprocal relationship between thinking, feeling, and behaving (Bandura, 1986). Kazdin (2001) makes a case for why a cognitive model, specifically self-regulation strategies, may be preferable to a purely behavioral model: (1) Self-regulation better generalizes behavior, (2) people tend to perform better when they do so by their own choice rather than an imposition by others, and (3) people know better than others which of their behaviors might be of concern.

The cognitive model explained here should not be confused with cognitive developmental theory (e.g., Piaget, 1952; Vygotsky, 1978), which explains children's intellectual development as a function of biological motivation and physical and social interactions. Although educators use many strategies derived from cognitive developmental theory (e.g., scaffolding, Montessori techniques), cognitive developmental psychologists do not try to explain why individuals suffer emotional disturbance and display disordered behavior. In contrast, the cognitive and cognitive-behavioral theorists discussed in this chapter are interested in abnormal psychology and have explained abnormal behavior by focusing on problematic cognitive processes.

The *cognitive model* assumes, as do the biophysical and psychodynamic schools, that covert human processes are the primary cause of disturbance and disorders. Cognitive psychologists also believe that external events are important. However, the key component of the cognitive explanation lies in people's perceptions and thinking and their ability to regulate their own behavior. Bandura (1978) depicts the cognitive school of thought when he explains that individuals are "highly motivated to accept responsibility for changes" (p. 305) and that people have the capacity to engage in reflective thought and thus have the ability to create and plan a course of action, rather than merely suffering the "consequences of thoughtless action" (p. 345).

Cognitive theory holds that external events alone are not the cause of negative emotions and behavior; rather, people's beliefs and biased thinking about these external variables make them unhappy and/or fearful (Beck, 1964; Haaga & Davison, 1991). Beck (1964) writes of troublesome cognitive events or automatic thinking that centers on (1) a negative view of oneself, (2) insurmountable obstacles in life, and (3) a hopeless future. These cognitions are thought to cause dysfunctional feelings and unhealthy behavior. The following scenario illustrates this model.

> Two people have been fired from similar jobs with the same company. One becomes very depressed and the other sets about finding another job. If asked to record their reactions to being fired, the depressed individual writes, "Things like this always happen to me. I must be a terrible employee. I've never been good at anything." The second individual records, "The company must be in dire financial difficulty. I'm sure it was difficult for my boss to fire me. We always got along well, and I'm sure if she could have, she would have found another job for me in the company."

Since the precipitating events are identical, the cognitive psychologist would focus on analyzing the differences in the individuals' perceptions of being fired as the cause of the first individual's subsequent depression. Assessment of thoughts primarily relies on self-report and questioning techniques. Treatment of the depression, from a cognitive restructuring model, would attempt to change the individual's self-defeating cognitions.

Cognitive-behavioral theory more narrowly relates internal processes to the regulation of one's behavior, essentially ignoring emotional aspects (Karoly, 1993). For someone displaying disturbing behavior it might be assumed from a cognitive-behavioral viewpoint that he or she lacked the ability to self-regulate or needed to learn self-control strategies. Self-regulation, according to Karoly (1993), "may be said to encompass up to five interrelated and iterative component (internally governed) phases: (1) goal selection; (2) goal cognition; (3) directional maintenance; (4) directional change or reprioritization; and (5) goal termination" (p. 25). Self-control strategies primarily include self-monitoring, self-evaluation, and self-reinforcement (Meyers, Cohen, & Schleser, 1989).

Etiology and Development of Disordered Behavior

To be able to analyze cognitive processes requires some understanding of typical thinking patterns. Rosenhan and Seligman (1989) divide cognitive processes into two categories: (1) short-term conscious cognitive processes, such as expectations, appraisals, and attributions and (2) long-term, typically unconscious cognitive processes, such as a belief system that affects the short-term processes.

Short-Term Cognitive Processes

Most people are either aware of their own short-term thinking, or they can be taught to become aware of these thoughts. Even so, certain expectations, appraisals of one's own actions, and attributions (perceptions of causal factors) are thought to cause anxiety (Beck, 1976), depression (Abramson, Seligman, & Teasdale, 1978; Beck, 1964), and other disorders (Garner & Bemis, 1982). In a recent review of the literature on cognitive interventions used with young people diagnosed with depression, the most prominent treatment was some form of Beck's (1967) cognitive restructuring therapy (Maag & Swearer, 2005). Chapter 9 contains more detail about the cognitive explanation of internalizing disorders.

Expectations. When people anticipate future events, they form expectations, usually about the consequences of what is happening or what might happen. For example, in the employment termination scenario, the individual suffering from depression anticipated that he would never be a good employee and that negative things would probably always happen to him. The notion of expectations affecting behavior was first studied by Bandura (1977b, 1978) as they were related to his social learning theory, which is described in Chapter 7. Bandura found that people not only learned to do things when they were directly reinforced, but that they also learned to do things for which they saw others reinforced. That is, expecting to be reinforced for the same behavior, they would likely display it. Bandura (1977b) further defined expectations as outcome expectations and efficacy expectations.

Outcome expectations are anticipations that certain behavior will lead to certain outcomes. For example, students who expect to be rewarded for good grades have positive outcome expectations and will probably work hard for the good grades. Efficacy expectations have to do with the belief that one is capable of performing a certain way. "People tend to avoid tasks and situations they believe exceed their capabilities, but they undertake and perform assuredly activities they judge themselves capable of handling" (Bandura, 1977b, p. 393). Thus, even though the student perceives that rewards will follow good grades, if she does not believe that she can perform well enough to get good grades, she will likely not be motivated to try. Efficacy expectations affect whether individuals initiate responses, whether they expend much effort in performing if they do initiate them, and whether they will persist in their performance when faced with obstacles (Bandura, 1977b).

Negative outcome and efficacy expectations have been linked to anxiety and phobias (Kane & Kendall, 1989; Lang, 1967). Individuals who are anxious or phobic expect something undesirable to happen. For example, someone who is convinced that a plane will crash will experience extreme fear when boarding it, may break out into a cold sweat (somatic symptoms), and, in extreme cases, flee from the airport. Kendall (1994) evaluated a program consisting of cognitive therapy, relaxation training, and systematic exposure to anxiety-provoking situations with 47 children diagnosed with anxiety disorders. Called the Coping Cat program, it was found that the group of treated children fared better than a group of matched children on a waiting list and maintained treatment gains after 7 years (Kendall, Safford, Flannery-Schroeder, & Webb, 2004). Bandura (1977a) believed that systematic desensitization and modeling therapies used to treat phobias are successful due to changes in self-efficacy expectations (Bandura, 1982; Biran & Wilson, 1981). In one study, these authors were able to raise efficacy expectations in patients suffering from snake phobia. The higher the efficacy expectation, it was found, the more likely the individual was to approach a boa constrictor.

Appraisals. Appraisals are evaluations of (1) what happens to us and (2) what we do (Rosenhan & Seligman, 1989). Sometimes these self-evaluations are obvious to us and at other times they occur automatically. Beck (1964) outlines several cognitive assumptions that predispose an individual to negative appraisals and depression.

1. In order to be happy, I have to be successful.
2. To be happy, I must be accepted by everyone at all times.
3. My value as a person depends on what others think of me.
4. If I make a mistake, it means I am inept.

Beck proposes that if individuals ascribe to these assumptions they will negatively appraise themselves quickly and habitually, causing extreme sadness and hopelessness. The following is an example of the depressive effect of negative appraisals.

> A mother of three found that her depression was at its worst from seven to nine in the morning when she prepared breakfast for her children. She was unable to explain this until she was taught to record her thoughts in writing as they occurred. As a result, she discovered she consistently compared herself with her mother, whom she remembered as irritable and argumentative in the morning. When her children misbehaved or made unreasonable requests, the patient often thought, "Don't get angry, or they'll resent you," with the result that she typically ignored them. With increasing frequency, however, she "exploded" at the children and then thought, "I'm worse than my mother ever was. I'm not fit to care for my children. They'd be better off if I were dead." (Beck, Rush, Shaw, & Emery, 1979, cited in Rosenhan & Seligman, 1989, p. 335)

Kroll, Harrington, Jayson, Fraser, and Gowers (1996) used cognitive therapy based on Beck's work together with social problem solving and activity scheduling with 29 adolescents diagnosed with depression in a psychiatric hospital. These researchers found that fewer youth receiving this treatment relapsed into depression than from the control group.

Attributions. An attribution is an individual's concept about why things have happened (causal factors). For example, a student who fails a test may blame the teacher for her poor performance by saying that the test was badly written or unfair. People may make external or internal attributions (Rotter, 1966). Since the student in the example attributed the cause of test failure to someone other than herself, it was an external attribution. If the student had attributed failing the test to her own ignorance, the attribution would then be internal. Attributions can also be stable or unstable (Weiner, 1974). A stable cause is one that is maintained over time; an unstable cause is transient. For example, if the student believed that she had never been nor would ever be able to take tests well, the attribution is a stable one. If she believed that not studying for the test was the cause for failure, then she had an unstable attribution. Finally, attributions may be global or specific (Abramson et al., 1978). Global attributions are displayed across situations, whereas specific attributions pertain to only one task or event. For example, if the student believes that she has always done poorly on all school tasks, she would have a global attribution. If she believed that she failed to study adequately for this one test, then she provided a specific attribution.

Attribution style may determine whether an individual is prone to certain psychological disorders (Abramson et al., 1978). For example, those who attribute failure to internal, global, and stable factors and attribute success to external, unstable, and specific factors may be predisposed to depression (Peterson, Luborsky, & Seligman, 1983; Stark, Sander, Yancy, Bronik, & Hoke, 2000). A combination of problematic expectations and attributions may be found in literature pertaining to the notion of learned helplessness (Overmier & Seligman, 1967). These researchers found that when dogs were shocked and not allowed to escape they ceased trying to escape the pain, even when it was possible to do so. Furthermore, even after the dog successfully escaped the shock, it failed to learn that the same response would result in escape in the future. Similar helpless behaviors were found in experiments on humans (Hiroto, 1974) when people exposed to inescapable noise would sit passively even when escape was possible. Conclusions from such research indicate that some individuals may have learned to be helpless in the face of everyday challenges. These individuals show deficits in the motivation to respond and the ability to learn that outcomes are contingent on responding (Seligman, Walker, & Rosenhan, 2001). From a cognitive viewpoint, this finding is explained by the assumption that helpless individuals expect that bad events will occur and believe there is nothing they can do about it (negative internal, global, stable attribution). Stark et al. (1991, 2000) taught elementary students diagnosed with depression to attribute failure to more external, unstable, and specific factors and make attributions for success to more internal, stable, and global factors in order to reduce learned helplessness and found significant improvement on measures of depression.

Long-Term Cognitive Processes

Long-term cognitive processes are hypothetical constructs and inferred dispositions that govern conscious cognitions (Seligman et al., 2001). One example is a set of general beliefs. Ellis (1962) put forth the theory that psychological disorder stems largely from irrational beliefs that, in turn, shape short-term expectations, appraisals, and attributions. Subsequently, he developed rational emotive therapy (RET), later changed to rational emotive behavioral therapy (REBT) as a method of restructuring faulty belief systems in order to cure various disorders.

Ellis (1980) distinguishes between rational and irrational beliefs: rational beliefs are characterized by responsibility to oneself and society; irrational beliefs lead to conflict with other individuals and with society. Ellis contends that people are socialized to adhere to irrational beliefs through messages in the media and from significant people in their lives. Ellis promotes the ABC model for disputing irrational beliefs. The A represents an activating event, which is unpleasant or bothersome; the C represents consequences, which are negative emotions, behaviors, or actions. Most people believe that consequences or emotions (C) are a direct result of an event (A). Ellis insists that there is a B, an intermediate step that represents the beliefs one holds about the event and that it is these beliefs that actually cause the emotional and behavioral consequences. These B statements may be rational statements about the event, which lead to positive or neutral consequences, or may be irrational statements about the event, which generate negative consequences. In REBT the individual learns to recognize and dispute (D) irrational beliefs and to replace them with more adaptive and effective (E) rational beliefs and outlooks (Neenen & Dryden, 1999). The following example illustrates the Ellis' relationship of A, B, and C:

A (Event) →	**B → (Belief)**	**C (Emotional and behavioral consequence)**
Upcoming final exam	Irrational: "I'll die if I don't make an A on this exam; nothing is more important"	Extreme anxiety and poor performance on the exam
	Rational: "I'd like to do well on this exam and it would be nice to get an A, but my personal worth does not depend on it"	Slight anxiety, confidence, better performance on the exam

REBT has been found to be an effective counseling technique (Aust, 1984; Clarke et al., 1995; Ellis, 2002; Gonzales et al., 2004). Gonzalez and his colleagues (2004) conducted a meta-analysis on 19 studies using REBT with children and adolescents and found a positive and significant effect size (Z_r = .50) indicating that the average young person scored better on outcome measures than approximately 69 percent of untreated control subjects. Effect size is the relative effectiveness of the strategy averaged across all studies. Positive effects were shown for self-concept, anxiety, irrationality, and grade point average, with the largest positive effect size for disruptive behavior.

This meta-analysis also found that REBT appeared effective for young people regardless of whether they were identified as having problems, indicating that it might be useful for prevention as well as intervention purposes, although longer-duration treatments produced more positive results. Surprisingly, non–mental health professionals produced greater effect sizes than mental health professionals. Finally, children tended to benefit more than adolescents. Clarke et al. (1995) taught 150 adolescents in high school groups through role play and group discussions to challenge irrational beliefs and found significantly fewer cases of depression as measured on two depression scales. It is important to note, however, that Ellis (1980) claims success only with populations who have mild emotional difficulties and who are motivated to change their behavior.

Cognitive Interventions

Based on the assumptions of the cognitive model, several types of cognitive restructuring therapies, including REBT, have been developed (Haaga & Davison, 1991; Kanfer & Gaelick-Buys, 1991; Kendall, 2000; Salovey & Singer, 1991). Each assumes that either faulty thinking patterns cause feelings that in turn influence behavior, or effective self-regulation skills are lacking. Based on this assumption, cognitive restructuring therapists "draw out, analyze, then change the individual's thoughts, hoping to discover, and then revise" the problematic thoughts that caused the disorder (Rosenhan & Seligman, 1989, p. 120). Cognitive therapists often begin by ruling out the hypothesis that the locus of a problem lies in external events. For example, if someone loses a loved one, a normal reaction is to be sad. However, if an individual remains depressed for months, refusing to see people and sleeping all the time, then the therapist sets about identifying and disproving possible dysfunctional cognitions through cognitive restructuring techniques.

Cognitive restructuring techniques are widely used in clinical situations (Haaga & Davison, 1991; Mayer et al., 2005), often targeting automatic thoughts (Beck, 1976; Maag & Swearer, 2005). Cognitive restructuring may also include reattribution training (Dweck, 1975; Forsterling, 1980), relaxation training (Barlow, Craske, Cerny, & Klosko, 1989), positive imagery procedures (Ellis, 1980, 2002), assertiveness training (Lazarus, 1976), corrective self-talk and instruction (Meichenbaum, 1986), thought evaluation (Haaga & Davison, 1991), reverse role play and reframing thoughts (Abelson, 1986), self-efficacy training (Biran & Wilson, 1981), and problem-solving therapy (Spivak, Platt, & Shure, 1976; Mayer et al., 2005). Although cognitive therapy is typically applied in clinical situations, many aspects of these approaches have been used in the schools. The last section of this chapter highlights some of these school-based techniques.

As with any treatment attempting to change internal variables, cognitive therapies are more difficult to substantiate as efficacious. Kendall and Choudhury (2003) raised concerns about, among other things, varying outcome measures across studies, simplistic definitions of patient improvements, difficulties with self-report measures, unclear understanding about moderating and mediating variables, treatment fidelity, and lack of generalizability. Measurement of treatment efficacy presents a particularly challenging problem because we can only surmise that, if therapy is provided and the individual's behavior changes for the better, some aspect of the therapy facilitated that change. Exactly which therapy component affected feelings and behavior is difficult to determine. Furthermore, it is difficult to determine whether altered thinking contributed to the outcomes. However, Gonzalez et al. (2004) found positive effects of REBT for children and youth and others have used cognitive therapy in combination with medication to treat substance abuse ("Is Cognitive Therapy Useful. . . ," 1995), eating disorders (Leitenberg & Rosen, 1988), and panic disorders (Barlow et al., 1989).

When cognitive therapists subscribe to both the behavioral and cognitive models of disturbance, believing that disturbance is both a function of faulty learning and faulty cognitions, they attempt to teach new, more functional behavior, as well as to change the individual's thinking patterns. The combination of both techniques is called *cognitive-behavioral therapy (CBT)* or *cognitive behavior modification (CBM)* (Mayer et al., 2005). Cognitive-behavioral therapy teaches individuals new cognitive strategies to mediate their own behavior through self-talk or self-instruction (Meichenbaum, 1977), often in the form of problem solving (Salovey & Singer, 1991). CBT also targets teaching individuals to apply behavioral techniques (i.e., setting goals, monitoring performance, reinforcement, and evaluation) to one's own behaviors. CBT chiefly attempts to promote self-management or self-regulation, rather than solely to restructure thoughts; however, CBT and cognitive restructuring strategy combinations are common (Maag & Swearer, 2005). Typical CBT strategies used in schools with students with EBD include self-instruction, self-monitoring, problem solving, and self-evaluation (Levendowski & Cartledge, 2000; Lloyd, 1980; Mayer et al., 2005). Lloyd (1980) extracted four common attributes of CBT procedures as they are applied to classroom behavior:

1. A self-imposed treatment is taught, for example, self-instruction, self-control, self-evaluation, or self-monitoring.
2. Verbalization is usually a part of the technique.
3. A problem-solving strategy is identified.
4. Modeling is used to teach the technique.

Individuals who are skilled in self-management or self-regulation are much more likely to display appropriate behaviors in a variety of settings. Cognitive psychologists use this premise to promote cognitive interventions over purely behavioral ones (Kazdin, 2001). Singular behavioral interventions, discussed in Chapter 7, often fail to result in generalization of behavior under different conditions. Thus, cognitive and behavioral techniques are often recommended in tandem in order to strengthen the benefits of both (Goldstein, 1988; Kazdin, 2001).

In schools, cognitive-behavioral techniques have been shown to improve both social and academic performance (Falk, Dunlap, & Kern, 1996; Gerber & Solari, 2005; Harris, Friedlander, Saddler, Frizzelle, & Graham, 2005; Reid & Lienemann, 2006; Reid, Trout, & Schartz, 2005). With students with emotional/behavioral disorders, CBT has been shown to improve social adjustment (Larson & Gerber, 1987) and attending to task (Webber, Scheuermann, McCall, & Coleman, 1993), and to decrease aggressive behaviors (Etscheidt, 1991; Smith, Lochman, & Daunic, 2005; Smith, Siegel, O'Connor, & Thomas, 1994). CBT techniques have been reviewed as promising for social behaviors with this population (Ager & Cole, 1991) and have been used with school-age children to treat social anxiety, test anxiety, school phobia, depression, impulsivity, and hyperactivity (King, Heyne, & Ollendick, 2005; Maag & Swearer, 2005; Reid et al., 2005). Cognitive approaches have also been used to improve academic behaviors, including memory, metacognition, reading comprehension, handwriting, and arithmetic (Gerber & Solari, 2005; Harris et al., 2005; Levendowski & Cartledge, 2000).

Establishing efficacy for CBT interventions is also difficult. Gresham (1985) reviewed 33 studies of cognitive-behavioral interventions to improve social skills and cited limitations in subject characteristics, treatment specifications, outcome measures, and generalization/maintenance of treatment gains. Although, in a recent review of several meta-analyses of studies using cognitive-behavioral therapy with children and adolescents, Gresham (2005) found approximately 65 percent of the young people improved compared to only 35 percent of controls, he once again questioned the role of cognition in treatment outcomes and the general lack of measures for treatment integrity. Nevertheless, CBT, particularly in combination with external contingencies, appears to promote positive outcomes for students with EBD.

A final view of the cognitive model lies in Bandura's (1986) notion of reciprocal determinism. In Chapters 7 and 8, you will read that behavioral and ecological theorists believe an individual's behavior and related contextual variables (things, people, events) have a reciprocal effect on each other. This reciprocal effect means that one's behavior affects people and the environment and, in turn, the context affects individual behavior and development. For example, a student may yell (behavior) obscenities at a teacher (context), causing the teacher to become angry and call the student a name. The name calling (context), in turn, embarrasses the student, who then throws a chair (behavior). The student is suspended (context) and chooses to sleep for 3 days (behavior) while falling behind in schoolwork (context). Having fallen behind in schoolwork, the student continues to act up (behavior) in school upon returning, and so forth.

Bandura added cognitions into this equation. Thus, he proposed that behavior could affect cognitions, and cognitions could affect behavior; cognitions also affect contextual variables, and the context influences cognitions; finally, contextual factors influence behavior, and vice versa. Reciprocal determinism implies that treatment should be comprehensive, targeting cognitive and behavior change while altering problematic aspects of the environment whenever possible. Interventions based on this approach are reflected in functional behavior assessment (FBA) and positive behavioral supports (PBS) strategies, which will be discussed further in Chapters 7 and 12.

Cognitive Evaluation Procedures

Cognitive assessment is based on the theoretical assumptions that (1) individuals strive to make sense of their experiences, (2) their resulting conditions affect their emotions and behavior, and (3) educators and clinicians are in a better position to help individuals reach their goals by understanding their cognitions or patterns of thinking. Therefore, cognitive assessments explore how individuals perceive and interpret information. There is a basic assumption that the individual being assessed possesses sufficient intelligence and verbal skills to describe his thoughts accurately. Cognitive assessment has been applied with individuals experiencing academic difficulties and to the diagnosis and treatment of emotional or behavioral difficulties.

Although a variety of specific cognitive assessments has been developed, many depend on a specific theoretical orientation, for example, depressed cognitions and their role in maintaining depressive symptoms or anxious cognitions and their role in maintaining anxiety. A thorough review of the perspectives on cognitive assessment is presented by Clark (1997); however, a brief review of the most common methods is presented here.

Questionnaires

Self-report in the form of a questionnaire is often used as a cognitive assessment tool because it is convenient and usually sensitive to treatment effects. One example is the *Cognitive Triad Inventory for Children* (CTI-C: Kaslow, Stark, Printz, Livingston, & Tsai,

1992). It is based on Beck's theory of the negative cognitive triad, which consists of negative thoughts of the self, the world, and the future (Beck, 1967). The CTI-C has 36 self-statements that relate to one's feelings and ideas about the self, the world, or the future; respondents are asked to answer based on their thoughts and feelings "right now." Thus it aims to get at current thoughts. Total scores and subscale scores are available; the CTI-C has been used extensively as an outcome measure in depression research with children and adolescents.

Thought Listing. Questionnaires are obviously restricted in their content to the ideas that the developer thinks may be important. In contrast, thought listing is an open-ended cognitive technique in which an individual is asked to list everything she was thinking about during a specified time or activity. Responses are often scored only on the ratio of positive to negative thought content, but more in-depth analyses can be done "by content analyzing the individual's reported thoughts, ideas, images, and feelings" (Cacioppo, von Hippel, & Ernst, 1997, p. 929).

Think Aloud. Think aloud is another open-ended cognitive assessment technique. As described by Ramirez (2000), one application of the think aloud is to present simulated situations on audio tape and then ask subjects to respond as if they were experiencing the situation and to verbalize what is going through their minds. The verbalizations are taped and transcribed for raters to code for content. Think aloud has been used to study cognitive factors in a number of problem areas such as depression and family conflict; it has also been applied to academics. For example, students may be asked to verbalize what they are thinking as they try to solve a math problem, and the teacher can then determine where the breakdown, if any, is occurring.

Haaga and Davison (1991) recommended that assessment responses be analyzed in several ways. First, in addition to the frequency of cognitions reported, they recommend counting the number of spontaneous reported cognitions. Thought listing could serve this purpose. Second, they recommend analyzing the sequence of cognitions. For example, progress may be detected if an individual follows negative appraisals with problem-solving cognitions, rather than a longer list of negative appraisals. Third, assess the strength of an individual's belief in a particular thought. Rigid adherence to a thought might indicate depressive predispositions (Segal & Shaw, 1988). Fourth, rather than a literal interpretation of cognitions, assess what the cognitions mean to the individual being assessed. Cognitions can often be misinterpreted by the assessor. Fifth, positive cognitions should be assessed as well as negative ones. Typically, more positive cognitions than negative ones indicate better coping ability.

Finally, it might be necessary to simulate a negative situation in order to generate cognitions that might be problematic. The think aloud method allows for such an analysis. For example, an individual might imagine a stressful situation and then report what he or she is thinking. Teachers may learn more about how children think by having them tell or write stories, act in skits, role-play, and/or participate in puppet activities and discussions. These same activities may be used to change the way that they think and view the world. The next section of this chapter covers various cognitive strategies as they apply to children and youth at risk or with emotional and behavioral disorders.

Educational Applications

Various cognitive techniques are used in schools to improve learning and social behavior. For example, students may be taught learning strategies, such as talking themselves through difficult tasks, using a multistepped approach for solving problems, memorizing mnemonic devices to guide performance, and/or recording their progress. They may be asked to set academic and social goals for themselves, to monitor and evaluate their performance, and to administer their own positive consequences. They may be provided signs and sayings to inspire positive thinking and attitudes. The common factor is that students are asked to think about their own thinking, feelings, and behavior and in many instances to change them. This section reviews strategies based on the cognitive model that have been applied in school settings.

Rational Emotive Behavior Therapy (REBT)

Facets of Albert Ellis's (1980) rational emotive behavior therapy have been recommended for use with students with EBD (Gonzalez et al., 20004; Zionts, 1998). School curriculum based on REBT is often called rational emotive education (REE). Zionts (1998) recommends using REBT as a mental health curriculum or as a therapeutic intervention. REBT can also be used as a problem-solving procedure for students who are faced with problems or situations that they cannot change. With a problem-solving approach, students are taught to either change problematic situations or to change their thoughts about them. When REBT is applied as a mental health curriculum and therapeutic intervention, students are taught to change their philosophy about life.

Center (1989) outlines the major objectives of a REE curriculum.

1. Teach students about their emotions and related definitions.
2. Teach students about the dimensions of emotion (frequency, intensity, and duration).
3. Teach students about the triggers for various emotions.
4. Teach students that thinking can be a trigger for emotions.
5. Teach students about thinking errors and the most common irrational beliefs.
6. Teach students to determine causal thinking by working backward from an effect.
7. Teach students to refrain from magical thinking or the notion that things just happen.
8. Teach students to distinguish between fact and opinion.
9. Teach students to distinguish between desires and need.

REE curriculum often relies on worksheet exercises, group and individual activities and games, discussion, self-monitoring, humor, shame-attacking exercises, reframing, imagery, behavioral rehearsal, problem-solving exercises, self-evaluation, singing, homework, and self-talk exercises (J. Anderson, 1981; Gonzalez et al., 2004; Zionts, 1996). Many of the exercises provided in REE curricula teach students how to recognize and dispute their own irrational thinking (Zionts, 1998). For example, a student who thinks that "everyone hates me" would be taught to ask herself, "Prove that everyone hates me. Where is the evidence that everyone hates me?" Some common irrational beliefs found in children and adolescents include the following:

- "It's awful if others don't like me."
- "I'm bad if I make a mistake."
- "It would be awful to be a social loser."
- "It's my parents' fault that I'm so miserable."
- "Adults should be perfect." (Center, 1989, p. 185)

Students are also taught to change their self-talk, particularly from demands to preferences. For example, a student who says to himself that he must win a game or else he will be seen as stupid could be taught to tell himself "I would prefer to win the game, but if I don't, it doesn't mean that I am stupid. I had fun just playing." Students are taught to assess life events for what they are and to avoid making mountains out of molehills or overgeneralizing (Vernon, 1989b). Zionts (1998) points out that students must be cognitively ready to fully participate in a rational disputation process. Those who are not ready can participate in behavior and self-talk rehearsals and REBT readiness strategies (Vernon, 1989a). As students begin to comprehend that they can control how they think about things and that thinking affects their behavior, teachers are encouraged to provide disputation and rational statements for them. Finally, once students understand the disputation process, they can assume responsibility for disputing and changing their own thought processes. Figure 6.1 illustrates an example of a REE worksheet for an older student.

Several REE curricula are available and are often recommended for students with emotional and behavioral disorders. Table 6.1 provides a curricular list for teachers and other school personnel. Additionally, Zionts (1996) and Goldstein (1988) included REBT as a major component of their comprehensive program recommendations for the treatment of students with emotional and behavioral disorders.

Research on the efficacy of REBT and REE has been difficult chiefly because various combinations of techniques are used in different situations. If REBT does work, it is often not clear why it worked (Haaga & Davison, 1991). However, the previously mentioned meta-analysis of REBT studies with children and youth found support for REBT as prevention and treatment for anxiety, disruptive behaviors, and irrational thinking patterns (Gonzalez et al., 2004). REBT has also been found to be somewhat effective in treating depression (Clarizio, 1985), anger management, and social phobia (Conoley, Conoley, McConnell, & Kimzey, 1983; McKnight, Nelson, Hayes, & Jarrett, 1984).

Bernard and Joyce (1984), in their review of the literature on the use of REE with children, found that (1) students of various ages can learn the basic principles, (2) REE can result in reduced emotional difficulties and aid in emotional adjustment, (3) programs using multiple techniques produced better results, (4) little is known about the interactive effects of REE and demographic variables, (5) personality measures do not substantiate major change from REE interventions, and (6) more research is warranted. Gonzalez et al. (2004) recommend more research linking demographic variables to outcomes to establish the types of children who respond best to REBT, and a component analysis to determine which REBT components are linked to positive outcomes. REBT can also provide teachers, particularly those who are working in stressful situations, with a functional philosophy and psychological resilience (Webber, 1994, 1997b; Webber, Anderson, & Otey, 1991; Webber & Coleman, 1988). Teachers who adopt a rational worldview and who learn to dispute their own irrational thinking might better tolerate the disturbing behavior of their students.

Describe a negative feeling you experienced this past week. For example: "extreme anger," "frustration"	
Describe what happened right before you felt the negative feeling. For example: "My friend called me a name and refused to give me my books."	
List your thoughts after the situation occurred. For example: 1. Boys who are afraid are not men. 2. People don't like me.	
List things you said to yourself after the situation. For example: 1. "I must be stupid." 2. "I'm going to lose my friend." 3. "I have to be tough all the time."	
Circle the thoughts and self-talk that are irrational, meaning they are overgeneralizations, catastrophic thinking, negative appraisals, demands, or cop-outs.	
List rational beliefs and rational self-talk that make sense for the target situation. For example: 1. "Being afraid is human nature and nothing to be ashamed of." 2. "I don't like being afraid but it doesn't make me a bad person and in some situations it may be wise to be afraid." 3. "Maybe this isn't the kind of friend I want to have."	

FIGURE 6.1 Sample REE Disputation Worksheet for Older Students.

Interpersonal Problem Solving

It is thought that teaching students to solve their own problems provides a basis for social adjustment and independent functioning. Interpersonal problem solving is often a component of REE, but it is also delivered as a separate curriculum (Nichols, 1996; Shure, 1992; Shure & Spivack, 1982). Deficits in problem-solving ability have been linked to aggression (Asarnow & Callan, 1985), emotional disturbance (Siegel & Platt, 1976), social rejection (Renshaw & Asher, 1982), impulsivity (Spivack & Shure, 1974), and suicidal behavior (Portnor, 2000a). These deficiencies may be manifested in an inability to (1) generate more than one solution for a problem (alternative thinking), (2) foresee consequences for specific actions (consequential thinking), and (3) plan or execute steps toward a goal (means–end

TABLE 6.1 Sample REE Curricula for Use with Children and Adolescents

Developing Self-acceptance (Dryden, 1998).
Think good-Feel good: A cognitive behavior therapy workbook (Stallard, 2002).
Rational Behavior Skills (Patton, 1995).
Rational-emotive Education: A Manual for Elementary School Teachers (Knaus 1974).
Rational-emotive Therapy with Children and Adolescents (Bernard & Joyce, 1984).
Thinking, Changing, Rearranging (Anderson, 1981).
Thinking, Feeling, Behaving: An Emotional Education Curriculum for Children (Vernon, 2005).
Thinking, Feeling, Behaving: An Emotional Curriculum for Adolescents (Vernon, 2005).
Thinking Straight and Talking Sense (Gerald & Eyman, 1984).
The Passport Program Series (Vernon, 1998).

thinking) (Spivack et al., 1976). Interpersonal problem-solving training has been implemented with large groups of students as a preventive program (Shure & Spivack, 1982), as well as with individual students displaying emotional and behavioral disorders (Larson & Gerber, 1987; Nichols, 1997; Vaughn, Ridley, & Bullock, 1984).

From a cognitive point of view, the inability to problem solve is seen as a cognitive deficit; that is, students have deficiencies in their covert thinking processes (Coleman, Wheeler, & Webber, 1993). Note that a cognitive deficiency differs from cognitive distortions that are assumed in REBT. A cognitive deficiency implies that an individual must learn a new cognitive strategy or skill, whereas cognitive distortions must be restructured. Thus, most problem-solving training aims to teach a series of problem-solving steps, while enhancing the ability to engage in the various types of thinking mentioned above (i.e., alternative, consequential, and means–end thinking) (Urbain & Kendall, 1980). The most typical problem-solving sequence or strategy usually includes the following steps:

1. Identify and define the problem.
2. Generate many possible solutions: alternative thinking.
3. Analyze each solution in terms of possible immediate and future consequences, and the amount of effort or resources to be expended: causal and consequential thinking. Also determine how the solution will affect others: perspective taking.
4. Choose a solution and list the steps to that solution: means–end thinking.
5. Implement the chosen solution and evaluate the results: self-evaluation. (Nichols, 1996; Spivack et al., 1976)

Typically, students are taught the prescribed problem-solving steps and thinking skills through the use of worksheets, individual and group activities, and discussions. For example, students may view a videotape or listen to an imaginary scenario involving others their age who face a dilemma. They may then be asked to discuss or write about what the person should do and what the results of that action might be. Figure 6.2 is a problem-solving worksheet from a cognitive-based mental health curriculum that has been utilized with adolescents with EBD (Nichols, 1996). Note that in filling out the sections of the worksheet a student engages in several types of thinking while completing the problem-solving sequence.

Getting a problem under control . . .

Name the problem:
This kid at school calls me sewer names

Ask: "What do I want that I don't have now?"
I want him to leave me alone

Think: "If I **want** something, I have to **do** something." Consider the possibilities:

- tell a teacher
- beat him up
- ask him to please knock it off
- call him something worse
- get my friends to talk to him
- bring a knife to scare him with (circled)
- stay home from school
- get my brother after him
- have my dad call his dad
- play deaf like I don't hear him
- write him a note
- make a joke about it

Circle a choice. Predict its consequences . . .

	NOW right this minute	LATER today or tomorrow	MUCH LATER next week, month, year . . .
COST	I could get caught Sewer mouth or some other kid goes to the office and makes a big deal out of it	I get sent home They call my mom -- she yells at me Sewer mouth brags that he got me in trouble His brother comes after me.	I get expelled, so I can't go to school & I can't get a job -- I'm put on probation Kids' parents say I'm a troublemaker, won't let me come over Sewer mouth's brother and friends laugh at me, & still call me names
PAYOFF	He's scared and shuts up It feels good to stand up for myself My friends stick up for me	People say I've got guts. I'm sent home, I miss a science test The kid knows he better not mess with me.	I get to sleep late and watch MTV

So, is it likely to **make things better**? Yes___ No_X_ Is it **honorable**? Yes___ No_X_ **Safe**? Yes___ No_X_
If I did my choice, what's the **worst** *that could happen?*

Get expelled, parents fed up, send me away to work on my uncle's farm in Iowa

How **likely**: *how many chances out of 100 that the worst that* **could** *happen* **would** *happen?* _83_ /100
What would I **do** *then?*

Maybe stick it out, maybe run away

What's the **best** *that could happen? How likely?*

I could earn some money to buy a car, go off on my own -- 20 chances out of 100

So, is it **worth a try**? *Yes___ I'll make a plan and do it. No_X_ I'll make a choice with longer, stronger payoffs.*

FIGURE 6.2 Sample Problem-solving Worksheet.

Source: From *Whispering Shodows* (p. 26), by P. Nichols and Martha Shaw, 1996, Iowa City, IA: River Lights Publishers. Copyright 1996 by River Lights. Reprinted with permission.

Once students learn a problem-solving process, they will more likely be able to "mediate socially competent behavior and behavioral adjustment over a wide variety of situations and contexts" (Denham & Almeida, 1987, p. 392). The assumption that teaching covert cognitive processes better ensures generalization of behavior is central to the cognitive model. However, initial claims that cognitive therapies produced greater levels of generalization might have been overblown and empirically unjustified (Quinn, Kavale, Mathur, Rutherford, & Forness, 1999). Just as behaviorists realized the need to incorporate specific generalization strategies into an intervention package, so too have proponents of cognitive interventions been investigating factors that enhance generalization (Mayer et al., 2005).

The efficacy of interpersonal problem-solving training has, unfortunately, not been proved with research. In a review of interpersonal problem-solving literature, Coleman and her colleagues (1993) found that students demonstrated cognitive gains after interpersonal problem-solving training (i.e., they demonstrated knowledge of problem solving when asked to role-play or respond to hypothetical problem situations). However, the students generally were not successful at applying their problem-solving skills to actual behavior or to other social situations or settings. This finding led the authors to concur with other researchers that interpersonal problem-solving training alone is not enough to produce social competency in populations with problem behavior.

Self-Management or Self-Regulation

Although rational emotive education and interpersonal problem solving aim to teach individuals to manage their own emotions and behavior, some cognitive-behavioral techniques more directly target skills for regulating one's behavior with a minimum of external guidance. Three of the most notable self-management strategies are self-instruction, self-monitoring, and self-evaluation. Such self-management or self-regulation techniques have been used in schools to improve attention to task (Harris et al., 2005), task completion (Maag, Rutherford, & DiGangi, 1993), disruptive behavior and anger control (Moore, Cartledge, & Heckaman, 1995), impulsive behavior (Meichenbaum & Goodman, 1971), academic performance (Carr & Punzo, 1993; Harris et al., 2005), and generalization of appropriate behavior (Rhode, Morgan, & Young, 1983).

Self-Instruction Training (SIT). Self-instruction is the process of talking to oneself for the purpose of regulating one's own behavior (Meichenbaum & Goodman, 1971). Self-instruction is also referred to as cognitive self-guidance, private speech, verbal or self-mediation (Jenson, 1966), and verbally mediated self-control (Bornstein & Quevillon, 1976). Self-instruction training consists of teaching students to use private speech for the purpose of guiding and controlling their own academic and social behaviors. This training process usually consists of first teaching students to match their behavior to someone else's verbalization, after which they learn to provide their own verbalizations and match their behavior accordingly.

Self-instruction training evolved from early work by Luria (1961) and Vygotsky (1962), who proposed that children proceed through several developmental phases before acquiring the ability to use covert language to guide their behavior. This developmental process moves sequentially from external to internal verbal mediation in three steps: (1) the child matches his behavior to adult verbalizations, (2) the child uses overt self-talk to guide his own behavior, and (3) the child internalizes self-talk, guiding his or her behavior covertly at about 5 years of age (Luria, 1961).

Children who do not develop functional self-mediation skills may also manifest language problems, learning disabilities, intellectual disabilities, and behavioral problems (Harris, 1986; Torgeson, 1982). Meichenbaum and Goodman (1971) used self-instruction training for the purpose of teaching young impulsive children to slow down and think before they acted. These authors explain the failure to successfully self-mediate as a function of failing to (1) develop self-talk, (2) listen to one's self-talk, or (3) match one's behavior to self-talk, even when attending to it.

Meichenbaum and Goodman (1971) recommend a five-step teaching strategy to train covert self-mediation for the purpose of improving student behavior.

1. Teacher talks aloud and performs a task matched to the verbalizations while student observes.
2. Student performs the same task as the teacher verbalizes instructions.
3. Student performs the task while verbalizing, out loud, the instructions.
4. Student performs the task while whispering instructions.
5. Student performs the task with covert verbalizations.

As with other cognitive interventions, research on the effectiveness of self-instruction training is mixed. SIT has been used successfully to increase attention to task (Bornstein & Quevillon, 1976), reduce impulsive behavior (Meichenbaum & Goodman, 1971), increase task accuracy and completion (Fish & Mendola, 1986; Leon & Pepe, 1983), and reduce aggression (McGillivray, Cummins, & Prior, 1988; Smith et al., 2005). Although some research results are encouraging, often SIT alone fails to produce desired changes in target behaviors without additional interventions. Questions also remain about which specific conditions positively affect training outcomes.

Self-Monitoring. One of the most efficacious self-management strategies is self-monitoring. Self-monitoring is the process of having individuals record data regarding their own behavior for the purpose of changing the rate (Nelson & Hughs, 1981). Thus, in schools, self-monitoring has been found to increase rates of learning behaviors such as attention to task, task completion, reading, writing, and math strategies (Carr & Punzo, 1993; De La Paz, 1999; Gardner & Cole, 1988; Levendoski & Cartledge, 2000; McDougall & Brady, 1998; Nelson, Smith, Young, & Dodd, 1991) and to decrease rates of inappropriate behavior (Kern, Dunlap, Childs, & Clark, 1994; Smith, Young, West, Morgan, & Rhode, 1988).

Self-monitoring typically refers to a process of self-recording by which students are taught to observe their own behavior and note whether a target behavior occurred. Not only does this process result in useful observational data, but it has also proved to produce positive student outcomes, even for students with emotional and behavioral disorders (Carr & Punzo, 1993; Gresham, 2005; Levendoski & Cartledge, 2000; Nelson et al., 1991). Behavioral changes as a result of self-monitoring can be explained from two different theoretical models. Cognitive psychologists explain the behavior change as a function of the fact that recording one's behavior leads to awareness of the behavior, which leads to self-regulation and covert self-administered consequences (Kanfer, 1977; Snider, 1987). Behavioral psychologists, however, explain the change as a function of the act of recording that cues certain behaviors that are under the control of external consequences (Rachlin, 1984). In either case, self-monitoring seems to be a viable intervention for use with special education students (Forness, Kavale, Blum, & Lloyd, 1997).

Self-monitoring may require students to tally the number of actual appropriate behaviors, such as task completion, positive statements, following directions, steps in a sequence, accurate work, positive classroom behaviors, or goal attainment; they may also be required to mark time intervals during which certain behaviors occur (McConnell, 1999; Webber, et al., 1993). Students may be taught to record these behaviors by making hash marks, check marks, or other notations; coloring in dot-to-dot figures or squares; circling numbers or yes–no responses; graphing; or placing objects in a container for each occurrence or interval of the behavior that they are counting. Four sample self-monitoring forms are illustrated in Figure 6.3.

Teaching students to self-monitor behaviors is similar to other skill training. Typically, the strategy is taught using direct instruction with modeling, practice, and feedback. Often self-monitoring is combined with an external reinforcement system whereby the student is rewarded for a high frequency of appropriate behavior and often for accurate recording (Barkley, Copeland, & Sivage, 1980; Webber et al., 1993).

Research indicates that self-monitoring has consistently produced improved academic performance and classroom behavior. In a review of the literature on self-monitoring

Name ______________________________ *On-Task Behavior*

Week ______________________________

Each time you hear a signal, circle the signal number if you have been on-task since the last signal.

	M	*T*	*W*	*Th*	*F*
Signal	1	1	1	1	1
	2	2	2	2	2
	3	3	3	3	3
	4	4	4	4	4
	5	5	5	5	5
	6	6	6	6	6
	7	7	7	7	7
	8	8	8	8	8
	9	9	9	9	9
	10	10	10	10	10

FIGURE 6.3 Sample Self-Monitoring Forms.

Name ______________________ *Following Directions*

Week ______________________

For each period, place a check (✔) each time I give you a direction and you follow it within 5 seconds.

Period	*M*	*T*	*W*	*Th*	*F*
1					
2					
3					
4					
5					
6					
7					
Total	____	____	____	____	____

Name ______________________ *Spelling Accuracy*

Color in the number of correct spelling words each week.

10										
9										
8										
7										
6										
5										
4										
3										
2										
1										
Weeks	1	2	3	4	5	6	7	8	9	10

FIGURE 6.3 Continued

Name ______________________________ Math Computation 2-Digit Addition

Step Problem number

	1	2	3	4	5	6	7	8	9	10
1. I copied problem correctly.										
2. I added numbers on right.										
3. I carried if the sum was greater than 9.										
4. I added numbers on left (including carried number).										
5. I checked my addition by adding from the bottom-up.										

Place a check (✔) beside each step as you complete it for each problem.

FIGURE 6.3 Continued

procedures, Webber and colleagues (1993) concluded that the use of self-monitoring was effective in increasing attention to task and time on task, as well as for generalization of appropriate behavior to other settings. Increases in academic production have been shown in more recent studies (Harris et al., 2005; Levendoski & Cartledge, 2000; Reid et al., 2005). In an analysis of meta-analyses of special education interventions, Forness et al. (1997) reported that cognitive behavior-modification techniques, primarily self-monitoring studies, resulted in a convincing effect size. Compared to the other 19 special education interventions, cognitive behavior modification ranked fifth with an effect size of 0.71. The authors concluded, however, that these interventions appeared to produce better outcomes for controlling hyperactivity than for managing aggressive behavior. Finally, numerous studies have shown that cognitive strategy instruction, which often includes self-monitoring, improves performance in phonics, reading comprehension, vocabulary, writing, spelling, math, and science (Harris, et al., 2005; Pressley, 2002; Reid, Schmidt, Harris, & Graham, 1997). More information about the use of cognitive strategy instruction for the improvement of academics is provided later in this chapter.

Self-Evaluation. Self-evaluation is related to self-monitoring and self-instruction. It is also related to short- and long-term cognitive processes. Self-evaluation involves observing one's behavior and assessing it according to some predetermined goal and/or standard (Rhode et al., 1983). Ideally, individuals set their own standard, monitor their behavior toward a goal, evaluate whether they met the goal, and then praise themselves if their performance was desirable. Such a self-regulation process would likely promote healthy cognitions, emotions, and behavior (Kanfer & Gaelick-Buys, 1991). However, most often individuals aim for externally established goals and standards, neglect to monitor their own behavior, and engage in automatic and often negative self-evaluations based on biased thinking (Beck, 1964).

Individuals with emotional and behavioral problems typically have a tendency to evaluate their performance inaccurately, often by providing highly negative appraisals or by ignoring their performance altogether (Rosenhan & Seligman, 1989). Thus, it is recommended that self-monitoring be included as a component of self-evaluation so that accurate data about one's performance is readily apparent. Self-evaluation has both feedback and feedforward effects (Kanfer & Gaelick-Buys, 1991). Meeting or not meeting self-evaluative criteria has covert reinforcing or punishing properties that make the future occurrence of the target behavior more or less likely to occur. Self-evaluation also affects self-efficacy (Bandura, 1982).

In a study with students with EBD, Rhode and her colleagues (1983) applied a self-evaluation procedure to improve appropriate classroom behavior and to generalize the treatment gains. Six elementary-age students with EBD were taught to rate their own behavior after certain time periods on a 0- to 5-point card. An excellent rating (5) was given if the student followed all classroom rules for the entire interval and if work was 100 percent correct, and a 0 was given for violating one or more rules throughout the entire period with no work or all incorrect work. Ratings of 1–4 represented increments in between the two extremes. The students were externally rewarded for points resulting from the ratings and for producing accurate ratings. Accuracy was defined as student ratings' matching teacher ratings. Students were punished in the form of lost points for inaccurate ratings. Teacher reliability checks were gradually faded, and during the last experimental phase, students were required to self-evaluate in general education classrooms. In this study, student behavior improved and generalized to the general education classroom. Furthermore, students were able to match their ratings to teacher ratings about 90 percent of the time.

The effects of self-evaluation and videotape feedback used with 18 elementary students, 6 with externalizing problems and 6 with internalizing problems, were evaluated for effect on social interactions (Falk et al., 1996). The intervention resulted in substantial increases in appropriate interactions for the internalizing group and decreases in inappropriate interactions for the externalizing group. In summary, the purpose of self-evaluation lies in the student's motivation to change or maintain future behavior. It is recommended that self-evaluation procedures in classrooms teach students the following:

- To observe and evaluate their own behavior relative to some criterion
- To match their self-evaluation to an external evaluation by the teacher
- To determine consequences for appropriate and accurate responses
- To gradually work with less external guidance and fewer external reinforcers. (Smith, Young, Nelson, & West, 1992)

Teaching students to conduct accurate self-evaluations, from a cognitive viewpoint, results in a slower and more accurate thought process and a comparison of one's performance to a standard that should be important to the individual (Kanfer & Gaelick-Buys, 1991). This more accurate thinking process, in turn, results in healthier emotions (Rosenhan & Seligman, 1989). From a behavioral viewpoint, self-evaluation activities cue and reinforce appropriate behavior. In any case, self-evaluation procedures have been shown to result in improved behavior for students with EBD, although more research is warranted (Mayer et al., 2005; Nelson et al., 1991).

Cognitive Strategy Instruction (CSI). Cognitive strategy instruction incorporates self-instruction, self-monitoring, and self-evaluation. Basically, cognitive strategies are defined as "goal directed and consciously controllable processes that facilitate performance" (Reid & Lienemann, 2006; Reid et al., 1997). The use of cognitive strategies for the purpose of enhancing academic performance has been well documented (Pressley & Associates, 1995). Students with disabilities have shown improvements in such skills as reading comprehension, test taking, math performance, and memorizing and retaining information as a result of cognitive strategy instruction (Special Education Works!, 1999).

Cognitive strategies can be as simple as making lists and crossing off tasks as they are completed or memorizing a math rule. Cognitive strategies have been developed for such activities as test taking and studying, writing and composition, reading, listening, memorizing and retention, and academic content mastery. CSI works because students are taught to think about their thinking and to develop flexible, habitual, and automatic thinking that assists them in learning (Reid et al., 1997).

One of the most efficacious types of CSI methods is the use of mnemonic strategies (Forness et al., 1997; Mastropieri & Scruggs, 1994). Mnemonic pertains to the improvement of memory. In fact, Forness and his colleagues found that mnemonic strategies had the largest effect size of 19 special education interventions analyzed. The evidence is very convincing that these cognitive strategies help students to learn. Mastropieri and Scruggs (1994) described three mnemonic strategies for linking unfamiliar information to familiar or concrete information for the purpose of remembering the new information: (1) keyword methods, (2) pegword methods, and (3) letter strategies. Keyword methods are typically used to improve memorizing content area information. The teacher finds key words in a name and makes pictures to assist with remembering this information. These authors provide an example of helping students to remember that Thomas Paine wrote *Common Sense* by drawing a picture of a man writing, who states that he has a "pain" from writing, and a woman, who says, "if you had common sense you would stop writing" (p. 267).

Pegwords are used to help students to link numbers or colors to new information. First, rhyming words are linked to numbers and then paired with new information, usually in the form of pictures. For example, to assist with remembering that the Nineteenth Amendment gave women the right to vote, provide a picture of a knight (19, "knighting") taking women to a voting booth (Mastropieri & Scruggs, 1994, p. 270). Letter strategies are often used to help in memorizing lists or categories of information and/or steps in a procedure. For example, students may be taught the CAST method of writing a book report (Character, Action, Setting, The end) or the LISTEN strategy for improving listening skills (Look, Idle your motor, Sit up straight, Turn to me, Engage your brain, Now) (Bauwens & Hourcade, 1989).

Successful application of cognitive strategies involves not only memorizing the strategy, but also learning how to select appropriate strategies, where and when to use them, and knowing why they are desirable (Reid et al., 1997). Harris and Graham (1996) have developed a framework for teaching cognitive strategies. Self-regulated strategy development (SRSD) includes six stages:

1. Develop students' background knowledge and prerequisite skills (e.g., learn addition before learning a strategy for carrying in subtraction).
2. Discuss the strategy with the student and get a commitment to learn it. Allow the student to take ownership of the learning goals and the notion that this strategy will help to achieve these goals.
3. Model the strategy: the teacher engages in the strategy out loud.
4. Memorize the strategy: assist the student to memorize the strategy steps with the goal of developing automatic thinking.
5. Practice the strategy with teacher guidance in small or large groups. Prompt and cue students until they can perform the strategy independently.
6. Allow independent practice: the teacher continues to monitor the student's use of the strategy and subsequent academic performance (De La Paz, 1999; Reid et al., 1997).

The SRSD model also combines goal setting as it relates to academics (e.g., the goal of writing a story) with self-monitoring and self-reinforcement. Reid and Lienemann (2006) used SRSD to improve length, completeness, and holistic quality of written narratives of students with ADHD with positive outcomes on all three measures. It is also recommended that teachers shape strategies that students may have already developed. Thinking about thinking and learning appears to reliably result in better academic and social outcomes.

Additional Cognitive Techniques. It is beyond the scope of this book to review all the cognitive techniques and programs that might be used with students with EBD. However, the reader is encouraged to research some of the following: stress inoculation training (Meichenbaum & Cameron, 1973; Meichenbaum & Turk, 1976), role taking or perspective taking (Kendall, 1991; Kendall & Braswell, 1985), thought stopping (Rimm & Masters, 1974), desensitization and relaxation training (Hughes, 1988; Morris, 1991), guided imagery (Bagley & Hess, 1984), impulse control intervention (Rezmierski, 1984), use of therapeutic signs and sayings (Long, 1984), attribution training (Dweck, 1975; Yasutake, Bryan, & Dohrn, 1996), and managing resistance (Maag, 1999). There are also CBT program packages using combinations of various cognitive strategies that can be very useful for teachers such as:

1. *Coping Power Program* (Lochman & Wells, 2001)
2. *Tools for Getting Along Curriculum* (University of Florida, http://education.ufl.edu/web/files/38/File/TFGA_Intro.pdf)
3. *Second Step* (Grossman et al., 1997)
4. *The Incredible Years* (Reid & Webster-Stratton, 2001)
5. *Anger Coping Program* (Lochman, Whidby, & FitzGerald, 2000)
6. *Fast Track Project* (Conduct Problems Prevention Research Group, 2002)
7. *Adolescents Coping with Depression Program* (CWDA) (Clarke, DeBar, & Lewinsohn, 2003)
8. *Promoting Alternative Thinking Strategies* (Greenberg, Kusché, & Mihalic, 1998)

Some cognitive restructuring activities are very easy and quick to administer. Box 6.1 shows an example of a cognitive restructuring technique, the "Awful Scale" used with Thomas to diffuse an anger episode. Paired with a problem-solving model and positive

BOX 6.1
Thomas Changes Perspective

Thomas, a 13-year-old seventh grader, had a history of aggression, outbursts, and immature behavior. He had been removed from his parents' custody at age 7 and spent several years moving from foster family to foster family. At the time, Thomas was labeled EBD and in my special education class at a residential facility because his latest foster family could not manage his angry outbursts. Generally, Thomas was compliant and, although he was behind in all academic subjects, he would try to do some work every day. Thomas would display aggression and disruptive behavior only when provoked. However, it often did not take much to provoke him.

One day Thomas swept into the classroom, knocking over two chairs on his way in. He was muttering under his breath with multiple curse words, slamming his books on his desk, and glaring at everyone in the class. Once he sat down, I asked him what had happened to upset him and he said his "girl" had "dumped him" for someone else. At this point I asked Thomas just how awful that event was in his life. He said it was the "worst thing that ever happened to him." I asked him to come to the board with me and I made a horizontal line with a #1 on the left end and a #10 on the right end, labeling it the "Awful Scale." I told him he had to rate the event on the Awful Scale and could not exceed a 10, which was the most awful thing that could happen to him.

By this time, Thomas had calmed down a bit and quickly put a mark by the #9, slamming down the chalk when he was done. He thought that the girl dumping him rated as an extremely awful event. I then asked him how he would rate a situation where he broke his leg, someone stole his favorite CD, and his girlfriend dumped him. He thought for a moment and gave that a #10. I asked about a situation where he broke both his legs, had to use a wheelchair, could not play football, had all his CDs stolen, and his girlfriend dumped him. After looking at me curiously he erased his former marks, making the last situation a #10 and moving the other two down on the scale.

This type of questioning continued until the girlfriend dumping him registered about a #5 on the 10-scale. At this point, I told Thomas that if the event was only a #5, then he should treat it like a #5 and not a #10. He should not use up his #10 reactions (throwing chairs, cursing, stomping, slamming books, etc.) on #5 events. "It's OK to be upset, but #5 events probably just warrant you feeling frustrated or sad, writing about it in your journal, and pondering what would be best to do next." Thomas laughed, told me I was crazy, sat down, and began his math work.

Changing the way students perceive the world does not need to be a time-consuming task. Often the cognitive restructuring strategies are fun and humorous. Once perception and perspective do change, behavior change usually follows. Thomas continued to use the "Awful Scale" whenever he was upset and even taught it to a few of his classmates.

---

self-statements, Thomas might well learn to better diffuse his own anger and improve his interpersonal relationships.

Summary

Cognitive psychologists believe that disordered behavior results from a relationship between cognition and affect; faulty or deficient thinking patterns lead to unhealthy emotions. Faulty thinking is manifested in negative expectations and self-appraisals, inaccurate attributions, and irrational beliefs. Deficient thinking skills are manifested in cognitive processes that are

TABLE 6.2 Summary of the Cognitive Model

Etiology	Evaluation Procedures	Educational Applications
Dysfunctional thinking manifested in negative expectations, appraisals, attributions and irrational beliefs Deficits in self-management or self-regulation skills	*Cognitive Triad Inventory for Children* (Kaslow et al., 1992) Questionnaires Thought recording Think aloud techniques	Cognitive Restructuring Rational Emotive Behavior Therapy Interpersonal Problem Solving Self-Management Self-instruction training Self-monitoring Self-evaluation Cognitive strategy instruction

yet to be learned. Assessment of thinking patterns typically takes the form of self-report questionnaires, thought listing, and think-aloud procedures. Once faulty thinking or cognitive deficiencies are identified, alternative cognitions or new thinking strategies are taught and reinforced, resulting in milder emotions and more appropriate behavior.

Cognitive-behavioral therapy (CBT) combines the notion of thinking with the application of behavioral principles for the purpose of self-regulation and self-control. Teaching children to think differently has spurred the development of several cognitive restructuring, CBT, and cognitive strategy training programs, many for violence prevention. Teachers are encouraged to further review literature on cognitive therapy, rational emotive education, problem-solving training, cognitive-behavioral techniques, and cognitive strategy instruction. Although research is mixed regarding the effect of cognitive restructuring techniques, meta-analyses of various studies of cognitive-behavioral and cognitive strategy instruction techniques have shown convincing effects in terms of improved learning and behaving. The cognitive model is summarized in Table 6.2.

Conclusions

Viewing disordered behavior as a function of internal cognitive processes implies, as with biological and psychodynamic views, that assessment and intervention focus primarily on the individual. Relatively new to the field of psychology, cognitive treatment often includes behavioral principles of learning, such as behavior rehearsal, reinforcement, and behavior monitoring. However, the treatment focus of the cognitive model is on teaching self-management or self-regulation of thoughts, emotions, and behavior, as opposed to altering external variables for behavior change, as you will learn in Chapter 7. Self-regulation is accomplished by restructuring cognitions and/or training new cognitive skills. Some of these approaches, especially self-monitoring and cognitive strategy instruction, have proved to be very effective with special education students for the improvement of behavior and learning. Whether improvement is a function of altered thinking remains generally unconfirmed. However, cognitive techniques are well enough established in the literature to recommend their use, particularly in combination with other interventions and treatments, for students with EBD.

KEY POINTS

1. The basic premise of cognitive theory is that dysfunctional thinking patterns and deficient cognitive strategies are at the root of emotional disturbance and disordered behavior.
2. Cognitive psychologists propose that emotional disturbance can be lessened by changing people's perceptions of the world and their cognitive processes through cognitive restructuring techniques and cognitive-behavioral therapy (CBT).
3. Assessment of cognitive patterns relies on self-reported thoughts.
4. Rational emotive behavior therapy (REBT) is used in both clinics and schools for the purpose of restructuring cognitions.
5. Cognitive-behavioral therapy incorporates both cognitive restructuring and behavioral skills training techniques.
6. Application of cognitive-behavioral therapy in the schools includes self-instruction, self-monitoring, self-evaluation, and cognitive strategy instruction.
7. Self-monitoring and cognitive strategy instruction have been shown to be effective in enhancing academic and social behavior with special education students.
8. Although cognitive interventions appear to produce positive student outcomes, it is not clear whether cognitive therapies and techniques work because cognitions change or because of the influence of external variables.
9. Learning to regulate one's own behavior could potentially result in better generalization of appropriate behavior.
10. Teachers of students with EBD would do well to review various cognitive techniques and cognitive-based curricula and programs used with children and youth and to apply them in combination with other best practices.

HOMEWORK QUESTIONS

1. Find one of the educational programs listed at the end of the chapter on the World Wide Web and evaluate it in terms of age-range of students, cost, components, and studies to support it.
2. Albert Ellis writes of the irrational beliefs (e.g., I must be perfect, I must be loved, life must be easy) promoted by popular media. List 5–10 irrational beliefs that you can find in songs, commercials, or magazines and tell how you might dispute them.
3. Try self-monitoring one of your behaviors for a week. Develop and use a recording form. Evaluate your performance with a rating scale that you construct.
4. Briefly describe how your worldview was affected by what happened on September 11, 2001. Has your behavior changed as a result? If so, explain.
5. What types of events might affect students' worldviews in terms of both a more positive and more negative stance? How do teacher behaviors figure into this equation?
6. Think of a time when you felt depressed or anxious. What were you thinking? Describe a way to change your thinking that might have resulted in better feelings. Discuss briefly in a one- to two-page paper.

ADDITIONAL READINGS AND RESOURCES

Beyond behavior modification: A cognitive-behavioral approach to behavior management in the school (Kaplan & Carter, 1995) and *Child and adolescent therapy: Cognitive-behavioral procedures* (3rd ed.) (Kendall, 2005), for information about how to teach students with EBD to use problem-solving and cognitive-behavioral strategies.

Clear thinking: Clearing dark thought with new words and images: A program for teachers and counseling professionals, by Polly Nichols, Iowa City, IA: Riverlights, 1996, for many ideas, activities, forms, and procedures for changing the way students with EBD think and view the world.

Cognitive strategy instruction that really improves children's academic performance, by M. Pressley & Associates, Cambridge, MA: Brookline, 1995, for an overview of various cognitive strategy techniques that improve academic performance.

SOS Self-Help Programs, Parents Press (*http://www.sosprograms.com/*), for games, videotapes, workbooks, stories, audiotapes, and puppet theaters for use with children and youth to teach REBT techniques and cognitive-behavioral strategies.

Reclaiming Children and Youth, 6(2), 1997, for an entire journal issue about cognitive interventions for special education students, particularly those with EBD.

Behavioral Disorders, 30(3), 2005, for an entire special journal issue about cognitive-behavioral interventions and students with EBD.

Teacher mindsets for surviving in BD classrooms, by Jo Webber, Tom Anderson, and Laura Otey, *Intervention in School and Clinic, 26*(5), 1991, for an overview of positive cognitions that will help teachers to survive day to day with challenging students.

Teaching disturbed and disturbing students: An integrative approach, by Paul Zionts, Austin, TX: Pro-Ed, 1996, for ideas about how to use rational emotive therapy in classrooms for students with EBD.

Teaching self-management strategies to adolescents, by Richard Young, Rich West, Deborah Smith, and Dan Morgan, Longmont, CO: Sopris West, 1991, for procedures and forms to teach secondary students to self-monitor and self-evaluate.

Using rational emotive therapy to prevent classroom problems, by Jo Webber and Maggie Coleman, *Teaching Exceptional Children, 21,* 1988, for a short, practical article written for teachers who would like to try REBT on themselves to improve classroom management skills.

Rational emotive behavioral approaches to childhood disorders, by Albert Ellis and Michael Bernard (eds), NY: Springer, 2006, for information about using REBT for specific childhood disorders.

The Albert Ellis reader: Rational emotive behavior therapy: A guide to well-being, New York: Citadel Press, 1998, for a guide for using REBT strategies.

Cognitive-behavioral interventions in educational settings: A handbook for practice, by Rosemary B. Mennuti, Arthur Freeman, and Ray W. Christner (eds.), New York: Routledge, 2005, for cognitive-behavioral therapy (CBT) applications in school settings.

The Association for Behavioral and Cognitive Therapies (*http://www.aabt.org/*) for research and information pertaining to cognitive and cognitive-behavioral therapies and research.

CHAPTER 7 Behavioral Model

QUESTIONS TO CONSIDER

- What are the major assumptions of behavioral theory?
- What is meant by external or contextual variables?
- What is the definition of applied behavioral analysis (ABA)?
- How do we know something is a reinforcer for someone?
- What is functional behavioral assessment (FBA) and why is it difficult to conduct in schools?
- Can someone have an "emotional disturbance" under the behavioral model?
- How would a behaviorist define teaching and learning?

Orientation

Unlike biophysical, psychodynamic, and cognitive models that presume problems originate within an individual, behavioral theory assumes that disordered behavior is a function of environmental influences and past experiences. Thus, disturbance is generally viewed as a repertoire of inappropriate behaviors that have been learned as a result of reinforcement and punishment history. Behaviorists believe that such inappropriate behavior can be suppressed and a new functional repertoire of behavior acquired. Many instructional and disciplinary strategies are based in behavioral theory, also called applied behavior analysis (ABA).

Overview

According to behavioral theory, or ABA, disturbed behavior is thought to arise from faulty learning. Behavioral theorists are interested in how a person acts, rather than how he feels or thinks. According to this model, there are few internal human elements that cannot be expressed as observable behaviors, and only observable behaviors should be addressed. Professionals ascribing to the behavioral model have attempted to have the special education label changed from seriously emotionally disturbed to behaviorally disordered for this reason. Since disordered behavior is viewed as a function of specific environmental influences, assessment and treatment primarily target contextual variables. It is believed that if designated contextual variables change, so will human behavior.

Definition and Basic View

> Emotional disturbance consists of maladaptive behavior (Ullman & Krasner, cited in Russ, 1974). As a learned behavior, it is developed and maintained like all other behaviors. (Russ, 1974, p. 102)

This definition indicates that behaviorists view disordered behaviors as learned responses that are subject to principles that govern all behavior. Behaviorists assert that the only differences between many disordered behaviors and normal behaviors are the frequency, magnitude, and social "adaptiveness" of the behaviors; if certain behaviors were less frequent, less extreme, and more adaptive, they would not be labeled disordered. Therefore, behaviors are not viewed as intrinsically deviant but rather as abnormal to the extent that they deviate from societal expectations and usually are seen as disturbing by others.

Behavioral theory is based on principles of learning established primarily in laboratory studies with animal subjects. Behavioral theories are by no means unitary and may appear to have more differences than similarities. Although the differences are unreconciled and there are divisions within divisions of the major theorists, the following assumptions are common to most behavioral theorists:

1. Behavior is defined as responses or actions that can be observed, analyzed, and measured.
2. With few exceptions, all behavior is learned.
3. People behave as a function of external variables (i.e., antecedents and consequences).
4. Behavior can be changed with reinforcing (rewarding) and punishing consequences; therefore, behavior is modifiable through learning, thus the term *behavior modification.*

These assumptions are the basis for a number of distinctive features of the behavioral model. First is the very basic proposition that most human behavior, including maladaptive behavior, is learned and therefore can be "unlearned" and new behaviors learned in its place. Second is the central role of the environment in eliciting and maintaining behaviors. Behaviorists place the utmost importance on the setting in which the behavior occurs and on events immediately preceding and following behavior. Third, behaviorism is a method that stresses observable behavior; it is not concerned with explaining intrapsychic forces or other reckonings internal to the individual. In this stance, the behavioral model is in direct opposition to the psychodynamic model, which is concerned with concepts of personality growth and the subconscious forces that determine behavior.

Etiology and Development of Disordered Behavior

The simplest and perhaps the most practical way to understand behavioral theory is through its three major divisions: respondent or classical conditioning, operant conditioning, and social learning or modeling.

Respondent (Classical) Conditioning

Three classic experiments are almost always cited as the bases for development of behavioral principles and the applications of those principles to treatment. In 1902, the Russian physiologist Ivan Pavlov observed that dogs in the laboratory began to salivate at cues that it was mealtime, that is, at the sight of the food dish or upon hearing the approach of the person responsible for feeding. Under experimental conditions, Pavlov established that dogs could be conditioned to salivate by pairing a neutral stimulus, a bell, with an unconditioned stimulus, meat powder. An unconditioned stimulus is an event or object that elicits an involuntary or respondent response, in this case, salivation. After several pairings, the bell alone elicited salivation in the dogs. Thus, the classical conditioning paradigm was established: an unconditioned stimulus (meat powder) could be paired with a previously neutral or conditioned stimulus (sound of a bell) to elicit a conditioned respondent response (salivation). Learning was defined as the process of conditioning or the association of the bell with food.

The second classic experiment was undertaken by Watson and Raynor (1920) with a child known as "little Albert." At the age of 11 months, little Albert was unusually fearless and showed a fear reaction only in response to loud sounds. By presenting a white rat (neutral or conditioned stimulus) simultaneously with a loud sound (unconditioned stimulus), the experimenters soon induced fear responses (conditioned response) in the child by presentation of the rat alone. The fear response was demonstrated after only seven pairings and generalized to other objects such as a rabbit, a dog, a fur coat, and a Santa Claus mask. The fear response was demonstrated for over a month and in a variety of settings. Learning was again defined as conditioning or association of the rat with the fear-inducing loud sound.

The third classic experiment was conducted by Jones (1924) who worked with Peter, a 2-year-old who already feared essentially the same objects that Albert had been conditioned to fear: rabbits, rats, and fur objects. By utilizing a conditioning technique of pairing the presentation of a rabbit with the pleasant activity of eating, over a period of time the experimenter taught Peter to lose his fear response. These experiments involved reflexive or respondent or involuntary responses such as salivation and the startle response, over which the individual or animal had no control. Both Pavlov and Watson believed that all learning takes place through classical conditioning, in which a new stimulus occurs simultaneously with a stimulus already eliciting a reflex response. After numerous pairings, the new stimulus alone will elicit the desired response and thus the organism is said to have learned to respond to novel stimuli or new situations.

Operant Conditioning

E. L. Thorndike and B. F. Skinner have been especially instrumental in establishing and developing operant conditioning theory. Around the turn of the century, Thorndike began a series of laboratory tests with animals, which established the basic principles of operant learning. Thorndike placed hungry chickens, dogs, and cats in a "puzzle box" from which they could learn to escape by manipulating levers. Once the animals escaped, they were rewarded with food. From observing and recording the animals' learning on successive trials, Thorndike formulated a law of effect, which states that a behavior is likely to recur when followed by rewarding consequences and is unlikely to recur when followed by unrewarding consequences or punishment. Thorndike (1932) later rejected the punishment part of this law and retained only the positive part.

B. F. Skinner, a Harvard psychologist, developed Thorndike's early formulations to the extent that Skinner's name has become almost synonymous with the term *operant conditioning.* Although Skinner recognized that respondent conditioning plays a role in learned behavior, he believed that the majority of behaviors, those under an individual's control, are developed through operant conditioning, in which new responses are generated by reinforcing consequences. Operant behavior is a voluntary response that operates on the environment to bring about certain desired consequences (the reinforcement) and to avoid or escape aversive consequences.

In operant conditioning, the emphasis is on consequences for behavior. In contrast, respondent behaviors are involuntary and elicited by a stimulus that occurs before the behavior occurs. Reinforcement and punishment are central concepts of operant conditioning theory. The most basic Skinnerian tenet is that the strength of a response increases with reinforcement and decreases without reinforcement or under punishment conditions (the same as Thorndike's original law of effect). According to Skinner (1953), reinforcement is the application of an event (e.g, giving food) or the removal of something unpleasant (e.g., reduced amount of homework) that results in an increased probability of future responding. Punishment is the application of a negative event (e.g., electric shock) or the withdrawal of a positive event (removal of food) that decreases or eliminates the probability of responding. Consequently, behavior change, defined as learning, occurs as a result of the manipulation of reinforcers and punishers.

Skinner rejected the importance of hypothetical inner causes of behavior, which can neither be proven nor disproven. Although he did not deny the existence of such inner states, he believed that they are useless concepts in behavior change. He further asserted that most deviant behaviors are simply learned through operant conditioning but are deemed pathological by society. Therefore, intervention involves identifying and changing the reinforcers that are maintaining these deviant behaviors. ABA is simply the application of B. F. Skinner's operant conditioning theory for various purposes. ABA is defined as:

> the process of applying sometimes tentative principles of behavior to the improvement of specific behaviors, and simultaneously evaluating whether or not any changes noted are indeed attributed to the process of application. (Baer, Wolf, & Risley, 1968, p. 91)

Note that this definition includes three major components: (1) the application of behavioral principles, (2) the ethical mandate that these applications should improve behavior, and (3) an accountability portion requiring simultaneous evaluation of treatment effects. Rigorous monitoring and evaluation of intervention effects is a hallmark of ABA and the behavioral model. Behaviorists often criticize other models for the lack of robust measurement and evaluation procedures. ABA techniques based on Skinner's concept of operant conditioning are widely used in psychology, economics, industry, animal management, and education, including special education. Educational applications of ABA will be reviewed in the "Educational Applications" section of this chapter.

Social Learning (Modeling)

Social learning or modeling is a third learning paradigm proposed by behaviorists. In this type of learning, individuals may acquire new responses by observing others who are being reinforced or punished, and subsequently imitating the behavior (models) of others or decreasing or eliminating their own similar behaviors. Social learning differs from operant and respondent conditioning in that individuals are not required to perform the behavior themselves and no direct reinforcement or punishment is necessary for learning to occur (Bandura, 1965a, 1965b).

After watching a model, the observer may be affected in one of three ways: new responses may be acquired, behaviors may become inhibited or disinhibited, or previously learned responses may be facilitated. For example, modeling is often used with students with EBD to teach a new social skill such as raising one's hand before speaking out in class. After learning how to raise hands, the behavior may become inhibited if the teacher responds inconsistently or negatively to others in the class who raise their hands before speaking out. If the hand-raising behavior was previously learned but not being used by an individual, the teacher's consistent positive recognition of others' hand raising may encourage the individual to use the behavior again.

The extent to which the observer is affected depends on the extent to which identification with the model has occurred. Some of the variables influencing this identification process are age, gender, sex, and status or prestige of the model (Bandura, 1965a). Other factors affecting social learning are whether the model is live or on film or TV (Bandura, 1965a), whether one or more models are observed, and whether the model is punished or reinforced (Bandura, 1977b). According to social learning theorists, negative or maladaptive behaviors as well as positive ones can be learned through exposure to a model. In other words, fears, phobias, and aggressive behavior can be learned vicariously.

The relationship of aggressive behavior to social learning is particularly prevalent in discussions and research pertaining to the effect of television watching and video game playing on children's behavior. Because young children do not easily differentiate between what is real and what is not real on TV and because they fail to connect behavior and motives to televised consequences, they are especially likely to be influenced by what they see on television (Berk, 2005). Since about 57 percent of TV programs between 6:00 AM and 11:00 PM contain violent scenes (Center for Communication and Social Policy, 1998), it might be assumed that imitation of violent acts would be prevalent among children. In fact, longitudinal studies found that time spent watching TV in childhood and adolescence predicted aggressive behavior in early adulthood (Huesmann, Moise-Titus, Podolski, & Eron, 2003; Johnson, Cohen, Smailes, Kasen, & Brook, 2002). Even for nonaggressive children, violent TV sparks hostile thoughts and behavior, although aggressive children are more intensely impacted (Bushman & Huesmann, 2001). "Violent media images modify children's attitudes toward social reality so they increasingly match what children see on TV" (Berk, 2005, p. 379).

Another pertinent area of social learning is that of self-reinforcement in which reinforcement is derived when an individual thinks about his own attitudes and behaviors in positive ways (Bandura, 1968). Thus, the individual's own judgments and personal feelings of merit become important factors in continuation of behaviors not reinforced by others or the environment. Indeed, Bandura believes that an individual's own thoughts and feelings may be powerful enough to override reinforcers readily available in the social environment. In this way, Bandura's theory bridged the behavioral and cognitive models. Self-reinforcement, as you learned in Chapter 6, can be systematically taught to students as a behavioral self-control technique (Kanfer & Gaelick-Buys, 1991).

In summary, social learning theory proposes that new behavior can be learned through observation and vicarious reinforcement, while behavior can be suppressed through observation and vicarious punishments. A separate dimension is added to behavioral theory by the inclusion of such concepts as vicarious learning and self-reinforcement. These concepts are based on internal mediation processes of the individual; hence, the environmental events that evoke behaviors are not as easily identified as in operant and respondent conditioning.

Evaluation Procedures

In contrast to the biophysical model in which medical personnel and the psychodynamic model in which clinical personnel are primarily responsible for diagnosis of disturbance, the teacher and/or school psychologist occupy a central role in the evaluation process of the behavioral model. Bower (1980) aptly describes the situation:

> The myth still exists that someone, somewhere, somehow, knows how to assess behavior and/or mental health as positive or negative, good or bad, healthy or nonhealthy, and independent of the social context wherein the individual is living and functioning. It is possible that the teacher who focuses on the child's observable behavior in school is closer to an operational reality of mental health than can be determined in an office examination. What a teacher is judging is how a specific behavior affects him as a professional person in a primary social system and how well a child can play the role of student in school. (p. 124)

Checklists and Behavior Rating Scales

Teachers are most often involved during screening in which they are asked to judge whether a student is in need of further evaluation. In addition to direct observation and behavior recording, behavior rating scales and checklists (reviewed in detail in Chapter 3) can act as primary aids to the teacher in making such a judgment. These measures provide a specific, somewhat objective structure for rating a student's behavior and also may help identify withdrawn, depressed, or passive children who may be easily overlooked in the classroom.

As you learned in Chapter 3, several published checklists and rating scales that provide the user with data for comparisons are available. Generally, raw scores are converted into standard scores, which allow comparisons among individuals by establishing a range of normalcy. One example, not mentioned in Chapter 3, is the *Devereux Scales of Mental*

Disorders (DSMD; Naglieri, LeBuffe, & Pfeiffer, 1994). The DSMD consists of 111 items rated on a 5-point scale ranging from "never" to "very frequently." There is one scale with different levels for children (ages 5–12) and adolescents (ages 13–18). The DSMD offers various subscales (e.g., depression, anxiety, attention, conduct) that fall under the broader classifications of Internalizing or Externalizing. In addition, the DSMD offers a third classification, Critical Pathology, that includes the autism and acute problems subscales. Figure 7.1 shows the profile form of the adolescent version.

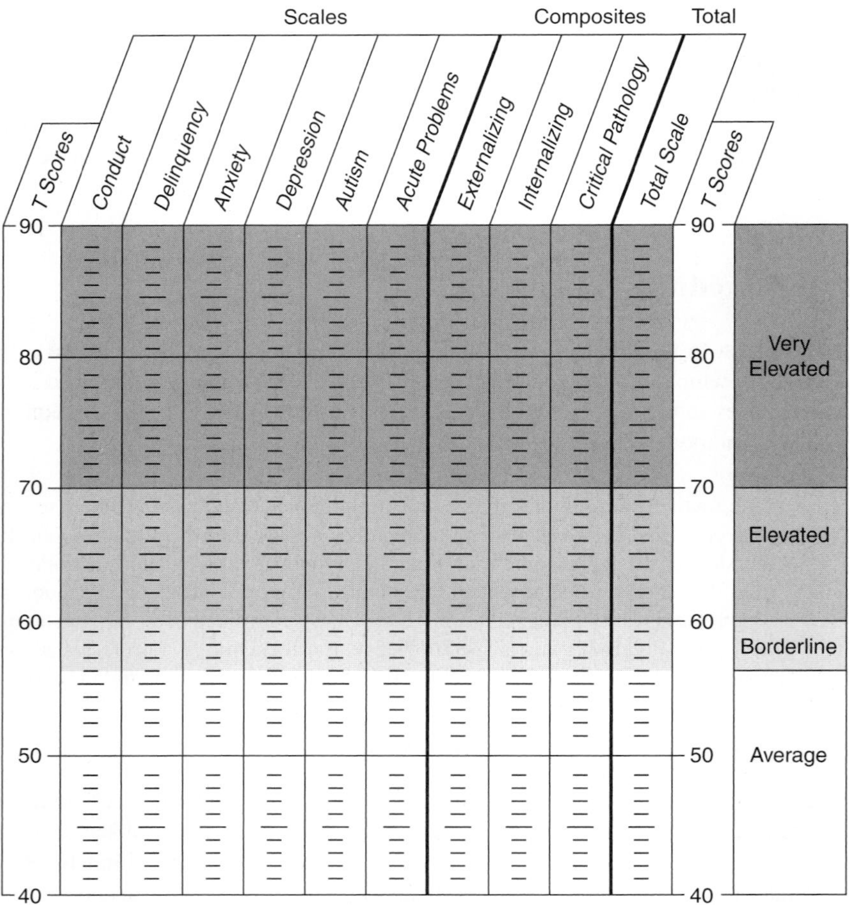

FIGURE 7.1 Profile for the Devereux Scales of Mental Disorders (DSMD), Adolescent Form

Adapted from *Devereux DSMD* Answer Sheet, by J. A. Naglieri, P. A. LeBuffee, & S. I. Pfeiffer (1994). San Antonio: The Psychological Corporation. Reprinted by permission of the publisher and the authors.

Behavior Recording

Behavior observation and recording is another method utilized by behaviorists to identify students with EBD and to determine the best treatment/intervention. Such recordings are often used as supplemental information to both informal and formal testing procedures. The referring teacher may be asked to keep anecdotal records, but assessment personnel generally are responsible for observing and recording behavior of the student in question. Recording involves direct observation of the student in the environment in which maladaptive behavior occurs, usually the classroom setting. For example, with the technique of time sampling, the observer chooses several time periods to observe and then records occurrences of one or more specified behaviors. A more difficult and generally less reliable technique is to record every behavior that occurs within very short time periods or intervals.

Recording obviously involves only behaviors that are observable and measurable. Such characteristics of behavior as frequency, duration, and topography should be considered. For example, if a teacher complains about a student's behavior, it may well be that it is the topography of behavior (e.g., spitting in someone's face) that makes it maladaptive or deviant rather than the frequency or number of times it occurs; conversely, the important consideration may be the duration rather than the topography of behavior (temper tantrums lasting 20–30 minutes versus temper tantrums lasting 4–5 minutes). In addition to frequency, duration, and topography, other considerations when judging maladaptiveness are whether the behavior is developmentally or age-appropriate and whether the behavior is situation-specific or occurs across settings. Of particular interest to behaviorists is the relationship of behavior to contextual variables. Behavioral recording in conjunction with other assessment information provides essential information for indentifying such relationships (Heckaman, Conroy, Fox, & Chait, 2000).

Functional Behavioral Assessment and Analysis (FBA)

The most fundamental behavioral assessment process is based on the notion that challenging or disordered behavior serves a function or purpose for individuals (Durand & Carr, 1985; Gresham, Watson, & Skinner, 2001). In trying to understand extreme problem behavior (e.g., self-injurious behavior), researchers discovered that the behavior of individuals, even those with severe retardation, tends to serve three general purposes: (1) to get something (positive reinforcement hypothesis), (2) to get out of something (negative reinforcement hypothesis), and/or (3) to obtain sensory stimulation (automatic reinforcement hypothesis) (Iwata, Dorsey, Slifer, Bauman, & Richman, 1982). It is also thought that many problem behaviors are simply methods for communicating about one of these functions (Carr & Durand, 1985a, 1985b). Through a detailed process of assessment (known as functional behavioral assessment, or FBA) whereby data are gathered directly linking problem behavior to specific triggers and reinforcers, and a subsequent analysis of the data (known as functional analysis, or FA) including hypotheses testing, the exact purposes for the behavior can be determined.

With knowledge about the function and about controlling antecedents (triggers) and reinforcers, effective functional-assessment-based intervention programs can be developed

(Gable, Quinn, Rutherford, Howell, & Hoffman, 2000; Lane, Umbreit, & Beebe-Frankenberger, 1999; Newcomer & Lewis, 2004; Sugai, Horner, & Sprague, 1999) and will be more likely effective than programs designed without FBAs. Function-based interventions usually include (1) teaching appropriate replacement behaviors that serve a similar function, (2) the elimination or alteration of controlling antecedents, and (3) reinforcement for replacement behaviors, but never again for the inappropriate behavior (Gable et al., 2000). In other words, functional assessment and analysis allows for "hypothesis-driven treatment" (Dunlap, Ferro, & Deperczel, 1996, p. 126), for which intervention is designed based on the exact relationship of specific behavior to its context.

Recommended methods for conducting functional behavioral assessment and analyses include: (1) informant-based methods (e.g., interviews, rating scales, questionnaires, record review), (2) descriptive analyses or direct observation (e.g., ABC and scatter plot analysis), and (3) experimental analysis (environmental manipulations, experimental design) (Alberto & Troutman, 2006; Dunlap et al., 1996; O'Neill et al., 1997).

Informant-based methods typically consist of FBA rating scales and/or interviews or interview forms. Two common FBA rating scales are the *Motivation Assessment Scale* (MAS; Delaney & Durant, 1986) and the *Problem Behavior Questionnaire* (PBQ; Lewis, Scott, & Sugai, 1994). The MAS is designed to determine which of four possible functions a particular behavior might serve. This is done with 16 questions requiring a rating on a 7-point Likert-type scale. Total numeric ratings and mean scores result in relative rankings to establish that category with the highest mean. Although the scale was developed for individuals with developmental disabilities and severe challenging behaviors and reliability across raters varies (Conroy, Fox, Bucklin, & Good, 1996), the MAS is often used in schools for milder forms of behavior problems (Barton-Arwood, Wehby, Gunter, & Lane, 2003).

The PBQ was primarily developed for individuals with mild behavior problems and has 15 context-specific situations also to be rated on a 7-point Likert scale. Ratings are loaded to indicate probability of five different functions: (1) access to peer attention, (2) access to teacher attention, (3) escape from peer attention, (4) escape from teacher attention, and (5) setting events. Technical adequacy of this tool has not been established (Barton-Arwood et al., 2003).

The FBA interviews completed with or by parents, teachers, teaching assistants, and sometimes the student himself ask the informant to do the following:

1. List specific challenging behaviors and, for each behavior, describe its frequency and intensity.
2. Describe "setting events" (those things happening long before a behavior occurs that might trigger it) such as sleep and eating patterns and medications that might be contributing to the problem behavior.
3. Tell when, where, and with whom the behavior is likely to occur.
4. Describe the conditions under which it is most and least likely to occur (e.g., what activity, type of instruction, materials).
5. List the consequences that are usually administered when the behavior occurs (i.e., what does the student get or get out of).
6. Speculate whether the behavior is communicative.
7. List possible effective reinforcers (O'Neill et al., 1997)

These extensive interviews also provide a basis for an initial hypothesis about why the behavior is occurring (i.e., which contextual variables are influencing the behavior and what purpose it is serving).

Additionally, it is recommended that a FBA include direct observation with behavioral recording techniques. The most common format for gathering this information is an ABC chart on which challenging behaviors are noted in the behavior column (B) and immediately preceding antecedents (A) and consequences (C) for that behavior are also noted (Sugai et al., 1999). This type of data more specifically illustrates the relationship of the behavior to specific environmental variables. Scatterplots or more detailed observation forms are also useful for descriptive assessment (Alberto & Troutman, 2006; O'Neill et al., 1997; Sugai et al., 1999). Figure 7.2 provides a sample scatterplot. Note in this example that Raymond's behavior seems to occur most often in English class. Apparently, there is something about this time of day, the subject matter, or some other situation in this class that seems to be precipitating the inappropriate behavior. At this point in the FBA, more specific descriptive data are usually gathered, perhaps with a scatterplot relating behavior to specific activities in the English class.

The major goal of functional behavioral assessment is to gather enough data to formulate an informed hypothesis about what might be cueing the behavior and what might be reinforcing the behavior (i.e., the function or purpose). After formulating hypotheses, it may be necessary to test them using experimental analyses (FA). Typically, this type of analysis consists of manipulating the conditions under which the behavior is occurring and recording the effect on the target behavior (Alberto & Troutman, 2006). The analysis can become very detailed, with one or more single-subject designs so as to pinpoint the function of inappropriate behavior with certainty. The analysis component of FBA is probably the most controversial because it requires knowledge that the typical classroom teacher may not possess and might discourage data collection (Nelson, Roberts, Mathur, & Rutherford, 1999; Scott & Nelson, 1999).

Student: *Raymond*

Behavior: *Cursing/Talking Back*

Date: *December 1–5*

Activity	Time	Days 1	2	3	4	5
Math	8–9:00					///
English	9–10:00	///	////		//	
PE	10–11:00					
Science	1–2:00					

FIGURE 7.2 Sample Scatterplot Used for Functional Assessment

The recommended *Extended-Functional Analyses,* usually conducted in clinical settings and taking many days to complete, have proved unrealistic for most school purposes (Alberto & Troutman, 2006). Fortunately, a *Brief-FA* was developed to make the process more efficient (only 90 minutes) (Broussard & Northup, 1995). It has been found that Brief-FAs yield similar and valid functional data as compared to Extended-FAs, yet with much more efficiency (Wallace & Iwata, 1999; Wallace & Knight, 2003), increasing the probability that hypotheses testing will occur more often as a component of school-based FBAs.

FBA procedures were mandated in the 1997 amendments to the Individuals with Disabilities Education Act (IDEA) in relation to the provision of positive behavior supports for students whose behavior violated school codes of conduct and/or were outside personal or interpersonal norms of acceptable social behavior. However, no specific guidelines for FBAs were issued, and, some speculated, there was not enough research to warrant their inclusion in the regulations (Nelson et al., 1999). These authors maintained the following:

1. There is little agreement in the field of ABA regarding which techniques constitute an adequate FBA.
2. A review of the literature reveals limited external validity for FBA, particularly with regard to sample characteristics (most studies were conducted with individuals with severe disabilities), settings (most studies took place in clinical settings rather than in schools), and professional characteristics (few, if any, teachers conducted FBAs in the research studies).
3. It is doubtful that FBA will become a common practice in the classroom because it requires extensive knowledge of ABA and more time than most teachers can devote to it.

Subsequent to the mandate to conduct FBAs, individual school districts have developed various versions of FBA procedures with little or no attention to empirically defined procedures (Watson & Steege., 2003), and few teachers or school psychologists are adequately trained to carry out FBAs with fidelity (Fox & Conroy, 2000; Scott et al., 2004).

Nevertheless, Sasso, Conroy, Peck-Stichter, and Fox (2001) stated "from both a conceptual and a theoretical standpoint, systemic analyses of the function of behavior should be considered best practice for children with behavior and learning problems" (p. 283). Thus, it is desirable that FBAs become an integral component of educating students with EBD because they include various types of direct and indirect assessment procedures from many sources, relate student problems to the context, provide useful data for designing interventions, and allow for ongoing evaluation of students' behavior. A plethora of journal articles and books have been developed describing various FBA techniques (e.g., O'Neill et al., 1997; Ryan, Halsey, & Matthews, 2003; Sugai et al. 1999). Further effort must be provided for preservice teacher and assessment personnel training, adequate technical support, and continued research to ensure efficacious use (Scott & Nelson, 1999; Scott et al., 2004).

Educational Applications

Behavioral techniques are the most commonly used interventions in classrooms for students with emotional/behavioral disorders. Behavioral techniques can be used in conjunction with other methods; even programs with a heavily psychodynamic or cognitive orientation will often use contracting or a token economy to improve academic and social performance. It is perhaps this flexibility plus generally positive results that account for the popularity of behavioral interventions. Although it is beyond the scope of this book to review the massive body of literature on behavioral technology, treatment, and interventions, we will look at the most common applications of behavioral principles to classrooms for students with EBD.

Behavioral techniques are used in the classroom for both instructional purposes and behavior management. In either case, behavioral applications include certain components:

1. *Setting goals:* The behavioral model dictates that instruction be directed by the teacher, rather than by the student. The teacher decides what a student needs to learn and the level of knowledge or competence that needs to be mastered. This differs from the psychodynamic model, which assumes that, given a supportive environment, individuals will choose what they need to master and set about doing so, but is comparable to the cognitive-behavioral model that promotes self-goal-setting (see Chapter 6). In an ABA model, the teacher first must identify broad academic and/or social goals.
2. *Assessing for current level of functioning:* Once the teacher has decided what the student needs to master, it must be determined which part of this curriculum the student has already completed and whether the prerequisites have been attained. Assessment strategies usually consist of curriculum-based assessment (CBA) (Mager, 1997; Mastropieri & Scruggs, 1994) in which the student is asked to perform academic or social tasks indicative of curricular mastery in order to determine which content or behaviors have yet to be mastered. In the case of social behavior, this assessment may include observational recording and functional behavioral assessment.
3. *Specifying learning objectives in behavioral terms:* Behavioral objectives contain essential information indicative of the behavioral model (Alberto & Troutman, 2006; Mager, 1984). A learning objective contains (1) a conditions statement that specifies antecedents required for student performance (e.g., "Given 10 word cards from the first-grade reader"), (2) the target behavior specified such that it can be observed and counted (e.g., "will read aloud"), and (3) a criterion statement providing information about the mastery level (e.g., "each word with no assistance for 3 consecutive days"). Sometimes these objectives are broken into smaller chunks of learning (task analysis). Task analysis is a common component of the behavioral model (Moran & Malott, 2004).
4. *Planning:* The behavioral model dictates that teachers plan instruction, as opposed to following a child's interest or current needs—a technique indicative of developmental models. Teachers are usually required to prepare lesson plans containing information about goals, objectives, learning activities and materials, and evaluation procedures.
5. *Implementing instruction:* The behavioral model of instruction has been used extensively in special education in the form of programmed instruction, direct instruction (DI), computer-assisted instruction, drill-and-practice activities, individualized instructional programs (e.g., individually guided education), role-playing, modeling, prompting techniques, precision teaching, incidental teaching, discrete trial teaching,

behavioral rehearsal, structured interactions, test–teach–test, and mastery learning (Adams & Engelmann, 1996; Cipiani & Spooner, 1994; Forness et al., 1997; Gardner et al., 1994; Marchand-Martella, Slocum, & Martella, 2004; Moran & Malott, 2004; Scheuermann & Webber, 2002; Tarver, 1998; Wehby, Symons, & Canale, 1999). We will not review and describe each of these applications here; virtually all special education methods textbooks provide such information. The point is that behavioral applications have been researched extensively and appear to be, as a group, among the most effective special education instructional strategies (Forness et al., 1997).

6. *Monitoring student performance:* The teacher keeps some record of the learner's progress on each learning objective through observational recording techniques (Moran & Malott, 2004) and/or test construction (Mager, 1997). Progress monitoring, referred to as formative assessment, is a key component of applied behavioral analysis.
7. *Evaluating student performance:* The teacher judges whether the learner's progress is appropriate and decides when to move to the next learning objective. Often evaluation procedures include data graphs, CBA, and other performance assessment strategies. Measuring student behavior to indicate progress differs significantly from the psychodynamic and cognitive models, for which it is often assumed that by virtue of participating in the activity the student has made progress.

Social skills instruction, often found in classrooms for students with EBD, is an excellent example of the behavioral model in practice. The premise of social skills instruction is that students with poor social skills do not know the proper way to act and need to be taught. Social skills curricula such as *The Walker Social Skills Curriculum: ACCESS Program* and *ACCEPTS Program* (Walker et al., 1983, 1988), and the *Skillstreaming* series (Goldstein, Sprafkin, Gershaw, & Klein, 1980; McGinnis & Goldstein, 1984) contain lists of discrete skills for getting along with others, surviving in school, managing stress, and handling anger and frustration. Each curriculum contains a curriculum-based assessment instrument and individual lessons for each skill. A direct instruction approach is used to teach each skill. Sometimes videotaped models are provided. Typically, lessons are taught to small groups of students that may include appropriate peer models. Lessons may include homework and self-monitoring procedures.

Although social skills training grew in popularity during the 1980s, many questions about its effectiveness have arisen (Gresham, 1998; Sasso, Melloy, & Kavale, 1990). One criticism addressed the fact that many of the skills were not functional for individual students nor valued by others in their environment, thus students would not perform them (Meadows, Neel, Parker, & Timo, 1991). Another criticism addressed the fact that learning social skills did not seem to increase students' acceptance by peers (Walker, Colvin & Ramsey, 1995). Last, social skills instruction has apparently not often resulted in lasting and generalized use of the acquired skills (Gresham, 1998). Students' failure to transfer learning to other settings and other conditions is a major issue for all behaviorally based programs.

A meta-analysis of 35 studies assessing the effects of social skills interventions with students with EBD showed disappointing results (Quinn et al., 1999). However, the authors recommended that we "refine and customize" training rather than eliminate it. Recommendations for improving the effects of social skills training include: (1) modifying skills to match the value system and culture of a specific student, (2) recruiting peers to participate in the training and to reinforce skill performance, (3) directly teaching to generalization, and (4) integrating social skills across the school curriculum and outside the classroom (Gresham, 1998; Quinn et al., 1999).

The notion of directly teaching socially appropriate behavior to students with EBD is a basic tenet of the behavioral approach to treatment. With this approach, the emphasis is on behavioral change. In fact, many believe that students with EBD, who usually display excessive amounts of disturbing behavior, need to be taught how to act right before they can be taught academics. For the purpose of managing disturbing behavior, most believe the primary goal to be the replacement of inappropriate responses with appropriate ones such as social skills (Gable et al., 2000; Sugai et al., 1999; Walker et al., 1996). Other behavioral tools for managing challenging behavior are reviewed in the next section.

Behavior Management and Behavioral Principles

Behavior theory is not only applied for the purpose of teaching new behavior (academic and/or social), it is also applied to reduce problem behavior. To accomplish this, the following techniques are generally recommended, based on data obtained from an FBA and FA:

1. Contributory antecedents should be altered (e.g., add structure and organization; modify schedules, materials, and curriculum; change the pace of instruction; keep student on task).
2. Alternative, preferably replacement (i.e., behavior that serves the same function as the target inappropriate behavior), behavior should be taught.
3. Existing consequences should be altered such that appropriate behavior is reinforced, while inappropriate behavior is not (i.e., differential reinforcement and extinction procedures).
4. Punishers should be added only as necessary.
5. The behavioral intervention should be monitored and evaluated (Alberto & Troutman, 2006; Gable et al., 2000)

Many of the specific tools and techniques used in this model are reviewed in this section.

Methods for Increasing Behaviors

Reinforcement. Reinforcement is any consequence of a targeted behavior that results in the maintenance or increase of that behavior (Flora, 2004). Reinforcement is the application of a reinforcer. For example, a student finishes a seatwork assignment (targeted behavior) for free time (reinforcer) and is offered 10 minutes on a computer by the teacher (positive reinforcement). The success of almost all behavioral intervention programs depends on effective use of reinforcers. There are two types of reinforcement: positive and negative. Positive reinforcement occurs when something (a reward) is presented as a consequence and behavior increases or maintains. Negative reinforcement occurs when something (an aversive) is removed and behavior increases or maintains. For example, a teacher hands a student a worksheet and stands right over the student until she starts work. The teacher then moves away (removing proximity to reinforce beginning work).

Positive reinforcement has two major classes: primary and secondary. Primary reinforcers are those biologically satisfying to an individual, such as food and liquids. Ice cream, raisins, cookies, crackers, popcorn, fruit, soda, and the ever-popular M&Ms are examples of primary reinforcers often dispensed in classrooms. Whereas primary reinforcers may be necessary with students who are younger or have more severe disabilities, secondary reinforcers usually work with students who are older or have milder disabilities. Secondary reinforcers have a value that is learned rather than biological or innate; examples are activities, social rewards, stamps, stickers, and tokens, which may be exchanged for something desirable. Use of secondary reinforcers is usually preferable to use of primary reinforcers in schools because the goal is eventually to fade planned external reinforcement for appropriate behavior.

Preferences for rewards are highly individualistic and the teacher should never assume that a particular reinforcer will be effective with every student. Teachers often prepare a list of acceptable reinforcers (a reinforcement menu) and let the students choose from the list. (Refer to Table 7.1 for examples of reinforcers.) However, the ultimate evaluation of whether something is reinforcing is the effect it has on the target behavior. Only after a reinforcer has been applied and has the desired effect can it be evaluated as truly successful or reinforcing: If behavior increases or maintains, it was a reinforcer, and if it decreases, it was not a reinforcer.

All teachers of students with EBD should become proficient at using reinforcement. These students often have a history of failure and punishment in the school setting, and the idea of being rewarded for positive deeds rather than punished for negative ones may be novel to them. Unfortunately, most teachers prefer to use punishers such as removal from classrooms, suspensions, scolding, fining systems and grade reductions, and expulsions for behavior management purposes (Maag, 2001), perhaps because they misunderstand ABA terminology and concepts and/or because our society as a whole seems to promote punishment. Maag recommends that teachers: (1) catch students being good and praise them, (2) shape appropriate behavior by reinforcing small steps, (3) establish a group management plan by setting class expectations and reinforcing students who meet them, and (4) use peer social reinforcement to encourage appropriate behavior. Contingency contracting and token economies are two methods of applying positive reinforcement in the classroom.

Contingency Contracting. Contingency contracting is a form of instructional or behavior management in which an "if . . . then" contract is made; if the student performs a specific behavior, then a specific reinforcer is given. Contingencies are based on the Premack (1959) principle or Grandma's law, "First you eat your meat and potatoes" (less probable behavior) "and then you may have dessert" (more probable behavior). Thus, high-frequency or valued activities are used to reinforce low-frequency or less-valued activities. Contingency contracting can be verbal and informal, such as an agreement on how many problems must be completed before free time is allotted. Contracts can also be formal and more complex, such as a written document specifying the behaviors that are disallowed and/or the behaviors that must be demonstrated to earn the reinforcer. The terms of such a contract are usually negotiated between teacher and student, who then sign the contract as a pact.

Contracting is widely used in special education settings with a variety of behaviors with students of all ages (Alberto & Troutman, 2006). However, research studies attempting to validate contracting have generally suffered from methodological flaws. In a review

TABLE 7.1 Reinforcers

Primary			
cereal peanuts chips ice cream	Coke raisins fruit	popcorn crackers candy	M&Ms juice other food and drink
Secondary			
		Tokens	
poker chips other colored plastic chips	stars checks happy faces	points ink stamps play money	hole punch paper clips
		Materials	
balloons ink stamp pad pennies stars bubbles liquid	badges books magazines play dough bookmarks	calendars puzzles	flash cards bean bags art supplies

Activities/Privileges		
grade or staple papers teacher's helper for the day tutor others janitorial tasks in class sit with teacher sit in special spot pass out snacks read to the class choose story for teacher to read class librarian	distribute and collect materials being first in line run errands leading an activity free time typing listening to music with headphones using tape recorder painting or drawing	drawing on chalkboard skipping nap time writing a letter taking photographs skipping an assignment or test playing with board games playing with puppets class snack break

of 35 studies using contracting with students who were delinquent or EBD, Rutherford and Polsgrove (1981) found a number of such flaws but reached the tentative conclusion that contracting had been effective in aiding behavioral change in many situations. An example of how a simple verbal contract with reinforcement was used with an 8-year-old in a residential treatment center is presented in Box 7.1.

Token Economies. Token economies are often used successfully in the classroom to improve social and academic skills. Tokens play the role that money plays in society, that is, tokens are inherently worthless; it is what they can buy or be traded for that makes them valuable. Tokens can be poker chips, play money, check marks, stars, points, or any number of other inexpensive, durable objects.

In a token economy, the teacher sets up a system in which accumulated tokens earned for specified behavior can be traded in for selected reinforcers (e.g., finishing three math

BOX 7.1
Robert's Contract

On the day of admission, Robert broke the psychologist's glasses. Apparently frightened, he would not venture into the open space of a room. Instead, he crouched behind the furniture at every opportunity. This small, blonde, 8-year-old had scratched his own face so badly that there were long, red marks deep in his flesh.

The two teachers to whom Robert was assigned typically "loved" their students into wellness, while teaching them everything from academics to manners to gardening. They were astounded by Robert and his lack of response to them and his classmates, however, they were determined that he would receive all the benefits they had to offer.

Since Robert chose to sit outside the classroom on the floor in the hallway, it was difficult to reward him with his favorite things. Through trial-and-error, it was eventually discovered that Robert responded positively when given certain color crayons—red, blue, black, and green. It was also ascertained that Robert had been severely abused and that his unresponsiveness was primarily due to fear. Therefore, the statement. "It is safe here" was reinforced with Robert as often as possible.

The contract that was implemented was simple: whenever Robert responded positively to his teachers or classmates, he was able to use his favorite crayons. Slowly, but surely, Robert began to respond to others, but he still preferred his safe hallway to the classroom. Still reinforcing, "It is safe here," the teachers placed a desk in the hallway and daily moved it closer to the door of the classroom. Robert's safety net was slowly changing, and he was accepting it.

After 6 months of concentrated effort on the part of the teachers, psychologists, and classmates, Robert was able to stay in the classroom. He began to indicate a readiness to learn and an eagerness to participate at an age-appropriate level. We extended the "It is safe here" assurance to other parts of Robert's world, and we emptied the stores of red, blue, black, and green crayons for months!

Throughout my work with a population with emotional/behavioral disorders, the behavioral contract has been a lifesaver. We all have things for which we are willing to work. This basic principle helps eliminate undesirable and inappropriate behaviors, replacing them with socially acceptable ones and providing the client with a chance for a better life in the future.

It is often difficult to identify something for which a child is willing to change a behavior, particularly when that behavior is one that has been a successful tool for him in the past. To be successful in implementing a contract, you must find a meaningful reward, set reasonable expectations for earning the reward, and implement the contract consistently. This simple idea works—don't we all meet certain daily expectations and occasionally modify our behavior so that we can receive our paychecks on a regular basis? I know I do!

Contributed by Sue N. Baugh, M.Ed, Coordinator of Rehabilitation Services, The Deverux Foundation, Victoria, Texas.

---

assignments with 90 percent accuracy is worth 6 points that can be traded in for a privilege such as skipping an assignment). Teachers of students with EBD often set up token economies in the classroom and then negotiate specific behavioral contracts with individual students.

Advantages of token economies are their flexibility and applicability in a wide range of settings. For example, token economies are often employed in institutional and other residential settings because they can be used by teachers, therapists, and childcare workers to reinforce targeted behaviors during school, during therapy, and on the unit. The specific reinforcers and contingencies would obviously differ according to age and sophistication of the students. The variety of reinforcers that can be offered adds longevity to the technique, as the reinforcement menu can be changed as frequently as necessary to sustain interest. Kazdin (2001) and Alberto and Troutman (2006) report that token economies have been used successfully with a wide variety of populations in special and general education classrooms for teaching academic skills, communication and language skills, play skills, self-management skills, on-task behavior, and in inclusion programs. For more about establishing a token system and point cards, the reader is referred to Alberto and Troutman (2006).

Level Systems. In classrooms for students with emotional and behavioral disorders, token systems are often organized into a level system (Smith & Farrell, 1993). A level system is a hierarchy of behavioral expectations matched to corresponding reinforcers. Students who display the appropriate behavioral expectation can access the reinforcers at that level and at some point be promoted to the next level, where expectations are theoretically more difficult and reinforcers are more desirable. Many level systems also include a punishment aspect whereby students lose a level or cannot access reinforcers for a period of time for behavioral infractions (Alberto & Troutman, 2006). Sometimes level systems include cognitive and psychodynamic components such as self-monitoring and goal-setting and journal writing (Barbetta, 1990).

Level systems, many of them published, are widely employed with students with EBD with little research to support their efficacy (Smith & Farrell, 1993) and many questions about their legality (Scheuermann, Webber, Partin, & Knies, 1994). It is speculated that teachers prefer level systems because they provide a standardized behavior management system. However, the application of standardized practices to special education students is always legally suspect. The IDEA provides that special education students must be provided individualized instruction in the least restrictive environment. Yet many teachers place students into a level system based on their label, rather than on individualized assessment, and move them forward and backward within the system with little regard to individual curricular goals and objectives. Furthermore, many level systems include access to the general education classroom at the top level as a privilege to be earned, rather than a given within the law, a blatant infraction of the IDEA specifications (Scheuermann et al., 1994).

The benefits of level systems may not outweigh the legal ramifications and may be discouraged as a behavior management tool (Scheuermann & Webber, 1996). If level systems are used, These authors recommend that students be placed within the level system based on individualized assessment, preferably functional behavioral assessment, and that behavioral progress be monitored frequently using observational recording techniques. Access to general education classes should never be included as a reinforcer, but should be deliberated by IEP teams based on individual formative assessment data.

Methods for Decreasing Behavior

Differential Reinforcement. Differential reinforcement, known as a positive reductive technique, uses deliberate reinforcement of some behaviors in order to reduce others (Alberto & Troutman, 2006; Webber & Scheuermann, 1991). There are several differential reinforcement strategies that can be used in combination or as separate interventions. It is usually recommended that, if other aversive reductive techniques are used, differential reinforcement can also be used.

One way to implement differential reinforcement is to reinforce time periods during which no targeted inappropriate behavior occurs (Differential Reinforcement of Other behaviors, or DRO). This means, in essence, that all other behaviors are reinforced during that time. For example, for every hour without hitting, a student will receive 5 points on his point card. A second strategy is to reinforce behaviors that are mutually incompatible with the target inappropriate behavior (Differential Reinforcement of Incompatible behaviors, or DRI). It is not always possible to find an incompatible behavior for the inappropriate target, but this is a strong reductive technique provided that the reinforcers are effective. For example, a student may be reinforced for each 10 minutes that she is in her seat in order to reduce out-of-seat behavior. In this case, in-seat and out-of-seat behavior are mutually incompatible.

A third differential reinforcement technique is that of reinforcing lower rates of an inappropriate behavior (Differential Reinforcement of Lower rates of behavior, or DRL). A student may be given points for reducing shout-outs from 15 per hour to 10 and then five per hour. This technique is best used with behaviors that are not dangerous or contagious. Differential Reinforcement of Communicative behavior (DRC) is a strategy for reinforcing communicative behaviors. If a student, for example, states, "Please don't tease me anymore," as opposed to hitting another, he would receive reinforcement. Differential Reinforcement of Alternate behaviors (DRA) is an umbrella strategy whereby students are reinforced for any alternative behavior, but not for targeted inappropriate behavior. Differential reinforcement has been used successfully for the reduction of many challenging behaviors in schools and clinics (Alberto & Troutman, 2006; Durand & Carr, 1985; Horner & Day, 1991; Neel & Cessna, 1993; Repp, Felce, & Barton, 1991; Symons, McDonald, & Wehby, 1998).

Punishment. Punishment is liberally defined here as a consequence resulting in a decrease of behavior, usually an unwanted behavior. As with reinforcement, however, the "proof is in the pudding": an act is truly punishing only if it has the desired effect of decreasing the behavior. Consider, for example, spanking. While universally considered an aversive or punishing act, if spanking does not decrease the behavior the child was spanked for, it was not truly a punisher for that child. In fact, if behavior continues, it was, by definition, a reinforcer.

Child development experts offer many reasons for avoiding use of punishment primarily because it does not teach children the correct way to behave, only what not to do. Among the reasons often cited are (1) that punishment serves to extinguish behavior for only short time and in the presence of the punisher and (2) that punishment offers no positive models of what is expected (Alberto & Troutman, 2006). Regardless of its effectiveness, punishment is often used in public schools as a means of discipline (Maag, 2001). Its use with students with EBD has been questioned and school districts have been sued over its appropriateness with this population. The following sections address punishment techniques aimed at decreasing behavior that are commonly used with students with EBD: response–cost, timeout, in-school suspension, Interim Alternative Education Programs, corporal punishment, and physical restraint. Many of these techniques have been questioned in the courts, and the resulting legal constraints are discussed in Box 7.2. It is usually recommended that if these strategies are to be used, they be used in conjunction with differential reinforcement systems (Alberto & Troutman, 2006).

Response–cost. Response–cost is the removal of something reinforcing that results in a decrease in the prior behavior. For example, if a student yells out in class, the teacher may remove recess time as a punisher. It is important to note that whatever is removed must be a reinforcer to the individual. In the above example, it is assumed that the student likes recess and would not like losing it, thus the loss is a punisher. For students with EBD, response–cost procedures are often in the form of a fining system paired with token or level systems. Students earn tokens or level advances for appropriate behavior and have to "pay up" or lose tokens/levels for inappropriate behavior. We lose tokens (dollars) for traffic violations or other failures to obey the law.

Recommendations for using response–cost include the following: (1) Make sure students are earning more than is being deducted, (2) refrain from removing all reinforcers away may escalate problems because students then have "nothing more to lose," (3) be able to remove reinforcers without a fight, (4) post earnings and fines before behavioral infractions occur, (5) using tokens and reinforcers that can easily be retrieved if an infraction occurs, and (6) choose fines that match the level of infraction. Response–cost procedures have been effective with student groups as well as individuals (Mowrer & Conoley, 1987) to reduce off-task and disruptive behavior (Higgens, Williams, & McLaughlin, 2001), aggressive behavior (Reynolds & Kelley, 1997), and obscene vocalizations (Facomata, Roane, Hovanetz, Kettering, & Keeney, 2004). Often, response–cost procedures are the preferred punisher because they work well with token reinforcement systems and often do not have the negative side effects of other forms of punishment (Kazdin, 1972).

Time-out. Time-out is the removal of an opportunity to receive reinforcement. For example, a student may have a red card placed on his desk to signal that he cannot receive points for 5 minutes as a punisher for poking the student next to him. Time-out can also be seclusionary or exclusionary with the student removed from presumably reinforcing situations (e.g., the classroom) to a time-out space or room for specified time periods (Rortvedt & Miltenberger, 1994). Time-out is frequently used in programs for students with EBD because it is recommended for aggressive behaviors. One survey of EBD teachers in two states found that 70 percent of the respondents used time-out with their students. Reported use decreased with the age of students, with 88 percent of preschool teachers reporting use of time-out, 65 percent at the junior high level, and 51 percent at the senior high level (Zabel, 1986).

Some programs have a time-out section in the classroom, screened with a partition from the rest of the room (exclusion). However, a separate time-out room (seclusion) may be needed for students who occasionally need to be physically separated from their peers until they regain control of their emotions and behavior. Also, if students continue to create a disturbance for the teacher or the remainder of the class after being placed in time-out, then the concept of removal from reinforcement is undermined. Time-out should be used for behaviors that are specified beforehand and only for brief periods of time (e.g., 5–15 minutes depending on age and cognitive ability). For a review of recommended time-out procedures, see Yell's (1994) legal analysis of the technique.

BOX 7.2

Punishment for Students with Behavior Disorders: Is It Legal?

Several punishment techniques commonly used with students with behavior disorders have been questioned in the courts. Time-out, in-school suspension, and corporal punishment have all been tested. Following is a summary of the courts' findings, along with recommendations for implementation if punishment procedures are to be used:

Time-out

In 1987 *Dickens* v. *Johnson County Board of Education* was a test case for exclusion time-out, and *Hayes* v. *Unified School District No. 377* was a test case for seclusion time-out. According to Yell's (1990) analysis of these court decisions, time-out was sanctioned by the courts under the following conditions: schools must have clear, written guidelines for time-out, facilities must be adequate, and time spent must be brief and proportionate to the offense. Long periods in time-out without provisions for the student's education would constitute a violation of student rights.

In-school Suspension (ISS)

In *Hayes* v. *Unified District No. 377,* the court upheld ISS under appropriate conditions: that written procedures outline which behaviors are punishable by ISS and how it will be carried out, that length of time in suspension is related to the offense, and that educational opportunities are provided during the suspension (Yell, 1990). Suspensions of up to 5 days have been upheld as long as other provisions were met.

Corporal Punishment

In *Cole* v. *Greenfield-Central Community Schools* in 1986, the court upheld the use of corporal punishment (in this instance, three strokes with the paddle and tape over the mouth). When using corporal punishment, schools must prove that it is part of a comprehensive disciplinary plan that serves an educational function (Yell, 1990). It also must not be excessive in relation to the offense. Although not yet prescribed by the courts, corporal punishment is still controversial and not advocated by a number of professionals concerned with the welfare of students with emotional/behavioral disorders. Use of corporal punishment for EBD students in public schools is questionable at best and could lead to further litigation.

Legal Principles for Interventions Entailing Punishment

Yell (1998) has analyzed relevant case law and extracted six principles that should be followed when applying punishing procedures with students with EBD. These principles represent legality as determined by court proceedings to date; moral and ethical issues are less clearly defined. Yell's six principles are as follows:

1. When using punishment, do not violate the student's due process rights. Clearly define the behavior to be punished and the punishing consequences to the student and parents beforehand. Use of a warning to the student before punishment is administered is also advisable.

2. When using punishment, do not violate the educational rights of students. Punishments such as expulsion, serial suspensions, prolonged time-outs and prolonged in-school suspensions have been considered changes in placement by the courts and are therefore illegal.

3. The punishing procedure must have a legitimate educational function. Written guidelines should describe the rationale, specify the intervention, and discuss the anticipated outcome.

4. The punishment must be reasonable. Although open to interpretation, the concept of reasonableness may be satisfied if the rule being enforced was reasonable, the punishment was suited to the offense, the amount of force was not unreasonable, and the punisher demonstrated no personal ill will toward the student.

5. Punishment should be used only if less intrusive interventions have failed. Documentation of this principle helps meet the courts' requirement of reasonableness.

6. Caution is necessary in interpreting case law. Court decisions are not nationally binding unless decided by the Supreme Court.

Although these principles are based on case law, it is advisable for school administrators to consult with school attorneys for updated or locally based information regarding use of punishment with students with EBD. It is clear that school districts should develop written policies that specify behaviors that are punishable and then detail punishment procedures to be used for these behaviors. To date, courts have upheld punishment procedures that are reasonable, do not interfere with educational rights, and have an educational function.

Time-out has generally been effective with students who exhibit disruptive or aggressive behavior and with students with moderate to severe emotional/behavioral disorders. According to a review by Nelson and Rutherford (1988), factors affecting success include level and duration of timeout, whether a warning signal was used, the schedule under which it was administered, and the procedures under which a student is placed in and removed from the time-out setting. As with any behavioral technique, specific procedures must be tailored to fit the individual based on initial assessment data and targeted goals and should result in improved behavior. Sending students who already lack social skills for long periods of time to socially isolated rooms makes no instructional sense. Time-out is often overused because teachers are able to "get rid" of a disturbing student for some amount of time (negative reinforcement for the teacher) regardless of the effect on the student (Maag, 2001).

At least three states have developed regulations for the use of time-out with special education students (Couvillon, 2003). In Texas, for example, special education students cannot be put into a locked box, closet, or room less than 50 square feet in area. Furthermore, if time-out is used, it must be used in conjunction with other positive behavioral intervention strategies and each use documented by the teacher. Some programs with separate time-out rooms allow students who are upset to voluntarily put themselves in time-out in order to allow a cooling-down period before returning to classes. In these instances, time-out is not used as punishment but as a self-control technique.

In-school suspension. As suspension from school as a disciplinary technique for students with disabilities has become controversial and more students with EBD are now included in general education, in-school suspensions or removal to "planning" classrooms have become more common. Application of in-school suspensions (ISS), a type of time-out, varies, but generally a classroom is designated for ISS with a full-time teacher or aide who supervises the students who bring their regular class assignments to complete while in ISS. Students are usually not allowed to interact with other students in ISS; otherwise, the ISS loses its punishing feature of removal from interaction with peers. The effectiveness of in-school suspension has not been well researched, but its legality with students with EBD has been upheld, with certain restrictions, in court (Gushee, 1984).

As an alternative for students with EBD who are included in general education settings, a SPED planning or crisis classroom and teacher might be designated to support them in the inclusion environment. If the students experience emotional or behavioral problems in the inclusion classroom, they may be removed to the planning or crises classroom to discuss the problems, finish work, and make a plan for returning.

Interim Alternative Education Programs (IAEP). For students who are extremely disruptive or who are involved with drugs or weapons, a more potent punisher has been established. Due to the federal Drug-free Schools Act and the Gun-free Schools Zone Act, which were adopted as part of the 1997 Elementary and Secondary Education Act (ESEA), and various subsequent school shootings, many school districts adopted zero-tolerance policies toward students found with weapons or drugs (Phi Delta Kappa, 1998). Typically, these students were suspended or expelled (time-out) for long periods of time. However, many school district personnel reasoned that putting violent youth on the street with no supervision was not a practical solution. As a result, disciplinary alternative education programs were established in many states. Additionally, protection for special education students in terms of a free appropriate public education makes IAEPs viable.

IAEPs vary in terms of structure, but most are housed in buildings separate from the regular campus. Students are placed in these programs temporarily until it is deemed appropriate to allow them back into their home school. Special education students, including those with EBD, may be sent to IAEPs according to the discipline provisions of the 1997 amendments to the IDEA and IDEA 2004; however, they must continue to receive an education commensurate with their IEPs, presumably delivered by a special education teacher (Mandlawitz, 2006).

IAEPs are not to be confused with separate special education programs for students with EBD, which are part of the special education service continuum. In a SPED program model, students would be sent to separate special education programs not for punitive reasons, but because the IEP team decides that placement in a more restrictive setting with lower student–teacher ratios and less stress is the appropriate education. Many separate EBD programs are structured around a psychodynamic model whereby punishment would not be a major component of the program. However, IAEPs, developed from a general education program model, are clearly punitive (based on a behavioral model) and designated for the purpose of reducing severely disruptive behavior. To date, there is little research to support the efficacy of IAEPs in terms of behavior improvement. However, the practice, as with many punitive techniques, is popular, because the student is removed from the general education campus, no longer endangers others, nor is an annoyance to teachers and administrators.

Corporal punishment. Corporal punishment of students in schools is prohibited by law in many states. Some boards of education prohibit its use regardless of state sanctions. Despite its controversial nature, Rose (1984) found that corporal punishment was still being widely used with students with EBD in the mid-1980s.

Corporal punishment is generally equated with spanking, although slapping, pinching, and shaking may also be considered in this category. Other physically aversive techniques such as application of aversive tastes and odors and electric shock have been used for severely maladaptive behaviors such as self-injurious behavior in individuals with severe disabilities. While physically aversive techniques have been instrumental in reducing such severe behaviors, their use has been questioned from an ethical standpoint by many parents and professionals (Goldstein & Conoley, 1997; Walker et al., 1995).

Physical restraint. Physical restraint is defined here as the application of force to an individual with the purpose of either restricting or redirecting his movement. While it may not be intended to be punitive, it does fit our definition of punishment. This procedure is typically used in medical and psychiatric facilities, correctional facilities, and in schools as a means to prevent an individual from hurting him- or herself or others (Ryan & Peterson, 2004). One survey indicated that 71 percent of teachers of students with EBD used physical restraint with students who display aggressive behavior toward others (Ruhl & Hughes, 1985).

Although there are limitations with this procedure, many professionals believe that it is justifiable under two conditions: (1) to prevent harm either to the student (self-injurious behavior) or others and (2) to enforce prearranged contingencies, such as removal to a time-out area (Schloss & Smith, 1987). Other professionals do not believe that physical restraint or any type of force should be used to enforce time-out.

The Children's Health Act of 2000 established national standards for use of physical restraint with children in psychiatric facilities, but to date, no similar standards have been passed for schools at the national level. Five states (Texas, Massachusetts, Colorado, Illinois, and Connecticut) have passed legislation outlining the proper use of restraint and the conditions that would warrant its use in schools (e.g, Couvillon, 2003). For example, in Texas, restraint cannot be used for noncompliance or verbal disruption, only specific emergency situations where behavior poses a threat of imminent, serious physical harm to self and/or others, or imminent serious property destruction.

Unfortunately, lack of personnel training in ABA, improper application of the restraint procedures, and lack of monitoring of its use result in serious injuries to students and even death (e.g., "National Restraint," 2003; Rodriguez, 2002). If physical restraints are to be used, there should be written procedures and adequate staff training not only for the restraint procedure, but also for behavioral techniques that will prevent aggressive behavior rendering the need for physical restraint unnecessary (Ryan & Peterson, 2004). These authors fear that the move to include more students with EBD in general education has actually resulted in more use of exclusionary time-outs and physical restraint with them. The use of any punisher should be for the purpose of improving behavior of the target student and in that student's best interest. Progress data should confirm that is the case.

Positive Behavioral Supports

As a result of the inappropriate and overuse of punishment, particularly exclusionary time-out and physical restraint, for SPED students in general, and those with EBD specifically, researchers developed an ABA model of discipline based on proactive and preventative approaches (Sugai & Horner, 2002). This model came to be known as Positive Behavioral Supports (PBS). The main premise of PBS is that by constructing a supportive context for students (e.g., clear expectations, prompting and reinforcing appropriate behavior, use of effective instructional techniques), and using FBA data for discipline planning, then most student problem behavior will be prevented, reducing the need for punishers. PBS blends ABA with the ecological model (Chapter 8) in that the principles are applied with a systems approach: schoolwide, classwide, and with targeted students. The U.S. Office of Special Education Programs (OSEP)–funded National Technical Assistance Center for Positive Behavior Interventions and Support (www.pbis.org) provides technical assistance and training to states, regions, and local school districts across the country. PBS has even been recommended for juvenile justice facilities (Nelson, Sugai, & Smith, 2005). We will discuss PBS in more detail in Chapter 12.

Summary

Behaviorists view disordered behavior as learned maladaptive responses. According to this model, behavior has a lawful relationship to the environment, as illustrated by the principles of operant and respondent conditioning. Whereas respondent conditioning dealt with pairing antecedents to reflexive behavior, operant conditioning pertains to voluntary behavior and is focused on events following behavior (consequences). Behaviorists believe that by manipulating antecedents and consequences (teaching), behavior can be altered (learning). The impact of social learning, or observation and imitation of others' behavior, is also emphasized. Applied behavioral analysis (ABA), the application of operant conditioning, is widely used in schools and for various other purposes. It is recommended that schools move away from overreliance on punitive techniques to control behavior to a positive support model for teaching and promoting appropriate behaviors. A summary of the behavioral view of etiology, typical evaluation procedures, and educational applications is presented in Table 7.2. Box 7.3, Victor Learns to stay in His Seat, provides an illustration of several components of the behavioral model used with a student with EBD. The reader is encouraged to attempt to answer the homework questions related to this case study.

TABLE 7.2 Summary of the Behavioral Model

Etiology	Evaluation Procedures	Educational Applications
Respondent (classical conditioning)	Checklists	Social Skills Instruction
Operant conditioning	Behavior rating scales	Techniques for increasing behaviors:
Social learning (modeling)	Behavior recording	Use of reinforcers
	Functional Behavioral Assessment and Analysis (FBA)	Contingency contracting
		Token economies
		Level systems
		Techniques for decreasing behaviors:
		Differential reinforcement
		Response-cost
		Timeout
		Punishment
		In-school suspension
		Interim alternative education programs
		Corporal punishment
		Physical restraint
		Positive Behavior Supports

BOX 7.3

Victor Learns to Stay in His Seat

Victor, a 6-year-old first grader, born prematurely, was placed in special education as EBD because of failing school subjects, extreme distractibility, and disruptive behaviors. At this young age, Victor is behind in math and reading and receives speech intervention for a mild speech problem. Victor spends the entire day in a general education classroom with special education support; however, his teacher is concerned about his constant out-of-seat behavior and loud talking during independent work time. Because of the first two behaviors, Victor seldom completes his assignments, thus falling further and further behind academically.

A functional behavior assessment was conducted using an interview, ABC chart, and behavioral recording of the target behaviors. The FBA teacher interview concluded that the behaviors were most likely to occur during midafternoon during reading, writing, and phonics lessons and that his behavior was best in the mornings when he had more freedom to choose his own activities. The teacher speculated that other children being off task resulted in Victor increasing his problem behaviors and that he generally demonstrated more problems during activities that required structure, independent work, and more intense concentration.

The ABC data during independent reading time showed that Victor went to the bathroom for several minutes, played with a piece of paper, shouted out of turn, and looked at pictures on the wall even though the teacher occasionally provided him with redirection, prompts, and individual instruction (see Figure 7.3). The hypothesis that Victor was displaying these behaviors in order to get teacher attention was tested by having the teacher provide high-frequency attention and very little attention for alternating 10-minutes intervals during an independent work time. The high-attention periods resulted in one talk-out and two times out of seat. The low attention periods resulted in three talk-outs and four out-of-seat behaviors so it was assumed that Victor was behaving badly to obtain teacher attention.

A second hypothesis stated Victor left his seat to obtain desirable activities and materials scattered about the general education classroom. This was tested by observing Victor working independently in the special education classroom where such stimuli were not visible. It was found that Victor displayed fewer problem behaviors under the low-stimulation condition so we might assume that Victor was inattentive to schoolwork because he wanted to be engaged in the more desirable activities.

A baseline observational recording during 70-minute independent work periods showed that on average, Victor spent 18 minutes out of his seat compared to an average of 9 minutes for a comparison student in the classroom. Furthermore, he completed only 13 percent of his work compared to an average of 68 percent completed by the other student (see Figures 7.4 and 7.5 for graphs). A reinforcer survey indicated that Victor was particularly fond of Jimmy Neutron stickers. It was decided to establish a token reinforcement system to reward Victor for the replacement behavior of raising his hand to get teacher attention and to leave his seat (see Figure 7.6); he would also receive reinforcement for the alternate behaviors of staying on task and in seat.

A simple point card was developed (see Figure 7.7) and the teacher marked each 5-minute interval when Victor displayed one of the three target behaviors. The marked boxes were then cashed in for Jimmy Neutron stickers at the end of the day. After 10 days, Victor was raising his hand 100 percent of the times he wanted to get out of his seat or talk to the teacher (figure 7.6), was completing an average of 86 percent of his work tasks, (Figure 7.4), and had reduced his out-of-seat behavior to an average of 2 minutes in the 70-minute period (Figure 7.1). It was hoped at the time that the simple FBA and token intervention would further result in improved academic achievement and continual success in the general education environment.

(*continued*)

BOX 7.3 continued

Setting: First Grade Classroom Observation Date: January 15th
Student: Victor

Time	Antecedent Events	Child Responses	Consequent Events
10:32 a.m.		1. While sitting at his table, V. begins to shake a piece of paper around & hits the girl with the paper to the right of him.	
			2. Teacher: "Throw that paper away in the trash and begin reading."
		3. V. "OK." He walks over to trash and mimics slam dunking paper into trash, then walks back to chair.	
			4. T: at her desk looking over papers.
		5. V. begins enveloping his face in his book.	
	6. T: "V., begin reading your story."		
		7. V. opens his book and then begins talking to the girl to his right.	
			8. T: "Don't interrupt S., V., read your pages."
		9. V. gets out of his seat, and walks to the class bathroom.	
			10 T. at her desk looking over papers.
10:40 a.m.		11. V. walks out of the bathroom, proceeds to wash hands at sink, dry hands, walks over to the class door, blows his nose while looking at a picture on door, then walks back over to his chair.	
			12. T. at her desk correcting papers.
		13. V. begins talking to girl on his right.	
	14. T: "Read your story, I'm about to come over & ask you some questions."		
		15. V: "Aye, aye, Captain!"	
	16. Classmate closed bathroom door.		
		17. V: "Who's in the bathroom?"	
			18. T. looked at V. & signaled "Shhh!"
10:42 a.m.	19. T. walks over to V, points to a line in book and says "Read this line."		
		20. V. reads line correctly.	
			21. T: "Very good V. Read these next two lines for me."
		22. V. reads next two lines correctly, phonetically sounds out last two words "here" & "again."	
	23. T: "What does Tiny do for his job?"		
		24. V. answers T.'s question correctly	
			25.T: "Good job V. Keep reading like you have been with me."
10:44 a.m.	26. T. walks to next table over		
10:45 a.m.		27. V. closes his book, walks over to get some Kleenex, and begins reading the sign on the classroom door.	

FIGURE 7.3

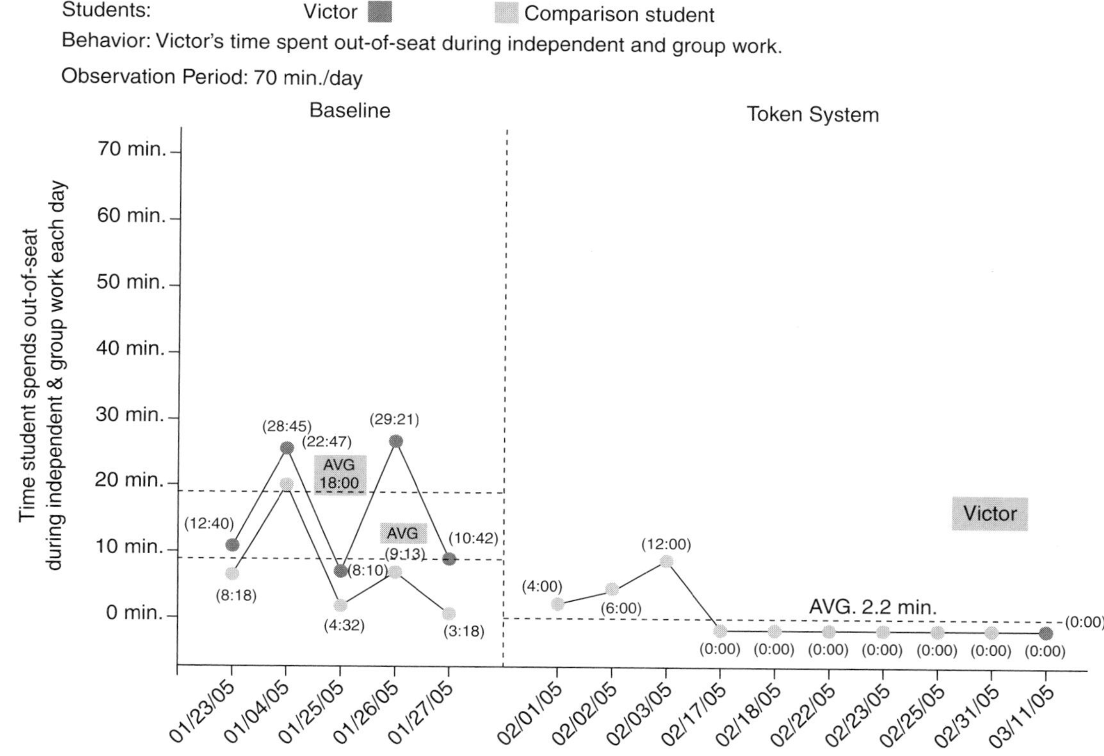

FIGURE 7.4

(continued)

BOX 7.3 continued

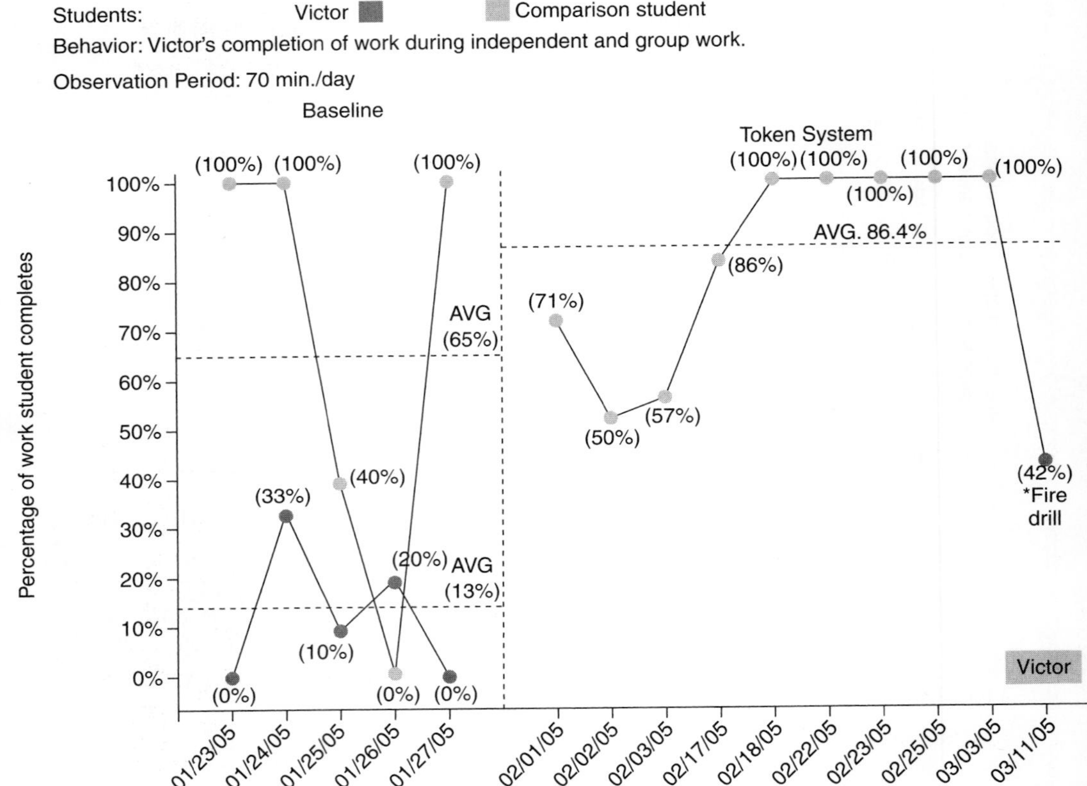

FIGURE 7.5

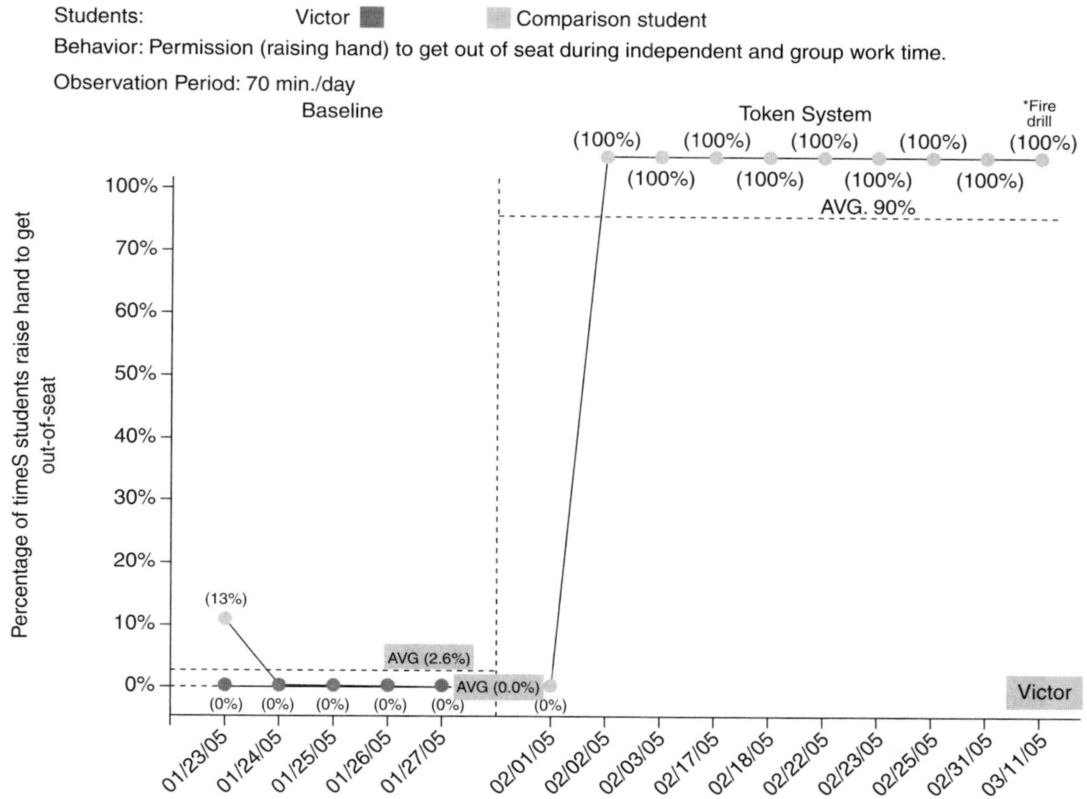

FIGURE 7.6

(continued)

BOX 7.3 continued

Name: Victor Date: Feb 17

I can be Jimmy Neutron!

EXPECTATIONS

Quiet Hand Raising: Raising hand without saying anything and continue working while you wait for the teacher to call on you or come to you.

Staying On Task: Working on what we are doing in class at all times.

Staying in your seat: Staying in your seat during class time.

	5 min	5 min	5 min	5 min	5 min	5 min	5 min	5 min	5 min	5 min	5 min	5 min	5 min	5 min
Staying on Task	+	+	+	+	+	+	+			+			+	+
												Total	50	min.

+ = 5 mins with behavior

	5 min	5 min	5 min	5 min	5 min	5 min	5 min	5 min	5 min	5 min	5 min	5 min	5 min	5 min
Staying in your seat	+	+	+	+	+	+	+			+	+	+	+	+
												Total	65	min.

	5 min	5 min	5 min	5 min	5 min	5 min	5 min	5 min	5 min	5 min	5 min	5 min	5 min	5 min
Raising your hand														
												Total	0	

You will earn!!!

On task:	7 +'s	= 1 sticker
	8 +'s	= 2 stickers
	10–14 +'s	= 3 stickers
In seat:	10–11 +'s	= 1 sticker
	12–13 +'s	= 2 stickers
	14 +'s	= 3 stickers

FIGURE 7.7

Conclusions

Understanding disordered behavior from a behavioral perspective allows teachers to employ a variety of successful interventions in the classroom. Taking data and manipulating either antecedents or consequences to effect behavior change are basic skills needed by all teachers of students with EBD. Behavioral interventions should not be viewed as a panacea because many useful techniques may stem from other models. For example, a blend of the behavioral and cognitive models, cognitive-behavioral modification, is receiving increasing attention for individuals with a number of different emotional and behavioral disorders. And a blend of the behavioral and ecological models has inspired Positive Behavior Interventions and Supports (PBIS), widely used as a replacement for punitive discipline systems in the schools.

KEY POINTS

1. The basic tenet of behavioral theory is that all behavior, including maladaptive behavior, is learned and therefore can be "unlearned" and new behavior learned in its place.
2. Another basic assumption of behavioral theory is that behavior is related to the environmental context. It does not occur in a vacuum. Thus, it is imperative to assess the contextual contributors to challenging behavior.
3. Behavioral theorists effect behavior change by manipulating environmental events that precede or follow the targeted behavior.
4. To teach new behavior, such as academic skills and social skills, behavioral techniques such as direct instruction, prompting, and reinforcement are recommended. Social skills training, precision teaching, and mastery learning are good examples of educational applications of the behavioral model.
5. Positive reductive techniques such as differential reinforcement are usually recommended in lieu of punishment.
6. Common punishers for students with EBD are in-school suspension, interim alternative education programs, time-out, and physical restraint.
7. The Positive Behavior Support (PBS) model was developed to provide schools with training and knowledge of ABA techniques that prevent problem behavior and promote appropriate social behavior.
8. All teachers of students with EBD should be adept at using behavioral techniques to increase desired behaviors and to decrease undesired behaviors in the classroom.

HOMEWORK QUESTIONS

1. List as many components of the behavioral model that you can find in the case study about Victor. In your own words, define each component.
2. Two differential reinforcement techniques were used to correct Victor's behavior. Define those techniques and give an additional school-based example of each. What other differential reinforcement technique might the teacher have used with Victor?
3. Discuss Victor's graphs with regard to school accountability and progress monitoring. What are some pros and cons of graphing behavioral data?

4. What will Victor's teacher have to count to show that Victor's academic performance and success in general education was positively impacted by the behavioral intervention?

5. Discuss why you think teachers would be reluctant to use behavioral techniques in their classroom, even when they have been proven effective.

6. Visit the websites for CECP and PBIS and choose one document or material based in the behavioral model to report about to your class. Explain what the material contains, what purpose it might serve, how useful it might be to school personnel, and why you chose to download that document. What aspect of the behavioral model does this document address?

7. List and discuss at least five common contextual variables in typical classrooms that might negatively affect student behavior. How might these variables be structured to positively impact student behavior?

8. Find one or two journal articles pertaining to Direct Instruction and report the contents to your group or class. Discuss how the components of Direct Instruction relate to ABA principles.

ADDITIONAL READINGS AND RESOURCES

Applied analysis for teachers, by Paul Alberto and Anne Troutman, Columbus, OH: Prentice Hall, 2006, for practical suggestions for implementing numerous behavioral techniques in general and special education classrooms.

Applied behavior analysis, by John Cooper, Tim Heron, and Bill Heward, Columbus, OH: Merrill, 1987, for a definitive text on applied behavior analysis.

Behavior analysis in education: Focus on measurably superior instruction, by Ralph Gardner and colleagues, Pacific Grove, CA: Brookes-Cole, 1994, for readings and research regarding applications of ABA in schools.

Evidence-based educational methods, by Daniel Moran and Richard Malott, San Diego, CA: Elsevier, 2004, for a summary of evidence-based educational methods that work in schools.

The psychology of B. F. Skinner, by William O'Donohue and Kyle Ferguson, Thousand Oaks, CA: Sage, 2001, for an illumination of Skinner's contributions to psychology and the applications that emerged from them.

The power of reinforcement, by Stephen Flora, Albany: State University of New York Press, 2004, for a defense of the use of reinforcement principles against a variety of challenges.

Functional assessment and program development for problem behavior: A practical handbook, by Rob O'Neill and colleagues, Pacific Grove, CA: Brookes-Cole, 1997, for a manual with forms to guide practitioners in the use of FBAs for behavior planning purposes

The entire issue of *School Psychology Review, 30*(2), 2001, National Association of School Psychologists, for a mini-series on issues and procedures for implementing functional behavior assessments in schools.

The entire issue of *Preventing School Failure, 44*(4), 2000, Heldref Publications, for articles addressing issues regarding the use of FBAs for students with EBD.

The entire issue of *Journal of Emotional and Behavioral Disorders, 10*(3), Fall 2002, Pro-Ed, for a special series on positive behavior support in schools as applied with students with EBD.

Journal of Direct Instruction of the Association for Direct Instruction, Eugene, OR: ADI Publications: *http://www.adihome.org,* for research pertaining to applications of ABA for academic progress in the schools.

Center for Effective Collaboration and Practice (CECP): *http://cecp.air.org/* and the National Technical Assistance Center for Positive Behavior Interventions and Supports (PBIS): *www.pbis.org,* for multiple technical assistance documents and articles pertaining to FBA and applications of PBS in schools.

The Association for Behavior Analysis (ABA): *www.abainternational.org,* for information, online bookstore, and training information regarding applications of ABA and their journal, the *Journal of Applied Behavior Analysis* (JABA), for research validating ABA applications.

Education and Treatment of Children (ETC): *http://www.educationandtreatmentofchildren.net/,* for a journal dedicated to researching educational applications of ABA.

CHAPTER 8 Ecological/Systems Model

Ecological Theory
- Definition and Etiology
- Evaluation Procedures
- Educational Applications

QUESTIONS TO CONSIDER

- Why would an ecological/systems model be preferred for students with EBD?
- Which ecological systems impact a child's development?
- What agencies are available to help schools address children's mental health and social needs?
- Why would the juvenile justice system be called a "default" system for students with EBD?
- What new mental health service delivery models have been developed in the past 25 years?
- What are common barriers to ensuring adequate mental health services to children and youth who need them?
- What roles do teachers play in a systems model?

Orientation

Ecological/systems theory has become a popular premise for explaining human development and social ills, such as school violence. This theory is important because it reminds us that to understand human behavior we must assess not only the individual but also the context in which that individual lives and the interactions of both. Treatment also assumes that we not only target the individual for change, but also the systems and situations with which the individual interacts.

Overview

Like behavioral theory, ecological/systems theory assumes that the source of deviance lies in the interaction between an individual and the environment. Ecological theorists view disturbance as a function of personal characteristics, environmental systems, and the reciprocal influence of each on the other. The major implication of this view is that a singular approach to assessment and treatment will be ineffective. Instead, the focus must be on assessing and changing individual characteristics, environmental systems and contexts, and subsequent interactions between them.

Definition and Basic View

> Behavioral disabilities are defined as a variety of excessive, chronic, deviant behaviors ranging from impulsive and aggressive to depressive and withdrawal acts (a) which violate the perceiver's expectations of appropriateness and (b) which the perceiver wishes to see stopped. (Graubard, 1973, p. 246)

Graubard's definition expresses the ecological view in its emphasis on both the perceiver of behavior and the behavior being perceived. The definition establishes that there are two parts to defining problem behavior: some type of behavior must be exhibited and someone must be offended by such behavior. Theorists of this model espouse the view that deviance lies in the interaction of an individual with others (the perceivers) in the environment, hence the term *ecological.*

As applied to human behavior, the ecological/systems model implies that it is meaningless to discuss problems of behavior in isolation from the contexts in which these behaviors arise, since it is these very contexts that define the behavior as a problem. Rhodes (1967) states that the disturbance often lies in the behavioral expectations of those with whom the child must interact. A child may be judged disordered by one person while appearing normal to another, or the child's behavior may be seen as abnormal in one setting but quite normal in another. The predictable result is that children who are judged to be the most disordered are those who uniformly arouse negative reactions in the environments in which they interact with others. Therefore, within the ecological model, behavior is viewed as "disturbing" rather than inherently "disturbed," and emphasis is placed not only on the child but also on other individuals and factors in the child's ecosystem. Therefore, ecological interventions call for a systems approach to treatment.

Etiology and Development of Disordered Behavior

Theory

In terms of applying ecological/systems theory to children with emotional and behavioral disorders, William Rhodes (1967, 1970) has been a vocal spokesperson. His arguments are persuasive but largely philosophical, as disturbances in ecosystems are difficult to define and assess operationally. According to Rhodes (1970), certain environments may be unable to accommodate the unfolding nature of children, thereby generating disturbance in the ecosystems. This view is in direct opposition to more traditional views that the child should accommodate to the environment rather than vice versa. Rhodes states that a major sign of disturbance is an increase in the amount and intensity of energy that is required by others to interact with the child, or a disturbance in the equilibrium of the ecosystem that calls attention to the child.

To operate from an ecological framework, one must accept that ecosystems rather than children are disordered, and that ecosystems are directly influenced by the culture in which they exist. Rhodes (1967) translates these assumptions into intervention goals: the short-term goal is to intrude into the disordered situation and help modify it, and the long-term goal is to expand the education process to develop functional yet individualistic members of society. Above all, Rhodes (1970) is adamant that we cannot hope to provide effective intervention if we "pluck" a child from a context of disturbance, attempt to fix or change him, and then place the child back into the unchanged environment from which he came.

Uri Bronfenbrenner, an American psychologist, developed an ecological systems theory to explain human development (1979, 1989, 1993). Bronfenbrenner assumes that a child's biological characteristics (e.g., gender, IQ, physical appearance) combine with environmental forces within multilevel systems to mold development. The reciprocal interactions between the child and those in his or her immediate environment (e.g., parents, teachers), between the child and more distant environments (e.g., federal government, cultural standards), and the interaction of those variables within systems (e.g., parents with teachers) will all affect the individual's growth and development. Note that because interactions are bidirectional, the environment not only changes the child, but the child affects the environment.

The explanation for abnormal human development, according to ecological/systems theory, is that the interactional processes between individuals and the changing properties of the settings in which they operate are not functioning in healthy ways. Bronfenbrenner divides the ecological context into layers or systems, each farther removed from day-to-day contact with the individual (Berk, 1999). The immediate environment (the microsystem) includes activities and interaction patterns with people close to the individual. For example, a child who is distractible and cries frequently, if born to parents who are impatient, might be subjected to negative interactions in the microsystem, which, in turn, will affect social and emotional development.

The second level of the environment (the mesosystem) includes interactions among those in the microsystem. For example, one student's parents may be at odds with school personnel, verbally criticizing teachers and administrators. On the other hand, a student's parents may be cooperating with the teacher in terms of a behavior management contract and reinforcers. The child in this second scenario is more likely to experience healthy interactions and be affected positively. The third system, the exosystem, includes settings not directly interacting with children, but nevertheless affecting their development. For example, the exosystem may contain the parents' workplaces, health and welfare agencies, or other community agencies. Whether a child's parents receive insurance benefits or maternity leave will affect child development even though children do not directly interact with the parents' workplace. Finally, the macrosystem pertains to the values, laws, customs, and resources present in a particular culture. For example, in countries with stringent gun laws, child injuries and deaths are considerably fewer.

According to Bronfenbrenner (1993), environmental systems are dynamic and affect individuals in different ways. The timing of key events and interactions, as well as the child's personal characteristics, are as important as the variables themselves. For example, the birth of a new sibling may affect a child one way if the child is 2 years old, but a very different way if the child is 14 years old. Or a baby with a low IQ affects a family one way, whereas an adolescent who acquires brain damage may affect his family very differently. This temporal dimension of ecological/systems theory is referred to as the *chronosystem* (Bronfenbrenner, 1989). It is important to remember that children are both products and producers of their environment. To illustrate this reciprocal interaction, Bronfenbrenner recently redefined his model as a *bioecological* model (Bronfenbrenner & Evans, 2000). Thus, to be effective, assessment and treatment approaches must address the entire bioecological system.

Typically, ecological/systems theory is depicted as a series of connected circles (shown in Figure 8.1). Students with emotional and behavioral disorders operate within all of these systems in unique ways. Analysis of variables in a child's ecosystem is important

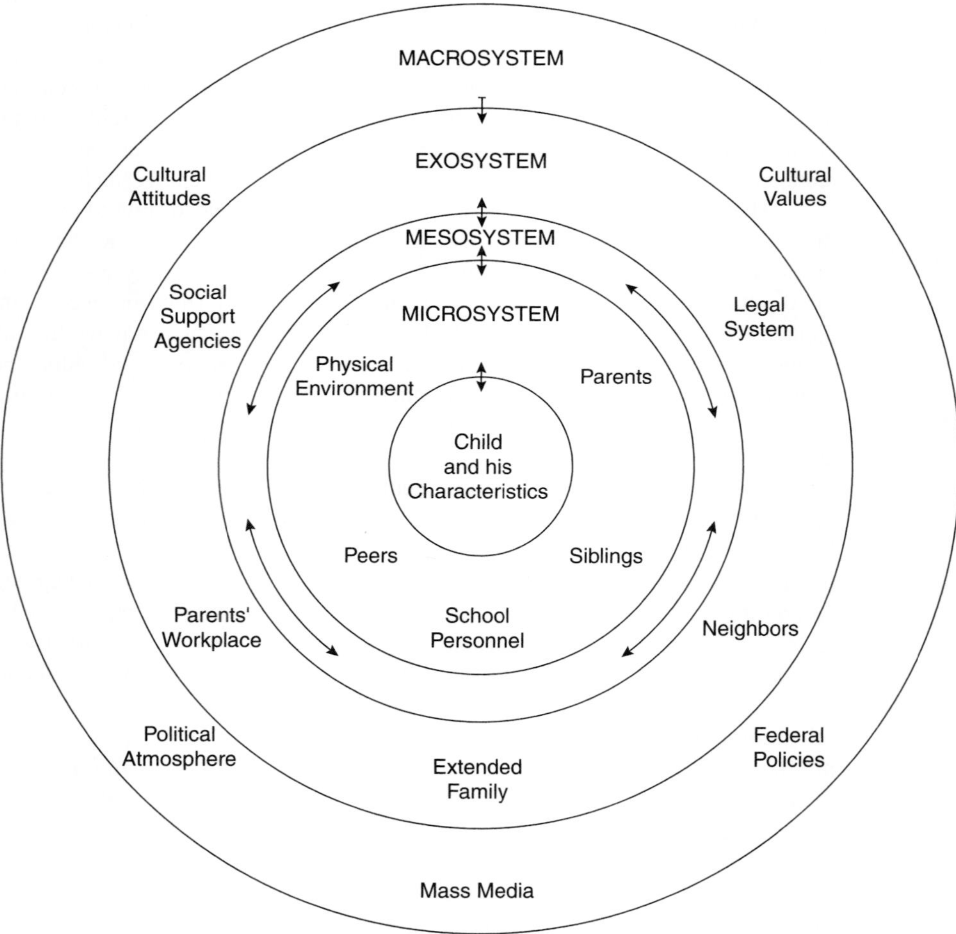

FIGURE 8.1 Bronfenbrenner's Ecological/Systems Model

for two reasons: (1) to determine whether the variables are contributing to the disturbance, and (2) to determine which contributing variables are amenable to change so that appropriate intervention can be planned. For example, it might be determined that Timothy's father's unemployment is causing anxiety in the home, which is having an effect on Timothy's frustration tolerance and academic functioning in the classroom. Although dealing directly with parental unemployment (exosystem) is outside the domain of education, an analysis of the classroom situation might reveal that Timothy would benefit from temporary help, such as adjusting the length of required assignments and/or providing individualized tutoring (microsystem adjustments).

Much educational research has been devoted to identifying specific microsystem variables that positively and negatively affect student learning and behavior. For example, certain teacher attitudes and expectations, curriculum choices, classroom structure, and lesson design (i.e., direct instruction) positively affect student learning (Forness et al., 1997; Mastropieri & Scruggs, 1994; Viadero, 1999). On the other hand, noise, crowding, unpredictable schedules, abusive and coercive interactions, oversleeping, long bus rides, scholastic failure, unstructured transitions, irrelevant curricula, and negative teacher attitudes and expectations have been found to promote inappropriate student behavior (e.g., Dunlap et al., 1994; Mayer, 1995; Myles & Simpson, 1994; Sugai & Horner, 2002). Identifying the potent ecological variables for particular students provides us with the opportunity to change them.

Students also contribute to the workings of ecosystems. Of all the student characteristics that have been shown to influence teacher attitudes and expectations within the classroom, challenging behavior may be the most potent (Kedar-Voivodas & Tannenbaum, 1979; Trevor, 1975). The behaviors that teachers find most disturbing are best described as defiant-aggressive (Algozzine, 1977; Gersten, Walker, & Darch, 1988; Walker, 1979). Such behaviors engender negative attitudes that are often translated into negative teacher–student interactions, thus setting into motion the rippling effect through the ecosystem described by Rhodes and Bronfenbrenner.

One of the major criticisms of the ecological theory of disturbance is that related strategies are difficult to apply. The next two sections offer examples of ecological assessment and of ecological applications.

Evaluation Procedures

Ecological Assessment Techniques

Basically, ecological assessment refers to the gathering of information from all environments or ecosystems in which a student spends a significant amount of time. A good ecological assessment (1) describes the environments; (2) lists the demands on the student, including expectations of others in those environments; and (3) defines the skills and behaviors needed by the student to be successful in those environments. Such environments include the home, the neighborhood, the school, and each of the classrooms that a student attends. Some ecological assessments focus only on the classroom environment. Examples of these are the *Instructional Environment Scale* (TIES; Ysseldyke & Christenson, 1987) and *Analysis of Classroom and Instructional Demands* (ACID Test; West, 1990). Both of these measures offer a structure to identify the demands of a particular classroom, including such variables as instructional content and presentation, class rules and teacher expectations, types of evaluations, and grading procedures. The information from these measures can then be used to modify certain aspects of the demands to fit an individual student's abilities or to offer the student additional help in meeting those demands. Educators can conduct their own informal assessments of classroom learning environments without using published measures, but it may be helpful to use these or other measures that have already identified important instructional, motivational, and management variables.

Some believe that functional behavioral assessment (FBA), described in depth in Chapter 7, is an assessment procedure more indicative of ecological theory than of behavioral theory (e.g., Lane, Umbreit, & Beebe-Frankenberger, 1999). Indeed, if the result of such assessment is a treatment approach primarily targeting micro- and mesosystem variables rather than the student alone, then the procedure seems well founded from an ecological perspective.

The *Behavioral and Emotional Rating Scale (BERS): A Strength-Based Approach to Assessment* (Epstein & Sharma, 1998) is based on the assumption that assessing for student strengths will better result in appropriate educational plans. The authors define strength-based assessment "as the measurement of those emotional and behavioral skills, competencies and characteristics that create a sense of personal accomplishment; contribute to satisfying relationships with family members, peers and adults; enhance one's ability to deal with adversity and stress; and promote one's personal, social and academic development" (Epstein & Sharma, 1998, p. 3). The 52-item scale assesses Interpersonal Strengths, Family Involvement including student–family relationships, Intrapersonal Strengths, School Functioning, and Affective Strength. The authors recommend the BERS be used to plan treatment programs and to evaluate the outcomes of services (Epstein & Sharma, 1998). The BERS is not only used by school personnel but also by other systems units (e.g., mental health programs, child welfare agencies, managed care companies), illustrating its systems and ecological perspective.

Such assessments and interventions are ecological in scope because they avoid only putting the burden upon the student to adapt to the environment; rather, the importance of a fit or a match between the student and the classroom or family demands is emphasized. Ecological assessments can be very helpful with all students with EBD, but may be particularly important when reintegrating or including these students in general education classrooms from more restrictive settings.

There are also instruments that seek information about an individual from a number of sources and from environments other than the classroom. The *Behavior Rating Profile-2* (BRP-2; Brown & Hammill, 1990) is such an instrument. According to its authors, the BRP-2 is an "ecological/behavioral assessment device" that allows behaviors to be examined in a variety of settings and from several points of view. There are six components of the BRP-2: three Student Rating Subscales in which the student responds to a total of 60 self-descriptive items in the areas of home, school, and peers; a Teacher Rating Scale of 30 items; a Parent Rating Scale of 30 items; and a sociogram. Table 8.1 shows these components and respondents. The BRP-2 is flexible in that one may either utilize input from all the scales or may use any of the scales independently. The instrument can be helpful in defining deviant behavior that is specific to one setting or to one individual's expectations.

TABLE 8.1 Respondent and Ecology Associated with the BRP-2 Components (Brown & Hammill, 1990)

	Respondent				Ecology		
BRP Component	**Student**	**Teachers**	**Parents**	**Peers**	**Home**	**School**	**Interpersonal**
Student Rating Scale: Home	X				X		
Student Rating Scale: School	X					X	
Student Rating Scale: Peer	X						X
Teacher Rating Scale		X				X	
Parent Rating Scale			X		X		
Sociogram				X			X

Used with permission of the publisher, Pro-Ed, 8700 Shoal Creek Blvd., Austin, TX 78758.

The *Behavior Assessment System for Children—2* (BASC-2; Reynolds & Kamphaus, 2004), presented in Chapter 3, is another example of an ecological assessment technique. The BASC-2 includes parent and teacher rating scales for children, a comprehensive self-report assessment for children and adolescents, a structured developmental history, and a student observation system. It assesses student strengths and adaptive behaviors and is easy to relate to IDEA criteria. The BASC-2 is one of the few measures that provides an integrative approach to assessment, with multiple informants (Sattler, 2002). The *Achenbach System of Empirically Based Assessment* (ASEBA; Achenbach & Rescorla, 2001), also discussed in Chapter 3, is a collection of several rating scales, self-report forms, semi-structured interviews, and observation forms for parents, teachers, and the children themselves. A strength of this system, as with the others mentioned above, is its emphasis on cross-informant assessment of an individual's behavior (Sattler, 2002). For all of these assessments, the inclusion of multiple informants and assessment formats provides a systems view for school personnel who conduct comprehensive assessments and plan educational programs.

Ecological/Systems Units and Their Educational Applications

Every child is an inseparable part of a complex web of interrelated systems. For "normal" children, these mini social systems function appropriately and may be defined as congruent or balanced. When the systems break down, we term them *incongruent* or *unbalanced.* We also tend to place the blame for such incongruence on the child, rationalize our action by labeling the child as emotionally disturbed, and plan our interventions to focus on remediating the identified child's emotional disturbance while neglecting the other aspects of the system (Apter, 1982).

Many educators, psychologists, social workers, medical personnel, and other child-care specialists recognize the futility of treating the child while ignoring the systems in which he functions (Apter & Conoley, 1984; Biglan, 1995; Department of Health and Human Services [DHHS], 2001; Hobbs, 1982; Mayer, 1995; Rhodes, 1970; Webber, 1997a). Instead, many professionals advocate a systems or an ecological approach to treatment, which focuses on imbalances or disturbances in systems. The child is seen as a part of the disturbance, and interventions are aimed at promoting changes not only in the child but also in other people and factors in the environment. The 2001 *Report of the Surgeon General's Conference on Mental Health* (DHHS, 2001) stated that responsibility for children's mental health care was dispersed across many systems: schools, primary care, juvenile justice, child welfare, substance abuse agencies, and families. A major component of the subsequent recommendations and vision set forth in this conference was to integrate family and child mental health services into all systems that serve children and youth, a systems vision.

The goal of a systems approach is to reduce the discrepancy between environmental expectations for a child and the capabilities of that child to fulfill those expectations. According to Apter (1982), such programs are based on the following assumptions:

1. Each child is an inseparable part of a small social system.
2. Disturbance is not viewed as a disease located within the child, but rather as discordance (a lack of balance) in the system.
3. Discordance may be viewed as a disparity between an individual's abilities and the demands or expectations of the environment— "failure to match" between child and system.
4. The goal of any intervention is to make the system work, and to make it work ultimately without the intervention.
5. Improvement in any part of the system can benefit the system.
6. This broader view of disturbance gives rise to three major areas for intervention:
   a. Changing the child
   b. Changing the environment
   c. Changing attitudes and expectations. (p. 69)

The focus of the first section is the family, which is the most influential system of a child. The focus of the second section is the education system, which is the second most influential system of a child. The third section emphasizes the community systems that impact the lives of students with EBD: social welfare, juvenile justice/correctional, and mental health. The teacher's role in working with individuals within these systems involves knowledge acquisition, consultation, and effective communication.

The Family System

Perhaps with no other exceptionality does successful intervention depend so heavily on parent involvement. Many educators have discovered the futility of trying to change behaviors exhibited at school that are being maintained in the home environment. In contrast, if inappropriate behavior patterns are consistently discouraged in both the home and in school, the student is more likely to choose more appropriate ways of behaving. Cooperative parents and teachers make a formidable team that provides consistency and prevents pitting home against school. For elementary and middle school students, the family is still a significant source of influence and control. Changes are most easily made in these formative years before loyalties shift from parents and teachers to peers. Parental involvement also enhances counseling efforts with youngsters. Many theorists view parental involvement in counseling sessions with children with emotional and behavioral problems as a necessity.

While recognizing the need to provide consistency between the home and school, teachers must also realize that communicating with parents may not be easy. Psychologists and educators historically have been willing to blame disordered behavior on disordered homes and poor parenting. Thus, interactions between parents and educators often have been undermined by issues of guilt and blame. Parents of students with emotional problems often feel responsible for or guilty about their child's problems. Educators may unwittingly exacerbate such feelings by pointing out inadequate discipline or management practices in the home, thus setting into motion a guilt–blame cycle that may be difficult to overcome. Teachers of students with EBD need to understand these dynamics, as well as research on the role of parenting in the development of behavior problems in children.

Research on Parenting. Considerable effort has been directed toward identifying parental characteristics and childrearing practices that are conducive to healthy development. Baumrind's (1971, 1977) classic research identified three basic parenting styles: permissive, authoritarian, and authoritative. Permissive parenting is characterized by a loose, nondemanding style similar to that promoted by the famous pediatrician Benjamin Spock in the 1950s. Permissive parents do not set limits and rarely use punishment, but they may reason with their child. At the other extreme, authoritarian parents value obedience and conformity to a set of standards that is usually based on religious or political beliefs; these beliefs are rigidly adhered to, and little room exists for individual choice or personal freedom. Between these extremes is authoritative parenting, marked by a concern for both obedience and expression of individuality. Authoritative parents often use reason and allow for discussion from the children when setting rules.

These parenting styles have been linked to subsequent behaviors in children. Overly permissive parenting, characterized by few demands or limits, has been linked to children who are highly aggressive with low impulse control. Parents who use severe punishment (especially physical punishment) as a parenting style may be more likely to produce offspring with higher rates of aggression and delinquency. When punishment is paired with perceived parental rejection, the relationship to aggression and delinquency is even more marked. Conversely, when parenting is marked by warmth, children are more likely to exhibit good social adjustment and to possess high self-esteem. Warmth is characterized by commitment and sensitivity to the child's needs, willingness to spend time with the child, and enthusiasm about the child's accomplishments.

Notably, antisocial children often come from families characterized by divorce, poverty, substance abuse, unemployment, abuse, and other sources of conflict. Under such adverse conditions, effective parenting often falls by the wayside. Patterson, Reed, and Dishion (1992) have identified parenting practices that have been linked with positive social development in children; furthermore, the inability to carry out such practices has been linked to early development of antisocial and aggressive behavior in children. The five practices include (1) fair, consistent discipline; (2) monitoring of the child's whereabouts and activities; (3) positive and supportive behavior management techniques; (4) parent involvement in the child's daily life; and (5) problem solving that models how to deal with conflicts and crises.

C.W. Anderson (1981a) also lists several parental variables that have been shown to promote positive social behaviors in children: warmth and responsiveness, consistent discipline, demands for responsible behavior, and purposeful modeling, teaching, and reinforcement of desired behaviors. What parents do with their children may be more important than global personality or attitudinal variables. Anderson also emphasizes the reciprocal nature of parent–child interactions. Not only do parents influence their children, but children also shape their parents' behavior: "The child is seen as an elicitor of parent behaviors and as responding in ways which may serve to positively or negatively reinforce parent behavior, or to extinguish or punish it" (Anderson, 1981b, p. 83).

The reciprocal nature of parent–child interactions is particularly applicable to students exhibiting hyperactivity or behavioral excesses. Researchers have found that hyperactive or overactive children tend to elicit more severe disciplinary or controlling behaviors from their parents than do their normal peers (Campbell, 1973, 1975; Stevens-Long, 1973). In studying parent–child interactions of aggressive children, Patterson (1975; Patterson & Cobb, 1973) observed that an aversive behavior from either party elicits an aversive response and results in a gradual escalation of aversive exchanges. Parents are likely to respond to high-frequency or intense behaviors by increasing their efforts at control; in turn, increasing parental control often elicits the child's control behaviors, and a negative pattern becomes established over time.

Although these linkages between parental behavior and child behavior have been consistently demonstrated in research, it should be noted that no parent personality characteristic has been shown to cause behavioral pathology. Many children who should be at risk for developing pathology according to the research in fact turn out to be well adjusted (Rutter, 1987; Werner & Smith, 2001). The research on resilient children has found that three major factors appear to offer protection against effects of major life stressors: (1) personal characteristics such as high intelligence, socially valued talents, easygoing sociable disposition, optimistic outlook, adaptable to change (Masten & Reed, 2002); (2) a strong bond to someone outside the immediate family who is competent and caring such as a teacher or a grandparent; and (3) a strong community with multiple activities for children and youth such as scouting or religious groups (Berk, 2005). In the real world, many factors may interact to produce, maintain, or inhibit the development of behavior problems or emotional pathology, and the reciprocal nature of individual characteristics and environmental situations appears important. For example, a child with EBD who is irritable and aggressive and dislikes change might have a more difficult time finding a competent, caring adult and may be excluded from community activities by virtue of the disturbing behavior.

Although it has been useful to study families from a dyadic perspective, that is, the study of two-person relationships, other theorists promote a triadic perspective. This perspective recognizes that many complex factors affect the parent–child relationship. For example, in traditional two-parent families, the mother and father are a social unit of husband and wife whose marital relationship will have an indirect bearing on the child. In single-parent families, the presence or absence of an adult partner will also influence the parent and his or her relationship with the child. These indirect effects may interact in complex ways to affect family functioning. Recognition of this complexity has led to study of the family as a system.

A Systems Approach to Families. Many professionals advocate a systems approach to working with parents and their children, in which the functioning of the family as a unit is studied. According to Simon and Johnston (1987), many researchers believe that the occurrence of a child's behavioral symptoms are usually related to a change in the family system that disturbs the "delicate balance of daily family functioning" (p. 82). Such changes include the family stresses of divorce, marital conflict, illness, death, and loss of employment. One study cited by Simon and Johnston as support of this theory was conducted by Abelsohn (1983) who found that acting-out behavior was a frequent result of parental separation or divorce. "A Mother's Story" presented in Box 8.1 illustrates how an adolescent girl eventually was placed in a residential treatment center partially as a result of her reaction to conditions surrounding the divorce of her parents. In working with families and family systems, Becvar and Becvar (1988) identified six characteristics of healthy families:

1. A legitimate source of authority, established and supported over time
2. A rule system, consistently enforced
3. Stable, consistent nurturing behavior
4. Effective childrearing and marriage-maintenance practices
5. A set of goals toward which each member of the family works
6. Flexibility to adapt to normal developmental changes as well as crises

In addition, researchers have established that healthy families demonstrate shared roles and responsibilities, distinct boundaries (parents are not afraid to act like parents and they allow children to be children), respect for privacy, and opportunities for expression of independence and a wide variety of emotions (Kaslow, 1982). Healthy families also typically have many friends and social relationships outside the immediate family, and such relationships are encouraged for the children. Social isolation, or the absence of such relationships, is common in families that abuse.

A final characteristic of healthy families is clear and congruent communication (Becvar & Becvar, 1988). In these families, verbal and nonverbal communications match so that children do not receive conflicting messages. Disagreement is allowed and individual differences are respected. Effective communication is modeled so that children learn to interact in positive ways with family members and others outside the family.

Systems approaches to developing healthy family relationships can be carried out in a number of ways. Family therapy is one avenue; parent involvement in school programs for parents of students with EBD is another. For example, in the On Campus model described by Simon and Johnston (1987), the student and parent(s) had to meet with program personnel prior to the student's enrollment. At this orientation meeting, the role of parents and their relationship to the school was outlined; communication and problem-solving procedures were emphasized. After the student was enrolled, family conferences that focused on problem solving and action plans for home and school were held by program personnel as needed. These family conferences were the key systems facet because (1) they recognized that many behaviors are exhibited in both settings; (2) they emphasized

BOX 8.1

A Mother's Story

Ms. Brown entered the admissions office, visibly shaken by the procedure she was about to complete. Mary Ann stood close behind her mother with a sullen look on her face. She refused to acknowlege the admissions officer; instead, she gazed out the window in disbelief of what her mother was about to do. Upon request, mother and daughter were seated, and the formalities of the day began. Ms. Brown's hand shook as she signed the forms admitting her daughter into the residential treatment center. Although for a moment she considered backing out, she knew that Mary Ann had already been given too many second chances, and that, as a single parent, her options were limited. She told her story to the admission officer, unaware that her story was typical of the thousands of U.S. teens in psychiatric hospitals and treatment centers across the country.

The Browns had divorced when Mary Ann was 10, concluding several turbulent years of marriage. Mary Ann and her brother Robert remained in their home with their mother, and the father moved into an apartment down the street. The divorce was amicable, and everyone seemed relieved that the new living arrangements were working out so well. For the first year, Mr. Brown sent child support checks regularly and the children spent every weekend with him. At the end of a year, however, Mr. Brown accepted a job in another state. Although he assured the children that they would still come to visit on holidays and summer vacations, they took the news hard.

At first, Mr. Brown did keep in touch through phone calls and packages in the mail. After several months, however, the contacts ceased. At the same time, word drifted back to Ms. Brown that her ex-husband had remarried and was expecting a child with his new wife. Over the next few months, child support checks arrived irregularly. In telephone conversations, Mr. Brown made it clear that he had made a new life for himself that left little room for Robert and Mary Ann. Feeling financial pressure, Ms. Brown took a weekend job to supplement her pay. Mary Ann, now 12, was left to care for her younger brother. After 6 months of struggling to make ends meet, Ms. Brown was forced to sell the family home and move across town to more affordable housing. The children protested, not wanting to leave their neighborhood friends. A sense of loss and abandonment was felt by mother and children.

The difficulties with Mary Ann began on her 13th birthday. Ms. Brown hoped to make up for some of the disappointments of the past year by throwing a birthday party for Mary Ann and inviting some of her "old" friends from their former neighborhood. This idea proved disastrous, as Mary Ann refused to invite her friends to the new home, voicing anger and embarrassment over their predicament. She blamed her mother for the divorce and the loss of her father. Ms. Brown was unprepared for this outburst, as she had hoped to be appreciated for working seven days a week and making sacrifices of her own to keep the family together. After a bitter argument, Mary Ann fled the house.

Things in school were also deteriorating. Although previously an A student, Mary Ann now made B's and C's with occasional D's. After receiving a call from the principal at work one day, Ms. Brown also learned that Mary Ann had been skipping school. When confronted, Mary Ann lied and stormed to her room, refusing to come out. The next morning Ms. Brown discovered that Mary Ann's bed had not been slept in, Frantic, Ms. Brown called the police to report Mary Ann as a runaway. However, Mary Ann returned of her own accord at midmorning. Another scene ensued, and Ms. Brown decided that she needed help in dealing with her daughter.

She made an appointment with a counselor at the local mental health clinic. Although Mary Ann begrudgingly accompanied her mother, she refused to cooperate with the counselor. The next several months were difficult. It appeared that Mary Ann no longer wanted to be part of the family. Upon her return from school each day, she would shut herself in her room and listen to loud music or watch television. She rarely ate with the family, preferring to take a plate of food to her room and eat by herself. Although there had been no more incidences of truancy or running away, Ms. Brown continued to worry about her daughter's emotional well-being. Counseling sessions were fruitless. Ms. Brown worried about leaving Mary Ann alone during the days of the upcoming summer vacation; she therefore made arrangements for Mary Ann to spend the summer with her father. This living arrangement proved unsatisfactory from the start. Mary Ann was jealous of her new sister and stepmother. She once again retreated into her room to listen to music. Determined not to fit in and to get back home, she refused to clean up after herself. When her father attempted to set limits, she expressed her anger and hatred toward him, which he in turn blamed on his ex-wife's parenting. Mary Ann began to come and go as she pleased, with grounding proving ineffective because she would sneak out of her window and not return until the early morning hours. On several occasions, Mary Ann took the family car and went joy-riding with several friends who were older than she. Mary Ann was sent back to her mother the day after her stepmother returned to the house to find it full of smoke, loud music, and a number of young people she did not know.

Upon her return home, Mary Ann at first appeared to be doing well at home and school. Her grades improved slightly. In October, however, Ms. Brown made an unannounced home visit at lunch time; there she found Mary Ann and a disreputable older boy in her bedroom smoking pot. After a physical confrontation with her mother, Mary Ann ran away and was not found by the police for several days. It was from the juvenile detention center that Ms. Brown had picked up Mary Ann to bring her to the treatment facility.

When it was time to say goodbye, Mary Ann pleaded with her mother not to leave her: when it was obvious that she would indeed have to stay, her pleas turned to anger. She called her mother obscene names, stating that she would never see her again, and for her not to bother to come visit. As Ms. Brown watched her angry daughter disappear behind the locked door of the unit, she succumbed to the familiar sense of pain and loss that had been so prevalent over the past few months. She wondered what had gone wrong and where she had failed. Their lives were not supposed to have turned out this way.

Contributed by Sarah Sims, M.Ed., Psychological Associate. The Devereux Foundation, Texas Center, Victoria, Texas.

---

an action plan, a written contract specifying everyone's responsibilities and consequences; and (3) they reinforced the partnership aspect of school–home. To further communication, phone calls were made to parents reporting any cuts or absences. Calls were also made to inform parents of good performance and progress. Academic and behavioral reports were sent to parents as needed: once every 3 weeks for those students making satisfactory progress, and either daily or weekly for those students needing more support.

In summary, many professionals, including the U.S. Surgeon General, have concluded that the most effective approach to working with students with EBD is a systems approach (DHHS, 2001). Applied to families, this approach means that educators need to recognize that a student is part of a family unit that strives to maintain its balance. Working with the family as a unit can be undertaken not only in family therapy sessions, but also in school programs. Refer to Box 8.2 for an example of family counseling undertaken by a school psychologist.

Educational Application: Strategies for Parent Involvement. If special educators are to establish viable teacher–parent relationships, they must accept and abide by two basic

BOX 8.2

Paul's Family: Crisis Counseling in the Schools

As an interning school psychologist in a large urban district, I was asked to work with Paul and his family. Paul was a 13-year-old seventh grader who was diagnosed as learning disabled. He had difficulty with verbal skills, as evidenced by his speaking in phrases and short sentences in a soft, almost inaudible voice. He had been referred for family counseling due to failing grades and recent incidences of fighting at school. He had also expressed suicidal thoughts to his mother and to school personnel. Paul's drawings were artistic but often depicted violent and bloody death scenes.

Paul's two older brothers, ages 16 and 17, were both in special education classes. The older brother was on probation from juvenile court and had returned to school after dropping out. The younger brother was attending an alternative school for repeated aggressive acts toward others. The only family member apparently doing well in school was the 9-year-old sister. After several attempts, the mother had severed her relationship with the father, a drug and alcohol abuser who was at the time imprisoned on drug charges. My role as therapist was crisis oriented, geared to a brief therapy problem-solving model of dealing with family needs in six sessions. The intent of this model is to help family members learn how each contributes to preferred behavior (which is the exception), and then to help make these instances commonplace.

It became clear to me very early in the first session that nothing would be easy in this family. The hope of getting a family consensus on a goal for the six sessions was lost in the quagmire of individual concerns. All family members except the daughter seemed depressed. Finally, the mother decided upon a goal: getting Paul to do his chores and his homework. Upon hearing this goal, Paul's brothers retreated into self-absorbed silence and Paul began muttering to himself about "killing someone." Through the remainder of the sessions. I tried to help the mother see Paul's acting-out behavior as his cry for her to provide some stability in his life by demanding that he behave better.

I would like to say that at the end of the counseling sessions, Paul's grades improved, he was getting along better at school, and that his mother had reaffirmed her leadership role in the family. In reality, Paul's grades continued to lag and he was suspended several times for bringing weapons to school. The mother did not appear to have the energy to deal with Paul's challenges or to maintain consistency in discipline. She did indicate, however, that she was able to initiate more conversation of a personal nature with her son; as one example, she was able to talk with him about a situation in which his feelings were hurt. Paul's story does not stop here. When his case was reviewed by school personnel, it was determined that his primary handicapping condition was emotional disturbance. He was placed in a self-contained affective learning class at another school, which allowed him to get a fresh start in a new environment with an empathic teacher. Meanwhile, I have picked him up in rational emotive therapy (RET). We are working to expand his understanding of feelings and developing more vocabulary to express those feelings. Through RET, Paul is learning to understand the irrationality of much of his anger and how he creates it. Progress is slow, but Paul wants to change. His teacher is pleased with his schoolwork. In the 2 months since his reassignment, Paul has missed only one day of school and has not been in any fights.

He may make it yet.

Contributed by Barbara Yonan, who at the time was completing an internship as part of the doctoral requirements in school psychology.

tenets: (1) their role with parents is a consultative one and (2) parents should be viewed as individuals, not as a homogeneous group.

The first tenet is that parents must be recognized as experts on their children, while educators must learn to be consultants to parents. Regardless of educational level or parenting skills, almost all parents can offer valuable insights about their child's development and level of functioning. Information on early development, stressful family relationships, and unusual environmental influences may prove crucial in helping the teacher understand the student's current functioning. When information is solicited from parents and their opinions are treated with respect, a bond of trust can be established that lays the groundwork for cooperative planning.

The second tenet is that parents of children with disabilities are not a homogeneous group. Parents differ greatly in the degree to which they participate in educational programming for their children. All parents of students with disabilities have a legal right to participate in decision making regarding their child's placement in special education services and in developing an individualized education program. While some parents communicate regularly with school personnel and are heavily involved throughout special education procedures, others may waive their rights to be actively involved. Similarly, some parents may know very little about alternative special education programs and placements, due process procedures under laws governing special education, and other legal issues; other parents may be well informed about the law and have definite ideas about what their child's educational program should entail. Some parents are knowledgeable about their child's difficulties and very skilled at managing their child's behavior, whereas others may need training to develop management skills. The point is that parents have differing levels of awareness and skills that teachers must accommodate when involving parents in education. Teachers will need to individualize their expectations for parents, just as they do for children.

Whose Fault Is It? Although the issue of blaming parents was alluded to earlier, it warrants additional attention. Often educators can fall into the trap of "if only." If only the parents were more interested; if only the parents would be consistent in discipline; if only there were a father in the home, and so on. These statements represent a subtle form of blame; that is, if only the parents were somehow different or better parents, then teaching students with EBD wouldn't be so hard. While this may be partially true, engaging in this type of thinking may also predispose the teacher to seeing the parent as an adversary rather than a partner. The teacher may also be tempted to absolve himself of responsibility for helping students achieve their behavioral and academic potential.

Simon and Johnston (1987) offered a good example of this blaming cycle. As they describe it, school personnel may easily fall prey to common misperceptions about single parents. Realizing that single parenting is often fraught with difficulties, school personnel may view the single parent as responsible for many of his child's behavior problems. This perception may be cemented when the single parent inevitably has difficulty scheduling and even making conferences; the parent then becomes labeled as indifferent or irresponsible. As the relationship between the home and school deteriorates (the mesosystem), the child is caught in the cycle: the school becomes more frustrated, the parent is viewed as more uncooperative, the child shows more behavior problems, and the school complains more about the parent.

Special Considerations for Nontraditional and Multicultural Families. Single-parent families have become the status quo rather than the exception. At any given time, 25 percent of U.S. children live in single-parent households, 12 percent of those with single fathers and 10 percent of American children live with a single parent who has never been married (Heatherington & Stanley-Hagan, 2002; U.S. Census Bureau, 2003). Single-parent families often experience many difficulties, including lack of emotional support from a partner, absence of a same-gender role model for children to emulate, and severe financial stress. Financial stress is worst in households headed by single mothers. Many children in single-mother homes display adjustment problems associated with economic hardship (Lipman, Boyle, Dooley, & Offord, 2002).

Other "nontraditional" family configurations that have become more common are families in which both parents work and blended families. More than 75 percent of mothers with school-age children are employed (U.S. Census Bureau, 2003). Finding adequate and affordable childcare for preschoolers and after-school care for older children becomes stressful for many families. Extended care also puts additional demands on the children to behave themselves in settings outside the home for most of their waking hours. Additionally, divorced or single parents usually remarry and children must learn to respond to stepparents' (usually stepfathers since mothers typically have custody of children) different childrearing practices. In blended families, children and youth may need to learn to share and interact with stepsiblings who also may be unhappy with the living arrangements. Most children in blended families have more problems than children in stable, first-marriage families (Hetherington & Kelly, 2002). Sensitivity to the special issues in these nontraditional families is essential in building partnerships between home and school (Berk, 2005; Coontz, 1995; Webber, 1997a).

Working with families of different ethnic, racial, or cultural backgrounds also calls for special consideration from teachers. Unfortunately, children from minority subcultures are too often living in poverty and in single-parent families. The Children's Defense Fund (2006), a renowned children's advocacy organization, states that "poor and minority children face risks and disadvantages that often pull them into a 'Cradle to Prison Pipeline.' This Pipeline leads children to marginalized lives and premature deaths" (p. 1). Furthermore, children and youth from African American and Hispanic homes may be overrepresented in classes for students with EBD in various parts of the country (Bradley & Monfore, 2004), possibly indicating a lack of sensitivity on the part of the educational system in dealing with these youth. Each of us is so socialized by our respective cultures that it becomes difficult to judge our own sensitivity to others' cultural practices. For example, the following have been suggested as basic values promoted by the dominant United States culture:

1. Importance of individualism and privacy
2. Belief in the equality of all individuals
3. Informality in interactions with others
4. Emphasis on the future, change, and progress
5. Belief in the general goodness of humanity
6. Emphasis on the importance of time and punctuality
7. High regard for achievement, action, work, and materialism
8. Pride in interaction styles that are direct and assertive (Althen, 1988)

These values are general but may affect a teacher's interactions, her behavior, and her assumptions about others' behavior. Some of these values also have direct implications for classroom performance. Experts in cross-cultural competence assert that the first step in becoming culturally sensitive is to be aware of one's own culture and its impact on beliefs, attitudes, and actions. Cultural self-awareness then becomes a bridge to understanding other cultures (Lynch, 1992).

The culturally competent individual also understands that communication style often differs from culture to culture. Particularly important are nonverbal behaviors and the meanings attributed to them by various cultures. Eye contact, facial expressions, proximity and touching, gestures, and other body language such as posture and body position may have very different meanings for persons from different cultures. For example, one researcher found that although members of different cultures claimed to recognize 70–100 percent of gestures from other groups, these members correctly interpreted the gestures at rates as low as 30 percent (Schneller, 1989).

Lynch (1992) offers a number of suggestions for improving cross-cultural communication:

- Respect individuals from other cultures
- Make continued and sincere attempts to understand the world from others' points of view
- Remain open to new learning
- Be flexible
- Have a sense of humor
- Accept ambiguity
- Approach others with a desire to learn (pp. 51–52)

These suggestions for involving parents are applicable to families of all cultural backgrounds. Although it may be important to understand the influence of certain aspects of an individual's cultural background, it is equally important to avoid stereotyping on that basis. As mentioned, successful teachers individualize expectations for parents and avoid blaming parents for their children's difficulties.

Staying in Touch. Teachers can encourage parental involvement in many ways. For parents who are interested in learning more about management techniques, teachers can be instrumental in setting up parent education groups. Parents who are experiencing high levels of stress may improve their coping skills by participation in a support group or in counseling. Each of these options is discussed in the following pages.

Staying in touch on a routine basis is essential. Ideally, parents should be involved in their child's school program in an ongoing, systematic way. While this degree of involvement is not always possible, there are some creative ways to stay in touch with parents. Taking advantage of technology can save time; examples are using computers to generate daily or weekly parent reports and using telephone answering machines or a website to record daily assignments. In the former case, parents call a number to get the day's class work or homework assignment; these tactics can be effective when students are especially "forgetful."

Many teachers find it helpful to make the student responsible for a daily notebook to be carried between home and school each day. Notes of communication and assignments are written in this notebook; teachers and parents can sign it each day to ensure its passage back and forth. Contingencies (penalties) can be set up for students who fail to keep the notebook updated.

Parent Groups. Organized parent groups are usually one of two types: (1) support groups, established to provide a support system among parents who have similar concerns, or (2) educational groups, established for the purpose of giving information or teaching specific skills. Support groups serve the function of getting parents together, often on an informal basis, to discuss concerns and frustrations relating to parenting and the education and management of their children. The impetus of support groups may come either from teachers or parents, but can be successful only if parents take an active role in sharing their needs and concerns. It is often a good idea for teachers to take very passive roles in parent support groups so that parents feel free to provide their own leadership. Support groups can also be structured according to the needs and desires of the group; for example, parents may want to bring in guest speakers on a certain topic and then break out into smaller discussion groups (Miller & Hudson, 1994).

Educational parent groups are usually conducted much like classes or workshops, with a specific agenda and a set number of meetings at a regular time and place. Educators, psychologists, social workers, and other child specialists are generally responsible for organizing and conducting these groups. Topics such as behavior management in the home and improving parent–child communication are offered.

Parent Counseling. Many parents need more support than can be provided by empathetic teachers or by parent groups. Individual or family counseling may be particularly indicated for parents of students with EBD, who usually face stressful situations on a daily basis. Parents may become so overwhelmed by financial problems, marital stress, or the day-to-day responsibilities of managing a family that the additional stress of their child's behavior problems becomes too much to handle (e.g., recall Mary Ann from the case study in Box 8.1).

Although teachers should lend a sympathetic ear to parents, it is beyond the scope of teacher responsibility—and training—to provide counseling services. However, the teacher is often in a position to be the first to recognize a plea for help and can be instrumental in making a referral. The following are signals that may indicate a need for professional counseling:

- Parents are experiencing a period of unusual financial difficulty, marital discord, or other emotional upheaval
- Parent(s) routinely expresses feelings of helplessness or depression
- Parent(s) feel(s) out of control of the child
- Child is habitually in trouble with the juvenile authorities
- Parent(s) chronically appear to be under a high level of stress
- Parent(s) is beginning to impose upon the teacher's time (at home or at school) with personal problems

To make appropriate referrals, teachers should become familiar with community resources that offer counseling and other psychological services. It is a good idea to know the background and training, credentials, and theoretical orientation of counselors and therapists to whom referrals are made. Many counselors and therapists specialize in school-related problems, child psychology, or family therapy; it is best to match parental needs to the specialty area of professionals. Teachers can be of most benefit to parents by helping them gain a realistic picture of their child's capabilities and behavior relative to school functioning, which might best be accomplished in face-to-face conferences.

In summary, teachers who view parents as partners in the educational process are likely to effect changes in a student's life at home and at school. All educators need to be skilled at communicating with parents. Other opportunities for parent involvement should be individualized to match the capabilities and interests of parents. In keeping with systems theory, the goal of parent involvement is to make adjustments in the home and with the family as a unit that will accommodate the child and make the system work more smoothly. Parents and teachers together should decide whether participation in activities such as parent groups will be both realistic and beneficial.

The Education System

The education system may be the second most important system in the lives of students with EBD because of the potential for impacting their daily lives. This section describes the difficulties in moving students from one educational placement to another. The education system can also be changed within individual classrooms.

An Educational Application: Reintegration. The ultimate goal for any program serving EBD students should be to ensure that individual students can function in the setting that is least restrictive for them. Thus, special education teachers must address the potential for each student's placement: If the setting is a hospital or residential school, perhaps the next step is to help the student function in a day school or self-contained classroom. If the setting is a self-contained classroom, the next step for students may be integration into a resource class or a general education class with consulting services. With the Highly Qualified Teacher requirements from the NCLB Act and related mandates to test the majority of special education students with grade-level academic achievement tests, ever more students with EBD are being reintegrated into general education settings. Any experienced special education teacher can attest that although these goals are worthwhile, they are not easily attained. Barriers to reintegration and some guidelines to aid the process are discussed in the next sections.

Barriers to Reintegration. Research over the years consistently shows that students with EBD are rated as the least accepted and the most negatively stereotyped of all exceptionalities (Haring, Stern, & Cruickshank, 1958; Kingsley, 1967; MacMillan, Gresham, & Forness, 1996; Parish, Dyck, & Kappes, 1979; Vaac & Kirst, 1977). Among the beliefs held by general education teachers were that they would be unable to manage students with EBD in their classrooms, and that these students would have a detrimental effect on their peers without disabilities.

These results are consistent with research on teacher attitudes toward consultation services. When teachers perceive that the problem lies within the child, they often want the child to be removed from the general education classroom rather than to be asked to make modifications or adjustments (i.e., change contextual variables). Resistance by teachers and administrators has been cited by experts as a major barrier to consultation services and successful reintegration of SPED students (Idol, 1997).

One study (Algozzine & Curran, 1979) showed that when teachers were asked to predict the school success of hypothetical EBD students in an inclusive setting, their responses varied as a function of their tolerance levels for behavior. The authors concluded that a "goodness of fit," the matching of teacher attitude to child behavior, could greatly influence the child's chances for success in that classroom.

Guidelines for Reintegration. Montgomery (1982) offered one set of guidelines for teachers whose goal is to reintegrate their students into a less restrictive setting. According to Montgomery, the program itself should be structured to foster student growth along four dimensions:

1. *From rigid to flexible scheduling:* As the student is able to handle independent learning situations, more free time is allowed and the schedule becomes more flexible.
2. *From external to internal control:* Initially, external reinforcers may be necessary; heavy supervision and planning are done for the student. Structure is lessened as the student displays appropriate behaviors.
3. *From short-term to long-term goals:* The student may initially be able to complete only short assignments or to work for very short periods of time. Extension of work periods to approximate those in general education classrooms and delay of rewards become program objectives.
4. *From segregation to integration:* Although the student may initially need the structure and control imposed in the segregated classroom, the long-term goal is to wean the student from dependency on external controls so he or she can function in integrated settings. Some school districts are attempting to ease the reintegration process through transition classes. These classes focus on independent behaviors and socialization skills that should facilitate a student's transition from a segregated class with a small teacher–pupil ratio to an integrated setting in which a student must be more independent.

Unfortunately, the NCLB Act and IDEA 2004 have often resulted in poorly planned and rapid reintegration, perhaps to the detriment of students (Kauffman et al., 2002; Mooney & Gunter, 2004).

Following the "goodness of fit" idea, special education teachers also can attempt to match student skills with the demands of the setting into which they are to be integrated, while keeping in mind the main goal may be to improve the students' mastery of academic curriculum. Most teachers are pleased to identify the crucial skills that are needed for success in their classrooms and discussions with the teacher can help to plan necessary supports for success.

Structured inventories with detailed questions about classroom rules and requirements for success have been published (Fuchs, Fernstrom, Scott, Fuchs, & Vandermeer, 1994; Welch, 1994). In addition, Walker and Rankin (1980) devised an assessment instrument for the specific purpose of facilitating inclusion for students with EBD. *Assessment for Integration into Mainstream Settings* (AIMS) was designed to help to identify (1) the skills required in the receiving setting, (2) maladaptive social skills that the receiving teacher finds unacceptable, and (3) technical assistance needed by the receiving teacher in order to teach and manage the child's behavior. Walker and his associates also developed a corresponding social skills curriculum, mentioned in Chapter 7, the *Walker Social Skills Curriculum: ACCESS and ACCEPTS programs* (Walker et al., 1983, 1988), aimed at teaching behaviors needed for functioning in integrated settings. Skills taught in the *Walker Social Skills Curriculum* are one of two types: those identified by teachers as critical to "successful classroom adjustment" or those that contribute to "social competence and peer acceptance."

A teacher of students with EBD may be employed in any one of the settings from a continuum of services and therefore will probably deal with the issue of helping students make the transition into a less restrictive setting. Planning for these transitions on both an individual basis and a programwide basis is essential to the success of the program. Sugai and Horner (2002) describe elements of classwide Positive Behavior Supports (PBS) to encourage all students to behave appropriately and progress academically. These same elements also can support students with EBD in less restrictive settings:

- Maximize instructional time (downtime is deadly in terms of behavior management)
- Arrangement of instructional time to emphasize successful academic engagement and student achievement
- Active supervision of all students (teacher proximity and mindfulness)
- High rates of positive teacher–student interactions
- Use of precorrection to prompt students to respond correctly before mistakes are made
- Clear classroom expectations and rules taught and practiced
- Positive reinforcement to promote meeting classroom expectations and rules
- Clear consistent scheduling and routines with time limits for all daily activities to provide structure and help students learn to manage time efficiently

Individual adaptations based on ecological assessments can also be made. In such classrooms, the teacher aims to create an atmosphere of acceptance and success rather than the expectation for failure that often surrounds the student with EBD. More detailed information about inclusion of students with EBD and Positive Behavior Supports will be provided in Chapter 12.

An Educational Application: Ecological School Program. Project Re-ED, first mentioned in Chapter 2, was founded in 1961 as a model program for students with EBD that is ecological in scope. The program was conceived by a number of theorists but headed by Nicholas Hobbs, who was motivated by disenchantment with psychiatric programs for children and adolescents Concerned with the high financial cost and lack of personnel to adequately staff such programs, Hobbs questioned the efficacy of the psychiatric approach:

> There is a real possibility that hospitals make children sick. The antiseptic atmosphere, the crepe sole and white coat, the tension, the expectancy of illness may confirm a child's worst fears about himself, firmly setting his aberrant behavior. (1966, p. 1105)

Hobbs opened Cumberland House in Nashville, Tennessee, and the Wright School in Durham, North Carolina, in the early 1960s. Several programs throughout the country operate according to Re-ED principles. Some are day programs or have day program components and some are short-term, residential programs based on the supposition that the most effective treatment is one that intervenes in all ecosystems. The goal, therefore, is not to fix the child and return her to the community, but to make the child's ecosystem fit together more smoothly. The targets for intervention include the child, the child's home, neighborhood, school, social agencies, and community (Fields, Farmer, Apperson, Mustillo, & Simmers, 2006; Hobbs, 1966).

Re-ED's treatment philosophy basically views children as capable of controlling and changing their own behavior to more adaptive ways. Trust in adults and competence in school and other life skills are viewed as the necessary bases from which changes can be made. The child's feelings are recognized and the youngster is taught to express both positive and negative feelings in socially acceptable ways.

Teacher-counselors implement school interventions. The teacher-counselor during the day functions much as a public school teacher in academics but performs the additional role of counseling and working to modify maladaptive behaviors. Education takes precedence over psychotherapy, as the ability to achieve academically is considered essential for making the child's school ecosystem work successfully. In residential programs the night teacher-counselor takes over after school hours and is primarily a support person who supervises group activities and extracurricular activities. Almost all activities are undertaken in small groups, which are considered an important source of both motivation and control.

Another important role in Re-ED programs is played by the liaison teacher-counselor who assesses the home, school, and community and helps them support or prepare for the return of the student. In the school, the liaison teacher-counselor collects extensive historical information such as past academic and behavioral records, successful and unsuccessful program modifications, relationships with various school personnel, and so forth. The goal is to plan cooperatively for a smooth reentry from a residential program or for supports during out-of-school time. The liaison teacher-counselor is also available as a consultant after reentry into less restrictive settings. Similar tasks are undertaken in the home and community. Parents are viewed as collaborators in effecting long-term change in their child's life. In residential programs, beginning with the child's weekend visits, the liaison teacher-counselor maintains close communication with parents and helps them plan changes that will aid the child's adaptation in the home and community. The liaison teacher-counselor also coordinates services with community agencies such as social service departments or mental health centers, which may be essential links to the child's support plan. Thus, the liaison teacher-counselor seeks to establish a supportive network in the child's major ecosystems that are conducive to healthy and adaptive functioning. Today, 16 agencies nationwide base their treatment programs on the Re-ED model (Fields et al., 2006).

Social Systems

Three major systems other than the family and education may affect the lives of students with emotional/behavioral disorders: social welfare, juvenile justice correctional, and mental health (see Figure 8.2). If teachers are to take a systems approach to programming, they should know something about how these systems work.

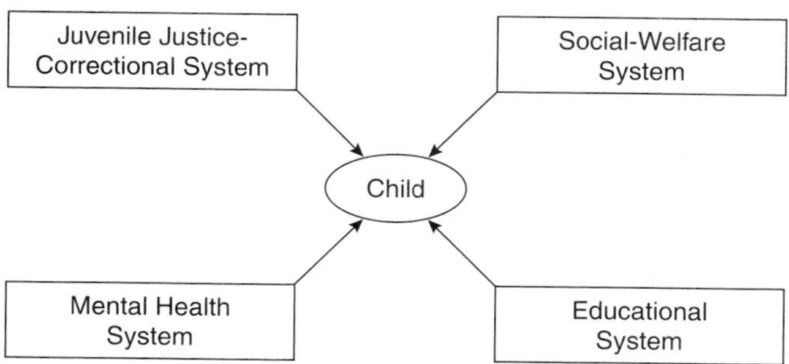

FIGURE 8.2 Systems Affecting Students with Emotional/ Behavior Disorders

Adapted with permission from *Troubled Children/Troubled Systems* by Stephen J. Apter. Copyright 1982, Pergamon Press.

Social-Welfare System. A variety of social services are provided to eligible families, including health services, family planning, housing services, emergency aid, and protective services for minors. Children may come to the attention of the social-welfare system due to abuse or neglect, parental substance abuse, unmet mental health needs, and domestic violence (CDF, 2006). Services are delivered primarily through caseworkers who decide eligibility and devise service plans for families. Children are rarely direct recipients of social services unless it is protective services that may result in legal removal from the home and placement into foster care. Each year about 800,000 children are served in foster care and children of color enter foster care at a higher rate than white children even when controlled for family variables (CDF, 2006).

Social caseworkers are more likely to be interested in a child's school functioning if abuse or neglect is suspected or if parental custody is in question. Because the teacher is in the position to observe on a daily basis, the teacher may be asked to make judgments about the child's general emotional state or physical welfare. Also, in most states teachers are required by law to report suspected abuse to child protective services. Alarming rates of child injury and death due to family violence should serve as the impetus for complying with such laws. Although no reliable statistics are currently available on the percentage of youngsters with EBD who have been physically or sexually abused, it is common for therapists to uncover instances of abuse with their clients who have been brought to therapy for other presenting problems. Children in the juvenile justice system and poor children are more likely to have been or are victims of abuse and neglect (CDF, 2006). Concerns about physically abused children relative to a systems perspective are discussed in Box 8.3.

Teachers and caseworkers together can gain a clearer picture of the child's total environment and be better equipped to plan interventions. Although their duties vary, many caseworkers coordinate all social services received by a family; therefore the caseworker generally has a network among other agencies that can be valuable when searching for resources to provide additional services to a child or adolescent. Teachers should not be reluctant to contact caseworkers to help find pertinent community resources and discuss effective school supports.

BOX 8.3

Child Abuse: Whose Responsibility?

We have all had the experience of reading about specific instances of child abuse that have occurred in our communities; some of us also have either read about or known children who died as a result of abuse. When these deaths occur, the media really gets interested: What were the circumstances? What was the psychological profile of the person who killed the child? How many times had this person abused the child before? Had it ever been reported to child protective services? Why wasn't the child removed from the home? etc.

Unfortunately, we know the answers to these questions because they are identical for so many cases in which children are routinely or severely abused. For instance, we know that many abusers were themselves abused as kids, that they tend to be immature and not prepared for the responsibility of taking care of children, that they suffer from frequent personal crises, and may use drugs or alcohol. We know that abusers tend to repeat the abuse when stressed. We know that in many cases, suspicion of child abuse was reported to the authorities who may have investigated but not found just cause to remove the child from the home. (Although parents are the most frequent child abusers, relatives and the parent's friends and lovers also abuse.) In many instances, child protective workers are so overworked that they can investigate only those reports in which the child's life is reported to be endangered.

When children die from repeated abuse, it is easy to point a finger—at the killer, at child protective services, at society, at the "system" that can allow such a thing to happen. We have discussed a systems orientation in this chapter. An important facet of a systems orientation is not allowing children to "fall through the cracks" because we think it is someone else's responsibility. How much responsibility beyond reporting it can teachers take when they suspect child abuse? What can teachers do about suspected sexual abuse, neglect, and emotional abuse? Whose responsibility is it?

Juvenile Justice/Correctional System. For about 10 years beginning in the early 1990s, an alarming trend of increasingly violent crimes being committed by increasingly younger children swept the nation, leaving few communities immune. Even small towns, once considered refuges from "big-city" crimes, were shocked by episodes of children killing other children and school shootings. It has been theorized that youth today are (1) more likely to respond with rage reactions when violated or victimized, (2) have a lower anger flashpoint, and (3) feel an obligation to retaliate for perceived wrongs (Walker, Ramsey, & Gresham, 2004). However, with zero-tolerance policies passed by schools and general attention to homeland security since the terrorist attacks on September 11, 2001, the number of violent offenses committed by youth began to decrease (e.g., Texas Juvenile Probation Commission, 2005). Nevertheless, in Texas, the total number of delinquent offenses rose 2.6 percent from 2002–2003, with 107,338 referrals. Figure 8.3 illustrates the frequency of all crimes committed by juveniles in Texas during the course of 1 year.

Analysis of juvenile referrals suggests that the continual delinquency rate may be directly related to two factors: growth in gang-related crimes and increased substance abuse–related crimes. We will return to the important issues of gangs and substance abuse in Chapter 11 and to school violence in Chapter 12. The Children's Defense Fund (2006) reports that each day in America, 4,356 children are arrested, 181 for violent crimes and 380 for drug abuse.

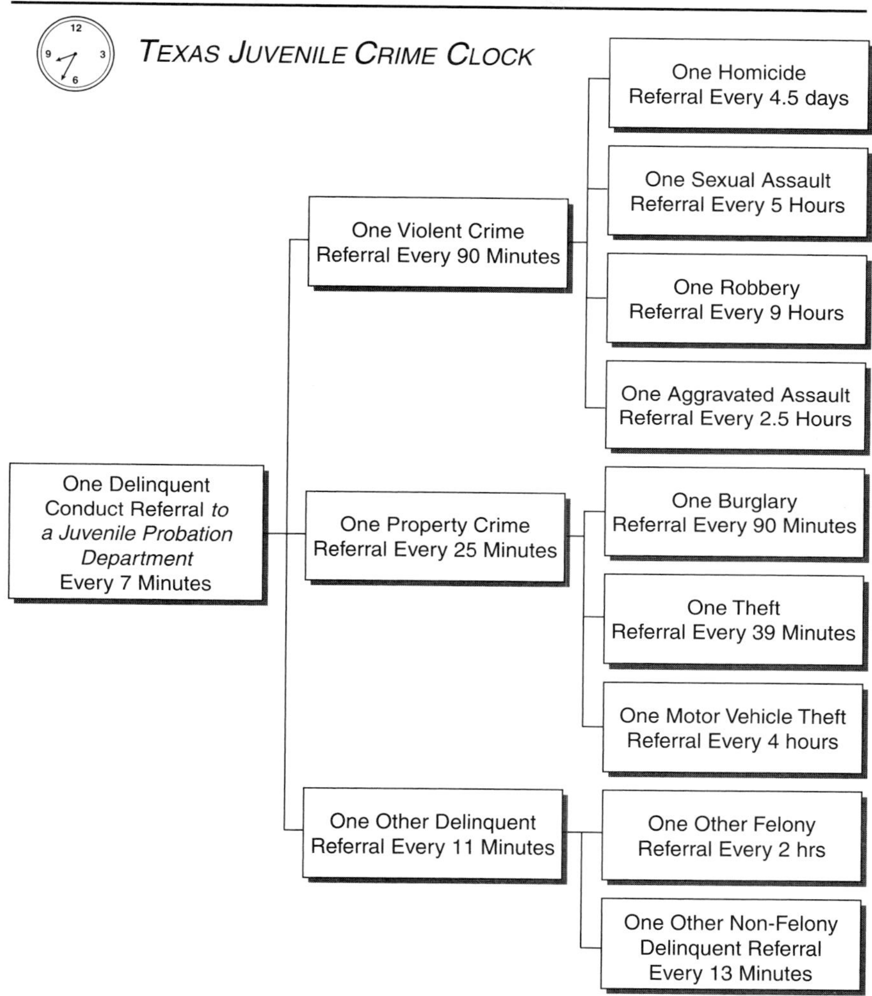

FIGURE 8.3 Frequency of Juvenile Crimes in Texas

From Texas Juvenile Probation Commission. The State of Juvenile Probation Activity in Texas, Calendar Year 2003, Austin, TX.

Many youth with EBD have histories of arrests or other incidences of lawbreaking. Wagner et al. (2003) reported that 35 percent of youth with EBD had been arrested, as compared with 13 percent of students without disabilities. The police and the courts have discretionary powers that allow great latitude in dealing with juvenile offenders. Before making a court referral, police can use a number of alternatives, such as verbal warnings with release to parent custody, referral to a social agency, or temporary custody at the police station. When a juvenile is taken to court for an offense, the judge may let him off with a warning, give him probation, or assign him to a restricted setting such as a group home, halfway house, detention center, or correctional facility. For example, in 2003 in Texas, 107,338 juveniles ages 10–17 who were arrested for offenses were handled in the following ways: 73 percent were counseled, cautioned, deferred, or dismissed by juvenile probation authorities; 25 percent were assigned to probation or modified probation by the court; 2.3 percent were committed to the correctional system; and 0.1% were certified to the adult court (Texas Juvenile Probation Commission, 2005). Thus, by the time a juvenile offender is assigned to probation or a correctional facility, he or she has usually been arrested and/or taken to juvenile court several times.

Depending on the severity and chronicity of their offenses, many juvenile offenders are still placed in detention centers (short term) or youth correctional facilities (long term). As in adult correctional facilities, the alleged goal of these juvenile treatment centers is rehabilitation of the individual for a productive life in the mainstream of society. Unfortunately, institutionalized youth often become more antisocial during their incarceration, resulting in low rates of rehabilitation and reincarceration (Bullis, Yovanoff, Mueller, & Havel, 2002). These authors found that about 40 percent of juvenile offenders returned to a correctional setting within 12 months of release and that juvenile offenders with disabilities were 2.8 times more likely to do so than their counterparts without disabilities. Recognizing the ineffectiveness of incarceration as a rehabilitative experience, many correctional programs are offering alternatives such as group homes, juvenile boot camps, and intensive supervision programs marked by close surveillance, home detention, and electronic monitoring.

The public education system is usually responsible for youth placed in community-based programs. The teacher often will need to work with parents, house-parents, or probation officers on matters of school attendance and other conditions of probation. The correctional system is responsible for the education of juveniles placed in institutional settings. For juvenile offenders who are identified as disabled, state education agencies are legally responsible for monitoring the quality of education and ensuring that the safeguards of federal law are met. However, in many states, educational programs within correctional facilities are the responsibility of corrections, mental health, or human service agencies other than education (Drakeford & Staples, 2006; Rutherford & Nelson, 1995; Walker et al., 2004). Teachers should be aware of the potential clash between the custodial and educational functions of the correctional system, which may exacerbate the difficulties in ensuring delivery of quality education for the offender with disabilities.

A comprehensive database detailing the state of the art for special education in juvenile corrections has not been established, although it is estimated that between 40 and 70 percent of incarcerated youth manifest some type of disability or mental health disorder (Unruh & Bullis, 2005; Wolford, 2000). Still pertinent, a study by Rutherford et al. (1986) cited several problems based on a survey of 15 state directors of correctional education. There was considerable variability among states in the numbers of certified special education teachers employed, and a shortage of certified teachers relative to the population with disabilities. Also cited were a lack of special education assessment procedures and lack of functional skills curricula. Three special education program prototypes were reported: self-contained, resource, and inclusion with general correctional education.

In 2005, the National Association of State Directors of Special Education and the National Association of Protection and Advocacy Systems organized an effort to develop a

BOX 8.4

The Independent Living Program: Assistance for Youth Needing Homes

In Washington D.C., the Center on Juvenile and Criminal Justice (CJCJ) determined that there was a great need for alternative placements for homeless youth and those from dysfunctional or unsafe home environments. The Independent Living Program (ILP) was opened in 1999 for youth diverted from or returning from residential detention because they had no supportive home environment. CJCJ can house up to 15 young adults age 17–21 in furnished apartments. The program gives them the necessary skills for independent living.

In addition to housing, the youth receive a weekly allowance and 24-hour monitoring and support. The residents in conjunction with staff develop their own individualized "life plan" that involves accessing the particular support services that they need. The ILP maintains a network of education services, substance abuse counseling, vocational training, mental health counseling, and other community-based services. Case managers carry small caseloads so they can monitor youth as they become more self-sufficient and independent.

While progressing through their life plans, residents attend weekly life skills seminars, each hosting several in their own apartments. These weekly classes are taught by outside facilitators targeting basic living skills, such as budgeting and banking, nutrition, food preparation, personal hygiene, and housekeeping techniques. Since 1999, the Independent Living Program has helped many young people formerly at-risk to become successfully independent and self-reliant.

Adapted from Center on Juvenile and Criminal Justice, 1234 Massachusetts Avenue, NW, Suite C1009, Washington, DC, 2005 website. Retrieved from *http://www.cjcj.org/* September 29, 2006.

---

national agenda to address the problem of youth with disabilities and serious mental health problems in the juvenile justice system, sometimes called the "default system" because other systems had failed to address the children's needs (Nelson, 2005). The basis for this agenda was to be a systems approach to providing effective community planning and cross-agency services to address the problem. One model program utilizing a systems approach to educating and rehabilitating delinquent youth is described in Box 8.4.

Mental Health System. It is a certainty that teachers of students with emotional/behavioral disorders will at some time come in contact with members of the mental health system. Psychologists or psychiatrists are usually responsible for diagnosing emotional/behavioral disorders; they may subsequently see students in individual or group therapy. In many states, social workers also are licensed therapists, as are licensed professional counselors (LPCs). Some school systems contract with therapists in private practice for such services, while others depend on the personnel in their local mental health centers for these services. The centers are usually staffed by psychologists, psychiatrists, social workers, and LPCs, who may vary widely in background, training, and theoretical orientation. Outpatient services also vary but usually include diagnostic services, psychotherapy or counseling, medication, group therapy, and consultation to parents and local school systems. Many centers have outreach programs aimed at promoting mental health and preventing alcohol and drug abuse. Mental health agencies are increasingly turning to schools as the site of services delivery, especially support groups and substance abuse prevention groups. Depending on local resources, inpatient services may be provided in hospitals, halfway houses, or other residential settings.

Two mental health interventions for children and youth with EBD that have been popular over the years are hopitalization or placement in residential facilities and use of medication. Based on the recommendation of child specialists, youngsters with EBD may still be placed in psychiatric hospital or residential settings or prescribed psychotropic medication. As Hobbs (1982) pointed out, these practices are contrary to a systems orientation because each isolates the child as the sole focal point of intervention.

> Often wisdom lies simply in not doing something that may impede the restoration of the ecosystem, such as institutionalizing the child or prescribing tranquilizing drugs. Both of these acts create abnormal situations; they cut off or distort feedback of information needed to modify or redirect behavior, and thereby impair an essential component of the regulatory process in all living systems. From an ecological perspective, the widespread practice of sending disturbed children out of a state for treatment elsewhere makes no sense at all. This convenient but expensive practice makes it impossible to build a sustaining ecosystem for the child and thus impedes a return to normal patterns of development. (p. 186)

Of course, there are exceptions such as suicidal, violent, or other maladaptive behavior that indicate an urgent need for drastic measures such as hospitalization or medication. However, the conventional wisdom has changed in favor of keeping children in the home environment and local community whenever possible by providing the family and schools with sufficient support and resources needed to maintain the child at home (Pumariega & Winters, 2003). Backed by federal legislation and public health funding, family preservation programs are available, but not limited, to children with emotional difficulties. Services falling under family preservation include developmental screening, information and referral, improvement of parenting skills, family therapy, case management services, parent support groups, drop-in centers, and emergency and routine respite care. Family preservation programs established the basis for comprehensive service delivery involving all social systems.

Systems Changes

A number of obstacles inherent in the education, social, juvenile justice, and mental health systems have traditionally impeded services delivery to children and youth with EBD.

- Services not tailored to the needs of individual clients
- Poor working relationships among agencies
- Decision makers who do not perceive the need for services
- Lack of appropriate planning for services
- Prohibitive cost of mental health services
- Inability to reach potential clients
- Political and social resistance to change
- Medical model that focuses on pathology rather than preventative services
- Lack of clear definition of mental health

- Services that dehumanize and frustrate clients
- Lack of interagency coordination
- Vague policies regarding target populations
- Blaming others. (Apter, 1982; National Mental Health & SPED Coalition, 1989; Stroul & Friedman, 1986)

In order to improve services, the various systems needed to change the way they did business. In the mid-1980s, changes were initiated on behalf of those children and youth with the most severe EBD.

Systems of Care: The Child and Adolescent Service System Program (CASSP). The need for systems changes, that is, changes in the ways in which services are conceptualized and delivered, garnered national attention. In 1984, the National Institute of Mental Health (NIMH) funded a technical assistance program, the Child and Adolescent Service System Program (CASSP), to guide the work of states and communities trying to effect systems change in mental health services for children (Kutash, Duchnowski, & Friedman, 2005; Stroul, 1993). The CASSP model was based on a set of principles for planning and delivering a system of care to children with EBD and their families:

- The system of care must be child centered and family driven
- Services should be community based and linked among agencies
- Real interagency coordination and cooperation are essential
- Services must be culturally sensitive and individualized
- The youngsters with the most severe disorders must be served by the system
- A balance of least restrictive to most restrictive options should be maintained
- Advocacy and case management should be promoted and provided

In addition, CASSP guiding principles promote early identification and prevention services and an emphasis on transition to adult service systems. Through modest state development grants, CASSP initially aided in systems changes by attacking the very obstacles just outlined. Subsequently, private foundations such as the Robert Wood Johnson Foundation joined the federal government in promoting community-based children's mental health programs. In a 20-year follow-up, Kutash and her colleagues (2005) conclude that the system of care based on the CASSP model is a viable program model for children's mental health. Furthermore, the 1999 Surgeon General's Report (DHHS) agreed that "The multiple problems associated with 'serious emotional disturbance" in children and adolescents are best addressed with a 'systems' approach in which multiple service sectors work in an organized collective way" (p. 193). Figure 8.4 illustrates the child-centered, multisystems CASSP approach to supporting children and adolescents with EBD and their families.

One of the more challenging changes needed for the various systems was a more effective use of resources. One-to-one treatment programs reach only a small segment of the population and are not cost-effective. There could never be enough trained specialists in any of the systems to deal on an individual basis with the social, legal, and mental health problems existing in our society. Some school systems and mental health systems

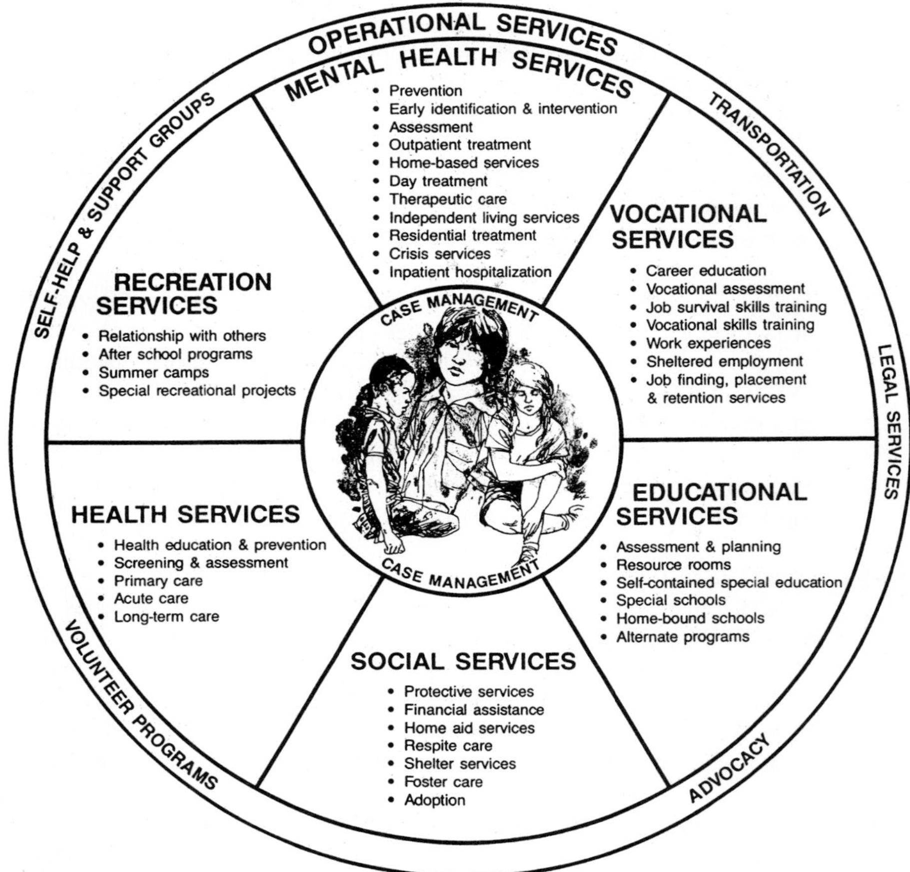

FIGURE 8.4 Dimensions of the CASSP Model

From *Invisible Children Project: Final Report and Recommendations of the Invisible Children Project,* prepared by Chris Zeigler-Dendy, 1989, Alexandria, VA: National Mental Health Association. Copyright National Mental Health Association. Reprinted with permission.

attempted to combat this problem by shifting to a consultation model in which trained personnel give direct services to a mediating person (such as a teacher or counselor) who can then use the acquired skills with a number of others. The purpose of the consultation model is to build a broader base of expertise within the system.

The Wraparound Model. A consultation model, which was based on wrapping services around children in need, particularly those with EBD, and their families, has been implemented in many states and communities in conjunction with the CAASP principles (Eber,

1996; Eber & Nelson, 1997; Eber, Nelson, & Miles, 1997). Wraparound planning and programming often provide school-based services, and result in unique and flexible child and family service plans encompassing multiagency, multilevel supports (Eber & Nelson, 1997; Stroul, 1993; VanDenBerg & Grealish, 1996). Training, technical assistance, and research are components of most wraparound models.

The wraparound model is an approach, rather than a program, and assumes an attitude of creativity toward blending services (Eber et al., 1997). This systems approach to treatment produces plans that encompass far more than the school day and considers several life domains (e.g., safety, legal problems, cultural differences, living arrangements, family factors, social contacts, emotional and behavioral problems, financial concerns, and transportation). The treatment plans often include nontraditional supports, such as community mentors, respite providers, and parent partners (Eber & Nelson, 1997). As with most special education services, this multiagency treatment approach is driven by child and family needs, rather than what services are easily available. The IEP may be one component of such a treatment plan.

The wraparound process includes teachers as primary stakeholders (Eber et al., 1997) who often benefit from the intensive supports and services. School-based goals should target improved academic and behavioral functioning, and the teacher's role should consist of communicating student strengths and needs, regularly communicating with team members prior to meetings, and productively participating with team members in planning meetings (Eber et al., 1997). Furthermore, all teachers should engage in regular screening procedures to identify children at risk for EBD and should include curriculum aimed at preventing emotional and behavioral problems (Dwyer, 1999). Most special and general education teachers will require technical assistance and training in order to become effective participants in wraparound programs.

Typically, mental health agencies take the lead in wraparound planning; however, educators are key players. The advantage of participating in this systems process is access to well-trained personnel and support services, with the result of more holistic, integrated services. Many believe that, because schools have daily access to children and youth with problems, most services should be delivered in and around the school—one-stop shopping (Eber, 1996; McLaughlin et al., 1994). However, school personnel need to be willing to change the way services are organized and delivered during school hours. In such a scenario, parents could access childcare and welfare benefits in school-based offices, students could access probation officers and mental health counselors, and the entire family could access health services. Transportation would cease to be a barrier to obtaining services, and coordination would be improved. By adopting a wraparound model, school districts can make inroads toward changing the system to better accommodate not only students with EBD, but also students with other special needs.

The wraparound model appears to address those factors that have historically contributed to social system failures for children with emotional and behavioral disorders (Duchnowski, Kutash, & Friedman, 2002; Knitzer et al., 1989; Kutash et al., 2005; Saxe, Cross, & Silverman, 1988) and seems to have effected positive outcomes such as increased access to services, more interagency collaboration, increased satisfaction by families regarding services, reductions in restrictive psychiatric placements, and reduction in costs (Clarke & Clarke, 1996; Eber & Nelson, 1997; Kutash et al., 2005; Louri, 1994). Unfortunately, definitive studies showing the wraparound model's superiority to traditional mental health models in terms of clinical outcomes for young people with EBD are still lacking, and mental health service delivery to children is still in need of improvement (DHHS, 1999).

Teacher as Part of a Social System. As an important part of a wraparound model or a system of care model, the education system and teachers in particular have key roles to play. Woodruff et al. (1999) offer several suggestions for school-based systems of care to ensure a successful and learning-focused system:

- Build support and maintain flexibility
- Build on opportunities strategically
- Have a system of coordinated leadership
- Provide continuity of school-based staff
- Involve and empower families
- Provide prevention and intervention programs
- Offer nontraditional learning environment
- Ensure institutionalization of the program (p. 84)

For teachers, Nelson (1983) and Eber et al. (1997) articulated a number of suggestions to ensure effective collaboration outside of the school itself. Students will benefit most when their teacher creates a perception of credibility and stays involved with other systems partners.

1. *Be aware of political realities.* Although it is natural for dedicated teachers to assume that they are primarily responsible for their students' salvation, this view is not generally held by human service agencies. Credibility must be established through helping these systems attain their goals and refraining from designing interventions that may conflict with those of other agencies.
2. *Practice underdogmanship:* Give credit to others even when you have been instrumental in a student's success. For example, credit the probation officer even if you devised a successful plan to decrease shoplifting.
3. *Avoid language barriers:* All human service systems are full of technical language and acronyms that serve as a type of shorthand within the system but are alienating to professionals outside the system. For example, practice not saying "IEP" or using the term *task analysis* when talking to other professionals outside education.
4. *Take the responsibility to initiate and maintain contact with other agencies:* Don't wait for others to contact you and inform you about what's happening with your students. Be persistent in maintaining contact and don't mistake others' lack of initiative as indifference. The caseloads of social workers, child protective caseworkers, probation and parole officers, and publicly funded mental health workers often approach the impossible.
5. *Clarify the roles and responsibilities of various agencies in writing:* Have a multiagency committee devise an individualized, written plan outlining what services are to be provided to the student, who is responsible for following through, and timelines.

In summary, if mental health services for children and youth with EBD are to improve and be effective, a systems approach is clearly needed. This approach should be one that views (1) emotional/behavioral disorders as the shared responsibility of child–environment and (2) treatment as the shared responsibility of a number of different systems offering a continuum of coordinated services. These agencies or systems include education, mental health, social services, and juvenile justice. Models for establishing such a systems approach have been developed and fairly well evaluated over the past 20 years. The U.S. Department of Health and Human Services (2001), in response to a call for more effective and comprehensive children's mental health services, put forth the following vision:

> Mental health is a critical component of children's learning and general health. Fostering social and emotional health in children as a part of healthy child development must therefore be a national priority. Both the promotion of mental health in children and the treatment of mental disorders should be major public health goals. To achieve these goals, the Surgeon General's National Action Agenda for Children's Mental Health takes as its guiding principles a commitment to:
>
> 1. Promoting the recognition of mental health as an essential part of child health;
> 2. Integrating family, child and youth-centered mental health services into all systems that serve children and youth;
> 3. Engaging families and incorporating the perspectives of children and youth in the development of all mental healthcare planning; and
> 4. Developing and enhancing a public–private health infrastructure to support these efforts to the fullest extent possible. (p. 4).

We will return to these issues and the ecological/systems approach, with regard to treatment of youth violence, in Chapter 12.

Summary

Ecological theorists believe that it is impossible to define disordered behavior in isolation from the contexts in which the behavior occurs. Disordered behavior is viewed as a disturbance in the equilibrium of a system; therefore, the child is viewed as a part of the problem rather than the owner of the problem. In theory, all components of the disturbed system should be analyzed for contributing factors and then targeted for intervention along with the child. In practice, analyzing and intervening in disturbed systems is difficult, time-consuming, and difficult to evaluate. A systems approach to serving this population has been touted by the National Mental Health and Special Education Coalition, the Center for Effective Collaboration and Practice, and the U.S. Department of Health and Human Services, which have called for effective interagency cooperation and a true continuum of services that includes family support. The ecological model is summarized in Table 8.2. Box 8.5 provides three case studies of students with EBD. Read these case studies and answer the questions provided in the box pertaining to an ecological/systems model of treatment.

TABLE 8.2 Summary of the Ecological/Systems Model

Etiology	Evaluation Procedures	Educational Applications
Disturbances in the ecosystems of: Home School Community Society	*Analysis of Classroom Instructional Demands* (West, 1990) *The Behavior and Emotional Rating Scale* (BERS) (Epstein & Sharma, 1998) *Behavior Rating Profile-2* (Brown & Hammill, 1990) *The Behavior Assessment System for Children* (BASC-2) (Reynolds & Camphaus, 2004) *The Achenbach System of Empirically-Based Assessment* (ASEBA) (Achenbach & Rescorla, 2001) *The Instructional Environment Scale* (Ysseldyke & Christenson, 1987) Functional behavioral assessment (FBA)	Parent involvement, support, and training groups Reintegration & Transition Programming Project Re-Ed CASSP model Wraparound & Systems of Care services

BOX 8.5

Case Studies

Lance

Lance is a ninth grader, for the third year. While he is currently in a self-contained classroom for students with EBD, he has made no measurable progress behaviorally or academically. Since eighth grade, Lance has spent a large part of each school year at the school district Alternative Learning Center for drug offenses or persistent misbehavior. His behavior is consistently inappropriate across all settings and all teachers.

Lance seems to detest school. He seldom attends and when he does come to school, he usually walks out by lunchtime. He is easily frustrated with his academic tasks, even though he is capable of the work. Lance will begin an assignment, make one error, and rip the rest of it to shreds. To date, no reinforcer, level system, point sheet, or other behavior-modification system has been found to be successful in reducing his behaviors, which include walking out of class at will, profane language, sexually inappropriate comments, and destroying property belonging to his teachers and classmates. He has been physically aggressive toward peers and staff, assaulting a student with "brass knuckles" and kicking the school police officer in the groin.

Lance's family appears to enable his negative behavior. At a removal hearing, his adult brother claimed that the marijuana found on Lance belonged to him, not Lance. At this same meeting, the father said that the teaching assistant had lied when she reported to have witnessed Lance exchanging a baggie of marijuana. The mother, who works in the school district, forged a document referring him for a homebound teacher.

Lance is a difficult student to enjoy. Teachers report that they are almost relieved when he is not in attendance. He requires so much teacher attention that other students are often ignored. He has not appeared to form a bond with any teachers or students. He encourages others to misbehave or leave campus with him so other parents have complained about their child's association with him.

Lance's sporadic attendance and confused family life create great hurdles in establishing consistency and effective programming.

Steve

Steve, with a street name of Zenor, has a serious conduct disorder. He uses his large size, over 400 pounds, to intimidate other students and even his teachers. He wears gang insignia as a member of a well-known street gang. Steve has an educational classification as a student with an emotional disturbance, however, because of his gang involvement, an independent evaluation was done to attempt to rule out ED and dismiss him from special education services.

Steve "bullies" his peers. He takes their belongings including things he does not even really want. He grabs backpacks and goes through them, tossing unwanted items into the trash. While other students certainly do not enjoy this invasion, they do not overtly say so. They retrieve their discarded items without much comment, and seldom report such incidents. Steve threatens to physically harm them if they report him.

Steve spends his class time disturbing others with his loud voice, poking fun at students, and heckling the teacher. He rarely completes assignments, even though he is capable of the work. He prefers the role of class clown. He teases others, yet dislikes any insult directed at him.

Steve's teacher has noticed that at times, he was attempting to be playful. His efforts are often so immature that he seems more like an upper elementary student rather than a high school freshman. His teacher attempted to capitalize on his sense of humor by allowing him to tell a joke to the class. However, he turned these events into a forum for telling inappropriate and crude stories. Steve was recently sent to the school district Alternative Learning Center for writing gang-related graffiti on the walls and lockers.

Bobby

Bobby is in a general education fourth-grade class. However, his behaviors are very different from his peers. He resides with his paternal grandparents, as both parents are currently incarcerated. His grandmother reports that she has to physically carry and force him into the car to bring him to school. Once at the school she pulls him, crying, from the back seat while a school monitor assists her efforts. While the grandmother drives away, Bobby stands yelling for her to come back. The monitor walks Bobby to his classroom and then gets his breakfast tray. The monitor used to walk Bobby to the cafeteria; however, at the cafeteria doors he would turn and run away.

When breakfast is delivered, Bobby will take the tray and go sit on the floor in a corner of the room facing the wall, eating in silence, occasionally rocking his body back and forth. When the bell rings signaling the beginning of class, Bobby has to be physically escorted to his desk. He sinks to the floor beside his desk and crawls underneath, his head in his hands, sobbing. He picks at any sore on his body and has chewed his fingernails to the quick. He pulls at his hair and pokes his fingers into his eyes.

About 10:00 AM, Bobby will emerge from the sanctuary beneath his desk and return to his seat. He keeps his head down on his desk and seldom looks around. Bobby has passed both vision and hearing tests, and intellectual testing places Bobby in the below-average IQ range. His academic work is sloppy and carelessly attempted. After lunch, which is served to him in the office, Bobby repeats his morning routine, going back under his desk and emerging about an hour before dismissal. Although he is happy to be going home, no one remembers him smiling.

Read each of these case studies and discuss these students' problems from an ecological/systems perspective. Which systems need addressing? How might a wraparound or systems of care model work to improve these students' outcomes? Which other systems, in addition to education, might you involve? What services might they be able to provide? What would be the challenges to accessing these services?

Information contributed by Glenna Billingsley, a high school teacher of students with emotional and behavioral disorders in Austin, Texas.

Conclusions

Viewing disordered behavior from an ecological perspective takes some of the pressure off the children to do all the changing. Although ecological interventions may be difficult to effect and evaluate, the philosophy underlying this model is an essential one for teachers: only when we truly believe in a systems approach to working with children with EBD and their families will we begin to make inroads in their treatment.

An ecological/systems approach to intervention requires changes in students' homes and in their communities. Although working with parents of students with EBD may not be easy, it is important that teachers work with parents whenever possible by offering several alternatives for involvement. Also, many of these students have multiple problems that necessitate the involvement of several community systems. Professionals from all systems have recognized the futility of providing fragmented services and have been very vocal about providing a community-based continuum of services that is coordinated by case managers. Systems of care and wrap-around programs based on a child-/family-driven and multiagency service delivery model have been operating for 20 years with promising results. To operate effectively within systems, teachers must be aware of political realities, both within the school and relative to other community agencies.

KEY POINTS

1. Ecological theorists believe that deviance results from the interactions of an individual with others in the environment; hence, ecosystems rather than individuals are viewed as disturbed or disordered.
2. If ecosystems are disturbed, then we must assess and intervene in the various systems in which students live and interact: school, home, community, and social systems.
3. Although systems changes are difficult to effect, many professionals now agree that we must provide and coordinate a variety of community-based services to students and their families if we are to truly make changes in their lives.
4. A systems approach to working with families assumes that the child with EBD is a symptom of difficulties with the family system that can best be rectified through working with all family members as a unit.
5. Within the education system, reintegration of students from more restrictive to less restrictive settings is fraught with difficulties.
6. CASSP spawned child-/family-driven, multiagency systems approaches for children's mental health services in the 1980s. There is general agreement that these approaches hold the most promise for improving children's mental health services.
7. The ability to work with professionals from other community systems is an important skill for teachers of students with EBD.
8. Effective special education teachers recognize their place in the mini social system of the school and are able to create their own bridges to other people and resources within the system.
9. Treatment for children and youth with EBD across systems is still inadequate and lacking in availability, quality, and coordination, thus it remains a national priority.

HOMEWORK QUESTIONS

1. Read one of the case studies in Box 8.5 and describe at least one cognitive, behavioral, psychodynamic, and ecological intervention that you might recommend for the student.
2. In no more than two pages discuss why you think the ecological/systems model is preferred for students with EBD. Why do you think it might be the most difficult model to implement?
3. Locate websites in your state for mental health services for children, juvenile justice programs, social services, and vocational services. Browse these websites and report about your findings (e.g., interesting statistical information, program descriptions, eligibility requirements).
4. Interview someone who works for a community agency that serves children and/or youth with emotional and behavioral disorders. Create an interview form with no more than 10 questions that will provide you with enough information to discuss the agency's services in a school team meeting.
5. Visit the Children's Defense Fund website and review statistics about children and youth in America. In no more than three paragraphs, relate that information to possible causes of emotional and behavioral disorders in children from an ecological/systems perspective.
6. With no more than one single spaced page, each, list as many issues as you can produce regarding: (1) mental health services for children and youth, (2) the juvenile justice system, (3) educational services for students with EBD, (4) multiagency service coordination (one topic per page).
7. Why would Bronfenbrenner rename his theory a bioecological theory? Discuss in no more than two paragraphs.

ADDITIONAL READINGS AND RESOURCES

Report of the Surgeon General's Conference on Children's Mental Health: A National Action Agenda, U. S. Department of Health and Human Services, 2001, for recommendations about what we should be doing to provide needed mental health services to our children.

School Mental Health Services in the United States, 2002–2003, U.S. Department of Health and Human Services, for a first-ever survey of mental health services in the approximately 83,000 public schools and their associated school districts.

Blueprint for change: Research on child and adolescent mental health, 2001, National Institutes of Health, for the National Advisory Mental Health Council's Workgroup on Child and Adolescent Mental Health Intervention Development and Deployment Report outlining recommendations for future research in the field.

Claiming Children, the newsletter of the Federation of Families for Children's Mental Health, Alexandria, VA, for articles pertaining to family participation and support in a System of Care.

Collaboration basics: A companion guide, by Deborah Stark, National Technical Assistance Center for Children's Mental Health, Georgetown University, Washington, DC, 1999, for a description of six communities engaged in collaborative efforts among families, child welfare, and children's mental health agencies.

The School Connectedness—Improving Students' Lives monograph, at the Johns Hopkins Bloomberg School of Public Health, 2006, for a monograph highlighting the best and promising practices for schools in terms of successful approaches for improving "school connectedness"— the belief by students that they are a valued and integral part of their school.

Doing things differently: Issues and options for creating school linked services for children and youth with emotional and behavioral disorders, by Margaret McLaughlin, Peter Leone, Sandra Warren, and Patricia Schofield, Center for Policy Options in Special Education, University of Maryland, College Park, 1994, for an overview of the components of a school-based system of care model.

Effective behavior support: A systems approach to proactive schoolwide management, by Tim Lewis and George Sugai, *Focus on Exceptional Children, 31*(6), 1999, 1–24, and *Effective school consultation: An interactive approach,* by George Sugai and G. Tindal, Pacfic Grove, CA: Brooks-Cole, 1993, for a schoolwide systems view of management and treatment of students with EBD.

Focal point: A national bulletin on family support and children's mental health, Research and Training Center on Family Support and Children's Mental Health and the Center for Effective Collaboration and Practice, Portland State University, for a publication pertaining to mental health and school-linked services for children and youth with emotional and behavioral disorders.

Helping disturbed children: Psychological and ecological strategies, by Nicholas Hobbs, *American Psychologist, 2,* 1966, 1105–1115, for a classic introduction to Project Re-ED.

Special education in juvenile corrections, by Peter Leone, Rob Rutherford, and Mike Nelson, Reston, VA: Council for Exceptional Children, 1991, for a summary of the challenges of providing educational services to youth with disabilities in correctional facilities.

Integrating services for children and youth with emotional and behavioral disorders, by C. Michael Nelson and Cheryl Pearson, Reston, VA: Council for Exceptional Children, 1991, for a handbook describing some of the issues (and solutions) to interagency programming for students with EBD.

Kids of survival: Real-life lessons in resilience, *Reaching Today's Youth: The Community Circle of Caring Journal, 2*(3), 1998, for articles relating to building children's resilience from an ecological perspective.

Macro-social validation: Referencing outcomes in behavioral disorders to societal issues and problems, by Hill Walker and his colleagues, *Behavioral Disorders, 24*(1), 1998, 7–18; and The present unwrapped: Change and challenge in the field of behavioral disorders, by Hill Walker and his colleagues, *Behavioral Disorders, 24*(4), 1999, 293–304, for an ecological systems view of the field of special education and behavior disorders specifically.

School violence intervention: A practical handbook, edited by Arnold Goldstein and Jane Close Conoley, New York: Guilford Press, 1997, for an ecological approach to addressing school violence.

Outcomes for children and youth with emotional and behavioral disorders and their families: Programs and evaluation best practices (2nd ed.), by Mike Epstein, Krista Kutash, and Albert Duchnowski, Austin, TX: Pro-Ed, 2005, for a series of articles summarizing and evaluating the effects of systems of care over the past 20 years.

Handbook of school mental health: Advancing practice and research, by M. Weist, S. W. Evans, and N. A. Lever (eds.), New York: Kluwer, 2003, for an overview of systems of care, policies, and recommendations.

The role of education in a system of care: Effectively serving children with emotional or behavioral disorders, by D. W. Woodruff and colleagues, Washington, DC: American Institutes for Research, 1999, for a comprehensive look at education's part in the systems of care model.

The disturbing child: A problem of ecological management, by William C. Rhodes, *Exceptional Children, 33,* 1967, 449–455; and A community participation analysis of emotional disturbance, also by Rhodes, *Exceptional Children, 36,* 1970, 309–314, for seminal writings on the ecological perspective.

The myth of mental illness, by T. Szasz, New York: Hoeber-Harber, 1966, for writings of an author who believes that society creates disturbance in individuals.

Multisystemic treatment of antisocial behavior in children and adolescents, by Scott Henggeler and colleagues, New York: Guilford Press, 1998, for a book recommending family and community involvement as a method of treatment for antisocial children and youth.

Children's Defense Fund: http://www.childrensdefense.org/, for reports, statistics, and advocacy efforts related to children and youth, particularly minority children and those with disabilities in the United States.

Bazelon Center for Mental Health Law: http://www.bazelon.org/, leading legal advocates for children and adults with mental disabilities, for policy analysis, public information, and technical support for local advocates.

For more information about wraparound and systems of care models the reader is referred to the following:

National Technical Assistance Center for Children's Mental Health, Georgetown University Child Development Center: http://gucchd.georgetown.edu/programs/ta_center/index.html

Center for Effective Collaboration and Practice: http://cecp.air.org/

Research and Training Center on Family Suppport and Children's Mental Health, Portland State University: http://www.rtc.pdx.edu/

Research and Training Center for Children's Mental Health, Florida Mental Health Institute, University of South Florida: *http://rtckids.fmhi.usf.edu/*

CHAPTER

9 Internalizing Disorders

A Developmental Framework

Depressive and Anxiety Disorders

Definition and Prevalence, Subtypes and Characteristics, Etiology, Treatment, Implications for Teachers

QUESTIONS TO CONSIDER

- How does developmental age impact the display of depressive and anxious symptoms in children and adolescents?
- How are internalizing disorders defined?
- What are the common characteristics of depression, dysthymia, and bipolar disorder and how would those characteristics affect functioning in the schools?
- What are the defining features of anxiety disorders?
- What therapeutic interventions are supported by research for internalizing disorders?
- What is the role of the classroom teacher in identifying, assessing, and intervening with internalizing disorders?

Orientation

Childhood traditionally has been considered a happy, carefree time devoid of the fears and anxieties that are the domain of adults. However, with increased pressures to live between households of divorced parents or with single parents, to "just say no" to drugs, cope with cyber-bullying, and to otherwise grow up fast, children and adolescents are showing the strain. Children who experience fears, phobias, anxiety, and depression need adult support; for those who cannot function routinely, clinical interventions may be required. Teachers need to be especially keen observers of these characteristics because children are often unable to identify or label internalizing disorders by themselves.

Overview

This chapter addresses internalizing disorders of childhood and adolescence. These disorders tend to be introversive or intrapersonal in nature; in the past, they have been termed *overcontrolled* and *personality disorder.* Students with these disorders do not ordinarily present problems of discipline or conformity and therefore historically have not received as much attention in the school setting as have students with externalizing disorders. However, both educational and mental health professionals are recognizing the debilitating effects of anxiety and depression upon the normal development of children and adolescents. Depression and anxiety disorders are the most prevalent of the internalizing problems. For each of these disorders, this chapter presents an overview of (1) definition, (2) characteristics and symptoms, (3) theories of etiology, (4) predisposing factors, and (5) intervention and treatment strategies. Initially, however, a developmental framework for internalizing disorders is presented.

A Developmental Framework for Internalizing Disorders

Based primarily on their work with children who are socially isolated or socially withdrawn, Rubin and Mills (1991) proposed a model that partially explains the development of internalizing problems. The model has three major components that, when interacting in certain ways, lead to problems of an internalizing nature. These three components are (1) the temperament of the child, (2) socialization experiences (parent–child interactions), and (3) environmental or setting conditions that affect the family. To illustrate how these components interact, Rubin and Mills have used the Fantasyland scenario to explain optimal conditions and the Temple of Doom scenario to explain detrimental conditions. In Fantasyland the child has an even-tempered, easy disposition; parents are responsive and sensitive to the child's needs; and there are no major stresses or crises in the family during the child's infancy and early childhood years. These optimal conditions lead to secure parent–child attachments, which in turn lead to positive socioemotional adjustment.

In the Temple of Doom scenario the child shows hyperarousal tendencies that make him difficult to soothe and comfort as an infant, parents react by being nonresponsive or even hostile, and the family lives under stressful and difficult conditions such as poverty or unemployment. Thus, these detrimental conditions can interact to produce insecure attachment or, as Rubin and Mills (1991) call it, felt insecurity.

Felt insecurity is a key concept in this model because it predicts that the child will shrink from her peers and become socially inhibited. Thus deprived of normal peer interactions, the child fails to develop social competence and by mid- to late childhood will likely become rejected and unpopular. Rubin and Mills go on to discuss research linking the various components of their model to the development of various internalizing problems.

This model is consistent with the classic temperament research, discussed in Chapter 4, conducted by Thomas and colleagues (Thomas & Chess, 1977; Thomas et al., 1969). These researchers found three patterns of temperament that characterized 65 percent of the sample in infancy and were stable over time. However, their longitudinal studies showed that children with difficult temperaments (poor adaptability and negativity) did not necessarily develop problem behaviors; conversely, some children with easy temperaments (adaptability, positive approach to new stimuli) did develop problem behaviors. Thomas and colleagues believed that parental interaction patterns and environmental influences were the keys in determining which direction the children would take in their socioemotional development.

These models clearly demonstrate the complexity of the related factors in the development of internalizing disorders. We agree with Rubin and Mills that two fertile areas for additional research are (1) longitudinal studies that assess the causal relationships posited in their model and (2) further investigation of parenting patterns that contribute to internalizing difficulties.

Depression

The existence of depression in children and adolescents has relatively recently been accepted by the mental health community. It was not until the late 1960s that textbooks in psychiatry included chapters on childhood depression (Golden, 1981). Reasons for questioning its existence related to beliefs about etiology. Early psychoanalytic views held that depression is caused by an overly punitive superego, which results in self-directed aggression manifested in depression (Freud, 1957; Rochlin, 1959). As the superego was thought to become internalized some time during adolescence, preadolescents were thought incapable of experiencing depression.

Overwhelming evidence supports the contention that both children and adolescents experience depression severe enough to interfere with daily functioning. In addition to the traditional markers of sad affect, low self-esteem, and decreased energy level, depressed youngsters may experience apathy or loss of interest in their usual activities and routines, including schoolwork. The federal definition of emotional disturbance in the IDEA accounts for depressed children in the component, "a pervasive mood of unhappiness or depression." The first two sections of this chapter clarifies the defining characteristics of depression, its prevalence, and accompanying symptoms.

Definition and Prevalence

Depression may be defined as "a syndrome of abnormally dejected mood persistent over time that interferes with daily functioning" (Muse, 1990). The current perspective on childhood depression is based on the belief that children exhibit depressive symptoms paralleling those in adults (American Psychiatric Association, 2000; Kovacs & Beck, 1977; Puig-Antich, 1982). However, many researchers argue for a developmental perspective, which posits that depression manifests itself in different symptoms at different developmental stages (Carlson & Cantwell, 1986; Rutter, Izard, & Read, 1986). For example, as the child gets older, depressive behavior may become more overt and may be manifested in acting out, truancy, running away, and disobedience (Lesse, 1974). Until epidemiological research can clearly establish parameters for depressive symptoms at differing developmental stages, most professionals will continue to define childhood depression by the diagnostic criteria set forth for adults in the DSM-IV-TR (American Psychiatric Association,

2000). This approach is obviously based on the belief that childhood depression is a downward extension of adult depression.

Four primary diagnostic categories of depressive disorders are provided in DSM-IV-TR: Major Depressive Disorder, Dysthymic Disorder, Bipolar Disorder, and Depressive Disorder Not Otherwise Specified. These categories differ in number, severity, and duration of symptoms. Major Depression consists of a prominent and persistent depressed mood or loss of interest and pleasure in usual activities. Depressed mood is characterized by symptoms such as "sad, discouraged, down in the dumps," and "hopeless." Children, however, may seem predominantly irritable instead of sad. In addition, at least four of the following symptoms must be present almost continuously for a period of at least 2 weeks:

- Change in appetite or weight
- Insomnia or too much sleep
- Psychomotor agitation or retardation
- Loss of interest or pleasure in usual activities
- Loss of energy/fatigue
- Feelings of worthlessness/excessive or inappropriate guilt
- Inability to concentrate
- Recurrent thoughts of death. (American Psychiatric Association, 2000)

Furthermore, these symptoms must result in significant distress or impaired functioning. The DSM-IV-TR makes a few marked distinctions between childhood and adult depressive disorders. First, the DSM-IV-TR includes irritability as a childhood symptom in addition to or in place of pervasive sadness. While the inclusion of irritability as a childhood symptom has been helpful in increasing the scientific view of the uniqueness and specificity of childhood depression, it has also made diagnoses more difficult. As described previously, depression is often comorbid with externalizing disorders. The irritable attitude and temper that children with depression sometimes exhibit are also symptoms of externalizing disorders such as oppositional-defiant disorder and are therefore difficult to distinguish. The second depressive symptom that can be exhibited differently by children is loss of weight. Children can display a failure to make expected weight gains in place of a significant weight loss, which is sometimes evident in adulthood. Last, the DSM-IV-TR accounts for developmental differences in its duration requirements for dysthymia: only a 1-year period of symptoms for childhood dysthymia as opposed to a 2-year period for adults.

Another type of depression—bipolar disorder—has been diagnosed in adolescents and adults; recently, physicians have begun to diagnose it in increasing numbers of children, although it was previously thought to be rare. Bipolar disorder was formerly called manic-depressive syndrome because of extreme mood swings from a highly active, agitated, grandiose "manic" state of mind to a dysphoric, "depressed" one. According to research by Papolos and Papolos (1999), prepubertal children with bipolar disorder have a different symptom presentation than adolescents or adults. Children are noted to have rapid cycling mood swings. The extreme mood variability and symptom overlap between other disorders make bipolar disorder difficult to diagnose. It may be confused with other disorders, including attention-deficit hyperactivity disorder (ADHD), conduct disorder (CD), anxiety disorders, and schizophrenia. ADHD and bipolar disorder have share numerous features. In both disorders, children may display increased restlessness, emotional lability, agitation, aggression, sleep disruption, poor school performance, distractibility, impulsivity, and hyperactivity (Sarampote, Efron, Robb, Pearl, & Stein, 2002; Weckerly, 2002; Weller, Weller, & Fristad, 1995). The overlapping features between CD and bipolar disorder include hostility, impulsivity, and irritability (Kim & Miklowitz, 2002). Children with anxiety or bipolar disorder can be irritable, restless, distractible, and agitated. Childhood schizophrenia and bipolar disorder are similar in that children with both disorders may appear to have psychotic features such as auditory hallucinations, persecutory delusions, paranoia, loosening of associations, and cognitive problems (Faedda et al., 1995). Just as depression is difficult to diagnose in children, so is bipolar disorder. Table 9.1 illustrates the overlap of depressive symptoms in children with other common disorders.

Prevalence estimates of childhood depression vary widely, primarily due to variation in instrumentation and criteria that are used by researchers. Also, prevalence rates in the general population would be expected to be significantly lower than those in samples of children and youth in special education or clinical treatment. Table 9.2 summarizes a number of prevalence studies. Despite disparities in prevalence rates, these data indicate a few trends. In the general population, adolescents show much higher rates of depression (13–18%) than elementary-age students (1.8–5.2%). As expected, special samples show significantly higher rates than in the general population (elementary special samples range from 21 to 37%; adolescent special samples range from 21 to 50%). Predictably, studies using more stringent criteria (including DSM criteria and/or clinical interview) usually find lower prevalence rates. Peterson and colleagues (1993) reviewed the literature and found that 20–40 percent of youth report experiencing a depressed mood, 5 percent experience a depressive syndrome, and 3–8 percent are clinically depressed.

TABLE 9.1 Children's Depressive Symptom Set for Similar Psychiatric Disorders

Bipolar Criteria	ADHD	Anxiety	CD	Schizophrenia
Abnormally elevated, expansive, or irritable mood	✓	✓	✓	✓
Inflated self-esteem/delusions of grandeur			✓	✓
Decreased need for sleep	✓	✓		
Extreme talkativeness	✓			
Flight of ideas				✓
Distractibility	✓	✓		✓
Increased goal-directed activity	✓		✓	
Excessive involvement in activities				
Depressed mood/flat affect			✓	✓
Loss of interest in activities				✓
Weight loss or gain				
Insomnia or hypersomnia	✓			
Motor agitation or retardation	✓	✓		✓
Fatigue		✓		
Feelings of worthlessness or guilt				
Poor concentration	✓	✓		✓
Thoughts of death			✓	

TABLE 9.2 Prevalence Estimates of Depression in Children and Adolescents

Investigation	Sample	% Depressed
Kashani & Simonds (1979)	103 elementary general population	1.9
Kashani et al. (1981)	641 elementary general population	1.8
Kandel & Davies (1982)	4,204 adolescents general population	13.0
Reynolds (1984)	2,800 adolescents general population	18.0
Lefkowitz & Tesiny (1985)	3,020 elementary general population	5.2
Alessi (1986)	134 child psychiatric patients	37.0
Mattison et al. (1986)	158 special ed children	21.0
	128 special ed adolescents	50.0
Maag & Behrens (1989)	144 E BD adolescents	21.0
Lewinsohn, Clarke, Seeley, & Rohde (1994)	1,508 adolescents general population	24.0
Ford, Goodman, & Meltzer (2003)	10,438 5- to 15-year-olds, British population	<1.0
Saluja et al. (2004)	9,863 adolescents general population	18.0
Quijada et al. (2005)	379 adolescents Spanish population	10.3

Rutter (1991) identified several developmental differences in the prevalence of depression. He found that the rate of depression increases significantly during the early to middle adolescent years. Kazdin (1988) also found that younger children typically show lower incidence rates than older subjects. These age differences have been a source of much controversy and, along with other evidence, have been presented in criticism of the inappropriateness of applying adult depression models to children. Researchers question whether children experience a unique pattern of symptoms as a result of their immaturity, either cognitive (Cole & Turner, 1993) or biological (Ryan, 1992).

Rutter (1991) also found that twice as many girls as boys experience depression subsequent to the onset of puberty, while prior to this stage gender differences are insignificant. He offered several possible reasons for these developmental gender differences, including hormonal, cognitive, and interpersonal differences between girls and boys. However, differences could also be attributed to differences in the socialization of females or the greater incidence of abuse of young girls. Comorbidity could account for differences as well. Although depression is often comorbid with conduct disorder in boys, most prevalence studies examine "pure" depression. As a result, more male subjects could be excluded from the tally.

Characteristics and Symptoms

We often think of depression as manifested by feelings of pervasive sadness. While sadness is a primary symptom, depressed individuals commonly show other characteristics along with or in place of sadness. In addition to emotional symptoms, depressed individuals can show cognitive, motivational, and physical symptoms. These symptoms are described, along with the specific characteristics that children and adolescents tend to exhibit.

Emotional symptoms, such as sadness and feelings other than sadness, often occur as a part of depression. The major emotional symptoms common among young people are a loss of interest in activities (even those that were previously fun), boredom, irritability, and frustration. Children additionally experience feelings of worthlessness and guilt. The severity of emotional symptoms depends on the intensity and variability of these feelings. In diagnosing the severity, for example, does the child feel worse in the morning or afternoon, or do these feelings last all day? Is the child able to change to a more positive mood when someone tries to cheer him up or if he or she engages in fun activities? The degree of variation and change in mood is an indication of the degree of impairment, the level of distress, and the prognosis for treatment.

Cognitive symptoms of depression may go unnoticed. Depressed children often exhibit general cognitive symptoms that can be observed in school, such as inattention and an inability to concentrate. However, many cognitive symptoms are characterized by how children think about themselves. These include negative self-image, hypochondria, self-pity, pessimism, thoughts of hopelessness, helplessness, discouragement, and thoughts of death and dying.

Negative self-evaluation, guilt, and hopelessness are more prevalent among depressed children than among their nondepressed counterparts. Studies have shown that self-dislike and self-blame are common characteristics (Kashani & Simonds, 1979; Seligman et al., 1984), with one study reporting that 97 percent of the depressed sample exhibited negative self-evaluation (Brumbeck, Dietz-Schmidt, & Weinberg, 1977). Excessive guilt is linked to negative self-evaluation because children who perceive themselves negatively are likely to blame themselves or feel responsible when things do not go well. Hopelessness is related to the child's bleak expectations for the future: things will not change for the better, but they could get worse. It is important to recognize feelings of hopelessness because of the close association with suicidal ideation (Kazdin, French, Unis, Esveldt-Dawson, & Sherick, 1983).

Another cognitive symptom, inability to concentrate, was found in 77 percent of one sample of depressed adolescent males (Kashani, Heinrichs, Reid, & Huff, 1982). Depressed children may become preoccupied and unable to concentrate on their schoolwork, causing them to fall behind academically. Reported estimates of depressed children who are experiencing academic difficulties range from 48 to 62 percent (Carlson & Cantwell, 1979; Kaslow, Tanenbaum, Abramson, Peterson, & Seligman, 1983). It is not clear whether this difficulty is related to motivational deficits or inability to concentrate.

Motivational symptoms include social withdrawal and suicidal ideation. Children who are depressed tend to shy away from social interactions (Poznanski, Cook, & Carroll, 1979). The child who withdraws due to depression should be distinguished from the socially isolated child: the former would have been considered socially active prior to the onset of depression, and the latter's behavior would have been consistently withdrawn over time. One study found that over two-thirds of the sample of depressed children had demonstrated decreased social interaction (Brumbeck et al., 1977). Depressed children also tend to think and sometimes talk about suicide (Carlson & Cantwell, 1982).

Physical symptoms may be the most easily observed symptoms of depression in children. Chronic fatigue and depressed energy level may be evident. Depressed children often complain of headaches, stomachaches, and other pains. Sleep disorders may be the most common somatic symptom, as one group of researchers found that 92 percent of their sample of depressed adolescent males reported some type of sleep disorder (Kashani et al., 1982). Both insomnia and hypersomnia (sleeping too much) have been reported. Changes in appetite resulting in weight gain or loss are also a major characteristic. Psychomotor agitation or retardation, referring to abnormal rates in the child's movements, speech, and reaction times, may also be present. Semrud-Clikeman and Hynd (1991) reviewed developmental studies that showed that children age 6–12 were more likely to show sadness, sleep disturbance, psychosomatic complaints, and enuresis as initial signs. Children age 12–16 exhibited more restlessness, irritability, social withdrawal, and acting-out behaviors. Symptoms of depression in children are summarized in Table 9.3.

Related Conditions

In a review of literature on depression in children and adolescents, Hodgman (1985) listed several clinical conditions found to coexist with depression: conduct disorders, eating disorders, substance abuse, and anxiety disorders.

Two studies assessing major depression in samples of juvenile offenders with conduct disorders recorded incidences of 15 percent (Alessi, McManus, & Grapente, 1984) and 18 percent (Kashani et al., 1982). These findings may be important because depressive symptoms are not usually associated with acting-out behaviors such as are found in populations with conduct disorders. Thus, among this population, depression may be manifested in agitated symptoms rather than the classic depressed affective ones. Depression also has been associated with both anorexia nervosa and bulimia. One group of researchers (Katz, Kuperberg, & Pollack, 1984) has suggested that depression and anorexia nervosa are interrelated, perhaps interacting to sustain one another either psychologically or physically. Although patients with bulimia have shown a response to antidepressants (Pope, Hudson, & Jonas, 1983), studies linking bulimia to depression are mixed, failing to establish a clear relationship.

Substance abuse may represent attempts by depressed adolescents to cope with dysphoric mood, perhaps clouding the diagnosis of depression in this population. While substance abuse among depressed adolescents has not been sufficiently studied, according to one researcher, the coexistence of depression and alcoholism in many families "is suggestive" (Hodgman, 1985).

TABLE 9.3 Symptoms of Depression in Children and Adolescents

Affective/Emotional Symptoms
Often looks sad
Complains of feeling sad, blue, or tired
Cries easily
Inability to respond to humor
Loss of interest in previously pleasurable activities

Cognitive Symptoms
Negative self-evaluation
Self-dislike
Self-blame
Excessive guilt
Hopelessness
Difficulty with concentration
Forgetful, failure to complete schoolwork or chores

Motivational Symptoms
Social withdrawal
Suicidal ideation
Poor school performance

Physical Symptoms
Chronic fatigue
Depressed energy level
Insomnia, hypersomnia
Changes in appetite and weight

Anxiety disorders have also been associated with depression. In fact, the two share many common characteristics and diagnostic criteria, leading researchers and clinicians to wonder whether anxiety and depression are two distinct conditions or a common syndrome. Clark and Watson (1991) conclude that adult anxiety and depression share a common component, that of general affective distress; however, Clark and Watson also found that symptoms of physiological hyperarousal were unique to anxiety and that symptoms of anhedonia (defined as lack of positive affect) were unique to depression.

Stark and his colleagues (Laurent, Landau, & Stark, 1993; Stark, Humphrey, Laurent, Livingston, & Christopher, 1993) extended this question of differential diagnosis to children and young adolescents. In a sample of fourth through seventh graders, Stark et al. (1993) found that the two disorders are distinct and characterized by unique cognitive and social skills and family profiles. In another study with the same age group, the two syndromes were differentiated by a number of symptoms. Four symptoms were predictive of depression: feeling unloved, anhedonia, excessive guilt, and depressed mood. One symptom characterized anxiety disorder: worries, especially about future events and academic competence (Laurent et al., 1993). Thus, there is some preliminary evidence to suggest that despite the overlap in observable symptoms, anxiety and depression do constitute separate syndromes that are identifiable in children, potentially leading to different treatments.

From a medical perspective, Hodgman (1985) summarizes the research on related conditions by expressing concerns that an undetermined number of depressed youngsters may not be accurately diagnosed, leading to ineffective treatment attempts. From an education perspective, Forness (1988b) reviewed literature relevant to the school functioning of depressed children and adolescents and found it sufficiently lacking in methodological soundness to draw conclusions. Although teachers are not expected to diagnose clinical conditions, it is important to recognize that these conditions may coexist, so that symptoms can be brought to the attention of appropriate personnel.

Etiology and Development

Discovering the causes of childhood and adolescent depression has been difficult. Hammen (1988) concluded her review of the literature by identifying only three things that research has established unequivocally. First, family history is significantly related to childhood and adolescent depression. Often a cycle is demonstrated within the family. Research has indicated a link between parental depression and children exhibiting greater physical symptoms, greater loss of interest in activities, more psychological problems, and more incidence of clinical depression (Miller, Birnbaum, & Durbin, 1990).

Second, age of onset is significantly correlated with the severity of depression. While supported in research, this also makes intuitive sense. When experiencing a major depressive episode, a young person misses that portion of his or her development. Missing a grade in school often means giving up friendships, social status, and academic standing. A 6-month period of hospitalization can be a substantial block of time for a school-age child.

Third, a first episode predicts additional episodes. Reviews of the data indicate that major depressive disorder and dysthymic disorder diagnosed in prepubertal children are associated with an increased risk of depressive disorders over the next 5 years (Cantwell, 1990; Peterson et al., 1993). Thus, depression in young people is significantly linked to depression later in life.

Schools of thought related to the development of depression may be categorized into biophysical, behavioral, and cognitive models. A comprehensive model that incorporates several aspects of the other models is also presented.

Biophysical Model. The biophysical model includes theories that have explored both biochemical and hereditary etiologies. Biochemical studies with depressed adults have focused primarily on the role of neurotransmitters or chemicals in the brain that facilitate transmissions of neural impulses. These studies assess the effects of antidepressant medication, which act by increasing the availability of certain neurotransmitters at critical receptor sites in the brain. The two most frequently targeted transmitters are norepinephrine and serotonin. However, neither these transmitters nor other biological markers (e.g., hormones, metabolic secretions) have yielded conclusive results in research with children. Biophysical research with children and adolescents may be hampered by the many developmental fluctuations caused by normal growth and by changes during puberty (Sellstrom, 1989).

Genetic or hereditary factors have been implicated in childhood depression. Patterns of depression and other disorders have been documented in the families of depressed children (Keller et al., 1986; Weissman et al., 1987). A number of studies have assessed the genetic aspect of depression through studies of adoptions and of twins (identical vs. fraternal) and generally support the notion of a genetic predisposition to depression in adults (Hodgman, 1985; Kashani et al., 1981). For example, one such study found that identical twins have four to five times the likelihood of experiencing concurrent major depression than do fraternal twins (Kendler, Heath, Martin, & Eaves, 1986). A particularly strong genetic disposition has been found for bipolar depression (Strober & Carlson, 1982; Winokur, Clayton, & Reich, 1984) and for recurring depression. However, these researchers caution that environmental causes are likely necessary for depression to develop and that current research is inconclusive in identifying a reliable genetic marker (Cytryn, McKnew, Zahn-Wexler, & Gershon, 1986; Hodgman, 1985).

Behavioral Model. A behavioral explanation for the development of depression has been formulated by Lewisohn, Hoberman, and colleagues (Hoberman & Clarke, 1993; Hoberman & Lewisohn, 1985; Lewisohn & Gotlib, 1995). This model postulates that depression develops when individuals fail to receive positive reinforcement for social interactions with others, for example, either ongoing or after the breakup of an important relationship. The amount of positive reinforcement received by an individual is based on not only the amount of available reinforcement, but, more importantly, the individual's skill at eliciting it. Therefore, Lewisohn and his colleagues propose a causal link between social skills deficits and depression in adults.

This model postulates that when individuals receive a low rate of positive reinforcement for their social behaviors, they become increasingly more passive and nonresponsive, resulting in a dysphoric mood. The dysphoric mood can then lead to secondary symptoms such as low self-esteem, pessimism, and guilt.

Lewisohn and Arconad (1981) have shown that depressed persons do elicit fewer behaviors from others, receive less positive reinforcement, and demonstrate fewer social skills when compared to nondepressed peers. However, it should be noted that these behaviors may exist as a result of depressed behavior rather than as a cause.

Cognitive Models. Cognitive models of depression have been put forth by Seligman (1975) and by Beck (1967, 1974; Beck, Steer, Beck, & Newman, 1993). Seligman and colleagues have formulated a causal theory of depression based on the concepts of learned helplessness and attributions. Seligman's original model proposed that individuals become depressed when they believe that they cannot control outcomes in their lives, resulting in the cognitive, emotional, and motivational correlates of depression. This learned helplessness concept was investigated and subsequently reformulated by Seligman and colleagues (Abramson et al., 1978), who proposed that the key to the development of depression is the attributions about uncontrollable outcomes made by an individual. In other words, the individual must ask him- or herself why the outcomes seem uncontrollable, and the resulting reasons or attributions will determine whether depression will result. As you learned in Chapter 6, three dimensions of attributions are important in this schema: (1) globality, meaning that the individual believes that he or she is helpless in a variety of situations; (2) stability, meaning that the individual believes that he or she will become chronically helpless; and (3) internality, meaning that the individual will attribute reasons for failures to him- or herself.

Beck's cognitive model of depression is based on three related concepts: the *negative cognitive triad, negative schemata,* and *cognitive distortion.* The negative cognitive triad refers to the depressed individual's negative perceptions of the self, the world, and the future. These pervasive negative thoughts account for many of the symptoms of depression. Negative schemata refers to stable thought patterns about the self, the world, and the future, the most important of these being negative self-schemata. Cognitive distortion is based on the premise that individuals maintain their negative schemata by faulty information processing; depressed individuals fail to process information that is incongruent with their negative self-schemata. A systematic bias in processing information thus reinforces negative perceptions and tends to permeate the thinking of depressed individuals. Although much of the original research to support Beck's cognitive model was done with adults, clinicians have found the model helpful with children and have found correlations between depression and the following:

- Negative cognitive attributions (Dixon & Ahrens, 1992; Nolen-Hoeksema, Girgus, & Seligman, 1986)
- Cognitive errors (Cole & Turner, 1993)
- Negative self-schemas (Hammen, 1988)
- Low self-esteem (Gotlib, Lewinsohn, Seeley, Rohde, & Redner, 1993; Tems, Stewart, Skinner, Hughs, & Emslie, 1993)
- Social information processing (Quiggle, Garber, Panak, & Dodge, 1992)
- Perception of hopelessness (Abramson, Metalsky, & Alloy, 1989)

To summarize, Beck's model holds that depression develops as the individual moves from realistic self-appraisal to self-devaluing, from a realistic appraisal of the environment to a negative one, and from a hopeful appraisal of the future to a hopeless one. Various aspects of this model have been supported by research with both adults and children; however, it has not been determined whether negative cognitions precede or result from depressive symptoms. In other words, no causation has been established and, thus far, this line of inquiry has produced mixed results.

Comprehensive Model. Stark and his colleagues have extended the work of Beck and others in proposing a more comprehensive model of childhood depression (Stark, Humphrey, Crook, & Lewis, 1990; Stark, Rouse, & Livingston, 1991). Cognitive-behavioral in basic orientation, this model recognizes genetic predisposition, family environment, and the child's own adaptive skills in accounting for the core schemas that determine how the child ultimately will view him- or herself. Stark's research has indicated that depressed children do have negative self-schemata when compared to controls, and that they report receiving more negative messages from both parents about the self, world, and future than either controls or anxious children (Stark et al., 1993). From this framework, a multidimensional treatment has been developed that is described in the next section.

Predisposing Factors

One of the most consistently identified factors in childhood depression is a family history of depression or related psychopathology. Having a parent with depression is a major risk factor. Hammen (1991) summarized the literature, stating that children of depressed parents show higher rates of depressive symptomatology and clinical depression, as well as other psychiatric problems.

Although a genetic predisposition toward depression has been documented, most researchers believe that environmental factors act as catalysts in its development. Many of these factors are related to losses, stress, or significant changes in the family context (Muse, 1990). Major life events or losses refer to such events as death of family members and "loss" of a parent through divorce. Stresses include chronic illness in self or family member, parental unemployment, and family violence or discord. Examples of significant family changes are birth of a sibling and remarriage. Substance abuse by parents, and physical, sexual, or emotional abuse of the child also add to the risk of developing depression. These risk factors are summarized in Table 9.4.

Intervention and Treatment

Researchers have documented improvement with samples of depressed children and adolescents through psychotherapy, medication, and school-based interventions. A wide variety of psychological and psychosocial treatments is commonplace in mental health services for depressed children and adolescents. Some of the most frequently utilized interventions include individual and group cognitive-behavioral therapy, interpersonal psychotherapy, family therapy, and social skills training (Mufson, Weissman, Moreau, & Garfinkel, 1999; Peterson et al., 1993).

A special task force assigned to the American Psychological Association recently put together a list of the most efficacious psychotherapeutic treatments for the major diagnostic categories. For depression and related disorders, the task force indicated that interpersonal psychotherapy was the best supported treatment followed by cognitive-behavioral therapy and psychotropic medications (Society of Clinical Child and Adolescent Psychology & The Network on Youth Mental Health, 2006). However, studies regarding the most efficacious treatments are mixed.

Psychotherapy versus Medication. Medication is frequently used for the treatment of depression and dysthymia in hospitals, psychiatric centers, and residential treatment facili-

TABLE 9.4 Risk Factors for Depression in Children

Other Family Members with Mental Health Problems	*Chronic Stress in the Family*
Relatives with depression	Chronic illness in family member
Relatives with alcohol problems	Chronic illness in the child
Relatives who abuse drugs	Loss of parental job/unemployment
Relatives who have been in a psychiatric hospital	Problems with the law
Important Losses	*Child Abuse*
Death of parent	Physical abuse
Death of sibling	Sexual abuse
Death of other close family member	Emotional abuse
Divorce	
Loss of friends because of moving	*Significant Family Change or Stress*
"Loss" of mother if she returns to work	Birth of a sibling
Death of a pet	Remarriage
Loss of important objects	Family violence
Loss of home	Parental discord
	Suicide in family or friend

From Muse (1990). *Depression and suicide in children and adolescents.* Reprinted by permission of Pro-Ed.

ties. Selective serotonin reuptake inhibitors (SSRIs) are the most commonly used medication in the treatment of childhood and adolescent depression and dysthymia (Kratochvil et al., 2006; Sommers-Flanagan & Sommers-Flanagan, 1996). SSRIs are believed to block the reuptake of the neurotransmitter serotonin in the brain. There are many SSRIs on the market, such as fluoxetine (brand name Prozac), sertraline (brand name Zoloft), paroxetine (brand name Paxil), and venlafaxine (brand name Effexor). Research has only proven fluoxetine to be beneficial in the treatment of childhood depression and dysthymia (Emslie et al., 2002). Children diagnosed with bipolar disorder may also be treated with lithium, neuroleptics such as haloperidol (brand name Haldol) and risperdone (brand name Risperdal), and anticonvulsants such as carbamazepine (brand name Tegretol) (Ryan, 2003). Research support for the efficacy of medications for childhood bipolar disorder is mixed.

Side effects of antidepressants are similar among adolescents and adults. Although no side effects are consistent among all users, the most common side effects include nausea, headache, nervousness, and insomnia (Ryan, 1992). However, few cardiac effects have been indicated, even with overdoses. Side effects of lithium, neuroleptics, and anticonvulsants can be more problematic. The side effects include nausea, tremor, diarrhea, fatigue, tardive dyskinesia, loss of coordination, and vertigo (Kane, 1988, 1991; Ryan, Bhatara, & Perel, 1999).

Despite the promise of fluoxetine, the Food and Drug Administration (FDA) issued a black box warning against all SSRIs for children in October 2004 (Kratochvill et al. 2006). A black box warning means the FDA requires a message to be placed in the medicine's package insert warning against potential harm to the user. The black box warning was indicated because the FDA found an increase in suicidal ideation among children who had been prescribed SSRIs. Physicians still prescribe the medication, but only after weighing the risks and benefits of its usage (Kratochvill et al. 2006). The issue of suicidal ideation being tied to the medication is controversial because it brings to light the "chicken" or "egg" issue. That is, did the medication cause an increase in suicidal ideation among the children with depression or did the depression itself lead to greater risk for suicidal ideation?

Regarding psychotherapeutic treatment, psychotherapy for mildly depressed adults and adolescents has been promoted as equal to or superior to other forms of treatment, including medication (Kaplan & Sadock, 1988; Society of Clinical Child and Adolescent Psychology & The Network on Youth Mental Health, 2006; Wright & Beck, 1983). Muse (1990) suggested that for children whose depression is mild, has clear precipitating stresses, and has no biological base, psychotherapy is the treatment of choice. However, for instances of more serious depression, Puig-Antich and Weston (1983) found limited evidence for the effectiveness of psychotherapy for children and adolescents; they suggest that serious depression is not amenable to other treatments until first improved with medication.

Other randomized, placebo-controlled treatment studies have compared whether psychotherapy or medication is more beneficial in the treatment of childhood depression. One study, the Treatment for Adolescents with Depression Study (TADS), reported that the combination of cognitive-behavioral therapy and fluoxetine was the most effective treatment for the alleviation of symptoms of depression. Fluoxetine alone was also superior to placebo, but cognitive-behavioral therapy alone was no more beneficial than placebo (TADS Team, 2004).

School-Based Interventions. School-based interventions can be an effective component in the treatment of depression for children and youth. These interventions are usually one of two types: (1) those that focus on individual students or (2) those that utilize various group techniques. In both cases, treatment often involves a combination of counseling and teaching in the areas of problem solving, affective education, cognitive restructuring, relaxation training, and social skills training (Hart, 1991).

In a model of individual counseling, Ramsey (1994) defines treatment in terms of alleviating negative internal feelings of unworthiness. Ramsey argues that internal feelings create a need to seek support and praise from others; the stronger the negative internal feelings are, the greater the demands for attention and support. Ramsey believes that support does not help the student confront irrational feelings of worthlessness, helplessness, and hopelessness. Instead, she promotes exploring the student's depressive feelings and how they affect daily activities and relationships, helping the student to understand the physical as well as emotional feelings that are part of the depression, and considering the anger that is often an accompanying characteristic of student depression.

A number of group interventions have also proved successful in alleviating symptoms of depression, usually on measures of self-report:

- Cognitive-behavioral approach; also relaxation training (Reynolds & Coates, 1986)
- Social skills combined with problem solving; also a cognitive restructuring approach (Butler, Miezitis, Friedman, & Cole, 1980)
- Social skills training (Kratochwill & French, 1984; Schloss, Schloss, & Harris, 1984)

A more comprehensive approach is advocated by Stark and his colleagues. Stark's multidimensional treatment package combines behavioral, cognitive, and affective procedures with parent training and family therapy (Stark et al., 1991). Included in the treatment are procedures for cognitive restructuring, behavioral assignments, problem solving, self-instructional training, social skills, relaxation exercises, scheduling pleasant activities, anger coping, and games to identify and explore emotions. Both group and individual sessions are used to implement these strategies. Parent training focuses first on helping parents understand depression and then on involving them as collaborators in their child's treatment. Among other things, parents are taught to use positive behavior management skills, including praise. Family therapy sessions focus on communication, family problem solving, and conflict resolution. Specifically, family interactions that lead to and maintain the child's depressed cognitive schema are targeted for change. One interesting goal of this program is to teach the parents how to help their families have fun. An example of how these procedures were used to treat a depressed 10-year-old is presented in Box 9.1.

Implications for Teachers. Teachers of students with EBD will undoubtedly encounter depressed students in their classrooms. Furthermore, teachers should be aware that depression may be significantly underdiagnosed, especially in younger children. The coexistence of other problems such as anxiety, conduct disorders, or substance abuse may mask the accurate diagnosis of depression in older children and adolescents.

Although some students may manifest their depression through agitated behaviors, most depressed individuals will present problems of withdrawal and lack of concentration

BOX 9.1

Sherry

Sherry was a 10-year-old fourth grader who was enrolled in language arts and math classes for the gifted. She began seeing the school counselor on a regular basis during the second grade. She complained that she hated herself and was "fat, ugly, and stupid."

Unbeknownst to the counselor, Sherry had first manifested symptoms of depression at the age of 4 and expressed serious suicidal wishes at the age of 6. A visit to the family physician at that time was unproductive. He told Sherry that "you're not fat, you're built strong," and told her parents that there was nothing wrong with her. Unfortunately, Sherry's problems persisted. By the fourth grade, Sherry had very few friends due to her negativity and bad temper. She was seen as a tattletale, and generally had very poor social skills. Following an increase in her tantrum behavior and alienation from peers, Sherry finally was referred to the school psychologist. Her parents were at their wits' end, as they had tried everything they knew to help her.

An assessment of Sherry revealed that she was suffering from chronic dysthymic disorder. Although there were only 5 weeks left in the school year, cognitive-behavioral therapy was initiated in the school setting for five sessions, during which Sherry seemed to learn very quickly how to control her mood. She used self-talk to control her anger and engaged herself in pleasant activities as a way to control her dysphoric mood. Cognitive restructuring procedures were introduced, in which she learned to replace some of her negative self-talk with positive self-talk. Both Sherry and her parents noted improvement. Upon returning to school following summer vacation, Sherry's condition was greatly worsened. An episode of major depression was now superimposed on the dysthymia, and she was concurrently experiencing severe separation anxiety. Therapy was resumed;

(*continued*)

BOX 9.1 Continued

however, Sherry was extremely resistant to the psychological interventions and commonly spent much of her therapy time throwing a temper tantrum or crying for her mother. Systematic desensitization for separation anxiety was not possible since Sherry refused to engage in the relaxation and imagery exercises.

Due to the continued severity of the disorder and a multigenerational family history of depression, Sherry was evaluated for medication and subsequently placed on Prozac. Prozac was chosen because of the favorable response to it by other family members. It produced a marked improvement in her depressive symptoms and especially in her separation anxiety. However, the medication clearly did not eliminate the depressive symptoms; rather, it buffered them and made her much more amenable to psychological treatment. Although her symptoms abated, Sherry continued to miss her mother during school and frequently asked to go to the nurse because she was feeling ill.

Cognitive-behavioral therapy for depression was reinitiated. Sherry was once again taught to use engagement in pleasant activities as a means of coping with dysphoria or anger. A diary was constructed with one page for each day of the week; each page had a list of 25 activities that Sherry most enjoyed doing. In addition, there were five blank spaces for her to write in other pleasant activities. An 11-point Likert-type scale ("Worst Ever" to "Best Ever") was placed at the bottom of each page where she rated her mood for the whole day prior to going to bed. Sherry kept the diary with her and self-monitored her engagement in the pleasant activities each day by checking off the ones she engaged in. This activity also led to some cognitive restructuring, as she realized that she actually did a number of enjoyable things every day.

As themes in her thinking were identified, self-monitoring was combined with cognitive restructuring to change the way Sherry was mentally constructing her world. For example, she believed that she was not loved by her parents and, furthermore, that she was unlovable. Sherry generated a list of the criteria that would provide evidence that she was loved by her parents, and that she was in fact worthy of love. (Her parents and the psychologist were quick to note that she was deserving of their love just because she was their child, and if she exhibited all of these desirable behaviors, that was just frosting on the cake. It is important to note that her parents did, in fact, love her dearly.) These criteria were listed on one side of her diary pages. A parallel version of this diary was constructed for her parents. Each night Sherry and her parents were instructed to go through their respective diaries together and to check off the evidence that Sherry was loved and that her parents had in fact demonstrated their love.

In addition, Sherry was taught social skills during sessions and applied them in the classroom. She received quiet and discrete reinforcement from her teacher for engaging in prosocial behaviors.

Cognitive-behavioral family therapy was initiated after the psychologist noted that the parents expected Sherry to act like an adult rather than a 10-year-old. The mother inadvertently responded to challenges to her parenting by blaming Sherry. This tendency led Sherry to feel attacked and as though she were guilty of being a bad child. Other subtle communications that led to and maintained Sherry's negative self-schema were identified, and her parents were taught to change them. Concurrently, they were taught to be better listeners and to allow Sherry to have an individual personality and to act in a more childlike fashion.

Sherry's mood slowly but continually improved to the point that she generally felt good, her social behavior improved, and she began to like herself. At this writing, the plan is to continue her on the medication until the end of the school year and to discontinue it over the summer.

Contributed by Kevin Stark, PhD, Professor in the Department of Educational Psychology, University of Texas at Austin.

or motivation in the classroom. These problems likely will be manifested through low rates of social interaction and inability to complete schoolwork. Table 9.5 lists a number of symptoms of depression that may be manifested in the classroom.

For those depressed students being treated by medication, the teacher should routinely confer with the prescribing physician regarding behavioral fluctuations and potential side effects. For students receiving psychotherapy or counseling, the teacher and therapist should coordinate to reinforce one another's treatment goals. Teachers may want to team up with other school personnel (counselors, social workers, or psychologists) in teaching social skills or cognitive techniques in a group format. At this point in our understanding of depression in children and adolescents, a combination of relaxation training, cognitive-behavioral strategies, positive behavioral supports, and social skills training appears to hold the most promise for educators.

Anxiety Disorders

As with depression, fear and anxiety in children relatively recently came to be viewed as a clinical syndrome requiring treatment. As childhood fear and anxiety are often viewed as common and transient, their impact is easily overlooked (Strauss, 1987). However, as

TABLE 9.5 Symptoms of Depression and Their Impact in the Classroom

Symptom	Impact
Motivational impairment	Reduced interest in schoolwork
Anhedonia (lack of positive affect)	Behavioral reinforcers hard to identify
Fatigue	Difficulty finishing assignments
Impaired concentration	Difficulty attending and finishing assignments
Lack of persistence	Failure to complete work
Impaired social relationships	Lack of engagement with teacher or students
Sadness/tearfulness	Withdrawal, alienation from peers, lack of energy for learning
Cognitive biases	Overperception of failures; tendency to interpret feedback as negative; grades become reinforcers of negative set
Heightened self-consciousness	Difficulty participating in group activities
Irritability/aggression	Disruptive to rest of class; not engaged in learning process; failure to complete work
Withdrawal	Lack of engagement with others or process; tendency to be ignored

From Stark, Swearer, Delaune, Knox, & Winter (1995). Reprinted with permission of the senior author and John Wiley & Sons, Inc.

Strauss (1987) asserts, "anxiety in childhood can be intense, distressing, and persistent, thus requiring the attention of professionals" (p. 109).

Definitions and Prevalence

Anxiety may be defined as "an aversive or unpleasant state involving subjective apprehension and physiological arousal of a diffuse nature" (King & Ollendick, 1989, p. 431). Anxiety is also often characterized as either *state* (acute) or *trait* (chronic) (Spielberger, 1973).

The psychiatric community acknowledges only separation anxiety disorder under Anxiety Disorders of Childhood and Adolescence in its most recent version of the *Diagnostic and Statistical Manual of Mental Disorders* (DSM-IV-TR) (APA, 2000). This discussion also includes generalized anxiety disorder (formerly known as overanxious disorder), due to the amount of relevant research, and brief discussions of adult classifications that are seen to a lesser extent in children and adolescents: posttraumatic stress disorder, obsessive–compulsive disorder, panic disorder, and phobias. School refusal and other school-related phobias are addressed due to their obvious implications for school-age children and youth. According to Bernstein and Borchardt (1991), the essential features of these disorders are as follows:

- Separation anxiety: excessive anxiety about separation from parents or attachment figures
- Fears and specific phobias: specific, isolated, persistent fear of a particular stimulus; generalized anxiety disorder: excessive anxiety that is not focused on a specific object or situation and is not a result of a recent stressor
- Posttraumatic stress disorder: can result from exposure to a single traumatic event or to repeated trauma over a period of time, such as in physical or sexual abuse; features include insomnia, poor concentration, anxiety, nightmares, avoidance, and flashbacks
- Obsessive–compulsive disorder: characterized by either obsessions (current, persistent thoughts that are experienced as intrusive and senseless) or compulsions (repetitive, purposeful behaviors or rituals)
- Panic disorder: discrete panic attacks that occur unexpectedly and are characterized by somatic and psychological symptoms.

After a discussion of the prevalence and etiology of anxiety disorders in general, the characteristics and treatment of each of these specific disorders are described. Issues of comorbidity are also addressed.

Prevalence

During the 1980s and 1990s, a number of researchers attempted to establish the prevalence of anxiety disorders among children and adolescents. The resulting prevalence figures vary widely, depending on (1) whether the sample was referred for clinical problems or was a sample of the general population; (2) whether multiple sources of information were gathered, including more than one informant; and (3) whether an additional criterion of significant impairment in functioning was required for diagnosis. As would be expected, figures are very high for clinical samples, whereas figures from community-based, naturalistic studies and studies requiring multiple informants and impairment in functioning are much lower. Although some studies (e.g., Keller et al., 1992) have found equal prevalence of anxiety disorders among males and females, most studies suggest that anxiety disorders are more common among females than males, particularly in adolescence (Clark, Smith, Neighbors, Skerlec, & Randall, 1994).

A number of prevalence studies are summarized in Table 9.6. These studies suggest that a high percentage of clinical samples of children and adolescents have anxiety disorders, perhaps about half of which are "pure," that is, without accompanying disorders. Smaller naturalistic studies without stringent criteria found estimates from 6 to 18 percent in children and adolescents (Silverman & Kurtines, 2001). The most prevalent anxiety disorders are generalized anxiety disorder (formerly overanxious disorder), specific phobias, and separation anxiety disorder (Ramirez, Feeney-Kettler, Flores-Torres, Kratochwill, & Morris, 2006).

Etiology of Anxious and Fearful Behavior

It may be said with certainty that no one knows precisely what causes anxiety disorders. Research has established that genetic and environmental factors are contributors. Theories that have been advanced to account for the development of anxiety and fears include neurobiological, behavioral, and cognitive.

Genetic Factors and Environmental Stressors. Anxiety disorders tend to run in families. Children of parents with anxiety disorders are more likely to exhibit anxiety disorders than children of adults with other diagnoses or no diagnoses (Turner, Beidel, & Costello, 1987; Weissman, Leckman, Merikangas, Gammon, & Prusoff, 1984). Approaching the problem in the opposite direction, Last, Phillips, and Statfeld (1987) identified children with anxiety disorders and then evaluated the mothers. They found a significantly higher proportion of both current and lifetime anxiety disorders in mothers of anxiety disordered

TABLE 9.6 Prevalence Estimates of Anxiety Disorders in Children and Adolescents

Investigation	Sample	% Anxious
Anderson, Williams, McGee, & Silva (1987)	General population, 11-year-olds	2.4–3.6
Last et al. (1987)	Clinical; children and adolescents	76
Kashani & Orvaschel (1988)	Nonreferred adolescents	8.7–17.3
Bowen, Offord, & Boyle (1990)	General population, ages 4–16	2.4–3.5
Kashani et al. (1990)	Inpatients; children	21
Keller et al. (1992)	Nonreferred children	14
Ford, Goodman, & Meltzer (2003)	General British population, ages 5–15	3.5–4.0
Brosky & Lally (2004)	Court-referred adolescents, ages 12–18	5.8
Lynch, Mills, Doly, & Fitzpatrick (2006)	Ireland general population, adolescents	3.7
Bolton et al. (2006)	General population, 6-year-old twin pairs	2.8–10.8

Note. Anxiety disorders reported in the studies included separation anxiety disorder, overanxious/generalized anxiety disorder, simple phobias, PTSD, and a history of an anxiety disorder.

children when compared to psychiatric controls. Another study revealed a high prevalence of anxiety disorders among relatives of patients with panic disorder (Crowe, Noyes, Pauls, & Slymen, 1983).

As would be expected, environmental stressors appear to play a role in the development of anxiety symptoms. More negative life events have been reported by high-anxiety children and adolescents than by their low-anxiety counterparts (Kashani et al., 1990). Conditioning by environmental stress is thought by some researchers to be responsible for the development of specific phobias (Bernstein & Borchardt, 1991). Other researchers suggest that both biological bases and negative life events should be included in a model of the etiology of anxiety disorders (Kashani, Dandoy, & Orvaschel, 1991).

Although these studies indicate both a familial pattern and environmental stressors in the development of anxiety disorders, studies needed to determine the degree of hereditary contribution versus environmental contribution have yet to be conducted.

Neurobiological Theory. One of the most popular biological explanations of anxiety disorders was put forth by Eysenck (1981), who posited that individuals differ in their levels of cortical arousal, which is biologically determined. Individuals also differ in the reactivity of their autonomic nervous systems. According to Eysenck, anxiety results from the interaction of the two; that is, highly anxious individuals often have high resting levels of cortical arousal and high reactivity of the autonomic nervous system. Other, more complex neurobiological theories have also been advanced, some of which have been supported by studies linking specific neurotransmitters such as serotonin with anxiety (Kandel, 1983).

One distinguished group of researchers (Biederman et al., 1990) studied behavioral inhibition and its relationship to the development of anxiety disorders in children. These researchers define behavioral inhibition as a temperament category, in which there is a tendency to constrict behavior in unfamiliar surroundings. It is assumed to reflect low levels of limbic arousal. This tendency was reliably identified in a sample of children at age 21 months and found to be present in follow-up studies at ages 4, 5, and 7. Biederman and colleagues (1990) concluded that "inhibited children had increased risk for multiple anxiety, overanxious/generalized anxiety, and phobic disorders. It is suggested that behavioral inhibition may be associated with risk for anxiety disorders in children" (p. 269).

Behavioral and Cognitive Theories. The principles of operant conditioning, social learning, and classical conditioning have been used to explain the etiology of anxious behavior. According to operant conditioning principles, fearful and anxious behavior is shaped and maintained by positive environmental responses. For example, if a child evidences fear and receives excessive sympathy or is able to avoid an unpleasant task, the behavior will be strengthened. Bandura (1977b) wrote extensively on the social learning of fears, in which children observe peers or adults in situations and learn the fear vicariously. For example, a young child witnessing another child being bitten by a dog might vicariously learn to fear dogs. In this example, the child who was bitten could develop an excessive fear of animals through classical conditioning (i.e., the association of pain with the appearance of a dog). Depending on several variables, including the amount of trauma surrounding the event, both children could develop a phobia of dogs or generalize fears to other animals. Conditioning theories may only partially account for the development of fearful and anxious behavior. Cognitive theories also have been advanced; unfortunately, research on the role of cognitive factors has been conducted with adults, rather than with children or adolescents. Nonetheless, work in this area is important because of its treatment implications.

In his work with adults, Beck (1976) developed a cognitive model that explains pathological anxiety as arising from unrealistic perceptions of danger. One or more of four cognitive errors are considered responsible for these unrealistic perceptions.

1. Overestimating the probability of a feared event
2. Overestimating the severity of the feared event
3. Underestimating what one can do about it (coping resources)
4. Underestimating what others can do to help (rescue factors)

Beck believes that an individual's perception of danger, realistic or not, sets into motion an "anxiety program" that is a "complex constellation of cognitive, affective, and behavioral changes which we have inherited from our evolutionary past and which were probably originally designed to protect us from harm in a primitive environment" (Clark & Beck, 1988, p. 363). Cognitive therapy is based on this reciprocal relationship between the perception of threat and the resulting anxiety. Cognitive therapy therefore deals with one's fears about the cognitive, behavioral, and somatic symptoms of anxiety. The individual's thoughts about his own reactions are the focus of therapy.

In summary, although principles of conditioning may account for development of specific fears and phobias, many researchers believe that genetic predispositions, environmental stressors, and cognitive factors may also play a role in the development of anxiety disorders. However, the role of each of these factors relative to one another has yet to be specified by empirical research. Table 9.7 summarizes the etiological factors and theories presented in this section.

Clearly, excessive fears and anxiety disorders in children are complex and multifaceted. Therefore, characteristics and interventions will be discussed separately for each of the specific disorders most relevant to children and adolescents.

Separation Anxiety Disorder.

Characteristics. The essential feature of separation anxiety disorder (SAD) is excessive anxiety about separation from a parent or other attachment figure past the age when it is

TABLE 9.7 Summary of Etiological Factors and Theories of Anxiety Disorders

Genetic and family factors	Behavioral theories
Environmental stressors	Operant conditioning
Negative life events	Social learning (modeling)
Neurobiological factors	Classical conditioning
Reactivity of autonomic nervous system	Cognitive theory
Neurotransmitter differences	
Temperament factors	
Behavioral inhibition	

considered appropriate (Ramirez et al., 2006). It is further characterized by unrealistic worry and persistent, anxious mood. It differs from other anxiety disorders in that the anxiety is clearly focused on separation from the attachment figure. It also differs from school phobia: in separation anxiety disorder, school is only one of many settings in which separation is feared, and in school phobia, the fear is specific to the school setting. Many researchers and clinicians now use the term *school refusal* and differentiate two subsets of school refusers: those with separation anxiety disorder and those who are school phobic. We will return to this important distinction under the section on school refusal.

The prevalence of separation anxiety disorder in the general community ranges from 2.4 to 3.5 percent (Anderson, Williams, McGee, & Silva, 1987; Bowen, Offord, & Boyle, 1990). Lower socioeconomic status has been reported as a risk factor for developing SAD (Velez, Johnson, & Cohen, 1989). The average age of onset has been reported as 9 years old (Last, Hersen, Kazdin, Finkelstein, & Strauss, 1987). Although adolescents are diagnosed with SAD, it is more prevalent in children. Specific symptoms and worries seem to be developmental in nature. Francis, Last, and Strauss (1987) found the following differences among three age groups:

- Ages 5–8: worries and nightmares about harm befalling the attachment figure and reluctance to go to school
- Ages 9–12: excessive distress upon separation
- Ages 13–16: school refusal and somatic complaints

Specific types of fears are reported by children with SAD compared to children with other anxiety disorders. Ollendick (1983) found that children with SAD most frequently said they feared getting lost, bee stings, and germs/illness. In contrast, children diagnosed with generalized anxiety disorder (GAD) have overall fears about the future, their health, their safety, and their performance (Flannery-Schroeder, 2004). Also, the general population of children does not typically report these fears as strongly, if at all.

Separation anxiety in childhood or adolescence has been linked to the later emergence of agoraphobia. A number of studies indicate that a significant percentage of adults with agoraphobia reported histories of severe SAD in childhood (cited in Bernstein & Borchardt, 1991). Other studies indicate that the child may not meet SAD criteria in the future, but the child may display symptoms of another anxiety disorder (Kovacs & Devlin, 1998). However, longitudinal studies following children with SAD into adulthood are needed before a clear link can be established between SAD, agoraphobia, and other anxiety disorders.

Intervention. In theory, techniques used to treat separation anxiety focus on enabling the child to separate from the attachment figure (Phelps, Cox, & Bajorek, 1992). Behavioral interventions, such as modeling, relaxation training, cognitive-behavioral therapy, and family anxiety management have proven useful (Society of Clinical Child and Adolescent Psychology & The Network on Youth Mental Health, 2006).

Through modeling, the child learns new behaviors by observing a model (e.g., caregiver, therapist, teacher) successfully master a feared situation. Modeling techniques are based on the social learning principles that fears can be both learned and extinguished through vicarious experiences. Modeling procedures can involve videotape; live models, usually one's peers; and participant modeling. In addition to SAD, modeling has been successful in reducing the common childhood fears of dogs, snakes, and heights and of medical procedures such as surgery or dental work (Strauss, 1987).

Like modeling, relaxation training helps improve behavior by teaching new methods to use in anxiety-evoking situations. Relaxation training involves teaching the child how to relax the major muscle groups of the body to release physical tension and increase the level of mental calmness.

Cognitive-behavioral therapy through individual, group, and family modalities has also proved helpful with SAD (Mansdorf & Lukens, 1987; Ramirez et al., 2006). Individually and in group settings children learn to manage fear by learning to understand the relationship between their thoughts, feelings, and behaviors. Cognitive-behavioral therapy has many components, including psychoeducation, managing physical reactions, cognitive restructuring, and exposure (Albano & Kendall, 2002). The family can also be brought into treatment to build a support network for their child. The parents can be taught to reward (also known as contingency management) the child's attempts to face fears, while ignoring fearful behaviors and comments. Psychoeducation is an important variable in family anxiety management in that parents learn to handle their own emotions while becoming more adept at communication and problem-solving skills (Barrett, Dadds, & Rapee, 1996).

A few studies claiming successful pharmacological treatment of SAD children with antidepressants have been reported (Biederman et al., 1990; Gittelman-Klein & Klein, 1971, 1973). A study of fluoxetine (brand name Prozac) found that 81 percent of children with SAD showed improvement (Birmhauer et al., 1994). Despite these isolated successes, there is no definitive information on whether medications can be used to treat separation anxiety disorders.

Fears and Specific Phobias.

Characteristics. Specific phobias are marked by specific and persistent fear of a particular stimulus accompanied by active avoidance of that stimulus. It is important to remember that fear serves an adaptive function and that children experience fears in the normal course of development. Almost all children experience at least one fear and many children experience multiple fears. Normative data indicate that children's fears change over time from internal, global, and imaginary content (e.g., ghosts, monsters, the dark) to more external, specific, and reality-based content (e.g., school performance, social acceptance). Thus, the development of children's fears appears to parallel their cognitive development and increasing knowledge of reality (Campbell, 1986). Childhood fears may be temporary and are not necessarily precursors to adult fears, although adult phobics report having had more phobias as children than nonphobics (Solyom, Beck, Solyom, & Hugel, 1974). Duration (over 2 years) and/or intensity (sufficient to be debilitating to routine) can be used as markers to differentiate normal fears from those that need clinical attention (Graziano, DeGiovanni, & Garcia, 1979). The prevalence of phobic disorders in children is about 3–4 percent (King & Ollendick, 1989).

Some of the most common phobias in the general population are of dogs, snakes, insects, mice, closed spaces, heights, and air travel (American Psychiatric Association, 2000). When confronted with the stimulus, the individual has an immediate anxiety reaction, which often involves sweating, difficulty with breathing, and feeling panicky. A phobic individual will therefore go to great lengths to avoid the stimulus. (A well-known example is the television football commentator John Madden, who travels to football games across the country by bus or train due to his fear of flying.) Because of the tendency to avoid the phobic object or situation, phobias may go undetected at school unless a student is phobic about a stimulus in the classroom or the school setting. A list of common phobias is presented in Table 9.8.

Intervention. A number of interventions have been used successfully to treat children's fears and phobias, including systematic desensitization and cognitive-behavioral therapy linked with modeling, role-play, exposure, and relaxation training.

Systematic desensitization has been applied to a variety of fears, including loud noises, dogs, and the dark. In systematic desensitization, the principles of counterconditioning are used to alleviate fears and anxiety. This technique was developed by J. Wolpe in the 1950s and is based on three basic steps: (1) establishing a hierarchy of fear-inducing stimuli, (2) learning deep-muscle relaxation techniques, and (3) pairing the relaxation state with each of the stimuli on the hierarchy. This last step is accomplished by asking the individual to visualize the least-feared stimuli on the hierarchy while in a state of deep relaxation; in successive sessions, the individual works through the hierarchy until the highest-ranking fear is faced without the accompanying anxiety.

The behavioral intervention of exposure is a deconditioning procedure similar to systematic desensitization. In this method, the child has a prolonged exposure to the anxiety-provoking stimuli; the rationale is that the individual cannot maintain a high level of arousal and thus the anxiety response is weakened.

Cognitive-behavioral therapy (CBT) treatment programs such as the *Coping Cat Program for Anxious Youth* program by P.C. Kendall (2000) have been shown to have a promising impact on children's anxiety and phobic behaviors (Albano & Kendall, 2002). In 14–18 sessions, the program implements cognitive and behavioral strategies, such as focusing on the child's thoughts and feelings in a structured format. Behavioral interventions include relaxation training, reinforcement, role-play, exposure, and modeling.

Relaxation training (as previously described as a treatment for SAD) is also a treatment for phobias. Role-play is also beneficial. While role-playing, the child and therapist enact and prepare for events that will elevate feelings of anxiety. In addition, parents and children can utilize reinforcement strategies to increase positive behaviors. Reinforcement

TABLE 9.8 Common Phobias

Overall Population	**Children**
General: dogs, snakes, insects, public speaking, mice, closed spaces, heights, injury, the dark, air travel, procedures such as surgery	*General:* loud noises, dogs, snakes, other animals, bodily injury, heights, medical or dental work
	School related: riding on buses, physical education activities, fire alarms, weather changes, going to the toilet, test taking, public speaking and other performance-related activities, school phobia

can be implemented when the child demonstrates the ability to face his or her fears may involve praise, privileges, and other rewards the child finds appealing.

School-Related Fears and Phobias.

Characteristics. Fears become a problem when they are intense, chronic, and/or interfere with functioning. Children evincing excessive fear in an educational setting may suffer in both academic and social development. Common phobias in the school setting include riding on buses, public speaking, test taking, and physical education activities (King, Ollendick, & Gullone, 1991). Other phobias that may be manifested in school or on the way to school are of dogs and other animals, toilets, loud noises, fire alarms, and weather changes. Whereas younger children tend to fear objects and animals, older children and adolescents tend to exhibit test anxiety and fear of other performance-related activities.

Test-taking anxiety is the most common school-related phobia. Estimates of school-age children experiencing test anxiety run from 10 to 25 percent (Johnson, 1979). It has been well established that a high level of anxiety interferes with performance, thus possibly reinforcing the individual's fear that he or she will not perform well on the test. If the anxiety becomes debilitating and severe enough, the child or adolescent may refuse to attend school in order to avoid test-taking situations.

Intervention. More interventions have been reported for test anxiety than for other school-related fears because of its prevalence and its debilitating effects. Techniques include systematic desensitization and cognitive-behavioral techniques, sometimes in combination with other procedures. Relaxation training has also been used in attempts to alleviate test anxiety (Huberty & Dick, 2006). See Table 9.9 for a summary listing of interventions that have been reported as successful for children with school-related anxiety disorders.

School Phobia versus Separation Anxiety Disorder. *School phobia* has been used in the literature since the 1940s as the term of choice to refer to the behavior of all children who refuse to attend school. However, there is growing evidence that school refusers may be categorized into two separate and distinct groups: those with separation anxiety and those with school phobia. It has been estimated that of those children identified as school refusers, 75–80 percent manifest separation anxiety disorder (Gittelman & Klein, 1984). Characteristics distinguishing the two groups have been identified: children with SAD were more likely to be female, prepubertal, and from lower socioeconomic status (SES) families, whereas school phobics were more likely to be male, postpubertal, and from higher SES families (Last, Francis, Hersen, Kazdin, & Strauss, 1987).

Two important criteria in distinguishing separation anxiety from school phobia are (1) for separation anxiety disorder, the significance of the attachment figure and excessive fear upon separation and (2) for school phobia, persistent fear of a specific stimulus or situation within the school setting (Phelps et al., 1992). These differences have implications for treatment, which are discussed in the sections to follow.

School Phobia.

Characteristics. The essential feature of school phobia is chronic refusal to attend school accompanied by anxiety about the school setting. When pressed to attend, the school phobic is likely to become very agitated. Somatic complaints such as headaches, stomachaches,

TABLE 9.9 Summary of Treatment Techniques for School-Related Fears and Anxieties

Treatment	Presenting Problem
Systematic desensitization	School phobia, test anxiety, math anxiety, reading anxiety
Modeling	Social withdrawal
Positive reinforcement	Separation anxiety, school phobia
Cognitive-behavioral	Anxiety related to test taking, speech, academic performance, and evaluation
Psychodynamic therapy	Separation anxiety, school phobia
Social skills training	Social withdrawal

dizziness, nausea, diarrhea, and abdominal pain are common. These complaints are most often made in the morning before school, but may occur at school as well. The symptoms almost always disappear when the child is allowed to stay at home or go home from school.

Younger children may cry and cling to their mothers, whereas older children may experience either acute panic or apprehension that is slower to develop. School phobia occurs equally across intelligence levels and is no more prevalent among children with learning problems (Ollendick & Mayer, 1984). It may occur for the first time subsequent to changes in the child's life, such as after a move to a new school, illness of the child or mother, or divorce of parents.

Etiological theories of school phobia are largely behavioral; both classical conditioning and operant conditioning paradigms have been proposed to explain the development of school phobia. Classical conditioning theorists propose that anxiety develops as a conditioned response to some stimuli in the school setting or that the school setting becomes paired with fear of separation from the parent. Operant conditioning theorists suggest that the child who refuses to attend school receives both positive and negative reinforcement for nonattending. For example, children may feel reinforced by being able to stay home and watch television rather than go to school. Parents may inadvertently reinforce school refusal (e.g., through attention). Being removed from the aversive situation (the classroom) may serve as negative reinforcement. Or, as Kearney and Silverman state, "Simply put, the rewards for not attending school are greater than those for going" (1990, p. 343). Numerous interventions based on both classical and operant conditioning paradigms have been successful with children with school phobia and are reported in the next section.

Intervention. School phobia has been studied extensively, with interventions falling into two primary categories: behavioral and pharmacological.

Behavioral Interventions. A number of behavioral treatments have been applied to children with school phobia including classical conditioning techniques (systematic desensitization and flooding) and operant conditioning techniques. Social learning (modeling) and cognitive-behavioral techniques have also been used, but usually in conjunction with other techniques rather than as the sole treatment (Coleman, 1996).

As described in the section on separation anxiety disorder, systematic desensitization usually involves a combination of relaxation and visual imaging techniques to desensitize the individual to the fear-inducing stimuli—in this case, a particular stimulus within the school setting such as the classroom. Over the years a number of single-subject studies have reported success with this technique with children with school phobia (e.g., Houlihan & Jones, 1989; Miller, 1972; O'Farrell, Hedlund, & Cutter, 1986; Tahmisian & McReynolds, 1971). For example, Houlihan and Jones (1989) reported the following fear hierarchy with a 13-year-old boy who had refused to go to school for almost a year: walking the halls, sitting in the back of homeroom class for increasing periods of time, eating lunch, and finally, attending other classes. Attendance 1 year later was reported to be at 84 percent. It should be noted that the boy was accompanied through many of the initial steps by a psychologist, which is a typical procedure in cases of school phobia.

Flooding is another classical conditioning procedure used successfully with children with school phobia (Blagg & Yule, 1984; Kennedy, 1965). In contrast to the gradual successive approximations employed by systematic desensitization, proponents of flooding insist on rapid and immediate reentry into the school in order to avoid potential complications of prolonged absences. While support such as counseling may be provided, somatic or physical complaints are downplayed so that the child is given clear expectations for school attendance.

Pharmacological Treatments. In the early 1970s, two studies were conducted that successfully treated children with school phobia (with separation anxiety disorder) with the antidepressant imipramine. In oft-cited studies, Gittelman-Klein and Klein (1971, 1973) used a double-blind, placebo procedure in conjunction with behavioral counseling to effect school return in 81 percent of the sample. However, these results have not been replicated in subsequent studies by Klein, Koplewicz, and Kanner (1992) or others (Berney et al., 1981; Bernstein, Garfinkel, & Borchardt, 1990).

Although initially promising, antidepressants and other medications have not been found consistently useful in alleviating symptoms or returning children with school phobia to school. However, the reader should be mindful that most of these studies have not clearly distinguished between children with school phobia and those with separation anxiety disorder; most subjects had depressive symptoms as well. In addition, imipramine is currently out of favor for use with children due to its side effects (Coleman, 1996). Future research with children and adolescents with anxiety disorders will likely continue with newer antidepressants and with more careful diagnostic criteria for sample selection.

A Functional Approach to School Refusal. One final study of school refusal is reported because of its practical implications for educators and others who work with these youth. Kearney and Silverman (1990) used a functional model of school refusal to treat seven children and adolescents with a school refusal history of less than 1 year. The researchers believed that each individual child needed specific therapeutic strategies, depending on the specific aspects of his or her school refusal behavior. They hypothesized four categories of variables that maintain school refusal and designed an assessment instrument accordingly: (1) avoidance of a specific fear related to school (e.g., of riding the bus or test anxiety);

(2) escape from aversive social situations (e.g., high social anxiety such as speaking in front of the class); (3) attention-getting or separation-anxious behavior (e.g., tantruming in order to stay home with a specific person); and (4) tangible reinforcement (e.g., those who prefer to stay home and watch television, but who are not especially fearful). Treatment was then prescribed for each individual child based on his or her profile according to the four categories. Results of these prescriptive treatments were that six of the seven subjects were able to resume full-time school attendance at posttreatment and at 6-month follow-up.

The success of this model underscores the need to differentiate subtypes of school refusal behavior. However, the functional model does not depend on an "accurate" diagnosis according to DSM-IV-TR criteria; rather, it assesses the functionality of the behavior and the variables maintaining the behavior for each individual. Although additional studies are needed to determine whether this specific model can be replicated with larger numbers of school refusers, a functional approach to intervention seems warranted.

Generalized Anxiety Disorder.

Characteristics. First referred to as an overanxious reaction and later overanxious disorder, or OAD, the essential feature of generalized anxiety disorder (GAD) is excessive anxiety that is not the result of a recent stressor nor focused on a specific object or situation. Anxiety may be focused on more general elements, such as one's performance or competence, past behavior, or future events. Unrealistic worries about future events were especially characteristic of children with OAD. OAD has been dropped from the DSM-IV-TR as a diagnostic category for children; however, it is included in this discussion because researchers have studied children diagnosed with OAD for the past 20 years. Children with these characteristics are now labeled as GAD, which remains an adult classification under the DSM-IV-TR.

Children classified as GAD tend to be older than children diagnosed with separation anxiety disorder (Last et al., 1987). It is estimated that an equal number of males and females are diagnosed with GAD (Ramirez et al., 2006). The prevalence of GAD in the general community has been reported to be between 2.9 and 3.6 percent (Anderson et al., 1987; Bowen et al., 1990).

Compared to separation anxiety, GAD has been described as more severe, of longer duration, and with less likelihood of recovery (Keller et al., 1992). Both anxiety disorders appear to be long lasting. GAD may be underdiagnosed due to the fact that many of its characteristics are also reported by the general population.

Intervention. Studies assessing the effectiveness of treatments specifically for GAD cite that cognitive-behavioral therapy, family anxiety management, modeling, exposure, relaxation training, and contingency management are appropriate (Society of Clinical Child and Adolescent Psychology & The Network on Youth Mental Health, 2006). According to Flannery-Schroeder (2004), pharmacological treatment studies are still in their infancy, There are early indicators of the alleviation of GAD symptoms with fluoxetine (brand name Prozac) and busipirone (brand name Buspar). More research is needed in this area, however.

Posttraumatic Stress Disorder.

Characteristics. The essential features of posttraumatic stress disorder (PTSD) are persistent anxiety symptoms and intrusive recollections of a single traumatic event or repeated traumatic events. The event(s) must be clearly identifiable as distressing and not within the normal range of human experiences, for example, witnessing a violent act, the death of a close relative, or sexual or physical abuse. Stressors most likely to lead to PTSD include exposure to death and destruction, loss of significant others, and threat to life (Wilson, Smith, & Johnson, 1985). Survivors who were in close proximity to the shootings at Columbine High School near Denver in 1999 are prime candidates for posttraumatic stress disorder. In fact, nearly 1 year later, follow-ups by the media were beginning to report many PTSD symptoms in the survivors.

Exposure to violence is more traumatic to children than exposure to events such as natural disasters (McNally, 1993). Symptoms include insomnia, poor concentration, anxiety, nightmares, flashbacks, avoidance, and diminished interest in activities. The prevalence of PTSD in childhood has not been established. However, one study of school-age children ages 11–18 found a prevalence of 2 percent (Berna & Hyman, 1993).

Although the bulk of relevant research has been conducted with adults, particularly war veterans, some research on PTSD in children and adolescents exists. It appears that children and adolescents react differently and show different symptoms than adults. One study supporting this assumption was conducted with children involved in the Chowchilla school bus kidnapping. The children, ages 5–14, were kidnapped, held at gunpoint for hours, and then buried alive for 16 hours before being rescued. Follow-up studies 4 years later indicated that the children, unlike adults, did not experience amnesia or flashbacks; rather, they were likely to behaviorally reenact the scene, show a distorted sense of time, and feel that their futures were limited (Terr, 1981). Other researchers have substantiated that children tend to reexperience the traumatic event through nightmares or behavioral reenactment, rather than through flashbacks. A study of children exposed to a sniper attack on a school playground not only confirmed the presence of PTSD in the sample of children exposed to the sniper, but also found a relationship between the severity of symptoms and the proximity to the shootings (Pynoos, Frederick, & Nader, 1987).

Children who have suffered abuse may develop symptoms indicative of PTSD (Bernstein & Borchardt, 1991). Almost half of one sample of sexually abused children met criteria for PTSD (McLeer, Deblinger, Atkins, Foa, & Ralphe, 1988). In this sample, the closer the relationship of the abuser to the child was, the more likely the child was to demonstrate PTSD.

The symptomatology of PTSD in adolescents is less clear. Adolescent reactions to traumatic events range from mild symptoms to severe pathology, including depression, psychotic symptoms, anxiety, and conduct problems (Clark et al., 1994); therefore, differential diagnosis may be difficult. However, studies of adolescents who have clearly been exposed to trauma suggest that there may be unique adolescent responses to trauma: impaired identity formation, acting-out behavior, premature entry into adulthood, interpersonal difficulties, and poor work habits (Clark et al., 1994). Other reactions are to become compliant and withdrawn or aggressive, to become a substance abuser, and to act out sexually (Lyons, 1987). It is clear that adolescents who have been exposed to trauma should be assessed for symptoms of PTSD, which may be easily obscured by depression or some form of acting-out behavior.

Intervention. Research in the treatment of childhood PTSD is relatively new. Effective treatments take on a cognitive-behavioral approach combined with narrative, imaginary, and *in vivo* exposure; that is, the traumatic event is reviewed and reprocessed with the aid of a therapist in a safe and supportive environment. Narrative exposure is unique in that the child learns to retell their story to increase habituation (McKnight, Compton, & March, 2004). Therapeutic play therapy is particularly effective with younger children when they are not able to communicate their anxiety verbally (Gil, 1998). This type of therapy allows the child to express their inner feelings through the use of symbolic representations of their world (toys). As for pharmacological treatment, limited information is available in the literature regarding the impact of medication. An example of a case of a child with PTSD is presented in Box 9.2.

Obsessive–Compulsive Disorder.

Characteristics. In obsessive–compulsive disorder (OCD) obsessions are recurrent, persistent thoughts that are experienced as intrusive and senseless; compulsions are repetitive, purposeful behaviors, or rituals. Children and adults with obsessive–compulsive disorder apparently do not differ much in their symptoms. As many as half the adults with OCD report onset in childhood or adolescence. The range of average age of onset has been reported as nine to twelve years old (Bernstein & Borchardt, 1991). Children and adolescents are often secretive about their symptoms and may not report them until after several weeks or months of therapy. Some researchers have found a higher prevalence of males; others have found equal numbers of males and females with OCD.

The most common obsessions of children and adolescents are fear of contamination, fear of harm to self or significant others, thoughts of violence or aggression, and somatic complaints. These obsessive thoughts occurred in one-third to one-half of the samples identified as OCD (Flament, Whitaker, & Rapoport, 1988; Riddle, Scahill, & King, 1990).

The most common compulsions are washing and cleaning (e.g., hand washing), checking (e.g., checking to make sure that all electrical appliances are turned off), ordering (e.g., making sure that all the stuffed animals are in the same order on the bed), repeating (e.g., drawing a letter until it is "perfect" or going through every door a certain number of times), and straightening (e.g, every object in the room in the right place) (Flament et al., 1988; Riddle et al., 1990; Swedo, Leonard, & Rapoport, 1992). An important component of obsessive–compulsive behavior is that the child often believes that performing the ritual perfectly will somehow protect him or her and/or his or her loved ones from harm. Children having obsessive thoughts without accompanying rituals or compulsions ("pure obsessives") are rare, but "pure ritualizers" are not uncommon. For example, ritualizers as young as 6–8 years old may have elaborate checking or washing rituals without cognitive obsessions (Swedo et al., 1992). It is also common, especially among adolescents, to have multiple obsessions, compulsions, or rituals.

There is a possible biological link between obsessive–compulsive disorder and Tourette's syndrome: an increased rate of OCD has been found with children with Tourette's and their relatives (Bernstein & Borchardt, 1991). As Tourette's is known to be a gender influenced, dominant trait, OCD is thought by some researchers to be genetically mediated as part of the syndrome (Pauls & Leckman, 1986).

Intervention. Two primary interventions have been attempted with children and adolescents with obsessive–compulsive disorder: pharmacological treatment and cognitive-behavioral therapy.

BOX 9.2
Anthony

Anthony was a 7-year-old, first grader who was one of six siblings removed from the family home due to accusations of sexual abuse. While there was no evidence that Anthony experienced sexual abuse from his mother's boyfriend, his older sisters were alleged victims of the crime. Anthony was reported to be a witness to the incidents. Prior to the removal of the children from the home, Anthony was sexually acting out toward his younger brother. One evening he was found in the same bed with his brother making sexual advances.

After Child Protective Services were called to the residence, all six children were taken to foster care. Some of the siblings were placed in the same foster home, but Anthony was placed in a home without younger children due to his previous behavior. He was placed with an older couple with a teenage son named Jamal.

Anthony had a brief "honeymoon" period in which he was compliant and affectionate toward his caregivers. They placed him in public school within the regular education curriculum. Not long after his entry into the classroom, Anthony began to have behavioral difficulties. Teachers indicated that he was moody and explosive. He had trouble making and keeping friends, following directions, finishing school and homework, staying seated, and remaining in the classroom. Several times Anthony was found wandering around the school during lunch and he also left school grounds. During one episode, a teacher once found him in the librarian's office eating part of the librarian's lunch.

The foster parents were exhausted and confused by Anthony's behavior. The "honeymoon" period was also over at home, with Anthony running out of the house and displaying excessive affection toward Jamal. While not sexually acting out toward Jamal, the foster parents were concerned. In addition, Anthony told his caregivers he was having nightmares about his mother's boyfriend and he often woke up crying. Due to the distress of the caregivers and school staff, a special education referral for testing was initiated and outpatient therapy began.

Through outpatient therapy and psychological assessment it was determined that Anthony was likely experiencing posttraumatic stress disorder (PTSD). To assist the foster parents, behavioral parent training was initiated along with trauma-focused play therapy. The foster parents were in need of behavior management techniques and supports that could be utilized in the home. Anthony's case was unique for most parent training cases, because of the sensitive issues surrounding sexual abuse and PTSD. While it had not been legally or medically proven that Anthony had experienced sexual abuse, there was evidence of stress, relationship problems, and possibly reexperiencing the event(s); therefore, the play therapy intervention was deemed necessary.

A behavior improvement plan was also created by special educators and the school psychologist. Anthony was assigned a peer "buddy" and rewarded for compliance and work completion with a behavioral chart. Time on task improved and Anthony was able to remain in his classroom and the lunchroom without running off. Unfortunately, his mood waned and he would shift from a joyful child to a sullen, irritable child.

The outpatient therapist also integrated multisystemic therapeutic techniques in Anthony's treatment by visiting the school and home. This was implemented to approach Anthony's care from all angles. Eventually, the foster parents felt they were unable to care for Anthony's extreme behaviors and opted to have him placed with another family. They also feared for Jamal's safety.

Anthony was finally placed with a younger foster mother and he was allowed supervised visitation with his mother and siblings. Through integration of services between multiple providers (school, foster care, social workers, outpatient therapist), Anthony began to show progress academically and socially. He continues to participate in therapy in and out of school, while remaining in a highly structured and individualized special education program. As Anthony is still young and has difficulty communicating his feelings, cognitive-behavioral interventions may also be utilized in the future.

Tricyclic antidepressants and selective serotonin reuptake inhibitors have been used to treat OCD. In the past, clomipramine (a tricyclic antidepressant) was systematically studied in children and demonstrated improvement in the majority of subjects (DeVeagh-Geiss et al., 1992; Swedo et al., 1992). Selective serotonin reuptake inhibitors are more likely to be prescribed at present. The Food and Drug Administration has officially approved fluvoxamine (brand name Luvox) and sertraline (brand name Zoloft) for the treatment of childhood OCD (March, Franklin, Leonard, & Foa, 2004).

The literature has not overwhelmingly established psychotherapeutic treatment for OCD, but cognitive-behavioral therapy with response prevention and exposure is the most common treatment. Response prevention involves setting up conditions to prevent the compulsive behavior. It has been effective in a number of case studies of adolescents (Apter, Bernhout, & Tyano, 1984; Bolton, Collins, & Steinberg, 1983). However, there is some concern that young children may lack the cognitive capacity to participate in cognitive-behavioral therapy procedures. Controlled studies of behavioral treatments for children, especially in contrast to drug treatment, are clearly needed (Swedo et al., 1992).

Panic Disorder.

Characteristics. The essential feature of panic disorder is the occurrence of discrete panic attacks that are spontaneous or unexpected and defined by intense fear or discomfort. DSM-IV-TR (APA, 2000) also indicates that there must be persistent worry about attacks. Symptoms include palpitations, dizziness or faintness, sweating, nausea, trembling, hot and cold flashes, tingling, and fear of dying, going crazy, or losing control. Shortness of breath and depersonalization are also common.

Previously, panic disorder was thought to occur only in adults. It is now accepted that adolescents experience panic disorder as well. In fact, adults have reported that the peak age of onset was between 15 and 19 years (Von Korff, Eaton, & Keyl, 1985). Nearly one in 10 adolescents in an anxiety outpatient clinic was identified as having panic attacks (Last & Strauss, 1989). In contrast, a general community adult sample reported estimates of 0.6–1.0 percent (Von Korff et al., 1985).

Whether children actually experience panic attacks is controversial. Panic attacks have been reported in children of prepubertal age in several studies (Bernstein & Borchardt, 1991; Moreau, Weissman, & Warner, 1989; Vitiello, Behar, Wolfson, & McLeer, 1990). However, diagnosable panic disorder in children is rare for a number of reasons. First are the DSM-IV-TR criteria of spontaneity and of concern about future attacks. Apparently, children rarely experience spontaneous attacks, and they tend to attribute panic symptoms to external rather than internal causes (Bernstein & Borchardt, 1991). They may therefore not be especially concerned about future panic attacks and thus do not meet the DSM-IV-TR criterion for panic disorder. In addition, children with panic attacks may experience other disorders, such as depression and separation anxiety, possibly obscuring accurate diagnosis. A final reason for the reported low incidence of panic disorder in children is that most instruments used to identify anxiety disorders in childhood do not adequately screen for panic disorder (Bernstein & Borchardt, 1991).

As with other anxiety disorders, there is a family link in panic disorder. Relatives of patients with panic disorder have been shown to be at increased risk for panic attack and panic disorder compared to relatives of controls (Crowe et al., 1983). In addition, the concordance of panic disorder among identical twins is five times that among fraternal twins (Torgersen, 1983).

Intervention. Since children are generally thought to experience panic disorder rarely if at all, very little information about their treatment is available. According to the literature, there are no well-established or promising psychotherapeutic treatments for panic disorder. The literature is, however, replete with studies on pharmacotherapy and cognitive-behavioral therapy with adults with panic disorder, with some studies finding cognitive-behavioral therapy superior to drug therapy, some finding the reverse, and others finding a combination of the two the most effective. No clinical trials for the pharmacological treatment of panic disorder in children have been completed. Despite the lack of research with children, cited psychotherapeutic interventions often consist of cognitive-behavioral techniques, psychoeducation, and assisting the child in the reinterpretation of body sensations associated with panic attacks (Ollendick, Birmaher, & Mattis, 2004). Table 9.10 summarizes the numerous interventions reported in the literature for childhood anxiety disorders.

TABLE 9.10 Interventions Reported for Childhood Anxiety Disorders

Disorder	Intervention
Separation anxiety disorder	Modeling, cognitive-behavioral techniques, relaxation training, family anxiety management
Fears and simple phobias	Systematic desensitization, cognitive-behavioral techniques, modeling, relaxation training, role-play, exposure
Test anxiety	Systematic desensitization, cognitive techniques, relaxation training
School phobia	Systematic desensitization, flooding, modeling, operant conditioning, cognitive-behavioral in combination with other techniques, pharmacological interventions
GAD/OAD	Relaxation training, cognitive-behavioral techniques, family anxiety management, modeling, exposure, contingency management
Posttraumatic stress disorder	Cognitive-behavioral techniques with reexposure procedures, play therapy
Obsessive–compulsive disorder	Pharmacological, cognitive-behavioral therapy (e.g., response prevention)
Panic disorder	Very little intervention research with children; pharmacotherapy and cognitive-behavioral therapy used with adults

Comorbidity. Children and adolescents with anxiety disorders are often diagnosed with more than one specific anxiety disorder, and many have coexisting disorders, such as depression, alcohol abuse, and conduct disorders.

Multiple Anxiety Disorders. The percentage of children and adolescents in clinical samples reporting more than one anxiety disorder is significant: estimates range from 15 percent (McGee et al., 1990) to 70 percent. The latter percentage was reported for OAD/GAD and separation anxiety disorder dually diagnosed in preadolescent children (Strauss, Lease, Last, & Francis, 1988).

There are several possible explanations for the coexistence of multiple anxiety disorders in individuals. One is that the different anxiety disorders share a common etiology. For example, possible genetic underpinnings connecting different anxiety disorders are indicated by the family studies linking OAD with Tourette's syndrome and those linking SAD with both panic disorder and agoraphobia. Another explanation is that diagnostic criteria are not discrete, and thus overlapping symptoms lead to multiple diagnoses.

Anxiety Disorders and Depression. It has been well established that anxiety disorders and depression often coexist in children, adolescents, and adults. In fact, depression is the disorder most likely to coexist with anxiety disorders. Large epidemiological studies found 17 percent comorbidity among children with anxiety disorders (Anderson et al., 1987) and a range of 12–30 percent among adolescents (Clark et al., 1994; McGee et al., 1990). Among clinical samples, the degree of overlap is much higher, ranging from 40 to 86 percent (McGee et al., 1990; Mitchell, McCauley, Burke, & Moss, 1988). Supporting these dual diagnoses are studies using self-report measures that show high levels of both anxiety and depression (King et al., 1991).

Older children are more likely to have concurrent anxiety and depression. It is noteworthy that the symptoms of each disorder are more severe in children and adolescents with coexisting conditions than in those with "pure" anxiety or "pure" depression (Bernstein & Borchardt, 1991). It is also noteworthy that in one study of comorbidity the anxiety disorder preceded the depressive disorder in the majority of cases (Kovacs, Gatsonis, Paulauskas, & Richards, 1989), leading to the conclusion that anxiety disorders are not likely to be a consequence of depression.

The high degree of the coexistence of anxiety and depression has led researchers to explore the causes. Some believe in the unitary model, which posits that anxiety and depression are the same fundamental disorder, but represent opposite ends of the continuum (cited in Bernstein & Borchardt, 1991; Clark et al., 1994). Despite symptom overlap and frequent comorbidity, many experts conclude that the disorders are in fact distinguishable and should be treated separately. In contrast, others suggest that implications of the unitary theory for child behavior therapy have yet to be fully explored (e.g., King et al., 1991).

Anxiety Disorders and Alcohol Abuse. Evidence suggests a relationship between alcohol abuse and anxiety disorders, often beginning in adolescence. One subtype of adolescent alcoholism that represents a large percentage of cases is characterized by both anxious and depressive symptoms (Mezzich et al., 1993). There is also evidence that anxiety disorder may precede alcohol abuse in some adolescents (Clark & Jacob, 1992). While such studies do not prove a causal relationship, it can be concluded that anxiety disorders may contribute to alcohol abuse (Clark et al., 1994).

Anxiety Disorders and Conduct Disorders. A number of studies have established a relationship between anxiety and conduct disorders. Taken together, the studies indicate a positive correlation between anxiety and aggressiveness in adolescents. In addition, studies of clinical samples, including females, have found a strong coexistence of anxiety disorders and conduct disorders as well as other disruptive behavior disorders (see the review by Clark et al., 1994).

In summary, anxiety disorders often coexist with one another and with other disorders such as alcohol abuse, conduct disorders, and depression. Although researchers have established these links, none have been proved causal in either direction. The importance of coexistence lies in the fact that anxiety disorders may be obscured by other, more obvious problems, such as alcohol abuse or disorders of an aggressive or acting-out nature. Unless a child or adolescent is self-reporting anxiety symptoms, the problems may go undiagnosed and untreated. An implication of the coexistence of anxiety disorders and depression is that some experts are questioning whether the two are different manifestations of the same fundamental disorder.

Implications for Teachers. Teachers of students with EBD will probably work with many students who evidence anxiety disorders. However, students diagnosed with a "pure" anxiety disorder will be uncommon, unless it is school phobia or otherwise school related. Teachers are more likely to work with students who experience anxiety along with multiple related disorders, such as alcohol abuse, conduct disorder, or depression. Students with anxiety disorders are more likely to be older—that is, adolescents—although it is now commonly accepted that children also develop these difficulties. Teachers will undoubtedly encounter children and adolescents who experience posttraumatic stress disorder as a result of physical or sexual abuse.

Since accurate diagnosis of anxiety disorders in children has lagged behind the diagnosis of older populations, less is known about successful treatment. There are a number of promising pharmacological and behavioral treatments that will usually be handled by mental health clinicians or other support personnel within the school setting. Teachers may be asked to monitor medications for side effects and behavioral fluctuations and to assist with behavioral treatments that may be carried out in the classroom or school. Teachers can also be key in assisting with and reinforcing cognitive-behavioral interventions related to classroom functioning.

Conclusions

Although children with internalizing disorders do not typically demand adult attention as frequently or as vociferously as children with externalizing disorders, it is important to realize that children and adolescents do suffer from anxiety and depression. There are probably genetic predispositions for the development of both disorders, although environmental and nongenetic family factors may serve as catalysts. One developing body of literature suggests that the individual's cognitions (i.e., faulty information processing) play a role in the development of both anxiety and depression. It is heartening that a variety of treatment approaches is demonstrating that children with these conditions can be helped to overcome their symptoms. Psychotherapy, medication, and cognitive-behavioral approaches have been attempted, with mixed results, with students who are depressed. Successful treatments for anxiety disorders have included a variety of behavioral and cognitive techniques. In some cases, teachers may be asked to help to implement interventions in their classrooms; in other cases, the child may be treated by a therapist outside the school setting.

KEY POINTS

1. Although mental health professionals have not always believed that children are capable of experiencing depression, it is now commonly held that children and adolescents may experience depression in a manner very similar to that of adults.
2. It is likely that a combination of genetic predisposition, family environment, and the child's coping mechanisms interacts to cause depression.
3. Depression has been found to coexist with other disorders, including conduct disorders, eating disorders, substance abuse, and anxiety disorders; depression may therefore be significantly underdiagnosed in children and adolescents.
4. For students with severe depression and/or a family history of depression, medication may be indicated; for others, cognitive-behavioral therapy and social skills training appear promising.
5. Many studies suggest that both biological bases (e.g., familial pattern) and negative life events (e.g., environmental stressors) play a significant role in the development of anxiety disorders.
6. Behavioral and cognitive models have been used to explain and also to treat anxious and fearful behavior.
7. Anxiety disorders are composed of a variety of distinct disorders, each with unique characteristics and treatments: separation anxiety disorder, phobias, generalized anxiety disorder, posttraumatic stress disorder, obsessive–compulsive disorder, and panic disorder.
8. Systematic desensitization, modeling, operant conditioning principles, and cognitive techniques have all been applied with some success to anxious and fearful behavior in children.
9. Pharmacological treatment of anxiety disorders in children has met with mixed success and is a much-needed area of study.

HOMEWORK QUESTIONS

1. Speak with a school psychologist or psychologist and identify procedures and measures for assessing children for depression and anxiety under IDEA criteria for emotional disturbance.
2. Go to the website for effective child therapy (*www.effectivechildtherapy.com*) and review the research-supported treatments for disorders of depression and anxiety. Report the definitions of "well-established" and "probably efficacious" treatments. Describe one treatment for anxiety and one for depression that meet the "well-established" criteria.
3. Describe how you would intervene with a child displaying the following:
   a. Withdrawing from social situations, lack of motivation, expression of helplessness, and irritability
   b. Expression of nervousness prior to math tests, somatic complaints during math class, avoidance of homework completion for math assignments
4. *Consider the following case:* Jake is a 3-year-old male with erratic behaviors. Parents and preschool teachers indicated that Jake displays

mood swings, temper tantrums, oppositional behavior, hyperactivity, aggression, and noncompliance; however, he is also reported to be a bright child with no major motor delays.

Jake's case is suggestive of bipolar disorder, but what other disorders may be possible? Write a brief essay that reviews the possibilities of the following:

a. A medical or neurological condition (e.g., deafness)
b. An externalizing disorder (e.g., oppositional-defiant disorder or attention-deficit hyperactivity disorder)
c. Comorbid internalizing and externalizing disorders
d. No disorder/typical development

ADDITIONAL READINGS AND RESOURCES

Anxiety disorders in children and adolescents (2nd ed.), by T.L. Morris and J.S. March New York: Guilford Press, 2004, for information on etiology, diagnosis, and treatment of anxiety disorders in children.

Bipolar disorder in childhood and early adolescence, by B. Geller and M.P. Delbello (eds.). New York: Guilford Press, 2003, for research on bipolar disorder in children.

Depression and Related Affective Disorders Foundation: *www.drada.org,* for information on a community organization committed to providing assistance to individuals with affective disorders by forming self-help groups, providing education and training, and funding research.

On the edge of darkness, by Kate Cronkite, New York: Doubleday, 1994, for a book of interviews with a number of famous people on how it feels to be depressed.

Phobic and anxiety disorders in children and adolescents: A clinician's guide to effective psychosocial and pharmacological interventions, by T.H. Ollendick and J.S. March (eds.), New York: Oxford University Press, 2004, for information on treatment of anxiety disorders in children.

Raising a moody child: How to cope with depression and bipolar disorder, by M. Fristad and J. G. Arnold, New York: Guilford Press, 2004, for parenting techniques for parents of children with depression and bipolar disorder.

Depression in children, by J. Garber and J.L. Horowitz in I.H. Gotlib and C.L. Hammen (eds.), *Handbook of depression,* pp. 510–540, New York: Guilford Press, 2002, for information on depression etiology, diagnosis, and treatment.

American Academy of Child and Adolescent Psychiatry (AACAP): *www.aacap.org,* for information about the national organization for psychiatrists specializing in the treatment of childhood psychiatric disorders.

Anxiety Disorders Association of America: *www.adaa.org,* for information on a national, nonprofit organization dedicated to educating the public, legislators, and professionals about issues surrounding the diagnosis and treatment of anxiety disorders in children and adults.

Child and Adolescent Bipolar Foundation: *www.bpkids.org,* for information from a personal point of view.

National Alliance on Mental Illness, www.nami.org, for information on the largest grassroots organization dedicated to improving the lives of persons with mental illness. The organization's mission is to provide advocacy and education and to further research in the area of mental illness.

Juvenile Bipolar Research Foundation: *www.jbrf.org,* for information on a charitable organization devoted to research in early-onset bipolar disorder.

National Alliance on Mental Illness: *www.nami.org,* for information on the largest advocacy organization for individuals with mental illness.

National Institute of Mental Health: *www.nimh.nih.gov/healthinformation/depressionmenu.cfm,* for information on depression in adults and children.

National Mental Health Association: *www.nmha.org,* for information on a nonprofit organization devoted to advocacy, training, research, and service to the mental health community.

Society of Clinical Child and Adolescent Psychology—APA Division 53: *www.clinicalchildpsychology.org,* for information on the section of the American Psychological Association devoted to training, research, and clinical activities with children.

The treatment of depression during childhood: A school-based program, by K. D. Stark New York: Guilford Press, 1990, for a description of a school-based treatment program for depression.

CHAPTER 10 Externalizing Disorders

Attention-Deficit Hyperactivity Disorder and Conduct Disorders
Definition and Prevalence, Subtypes and Characteristics, Etiology, Treatment, Implications for Teachers

QUESTIONS TO CONSIDER

- What are the three core characteristics of attention-deficit hyperactivity disorder (ADHD)?
- Why is it essential that some symptoms be present before age 7 to make the diagnosis of ADHD?
- What are some of the major theories for the etiology of ADHD?
- What treatments have been found to be most effective for ADHD?
- How are the terms *conduct disorder, social maladjustment,* and *juvenile delinquency* related?
- What are some of the predisposing factors for conduct disorder?
- How do theories for the etiology of conduct disorder inform school-based interventions?
- How do comorbid diagnoses affect treatment considerations for externalizing disorders?
- How can positive behavioral support systems benefit children with externalizing disorders and what is the role of the special education teacher?

Orientation

The previous chapter dealt with children suffering from the internalizing disorders of anxiety, depression, and withdrawal, that is, the kids that hurt on the inside but may not show it on the outside. In sharp contrast are the students who let everybody know what's happening in their lives; in fact, they demand our attention. Children and youth with conduct disorders demand our attention through actions that are, at best, worrisome acting-out behaviors, and at worst, antisocial, aggressive acts that break the law. Hyperactive children demand our attention by twisting, wiggling, fidgeting, interrupting everyone, and performing poorly in school.

Overview

This chapter addresses externalizing disorders of childhood and adolescence. These disorders tend to be extroversive or interpersonal in their manifestations; in the past, they have been called undercontrolled and acting out. Aggressive and delinquent behaviors are often associated with hyperactivity and conduct disorders; thus, these students are often in constant conflict with authority, either in school or in the community. For both hyperactivity and conduct disorders, this chapter addresses definition and characteristics, etiology and development, and treatment interventions. The role of teachers is also addressed.

Attention-Deficit Hyperactivity Disorder

As with most other syndromes, this disorder historically has been called many names, including minimal brain dysfunction, minimal brain injury, hyperactivity, hyperkinesis, and the current label, *attention-deficit hyperactivity disorder* (ADHD). One writer at the turn of the century even labeled hyperactivity as a "defect in moral control" (Still, 1902). This discussion will highlight current thinking regarding the nature and etiology of ADHD.

Definition and Prevalence

Attention-deficit hyperactivity disorder is defined by its core behaviors of inattention, impulsivity, and hyperactivity. These behaviors generally occur across settings and are most noticeable when in-seat and attentive behaviors are required, as in the classroom. DSM-IV-TR (American Psychological Association [APA], 2000) describes these core behaviors as the essential features when making a diagnosis of ADHD. The following criteria are manifestations of these core behaviors; in order to make a DSM-IV diagnosis, six criteria for inattention or six criteria for hyperactivity/impulsivity should be evident for a period of at least 6 months and to a maladaptive degree:

Inattention

1. Fails to give close attention to details/makes careless mistakes
2. Has difficulty sustaining attention to tasks or play
3. Does not seem to listen when spoken to directly
4. Has difficulty following instructions (e.g., fails to finish schoolwork, chores)
5. Has difficulty organizing tasks and activities
6. Avoids tasks requiring sustained mental effort (e.g., homework)
7. Often loses things needed for home or school (e.g., toys, assignments)
8. Is easily distracted
9. Is forgetful

Hyperactivity

1. Often fidgets or squirms
2. Has difficulty remaining seated
3. Runs or climbs excessively

4. Has difficulty playing or engaging in leisure activities quietly
5. Often talks excessively
6. Is often "on the go"

Impulsivity

1. Often blurts out answers to questions
2. Has difficulty awaiting turn
3. Often interrupts or intrudes on others. (APA, 2000, pp. 83–84)

It is obvious that these behaviors must be viewed in a developmental context; that is, for any child to be diagnosed with ADHD, these behaviors must be present at a much higher rate than is typical and appropriate for the child's age and at least some of the symptoms must have been present before age 7. The symptoms must also persist to a degree that significantly impairs the child's functioning in at least two settings, such as home and school.

The DSM-IV describes three subtypes of ADHD: *predominantly inattentive, predominantly hyperactive–impulsive,* or *combined* (Forness, Walker, & Kavale, 2003–2004). Most empirical approaches to the classification of ADHD support the distinction between the predominantly inattentive type, in which the child's primary problems reflect inattention and disorganization, and the other subtypes, which include symptoms of hyperactivity and impulsivity (Hoff, Doepke, & Landau, 2001). For this chapter, the focus is on children with ADHD who have the features of hyperactivity and impulsivity that characterize externalizing behavior.

Barkley (1998) postulates that the major symptoms of ADHD (in the predominantly hyperactive and combined subtypes) can best be understood as manifestations of *behavioral disinhibition;* while the everyday demands of school and social settings require that students suppress or inhibit responses, children with ADHD are not able to inhibit behavior at a rate consistent with chronological age expectations. Barkley further describes this behavioral disinhibition problem as consistent with a primary deficit in *executive functioning,* or the ability to self-regulate behavior, thought, and emotion. Pennington (2002) reported that in a review of published studies regarding executive functions in ADHD (Pennington & Ozonoff, 1996), 15 of the 18 studies found a significant difference between ADHD subjects and control subjects on one or more executive function measures. Problems with working memory, internalization of speech, and construction of appropriate responses to external events also characterize executive functioning deficits (Hoff et al., 2001). In a similar conceptualization, Goldstein (1999) includes five components as defining ADHD: (1) impulsivity, (2) inattention, (3) overarousal, (4) difficulty with gratification, and (5) emotional lability and external locus of control.

Diagnostic guidelines issued by the American Academy of Pediatrics state that, in addition to the DSM-IV criteria, diagnostic procedures should also accomplish the following:

- Determine that symptoms are present in two or more of a child's settings (e.g., home and school)
- Determine that the symptoms adversely affect the child's academic or social functioning for at least 6 months
- Ensure that the evaluations are initiated by the primary-care physician

- Include assessment information from both parents and school professionals
- Include evaluation for coexisting disorders such as depression, anxiety, and learning disabilities. (Coles, 2000; Tanner, 2000)

Prevalence estimates have ranged as high as 20 percent, but a more realistic figure is between 3 and 5 percent (APA, 2000; Barkley, 1998; Forness et al., 2003–2004). This figure translates into about one hyperactive child per classroom, or between 1.5 and 2.5 million school-age children in the United States. ADHD is much more common in boys, with a male:female ratio of about 6 to 1 in clinic settings, and about 3 to 1 in community settings (Goldstein, 1999). The higher number of males referred in clinical settings may reflect the greater prevalence of comorbid disruptive behavior disorders in males, including oppositional- defiant disorder and conduct disorder.

Characteristics and Symptoms

Although problems with schoolwork are not listed as specific DSM-IV criteria, the reader can easily ascertain how such problems can arise as a result of these behaviors. The varied classroom manifestations of ADHD are dealt with in this section. The following clusters of behaviors are discussed: attending, hyperactivity, impulsivity, academic performance, and social interaction.

Attending. "He doesn't pay attention" has long been the hue and cry of parents and teachers working with children with ADHD. Research has supported this complaint, as the ADHD child appears to have problems with both selective and sustained attention (Douglas & Peters, 1979), resulting in behaviors such as distractibility, disorganization, sloppiness, irresponsibility, and intrusiveness (Hoff et al., 2001). Selective attention deficiencies interfere with the child's classroom functioning because he or she tends to either focus on inappropriate stimuli and/or to be easily distracted when paying attention to the proper stimuli. Both external and internal distraction may be operating. Examples of internal and external distraction commonly seen in the classroom were offered by Fournier (1987): An example of external distraction is the child who cannot be seated by the classroom door because he or she is distracted by every noise in the hall, even those that are easily screened out by the majority of the class. An example of internal distraction is the child who becomes preoccupied with doodling rather than the class assignment.

Larry Silver, a prominent spokesperson for ADHD, has aptly defined the distractibility of these children by describing them as being "at the mercy of their senses." The ability to sustain attention is another requirement for success in the classroom. The inability to sustain attention is illustrated by the child who completes three-fourths of a worksheet and "forgets" the rest, or skips every other row on a sheet of math problems. Poorer performance on repetitious tasks has been found for children with ADHD compared to controls (Hebben, Whitman, Milberg, Andresko, & Galpin, 1981), and the poorer performance is thought to reflect the child's lack of internal controls rather than lack of capability (Draeger, Prior, & Sanson, 1986).

One of the most puzzling features of the inattention component is that attending is often inconsistent (Attention Deficit Disorder—Part I, 1995). For example, many children with ADHD concentrate well on tasks in which they are extremely interested, but not on others, or may do fine on one week's homework, but neglect it the next week. Other research suggests that sustained attention may be influenced by external factors such as positive reinforcement (Devers, Bradley-Johnson, & Johnson, 1994), smaller groups (Attention Deficit Disorder—Part I, 1995), or presence of an authority figure (Draeger et al., 1986; Nuechterlein, 1983). Difficulty with executive functioning, as described earlier in this chapter, may help to account for the poor regulation of attention and the variability associated with external factors.

Hyperactivity. Increased motor activity may be manifested in a variety of classroom behaviors: being out of seat; wiggling, fidgeting, and constant leg-shaking when seated; pencil-tapping; frequent pencil-sharpening and difficulty keeping hands to self. The analogies to "a motor that is always running" or "an engine that only has one gear—high" appear to be appropriate. Such behaviors present classroom management problems for the teacher because the child is frequently breaking class rules, distracting others, and falling behind in schoolwork. The concept of disinhibition as central to ADHD (Barkley, 1998) appears relevant to the behaviors associated with motor hyperactivity. Pennington (2002) describes *intentional motor inhibition,* or the ability to consciously restrain a motor response, as a characteristic that appears to be impaired in studies of children with ADHD, and relates this impairment to an executive function deficit.

Impulsivity. Impulsivity refers to a tendency to act without thinking. Many of the DSM-IV criteria describe impulsivity: blurting out answers before the question has been completed, having difficulty with turn-taking, and interrupting others. Although impulsivity has implications for task completion both in the classroom and the home, its most detrimental effect may be on interpersonal relationships. Intrusiveness of verbal interaction (e.g., interrupting or otherwise intruding when socially inappropriate) was found to discriminate hyperactive from nonhyperactive children at a high degree of accuracy (Abikoff, Gittelman, & Klein, 1980). Hyperactive children were found to demonstrate intrusive behavior at higher rates and with greater intensity than nonhyperactive children (Vincent, Williams, Harris, & Duval, 1981). As stated by Goldstein (1999), "their limited capacity for self-control is quickly overwhelmed by their immediate need to act" (p. 159).

Academic Performance. There is little doubt that students with ADHD have academic difficulties (Hoff et al., 2002; Weiss & Hechtman, 1986). The core behaviors of hyperactivity, impulsivity, and attention problems likely interact to produce academic problems (Weiss & Hechtman, 1986). Documented academic problems of students with ADHD include failing grades (Barkley, 1998) and higher levels of grade retention (Cantwell & Satterfield, 1978). They are also prone to underachievement despite adequate intellectual potential. By high school, approximately 80 percent of children with ADHD fall behind in a basic academic subject requiring repetition and attention, such as basic math knowledge, written language, or spelling (Goldstein & Goldstein, 1998). DuPaul, Stoner, and O'Reilly (2002) observe that the academic achievement problems associated with ADHD appear to be generic rather than isolated to a specific subject.

Social Interaction. Difficulties in social relationships of children with ADHD have become an increasing concern. Research has established that they tend to be deficient in social skills and peer interactions, less compliant to requests, and display more explosiveness and argumentativeness (Barkley, 1998: Hoff et al., 2001). Whether their social interactions are difficult primarily due to their impulsivity and intrusiveness or to other related factors remains to be proved. Some research indicates that aggressive hyperactive children display negative attributional biases when interpreting social situations (Goldstein, 1999; Milich & Dodge, 1984). For example, ADHD aggressive children were more likely to interpret as hostile an ambiguous event such as being hit in the back with a ball. On the other hand, it has been postulated that hyperactive boys with social problems can adequately comprehend social situations but are deficient in generating and acting on adaptive solutions. Thus, both deficiencies in social perception and generation of adaptive solutions to problems could be contributing to the social problems of children and adolescents with ADHD.

In summary, the symptoms of children with ADHD include a number of problems with attention, impulsivity, and hyperactivity. These core behaviors interact to produce classroom problems in interpersonal interactions and in academic performance. It is important for teachers to recognize these symptoms and to seek help before a negative classroom interaction cycle is set into motion. The hyperactive child in the classroom often elicits teacher behaviors that are more intense, controlling, and negative than usual (Goldstein, 1999; Whalen, Henker, Collins, McAulliffe, & Vaux, 1979). Given the externalized nature of hyperactivity, it may be easy to overlook the internal turmoil experienced by these youngsters, as illustrated in Figure 10.1.

FIGURE 10.1 A Self-Portrait from a "Stressed-Out 7½ Year-Old with ADHD

From N. Nussbaum & E. Bigler (1990), Identification and treatment of attention deficit disorder, Austin, TX: Pro-Ed. Reprinted with permission of the publisher.

Assessment Procedures

Three types of procedures are used to diagnose ADHD: (1) developmental histories including data from home and school, (2) clinical procedures, and (3) observations and recordings of behavior. It is important to obtain developmental histories because certain factors such as low birth weight, respiratory problems after delivery, and a family history of learning problems have been shown to have an abnormally high occurrence among these children. It is important to rule out other psychiatric disorders, such as autism, depression, and anxiety disorders, because if identified, such disorders may take precedence over the diagnosis of ADHD (Forness et al., 2003–2004; Goldstein, 1999).

Most children with ADHD are described by their parents as being restless and inattentive and, to a lesser extent, disruptive, destructive, or temperamental during this period. Barkley (1998) considers teacher observations and school history to be more informative even than parental accounts or physicians' judgments because "hyperactivity reaches its peak in a sit-down, all-day classroom situation, an experience routinely observed only by the teacher" (p. 17). Within the school setting, off-task behavior, excessive motor activity, and negative vocalizations appear to be the most observable manifestations of ADHD (DuPaul, Guevremont, & Barkley, 1992).

Clinical procedures are used by pediatric neurologists, pediatricians, psychologists, and other child specialists to diagnose ADHD. Depending on the specialist, clinical procedures may include assessments of visual–motor skills, intelligence, achievement, memory, executive functions, and sometimes an electroencephalogram (EEG) and a pediatric neurological examination.

Observations and recordings of classroom behavior may be completed by a teacher or other school personnel using a behavior checklist or some type of behavior recording. There are a number of published checklists available for teacher use, including the *Conner's Rating Scales—Revised* (Conners, 1997), the *ADHD-IV Rating Scale* (DuPaul, Power, Anastopoulos, & Reid, 1998), and the *Behavior Assessment System for Children—2* (BASC-2; Reynolds & Kamphaus, 2004). On such measures, the teacher is asked to rate the degree to which a child shows characteristics and behaviors such as impulsivity, disturbing others, fighting, inattention, failing to complete work, tenseness and crying, temper tantrums, or other signs of frustration. Under optimal conditions, more than one teacher's rating on a particular child is obtained. To obtain a behavioral record, a person trained in systematic behavior recording observes the child in the classroom and other school settings. In this procedure, a number of behaviors such as out-of-seat or talking out are usually selected, and for short periods of time, each occurrence is recorded. Recordings of this type may be used to validate or supplement teacher ratings. Some authors caution against overreliance on behavioral rating scales for diagnosis of ADHD because of problems of rater bias, confounding contextual variables, and cultural differences in behavior and perception (Reid, 1995). It is important to obtain information about the child's behavior from many sources.

Diagnosing ADHD is problematic because of the reliance on subjective opinion and disagreement about what level of behavior constitutes a psychiatric disorder (Attention Deficit Disorder—Part I, 1995; Barkley, 1998; Reid, 1995). Since the level of inattention and impulsivity is often controlled by environmental factors (i.e., smaller groups, less stimulation, interesting activities, structured family interactions), it might be assumed that the locus of the problem lies with external sources. Differing cultural perspectives relative to normal behavior also confound diagnosis. ADHD is diagnosed far more often in the United States than in Europe, for example (Attention Deficit Disorder—Part I, 1995; Pennington, 2002), and most of the diagnostic instruments reflect the perspective of Western professionals. Thus, cross-cultural ratings may be invalid (Reid, 1995). Some have argued that ADHD is simply a social construct invented for children who are a nuisance by mainstream U.S. standards (e.g., Reid, Maag, & Vasa, 1994). Others believe that ADHD symptoms are primarily a result of an abnormal or unsuitable home and/or family environments on children with normal variation in temperament (Attention Deficit Disorder—Part I, 1995). Furthermore, the diagnosis is difficult because symptoms are inconsistent across individuals. Nevertheless, most mental health professionals believe that ADHD can be reliably diagnosed through multimethod strategies. To further complicate diagnosis, ADHD often occurs with other disabilities, such as major depression and anxiety disorders, conduct disorders, and learning disabilities (Attention Deficit Disorder—Part I, 1995; Forness, Kavale, Sweeney, & Crenshaw, 1999).

Assessment guidelines provided by Hoff et al. (2002) include the following: (1) identify the major concerns of referral sources and apply a developmental perspective, using interviews and rating scales; (2) operationally define target behaviors of concern and specify frequency, intensity, and duration as well as appropriate alternative behaviors; (3) observe across settings to determine where behaviors do and do not occur; (4) generate hypotheses about the function of behaviors, including use of a functional behavior analysis, if indicated; and (5) identify unique aspects of the case, including parent, teacher, child, and peer variables, that may impact treatment.

Table 10.1 provides information regarding the specialists who are qualified to diagnose and treat ADHD.

ADHD does not constitute a separate special education category. In the past, children and adolescents with ADHD were either labeled as "learning disabled" or "behavior disordered" in order to be eligible for special education services. Since 1991, however, they have been eligible for special education services under the category of "other health impaired" when all criteria have been met. Studies both prior to and after 1991 have found a substantial percentage (43–47%) of students in classrooms for EBD who have a primary psychiatric

TABLE 10.1 Professionals Qualified to Diagnose ADHD

Specialty	Can Diagnose ADHD	Can Prescribe Medications	Provides Counseling or Training
Psychiatrists	Yes	Yes	Yes
Psychologists	Yes	No, in most states	Yes
Pediatricians or family physicians	Yes	Yes	No
Neurologists	Yes	Yes	No
Clinical social workers	Yes	No	Yes

Adapted from National Institute of Mental Health (2003), *Attention Deficit Hyperactivity Disorder.*

diagnosis of ADHD (Mattison et al., 1986; Mattison, Morales, & Bauer, 1992). These findings suggest that regardless of specific identification policies, some students with ADHD will continue to be placed in classrooms for students with EBD.

Many students with ADHD, however, are not served as special education students because they do not meet IDEA eligibility criteria and do not need such intensive services to progress educationally. These students might qualify for accommodations in their general education classrooms under the mandates of Section 504 of the Rehabilitation Act of 1973, which specifies that a student cannot be denied public education participation or enjoyment of the benefits offered by public school programs because of a disability (Reid & Katsiyannis, 1995). Section 504 affords students many of the same services that IDEA provides, although not as extensive (e.g., child find, instructional modifications, free appropriate public education, procedural safeguards). Given the high incidence of this disorder, it is not surprising that there has been a reluctance to delineate ADHD as a separate category under IDEA for fear that the floodgates would be open to special education services.

Etiology and Development

Theories of etiology and development of ADHD can be categorized into (1) brain-related and genetic factors and (2) environmental agents. Pennington (2002) asserts that while the exact etiology of ADHD is still unknown, research has resulted in fairly clear evidence that ADHD is familial, moderately heritable, and influenced by two specific genes that affect dopamine transmission.

Theories of Etiology: Brain-Related Factors. The vast majority of research into the etiology of ADHD has centered on various brain-related hypotheses. You will recall that ADHD previously was called minimal brain injury and minimal brain dysfunction. The term *minimal brain injury* in particular captured the popular notion of the time that hyperactivity was caused by some type of ill-defined brain damage. It is now generally accepted that a very small percentage of hyperactive children show clear evidence of neurological damage, such as abnormal reflexes or loss of sensation (Attention Deficit Disorder—Part I, 1995; Rutter, 1977). However, some type of neurological dysfunction is still believed by many researchers to be a causal factor in ADHD. Among neurological dysfunction theories are those implicating neurotransmitters and biophysical development as causal factors.

Neurotransmitter disturbances have been hypothesized to underlie ADHD. The specific systems that have been implicated are the dopamine and norepinephrine systems, which contribute to arousal, alertness, and motor activity. Pennington (2002) discusses the functional "hypofrontality" hypothesis of ADHD. Reduced activity in the anterior frontal lobes (associated with executive functions) may, according to this theory, be caused by dopamine and/or norepinephrine depletion in the frontal lobes, resulting in central nervous system underarousal. However, both Goldstein (1999) and Pennington (2002) caution that current research does not support any single hypothesis of neurotransmitter deficit.

Biophysical development of the brain is another possible causal explanation for ADHD. For example, it is known that the brain matures in developmental stages and that the frontal lobes, which affect the regulation of attention and concentration, do not reach maturity until late adolescence or early adulthood. Therefore, this theory posits that the ADHD characteristics of impulsivity and inattention are related to a specific lag or deficit in frontal lobe development. For example, a 10-year-old child with frontal lobe immaturity may have the attentional capacity of a 6- or 7-year-old (Massman, Nussbaum, & Bigler, 1988). This theory underscores the age-appropriateness of behavior in diagnosing ADHD.

Some studies have found that certain regions of the brain (the frontal lobes) consume less energy than normal in individuals with ADHD (Attention Deficit Disorder—Part I, 1995; Pennington, 2002) and that the corpus callosum (the tissue joining the two hemispheres) contains less tissue than normal, which may affect the suppression of automatic responses. There have been various other findings of differences in brain structure, including lack of typical left–right hemisphere asymmetries and reduced volume (smaller size) of the structures in the basal ganglia, a set of subcortical structures known to be involved with motor behavior (Pennington, 2002).

Pennington (1992) and Goldstein (1999) report research findings that indicate ADHD is familial, with the rate of the disorder in affected families far exceeding the rate in nonpsychiatric control families, and a heritability estimate of about 70 percent. Additionally, it has been found that certain families that show a genetic resistance to the effects of thyroid hormones have an increased incidence of ADHD in the family (10–15 times higher than families without the thyroid disorder). Thyroid malfunctioning affects energy consumption and is often implicated in emotional disturbance (Attention Deficit Disorder—Part I, 1995).

A number of other familial variables are associated with hyperactivity in children. Some evidence suggests that hyperactive children more often come from families with higher familial alcoholism, antisocial behavior, and clinical problems (Cantwell, 1978; Halperin et al., 1997). Other research has assessed the social interactions of children with ADHD with family members, particularly mothers. Although earlier research showed that mothers of hyperactive children tended to be more controlling, commanding, and negative in their interactions than mothers of children with no ADHD, more recent research indicates that the controlling pattern of the mothers is likely a reaction to, rather than a cause of, their offspring's behavior. The latter research assessed the effects of medication on mother–child interaction styles and found that when the child's behavior improved, mothers' reactions were also less intense (Barkley & Cunningham, 1979).

Theories of Etiology: Environmental Agents. Allergic reactions to toxins and foods are considered under this category. Although sugar, food additives, and fluorescent lighting have all been held accountable for hyperactivity at one time or another by the lay press, none of these has been proven a causal factor for children with ADHD. A very small percentage of youngsters with ADHD have shown hyperactive allergic reactions to certain foods that can be controlled through diet; this topic is addressed in Chapter 4 under "Biophysical Interventions." Lead poisoning is one toxin that is associated with hyperactivity in children. Several studies have shown that, among children with elevated blood lead levels, 25–35 percent are hyperactive (Barkley, 1984). Although these incidence levels were much higher than in control groups, none of the studies addressed lead poisoning as a cause of hyperactivity. Goldstein and Goldstein (1998) provide a review of factors that have been reported to be associated with development of inattention and impulsivity, including exposure to various toxins, perinatal complications, medical problems (e.g., encephalitis, hypothyroidism), and radiation therapy.

In summary, etiological factors in the development of hyperactivity are usually assumed to be brain related or environment related, with increasing understanding of the genetic mechanisms that may be implicated in ADHD. These factors are summarized in Table 10.2. Various theories of brain dysfunction have logical appeal but insufficient evidence to establish them as causal factors, although evidence implicates differences in the frontal lobes and associated neurotransmitters. Theories implicating environmental agents also suffer from lack of evidence, although children with high levels of lead in their blood do show a marked increase in incidence of hyperactivity. Current research suggests that many children with ADHD inherit a central nervous system that predisposes them toward problems with attention and concentration (Levy, Hay, McStephen, Wood, & Waldman, 1997).

Related Conditions. The two primary conditions associated with ADHD are learning disabilities and conduct disorders. Poor school achievement is almost always associated with ADHD. Hoff et al. (2002) summarize research indicating that conduct problems, social concerns, and achievement difficulties are frequently associated with ADHD. They further note that since there is great heterogeneity in the ADHD population, assessment should go well beyond the primary features of the disorder. In their review, Weiss and Hechtman (1986) concluded that low school achievement is a common result of the core ADHD behaviors (i.e., impulsivity, inattention, overactivity). The prevalence of learning disabilities among children with ADHD has been estimated as high as 80 percent, but when

TABLE 10.2 Possible Causes of ADHD

Cause	Comments
Brain-related factors	
Brain dysfunction	Neurotransmitter imbalance
Biophysical development	Frontal lobe differences Corpus callosum differences Basal ganglia differences
Genetic factors	
Familial	Approximately 70% heritability Thyroid malfunction Candidate genes identified
Other associated factors	
Allergic reactions to foods, dyes, additives	Only a small percentage of children show allergic reactions
Environmental toxins/events	Lead poisoning, fetal alcohol exposure, pediatric brain injury

Adapted from N. Nussbaum & E. Bigler (1990), *Identification and treatment of attention deficit disorder.* Austin, TX: Pro-Ed. Reprinted with permission of the publisher.

stringent criteria for learning disabilities are applied, the estimate may drop to as low as 10–20 percent (Reeve, 1990). From a clinical perspective, Silver (1987) suggests that ADHD children are likely to have a specific learning disability in at least one area. Experts do not agree, however, on whether there is a common underlying dysfunction that causes both ADHD and learning disabilities, or whether the ADHD behaviors cause serious achievement problems.

The relationship between ADHD and conduct disorders also has been studied. It has been suggested that the child with ADHD is more prone to verbal and physical aggression than other children, thereby demonstrating some of the core behaviors of conduct disorders (Abikoff, Gittelman-Klein, & Klein, 1977; Attention Deficit Disorder—Part I, 1995). Also, lowered levels of self-control due to impulsivity may predispose these youngsters toward conduct disorders. In two long-term follow-up studies, Weiss and Hechtman (1986) found higher rates of conduct-disordered behavior and antisocial personality disorder among the hyperactive sample than among the controls. While these results would appear to substantiate that ADHD predisposes children to develop conduct disorders, other researchers have pointed out that the Weiss and Hechtman research failed to initially differentiate hyperactive children with conduct disorders from hyperactive children without conduct disorders in the original sample (Satterfield, Hoppe, & Schell, 1982). It is therefore possible that a proportion of the hyperactive sample was displaying concomitant conduct disorders at the time the study began.

Longitudinal studies by Lambert and her colleagues (Lambert, 1988; Lambert, Sassone, Hartsough, & Sandoval, 1987) also substantiate that hyperactive children are at risk for developing conduct disorders and have more problems with the juvenile authorities than their nonhyperactive peers. Children who exhibit hyperactivity with impulsivity and inattention and who also display conduct problems such as fighting, stealing, truancy, noncompliance, and arguing are referred to as "fledgling psychopaths" (Gresham et al., 2000, p. 83). Unfortunately, these fledgling psychopaths tend to be highly resistant to interventions. Studies have found that 30–50 percent of children with ADHD also have major depression or anxiety disorders (Attention Deficit Disorder—Part I, 1995).The research on related conditions can be summarized thus: we do not currently know whether some underlying common cause predisposes youngsters to develop these multiple conditions or whether one disorder causes the others. However, ADHD, conduct disorders, depression, anxiety, and learning disabilities do coexist at a high rate. Furthermore, it is likely that some students with all of these difficulties will find their way into classrooms for students with emotional/behavioral disorders. Box 10.1 provides a case summary for a child who exhibits ADHD with comorbid disorders and illustrates the complexity of diagnosis in these cases.

Intervention and Treatment

It is not an overstatement to suggest that hundreds and hundreds of studies have assessed treatment outcomes with ADHD youngsters. Its high prevalence relative to other disorders and the visibility of ADHD behaviors at school have likely contributed to this interest in treatment research. The majority of treatments can be categorized as medication therapy, behavior management, or cognitive-behavioral techniques. Many studies employed a combination of these techniques such as medication plus behavior management.

BOX 10.1
Maria

Maria is a 9-year-old second grader at Rolling Hills Elementary. She was retained in kindergarten. Her brother, who is a year younger, is also in second grade at this school. They both currently are eligible for special education as students with a learning disability. Maria's teacher, Mrs. Stalling, reported that Maria was showing poor progress in reading and math. Maria is also eligible for special education as a student with an emotional disturbance. A recent reevaluation indicated that she continues to qualify for special education under these two categories.

Maria entered the Preschool Programs for Children with Disabilities (PPCD) when she was 3 years old for a severe delay in language development. She also had a tendency to "space out" and exhibited fleeting eye contact and a shuffling gait. Overall, during her preschool years she exhibited delays in expressive language, social skills, and emotional/behavioral competencies. Maria also was taking medication during kindergarten for attention-deficit hyperactivity disorder (ADHD). Maria first met the criteria for a student with an emotional disturbance when she was 6 years old. She exhibited signs of anxiety, depression, withdrawal, attention problems, hyperactivity, aggression, and atypical behaviors.

Maria currently lives with her father and brother in a small mobile home. Her parents are divorced, and her father gained custody of the children when Maria was 4 years old after alleged abuse by the mother. She still sees her mother on a regular basis. In the hallways and to people in passing, Maria presents herself as a smiling and happy girl. People who interact with her frequently see her moody side and a tendency toward anxiety, sadness, and aggression. Mrs. Stalling, Maria's second-grade teacher, reported that Maria has frequent crying spells and, at times, enuresis. She also misbehaves in the classroom on a regular basis, hitting and pushing other students. Mrs. Stalling also noted a tendency for Maria to present a blank expression at unpredictable times.

During assessment it was noted that Maria appeared at times happy but would refuse to answer or would respond "I don't know" if testing became too personal. She often looked tired and sad. Maria reported that she didn't sleep well and had frequent nightmares. Maria also had difficulty with focused attention during the testing process. She frequently reported somatic concerns such as headaches, stomachaches, and hurting hands. The test results indicated clinically significant concerns in many areas, such as hyperactivity, conduct problems, withdrawal, attention problems, daily living, depression, and school problems. She also is reported to at times act strangely and show feelings that do not fit the situation. It appears that Maria is suppressing emotions that may be resulting in her outbursts of aggressive behavior and feelings of anxiety and depression.

The test results indicate that Maria demonstrates inappropriate types of behavior under normal circumstances, and has a general pervasive mood of unhappiness or depression. These characteristics have occurred over a long period of time to a marked degree and are adversely affecting her education performance. She therefore qualifies for special education services as a student with an emotional disturbance. She also qualifies as a student with a learning disability in the area of basic reading.

Academic recommendations for Maria include working in a smaller class size, resource room help for reading and writing, and access to individualized assistance for all subjects. It is recommended that she sit in the front of the classroom, be allowed more time to finish her assignments, and receive both visual and auditory directions. A behavior intervention plan should be implemented with frequent positive reinforcement for desired behaviors. Maria should also undergo an occupational therapy evaluation. Special education counseling using play therapy is recommended since Maria has a tendency to refuse to answer when a topic becomes too personal. Group counseling for self-esteem and life skills would also be beneficial. It is recommended that Maria participate in extracurricular activities to help improve her self-image.

Contributed by Kirstyn Jorgenson, School Psychology Intern, Texas State University—San Marcos.

Medication. The effects of medication, primarily stimulants, on ADHD behaviors have been widely studied. Stimulants are reported to improve symptoms in approximately 70 percent of hyperactive children (Attention Deficit Disorder—Part II, 1995; Barkley, 1990). In a more recent commentary, Pennington (2002) maintains that about 75–90 percent of children with ADHD exhibit a favorable response to stimulant medication, with safety and efficacy well established. Methylphenidate (Ritalin) is the most commonly prescribed and most studied stimulant. Dexedrine and Cylert are used to a much lesser extent. Table 10.3 outlines some of the major stimulant medications used to treat ADHD; a newer nonstimulant drug, Straterra, which affects the norepinephrine system, is included as well. It should also be noted that a new skin patch has been developed that can deliver a generic version of Ritalin (Daytrana) for children who have trouble taking pills (Heavey, 2006). Some antidepressants may be tried as alternative medications for children with ADHD who do not respond favorably to stimulants or Straterra.

Stimulants have been shown to have short-term effects on sustained attention, activity level, impulsivity, and classroom behavior (Forness et al., 1999; Rapport, 1987). Whether symptom improvement secondary to medication also leads to increased academic achievement is still a point of contention (Crenshaw, Kavale, Forness, & Reeve, 1999; Gadow, 1983, 1985; Rapport, Stoner, DuPaul, Birmingham, & Tucker, 1985). There is some evidence to suggest that research results on symptom improvement depend largely on which symptoms are studied and which measures are used to document improvement. According to Forness and his colleagues (Forness, Swanson, Cantwell, Guthrie, & Sena, 1992; Forness et al., 1999), many studies used only one or two measures and found improvement in one area (e.g., cognitive or behavioral) but not another. For example, higher doses of stimulants may be more effective in controlling classroom behavior but less

TABLE 10.3 Stimulant Medications

Trade Name	Generic Name	Approved Age
Adderall	amphetamine	3 and older
Adderall XR	extended release amphetamine	6 and older
Concerta	methylphenidate (long acting)	6 and older
Cylert*	pemoline	6 and older
Dexedrine	dextroamphetamine	3 and older
Dextrostat		
Focalin	dexmethylphenidate	6 and older
Metadate ER	methylphenidate (extended release)	6 and older
Ritalin	methylphenidate	6 and older
Nonstimulant for ADHD		
Strattera	atomoxetine	6 and older

Adapted from NIMH publication *Medications (2002).*

*Because of its potential for serious side effects related to liver function, Cylert should not ordinarily be considered as a first-line drug therapy for ADHD.

effective in improving learning than lower doses. On the other hand, lower dosages may not be sufficient to help control behavior (Gadow, 1986a). Forness et al. (1992) studied the effects of Ritalin on six measures of academic, cognitive, and social functioning with a sample of 71 boys with ADHD, ages 7 to 11 years. They concluded that although the disruptive behavioral symptoms do appear to improve significantly (e.g., response level of around 70%), measures of new learning and of oral reading produce favorable responses of only around 50 percent, and tasks such as reading comprehension less than 20 percent. These findings support the need to clearly differentiate the deficits or symptoms that are being targeted for improvement by use of stimulant medication.

In a more comprehensive study, the National Institute of Mental Health (NIMH) assessed various treatments for children with ADHD. The study involved 576 elementary school children in six different sites across the country (Greenhill et al., 1996). Four groups of children at each site were treated over a period of 14 months with a planned 2-year follow-up. One group received only medication and one received only psychosocial interventions (e.g., token economies, parent education, classroom shadow aide, social skills instruction, computer-assisted instruction). A third group received both medication and psychosocial intervention, and the fourth group acted as a control group. Initial findings suggest that across 15 outcome measures (e.g., behavioral, cognitive, academic, classroom observation, social skill, and consumer-satisfaction variables), stimulant medication was more effective than psychosocial treatment and was even more effective alone than psychosocial interventions combined with medication (Forness et al., 1999). Given these findings, Forness and his colleagues (1999) suggest that stimulant medication should be the key component of successful treatment for students with ADHD. Pennington (2002) also cites a growing body of research supporting this conclusion. This does not preclude the application of psychosocial interventions, but implies that correct diagnosis and careful prescribing by physicians should be seriously considered. As attention, motor coordination, and mood improve with these medications, social relationships should improve, which should make special education easier (Attention Deficit Disorder—Part II, 1995).

While the specific mechanism through which these medications work is currently unknown, the drugs appear to alter the catecholamine neurotransmitters, norephinephrine or dopamine, but the exact alteration is still speculative (Attention Deficit Disorder—Part II, 1995). Side effects of stimulant medication include headaches, stomachaches, insomnia, loss of appetite, irritability or mood swings, and growth inhibition. Most of the side effects disappear naturally within a couple of weeks or in response to adjustments in timing or amount of dosages (Forness et al., 2003–2004). Growth inhibition is thought to be related to decreased appetite, which can be ameliorated by giving the medication with or immediately after meals (Nussbaum & Bigler, 1990).

In addition to side effects, there are other drawbacks and criticisms regarding use of medication to treat ADHD. First is a concern regarding a nationwide tendency toward overprescribing, possibly because medication may be viewed as a "sure cure" or a panacea for a host of very difficult behaviors in children. A sharp rise in the number of preschoolers (ages 2–4) who were prescribed stimulants, antidepressants, and other psychiatric drugs (e.g., clonidine, a blood pressure drug) primarily for treatment of ADHD (Goode, 2000) occurred in the 1990s when it was estimated that about 12 in 1,000 preschoolers were taking Ritalin. However, in the last few years prescriptions have stabilized (see Chapter 4).

Diagnosing ADHD in children under age 5 is difficult, and Ritalin and other medications have not been approved by the Food and Drug Administration (FDA) for use in young children. Thus, many fear that these medications may be inappropriately prescribed and may result in abnormal brain development (Goode, 2000). Second, medication can become a crutch for the child and those working with him or her. For example, the child who becomes psychologically dependent may believe that he or she can't control him- or herself without the drug. There may also be concerns that children on prescription medication may be prone to later drug abuse, although this assumption has not been borne out by research (Loney, Kramer, & Milich, 1981). Parents and professionals may also tend to let medication replace their management responsibilities.

These concerns have led some professionals to question whether medication should be used only when other interventions have failed, while others believe that alternative interventions will be more successful when ADHD symptoms are first ameliorated with medication.

Behavior Management Strategies. Many behavioral strategies such as those described in Chapter 7 have been successful in improving the behaviors associated with ADHD. Programs using positive reinforcement as well as those using behavior reduction procedures have proven effective. For example, attending behavior of hyperactive children has responded positively to both social reinforcement and a response cost system (Rapport, 1987; Reid, 1999). On-task behavior has also been increased with a positive reinforcement system (Allyon, Layman, & Kandel, 1975). It is also often recommended that students with ADHD be given structure and routine. Task analysis, clear and consistent rules, quiet study areas, short study periods, repetitive verbal instructions, advanced organizers, and learning strategies such as underlining can help with attending problems and impulsivity (Reid, 1999). By bringing clarity and order to the environment, teachers can help these students function more effectively.

In addition, home-based contingency systems for appropriate classroom behavior have been implemented successfully with these students (Pelham, Schnedler, Bologna, & Contreras, 1980); however, Rapport (1987) cautions that home-based reinforcement may not be effective for those impulsive children and youth with ADHD who have difficulty in delaying gratification. Another potential difficulty with some behavioral programs was identified by Ross and Ross (1982) in their review. These authors concluded that, while many programs were initially successful in changing behavior, the positive gains were not always maintained. Reasons for diminished success were teacher disinterest in continuing the program, inadequacies in the program design, and/or habituation of the children to the reinforcers. One study showed that the teacher also needed reinforcement for maintaining the program: improvement in child behavior fluctuated according to whether the teacher was being reinforced (Brown, Montgomery, & Barclay, 1969). These studies point to the importance of system variables that may be overlooked when focusing only on the hyperactive child.

Given these concerns, a related intervention model, behavioral consultation, has been employed to help to improve student behavior while also supporting and strengthening the teacher's behavior management and instructional skills. In this model, the teacher becomes the "consultee"; the "consultant" is typically a school psychologist (Allen & Graden,

2002). The model provides for indirect service to children via the teacher's increased repertoire of tools and skills to deal with similar students in the future. The consultation program described in Box 10.2 is one example of such a program designed to address the problems of children with ADHD. The *Challenging Horizons Program* (Evans, Dowling, & Brown, in press; Schulz & Cobb, 2005) is another such example, with behavioral consultation used to assist teachers in effective intervention for children with ADHD. Both models are based on a ecobehavioral framework, which takes into account the environmental factors that affect individual behavior. The five steps involved in a behavioral consultation program are: (1) forging the consultative relationship, (2) identifying the problem, (3) selecting an intervention, (4) implementing an intervention, and (5) evaluating outcomes (Kratochwill, Elliott, & Callan-Stoiber, 2002).

Cognitive-Behavioral Interventions. These interventions are based on a combination of self-talk, self-monitoring, and problem solving; with children having ADHD the techniques are usually aimed at increasing attention and decreasing impulsivity. Ideally, interventions with a stronger self-management component are more effective than those managed primarily or exclusively by the teacher. The goal of such systems is to eventually train a child to monitor and reinforce his or her own behavior, without relying on constant feedback from the teacher (DuPaul et al., 2002). The child is usually taught a set of self-statements or a problem-solving sequence that she practices overtly, and eventually, covertly. Self-talk and self-monitoring have proved helpful to the hyperactive child in specific learning situations (Abikoff, 1985; Craighead, Meyers, & Wilcoxon-Craighead, 1985; Harris & Schmidt, 1997; Reid, 1996) and in general classroom and playground behaviors (Abikoff, 1985). However, researchers cite problems in maintaining acquired gains in other settings and over time. Effects of this research are also obscured by the coexistence of ADHD with conduct disorders and learning disabilities.

Combination of Treatments. Owing to the intractable and multifaceted nature of ADHD symptoms, the use of combined treatments has become more popular (Forness et al., 1999; Rapport, 1987; Reid, 1999). Combined treatments also address some of the issues raised by use of medication alone, particularly the tendency toward overreliance on drugs to control or "fix" the behavior.

The most common combination is use of stimulant medication with some behavior management, skill training, or cognitive-behavioral technique. While some studies have shown superior results with combined treatments, others have failed to increase gains by adding behavioral or cognitive therapy components (Forness et al., 1999; Greenhill et al., 1996). However, combined treatments appeal to both practitioners and researchers, and therefore probably will continue to be implemented.

In summary, medication appears to improve behavioral symptoms in a large proportion of children with ADHD; however, the drawbacks of side effects and potential overreliance on medication lead many parents and professionals to question its viability. A variety of behavioral and cognitive-behavioral techniques have also been shown to improve symptoms such as attention and impulsivity. Despite the popular appeal of combined treatments, they have not yet been demonstrated as clearly superior to treatments employing medication only. However, flaws in the studies rather than ineffectiveness of the combined treatments may be responsible for these findings. Based on several large-scale studies of

BOX 10.2

A School-Based Consultation Program for Students with ADHD

Because students with ADHD are challenging to most school personnel, Shapiro, DuPaul, Bradley, and Bailey (1996) implemented a consultation model for providing necessary services. The services were conceptualized at both a systems level (districtwide needs assessment, identification of systems impediments, and provision of districtwide inservice) and at the staff level (individualized training, monitoring, and support). The Lehigh University—Consulting Center for Adolescents with Attention Deficit Disorders was formulated with funding from the U.S. Office of Special Education and Rehabilitation Services for the purpose of addressing the training needs of teachers, related school personnel, and parents regarding middle school students with ADHD.

The model was based on a three-tiered approach: inservice training, on-site consultation, and advanced training with follow-up consultation. During the first level, the objective was to provide core knowledge across participants. This was accomplished with a 2-day inservice training program covering identification and assessment of ADHD, self-management strategies, behavior management, medication monitoring and intervention, social skills and problem-solving training, and home-based behavior management. This training was provided to various groups of participants depending on school district needs.

On-site consultation (level 2) was provided by trained doctoral students at various participating school sites. Services were provided based on a building needs analysis. Services might include student program development, direct inservice, consultation with building-level teams, student monitoring, communication and interaction with physicians, and further skills training for staff. The consultation phase-typically covered about 60 days of service delivery over a given year. Some districts used the service to formulate policies and procedures regarding students with ADHD.

The third consultation level consisted of advanced training regarding ADHD, widescale dissemination of the training program, and follow-up consultation and assessment. For example, Lehigh University developed a 1-week institute on ADHD, inviting staff from participating districts to hear national experts speak on the topic. Additionally, a training manual and video were developed and disseminated. Over three years, 169 school personnel from 57 school districts attended level 1 inservices. Consultation regarding about 170 students across these districts was also provided. Shapiro and his colleagues report that overall outcomes of the program were very successful in improving knowledge about adolescents with ADHD. However, the authors cautioned that the program needs to be replicated in rural settings and in settings with culturally diverse students. There were also no student outcome measures. However, the systems approach to managing students with ADHD seems to be a promising intervention component for these very challenging students.

---

efficacy, the best treatments for ADHD at the current time appear to be a combination of psychosocial and pharmacological approaches, with medication approaches receiving the most empirical support (Forness & Kavale, 2001; Goldstein, 1999; Pennington, 2002; Sinacola & Peters-Strickland, 2006).

Implications for Teachers. Teachers may be more involved in the assessment and remediation of ADHD than with any other of the internalizing and externalizing disorders. Unlike the other disorders, ADHD may cause more problems in the classroom than anywhere else. A teacher may be the first person to point out the age-inappropriateness of the child's behavior to his parents. Teachers may be asked to keep observational data, to complete checklists, and to monitor side effects of medication manifested in the classroom. These are all important tasks and especially necessary if the child is receiving medication. Physicians can only estimate the dosage needed by a particular child and will need feedback from teachers and parents in order to properly adjust the dosage. In a recent study (Snider, Busch, & Arrowood, 2003), researchers found when a random sample of 200 general educators and 200 special educators were surveyed, the teachers had limited knowledge about ADHD and the use of psychostimulant medication, even though their opinions about medication for ADHD were generally positive. The survey also confirmed prior findings that teachers were the school personnel most likely to refer for assessment for ADHD. These findings underscore the need for special education teachers to be knowledgeable about symptoms and the course of ADHD, as well as appropriate assessement and intervention options.

Teachers of youngsters with ADHD are also likely to be involved in behavior management programs aimed at improving attention, task completion, and ultimately academic achievement. Such programs may be based on a highly structured environment, positive reinforcement, a cognitive-behavioral approach, or a response cost system. One study of teacher attitudes toward ADHD interventions compared teachers' acceptability ratings of various techniques that could be implemented in their classrooms. Given a choice of a positive reinforcement approach, a cognitive-behavioral strategy, medication therapy, and a response cost strategy, teachers rated the response cost strategy for inappropriate behaviors as most acceptable in their classrooms (Fournier, 1987). Risk to the child, amount of record keeping, and usefulness of the intervention for other behaviors were among the variables influencing teacher ratings.

Goldstein (1999) provides guidelines for teachers derived from a review of classroom research data:

- Classrooms should be organized and structured, with a predictable schedule, clear rules, and separate desks.
- Rewards should be consistent, frequent, salient, and immediate.
- Response cost reinforcement systems are especially effective.
- Constant feedback from teachers is needed.
- Minor disruptions should be ignored.
- Tasks should be interesting and involve meaningful payoff.
- Academic instruction/materials should be matched to the child's ability.
- Transition times should be closely supervised.
- Close communication between parents and teachers should be maintained, especially in the lower grades.
- Teacher expectations should be adjusted to meet the child's behavioral and academic skills levels.
- Teachers should be educated regarding ADHD and should develop an appropriate repertoire of interventions.

Because of the incidence of the disorder, most teachers will encounter children and adolescents with ADHD in their classrooms. Although the social and emotional needs of these youngsters were not addressed in depth in this section, it is important to realize that these youth may need counseling to help them understand the nature and implications of their problems. Parents may need to increase their behavior management skills and/or may profit from a support group. Teachers may be the only link between some of these parents and the professional community; they are therefore in a position to refer students and their parents to helpful community resources.

Conduct Disorders and Aggression

Conduct disorder has been used as a catch-all term for a variety of acting-out, aggressive, and antisocial acts. It also has been equated with social maladjustment, thus eliciting debate regarding exclusion of youngsters so labeled from public school services for students with emotional/behavioral disorders. Many youth with conduct disorders get into trouble with the law, are adjudicated, and become labeled delinquent by the courts. It may be helpful to consider that *conduct disorder* is the term of choice for the mental health system, that *social maladjustment* may be used by schools, and that *delinquency* is used by the legal system for those brought before the courts. In addition, the term *antisocial behavior* is a general term used to denote a pattern of willful and repeated violations of societal standards; antisocial behavior is the most common reason for referral of children and youth to mental health services (Reid, 1993). Pennington (2002) notes that conduct disorders are of immediate concern, given the high rates of gun violence and incarceration in the United States and because of the relationships among legal, moral, and psychological explanations of behavior that affect intervention choices.

In this context, it is accurate to say that antisocial behavior is commonly exhibited by youth who are labeled conduct disordered, socially maladjusted, and delinquent. Despite the confusion over terms and eligibility, it is important to understand youngsters with conduct disorders because students with these characteristics do ultimately find their way into classrooms for students with emotional/behavioral disorders in the schools.

Definition and Prevalence

Conduct disorder (CD) is composed of a constellation of behaviors, but is best understood as a distinctive pattern of antisocial behavior that violates the rights of others. Some key behaviors are overtly aggressive such as fighting and destroying property, while other key behaviors are more covert such as stealing and lying. DSM-IV-TR (APA, 2000) emphasizes that individuals with conduct disorders break rules or violate major societal norms across settings: at home, in school, with peers, and in the community. DSM-IV-TR diagnosis lists the following criteria:

Aggression

1. Often bullies, threatens others, or initiates fights
2. Has used a weapon such as a knife, gun, bat, etc.
3. Has been physically cruel to people or animals

4. Has stolen with victim present
5. Has forced someone into sexual activity

Destruction of property

1. Has engaged in deliberate fire-setting or destroyed others' property

Deceitfulness or theft

1. Has broken into houses, buildings, or cars
2. Often lies or cons others
3. Has stolen without victim present (e.g., shoplifting)

Serious rules violations

1. Often stays out at night without parental permission, beginning before age 13
2. Has run away from home overnight more than once
3. Is often truant from school, beginning before age 13 (APA, 2000, pp. 98–99)

According to the DSM-IV-TR, three or more such behaviors must be present in the past 12 months, with at least one occurring in the last 6 months. The behavior pattern must cause clinically significant impairment in social, academic, or occupational functioning. If only three symptoms are present, the conduct disorder is described as mild, with moderate and severe conduct disorders characterized by increasing numbers of symptoms and increasing harm to others (Forness et al., 2003–2004). The DSM-IV-TR also specifies subtypes, including childhood onset (prior to age 10), adolescent-onset (no criteria prior to age 10), and unspecified onset (if age of onset is unknown). If the individual is 18 or older and meets the criteria for antisocial personality disorder, then the CD diagnosis is not given.

Oppositional-defiant disorder is a separate DSM-IV-TR diagnosis; however, it will be included in this section because it often coexists with conduct disorder and because little is written about the two as distinctly different conditions. Although quite annoying, oppositional-defiant behaviors are considered less serious than conduct disorders because they do not violate major norms or the basic rights of others. Oppositional-defiant behaviors include arguing with adults, losing one's temper, refusing adult requests, blaming others for one's own mistakes, and deliberately annoying others. Descriptive characteristics include terms such as touchy, angry, resentful, spiteful, and vindictive (American Psychiatric Association, 2000). After perusing these criteria, the reader can readily see that many students with emotional/behavioral disorders could be labeled as oppositional-defiant.

It may also be important to distinguish a subgroup of youth with conduct disorders who can be described as not socialized or lacking significant social attachments to family or friends. (As adults, they may be referred to as psychopathic or sociopathic.) The most salient characteristic of these individuals is their lack of internalization of societal rules, norms, or standards of appropriate behavior toward others; in other words, they do not apply such standards to themselves. They appear to have no conscience and little concept of right and wrong. They may further be described as operating at a low level of moral development: negative behavior is bad if one gets caught and subsequently punished; negative behavior is okay if one doesn't get caught or gets rewarded.

For such individuals authority and reciprocal relationships with others have little meaning. Due to such attitudes, these individuals are at highest risk for breaking the law, being adjudicated, and continuing persistent patterns of delinquent behavior. These behavior patterns often continue into adulthood, manifested in criminal activity and/or antisocial personality disorder. Several studies have found that aggression, noncompliance, and poor social relationships in children ages 6–10 were also evidenced in adolescence along with school failure and delinquency (Camp & Ray, 1984; Fergusson & Lynskey, 1998). Thus, once established, these behavior patterns are extremely difficult to change. Individuals who develop conduct disorders in childhood (before age 10) are more likely to continue the behaviors (and become labeled antisocial personality disorder) in adulthood than individuals who develop conduct disorders in adolescence (American Psychiatric Association, 2000). Pennington (2002) cites research supporting the distinction between two subtypes of conduct disorder: life-course persistent and adolescence-limited subtype, with the first subtypes more likely to be heritable. Therefore, early identification of the nature of the disorder and appropriate intervention are essential to working with this population.

Conduct disorders are defined by a number of covert and overt antisocial acts. Walker and Colleagues (2004) assert that antisocial children and youth follow one or more of three distinct paths in developing conduct disorders: covert, disobedient, or overt. A covert path is defined by stealth and is usually directed toward property (vandalism, stealing) or self (substance abuse). An overt path is defined by aggressive behavior and victimization of others (cruelty, fighting), and a disobedient path is characterized by oppositional behavior such as noncompliance with adult requests and rules. Although all three are disruptive and lead to adjustment difficulties, the specific developmental path taken by an individual may dictate a different treatment approach (Pennington, 2002).

The specific behaviors of conduct disorders tend to cluster; in other words, a child who engages in one of these behaviors is likely to engage in others as well. Although one child may not engage in all these behaviors, core behaviors include fighting, temper tantrums, theft, truancy, destroying property, defying or threatening others, and running away (Quay, 1986b). Refer to Box 10.3 for brief case studies illustrating the clustering nature of conduct-disordered behavior.

Other characteristics of conduct disorders are, not surprisingly, poor interpersonal relations (Carlson, Lahey, & Neeper, 1984) and academic deficiencies (Ledingham & Schwartzman, 1984). In addition, youth with conduct disorders have shown deficiencies in cognitive problem-solving skills such as perspective taking and identifying alternative solutions to interpersonal problems (Dodge, 1985).

Prevalence estimates depend on definition and the population studied, with rates of CD usually higher in urban than in rural communities (American Psychiatric Association, 2000). According to Pennington (2002), most epidemiological surveys do not distinguish between the life-course persistent and adolescence-limited subtypes, which probably inflates prevalence estimates. The prevalence of conduct disorders among children has increased. In 1987, it was estimated as ranging from 4 to 10 percent (Kazdin, 1987b). In 1994, it was estimated as between 6 and 16 percent for males, and between 2 and 9 percent for females (American Psychiatric Association, 2000). However, according to Pennington (2002), some research has suggested a lower rate of persistent CD, about 5.9 percent. Males most often exhibit conduct disorders prior to puberty, with an average age of onset between

BOX 10.3
Case Studies of Conduct Disorder

CASE STUDY 1: Jeremy

A husband and wife who could not have children adopted Jeremy when he was 3, Jeremy is now 15. He has been very difficult to handle while growing up. He is hyperactive and requires constant attention. When he was younger he got into everything, wrote on walls, hurt the cat, set fires, and broke various items in the house. Most recently, he has been oppositional and defiant at home. His parents suspect drug use. He is skipping school. He has also been breaking into cars with his peers. This is the first time these individuals have experienced parenthood. They are unsure how to handle this situation, and they do not know how concerned to be about this behavior. Jeremy's mother is worried, but his father is still hoping he will "grow out of it." His father recalls getting into trouble when he was young. The situation is difficult for both parents, and they are constantly in conflict. To make matters worse. Jeremy's father is traveling out of town more frequently on business. The mother cannot handle this situation by herself. She is tired, depressed, and feels abandoned by her husband. The child's behavior worsens as the mother's behavior changes. The problems begin to appear insurmountable to the mother, and she is having difficulty setting any limits.

CASE STUDY 2: Evelyn

Mrs. Harris is a single parent. Her husband left when her two children, Larry and Evelyn, were young. Both children did well in grade school, academically and behaviorally. Mrs. Harris had an opportunity for a better job and relocated her family when Larry was 13 and Evelyn was 16. The job is very stressful. Larry has adjusted well to his new home and school. Evelyn has had more difficulty adjusting. She was in her senior year when they moved. The school is more difficult for her and she has made few friends. She feels isolated and frustrated. Her mother is less available due to work. Mrs. Harris is also struggling with her own mother's recent diagnosis of Alzheimer's disease and has had trouble with anxiousness and depression. Evelyn began skipping school and smoking marijuana with a group of teens at school who had behavioral problems. She became sexually active, sneaking out at night. She kept these behaviors secret from her mother. She often lied. She began stealing clothing and cosmetics from a department store. When arrested for shoplifting, her mother was called to the police station. Mrs. Harris is very upset and does not know what to do. She feels overwhelmed and unable to make any decisions.

From M.K. Toth (1990), *Understanding treating conduct disorders.* Austin, TX: Pro-Ed. Used with permission of the publisher.

8 and 10; age of onset for females is later, usually between ages 13 and 15 (Toth, 1990). For the childhood-onset subtype, the male:female ratio is about 3:1; for the adolescent-onset subtype, the gender ratio is closer to equal (Pennington, 2002).

Children and adolescents with conduct disorders pose a tremendous challenge to society. According to Walker et al. (2004), they also represent one of the most costly groups not only in terms of vandalism and damage, but also because they tend to cycle in and out of the mental health and juvenile justice systems throughout adolescence and into adulthood. These social costs are compounded by the individual misery incurred by persons with antisocial behavior: the youngsters themselves often suffer, as do their families. And when the antisocial behavior takes a violent turn, the victims of crime also suffer. According to Kazdin (1987a), the crimes of murder, rape, robbery, arson, drunk driving, and spouse or child abuse are perpetrated at a much higher rate by individuals with a history of antisocial behavior than by those without such a history. It is important to remember that not all children and youth with conduct disorders are violent or break the law, but a significant portion of them do.

Etiology

Although much research has been devoted to identifying predisposing factors, only a couple of behavioral theories have been put forth to explain how conduct-disordered behavior (including oppositional behavior) develops. Because aggressive behavior also is so often a part of conduct disorders, theories relating to the development of aggressive behavior are explored in this section.

Theories of Etiology of Conduct Disorders. Patterson (1976) has developed a "coercion hypothesis" to account for the development and maintenance of behavior leading to conduct disorders. According to Patterson, infants have a repertoire of coercive behaviors that are highly adaptive in shaping parental responses (e.g., crying when hungry or uncomfortable to get parents' attention). As infants grow older, the majority learn other ways to get their needs met; however, if parents fail to reinforce appropriate social behaviors and/or continue to respond to coercive demands, then a pattern of ever more intensive coercive behavior and responses may be set into motion. For example: mother asks the child to put away his toys; the child whines and refuses; the mother then gives up and does it herself rather than listen to the whining, thus reinforcing the coercive behavior of the child. In a different scenario, if the mother escalates her demand by yelling and becoming aggressive rather than giving up, she may eventually get the child to comply; thus, she is reinforced for her aggressive behavior, and a pattern of negative coercion is still created. Over time, these interactions can establish a pattern of escalating coercion between parent and child that eventually determines the way the child will interact with others.

In-home observations of 27 aggressive and 27 nonproblem boys support this coercive interaction hypothesis, as the aggressive youngsters displayed significantly higher rates of coercive behaviors such as negative commands, disapproval, humiliation, noncompliance, negativism, teasing, and yelling (Patterson, 1976). In return, family members tended to retaliate with equally aversive responses such as criticism and threats.

Although offering a behavioral perspective, Patterson's model also encompasses a family systems orientation in that parents and other family members become a part of the continued coercive pattern over time and therefore become part of the problem, "setting in motion a vicious circle that potentiates the development of CD behaviors in children" (Pennington, 2002, p. 187). Such an orientation has implications for treatment of the entire family, a topic to which we will return later in this chapter.

Wahler (1976) believed that positive reinforcement can also play a role in the development of conduct-disordered behavior. According to this hypothesis, the child's disruptive behavior elicits either verbal or physical attention from the parent, thus inadvertently reinforcing the behavior. In the previous example, the mother might approach the child and quietly try to talk him into putting up his toys by reasoning with him; the positive attention afforded by his refusal would then serve to reinforce the refusal.

These models focus on parent–child interactions; although much less has been written about conduct-disordered behaviors in the school setting, these same principles can operate in teacher–child interactions in the classroom (Atkeson & Forehand, 1984). Reid and Patterson (1991) have offered reasons children who demonstrate aggressive and coercive behavior at home are very likely to exhibit similar problems at school. First, these children have developed aggressive methods for dealing with problems and confrontations and will likely repeat these behavior patterns elsewhere. Second, if aggressive behavior is being reinforced at home, schools have a more difficult time socializing the child. Third, the child's aggressive, coercive behavior will likely induce teachers and other school personnel to mimic parental interaction styles; thus the coercive process will continue in school. This process often results in peer rejection and less support from teachers (Campbell & Ewing, 1990; Ladd, 1990). Thus, it appears that once they enter school, "negative school experiences and social experiences further exacerbate the adjustment difficulties of children with conduct problems" (Webster-Stratton & Herbert, 1994, p. 21).

Theories of Development of Aggression. A number of models explaining the development of aggression have been proposed: (1) a social learning hypothesis, (2) a cognitive hypothesis, (3) a more comprehensive model including both cognitive and behavioral components, and (4) biophysical factors. In addition, society has contributed in a very concrete way to the development of aggressive and violent behavior patterns among our children and youth.

Social Learning. A social learning perspective was researched by Bandura (Bandura, Ross, & Ross, 1963), who demonstrated that young children learn aggressive behavior through imitation of aggressive models. These models can be peers, individuals on film, computer or video games, or television, and parents (especially those who use physical punishment). There is ample opportunity for today's youngsters to be exposed to aggressive models, particularly in the media. Box 10.4 summarizes several studies on the relationship between watching aggression on TV and subsequent levels of aggression in children and adolescents. Conclusions from these and other studies indicate that aggressive behavior is linked to watching violence on TV, although a direct causal relationship would be difficult to prove.

Cognitive Perspective. Cognitive models have also been developed to explain aggression. Novaco (1978) proposed a cognitive paradigm to explain the relationship of anger and aggression. Angry responses are explained in terms of external cues, internal arousal, cognitions about that arousal, and a behavioral reaction. Novaco stresses that external cues and events play only an indirect role because the cognitions and internal arousal are what eventually determine whether the individual becomes angry. Anger arousal then increases the likelihood of aggressive responses, although there are alternative responses. Children as young as kindergarten-age tend to cognitively appraise events that make them angry (Hill, 1989).

Comprehensive Models. Other researchers promote more comprehensive models suggesting that both cognitive distortions and deficiencies in social problem solving interact to encourage aggressive responding. For example, Dodge (1985) found that aggressive children have shown a tendency to attribute hostile intent to others' actions, especially when the social cues are ambiguous. Aggressive children perceive cues differently and make attributions differently than do nonaggressive children (Lochman, White, & Wayland, 1990).

BOX 10.4

Television, Social Learning, and Aggression

The National Television Violence Study, a large-scale survey of the amount, nature, and context of TV violence in the United States, concluded that violence pervades American TV. Fifty-seven percent of programs between 6:00 A.M. and 11:00 P.M. contain violent scenes, often in the form of repeated aggressive acts against a victim that go unpunished. In fact, most violent portrayals do not show victims experiencing any serious physical harm, and few condemn violence or depict alternative ways of solving problems. To the contrary, over one-third of violent TV scenes are embedded in humor, a figure that rises to two-thirds for children's shows. Violent content is 9 percent above average in children's programming, and cartoons are the most violent TV fare of all (Center for Communication and Social Policy, 1998).

Reviewers of thousands of studies have concluded that television violence provides children with "an extensive how-to course in aggression" (Comstock & Paik, 1994; Huston et al., 1992; Slaby, Roedell, Arezzo, & Hendrix, 1995, p. 163). The case is strengthened by the fact that research using a wide variety of research designs, methods, and participants has yielded similar findings. In addition, the relation of TV violence to hostile behavior remains the same after many factors that might otherwise account for this association are controlled, such as IQ, SES, school achievement, and childrearing practices (Donnerstein, Slaby, & Eron, 1994).

Violent programming creates both short- and long-term difficulties in family and peer relations. Longitudinal research reveals that highly aggressive children have a greater appetite for violent TV. As they watch more, they become increasingly likely to resort to hostile ways of solving problems, a spiraling pattern of learning that contributes to serious antisocial acts by adolescence and young adulthood (Slaby et al., 1995). In one extensive longitudinal study boys who watched many violent programs at age 8 were more likely to be rated by peers as highly aggressive at age 19 and to have committed serious criminal acts by age 30 (Huesmann, 1986; Lefkowitz, Eron, Walden, & Huesmann, 1972).

Television violence also hardens children to aggression, making them more willing to tolerate it in others. Heavy TV viewers believe that there is much more violence and danger in society, an effect that is especially strong for children who perceive televised aggression as realistic and relevant to their own lives (Donnerstein, Slaby, & Eron, 1994). As these findings indicate, violent television modifies children's attitudes toward social reality such that they increasingly match what children see on TV. They begin to see the world as a mean and scary place, where aggressive acts are a normal and acceptable means for solving problems.

From L. E. Berk (2000), *Child development* (5th ed.). Boston: Allyn & Bacon. Reprinted with permission of the publisher.

Aggressive youngsters also tend to readily label their internal responses to conflict-producing situations as anger (Garrison & Stolberg, 1983; Hinshaw & Anderson, 1996). In addition to these cognitive distortions, aggressive children are deficient in social problem-solving skills. Although findings are mixed as to whether the number or quantity of solutions to problems that are generated by aggressive youngsters is deficient, there is little doubt that they display problems with the content or quality of the problem solutions they generate (Lochman et al., 1990). In contrast to nonaggressive children, aggressive children consistently generate more action solutions and fewer verbal assertion solutions (Asarnow & Callan, 1985; Lochman & Lampron, 1986). In other words, these kids tend to solve problems by immediate action rather than by trying to talk, which leaves others few choices in interacting with them. Thus, cognitive-behavioral interventions focus on changing cognitive distortions and upon increasing problem-solving skills.

Biophysical Factors. Pennington (2002) discusses bioenvironmental variables, such as closed head injury, perinatal factors, lead exposure, and maternal smoking during pregnancy, as likely contributors to the development of CD, probably by increasing the risk for ADHD and other neuropsychological deficits such as language delay and lower IQ. Acquired brain damage, particularly in the frontal areas of the brain, appears to act more directly to influence the development of antisocial behavior in both adults and children. Pennington (2002) provides a review of research related to neurological mechanisms in the development and expression of CD, including low prefrontal brain volume, low autonomic arousal, and low serotonin levels.

Pennington (2002) also reviews research supporting gene-by-environment interactions in the development of CD, primarily from adoption studies. The presence of both biological risk factors (perinatal risk) and environmental risk factors (lack of maternal warmth) produced a higher rate of CD than either factor acting independently (Raine, Brennan, & Mednick (1997). Genetic or other biological risk factors appear to interact with environmental stress, particularly parenting factors, to greatly increase the risk for CD (Harvard Health Publications, 2005).

Social Factors. Societal factors have been implicated as contributing to the increases in youth-perpetrated violence. Of particular concern is that more violent crimes are being committed by younger children, in some cases, preteens. One study cited failures of both parents and schools as causal factors (Commission on Violence and Youth, 1993). The commission also cited societal factors such as easy access to firearms, increased use of drugs and alcohol, prevalence of gangs, and exposure to violence in the media. Concern has also been voiced about access to gory and violent video and virtual games and websites (Taylor, 1999). These factors are pervasive in urban and suburban settings, but have also spread to many rural areas that had previously considered themselves immune.

Conduct disorders are associated with poverty and neighborhood characteristics, although the relationships are not simple. Poverty itself does not dictate that a neighborhood will have high crime rates (Harvard Health Publications, 2005); rather, neighborhoods vary in the rate of CD among their youth according to both neighborhood cohesion (friendship networks, voluntary community organizations) and the extent of monitoring and supervision of adolescents by adults. Therefore, neighborhood and family variables can act as either risk factors or protective factors in relationship to the development of CD (Pennington, 2002).

Types of Aggression. Five different types of aggression have been identified by Walker and his colleagues (2004). In overaroused aggression, aggressive acts are seen as a side effect of a state of heightened arousal and activity levels such as are often found in youngsters with ADHD. Another type, impulsive aggression, is thought to be neurologically based, unpredictable, and most often manifested in brief episodes. A third type, affective aggression, is spawned by intense anger and rage, such as that suffered by children who have been abused; this aggression is likely to be manifested in violent episodes that may be dangerous and/or destructive. Predatory aggression is related to thought disorders involving paranoia in adolescents and adults; it may involve "settling scores" that are either real or imagined. A fifth type, instrumental aggression, involves the adoption of aggressive tactics to take advantage of others and to get one's way. It is used to intimidate and coerce others. Children and youth who adopt antisocial patterns of behavior (i.e., those with conduct disorders) tend to use instrumental aggression as a means of interacting with others, although affective aggression may be a factor as well. Well-developed, comprehensive intervention plans may help ameliorate all types of aggression. Nonetheless, understanding the specific type may lead to additional interventions such as individual or group therapy for children whose aggression stems from abuse, and use of medication for those whose behavior stems from impulsive or overaroused aggression.

Predisposing Factors. Two undisputed facts in the study of conduct disorder are (1) that the disorder tends to be stable across time and (2) that it runs in families (Kazdin, 1987b). Studies have established that aggression is very stable over a 10-year period: test–retest correlations for aggressive behavior range from 0.60 to 0.80 (Quay, 1986b; Reid, 1993). A longitudinal study of 1,265 children in a New Zealand cohort from birth through 18 years of age yielded the finding that children with conduct problems at age 8 had higher rates of substance abuse/dependence, juvenile offenses, and mental health problems at age 18 (Fergusson & Lynskey, 1998). Contributing factors appeared to be poor parental attachment, early substance use, and affiliation with substance-abusing or delinquent peers during adolescence.

Studies have also shown that antisocial behavior in one's childhood is a good predictor of antisocial behavior in one's offspring (Huesman, Eron, Lefkowitz, & Walder, 1984; Pennington, 2002; Robins, 1991). Interestingly, this trend continues across generations: children whose grandparents had a history of antisocial behavior are more likely to evidence antisocial behavior (Glueck & Glueck, 1968). One explanation for this cross-generational finding is Patterson's coercive behavior model: these patterns of family interaction become routine and are passed from one generation to the next if no intervention occurs. Other explanations are based on hereditary factors, and temperament and bonding issues. Hereditary factors in criminality have been the object of much research; in a review, Rosenthal (1975) concluded that heredity and criminality are connected. In reviewing adoption versus twin studies, he concluded that characteristics such as EEG abnormalities and sensitivity to alcohol that predispose one to antisocial and criminal behavior may be inherited. Other evidence suggests that children whose fathers show criminal behaviors and abuse alcohol are at greater risk for developing conduct disorders (Harvard Health Publications, 2005; Kazdin, 1987a). However, Rosenthal believes that environmental conditions including family factors and social learning are probably instrumental in eliciting the inherited tendencies. Pennington (2002) cites several studies that support this conclusion and adds that both abuse and harsh parenting increase the risk for CD in children, particularly when there is a family history of antisocial behavior.

Temperament and bonding problems in infancy have been associated with later conduct and behavior problems. Temperament is an inborn behavioral style that is also influenced by the environment (Teglasi, 2006). Defining characteristics of temperament include activity level, moodiness, intensity of reaction or emotionality, and ability to adapt to new stimuli (Thomas & Chess, 1977). Parental behavior and responses to the infant, especially the mother's, are influenced by the infant's temperament. Some evidence suggests that infants whose temperaments do not match their mothers' are at increased risk for developing conduct problems (Chess, 1967), perhaps because the quality and closeness of the mother–child interactions are affected. Bonding occurs during the first few months of life and, unfortunately, unless the mother seeks help with her difficult infant very early, the opportunity to intervene and improve the bonding process is lost. Parent and caretaker responses to a child's range of intense emotions has a profound impact on how a child learns to regulate those emotions. In addition, temperament research indicates that infants who have low adaptability and high intensity of emotional reactivity are more prone to develop behavior problems as they grow older (Earls & Jung, 1987; Teglasi, 2006). Thus, intense and inflexible temperaments are predictors of childhood problems (Toth, 1990), in the sense that having a greater number of risk factors reduces the likelihood of developing resources such as social competence (Teglasi, 2006).

According to DSM-IV-TR, difficult infant temperament is a predisposing factor to development of conduct disorders (APA, 2000). Research with the sociopathic subgroup of individuals with conduct disorders appears to contradict these findings. Some researchers believe that these individuals suffer from underarousal of the autonomic nervous system that is thought to cause sensory deprivation, resulting in a need to seek physiological stimulation. Therefore, these individuals turn to thrill seeking and other forms of adventuresome, usually socially unacceptable, behavior to relieve the tiresomeness of routine. Sociopathic individuals have been found to demonstrate lower reactivity and quicker adaptability to stimuli (Hare, 1970; Harvard Health Publications, 2005; Quay, 1977), as opposed to higher reactivity and slower adaptability cited in the earlier temperament studies. Pennington (2002) cites numerous studies demonstrating that low autonomic arousal is associated with antisocial behaviors in both children and adults. This apparent contradiction may be attributed to the fact that the temperament studies have been linked to problems of conduct, but not conduct disorders per se, and not to a subgroup of conduct-disordered individuals. Thus, considered together, the temperament and biological research points to inborn tendencies that may predispose an individual to develop patterns of conduct-disordered behavior; perhaps modeling and coercive patterns of adult–child interaction are environmental catalysts that bring this predisposition to the surface.

DSM-IV-TR lists a number of predisposing factors that are based on clinical observations about the development of conduct disorders: parental rejection and neglect, inconsistent management with harsh discipline, early institutional living, frequent shifting of parental figures (e.g., foster parents, stepparents), physical or sexual abuse, lack of supervision, difficult infant temperament, large family size, and association with a delinquent peer group (APA, 2000). Many of these factors can be construed as supportive of the research on parent–child interaction difficulties as well as temperament and bonding problems.

One underrated factor related to aggression and antisocial behavior is bullying behavior (Kimmel & Mahler, 2003; Sprague & Walker, 2000; Walker et al., 2004). Bullying involves coercion, intimidation, and threats, usually by a group of individuals toward one victim. Olweus (1987) found about 15 percent of the school population in Scandinavia were involved in bully–victim interactions. The problem is even worse in the United States, perhaps as a result of the apparent cultural acceptance of violence (Centers for Disease Control (CDC), 2004; Hoover & Juul, 1993). The CDC (2004) found that of over 16,000 students surveyed, 5.4% missed school for fear of being bullied or other safety concerns. Walker and his colleagues (2004) delineate three roles in a bully–victim interaction: victim, nonparticipant, and perpetrator. Most children choose to be nonparticipants, avoiding bullies and interaction with them. Antisocial youth and individuals with conduct disorders are most often the bullies, while children with physical differences are often involuntary victims. However, there is one scenario in which students with aggressive behavior and conduct disorders are usually the victims; this is at the hands of school personnel (Hyman et al., 1997). "Victimization of students by teachers, administrators, and other school staff members, most often in the name of discipline, is widely practiced and little recognized as a serious problem that contributes to student alienation and aggression" (p. 426). These authors maintain that the overuse of punishment causes emotional damage, which increases student hostility, anger, alienation, and actual aggression against school property, peers, and authorities. Furthermore, excessive use of corporal punishment is frequently associated with conduct disorders (Hyman & Gasiewski, 1992). It seems that the best practice would dictate that school personnel refrain from acting like the students whom they are trying to treat. Furthermore, many believe that because high rates of bullying in school indicate risk of violence, school personnel should make every effort to prevent such interactions (Olweus, 1991; Stephens, 1997; Walker et al., 2004). Box 10.5 describes a multilevel approach to bully–victim problems.

Related Conditions. ADHD, learning problems, depression, and anxiety have been linked with conduct disorders (Harvard Health Publications, 2005; Pennington, 2002). The impulsivity, distractibility, and agitated level of activity associated with ADHD can easily lead to problems with self-control, which may predispose the individual to a variety of problems in social and academic arenas. If exacerbated by some of the other predisposing factors (e.g., parental rejection and paternal alcohol abuse), these difficulties can turn into a pattern of antisocial acts. It has been estimated that a 50–60 percent overlap exists between ADHD and conduct disorders (Barkley, 1998). Learning problems have also long been associated with conduct disorders; however, whether one causes the other is a subject for conjecture. The relationship between specific learning disabilities and juvenile delinquency has been extensively studied, and two causal theories have been put forth: the school failure theory and the susceptibility theory. The school failure theory indicates that learning disabilities set in motion a chain reaction: learning disabilities cause academic failure that in turn offers motivation for delinquent behavior, that is, a chance to strike back at society (Keilitz & Dunivant, 1987; Post, 1981). The susceptibility theory posits that correlates of learning disabilities such as lack of impulse control, inability to anticipate consequences, suggestibility, and a tendency to act out directly influence the development of delinquent behavior (Murray, 1976; Post, 1981).

From a large, well-designed study commissioned by the U.S. Office of Juvenile Justice and Delinquency Prevention, researchers reported the following conclusions: (1) the relationship between learning disabilities and self-reported delinquency was significant, (2) the incidence of learning disabilities among adjudicated delinquents was high (36%), and (3) both the school failure theory and the susceptibility theories were supported (Keilitz & Dunivant, 1987). Thus a strong association between learning disabilities and the propensity to develop delinquent behavior has been established. Pennington (2002) observes

BOX 10.5

Multilevel Approach to Bully–Victim Problems

Intervention for problems with multiple causes and contributors such as bully–victim interactions usually demands an ecological perspective. Olweus (1991, 2003) offers suggestions for addressing such problems at the school level and the classroom level and with the individual him- or herself. The major assumptions according to Olweus are that (1) school and home environments should be warm and positive with adult involvement and include firm limits for unacceptable behavior; (2) inappropriate behavior should be consequated with consistent nonpunitive, nonphysical sanctions; (3) there should be regular monitoring of student activities in and around the school; and (4) adults should act as responsible authorities and role models in adult–child interactions, particularly during bullying interactions.

Olweus recommends that at the school level there be careful supervision at recess, inservice presentations on bully–victim interactions, meetings with staff and parents regarding the problems, formation of a Bullying Prevention Coordinating Committee, promotion of a positive school climate, attractive playgrounds, and parent study groups. Within classrooms, the recommendations include class rules against bullying, cooperative learning activities, regular class meetings to discuss feelings and conflict resolution, teacher–parent meetings, positive activities, and role-playing and readings regarding the prevention of bully–victim interactions. For bullies and victims themselves, Olweus suggests that teachers or counselors have serious talks with them and their parents, use neutral students to assist with positive interactions and problem solving, provide brochures with advice for parents, conduct group discussions with parents of bullies and victims, and perhaps change student classrooms or schools. Development of individual intervention plans is also recommended. It is easier to change the behavior patterns of young children, so early identification and treatment is indicated.

More information about the Olweus Bullying Prevention Program is available at *www.colorado.edu/cspv/blueprints/model/BPPmaterials.html.*

that there are several well-documented correlates of life-course-persistent conduct disorders, including lowered IQ, relatively more depressed verbal compared to nonverbal IQ, and executive function deficits. This pattern could contribute to both the learning problems and social judgment and impulse control deficits observed in individuals with conduct disorders.

In summarizing the development of conduct-disordered and aggressive behavior, we should first consider that a number of predisposing factors may be operating: inherited tendencies toward neurological problems and alcohol sensitivity; temperament, arousal, and bonding difficulties in early interactions between mother and child; later attachment problems with parents and significant adults; and other family and social factors beyond the child's control. Given a combination of these predisposing factors, children who then develop coercive interaction styles with their parents at home and in other settings may be at very high risk for developing conduct disorders. Exposure to aggressive models may also play a role in the development of aggressive behavior. The coexistence of ADHD, learning disabilities, depression, and anxiety with conduct-disordered and delinquent behavior should alert educators to the necessity of early identification and intervention with these youngsters. Box 10.6 describes a case in which a number of predisposing factors were present in a child with features of both internalizing and externalizing disorders.

Intervention and Treatment

In a review of treatment for children with conduct disorders, Kazdin (1987b) introduced the topic thus:

> The diversity of behaviors that conduct disorder includes, the range of dysfunctions associated with them, and the concomitant parent and family dysfunction present a remarkable challenge for treatment . . . the plethora of available treatments might be viewed as a healthy sign that the field has not become rigidly set on one or two techniques. On the other hand, the diversity of procedures suggest that no particular approach has ameliorated clinically severe antisocial behavior. (p. 187)

Furthermore, Mayer (1995), writing about the prevention of antisocial behavior in the schools, states that "our efforts should no longer emphasize 'treating' youngsters as though they are the source of the problem. Rather, our focus must be on identifying and correcting the factors that exist within their environments that promote antisocial behavior" (p. 475). These statements offer an insight about interventions with individuals with conduct disorders: that the complexity of factors contributing to the development and maintenance of these behaviors demands equally complex treatment. So far, we have been unable to find effective interventions that have clear implications for long-term behavior change. However, we have begun to recognize the complexity of the problem and to incorporate equally comprehensive interventions.

Comprehensive interventions must involve numerous people who routinely interact with the child in different settings. Since parents, teachers, and peers are the most important socialization agents in the lives of all children, then interventions should include these agents if we are to alter the path of antisocial children who are on their way to developing disorders (Sprague & Walker, 2000). From a systems point of view, schoolwide interventions and neighborhood-based programming have been indicated for the purpose of preventing antisocial behavior (Garbarino & Kostelny, 1997; Mayer, 1995). Strategies that include parents (i.e., parent involvement), school personnel, peers (i.e., social skills training), and communities will be reviewed in the remainder of this chapter and discussed again in Chapter 12 in the section on youth violence.

Families that are struggling with issues such as divorce, poverty, abuse, unemployment, and drug or alcohol abuse are susceptible to disrupted parenting practices, which in turn often lead to antisocial behavior in young children (Fergusson & Lynskey, 1998; Patterson, 1983; Patterson et al., 1992). Five parenting practices that, in combination with other factors, have been found to breed antisocial behavior are harsh and inconsistent discipline, failure to monitor the child's whereabouts, failure to invest time and energy in the child's life, failure to use positive management strategies such as support and limit setting, and inability to handle conflict within the family (Walker et al., 2004). Interventions with parents usually target these and similar unsuccessful parenting habits. Such interventions include parent training, family therapy, and parent involvement in the school program.

BOX 10.6
Eric

Eric is a 12-year-old seventh grader whose paternal grandparents requested a psychological assessment because they were concerned that he was falling behind academically, despite being served through special education since kindergarten as a student with a learning disability and emotional disturbance (general pervasive mood of unhappiness under normal circumstances). During her pregnancy, his mother experienced high blood pressure and Rh bloodtype incompatibility, but there were no known related complications. Eric's developmental history includes a long and difficult birth, milk-product allergies in infancy, and a pigeon-toed stance that necessitated a leg brace by age 1.

Eric's parents divorced when he was 7 years old and his father is the custodial parent. Both parents have remarried and Eric visits his mother's family on alternate weekends. Eric has a younger brother who lives with him and his father. His mother has a history of dyslexia and dropped out of high school. Her family history includes alcoholism, drug abuse, sexual abuse, and major depression. On the father's side, there is a history of alcohol and drug abuse and ADHD.

Recent concerns include Eric's stealing money from his stepmother, short temper and frequent, unprovoked fighting with his brother, once shooting him in the nose with a pellet gun, an action for which he showed little remorse. He exhibits mood swings and oppositional behaviors toward his parents. Eric also tends to hoard food in his bedroom and has gained a lot of weight over the past 3 years so that he is now significantly overweight. At the end of sixth grade, he and some friends vandalized school lockers and were suspended from school. Teachers described him as noncompliant, not taking responsibility for his work, and barely passing to seventh grade. School attention and motivation were described as minimal.

Consistent with past testing, his IQ score was in the superior range, while academic achievement was in the low-average to average range, with basic writing skills and written expression his areas of greatest weakness. His achievement scores were below what would be expected in all areas given his intellectual aptitude. This low achievement pattern appears to have been present throughout his school years. Personality testing indicated that Eric experiences chronic depression, poor relationships with peers and teachers, and inappropriate types of behavior and feelings under normal circumstances. Minimal empathy or insight into the effects of his behavior on others was evident. History and current behavior, based on grandparent and parent report, as well as parent and teacher behavior rating scales, are consistent with oppositional-defiant behaviors and ADHD, with clinically significant symptoms of inattention, hyperactivity, and impulsivity present in all parent and teacher behavior rating scales. At the time of this evaluation, he exhibited a sufficient number of symptoms to be diagnosed with a conduct disorder, with the pattern of antisocial behavior increasing over the past year. Without family involvement in counseling and a structured school behavior intervention plan, it appears likely that Eric will continue to be at risk for school failure, substance abuse, and an antisocial pattern of behavior, with underlying depression and ADHD.

Based on this evaluation, Eric continued to be eligible for special education services as a student with emotional disturbance and a learning disability. Recommendations included parent behavioral management training, a functional behavioral assessment and home/school-based intervention plan, behavioral consultation for the classroom teachers, individual counseling with Eric, medication consultation with a psychiatrist, and intensive remediation of academic deficits through special education.

Parent Training in Management Skills. Many variations of parent training exist, but most are focused on breaking the cycle of coercive interactions between parent and child. In accordance, parents must attempt to support prosocial behaviors rather than coercive ones by learning and implementing such skills as establishing clear rules for behavior, using positive reinforcement, negotiating compromises, and using only mild forms of punishment. In this treatment, parents are the clients, and no direct intervention with the child is attempted. Parents must be shown specifically how to use these skills, have a chance to practice them, and be given support and feedback. In other words, therapists model the behavior and rehearse the parents (Harvard Health Publications, 2005).

The effectiveness of parent training has been evaluated in hundreds of studies with children of varying ages and degrees of problem severity (Hester & Kaiser, 1998; Johnston & Chen, 2005; Kazdin, 1985). Johnston and Chen (2005), in a review of related studies, conclude that behavioral parent training has met the standard to be described as evidenced-based treatment for child disruptive behaviors and note that there is research evidence of benefit up to 14 years' posttreatment. Furthermore, parents tend to prefer this form of treatment over other options.

Patterson, Chamberlain and Reid's (1982) work with the families of over 200 aggressive youngsters is probably the most concerted effort to prove the effectiveness of parent training with this population. Several of these studies have shown that parent training does result in improvement of children's aggressive behavior (Kazdin, 1993). Parent training has been demonstrated as more effective in comparison to other treatments (Patterson, et al., 1982) in bringing the level of problem behaviors within normal range (Wells, Forehand, & Griest, 1980), and as sustaining improvements with noncompliant children up to 4 years later (Baum & Forehand, 1981). Siennick, Findling, and Guelzow (2005) conclude from their review of research that parent management training is one of the most effective strategies, in terms of durability of behavioral improvement across settings, for treating conduct disorders. Harvard Health Publications (2005) describes several demonstration programs that employ parent management training and are funded by the National Institute of Mental Health (NIMH). This reference is included in the "Additional Readings and Resources" section at the end of this chapter.

Factors that appear to limit effectiveness of parent training programs are length of treatment (optimally, up to 50 or 60 hours), lower socioeconomic status or single parenthood, and parental variables such as marital discord and psychopathology (Johnston & Chen, 2005; Kazdin, 1985; Strain, Young, & Horowitz, 1981). This treatment obviously makes many demands on parents, including time and a commitment to change habitual ways of interacting with their child. Therefore, parent training is not an option for those students with conduct disorders whose parents are unavailable, unwilling, or unable to make these commitments (Hester & Kaiser, 1998; Kazdin, 1987b). Longer-lasting programs appear to be more effective, especially when academic support is included (Harvard Health Publications, 2005).

Functional Family Therapy. A second, promising treatment approach involves the entire family in therapy. Functional family therapy is based on a family systems approach that presupposes that the problem behavior of the child is serving a function in the family, albeit a maladaptive one. The goal, therefore, is to get family members to understand these dynamics in their day-to-day interactions and to alter them to more adaptive ways of communicating with one another (Jacob & Doherty, 2006). More specific goals are (1) to increase positive reinforcement and reciprocity among family members and (2) to help them negotiate constructively and learn to identify alternative solutions to conflicts that arise. These goals are actively identified and worked on by family members during sessions with the help of the therapist. Outcome studies comparing the effectiveness of functional family therapy with other treatments is encouraging, but unfortunately scarce with youth with conduct disorders. Parsons and Alexander (1973) compared other types of family therapy to functional family therapy with a group of delinquents and found improved family interaction and lower recidivism rates to juvenile courts 18 months after treatment. Perhaps more impressively, follow-up data 2½ years later showed that siblings of the delinquent group had significantly lower incidences of juvenile court referrals (Klein, Alexander, & Parsons, 1977). Thus, the positive changes apparently "spilled over" or generalized to other family members as well as the targeted youth.

Parent Involvement in the School Program. The prognosis for positive results with antisocial behavior is greatly enhanced by early intervention that includes a family–school partnership (Reid & Patterson, 1991; Siennick et al., 2005; Sprague & Walker, 2000). Walker et al. (2004) outline a step-by-step approach for involving parents of antisocial children in the school program. Although these authors recognize the difficulties inherent in involving parents of families that are stressed by numerous problems, they also recognize the necessity of doing so. Their strategies include the following:

- Initiating and maintaining positive interactions through a variety of home–school communicators
- Using a written problem-solving sequence to cooperatively find solutions to problems
- Implementing home–school cards and contracts
- Helping parents with discipline and management strategies at home (specifically, the effective use of reinforcement, contracts, time-out, privilege removal, and work chores)

The emphasis throughout all activities is developing a partnership between teacher and parents so that students understand they cannot "get away" with antisocial behavior in either setting.

Recent reviews of parent–school programs have included the Families and Schools Together Track (FASTT) as a promising intervention model (Harvard Health Publications, 2005; Jacob & Doherty, 2006). In this program, which is funded by NIMH as a demonstration program, experts worked with parents and teachers of aggressive children beginning at age 6. Two years later, compared with controls, these children showed less aggression and reduced need for special education placement.

To summarize parent involvement strategies, the literature to date indicates that the most effective interventions help parents identify maladaptive interactions with their children and then offer a means to alter these interactions. Such interventions can be effected through parent training, family therapy, and increased parental involvement in school programs. Each of these techniques has yielded encouraging results, but youth with conduct disorders continue to pose one of the greatest challenges to all professionals.

School-Based Programming. Many propose that schools are a major contributor to antisocial behavior because they promote coercive and punitive environments, unclear rules, inconsistent consequences, and ineffective instruction (Goldstein & Conoley, 1997; Mayer, 1995). Furthermore, schools facilitate problems when they fail to consider individual differences among the students (Mayer, 1995). To prevent and treat antisocial behavior in the schools, contributory factors should be identified and changed. As discussed in Chapter 7, Mayer (1995) suggests that schools need to emphasize functional behavioral assessments and positive behavioral interventions and supports. This notion of positive behavioral supports (PBS) also mentioned in Chapter 7 and described in detail in Chapter 12, has gained increasing acceptance, as evidenced by the inclusion of PBS in the 1997 and 2004 reauthorizations of IDEA.

As you learned in Chapter 7, PBS is based on behavioral and ecological models of behavior and learning. This means that behavior management strategies target contextual variables as well as individual variables (Sugai & Horner, 1999). Usually, PBS includes the following:

- Functional behavioral assessments
- Alteration of home, school, classroom, and teacher variables based on assessment results
- Clear expectations and routines
- Skill training for alternative and replacement behaviors (i.e., behaviors that serve the same function as the targeted inappropriate behavior)
- Precorrection to prevent mistakes
- Differential reinforcement for promotion of correct behavior
- Data-based decisions
- Punishment only as necessary
- Applications at the school, classroom, and individual levels
- Strategies for involving parents and community in schools

Many believe that multilevel school-based programming is necessary to prevent antisocial behavior and respond to students with conduct problems; singular simplistic approaches appear doomed to fail (Goldstein & Conoley, 1997; Lewis & Sugai, 1999; Mayer, 1995; Van Acker & Talbott, 1999; Walker et al., 2004; Webber, 1997a). Although PBS was not developed specifically for students with conduct disorders, application of these strategies will likely result in less pathology and healthier students overall.

Social Skills Training. Students with conduct disorders almost always have well-established negative peer and teacher relations. Social skills training emphasizing teacher- and peer-related skills is another component of comprehensive treatment for this population. There are several points relative to social skills training with students with conduct disorders that bear mentioning.

1. Social skills training is an important complement to behavior reduction techniques in that it teaches positive alternatives to negative, coercive behavior (Walker et al., 2004). Many students with conduct disorder are totally lacking in positive interaction skills (Gresham, 2002).

2. Social rejection by peers and teachers is a very powerful contributor to the process whereby antisocial behavior develops into conduct disorders (Patterson, 1988). Unfortunately, there is a social perception bias held by peers against aggressive and antisocial students that is extremely difficult to change even after the aggressive behavior improves (Zaragosa, Vaughn, & McIntosh, 1991). Such findings underscore the need to involve peers in social skills and other interventions.
3. The difficulties in generalization and maintenance of newly acquired social skills are well established (e.g., Baer, 1981; Gresham, 2002; McGinnis & Goldstein, 1984). Together with the social bias and peer rejection factors described above, these difficulties point to the need to offer opportunities for practice and reinforcement within natural settings. For example, Walker et al. (1995) suggest a playground supervisor who roams the playground and, according to a well-defined set of rules, not only distributes points for positive behavior but also takes points away for instances of negative behavior. Students in each classroom are divided into four or five groups, and the incentive system is based on group performance. Thus, the playground supervision program offers daily opportunities for both reinforcing social skills and punishing negative behavior in a natural setting.
4. Gresham (1998), in synthesizing meta-analytic reviews, concludes that social skills training has produced weak effect sizes (has failed to produce targeted outcomes), particularly for students with EBD. He proposes that the reasons for this failure can be attributed to three factors: "(1) use of socially invalid and insensitive outcome measures; (2) failure to match social skills interventions to specific social skills deficits; and (3) failure to program for functional generalization" (p. 23). Gresham (2002) suggests that researchers use valid outcome measures and that practitioners match social skills training to particular deficits identified for each student through valid assessment. He further suggests that social skills training be conducted through incidental teaching strategies to promote generalization. Finally, social skills should be chosen as functional replacement behaviors that compete with the efficiency and effectiveness of targeted problem behaviors. In this way, problem behavior will likely be alleviated by mastery of the more effective prosocial behaviors.

Neighborhood-Based Programming. In keeping with a systems perspective of conduct disorders, Garbarino and Kostelny (1997) explored the contribution of neighborhoods to the problem of youth violence and conduct problems. They state that "The situation of neighborhoods that are at risk for child maltreatment because of a deterioration of economic and social supports bears a relationship to situations of acute disaster, in which there is a dramatic destruction of the infrastructure of daily life" (p. 383). For such neighborhoods, where stress is high and resources are low, typical neighborhood-based support programs will fail unless the negative momentum is first reversed. Garbarino and Kostelny identify seven factors that lead to individuals' healthy adaptability. These authors propose that neighborhoods play an important role in the development of such resilience. The seven factors that positively influence individual resilience are as follows:

1. Actively attempting to alleviate stress, rather than just reacting to it
2. An average level of intelligence

3. Experiences that lead to self-confidence and self-efficacy
4. Positive interpersonal relationship skills, rather than withdrawal
5. A stable emotional relationship with at least one adult
6. An open, supportive educational climate and positive parental modeling of coping strategies
7. Social support from adults other than the family

The last factor obviously applies to neighborhoods. Everyone needs to be responsible for all children. Unfortunately, families that are at high risk for unhealthy children are also unable to access neighborhood resources (Garbarino, 1977). Stable emotional relationships will develop when family members are taught to truly care for their children and are given the skills necessary to access needed resources. Teaching others resourcefulness and the ability to form emotional bonds demands complex strategies at multiple levels. Conduct disorders will not be alleviated through singular approaches aimed at individual students. Although effective neighborhood-based interventions for children and youth with conduct problems are not clearly defined and delineated, the concept of building community supports seems well founded and will certainly require special investments (Garbarino & Kostelny, 1997). Schools, as perhaps centers of the community, could play a key role in establishing a coalition of families, social agencies, elected officials, police, and the judicial system for the purpose of investing in and committing to particular research-based approaches for building resilient and healthy children, families, and communities (Conoley & Goldstein, 1997). School-linked support services were discussed in more detail in Chapter 8.

Medication. While there is no pharmacological solution for the behavior problems presented by conduct disorders, medications are sometimes prescribed for comorbid conditions, such as ADHD, depression, and anxiety (Forness et al., 2003–2004). Furthermore, sometimes medication interventions are needed for more severe aggression and mood swings. In such cases, antipsychotic drugs such as risperidone (Risperdal), anticonvulsants like valproate (Depakote), and mood stabilizers like lithium may be prescribed (Harvard Health Publications, 2005; Siennick et al., 2005).

Implications for Teachers. It is clear that teachers need to be primarily concerned about teaching their assigned students. However, teachers would do well to maintain a macro-perspective of the problem. More than any other disorder, conduct disorders demand such a perspective. Teachers should also try to establish a strong partnership with parents of students with conduct disorders. Unfortunately, parent involvement may not be feasible for a number of these youths. In such cases, it may be helpful to remember that many aggressive behaviors are maintained by coercive interactions with others, including teachers and peers. Therefore, breaking the coercive interaction cycle at school by refusing to engage coercively is one helpful intervention. Teachers can also implement social skills training that (1) focuses on teacher- and peer-related skills and (2) incorporates peers into both the training and reinforcement activities.

The literature on effective interventions with children with antisocial behavior or conduct disorder indicates that a combination of behavioral treatments is needed (Forness et al., 2003–2004), including limit-setting, careful monitoring, and a system of both positive and aversive consequences (Kazdin, 1987a; Mayer, 1995; Patterson et al., 1992). Special education teachers already employ a variety of behavioral techniques; teachers of students with conduct disorders may want to be certain that they include (1) a system for careful monitoring outside the classroom as well as inside the classroom and (2) principles and techniques associated with PBS. For further information, the reader is referred to an excellent, comprehensive school-based plan for treatment of these students titled *Antisocial Behavior in School: Evidence-based Practices* (Walker, Ramsey, & Gresham, 2004) included in the Additional Readings and Resources section.

Need for Early Intervention. The stability of antisocial behavior over time leads to the conclusion that early intervention in "budding" conduct disorders may be essential (Sprague & Walker, 2000). Young children displaying oppositional-defiant and other anti-social characteristics should be identified and worked with as early as possible, even in the preschool years. The child who gets kicked out of one or more preschools for aggressive behavior and who appears to be shaping his parents' behavior rather than vice versa is a good candidate for early intervention. In fact, the argument has been made that, if antisocial behavior has not come under control by the time an individual is 8 years old, then it should be viewed as a chronic condition like diabetes: it cannot be cured, but its symptoms can be managed and controlled only with careful intervention (Kazdin, 1987a).

Conclusions

Students with ADHD and/or conduct disorders pose a special challenge to teachers because of the provoking, often aggressive nature of their behavior. The coexistence of these disorders and learning, emotional, and social problems frequently requires a multifaceted approach to treatment. With ADHD children, a combination of medication and behavior management may prove most effective in ameliorating the symptoms, although these techniques will not "cure" the disorder. Conduct disorders, particularly those with onset before age 10, are stable, persistent, and resistant to treatment. However, early identification and multimodal treatment of the child in the context of family, school, and community interactions may prove to be effective in changing some of the coercive interaction styles of this population. Teachers can focus on parent involvement plus a combination of social skills and selected behavioral techniques that have proven partially effective with students with conduct disorders.

KEY POINTS

1. Children and youth with the diagnosis of ADHD and the core behaviors of impulsivity, inattention, and hyperactivity will find their way into classrooms for students with emotional/behavioral disorders.
2. Teachers may be called on to assist with the diagnosis of ADHD because of its observability in the classroom.
3. Most professionals now believe that children with ADHD inherit a central nervous system that predisposes them toward problems with attention and concentration.

4. Although studies of stimulant medication treatment for ADHD have proven effective in ameliorating symptoms, some professionals still believe that behavior management alone or in combination with medication is the preferred mode of treatment.
5. When a number of predisposing factors are present, a conduct disorder may develop out of a coercive interaction style between child and parent that is subsequently reinforced in the home and other settings.
6. Conduct disorders are stable, persistent over time, and tend to run in families. Conduct disorders with onset in adolescence are more likely to be time-limited, while those with early onset are more likely to be chronic, or life-course-persistent.
7. It is known that conduct disorders require interventions that are multifacted and comprehensive.
8. We have yet to discover how to effectively help individuals with conduct disorders change their behavior patterns, but promising interventions include early identification, family therapy, parent training, parent involvement in the school program, positive behavioral supports, schoolwide management systems, social skills training, neighborhood supports, and specific behavior management techniques.

HOMEWORK QUESTIONS

1. In the case study of Eric, consider the multiple diagnoses resulting from his evaluation (LD, ADHD, conduct disorder, ED [depression]). Select two of these diagnoses and describe your approach to them in a special education classroom. (two paragraphs)
2. How does the diagnosis of ADHD differ from that of oppositional-defiant disorder? Consider both overlap and differences in these diagnoses. What is the educational significance of these differences? (two paragraphs)
3. Consider the major current theories regarding the etiology of ADHD. If parents were to come to you for advice about assessment and treatment for their child with suspected ADHD, to whom would you refer them and why? (one paragraph)
4. Given what is known about the prognosis for childhood-onset conduct disorder, what interventions seem most essential to help a child with this diagnosis? What factors might increase positive outcomes? What factors might limit effectiveness of interventions? (two paragraphs)
5. Do you think that children with conduct disorder should be eligible for special education as EBD? Justify your answer. If yes, under what conditions? If no, why not? (two paragraphs)

ADDITIONAL READINGS AND RESOURCES

National Organization of Children and Adults with Attention-Deficit/Hyperactivity Disorder (CHADD) website: *http://www.chadd.org,* for resources and references for parents and teachers, as well as information regarding assessment, treatment, and legal issues.

Antisocial behavior in the schools: Evidence-based practices (2nd ed.), by Hill Walker, Elizabeth Ramsey, and Frank Gresham, Belmont, CA: Wadsworth, 2004, for a superb, comprehensive treatment of dealing with antisocial behavior and budding conduct disorders through school-based approaches.

Attention-deficit hyperactivity disorder: A handbook for diagnosis and treatment (2nd ed.), by R. Barkley, New York: Guilford Press, 1998, for a practitioner's approach to dealing with children with ADHD.

Classroom-based functional and adjunctive assessments: Proactive approaches to intervention selection for adolescents with attention deficit hyperactivity disorder, by R. A. Ervin, G. J. DuPaul, L. Kern, & P. C. Friman, *Journal of Applied Behavior Analysis, 31,* 1998, 65–78, for case studies of functional assessment strategies and related classroom interventions applied to the challenging behaviors of two adolescents.

Cormorbidity of conduct problems and ADHD: Identification of "fledging psychopaths," by F. Gresham, K. Lane, and K. Lambros, *Journal of Emotional and Behavioral Disorders, 8*(2), 2000, 83–93, for a literature review of issues surrounding identification and treatment of individuals displaying both externalizing disorders.

School violence intervention: A practical handbook, by A. P. Goldstein & J. C. Conoley, New York: Guilford Press, 1997, for a comprehensive view of the problem of school violence and a systems approach to dealing with it.

Psychiatric disorders and their treatment: A primer for school professionals, by S. R. Forness, H. M. Walker, & K. A. Kavale, *Emotional and Behavioral Disorders in Youth, 4*(1), 2003–2004, 3–6, 20–23 for medication treatment effects.

Pediatric psychoparmacology, by M. C. Kral, A. LaRosa, R. T. Brown, & T. Kubiszyn, in G. G. Bear & K. M. Minke (eds.), *Children's needs III: Development, prevention, and intervention* (pp. 1077–1088), Bethesda, MD: NASP, 2006, for an updated summary of commonly prescribed psychotropic medications for children and adolescents, along with indications for use, side effects, and the status of FDA approval.

Child and adolescent conduct disorder, *Harvard Mental Health Letter,* April 2005, for a discussion of parent management training programs and associated references and websites.

Conduct Disorders and Severe Antisocial Behavior by Paul J. Frick, New York: Springer, 1998, for clear guidelines for intervention with children and adolescents who display a severe pattern of aggressive antisocial behavior based on the most current research.

Journal of Emotional and Behavioral Disorders, 2002, 10(3) edited by George Sugai and Robert Horner for a special issue addressing positive behavior supports and functional behavioral assessments in schools.

Office of Juvenile Justice and Delinquency Prevention (*http://ojjdp.ncjrs.org/*) for reports on juvenile crimes and arrests.

U.S. Surgeon General's Office for various reports on the health and well being of children and youth (*http://www.surgeongeneral.gov/*)

American Academy of Child and Adolescent Psychiatry (*http://aacap.org*) for resources for families with children with externalizing disorders.

U.S. Department of Health and Human Services, Substance Abuse and Mental Health Service Administration (SAMHSA) (*http://mentalhealth.samhsa.gov/*) for mental health facts about children and youth with ADHD and conduct disorders.

Children and Adults with Attention-deficit/Hyperactivity Disorder (CHADD) (*http://www.chadd.org*) for an organization dedicated to education, advocacy, and support for individuals with AD/HD.

National Institute of Mental Health (NIMH) (National Institutes of Health) (*http://www.nimh.nih.gov/*) for information, booklets, and research on various disabilities including CD and ADHD.

CHAPTER 11 Adolescence

QUESTIONS TO CONSIDER

- How do the normal concerns and behavioral issues of adolescence differ from those observed in teens with emotional/behavioral disorders?
- What role do special educators play in the prevention of behavior patterns that lead to dropping out or school failure?
- What are the risk factors for alcohol/drug use? Gang involvement? Self-destructive behavior?
- How can special education teachers be involved in suicide prevention?
- What are the two major types of eating disorders encountered in adolescence?
- Why have special issues involving girls become more prominent in recent years?
- How are special educators involved in transition services and why are these services so important for adolescents?

Orientation

The fine line between deviant and nondeviant behavior during adolescence is implied by Morse's observation that "All secondary teachers are teachers of disturbed adolescents" (1969a, p. 442). It is common for today's adolescent to experiment with alcohol, drugs, and sex and to evidence many other forms of behavior that can be characterized as "borderline deviant." In addition to experimenting, which is a normal part of adolescence, adolescents with emotional/behavioral disorders evidence extremeness of behavior and maladaptive coping patterns, which result in their being diagnosed or labeled. If you plan to teach this population, you should be prepared to deal with numerous problems that are not as often found in younger children.

Overview

The mere use of the term *adolescence* generally evokes images of awkwardness, self-consciousness, and conflict. Adolescents typically experience a period of rapid changes in physical, cognitive, and social development, entering this period into as children and emerging as adults. The first section of this chapter explores some of the major issues affecting adolescents and causing friction between them and the adults in their lives. The primary adolescent issues that educators must deal with in the schools are related to dropping out, sex, social rejection, discrimination, drugs, gangs, and self-destructive behavior.

Experimentation is a natural part of adolescent development. The majority of adolescents experiment and then eventually adopt social behaviors that allow them to function as young adults in society. In contrast, adolescents with emotional/behavioral disorders may fail to learn coping strategies that allow them to adapt. Behavioral and counseling interventions are often necessary to help them learn more acceptable ways of coping.

Although development of educational services for adolescents with EBD has lagged behind services for children with EBD, many school systems have established successful model programs for this population. These programs typically include transition planning, behavioral interventions, and counseling techniques.

Defining Adolescence and Emotional/Behavioral Disorders in Adolescence

> Adults sometimes cynically regard adolescence as a "disease" that only time can cure, suggesting that parents would do well to bury their offspring at age 12 and dig them up again at age 20. At the same time, some critics contend that adolescence has become artificially prolonged as a "tribal subculture," so that there is little assurance of adulthood even at 20. (Atwater, 1983, p. 1)

Adolescence is a developmental period of the human growth cycle occurring between the ages of approximately 12 and 20. For most individuals, it is an awkward period in which they are no longer considered children but have not yet attained adult status. The onset of adolescence is generally considered to be marked by the rapid physiological changes occurring during puberty. The demise of adolescence is less well defined by markers such as legal independence and the acquisition of adult responsibilities. There is no clearly defined upper limit of adolescence, or age at which individuals officially pass over from adolescence into adulthood. Unlike many primitive cultures, which clearly separate childhood from adulthood by ceremonial rites of passage, our modern culture allows the individual nearly a decade of preparation for the responsibilities of adulthood. Adolescence is best defined as the period of transition from childhood to adulthood, a period of flux in which the adolescent may act as mature and responsible as any adult on one day and then revert to childish behavior the next. Adolescence is a time in which individuals redefine their identities based on rapidly changing potential in many areas of their lives.

Developmental Changes

Studies of the modern adolescent reveal upheaval in three developmental areas: physical, cognitive, and personal-social. Given that physiological changes associated with puberty generally occur early in adolescence, while cognitive and personal-social development continue into early adulthood, the period termed *adolescence* is both prolonged and complex.

Physical Changes. Rapid changes in physical development mark the onset of puberty and the adolescent period. Hormonal secretions from the hypothalamus and pituitary gland are responsible for physiological changes manifested in growth spurts of height and weight, and in sexual maturation. Girls generally become capable of reproduction between ages 11 and 13, with breast development occurring before age 10 (Tharinger, Wilkinson, & Lasser, 2006) and girls reach their approximate adult height and weight at about age 15 or 16. Boys mature sexually at age 13 or 14 and reach their approximate adult stature at age 17 or 18. Commensurate changes in skeletal and muscular structure also occur during this period.

Such drastic physiological changes in the adolescent require an adjustment in body image, which may be reflected in self-concept. As they attempt to adjust mentally to their rapidly developing physiques, adolescents can become preoccupied with physical characteristics and attractiveness. They are sensitive to societal standards of beauty and are often highly self-critical. Girls tend to be more concerned about their physical appearance than boys, who tend to be more concerned about physical competence or prowess. Another issue is the age at which an individual matures; while early maturers may be thrust into social situations that they are not yet prepared to handle, late maturers often experience undue anxiety about their development.

Cognitive Changes. In addition to physiological changes, the onset of puberty generally is accompanied by an increasing capacity for complex and abstract thought. In Piaget's theory of cognitive development, adolescence corresponds with the stage of formal operational thought. Formal thought is marked by the ability to think abstractly and to hypothesize. In contrast to the previous childhood stage of concrete thought, which is limited to perceived reality, formal thought encompasses hypothetical possibilities (Inhelder & Piaget, 1958). This shift from the real to the possible enables an individual to generate and discard hypotheses (hypothetico-deductive reasoning), much like the scientist does. For example, younger children usually generate a single explanation for an event based on their perception, and they are unable to discard this explanation even when subsequent experience proves them wrong; the child's perception is her reality. Adolescents in the formal operations stage are able to discard an explanation when it fails to fit the facts and are able to generate other possible explanations. Hypotheses are secondary to reality (Inhelder & Piaget, 1958). Other characteristics of formal thought include increased flexibility and imagination, and capacity for logic and propositional thought (if–then hypotheses).

Some implications of formal thought in adolescents are summarized by Atwater (1983):

> The emergence of abstract thought at this age helps to explain much characteristic adolescent behavior. For one thing, it helps to explain why adolescents become so idealistic and

> romantic on the one hand, yet more critical and cynical on the other. It also explains why adolescents are so busy clarifying their own identity, yet suffer from the accompanying conflicts and confusion. The newly discovered capacity for abstract thought may also explain the characteristic self-centeredness of this stage of life. (p. 72)

Although formal thought generally is acquired between the ages of 12 and 16, there is much variation among individuals in capability for formal thought. Some adolescents and adults never attain it. Most cognitive development theorists, including Piaget (1972), recognize that formal thought is not automatically attained, but can be facilitated through appropriate educational experiences. Effects of social class and intelligence on the acquisition of formal thought have been found to be negligible (Kuhn & Angelev, 1976; Neimark, 1975). The somewhat newer concept of executive functions, described in Chapters 5 and 10, in some ways parallels the construct of formal operations. However, executive functions are somewhat more broadly defined, affecting the regulation and control of both emotional and cognitive behaviors. Executive functions are also closely tied to brain development and are believed to continue to develop throughout adolescence and into young adulthood (Delis, Kaplan, & Kramer, 2001; Harvard Medical School, 2005). The outcome of increasing executive function is enhanced ability to plan ahead by considering options, organizing behavior toward goals, and monitoring/changing behavior as needed based on environmental feedback. These are some of the skills that may show wide variability in adolescent populations, particularly among those teens with emotional/behavioral disorders.

Personal and Social Changes. Along with physical and cognitive changes, adolescents experience tremendous upheaval in personal ideology and social relationships. The old rules of childhood suddenly don't work anymore. The adolescent is thrust into a period of experimentation with new rules, new roles, and an emerging concept of a new self. Three major personal-social changes that occur during this period are noteworthy: searches for identity, independence, and peer approval.

The search for identity involves the individual's attempt to integrate the old childhood self with potential for a new adult self. Erikson (1968) dubbed this phenomenon "identity versus role confusion" and included it as the fifth stage of the eight stages of psychosocial development, as discussed in Chapter 5. According to Erikson, the search for self is a normal developmental process that may reach crisis proportions but must be resolved if optimal personal growth is to be attained. Conflict, anxiety, self-doubt, and experimentation are all part of the process as adolescents try to find out who they are and what distinguishes them as individuals from their peers. This period is also marked by egocentrism or extreme self-centeredness, during which individuals may become painfully self-conscious. This acute self-consciousness is illustrated by Elkind's (1974) concept of the imaginary audience, in which adolescents feel as though they are constantly being watched and evaluated by everyone as if on stage and performing for an audience. A preoccupation with others' perceptions is the major outcome of this stage of egocentrism.

A certain degree of role confusion is unavoidable as the individual tries out various points of view and periodically adopts new styles of interacting, but role confusion is detrimental when it becomes so extreme that the individual loses the boundaries of self. As part of normal development, children's self-perceptions may be somewhat inflated in early childhood, but decline as they enter late childhood and early adolescence, consistent with growing ability to perceive differences between their real and ideal selves as reflected in the evaluations of significant others. However, self-esteem gradually increases through middle and late adolescence as increasing freedom allows for greater opportunities to participate in activities in which adolescents feel competent. Greater capacity to adjust behavior to meet social expectations and thus obtain support and positive response also contributes to increases in self-esteem in normally developing adolescents (Manning, Bear, & Minke, 2006). Harter (1999) posited that fluctuations in self-esteem characterize normal development in both males and females, across various dimensions of self-concept.

In contrast, extreme role confusion and loss of sense of self are frequently found among adolescents with severe disorders (e.g., psychosis). Another difficulty is the adoption of a negative identity, which often happens when adolescents have no positive role models to emulate (Hauser, 1972). Many youth from impoverished communities or unhappy homes turn to delinquency or gangs as ways to establish an identity, albeit an unacceptable one by society's standards.

A second major issue for adolescents is the development of independence or autonomy. While not wanting to jeopardize the emotional security provided by the home, the adolescent constantly struggles to establish a legitimate identity separate from parents. Increased self-sufficiency and decision making are a large part of independence, yet adolescents do not consistently manifest these skills even when acquired; rather, an individual may be unusually mature and self-sufficient in one moment and quite dependent the next. Such fluctuations make teenagers' behavior difficult to predict and sometimes exasperating for adults.

Open rejection of parental values and questioning of authority are classic symptoms of developing independence. The home is typically the focal point of conflict over independence issues, as the adolescent wants to have more decision-making power, to be afforded some privileges, and generally to take more control of his or her life. Issues that cause conflict in most families of adolescents are those pertaining to the quest for independence and intimacy, such as dress, use of the family car, dating, daily chores, school performance, and use of drugs (Atwater, 1983; Schickedanz, Schickedanz, Forsyth, & Forsyth, 1998). The parents' sense of authority and the adolescent's sense of increasing autonomy are challenged by the almost daily conflicts that arise over these issues. Various influences on parent–child conflicts are summarized in Table 11.1.

A third and extremely important change that occurs in the lives of adolescents is the shift in allegiance from family to peers. Peer approval supersedes most other social aspirations at this point in the individual's development (Tharinger et al., 2006). An inordinate amount of time is spent in cultivating friendships and dating relationships, and for many teenagers the telephone becomes an essential instrument for gathering information about the rapidly changing social scene at school.

The adolescent's emerging identity is closely allied with peer approval and acceptance. Social acceptance is generally based on social conformity; to be "in," one must speak, dress, look, and act like everyone else, or at least like a specific subgroup. Although the styles change over the years, each generation creates a fringe element, which is the ultimate adolescent statement of identity through conformity. (Consider the beatniks of the 1950s, the hippies of the 1960s, the preppies of the 1970s, the punks of the 1980s, and the

TABLE 11.1 Some Influences on Parent–Adolescent Conflicts

Age: Although the number of conflicts tends to decrease with age, older adolescents pose more serious conflicts involving the use of the car, sex, or drugs.

Sex: The frequency and type of conflict tend to vary by sex. According to one study, family problems made up 22 percent of the difficulties reported by adolescent girls, but only 10 percent of those reported by boys. Parents are more likely to have conflicts with their sons over taking care of property or use of cars.

Social Class: The type of conflict often reflects social-class values. Working-class families tend to worry more about their teenagers' being obedient, polite, and staying out of trouble in school. Middle-class families tend to be more concerned about their teenagers' taking the initiative, being competitive, and doing well in school.

Family Size: The larger the size of the family, the more parent–adolescent conflicts occur, and the more often parents use force in settling such conflicts. However, this is true mostly for middle-class families; the efforts to control conflicts do not vary with the size of working-class families.

Parental Authority and Family Atmosphere: An unhappy marriage or home life tends to increase parent–adolescent conflicts; unhappily married, authoritarian parents evoke the most conflicts.

Topics: Common sources of conflicts are dress, daily chores, use of the car, dating, and use of cigarettes or alcohol. Other conflicts of special concern to both generations are staying out late and school performance, especially failure at school. Some of the most heated conflicts occur over sex and drugs.

"grunge" groups of the 1990s.) The generation gap is often purposefully widened by use of lingo and slang.

In addition to seeking acceptance from the larger peer group, many adolescents seek further support from cliques, which are small, informal groups of friends who do things together. These cliques are loosely structured but usually identifiable within a school or neighborhood setting. While some cliques are based on common interests such as music or sports, others are based on popularity or status within the system. Gangs may also fulfill the adolescent need for peer acceptance.

Although all adolescents experience some degree of pressure from peers, the amount of needed peer approval varies widely. The ultimate resolution of the need for peer acceptance depends in part on the quality of the parent–adolescent relationship. With parents who are perceived as nonsupportive, rejecting, or punitive in other ways, the individual may respond with a total shift of allegiance from family to the peer group. For adolescents whose parents are perceived as understanding and supportive, a gradual transition can be made from total reliance on the family to a more balanced sense of self-acceptance, which includes but is not limited to peer approval (Jacob & Doherty, 2006). This transition may not be complete until the individual is well into adulthood. The need for peer approval has a strong impact on motivation and therefore has many implications for the classroom setting, which will be addressed later in this chapter. Box 11.1 provides more information about adolescent crowds and cliques.

BOX 11.1

Adolescent Crowds and Cliques

Some researchers suggest that high school students in the United States have a complex and structured culture that is as differentiated as adult social institutions (Youniss, McLeellan, & Strouse, 1994). *Cliques* are small friendship groups of three to ten adolescents who hang out together, usually have similar backgrounds, are in the same class in school, and live near each other. *Crowds* (there may be about five to seven in a school) are a larger group of peers, often with a label, that provides membership for the adolescents in a clique. Crowds are collections of 3 to as many as 160 adolescents identified by the attitudes, abilities, interests, and/or personal characteristics that they have in common (Brown, Mory, & Kinney, 1994; Urberg, Degirmencioglu, Tolson, & Halliday-Scher, 1995). Crowds serve to regulate social relationships among adolescents, and they foster individuals' identity or self-concept development (Brown et al., 1994).

Youniss and colleagues (1994) found that adolescents often claim membership in several different crowds, that shared interests and concerns may be held by members of different crowds, and that the peer culture tends not to be organized in opposition to adult society. They also found that female adolescents are more concerned with matters of interpersonal sensitivity and attractiveness, while males are more concerned with physical activities and athletic prowess.

Brown (1990) suggests that crowds may help adolescents to negotiate relationships with peers who are strangers or acquaintances. Brown and colleagues (1994) came to the following conclusions concerning adolescent crowds: (1) crowds categorize adolescents by individual interests and abilities; (2) the crowd system gives adolescents a language for understanding and expressing social relationships with peers; and (3) crowd affiliation and the adolescent's understanding of the crowd system affect the choice of peers with whom to associate.

Adolescents use the crowd system to make choices about close peers through proximity, permeability (receptiveness of crowds to outsiders), and desirability (status of the crowd). Belonging to friendship groups and crowds reduces feelings of rejection, loneliness, isolation, depression, and unpopularity. In addition, membership in cliques and crowds can help to develop interpersonal sensitivity, intimacy, mutual perspective taking, prosocial reciprocity, and feelings of acceptance and self-worth (Cohen, Reinherz, & Frost, 1994). Adolescents have portrayed various crowds, as "They all wear glasses and kiss up to teachers, and after school they all tromp uptown to the library, or they go over to somebody's house and play some stupid computer game until 9.00 at night—and they go right to bed 'cause their mommies make 'um!" or "You'd be crazy to walk down the 1-wing by yourself because the headbangers, they like attack you" (Brown et al. 1994, p. 128).

From J. A. Schickedanz et al. (1998). *Understanding children and adolescents* (3rd ed.) Boston: Allyn & Bacon. Reprinted with permission of the publisher.

In summary, the entire adolescent experience is best viewed as a normal developmental process of identity redefinition. As Schmid and Slade note, all adolescent behavior is an "experimentation to successfully adapt to the demands of life," and is meaningful when viewed in this context (1981, p. 369). The struggles between parent and teenager, and between teacher and teenager, over issues such as school attendance, grades, and social behavior are all part of adolescent experimentation. While most adolescents experience stress and exhibit some deviant behavior, they eventually learn the skills that will enable them to cope in an adult world. In contrast, adolescents with EBD often fail to develop these adaptive coping patterns.

The Adolescent with Emotional/Behavioral Disorders

What distinguishes adolescents with EBD from their peers? It is often difficult to determine exactly what constitutes maladaptive, disordered, or deviant behavior during adolescence. McDowell and Brown (1978) note that many definitions of emotional/behavioral disorders include inability to establish appropriate relationships with others and demonstration of behaviors that fail to meet the expectations of others. Because these characteristics are often found in normal adolescents, deviance in adolescents is more appropriately defined by the frequency or severity of the offending behavior (McDowell, 1981). As in childhood psychopathology, the extremeness of behavior can be considered an underlying characteristic of adolescent psychopathology.

Other researchers have attempted to define emotional/behavioral disorders in adolescents more clearly by identifying specific dimensions of problem behavior. In two studies, researchers asked parents of adolescents referred for mental health services to rate their children on behavior checklists. Results yielded two dimensions of problem behavior: internalizing (keeping feelings of distress inside, resulting in depression or psychosomatic symptoms) and externalizing (striking out at others or the environment), which have also been identified with younger children (Achenbach & Edelbrock, 1979; Miller, 1980). In another study, Epstein et al. (1983) asked teachers to rate the behaviors of adolescents with EBD and those without EBD on the Behavior Problem Checklist (BPC; Quay & Peterson, 1967). The BPC is composed of four dimensions: Conduct Disorder, Personality Problem, Inadequacy–Immaturity, and Socialized Delinquency; it has been used extensively with children with emotional/behavioral disorders. Epstein et al. found that adolescents with EBD were rated as significantly more maladjusted on the Conduct Disorder and Personality Problem dimensions only; there were no significant differences in ratings on Inadequacy–Immaturity and Socialized Delinquency. Conduct Disorder is characterized by aggressive, hostile, and contentious behavior, and Personality Problem is characterized by anxious, withdrawn, and introvertive behavior. These results are consistent with previous investigations with adolescents that found the two primary dimensions of externalizing and internalizing.

In another study, characteristic profiles of 128 adolescents referred for multiagency treatment in a system of care were examined (Rosenblatt et al., 1998). Using a two-step clustering procedure, the authors delineated four types of referral profiles: (1) Troubled, (2) Troubling, (3) Troubled and Troubling, and (4) At Risk. Troubled youth (internalizing disorders) showed primary difficulties in home and school settings, but not the community, with both internalizing and externalizing parent-rated behavior problems. These youth had few arrests and low substance abuse. Troubling youth (externalizing disorders) had low parent-rated problem behaviors, but high numbers of arrests and substance abuse impairments. They showed frequent difficulties in the community. Youth who were troubled and troubling had problems across home, school, and community settings, high substance abuse impairment, and a high number of arrests. At-risk youth were the least impaired, with minimal difficulties across settings, low levels of parent-rated problem behaviors, and moderate child-risk factors. This study confirmed that the internalizing and externalizing disorders often occur together (see Chapters 9 and 10) and that multiagency services are needed for all these youth.

Cauffman, Scholle, Mulvey, and Kelleher (2005) studied first-time involvement in the juvenile justice sytem of youth with EBD who were also receiving mental health services. This large-scale, 1-year study was completed with over 650 youth between ages 8 and 17 who resided in Pennsylvania. Among this group, those youth who were older, exhibited more externalizing behaviors, and came from minority backgrounds were more likely to enter the juvenile justice system. Cauffman et al. further noted that parents who have a hard time caring for children with mental illness may turn to the juvenile justice system for help, possibly because needed services were not otherwise available. These authors concluded that mental health and juvenile justice systems must be better integrated to address the high incidence of mental health problems of adolescents who find their way into the juvenile justice system.

In a review of long-term, follow-up studies, Safer and Heaton (1982) found that children with moderate-to-serious behavior problems were likely to manifest the same difficulties in adolescence and sometimes in adulthood. Murray (2003) reviews numerous studies that support the general conclusion that youth with high-incidence disabilities have poorer adult outcomes than peers without disabilities. Based on research to date, one might surmise that children with EBD grow into adolescents with EBD, and if the cycle is not broken, into adults with EBD. Some adolescents with EBD are also juvenile offenders (Cauffman et al., 2005) and this association is likely to be enhanced when substance abuse is a factor (Hoffmann, Abrantes, & Anton, 2003–2004).

Dealing with Adolescent Issues in the Schools

Taking into account the extremeness of behavior that is typical of students with EBD, educators should expect to be confronted with nonattendance, sex- and gender-related problems, social rejection, substance abuse, gangs, and delinquent and self-destructive behavior. Since the authors recognize that many of these problems, particularly substance abuse and suicide, are also relevant to preadolescents, the issues will be dealt with in a manner that is applicable to younger students as well as adolescents. Prevalence of the problems, ramifications, and possible interventions within the schools are addressed in this section.

Dropping Out

Although compulsory attendance laws have been in effect in most states for several decades, many adolescents do not attend school on a regular basis. Educators traditionally have been unable, through coercion or other means, to motivate a certain proportion of adolescents to regularly attend classes.

Estimates of the number of American adolescents who fail to complete high school have reached as high as 10–15 percent (Atwater, 1996; Cobb, 1995), with more recent estimates at about 5 percent (National Center for Education Statistics, 2006). This percentage declined through the 1970s and 1980s, but has been stable since 1987. However, in 2000, young adults in the lowest 20 percent of income were six times as likely as peers in the top 20 percent of income to drop out of high school. Almost half of the youth who leave high school early are of average or above-average intelligence. Reasons for dropping out include failing grades, nonstimulating classes, irrelevant curriculum, pregnancy, life stressors, home responsibilities, desire to earn money, low extracurricular involvement, and poor peer relationships (Bullock, 1992; Schickedanz et al., 1998). High school dropouts are likely to come from poor, single-parent families in which parents may have also dropped out of school (Garnier, Stein, & Jacobs, 1997; Reschly & Christenson, 2006). These students may exhibit antisocial behavior and use drugs. Dropout rates vary by ethnicity; about 6–9 percent of white students drop out of school, but about 13–15 percent of African American students and 27–29 percent of Hispanic students drop out. In 2000, 44.2 percent of Hispanic young adults born outside the United States dropped out of high school (National Center for Education Statistics, 2006).

In a study of adolescents with severe emotional/behavioral disorders, Hagborg (1989) found that only student SES and behavioral adjustment distinguished high attenders from low attenders. Gender, race, and age characteristics did not distinguish groups in this population as they did in the general population. High rates of absenteeism are accompanied by school failure and, eventually, high dropout rates. Unfortunately, the dropout rate for students with EBD is almost 60 percent, which means that we are losing one out of every two of these students before they graduate (Danielson, 2006; Wagner, Blackorby, Cameto, & Newman, 1993). This percentage is not only three times that of the general population, but it is also much higher than for any other special education category.

In an effort to keep students in school, many communities have aided schools in developing dropout prevention programs. Services provided through these programs vary but often include individual and peer counseling, tutoring, structured leisure-time activities, vocational training, and social services to families of high-risk students. Some communities offer special classes to teenage parents and on-campus day care services. In addition, many communities have alternative schools or alternative programs for students who do not fare well under the traditional educational system or who have dropped out and wish to reenroll. For students who have dropped out but wish to obtain the equivalent of a high school diploma, community colleges are a good resource. As students with EBD are at risk of dropping out, teachers should become familiar with dropout prevention/alternative programs offered in their own communities and schools. Numerous recent professional publications and newspaper and magazine articles address the problem of dropping out. One of the themes that seems to be emerging across major urban districts is the development of more flexible routes toward graduation, including allowing students more self-paced academic opportunities, including more flexible high school hours (Gehring, 2004). This opportunity may be most important for over-age ninth graders, who are most at risk for dropping out when they are required to repeat the entire grade.

Reschly and Christenson (2006) note that research regarding evidence-based practices for dropout prevention are in their earliest stages. However, based on available research, they advocate for programs that address in a comprehensive manner students' academic, cognitive, behavioral, and psychological engagement and the facilitators of student engagement, including peers, family, and schools. Of particular importance are interventions that include opportunities for academic success, relevant coursework, individual assistance, a positive interpersonal climate, resources for addressing students' personal problems, and early intervention with academic and behavioral problems.

Sex-Related Problems

It is estimated that in 2005, 47 percent of adolescents in 9th through 12th grades have had sexual intercourse; this number declined from 1991 (54%) to 2005 (U.S. Department of Health and Human Services, 2006). More permissive attitudes toward sex and trends toward accepting a greater number of options for sexual expression have permeated U.S. culture since the mid-20th century. Improved forms of contraception, including the birth-control pill, have made sexual experimentation more appealing to many adolescents. However, despite easier access to information and increasing availability of contraceptives to today's youth, the problems accompanying sexual activity such as premarital pregnancy and sexually transmitted disease have continued to be problematic. More than half of all sexually active teenagers, about 63 percent, used condoms during sexual intercourse in 2005; this percentage increased from 46 percent in 1991 (U.S. Department of Health and Human Services, 2006). These data, while indicating improvement in knowledge about and use of contraceptives, still indicate that many adolescents either remain ignorant about contraceptive information or do not seek out contraceptive devices for a number of reasons, including embarrassment, trusting to luck, and fear of adult reprisal.

Teen Pregnancy. Each year about 860,000 American girls become pregnant; in addition, the number of adolescents initiating sexual activity at 15 years of age or younger has risen (Stoiber & McIntyre, 2006). The teenage pregnancy rate in the United States far exceeds that of other industrialized nations. On the positive side, adolescent pregnancy, birth, and abortion rates have steadily declined over the past decade (Stoiber & McIntyre, 2006). The steepest declines have occurred among African American adolescents; between 1991 and 2001, the birth rate among 15-to 19-year-old African Americans decreased by 36 percent. The birth rate among Hispanic adolescents fell the least, with Hispanic females having the highest birth rate of the various racial and ethnic groups in the United States (United States Dept. of Health and Human Services, 2003).

Teen parents are obviously the least prepared emotionally or financially to provide for the needs of an infant or to provide a stable home environment for a growing child. More high-risk infants are born to adolescent mothers than to older mothers, thereby increasing the pressures of parenthood. The United States also has one of the highest adolescent abortion rates compared to other developed countries (Henshaw, 1997; Meyers & Landau, 2002). Another 13 percent of teenage pregnancies end in miscarriage. Seventy-five percent of teenage births are to unmarried females; thus, about 350,000 girls a year take on the responsibilities of parenthood (Berk, 1999).

Adolescent females most likely to get pregnant are from low-income families, perform poorly in school, and abuse drugs. Their mothers may be unmarried, unemployed, and school dropouts (Berk, 1999; Stoiber & McIntyre, 2006). One of the most consistent predictors of adolescent pregnancy is low academic achievement accompanied by low aspirations for employment. It is clear that many teenage mothers, once they drop out of school, do not return. Thus, they are at risk for additional pregnancies and are often unable to take care of themselves financially over the long term. Many experts on teen pregnancy therefore believe that sex education and prevention programs must include access to contraception, vocational training, and instruction in social competence (Allen, Philliber, Herrling, & Kuperminc, 1997).

Sexually Transmitted Diseases. Another problem associated with adolescent sexual activity is sexually transmitted disease (STD). Sexually active adolescents are at risk of contracting one of the three most common STDs: gonorrhea, chlamydia, or herpes. Gonorrhea is especially insidious because its symptoms may go unnoticed, resulting in infertility in women and sterility in men. Although a relatively new disease, chlamydia is now the most common STD, with estimates running as high as 10 percent of sexually active females (Centers for Disease Control and Prevention, 2004). Chlamydia is also insidious, often without symptoms in the early stages; although it can be treated with antibiotics, many women become infertile before the condition is diagnosed. Herpes is a viral infection that is also reaching epidemic proportions and can affect fertility and newborn infants. About 9 million teenagers contracted an STD in 2000 (Stoiber & McIntyre, 2006).

Acquired immune deficiency syndrome (AIDS) is another sexually transmitted disease that has reached epidemic proportions among segments of the U.S. population. The fact that AIDS often leads to debilitating illness and death has been well publicized. AIDS is acquired primarily through direct sexual contact or through injections with a needle contaminated with the virus. Experts assure us that the percentage of AIDS victims acquiring the virus through contaminated blood transfusions has decreased since the implementation of screening donors' blood before accepting it. Having several sexual partners increases the risk of contracting AIDS if precautions are not taken. Although many adolescents are knowledgeable about symptoms and effects of sexually transmitted diseases, a sizeable percentage do not know how to prevent its transmission or what treatment is available in most states without parental permission.

Sexuality Issues. Students with EBD may be more susceptible to difficulties with sexuality than their peers. The primary difference in sexual development between adolescents with EBD and their peers probably lies in the psychosocial domain (Adrian, 1990). While adolescents with EBD usually do not differ from their peers in physical development or the variety of sexual relations they experience, their psychosocial development may have been impaired by many factors, including difficult parent–child relationships, parental substance abuse, conflicting subcultural norms and values, and sexual abuse (Adrian, 1990). They also may experience more conflict than other adolescents over body image and attractiveness. Thus, relating to the opposite sex and developing healthy attitudes toward sexuality may be more difficult for these youth. Realmuto and Erickson (1986) found that adolescents with EBD tended to (1) equate the capacity for sexual intercourse with maturity, (2) equate sexual relationships with personal desirability, and (3) view contraception as an authoritative and punitive demand.

Delinquent sexual behavior among adolescents has not been sufficiently researched to draw many conclusions. Sexual misbehavior by females consists primarily of nonviolent contact with willing male partners, and the only distinctive form of sexual delinquency for female adolescents is prostitution (Erickson, 1984). On the other hand, delinquent sexual behavior by males may either be violent, as in rape, or nonviolent, as in exhibitionism. Child molestation is another sexual offense usually instigated by males. Although there are few empirical studies solely with adolescent sex offenders, there is some evidence that sexual assaults, including rape, are more linked to aggression and to antisocial tendencies than to specific sexuality problems (Erickson, 1984; Lewis, Shanok, & Pincus, 1979). This finding also holds true with adult offenders. Erickson (1984) argues that "there is little that is unique about sexual delinquency, male or female. Arguments in favor of specialized programs must be based on the inadequacy of regular programs [for juvenile offenders] in dealing with sexual matters" (p. 31).

Dealing with Gay, Lesbian, and Bisexual Issues. Inclusion of this topic is not meant to imply that gay, lesbian, or bisexual orientations constitute emotional/behavioral disorders. Rather, students with EBD who are also gay or lesbian are likely to experience additional stresses related to their sexual orientation. A frequently cited statistic is that 10 percent of the population is gay or lesbian (Tievsky, 1988); Lasser, Tharinger, and Cloth (2006) cite an estimate that over 1 million of the 45 million school-age children in the United States are gay, lesbian, or bisexual (GLB). It is almost a certainty that teachers of students with EBD will encounter many GLB students during their teaching careers.

The basic issue with regard to the emotional and behavioral adjustment of GLB youth is not what causes their orientation, whether it is right or wrong, better or worse than a heterosexual orientation; the basic problem is how society reacts to it (Mallon, 1992). The stresses associated with societal stigmatization make gay and lesbian youth especially vulnerable to psychological problems such as chronic depression, substance abuse, school failure, and relationship problems (Lasser et al., 2006; Mallon, 1992). Many leave their homes either by force or by choice and turn to foster homes or the streets to live. Also, it is estimated that 30 percent of adolescent suicides may have to do with sexual identity issues (Gibson, 1991). Lasser et al. (2006) cite numerous studies that document increased rates of mental health disorders, suicidal tendencies, substance abuse and other high-risk behaviors, school failure and dropout, and homelessness among GLB youth compared to heterosexual youth.

A recent survey conducted in a California high school with 1,800 students found that 6 percent of the students described themselves as homosexual or bisexual, and 13 percent indicated that they were not sure of their sexual orientation (Lock & Steiner, 1999). Students stating that they were homosexual or bisexual also indicated higher rates of mental health problems, health problems in general, eating disorders, and victimization. Youth who indicated that they were not comfortable with their sexual orientation also complained of more health problems and more sexual assaults (both as victim and perpetrator). The authors speculate that these youth may be suffering from internalized homophobia or self-hatred or just may be unhappy in many aspects of their lives.

Adding to these difficulties is the fact that sexual orientation usually emerges during adolescence, and many mental health professionals consider sexual experimentation with same-sex individuals a possible part of heterosexual identity development. Therefore, therapists and counselors may ignore such adolescent disclosures, or worse, may hasten to assure the adolescent that same-sex encounters are a "normal" part of heterosexual experimentation, thereby inadvertently confirming the "abnormality" of gay and lesbian orientations.

Another difficulty is that many GLB adolescents feel that they must hide their sexual identities, resulting in *visibility management* efforts that may preclude disclosure of sexual identity (Lasser et al., 2006). There is also the unique mistaken belief that GLB youth choose their orientation and therefore could change their sexual orientation if they so desire. Little wonder that most report feelings of extreme isolation (Ruenzel, 1999).

Following are excerpts from a newspaper article by a high school senior about the isolation of "growing up gay":

> Growing up gay and not being able to tell everyone is like hell. It's very hard to have to keep it to yourself. . . . My friends would look at girls and I would look at my friends. By then, I knew I could not tell them the truth. I had heard the jokes about gays and I was afraid of what might happen. I went through elementary and junior high school lying to all my friends, but the hardest thing was lying to my parents. My parents have a real problem with gays. My dad says they're sick and AIDS is what they deserve to get. It hurts me to think this is the way they feel. What they don't know is that they're talking about their own son. . . . I have to think twice before I do everything. I have to watch what I stare at, how I talk, what I say, and how I walk and behave. Trying to worry about these things and juggle my classes is too much to bear. ("Growing up gay," 1994)

The prejudice and resulting isolation has become so widespread in some locations that alternative programs or campuses have been set up for gay and lesbian youth. Examples are the Harvey Milk School, a segregated campus in New York, and Project 10, a dropout prevention program for gay and lesbian adolescents in the Los Angeles Unified School District. Project 10 offers nonjudgmental counseling, support, and information. Similar projects have been started across the country. School personnel have increasingly found themselves confronted with the task of protecting gay students from peer sexual harassment and discrimination and ensuring equal protection for these students under the U.S. Constitution (e.g., Doty, 2000; Ruenzel, 1999). The notion of protection is too often lost in extreme emotional reactions about homosexuality; thus, Doty (2000) explains, "issues involving gay students in public schools are complex and will continue to proliferate across the country. . . . Nevertheless, if people will lower their voices, and participate genuinely in an inclusive policy process focused more on listening than talking, anger can give way to collaboration. . . " (p. 47).

In a qualitative study of the school experience of GLB adolescents, Lasser and Tharinger (2003) conducted semi-structured interviews with 20 self-identified GLB and questioning youth age 18 or younger. The participants were recruited from an urban, nonprofit agency that provides peer support and education for GLB youth. The sample consisted of 12 females and 8 males, the majority of whom were Caucasian. Their findings included the general conclusion that GLB adolescents are continually engaged in *meaning making* in their lives, with their GLB experience as part of the larger context of reciprocal interactions with their environment. A theory of *visibility management* (referred to above) emerged from this study. In this context, visibility management refers to "a dynamic process of social decision-making, selective disclosure and ongoing monitoring and self-presentation" that may range from most restrictive (disclosing to very few or no people) to least restrictive (disclosing to most people) (Lasser & Tharinger, 2003, p. 241). The experiences reported by these adolescents indicate that they actively and continuously plan, monitor, and modify the extent to which they disclose their sexual orientation to others. In Box 11.2 are examples of the experiences of some of the students interviewed in this study.

What can teachers do? They can help by being sensitive to the particular problems experienced by GLB adolescents and by knowing local resources that are available to help ameliorate the feelings of isolation. One cannot assume, for example, that all counselors or therapists will handle gay and lesbian disclosures appropriately. Teachers should know which counselors are sensitive to these issues and then can make referrals when needed. Teachers can search out local support groups. In addition, discussion of successful role models would be helpful. Finally, teachers should neither model nor tolerate slurs, homophobic jokes, and other prejudiced remarks.

Sex Education. Many sex-related problems could be minimized if adolescents were better informed about sex-related issues. Although it is argued by some that the home is the proper place for such information to be dispensed, the majority of adolescent students

BOX 11.2
Experiences of GLB Youth

"I don't see why it's [sexual orientation] anyone's business at school. I mean high school can be a really tough time, for a lot of kids. And I don't think someone's sexual preference is anyone's business but them. That's just me personally. I don't think it's healthy to keep it bottled in for your whole life, but I think that the people you want to tell you should tell."—Derek, age 17

"Basically, the people I tell are the ones who . . . everyone goes through different kinds of problems and stuff, and the friends that have had really tough times, whether it's problems with their parents or a family member has passed away or there's a big project that's due . . . something where you have to be totally open with a person, like if they can rely on you to be there for them in their time of need, I tend to talk to tell them. As soon as I was sure I was gay I told them. If we can confide in each other with stuff like death, secrets, their own personal life, like things that are going on with them, I knew that they would still like me for who I was. That's basically when I tell people, when we have this different level of friendship. It's like a more personal, emotional thing."—Jaime, age 16

"I didn't tell any of my friends last year. I made some remarks that would hint at them, like I would tell them about all of my gay friends. I'd tell them about gay culture and see how they feel."

"Schools can be rough. They can be really bad for people. And so in some cases it's better to look at a wall than it is to look at somebody's fist. And to feel like hiding rather than to feel like everyone's against you . . . Kinda like a pro-and-con thing, like, well, I could feel like I'm lying to everybody or I could get beat up."—Denise, age 16

"You're trying to prove that you're not this. . . . You acquire all these friends and stuff and in the back of your mind you think, 'They're not really my friends because if they knew who I was they would drop me'."—Rebecca, age 18

Reprinted with permission from Lasser, J., & Tharinger, D. (2003). Visibility management in school and beyond: A qualitative study of gay, lesbian, bisexual youth. *Journal of Adolescence, 26,* 233–244.

report that their parents do not give them the information they need. Minimal information needed by adolescents includes facts on sexual anatomy and functioning, sexually transmitted disease, birth control, abortion, and informative discussions on such anxiety-provoking issues as masturbation and gay and lesbian orientation. Most experts agree that in addition to providing factual information, sex education programs should also explore sexual values and attitudes.

In the recent past, the majority of states had laws that either prohibited or restricted sex education in the schools, primarily due to a vocal minority of parents who did not want the schools to deal with sex education. The advent of AIDS has helped reverse this trend: In the 1980s, the number of states requiring sex education to be taught in public schools increased from 3 to 23 (Hackett, 1990). Stoiber and McIntyre (2006) observe that sexuality education is now common in public schools and is generally supported by the public. This mandate to teach sex education in many states is a distinct reversal from the earlier prohibitions and offers educators an opportunity to address sexuality as a part of basic human relationships. In many locales, Planned Parenthood organizations have sex education materials appropriate for use with adolescents. Sex education programs should encourage self-expression while teaching responsibility for one's sexual behavior (Knopp, 1982).

Additionally, sex education should be a part of all adolescent treatment programs. For male adolescent sex offenders, Erickson (1984) suggests that a well-trained male staff member take a detailed sexual history in order to demystify sexual issues and to establish a relationship in which the adolescent can begin to express sexual concerns. Erickson warns that with adolescent offenders, premature attempts to explore sexual issues in coeducational groups may increase resistance rather than promote growth. With groups of nonoffenders, however, coeducational discussion may facilitate more comprehensive understanding of sexuality issues.

Despite its controversial nature, sex education in the public schools should be addressed. Advocates believe that public school sex education can increase knowledge (Kirby, 1984), improve decision making (Gordon, 1983), improve self-esteem (Crooks & Baur, 1983), and ultimately decrease unwanted pregnancies (Zabin et al., 1988). A common argument against sex education, that increased knowledge leads to increased sexual experimentation, has not been validated. The decreases in incidence of adolescent pregnancy and abortion rates over the past 10–15 years attest to the effectiveness of sex education efforts. It should be clear to educators and parents alike that the ostrich approach of pretending that if we don't talk about sex the problems will go away is untenable.

Social Rejection

Gay and lesbian students are not the only young people to suffer from social isolation, peer rejection, and discrimination. Adolescents typically obtain their identity through their peer associations; therefore, they naturally migrate toward distinct peer groups (cliques and crowds) and in the process reject associations with others (Cairns & Cairns, 1994). Through this selective process, social hierarchies emerge, with some peer groups having greater social prominence than others (Adler & Adler, 1995). It is generally agreed that the groups with the greatest social prominence are those composed of athletes, cheerleaders, and their friends (Adler, Kless, & Adler, 1992; Cohen, 1999; Zimmerman, 1999), with male athletes generally "running" the school.

Conversely, many adolescents are considered outsiders. They, too, often form groups and may identify themselves through their bizarre attire. Eric Harris and Dylan Klebold, who gunned down 12 fellow students and a teacher at Columbine High School in Littleton, Colorado, in April 1999, were members of such a group. As a matter of fact, their social rejection by male athletes at the high school was cited as the primary reason for their murderous rage (Cohen, 1999; Zimmerman, 1999). Apparently, it is common practice for adolescents to enhance their own social status by ridiculing others who are different (Adler & Adler, 1995). Social isolation and peer rejection are related to dropping out of school, antisocial behavior, mental health problems, and, later, work adjustment problems (Waas, 2006).

Students with emotional and behavioral disorders are certainly at risk for peer rejection and social isolation because they are typically deficient in social skills and are not usually well accepted by their peers (Kauffman, 1997). Many think that youth who suffer from peer rejection and feel powerless are capable of horrible, aggressive acts (Cohen, 1999). Teachers and school personnel should be aware of peer interactions and attempt to facilitate inclusion and acceptance among all students. Bullying and teasing should be discouraged, while athletics should not be exalted over other extracurricular activities.

Reclaiming Youth at Risk. Some believe that the way to treat youth who feel alienated and powerless is to address the ecological hazards that make them feel that way (Brendtro et al., 1990). These authors identify four interactional influences that promote social isolation: (1) destructive relationships, (2) climates of futility and helplessness, (3) learned irresponsibility, and (4) loss of purpose and the search for meaning. These authors recommend that professionals build positive cultures in schools modeled after traditional Native American childrearing philosophies.

Based on the Circle of Courage, Brendtro and his colleagues (1990) provide various techniques for creating (1) a sense of belonging and significance through a cultural milieu, (2) a sense of mastery through opportunities to succeed, (3) independence and choice making, and (4) a preeminent value of generosity. Teachers are encouraged to attend to students and to show them affection, to give them many successful opportunities to create products of social significance, to encourage students to control their own behavior, and to teach students to give to others without expecting things in return. Table 11.2 depicts the descriptors of the four areas of the Circle of Courage.

Another educational strategy for addressing social isolation and hopelessness is to combine classroom work with community service and social action (Allen, 2003; Nathan & Kielsmeier, 1991). As discussed in Chapter 5, youth service programs are widespread across the country and include projects such as cleaning up hazardous waste, affecting environmental laws, establishing day-care centers, building new playgrounds, buddy programs, tutoring programs, fundraising, collaborative art projects, and assistance to homeless children (Hall, 1991; McPherson, 1991; Tenenbaum, 2000). The best youth service programs contain the following components:

1. Service opportunities that are significant and necessary
2. Planning and implementation primarily by the students

TABLE 11.2 Components of the Circle of Courage for Treatment of Alienated Youth

Belonging

Normal	Distorted	Absent
Attached	Gang loyalty	Unattached
Loving	Craves affection	Guarded
Friendly	Craves acceptance	Rejected
Intimate	Promiscuous	Lonely
Gregarious	Clinging	Aloof
Cooperative	Cult vulnerable	Isolated
Trusting	Overly dependent	Distrustful

Some youth who feel rejected are struggling to find artificial, distorted belongings through behavior such as attention seeking or running with gangs. Others have abandoned the pursuit and are reluctant to form human attachments. In either case, their unmet needs can be addressed by corrective relationships of trust and intimacy.

Mastery

Normal	Distorted	Absent
Achiever	Overachiever	Nonachiever
Successful	Arrogant	Failure oriented
Creative	Risk seeker	Avoids risks
Problem solver	Cheater	Fears challenges
Motivated	Workaholic	Unmotivated
Persistent	Persevering	Gives up easily
Competent	Delinquent skill	Inadequate

Frustrated in their attempts to achieve, children may seek to prove their competence in distorted ways, such as skill in delinquent activity. Others have learned to retreat from difficult challenges by giving up in futility. The remedy for these problems is involvement in an environment with abundant opportunities for meaningful achievement.

Independence

Normal	Distorted	Absent
Autonomous	Dictatorial	Submissive
Confident	Reckless/macho	Lacks confidence
Assertive	Bullies others	Inferiority
Responsible	Sexual prowess	Irresponsible
Inner control	Manipulative	Helplessness
Self-discipline	Rebellious	Undisciplined
Leadership	Defies authority	Easily led

Fighting against feelings of powerlessness, some youth assert themselves in rebellious and aggressive ways. Those who believe they are too weak or impotent to manage their own lives become pawns of others. These young people need opportunities to develop the skills and confidence to assert positive leadership and self-discipline.

TABLE 11.2 *Continued*

Generosity		
Normal	**Distorted**	**Absent**
Altruistic	Noblesse oblige	Selfish
Caring	Overinvolved	Affectionless
Sharing	Plays martyr	Narcissistic
Loyal	Codependency	Disloyal
Empathic	Overinvolvement	Hardened
Prosocial	Servitude	Antisocial
Supportive	Bondage	Exploitative

Without opportunities to give to others, young people do not develop as caring persons. Some may be involved in pseudoaltruistic helping or they may be locked in servitude to someone who uses them. Others plunge into lifestyles of hedonism and narcissism. The antidote for the malaise is to experience the joys that accrue from helping others.

Reprinted with permission from Brendtro, L. K., Brokenleg, M., & Van Bockern, S. (1991). The Circle of Courage, *Beyond Behavior, 2*(1), 11. Copyright by Council for Children with Behavior Disorders (CCBD), Council for Exceptional Children (CEC), 1920 Association Drive, Reston, VA 22091-1589.

3. School support
4. Community support
5. Specified student outcomes
6. Curriculum that includes preparation, supervision, and active reflection
7. Regular and significant recognition of the students and adult participants. (Nathan & Kielsmeier, 1991)

Although research on youth service is primarily qualitative in nature (Billig, 2000; Conrad & Hedin, 1991), indications are that students improved academic learning, problem solving, social and personal responsibility skills, social competence, and positive attitudes toward adults and that students reported feeling less isolated and alienated. Some studies showed lower levels of discipline problems. Conrad and Hedin (1991) state that "the case for community service as a legitimate educational practice receives provisional support from quantitative, quasi-experimental studies and even more consistent affirmation from the reports and testimony of participants and practitioners" (p. 749). As Barbara Lewis, a teacher in Salt Lake City, wrote:

> Solving social problems will bring excitement and suspense into your life. Instead of reading textbooks and memorizing what other people have done, you'll create your own history with actions you take. And here's a promise: As you reach out to solve problems in your community, you will not only design a better future, you'll also learn to take charge of your personal life. You'll become more confident in yourself because you'll prove to yourself that you can do almost anything. (1991, p. 2)

An additional source for ideas to reclaim alienated youth is literature pertaining to the enhancement of resiliency factors (Benard, 1991; Murray, 2003; Werner & Smith, 1982). Instead of focusing on risk factors that predispose adolescents to negative outcomes, these authors identify factors that seem to immunize children against life's stressors. These positive factors include the following:

1. At least average intelligence
2. Enthusiasm and a positive social temperament that elicit positive adult responses
3. Affectional ties with significant adults other than parents that facilitate trust, autonomy, and initiative
4. Consistent external support system, including churches, youth groups, and schools, that rewards competence

The premise is that if we teach youth with EBD to exhibit resilient traits and work to create consistent positive relationships between these young people and psychologically healthy adults, then we will enhance the adolescents' ability to survive many types of adversity (i.e., they will develop a self-righting tendency) (Blankenship & Bullock, 1998; Werner & Smith, 1982).

Substance Abuse

Prevalence. Experimentation with mood-altering drugs is often viewed as a hallmark of adolescence, although less attention may be paid to adolescents who choose to abstain from such experimentation. Unfortunately, drug use has crept downward into middle schools and even into the early elementary grades. Availability of many drugs on the street, tolerant attitudes toward underage drinking, and misuse of prescription drugs may account for much of the drug use among today's children and adolescents.

The drugs most widely used by high school students are alcohol, tobacco, and marijuana. Amphetamines, cocaine, crack, inhalants, and miscellaneous other drugs are used to a much lesser extent by this age group. Alcohol and drug use among American youth is higher than in any other industrialized nation. According to the U.S. Department of Health and Human Services (2003), the incidence of cigarette smoking has decreased over the past decade, after peaking in 1997. In 2002, about 11 percent of 8th graders, 18 percent of 10th graders, and 27 percent of high school seniors reported smoking cigarettes. Alcohol and illicit drug use have also decreased from 1990 to 2005, according to the National Youth Risk Behavior Survey: 1991–2005 (Centers for Disease Control and Prevention, 2006). Approximately 43 percent of high schoolers reported having drunk alcohol within the last 30 days, while about 20 percent reported using marijuana, and 3.4 percent reported cocaine use. A 2003 survey indicated that 51 percent of students in the United States had used a substance within the past year (Forman, Bry, & Urga, 2006), so despite recent declines, substance use among adolescents remains a significant problem.

Few would deny that drug use among adolescents is a cause for concern. Alcohol, which is legal after a certain age and socially acceptable by many standards, is the most widely used and misused drug by teenagers and even preteens. Recent surveys show that the first drinking experience in the United States today usually occurs around age 12, and that over a third of fourth graders report peer pressure to try beer, wine, or liquor (Genaux,

Likens, & Morgan, 1993). Not only are kids drinking at earlier ages, but also an alarming number of youth are drinking at a rate that suggests serious problems. In a survey of 27,000 New York junior and senior high school students, 13 percent admitted attending classes while "high" or "drunk" (Genaux et al., 1993). According to Finn, Willert, and Marable (2003), research indicates that somewhere between 6 and 25 percent of U.S. students have been under the influence of alcohol or marijuana during school hours. In 2005, 26 percent of high school students reported episodic heavy or binge drinking (Centers for Disease Control and Prevention, 2006).

In addition to the physical and psychological dependency caused by alcohol are the dangers of driving while intoxicated. Studies have shown that alcohol use has been a factor in almost half of all fatal car accidents, and the majority of these involve drivers under the age of 21. In 2005, 10 percent of high school students reported driving a vehicle within the past 30 days while under the influence of alcohol. Such statistics have encouraged states to raise the legal drinking age to 21; as of 1988, all states require a person to be 21 before he can legally purchase alcohol (Centers for Disease Control and Prevention, 2006).

Another legal and socially acceptable drug is tobacco, or more specifically, nicotine. Since the adverse publicity surrounding the Surgeon General's Report in 1965 linking cigarette smoking to lung cancer, the incidence of smoking among youth declined until 1992. Tobacco use still has a sizable following, although the prevalence of smoking in younger adolescence has declined. In 1995, 20 percent of American eighth graders said that they had smoked in the last month (U.S. Department of Health and Human Services, 1997), while in 2002, the reported rate was 11 percent (U.S. Department of Health and Human Services, 2003). Cigarettes are known to be physically addicting and to be highly carcinogenic, causing lung ailments and several forms of oral cancer.

Another drug favored by adolescents is marijuana. Popularized by hippies and the college crowd of the 1960s, marijuana became a common part of the U.S. drug scene. Although still illegal, it has become more socially acceptable and has been touted by many as less harmful than cigarettes or alcohol. However, marijuana use does have drawbacks. Habitual use often results in lowered academic performance because of its effects on concentration and memory. High levels of marijuana ingestion also impair motor performance and ability to maneuver a car in traffic. The most detrimental effect of marijuana is the psychological dependency it fosters, and for this reason many experts discourage its use by adolescents (National Institute on Drug Abuse, 1980).

Crack cocaine has made inroads into the child and adolescent population in past years. Previous to the development of crack, which is a low-grade, inexpensive form of cocaine, few adolescents could afford the higher-grade quality of cocaine, which was considered an upper-class drug due to its expense. In many locations, crack is now being sold to elementary and middle school students as well as high school students. Crack is especially dangerous because it is psychologically addictive and deprives the user of the normal drives to eat, rest, and take care of him- or herself.

Numerous other drugs are used by adolescents with less frequency than alcohol, tobacco, or marijuana, but with great potential for damage. "Hard" drugs such as heroin are not likely to be used frequently by this age group because of the expense. Amphetamines and sedatives are more likely to be misused by adolescents because of availability through prescriptions. Amphetamines ("speed," "uppers") are commonly prescribed for weight loss, and sedatives ("downers," barbiturates, and tranquilizers) may be prescribed to alleviate anxiety or to promote sleep. The prescribed use of sleeping pills and tranquilizers has become so widespread among middle- and upper-class families that many adolescents need only to shake down their mothers' purses or to raid the family medicine cabinets for a ready supply. In addition, mild amphetamines are available over the counter in the form of diet pills. The major dangers resulting from misuse of amphetamines and sedatives are physical and psychological addiction, overdosing, and potentially lethal effects of mixing the drugs with alcohol. Amphetamine use, although not physically addicting, can be psychologically addicting and can cause depression, aggressiveness, and other undesirable psychological states.

Risk Factors and Characteristics. A number of high-risk factors have been identified by researchers attempting to decrease drug abuse among adolescents. Several of these risk factors are associated with parental attitudes or parental use. For example, if there is a history of alcoholism in the family, the risk of an adolescent male's abuse of alcohol is doubled (Chassin, Curran, Hussong, & Colder, 1996). Risk factors outside the home include lack of commitment to school, academic failure (especially in grades 4–6), friends who use, and pronounced feelings of alienation and rebelliousness (Berk, 1999; Hawkins & Catalono, 1988). Finn et al. (2003) add to this list the degree to which schools provide opportunities for drug use, for example, by not sufficiently monitoring locations where students traditionally sell and use drugs. Antisocial behavior, evidenced in early childhood as well as in early adolescence, has a marked correlation with substance abuse. These and other characteristics are summarized in Table 11.3.

In addition to these risk factors are a number of characteristics of substance abusers that teachers can use to help identify individuals who may be abusing.

- Psychosomatic symptoms
- Poor diets
- Sleep disturbances
- Inability to handle social experiences
- High number of stressful life events
- Belief in the magical power of the substance
- Serious disturbances in moral and character development
- Risk-taking behavior and intellectual curiosity
- State-dependent learning, in which material learned while under the influence of chemicals is not available when sober
- Depression and suicidal ideation
- Low self-esteem. (Johnson, 1988)

These characteristics and risk factors bear a remarkable resemblance to characteristics of students with EBD, thereby placing these students at very high risk for substance abuse. One group of researchers surveyed drug and alcohol use by almost 300 high school students in both special education and general education settings. The researchers found that students with EBD in restrictive settings reported using a much wider range of drugs and were more likely to be currently using cigarettes, alcohol, and marijuana than their

TABLE 11.3 Risk Factors for Adolescent Substance Use

1. Family history of alcoholism, especially males (two times greater)
2. Family management problems
   - poorly defined roles
   - little monitoring
   - inconsistent and excessively severe discipline
3. Early antisocial behavior, hyperactivity
4. Parental drug use and positive attitudes toward use
5. Academic failure (grades 4–6)
6. Little commitment to school
7. Alienation, rebelliousness, lack of social bonding to society
8. Antisocial behavior in early adolescence
9. Friends who use
10. Favorable attitudes toward drug use
11. Early first use of drugs

Adapted from *Preparing for the Drug Free Years,* by J. D. Hawkins and R. F. Catalano. Seattle: Developmental Research and Programs, Prevention Resource Center, 1988.

peers in less restrictive settings and in general education classes (Leone, Greenberg, Trickett, & Spero, 1989). Additionally, numerous studies of adolescent psychiatric patients indicate a strong relationship between substance use/abuse and emotional problems such as depression (Leone, 1991; Luthar & Cushing, 1997). Some studies of the role of heredity in alcohol addiction suggest that there may be two types: (1) steady drinkers, who exhibit antisocial, pleasure-seeking personality types, and (2) binge drinkers, who exhibit depressed, anxiety-ridden personality types (Carlson, 2004). Certainly, similar descriptions of personality types are found in the literature describing internalizing and externalizing disorders that often result in EBD classification in schools.

Effects of Substance Abuse. The damaging effects of drug misuse are not limited to physiological side effects. For adolescents who are trying to learn to cope with life and who are struggling to become adults, the psychological side effects can be especially deleterious. Chronic or heavy use of drugs can postpone these struggles, which are an essential part of the transition from childhood to adulthood. Drug-dependent adolescents make little progress toward becoming responsible, functioning members of society. Students who are occasional users may suffer only temporary difficulties, but they are more likely than nonusers to have problems in school or on the job. Educators can play an important role in detecting and helping ameliorate drug misuse.

Substance Abuse Education. It is a temptation to react emotionally or moralistically to the topic of drug abuse among children and adolescents. The drug abuse programs of the early 1960s reflected this moralistic tone. Many of these school- and community-based programs utilized scare tactics such as having ex-addicts or police condemn the use of drugs. Often, misinformation or biased information was given in hopes of discouraging drug use. Unfortunately, the effect of most of these efforts was to undermine the credibility of drug education programs and to further entrench adolescents against "the establishment." Due to the shortcomings of early programs, subsequent programs began to avoid moralizing and to focus on providing accurate, unbiased information. Many programs also began to incorporate activities in values clarification in order to help students make their own decisions and take responsibility for them. More recently, programs have returned to a moralistic note, a campaign against any use of drugs.

Research on the effectiveness of substance abuse prevention has yielded few consistent results (Finn et al., 2003). According to Leone (1991), most prevention efforts have continued in the "just say no" vein; that is, prevention efforts focus on the individual to the exclusion of powerful contextual and cultural influences. Some researchers (Berk, 1999; Pentz et al., 1989; Wallack & Corbitt, 1990) argue that successful prevention efforts must expand to cover multiple environmental influences (schools, family, peer group, the community) as well as the individual. The National Institute on Drug Abuse (2001) identified two programs as showing positive results in promoting resistance, self-management, and social skills training: the Life Skills Training Program, a 3-year classroom program at the middle and junior high school level, and the Reconnecting Youth Program, which targets high-risk students in grades 9–12. One of the most widely used drug prevention programs is D.A.R.E. (Drug Abuse Resistance Education). Developed in 1983 in Los Angeles, D.A.R.E. programs have been implemented in a majority of the nation's school districts and in over 40 other countries (Drug Abuse Resistance Education, 2006). Lessons for Kindergarten through high school, lead by police officers, provide information and skills for resisting peer pressure and leading productive lives that are drug and violence-free. The program promotes the notion of community policing and creates positive relationships between law enforcement personnel and youth.

Wallack and Corbitt (1990) believe that effective prevention programs share the following characteristics:

- Drug problems are viewed as complex.
- An integrated approach is taken.
- Long-term planning is utilized.
- The idea is understood that information about drugs is necessary but not sufficient to change behavior.

In developing a substance use prevention curriculum specifically for special education students, Morgan (1993) reviewed the literature to determine successful strategies. Morgan found that effective school-based programs:

- Focus on knowledge, attitudes, and behavior that influence use
- Are based on theoretical models that include awareness of pressures to use, attitudinal inoculation to those pressures, and rehearsal of strategies to overcome those pressures
- Build general life skills such as communication, resistance, and decision making

- Target families and communities for intervention
- Recognize the need for long-term, intensive involvement for high-risk kids

In summary, the latest research on substance abuse prevention indicates that we must move beyond teaching decision-making skills and providing information about drugs, alcohol, and tobacco. Effective programs must also begin to (1) target the context as well as the individual, (2) offer specific strategies for resisting peer pressure to use controlled substances, (3) provide opportunities for youth to practice resistance skills, and (4) carefully monitor locations and situations in and around school settings that allow for selling and use of drugs. An example of a program that incorporates these principles is described in Box 11.3.

Most substance abuse education programs have a prevention focus and may not be suitable for students who are already into heavy or chronic drug use. In such cases, other intervention measures are necessary. Leone (1991) and Johnson (1988) take the hard-line position that teachers and other direct-care professionals are contributing to students' substance abuse problems when they ignore suspected use or abuse.

Jardin and Ziebell (1981) offer guidelines for teachers to follow when they suspect a student of having a drug problem. Before action is taken, however, Jardin and Ziebell warn that two things must be clearly understood by all involved parties. First is a clear statement of school policy about legal issues regarding drug possession and observed use of drugs on the school grounds. Second, when the student is only suspected of drug abuse, the issue is one of treatment and not of discipline. Once these issues are clearly articulated, teachers may take action in the following sequence.

> *Identification.* The most accurate clue to drug use is a drastic and sustained change in a student's attitude, temperament, work habits, work quality, or grades. The teacher should solicit information from other school personnel before a suspicion is voiced. The teacher should also describe the resulting unacceptable behaviors to the student and obtain the backing of an administrator before further action is taken.
>
> *Parent Conference.* The purpose of meeting with the student's parents is to define the problem, to obtain parental input about what steps they intend to take, to get the parents' opinion about the role the school should take, and to get a commitment to try a plan of action.
>
> *Family Conference.* A family conference that includes the student and a school representative should be held as soon as the parents come up with a plan of action. The proposed plan should be parent initiated and school supported.
>
> *Follow-Up.* If outside help for the student is part of the plan, the teacher should check on whether it has been obtained. Continued contact with parents is essential, and if representatives from the mental health or juvenile justice systems have become involved, the teacher should maintain periodic contact with them.

It is also worth noting that discipline policies, such as the zero-tolerance policies in which any use or possession of illicit substances on school grounds results in suspension or expulsion, may have the unintended effect of exacerbating drug use since those students most in need may not receive any counseling or drug treatment and may not be motivated to return to school (Finn et al., 2003).

BOX 11.3
RESIST: A Substance Use Prevention Program

RESIST is a curriculum to prevent the use of alcohol, tobacco, and other drugs by students in special education. It is one of the few prevention programs specifically for students with disabilities. Developed by Daniel Morgan and his colleagues at Utah State University, RESIST has both elementary and secondary curricula. RESIST is based on theoretical premises and on research about effective strategies in prevention. Among the premises are that an effective program must include (1) awareness of pressures to use alcohol, tobacco, and other drugs; (2) attitudinal inoculation to those pressures; and (3) active practice of skills and strategies to overcome these pressures.

RESIST emphasizes the following messages:

- Drug use is not normal or healthy behavior.
- Most youths do not use drugs.
- One can lead a full and exciting life with many friends without using.
- Students help themselves and their communities by staying drug-free.

Similar to many social skills curricula, RESIST is a combination of instruction, discussion, and practice of skills. Based on sound instructional principles, it incorporates the following: direct instruction, role-playing, homework, parent involvement activities, behavior management procedures, and correction procedures. A typical lesson includes all of these components.

One unique feature of RESIST is that it teaches and reinforces a number of resistance skills:

- RESIST with a reason ("I don't like the taste/smell").
- Say "no thanks."
- Use humor ("I can't afford to kill any brain cells.")
- Change the subject ("Did you see the game last night?").
- Leave the situation ("No" and walk away).
- Avoid the situation.
- Ignore.
- Be a broken record ("No thanks. . . . No thanks. . . . No thanks").
- Stalling for time ("Not right now/Maybe later").

In addition to basic resistance skills, lessons focus on information and practice in resisting each of the individual drugs: alcohol, tobacco, marijuana, cocaine, crack, inhalants, and hallucinogens. For example, the lesson overview on "Resisting Pressure to Use Alcohol," contains the following elements: review previous homework, address facts about alcohol and drinking, discuss reasons not to use alcohol, role play situations involving pressure to drink alcohol, quiz on alcohol facts, homework assignment, and handout for parents.

Parents, teachers, and participating students rated the program favorably. Pre- and posttests indicate that students both improved their attitudes and increased their knowledge of the risks of using alcohol, tobacco, and other drugs. Inconsistent results were obtained when students were asked to rate their own drug use in the past 30 days; however, there was a sizable decrease in self-reported recent use of alcohol among high school students with mild disabilities.

One interesting finding is that although RESIST specifically emphasizes the idea that most students do not use drugs, tobacco, and alcohol, the majority of students continue to overestimate drug use among their peers. According to the authors of RESIST, we need to direct more attention to student perceptions and expectations about peer drug use.

Sources: Morgan, D. P. (1993). *RESIST: A curriculum to prevent the use of alcohol, tobacco, and other drugs by students in special education.* Logan: Utah State University. And Morgan, D. Likins, M., Friedman, S. & Gonaux, M. (1994). *A preliminary investigation of the effectiveness of a substance use prevention program for students in special education programs.* Logan: Utah State University.

Gangs, Delinquency, and the Juvenile Offender with Emotional/Behavioral Disorders

In this section, we explore issues related to gangs and law breaking among adolescents. First, the research on juvenile offenders and the relationship between education and corrections is described. Next, the prevalence of gangs, reasons for joining gangs, and a few community-based solutions are discussed.

Juvenile Offenders with EBD

Research on the juvenile offender with emotional/behavioral disorders is scarce. The bulk of related research in special education literature is devoted to (1) the characteristics of juvenile offenders who are not specifically labeled EBD or (2) the necessity of coordinating services between the educational and juvenile justice systems.

Studies clearly identifying juvenile offenders with emotional/behavioral disorders are difficult to conduct, primarily due to the different classification systems used by the education, mental health, and correctional systems (Gilliam & Scott, 1987). For example, many juvenile offenders are labeled as conduct disordered by psychologists using the DSM-IV system; however, many professionals in the education system have equated "conduct disordered" with "socially maladjusted" and therefore can exclude these youth from special education services. Although there is a movement to prevent exclusion of the socially maladjusted in the educational definition, such problems with definition and terminology have historically hampered efforts to conduct prevalence studies of individuals with EBD among adjudicated populations.

If students are not labeled by the special education system prior to incarceration, then chances may be slim for their being referred for special education afterward. As Gilliam and Scott (1987) point out, correctional staff have little motivation to make such referrals because they may see few differences between inmates who are labeled and those who are not. In addition, the facility may not have segregated classes for students with EBD; therefore, both labeled and unlabeled students are likely to be served in the same classroom.

Despite these difficulties in identifying offenders with EBD, some prevalence estimates have been made. Surveys indicate that a high percentage of juvenile inmates are identified as having emotional/behavioral disorders (Eggleston, 1984; McIntyre, 1993; Nelson & Rutherford, 1989), with up to 20–50% of incarcerated juvenile offenders having a mental disorder (Cocozza & Skowyra, 2002). This estimate is certainly cause for alarm. When applied to the total estimate of 150,000 incarcerated youth under age 22 (Murphy, 1986), the resulting number of juvenile offenders with EBD falls between 25,000 and 52,500. Also, when compared to the general population prevalence estimates of approximately 2 percent, the magnitude of emotional problems among this population becomes evident. According to Burrell and Warboys (2000), as many as 20 percent of students with emotional disabilities are arrested at least once before they leave school.

The prevalence of EBD among juvenile offenders can also be implicated with statistics showing the relationship of mental illness to violent behavior. Among violent adults in prison, the rate of severe mental illness is higher than for the average population. A study of 600 prisoners in Cook County Jail in Chicago showed that the rate of psychiatric disorders (e.g., major depression, bipolar disorder, and schizophrenia) among this group was two to three times higher than among the general population (Violence and Mental Health—Part I, 2000). Violent acts are also more frequent among individuals with low intelligence, brain damage (especially from physical abuse), and personality disorders (Violence and Mental Health—Part I, 2000). Only a small percentage of violent acts are committed by individuals with mental illness, however; psychological disorders seem to put an individual at risk for antisocial behavior and possible adjudication.

Unfortunately, prevalence estimates shed little light on the characteristics of juvenile offenders with EBD and how they may differ from other populations. For example, although not all youth with conduct-disorders break the law, juvenile offenders may differ from youth with conduct-behavior disorders as a group primarily by the fact that the juvenile offenders have been caught breaking the law enough times to become adjudicated. One study examined the characteristics of 266 juvenile offenders and found differences between those with special education backgrounds and those without (Zabel & Nigro, 1999). Of the 266 offenders, 37 percent had been previously labeled for special education purposes; most were served as EBD (16%), learning disabled (14%), or both (5%). The authors' self-report survey indicated that youth with prior special education experience exhibited more risk factors than the other delinquents; they were more likely to be labeled with ADHD, to be male, to be African American, to need corrective lenses, to have taken medications for emotional problems, to have lived in foster placements, to have attended more schools, to have been in trouble in school (e.g., assault) and been suspended, and to have committed crimes at an earlier age. Zabel and Nigro (1999) recommend that the primary interventions for students with EBD in terms of preventing juvenile delinquency are (1) to keep them in school, (2) provide effective instruction and behavior management, (3) develop adult–adolescent relationships that provide buffers against adversity, and (4) utilize a multiagency approach for supporting the student and his or her family. Box 11.4 offers a teacher's point of view about managing students with EBD and juvenile offenders in the same classroom.

Once children are in the juvenile justice system, special education services must continue to be provided according to federal law. Of course, this requirement poses many challenges, given the difficulty in tracking the many children and adolescents who have mental health diagnoses and enter the juvenile justice system. Data gathered from the National Collaboration Project based at Florida State University suggests that educational oversight of juvenile offenders varies widely across states (Gehring, 2005), and that zero-tolerance policies and high-stakes testing may interfere with transition back to the public school system.

Gangs

The Problem. Adolescents with EBD, especially those with diagnoses of conduct disorder, are at risk for becoming involved in gangs or delinquency. A gang is a group of persons who identify with one another by a common name and sign, and who break the law or behave in antisocial ways (Donnelly & Suter, 1994). Once confined primarily to the largest cities in the United States, gangs have now spread into suburban and small communities in

Box 11.4

A Teacher's Experience

It was bound to be an interesting year for me because it was the first year I'd taught in a public school since my college days. For 3½ years I'd taught in a psychiatric setting with doctors, social workers, psychologists, nurses, nutritionists, child-care workers, and what would later seem like a cast of thousands for support services. That year I was teaching in one of the largest and poorest school districts in the state, in an area of town where people were highly transient. I was assigned to a self-contained classroom for junior high school students with serious emotional/behavioral disorders.

From the information in my students' folders I learned that I would have one of the most ethnically diverse groups imaginable, including a Polynesian American and an American Inuit. As it turned out, ethnicity was not a problem in developing cooperative work groups. The problem in group interaction seemed to arise from the fact that my students were evenly divided between those with a very tenuous contact with reality, and those who had a firm grasp on reality but chose to walk on the fine edge with the local police. The other little twist was that of my ten students, only one was female.

Early on, my aide and I knew that we would have to watch our delinquent group very carefully because they began to manipulate and "borrow" from the less discerning students. We addressed the problem through careful seating arrangement, giving each student a single desk with some sort of barrier to limit visual contact with other students where academic work was to be completed. We structured group activities so that the more vulnerable of our students never worked with our more cunning students unless they were under the direct supervision of the aide or the teacher. We also worked very hard to foster friendships between the students, and eventually some of our delinquent students became very protective of the others.

Our group activities had to be carefully designed so that competition did not become a destructive dynamic. Team members were chosen by the aide or the teacher. Most of the activities were cooperative, but those that were competitive had rules about such things as "seeing how long we can keep the ball in bounds" or giving points for assists. Some days, the electricity in the air was just too tense to try to involve the group in a game; on such days, science lessons might be adjusted to include a nature walk. The key element in all our planning was flexibility. There were a lot of beautiful lesson plans that were put on hold because the students' needs shifted so quickly.

The most difficult adjustment for me was dealing with the isolation and lack of support personnel. I was accustomed to working in a setting where everyone was dealing with children with disabilities and trying to promote each child's potential. In the public school setting, not only were there no psychologists, no social workers, no child-care workers, but there were no other special education teachers on my side of the building! I was the only faculty member who ate lunch with her students, and frequently the only adult to be seen in the cafeteria at noon. When I talked with the principal about mainstreaming my students, she painfully admitted that there were only three teachers in the building who would give my students a chance—and two of them taught the same subject.

There may be a dozen solutions to the problem of not having support personnel, but I only found one that worked—looking for help outside the school system. By the end of the fall semester, I knew most of the juvenile probation officers in that section of town. I met with or called the students' parents at least once a week, even if it was a chat at the curb or a 5-minute phone call. I checked with the local United Fund office to locate as many social service agencies as I could, and then I developed friendships with some of the staff members. Within my building, I used any excuse I could find to bring other teachers into my room so that they could see for themselves that we were just another class. When a student was having a good day, he might earn the privilege of running errands, not only for me but also for the other teachers in our

(*continued*)

BOX 11.4 Continued

area. Before too long, teachers on our hall were asking why such a nice child was in my class.

There weren't any miracle cures in our class, but there were some significant changes. All of the students managed to stay out of the juvenile detention facilities for the year. None of the furniture was damaged. One student gave up being a mountain lion during free time. One young man learned to eat with a knife and fork and to stop talking to the plastic alligator he kept in his pocket. Three of our students did go to mainstream class, but only one progressed to the point of not needing the support of a self-contained class the next year. Although we would have liked to have seen more progress, I know how hard all of us had to work to achieve these goals.

Contributed by Dona Stallworth, PhD, former teacher and current principal in central Texas.

---

almost all 50 states. The massive migration to smaller communities is believed to be related primarily to expanding the turf for drug trafficking (Huff, 1992). According to the National Youth Violence Prevention Resource Center (2006), there are more than 24,500 different youth gangs around the United States, and more than 772,500 teens and young adults are involved in gangs. The good news is that since 1996, the overall number of gangs and gang members has decreased; however, in cities with populations larger than 25,000, gang involvement is still near peak levels.

Youths who are most at risk for becoming involved in gangs and delinquency are those from neighborhoods in which poverty and crime are rampant, and from homes in which substance abuse and violence are routine. In addition, these youth often have established histories of behavior problems and academic failure in school. The average gang member is 17 to 18 years old, although some members are as young as 12. Only about 6 percent of gang members are female, although some researchers believe this estimate is low and that female membership may be as high as 38 percent (National Youth Violence Resource Prevention Center, 2006).

Gangs are popular and difficult to combat because they serve basic socialization and survival functions. When families and schools are unable to meet the needs of these children and youth, gangs become an attractive alternative. Youths join gangs for many reasons, including acceptance, recognition, sense of belonging, status, power, shelter, food, clothing, nurturing, and respect (Conley, 1993). Unemployment is also a large factor; in many cities where gangs are a problem, job opportunities for which potential gang members would qualify are scarce. In fact, Huff (1992) emphasizes that to combat gangs, legal job opportunities must not only be available, but also must be able to compete with illegal opportunities such as drug trafficking.

Solutions. Obviously there are no simple solutions to gangs and juvenile crime because they are intertwined with a myriad of societal problems. Arrest and prosecution of gang members have not proven to be a deterrent to gang membership; in fact, among some gangs, arrests are viewed as honors. A strategy that has been adopted by community-based programs is to identify active gang members and to try to supplant gang-related activities with positive activities and skills. Prevention programs are similar, except that they target youth who are at risk but have not yet joined a gang. A survey of gang-plagued cities concluded that the most effective approaches to date have been a combination of tight law enforcement, school safety plans, dress and behavior codes, provision of opportunities such as remedial education and job training, school staff training, and community mobilization in which a variety of neighborhood groups coordinate efforts to help (Kodluboy, 1997).

As discussed in Chapter 8, it is important to work with the various systems involved with these youth. On a personal level, teachers can help by establishing relationships with individuals from law enforcement and juvenile justice who are also working with students involved in gangs and delinquent activities. On a systems level, teachers who are concerned about their students' involvement in gangs can also volunteer for interagency task forces or community mobilization groups to help combat the problem. School buildings, playgrounds, and gyms are ideal places for community programs to offer after-school activities as positive alternatives to gang activities (e.g., midnight basketball).

Self-Destructive Behavior

Children and youth with EBD may be prone toward self-destructive behaviors such as suicide and severe eating disorders.

Suicide

The most extreme form of self-destructive behavior is suicide. The suicide rate for adolescents ages 15–19 has been placed at 11.3 per 100,000 (Suicide—Part I, 1996). Many more attempted suicides take place. However, more recent statistics suggest that the current youth suicide rate has been declining since 1992 and is at its lowest point in 20 years (Brock, Sandoval, & Hart, 2006). Despite this encouraging news, youth suicide rates are still three times higher than what they were in 1950 and suicide ranks as the third leading cause of death in individuals ages 20–24 (Centers for Disease Control and Prevention [CDC] 2005). While adolescent females attempt suicide more often than their male counterparts, adolescent males successfully kill themselves five times more often (CDC, 2005). The rate of suicide attempts is highest among adolescents and young adults, while older adults have the highest rate of completion (Brock et al., 2006).

In a study of suicide rates among students with EBD, Miller (1994) found that of 71 adolescents with EBD, 55 percent reported suicide attempts, compared to 18 percent of nondisabled adolescents (N = 72). Typically, girls in both groups reported more suicide attempts (50% of the girls with EBD and 30% of the nondisabled girls) compared with boys (29% of boys with EBD and 9% of nondisabled boys). Twenty-five percent of the girls with EBD reported more than one suicide attempt, whereas no other adolescents in the study reported frequent attempts. It is thought that the majority of young people who commit suicide have some type of diagnosable mental disorder, with one estimate suggesting that over 90 percent of people who engage in suicidal behavior have a psychiatric disorder. Mood disorders rank as the most common diagnosis among suicidal individuals, followed by substance abuse, disruptive behavior disorders, and anxiety disorders (Brock et al., 2006). Religious affiliation and social support act as protective factors (Poland & Lieberman, 2002).

Some speculate that, because adolescents are more prone to risk-taking behavior and often do not think about the consequences of their behavior, they are more vulnerable to thoughts of suicide. Furthermore, the move by schools to raise performance standards puts additional pressure on students (Portner, 2000a). Coupled with a lack of access to mental health services and, in many cases, a traditional family unit, and bombarded by violent media, many teens react impulsively and destructively. Gay students and students who are victimized by bullies are particularly at risk for self-destructive behavior (Brock et al., 2006; Poland & Lieberman, 2002; Portner, 2000b).

Researchers have attempted to identify factors contributing to adolescent suicide. The acute onset of so many developmental changes during the adolescent years may create increased susceptibility. Chronic depression has also been linked with suicidal behavior, although depression is likely a correlate rather than a cause of suicide. In other words, the factors that cause an individual to be depressed may also eventually lead to suicide. Another factor is alienation, or a feeling of irreparable aloneness, which may be manifested through broken romances, little contact with peers, poor communication or conflict with parents, and divorce of parents. Other recurrent themes in suicide victims are feelings of being helpless and powerless and unresolved feelings over loss of a parent or other close relative at an early age. Familial factors such as a family history of medical and psychiatric illness, significant family strife, parental separations, divorce, and remarriages, and lack of family cohesion and engagement have also been linked to suicidal behavior in adolescence (Poland & Lieberman, 2002). Psychotic adolescents also may be at high risk for attempting suicide, as auditory hallucinations commanding suicide have been reported among both psychotic adults and adolescents.

Suicide and attempted suicide may also have a genetic component. Adopted children whose biological parent committed suicide are six times more likely than average to commit suicide (Suicide—Part I, 1996). The concordance rate of suicide among identical twins is four times higher than among fraternal twins, indicating a genetic predisposition. It is speculated that the heritability factor may be related to a genetic predisposition toward depression, alcoholism, and other psychiatric disorders and/or that there may be a genetic factor related to the ability to control impulses under stress (Brock et al., 2006; Suicide—Part I, 1996).

Table 11.4 lists a number of risk factors that may predispose children and adolescents toward suicidal behavior. These risk factors include substance abuse, familiarity with suicide, recent loss of family member or friend, chronic illness, and access to lethal means. Also increasing the probability of suicide attempts are a history of physical or sexual abuse and close association with a person who has died by suicide (Brock et al., 2006; Suicide—Part I, 1996). Additional signals are progressive isolation from social contact and a long history of social problems that worsens in adolescence. While the risk factors are similar for males and females, notable differences exist in their relative importance. For boys the primary risk factors include a previous attempt, depression, disruptive behavior, and/or substance abuse, whereas for girls major depression and/or a previous attempt are the most important risk factors (Poland & Lieberman, 2002).

TABLE 11.4 Risk Factors for Suicide

Emotional/Behavior Problems
Depression
Impulsive personality
Alcohol abuse
Drug abuse
Other serious psychiatric illness

Decreased Inhibition
Alcohol intoxication
PCP intoxication
Hallucinogen intoxication

Suicide is Familiar
Suicide threats
Previous suicide attempts
Family member has attempted suicide
Completed suicide in family member
Recent publicized suicide in community

Severe Stress
Recent significant loss
Chronic illness
Public humiliation or threat thereof

Access to Lethal Means
Prescription drugs at hand
Street drugs easy to obtain
Guns and ammunition in home
Has time alone to carry out plan

Teachers and other significant adults in the lives of teenagers can play key roles in suicide prevention. Adolescents who talk about suicide must be taken seriously, as they are at higher risk for attempting it, especially if a specific method is mentioned. Experts caution that no suicide threat is an idle threat, because it is always a plea for help.

Adults in a preventive role must be able to maintain open, honest communication and to accept strong emotions, both positive and negative (Suicide—Part II, 1996). Guetzloe (1988, 1991) offers some pragmatic suggestions for school personnel in working with potentially suicidal youth. These youth may be overwhelmed by a series of events over which they have little or no control; by identifying specific areas and making even a small positive change, the students can be shown that all is not hopeless. For example, dropping a class, removing the threat of punishment, or entering into a peer support group may relieve some of the pressure perceived by the individual. Guetzloe also recommends addressing problems relevant to suicidal behavior in the individual education plan; for example, if the student is highly stressed, provide training in relaxation, problem solving, and other coping skills. Brock et al., (2006) recommend that school districts provide staff with periodic training in suicide prevention and intervention, especially since teachers are the school professionals who spend the most time with at-risk students and are most likely to observe warning signs.

One interesting note from research on suicide prevention is that students themselves are the most likely to know who among them is suicidal. This finding has led some schools to set up peer counseling programs, in which students are trained to make referrals within the school system. Although there is some evidence for "contagion," that is, one suicide encouraging others, research suggests that contagion is more likely to occur when the first suicide is not discussed openly, thereby denying adolescents the opportunity to voice their feelings and regain some sense of control (Davis, Sandoval, & Wilson, 1988). School personnel will also want to contact parents and refer to a mental health professional in the

TABLE 11.5 Warning Signs of Suicide

- *Threats:* may be direct ("I want to die", "I am going to kill myself") or indirect ("The world would be better without me", "Nobody will miss me anyway"). In adolescence, indirect clues could be offered through joking or through reference in school assignments, particularly creative writing or art pieces.
- *Plan/method/access:* lethality of method, availability of means, and level of sophistication of the plan are important variables
- *Previous attempts:* 15% of individuals with a history of one or more suicide attempts will go on to kill themselves
- *Final arrangements:* giving away prized possessions, goodbye letters
- *Depression:* may be especially significant when there are pervasive thoughts of helplessness or hopelessness
- *Sudden changes:* changes in behavior, friends, or personality

Adapted from Poland, S., & Lieberman, R. (2002). Best practices in suicide intervention. In A., Thomas, & J. Grimes (Eds.), *Best practices in school psychology IV* (pp. 1151–1165). Bethesda, MD: National Association of School Psychologists.

event of threatened or attempted suicide. It is important to remember that the single best predictor of subsequent attempts is whether the adolescent is able to maintain communication with others. Table 11.5 provides a list of warning signs for suicide. Teachers should be aware of such signs and refer at-risk students to school or mental health counselors (Poland & Lieberman, 2002).

Eating Disorders

Two self-destructive eating disorders, anorexia nervosa and bulimia, are more prevalent among adolescent girls (about 90% of all cases) and among whites than among other populations (Merrell, 2003). The incidence has steadily increased, with as many as 18–20 percent of school-age girls suffering from symptoms of one or both disorders (Eating Disorders—Part I, 1997; Phelps & Bajorek, 1991). The prevalence of individuals who meet the full DSM-IV-TR criteria for anorexia nervosa is lower, about 0.5–1 percent; with bulimia, prevalence estimates range from 1 to 3 percent of individuals in industrialized nations.

Anorexia nervosa is a self-imposed restriction of eating that results in severe, sometimes life-threatening, weight loss. It is 10 times more common in girls than in boys, and is most likely to occur in adolescent girls in the age range from 14 to 17. Unfortunately, mental health professionals are reporting increasing numbers of cases in preadolescents, including children as young as 7 (Phelps & Bajorek, 1991). If untreated, cases of the disorder are likely to continue into adulthood and may result in death. From 1953 to 1999, mortality rates for those diagnosed with anorexia were about 5 percent; of survivors, fewer than 50 percent recover (Cook-Cottone & Phelps, 2006).

The cause of anorexia is currently unknown, with associated factors including individual characteristics (physiological, gender, emotional regulation, self-concept), familial factors (low levels of communication, abuse, preoccupation with appearance) and cultural factors (media depictions of thinness as ideal) (Cook-Cottone & Phelps, 2006). Individuals with anorexia have been characterized as overcontrolled and meticulous and as coming from overcontrolled homes, which engendered emotional conflict. It is more practical to view anorexia as a phobia of being overweight or fat. Anorexia usually begins with dieting, which becomes an obsession; consequently, the individual loses all perspective of appropriate body weight. Even when abnormally thin, the individual cannot lose the fear of becoming fat and therefore does not resume normal eating habits. It has not been determined whether most are overweight before they begin dieting. Some studies have indicated that many were not overweight but began dieting for reasons of their own, without external suggestions or provocation. Anorexia is often comorbid with depressive disorders, obsessive–compulsive disorders, and personality disorders (Merrell, 2003).

There is some evidence that anorexia has an inherited biochemical basis, which also may be responsible for the anxiety and depression found in individuals suffering from anorexia (Eating Disorders—Part I, 1997; Fava, Copeland, Schweiger, & Herzog, 1989; Garfinkel & Garner, 1987). One study has found that individuals with anorexia and bulimia lack the ability to absorb zinc, a trace metal that is essential to a variety of internal processes (Warren, 1990). Subjects' symptoms improved with zinc supplements, suggesting that a biochemical abnormality may in fact be causally related to these eating disorders. Other studies have found changes in neurotransmitters and endorphins among adolescents with anorexia (Eating Disorders—Part I, 1997; Fava et al., 1989; Kaplan & Woodside, 1987). Treatment is complicated, usually involving behavioral interventions with a goal of realistic weight gain followed by cognitive-behavioral interventions aimed at changing irrational beliefs and distorted body image. Numerous drugs have been tried in treating anorectic symptoms; however, to date, no drug has been found effective in treating anorexia, although antidepressant medication may be helpful in relapse prevention (Cook-Cattone & Phelps, 2006; Eating Disorders—Part II, 1997).

Bulimia is an eating disorder in which the individual eats an abnormally large amount of food and then induces vomiting or uses laxatives to remove the food before it can be digested. For this reason, it is often called the "binge-and-purge" syndrome. The DSM-IV describes two types: the purging type (the person regularly engages in self-induced vomiting, laxatives, diuretics, or enemas) and the nonpurging type (the person uses other compensatory measures, such as excessive exercise or fasting). Bulimia differs from anorexia in that individuals are often of normal weight, thus their abnormal eating habits may not be known to others. Bulimia may be characterized as a form of obsessive–compulsive behavior: Individuals cannot rid themselves of the idea of going on a food binge (obsessive), and once the food has been ingested, cannot resist the urge to get it out of their system (compulsive). Although individuals with bulimia may be of normal weight and appear healthy, they can suffer a number of physical ailments related to constant vomiting and/or use of laxatives. In addition, persons with bulimia recognize their aberrant eating habits and therefore suffer more anxiety, depression, and guilt about the disorder than persons with anorexia (Johnson, Steinberg, & Lewis, 1988).

Researchers have found that a cognitive-behavioral approach (coupled with response prevention of vomiting) is highly effective in treating individuals with bulimia (Eating Disorders—Part II, 1997; Phelps & Bajorek, 1991). This approach is a step-by-step procedure aimed at eliminating the secrecy, gradually shaping dietary behavior through self-monitoring, and gradually introducing binge foods. Faulty cognitions regarding food and body image are also targeted (Eating Disorders—Part II, 1997). Some success has also been reported with drug therapy, particularly with antidepressant medications (Cook-Cottone & Phelps, 2006).

If teachers suspect that a student is experiencing either of these eating disorders, referral to a local mental health program specializing in these disorders should be made. Support groups for adolescents with eating disorders and their parents are also available in many communities. Cook-Cottone and Phelps (2006) summarize that recommended treatments for eating disorders involve a multidisciplinary treatment team to address health status and medication, nutritional counseling, and psychosocial needs. Prevention efforts should be geared toward development of resiliency and should include media activism, coping and self-regulation strategies, assertiveness and competence training, and development of a positive physical self-concept.

Troubled Girls

Many educational researchers have explored the possibility of gender bias in the public schools (American Association of University Women Educational Foundation, 1992; Brown & Gilligan, 1992). Others have speculated that gender bias also exists in terms of mental health diagnosis and treatment (Caseau, Luckasson, & Kroth, 1994). These researchers found that the number of boys identified as emotionally disturbed by schools far exceeded the number of girls. They also found that boys identified by the schools and served by private psychiatric hospitals outnumbered girls. However, they found that students not identified by the public schools, but served by private psychiatric hospitals, were predominantly girls. These girls exhibited depression, family conflict, suicidal ideation, and suicide attempts. Ninety percent of adolescents exhibiting eating disorders are girls, and the majority of attempted suicides are by females (Eating Disorders—Part I, 1997; Miller, 1994; Poland, 2003; Portner, 2000a). Caseau and her colleagues (1994) speculate that the IDEA definition and the procedures and instruments used to identify EBD may be biased in favor of identifying males, who typically exhibit externalizing disorders, resulting in unequal distribution of mental health services, at least in school settings.

Cullinan, Osborne, and Epstein (2004) report that girls make up about 15–25 percent of students with EBD. However, most research addresses the defiant, aggressive, and disruptive behavior in school, often with mainly male subjects, according to these authors. In a comparison study of females with and without EBD, they found that the females with EBD functioned significantly worse on all five characteristics identified in the federal definition of emotional disturbance. Furthermore, they also showed more social maladjustment and reduced overall competence compared to female peers without EBD. Nearly one-third of the females with EBD experienced two or more characteristics to an extreme extent. These authors, along with others, advocate for research that addresses the hypothesis that assessment procedures underestimate the degree to which girls qualify for EBD. They propose that typically used instruments and techniques may not adequately capture female forms of aggression and less obvious symptoms of depression.

The effects of gender and delinquency on emotional distress and suicide ideation (Liu, 2004) were studied with a national sample of 4,221 adolescents. The author found that (1) the experience of emotional distress predicts subsequent suicidal ideation or attempt and (2) delinquency predicts suicidal gestures among girls. For boys, these effects are present but not statistically significant. Another interesting finding was that girls who are both emotionally distressed and involved in antisocial or delinquent behavior are less suicidal than those who are emotionally distressed but are conforming to social rules. With girls, it appears that among those who exhibit emotional/behavioral disorders, those who are delinquent or engaged in antisocial behavior may be at a lower risk for suicide than those who are conforming to social rules, although both groups are at risk.

Ruffolo, Sarri, and Goodkind (2004), in a structured questionnaire study with 159 delinquent or high-risk adolescent girls, found that although most of the girls reported moderate to severe depression, only about one-third had received mental health services. Girls who experience a *double vulnerability,* defined as early physical maturation and living in a disadvantaged neighborhood, were found in one study to be at higher risk for engaging in violent behavior (Obeidallah, Brennan, Brooks-Gunn, & Earls, 2004). Other areas of research into associations between gender and mental health include studies of aggression in adolescent female relationships (Crothers, Field, & Kolbert, 2005), the link between depression and high-risk sexual behavior (Medline Plus, 2006), and the relationship between childhood victimization and later victimization in dating relationships (Gagne, Lavoie, & Hebert, 2005).

Reflecting the concern that troubled and troubling girls have not been adequately served by special education, Nichols and Steinberg (1996) devoted an entire journal issue to this topic. Their assumptions are that (1) there is an insidious assault on the minds of girls and boys about the basic worth of girls, (2) girls are often seen as sexual property, (3) girls are thought to be fundamentally inferior to men, and (4) girls are defined by their relationship to men. Therefore, many young girls become severely depressed, develop eating disorders, become sex objects in gangs, and are victims of sexual and physical abuse. Box 11.5 contains passages from the journal editorial (Nichols & Steinberg, 1996), a composition outlining what troubled girls need and how school personnel can help.

BOX 11.5

Voices of Courage

When asked whether we would edit an issue about troubled girls, something with a title like *Courage for Discouraged Girls,* we were intrigued by the opportunity to focus on how the world is treating and shaping girls and giving them resilience and courage. As we searched for contributors with perspectives and experiences to share, the interest grew from absorption to a sense of mission.

Many girls lose buoyancy and self-confidence as they near their teens. The erosion of female self-esteem and competence that begins at junior high is described in *Meetings at the Crossroads* (1992) by Lyn Mikel Brown and Carol Gilligan, *Reviving Ophelia* (1994) by Mary Pipher, *Failing at Fairness* (1994) by Myra and David Sadker, and *School Girls* (1994) by Peggy Orenstein. These books offer a new lens through which we look at yearbooks, soap operas, and fashion magazines and see the distorted view of life and self that is sold to girls every day.

Our writers report that 70 to 80 percent of the girls that they work with have histories of abuse. We, who have worked with children for

(*continued*)

BOX 11.5 Continued

years, are stunned at the sexual abuse that is now almost a constant in the stories of girls so troubled that they end up in hospitals, treatment programs, therapists' offices, and prisons. We wonder if this has always been true. Are people just now being open about secrets that they have always guarded? Or is there something more wrong with our world than in past times? Probably some of both, but still, most girls in the general population haven't been sexually abused, so what's the problem?

Girls as Objects: A Theme of the Times

We conclude that the core problem is an insidious assault on the minds of girls—and on the minds of boys, too, for that matter—about the basic worth of girls. We are shocked about girls being prostitutes in India, female fetuses being aborted in China, women being killed for infidelity in fundamentalist Islamic societies. But U.S. society reflects the same images of women as sexual property; as fundamentally inferior to men; as defined by their sexual role with, acceptance by, and relationship to men. Today, no storyline is too steamy or seamy for the shows our kids watch on TV any day of the week, and few women are allowed in front of the cameras who do not conform to the beauty myth. Not that our modern girls don't dream and realize dreams beyond the ken of most 1950s girls, but successful, smart women need all the more to prove their femininity. They are to be like Cosmo girls, Barbie in her astronaut suit. Jane Fonda in her aerobics togs, or at least like Sally Field—smart, forever thin, fit, and sexually appealing.

How does this affect girls? The authors in this issue of *Reclaiming Children and Youth* begin to tell us. Julia Graber and Jeanne Brooks-Gunn explain the devastating impact of eating disorders on ever-younger girls. Mara Benitez tells us of a girl who had to change schools because of rumors started about her, of another having her hair cut off because someone thought she was after her man, of boys' "gawking, the disrespectful stares and words," of the sexual harassment and cruelty about appearance that, according to newspaper polls, are virtually endemic to U.S. secondary schools. Heidi Solomon speaks of the extra pressures young girls feel that lead them to assert their power physically and sexually, ending up "in juvenile court or pregnant." Richard Garland describes girls who are initiated into gangs by sexual intercourse, their personhood defined as sex objects or fighters. There was a time when these issues seemed remote to most U.S. citizens. This no longer is true.

Girls need courage to hold out against the pressures they now endure, to speak out clearly and have their voices heard, to respect themselves even when they don't meet the sleazy standards reflected in the media. The other thing that they need is care—careful listening from meaningful adults, careful attention when they are in trouble, careful programming as soon as it is needed (long before their "quiet" problems become so disturbing to society that they are banished) and as long as they need it (long after they have experienced abuse or been abandoned to homelessness or put in jail).

Adapted with permission. Nichols, P., & Steinberg, Z. (1996). Voices of courage. *Reclaiming Children and Youth, 5*(2), *Courage for Troubled Girls* 64–67; Austin, TX: Pro-Ed.

Interventions for Adolescents with Emotional/Behavioral Disorders

Over the years, program development for adolescents with EBD has received much less attention than program development for younger children. One factor impeding program development for adolescents with EBD is the lack of clear-cut research on the effectiveness of specific approaches to dealing with important issues such as career preparation, sex-related problems, and drug abuse. Despite these factors, a growing interest in developing model programs and researching the efficacy of specific interventions for this population has become evident. The remainder of this chapter explores career education alternatives and behavioral and counseling interventions that hold promise for dealing with the adolescent with emotional/behavioral disorders.

Transition Planning

Transition planning is viewed as a comprehensive, multiyear program. In this section, a general transition model is discussed.

Transition Model. Transition services for special education adolescents are based on the assumption that what students are taught in school will affect their postschool work experiences. Levinson (2002) maintains that students in general, and students with disabilities in particular, are underprepared for work when they leave public schools. Initially, transition services included career education, job training, and community adjustment (Will, 1984). However, by 1990, the amendments to IDEA defined transition services in broader terms (cited in Bullis & Cheney, 1999, p. 1). Transition services means a coordinated set of activities for a student, designed within an outcome-oriented process, that promotes movement from school to postschool activities, including postsecondary education, vocational training, integrated employment (including supported employment), continuing and adult education, adult services, independent living, or community participation. The coordinated set of activities must be based on the individual student's needs, taking into account the student's preferences and interests, and must include instruction, community experiences, the development of employment and other postschool adult living objectives, and, if appropriate, acquisition of daily living skills and functional vocational evaluation (Witte, 2002).

Furthermore, the 1990 amendments mandated transition services and planning for all special education students ages 16 and older, stated that the services should be specified in an individualized education plan or individualized transition plan, and that local school personnel were responsible for including adult service providers and other pertinent agencies in the planning and implementation process (deFur & Patton, 1999). In the 1997 reauthorization of IDEA, all students were required to have an individual transition statement in the IEP by age 14, and a statement of needed transition services by age 16 (or younger as determined by the IEP team). Witte (2002) advocates for the development of IEPs that adopt a long-term lifespan approach that emphasizes functional life skills along with academic progress. Accomplishing such an approach under the NCLB mandates for academic-only curriculum maybe difficult.

Students with EBD who have poor social skills and often display violent and aggressive behavior have performed poorly on transition outcomes relative to other disability populations and to students without disabilities (Bullis & Cheney, 1999). In terms of postschool employment, 59 percent of students with EBD were unemployed less than 2 years after leaving school and 52 percent were still unemployed 3–5 years after leaving school (D'Amico & Blackorby, 1992). This is compared to students with LD, who were 40 percent unemployed 2 years after leaving school and 29 percent unemployed 3–5 years after leaving school. Thirty-one percent of students without disabilities were unemployed

3–5 years after leaving school. Basically, students with EBD had higher unemployment, lost jobs more often, worked fewer hours, and earned lower wages than other student groups (DeStefano & Wagner, 1992). Enrollment in vocational courses during high school tends to predict later employment success; however, 58 percent of students with EBD were enrolled in vocational classes, compared to 64 percent of students with LD and students without disabilities (Wagner, 1991b). Three years after leaving school, 26 percent of students with EBD had enrolled in postsecondary programs compared to 68 percent of the students without disabilities (Malmgren, Neel, & Edgar, 1998). In terms of living arrangements, 3–5 years after leaving school, 40 percent of students with EBD were living independently, compared to 37 percent of the general population, and 26 percent were parents themselves (Newman, 1992). Taken together with the fact that after school, students with EBD are 17 times more likely to be arrested compared to other student groups (Bullis & Cheney, 1999), the postschool outcomes for this population appear bleak.

Consistent with other interventions for this difficult and complex population, a systems approach to transition planning and vocational preparation appears indicated (Bullis & Cheney, 1999). These authors recommend that transition service delivery for students with EBD be a zero-reject program conducted away from the high school campus, with low student–teacher ratios and with well-trained transition or career specialists. Clark (1998) recommends that the transition specialist ensure that services (1) be individualized and encompass all transition domains; (2) be focused on individual characteristics, strengths, interests, and needs; (3) include a safety net of staff support for students; (4) be seamless in that continuity of effort and support is ensured; and (5) be outcome oriented.

Specifically, Bullis and Fredericks (2002) recommend that transition programs for students with EBD include the following components:

1. *Intake and functional skill assessment:* determine eligibility for services from educational programs and social service agencies and assess work and transition skills and interests. It is assumed that skills, rather than diagnosis, predict vocational outcomes.
2. *Personal futures planning:* a team of educators, family members, agency members, and the student meet and discuss options in order to form a vision for the student's successful transition.
3. *Community-based wraparound social services:* a coordinated system of care including schools, mental health agencies, vocational rehabilitation, social service agencies, and families plan and implement specific services to EBD adolescents and young adults. Management and funds are blended according to each student's needs.
4. *Competitive employment:* students are placed in jobs that provide opportunities to learn and practice productive skills, foster job-related social skills, and allow students to explore their own vocational interests. Job development should be a thoughtful, deliberate process.
5. *Flexible educational programming:* provide flexible academic scheduling, curriculum, learning environments, and course policies (i.e., earning credits) in order to ensure successful transition programs.
6. *Social skill training:* teach transition-related social skills through support groups and individual instruction using a social problem-solving approach.

7. *Long-term support and follow-up services:* contact graduates (preferably through phone contacts) at regular times to offer support and determine postsecondary outcomes.

The belief is that adolescents with EBD need not transition to the adult world without help and that the cost of intensive interagency support will be offset by earned wages and reduced social service costs to adults (Cheney, Malloy, & Hagner, 1998). Table 11.6 depicts

TABLE 11.6 Vocational Phases for Job Training

Phase I: Learning
Vocational trainer trains and supervises worker on all tasks and duties.
Worker learns various job tasks, maintaining 3 working hours per week.
Worker follows job site rules and practices skills seen on job site.
Trainer and worker explore transportation options.
Trainer collects data from job site.

Phase II: Responsibility
Worker begins to perform job tasks independently, with intermittent quality checks by trainer.
Worker establishes own vocational goals.
Worker travels to job independently.
Worker maintains 5 working hours per week with satisfactory performance ratings.
Worker begins to receive feedback from employer.
Trainer gathers data and continues to supervise worker.

Phase III: Transition
Trainer no longer at job site, making only intermittent quality checks.
Worker performs job independently.
Worker works toward goals and monitors progress.
Worker travels to and from work independently.
Worker maintains work quality equal to the regular employees for 10 hours per week.
Employer supervises worker.

Phase IV: Independence
Trainer performs quality checks by phone.
Worker is independent on all tasks, duties, and transportation.
Worker monitors own goals.
Worker maintains 10 hours per week with satisfactory employee performance.
Employer supervises worker.
Worker will be eligible for paid employment with trainer support.

Phase V: Employable
Trainer assists with administrative issues.
Employer trains and manages employee.
Worker reaches vocational goals.
Worker travels to work independently for 20 hours per week employment for 1 year.
Worker is able to independently gain paid employment.

Adapted with permission from Bullis, M., and Cheney, D. (1999), Vocational and transition interventions for adolescents and young adults with emotional or behavioral disorders. *Focus on Exceptional Children, 31*(7), 16, copyright Behavioral Institute for Children and Adolescents.

vocational phases for job training. Note that successful employment requires a gradual, supported process toward independence.

Behavioral Interventions

Utilization of behavioral techniques with adolescents warrants special consideration. It is generally not too difficult to find reinforcers for a child, and, between parents and teachers, the child's environment may be fairly easily arranged to control reinforcement. In contrast, adolescents have much more control over their environment, and many of the reinforcers that worked in childhood no longer work in adolescence. It may be difficult for teacher and student to mutually agree upon suitable reinforcers, as adolescents may name reinforcers that are either illegal or unethical (alcohol or pornography, for example). Another factor is the emergence of peer group influence as a major motivator for adolescents, which may diminish the adolescent's need for adult approval. Adolescents with EBD in particular often do not place a premium on the usual social incentives, which may further limit the range of possible reinforcers.

Despite these potential difficulties, token economy and contingency management systems appear to be useful with this population. Towns (1981) reviewed research in this area and found that token economies that were successful with adolescents fall into three categories: those utilizing home-based reinforcement systems, those using group contingencies, and those using self-determined reinforcement. Home-based reinforcement systems can have a powerful effect on in-school behavior if parents and teachers work out a cooperative plan. Typical targeted behaviors in home-based systems include completing homework and other study behaviors, and typical reinforcers include watching television and social privileges in the home and community. Due to the influence of peer pressure among adolescents, group contingencies may be more successful than individual contingencies (Alberto & Troutman, 2006). In group contingencies, reinforcement is dependent upon the cooperation of every member of the group: If any member fails to exhibit the agreed-upon behavior, then no one receives the reinforcement. Group contingencies have been applied successfully with adolescents with EBD to improve academic, social, and learning behaviors (Alberto & Troutman, 2006). Self-determined reinforcement allows students either to choose from a teacher-approved list or to negotiate reinforcers with the teacher. Although self-determined reinforcement is always good practice, it may be essential to getting adolescents "hooked" into a behavior management plan.

Token systems are based on contingency management, which is in turn based on the Premack Principle: that high-probability behaviors can be used to increase low-probability behaviors (Premack, 1965). High-probability behaviors of adolescents include listening to music, watching videos, eating, talking to one another, playing video games, and participating in sports or other recreational activities. Low-probability behaviors include studying, completing classwork, and finishing homework. Although token economies have been successful with adolescents with EBD, teachers may choose to forego tokens and implement a simplified contingency management system whereby the student is presented with an if–then proposition. ("If you finish your class assignment [low-probability behavior], then

TABLE 11.7 Typical Reinforcers for Adolescents

Doing nothing (true free time)	Play a game (cards, board games)
Reading magazines and newspapers	Using a camera
Writing a letter to a friend or a famous person	Time off from school
Peer tutoring	Coach's assistant
Listening to music	Run errands
Working on a hobby	Extra time in high-interest areas (shop, art, PE)
Watching a movie	Do clerical work in building
Drawing, painting, creating	Custodian's assistant
Acting as teacher assistant	Watch TV
Having class outside	Typing and computer games
Field trips	Attend sports events
Having a snack or soda	Food or treat coupons
Having a sport time (some play and some watch)	

you may listen to music" [high-probability behavior].) Table 11.7 provides a list of typical reinforcers for adolescents.

Often teachers of students with behavior disorders arrange their token and contingency management systems into level systems. Level systems are composed of a hierarchy of behavioral expectations matched to reinforcers. Behaviors at the lowest level are presumably easier and more basic, whereas those at higher levels require more skill. The reinforcers at the higher levels are presumably more powerful, thus students will perform better and more difficult behavior in order to acquire the preferred reinforcers. If inappropriate behavior occurs, students may lose access to the reinforcers by being bumped down a level or being put off-level. Teachers seem to like level systems because they present a standardized management system. However, because the system is standardized, the legality of level systems has been questioned (Scheuermann, et al., 1994). Additional information about token economies and level systems was presented in Chapter 7.

Another promising avenue for educators is teaching self-control and self-management techniques to adolescents as you learned in Chapter 6. Behavioral self-control and other forms of cognitive-behavioral management are especially important with adolescents because these techniques emphasize the shift from external to internal controls. The shift to internal controls becomes important as the individual matures and experiences more choices and options, while at the same time fewer restrictions are imposed by adults in the environment. Although tight environmental controls are used in the highly structured classrooms of many adolescent programs, the individual must learn to cope with increasing demands for independence if he or she is to be able to leave the program and be successful on his or her own. An emphasis on student self-control and student responsibility for outcomes also helps eliminate the power struggles between teacher and student so often found in adolescent classrooms.

Several self-management techniques have been implemented successfully with adolescents with EBD. Disruptive behavior was decreased with self-rating intervention (Smith et al., 1988) and on-task behavior was improved with self-recording (Blick & Test, 1987;

Lloyd & Hilliard, 1989; Smith et al., 1988; Webber et al., 1993). Although problems with generalization and maintenance of behavioral gains persist, self-management techniques with this population are promising.

Counseling Techniques and Classroom Groups

Techniques employed in individual therapy sessions vary according to the preference and training of the therapist, but most focus on some combination of self-understanding and the changing of behaviors that are maladaptive to the individual. Although family therapy has been available for years, only recently have researchers begun to view it as necessary for effecting long-term change in the life of a child. Because friction between parent and child is a normal part of the adolescent developmental phase, parent involvement in therapy is especially important for this age group. In fact, one study found a moderately high success rate for adolescents in therapy whose parents were involved in some part of the treatment plan, and a 100 percent failure rate for adolescents whose parents were not involved at all (Rosenstock & Vincent, 1979).

Another form of counseling especially effective with adolescents is group therapy. Group therapy may yield more satisfactory results than individual therapy for adolescents for several reasons. A strong allegiance to peers and need for peer approval is one factor. This strong identification with peers can be both a source of support and a source of pressure to conform to the group's ideas and values. With some adolescents, there is the additional factor of rebellion against adults or authority figures. Such an attitude, when coupled with an exaggerated need for privacy, often leaves an adult therapist with a sullen, noncommunicative client. Therefore, group therapy is often a better outlet for adolescents than individual therapy. Group therapy for adolescents usually focuses on a common theme, such as groups for individuals at risk for substance abuse or dropping out. Unfortunately, many students with EBD fail to receive counseling as a related service (Knitzer et al., 1989), even though it is typically recommended as an important treatment component (Walker et al., 2004). It is thought that the cost of such services, along with failure to document positive outcomes, discourages consideration. Once again, interagency cooperation and funding could alleviate the high cost of individual and group counseling (Maag & Katsiyannis, 1996) so that more students with EBD could receive such services.

Teachers can implement group sessions in the classroom on a routine basis. These groups should be considered class meetings rather than group therapy. Coleman and Webber (1988) suggest that groups can be used to accomplish two major goals: (1) groups allow students and teacher to openly deal with sources of conflict that may be causing surface behavior problems, and (2) groups help shift control from external (teacher) to internal (students themselves). In other words, a group process allows students to analyze and manage their own actions and reactions.

Students should feel that the meetings are a forum during which they may speak freely and honestly. The teacher should also take an active part and provide direction to the group and support to those who may feel threatened. Ground rules should always be established and maintained. Box 11.6 illustrates how one group incorporated a recalcitrant member into its ranks.

BOX 11.6

Ham Bone and the Group Process[1]

The group described below was part of a prevention program funded by the state commission on alcohol and drug abuse and administered by the local child guidance center in two middle schools. The purpose of the 8-week groups was to provide experiential exercises to enhance social skills, problem-solving skills, and self-esteem. Students can be referred by counselors, teachers, administrators, parents or self.

One group consisted of eight African American sixth graders. Groups typically have ethnic balance; however, referrals determined the group composition. During the first meeting, the students signed a contract establishing ground rules for the group. They also played some "icebreaker" games. Two of the male students were absent at this meeting, but both showed up for the second meeting. One of these was about 6 inches taller and much stockier than the rest of the group; during introductions, he announced that his name was "Ham Bone." During icebreaker activities, Ham Bone repeatedly called the other students "nigger" and other racial epithets. He was unnecessarily rough and refused to hold hands during one activity because he "wasn't a fag."

According to the group contract, put-downs were not forbidden, but it was agreed that the group would discuss them. When Ham Bone's slurs were discussed, the other students responded that it didn't matter because "words can't hurt."

At the third session, Ham Bone and another student refused to participate in a trust-building activity. At the next session, the group confronted both students about their refusal to participate and decided that those who refused to participate should return to their classes. Ham Bone did participate in that day's activity, which was another trust-building activity using a blindfold. He also followed the group rules and refrained from name-calling. During the following sessions, Ham Bone continued to participate and his bullying and other negative behavior continued to decrease. During a particularly challenging problem-solving activity, Ham Bone reverted to his old behaviors of dominating and name-calling, but the group acted protective toward him and scapegoated another male group member. At the last session, Ham Bone was a model of considerate and cooperative behavior. He expressed concern about another student, was attentive during discussion, and volunteered to do helpful tasks. He also expressed frustration that the girls, who were giggling and whispering among themselves, were not abiding by the group guidelines. Ham Bone and the group had come to terms with one another.

[1]The Texas Commission on Alcohol and Drug Abuse furnished financial support to the activity described in this publication. This does not imply the Commission's endorsement or concurrence with statements or conclusions contained therein.

Contributed by Beth Dennis, MSSW-CSW, and Rebecca Brown, MA, therapists with the Austin Child Guidance Center.

Conclusions

Children who are labeled emotionally/behaviorally disordered do not tend to "grow out of it" as they approach adolescence; in fact, their behaviors may become more intense and have more serious ramifications. All adolescents become more egocentric and experience identity crises; many experiment with behavior that is deviant. These experiences are intensified for the adolescent with EBD, who has even fewer coping skills than his or her peers. School may be the only place that many of these adolescents will have access to the help they need with issues related to staying in school, drugs, alcohol, gangs, social rejection, sex, and self-destructive behavior. Providing support while helping your students sort out all the confusion may be the most important thing you can do as a teacher. Viewing the adolescent as a child searching for an adult identity may be a helpful framework.

KEY POINTS

1. Adolescence is an awkward period in which individuals are no longer children and not quite adults.
2. Struggles for identity, independence, and peer approval are the hallmarks of normally developing adolescents.
3. Research has failed to document pathology in adolescence that differs from pathology in childhood, suggesting that children with EBD grow into adolescents with EBD.
4. Teachers of adolescents must routinely deal with problems related to dropping out, drugs, gangs, social rejection, sex, and self-destructive behavior such as eating disorders and suicide.
5. Girls' emotional problems may be under-identified and overlooked by school personnel.
6. Although the effectiveness of school-based substance abuse education in reducing actual consumption has not been established, it is essential that educators continue to deal with substance use and abuse.
7. The content of sex education programs in the schools is the subject of much controversy; however, with the skyrocketing incidence of sexually transmitted diseases and teenage pregnancies, schools must continue to deal with sex-related issues.
8. It is important to engage adolescents in meaningful activities in order to deter gang membership, alleviate social isolation, and prepare them for adulthood.
9. Recognizing the importance of peer approval to adolescents, teachers may want to use group sessions and group contingencies instead of individual ones.
10. Self-management becomes increasingly important during the teenage years, as parents, teachers, and other authority figures have less and less control over the adolescent's environment.

HOMEWORK QUESTIONS

1. Reflect upon your own experiences as an adolescent. How did your school address problems of substance use/abuse? How do you think the approach could have been improved? (two paragraphs)
2. If a student were to approach you regarding issues of sexual orientation, how would you respond? How is the concept of visibility management relevant to your response? (one paragraph)
3. Consider the warning signs of suicide outlined in Table 11.5. If you recognized several of these signs in one of your students, what specific steps would you take? (one paragraph)

4. If a child with an EBD also had an eating disorder, how might this information affect the development of the IEP?
5. How would transition planning for a student with an emotional disturbance help to guide instruction for the secondary special education teacher? What specific needs should be considered in preparing to leave the special education program?
6. Discuss 3–5 reasons why teaching adolescents with EBD differs from teaching children with EBD. Which do you think would be more difficult? Defend your answer.

ADDITIONAL READINGS AND RESOURCES

Alcohol and other drugs: Use, abuse and disabilities, by Peter Leone, Reston, VA: Council for Exceptional Children, 1991, for a handbook describing (1) the prevalence of these problems among exceptional children and youth, (2) strategies for practitioners, and (3) suggestions for program development.

Applied behavior analysis for teachers (7th ed.), by Paul Alberto and Anne Troutman, Columbus, OH: Prentice Hall, 2006, for detailed information about applying behavioral principles such as token systems and group contingencies in the classroom.

The tough kid book: Practical classroom management strategies, by G. Rhode, W. R. Jensen, and H. K. Reavis, Longmont, CO: Sopris West, 1992, for more information about reinforcement systems and token economies.

Assessment for transitions planning: A guide for special education teachers and related services personnel, by G. B. Clark, Austin, TX: Pro-Ed, 1998, for a discussion of assessment techniques, accommodations, and roles of various professionals in the transition process.

Individual transition plans: The teacher's guide for helping youth with special needs, by Paul Wehman, Austin, TX: Pro-Ed, 1995, for a collection of sample transition plans, including examples for adolescents with emotional and behavioral disorders.

Behavior problems? Try groups! by Maggie Coleman and Jo Webber, *Academic Therapy, 23,* 1988, 265–274, for an article written for teachers who would like to try groups with adolescent students.

Making the list: Understanding, selecting, and replicating effective teen pregnancy prevention programs, by J. Solomon and J. J. Card, 2004 Washington, DC: National Campaign to Prevent Teen Pregnancy, for a publication funded by the Centers for Disease Control and Prevention (CDC) that provides information for parents and providers on evidence-based teen pregnancy prevention programs,

Preventing drug abuse among children and adolescents: A research based guide by the National Institute on Drug Abuse (NIH Publication No. 04-4212[A], Bethesda, MD: National Institutes of Health, 2003.

Reclaiming youth at risk: Our hope for the future, by Larry Brendtro, Martin Brokenleg, and Steve Van Bockern, Bloomington, IN: National Education Service, 1990, for ideas for teaching troubled adolescents according to Native American values.

School violence intervention: A practical handbook, by Arnold Goldstein and Jane Conoley, New York: Guilford Press, 1997, for an ecological approach to dealing with gangs, building individual and community resilience, and school violence.

Talk about sex: The battles over sex education in the United States, by J. M. Irvine, Berkeley: University of California Press, 2003, for a history of the culture wars over sex education.

Teaching occupational social skills, by Nick Elksnin and Linda Elksnin, Austin, TX: Pro-Ed, 1998, for a book focused on teaching adolescents job-related social skills.

Transition and school-based services, by Sharon DeFur and Jim Patton, Austin, TX: Pro-Ed, 1999, for an interdisciplinary perspective for enhancing the transition process.

RELATED WEBSITES

http://www.drugabuse.gov

This website for the National Institute on Drug Abuse contains current information on prevention and treatment of substance abuse.

http://www.modelprograms.samhsa.gov

Describes programs that have been evaluated for effectiveness in preventing and treating substance abuse.

http://www.nationaleatingdisorders.org/

Offers curriculum and program materials for practitioners, along with information on eating disorders and research grant opportunities.

http://www.4girls.gov
This forum promotes healthy behaviors in girls between the ages of 10 and 16 by providing information on health issues and handling relationships.

http://www.teenpregnancy.org
Contains fact sheets, answers to common questions, and survey results regarding sexual activity, sexual attitudes, and pregnancy prevention.

http://www.ncsby.org
This website for the National Center on Sexual Behavior of Youth provides information on the management of sexual behavior problems in children.

http://www.nichcy.org
The National Information Center for Children and Youth with Disabilities site offers information regarding sexual education for children with disabilities.

http://www.glsen.org
The Gay, Lesbian and Straight Education Network provides details about forming gay–straight alliances as school clubs with the goals of making schools safe for GLB youth.

http://reclaiming.com
Provides resources, including conference information, training programs, research, and publications, for parents, professionals, and policymakers concerned with children and youth in conflict in their homes, schools, and communities.

CHAPTER

12 Special Issues in the Schools

QUESTIONS TO CONSIDER

- What factors promote a context in which children and youth commit violent acts?
- What was the impact of the Columbine High School massacre on public policies and perceptions? How might these policies and perceptions affect students with EBD?
- What is the relationship of youth violence to Positive Behavioral Interventions and Supports (PBIS)?
- What are the main components of PBIS? What are the challenges for those attempting to implement PBIS?
- Why are effective academic interventions important for students with EBD?
- How has the NCLB Act affected instruction of students with EBD in public schools?
- What are the most efficacious instructional strategies for special education students and students with EBD specifically?
- What are common strategies and models for supporting students with EBD in inclusive situations?
- What are the benefits and challenges of inclusion in general education curriculum and classes for students with EBD?
- Why is it important to advocate for students with EBD in today's schools?

Orientation

In this special issues chapter, we review four topics of interest to school personnel that are related to educating students with EBD. We begin with a section about **youth violence,** which has in the past decade become a source of great concern for all educators and for the public at large. The second section addresses one popular method of addressing school violence and planning for students with EBD from a preventative stance utilizing school- and classwide support strategies. **Positive Behavioral Interventions and Supports (PBIS),** or **Positive Behavior Support (PBS),** is a systems model for addressing student behavior in constructive ways. PBS has been initiated in school districts across the country; in some instances, whole states have ascribed to PBS programs. Related to the concept of violence prevention and positive approaches to discipline is the need for effective instruction and successful academic achievement. Students who do well in school seldom display inappropriate and violent behavior. Thus, the third section addresses **academic interventions** for students with EBD. Academic achievement for these students is particularly important due to its direct relationship to positive, long-term outcomes and behavior improvement. Academic instruction for students with EBD is often neglected in favor of behavior management programming. This interrelationship of academic instruction and behavior management is important for teachers to address. The final section reviews implications and strategies for successful **inclusion** of students with EBD in general education curriculum and classrooms. First promoted with the 1975 *Education for All Handicapped Children Act (P.L. 94-142),* inclusion is now common practice as a result of the NCLB Act and IDEA 2004, discussed in previous chapters. However, mass inclusion of special education students as a matter of policy continues to be a source of contention among advocates and school personnel.

Overview

Today's society offers unprecedented challenges in the field of education. For over a decade a series of tragic school shootings by students and by outsiders resulting in the death of innocent school children and their teachers have sent us searching for answers about why such violence occurred and about how we can prevent it in the future. Although none of the shooters were SPED students, psychological pathology appears evident in most of the cases. What would cause a young person to want to kill his peers and teachers? What would cause an adult to want to kill children? We explore these questions as they pertain to programs to prevent such violent acts and to teach students to engage productively in learning activities. We also explore how the IDEA 2004 and ongoing implementation of the NCLB Act have narrowed the focus of public education and in so doing changed the emphasis in educational programs for children with EBD from primarily addressing students' emotional well-being and social behavior to singularly targeting rigorous academic preparation. Evidence-based academic interventions are now mandated and promoted for all SPED students, with few exceptions, and are expected to increase gains across the standardized academic curriculum. Related to the shifted emphasis to academic achievement for students with EBD is the move to reintegrate these students into general education curriculum and classrooms in order to achieve the NCLB goals. What do we know about effective academic instruction, inclusion, and students with EBD? How can we create a balanced approach to inclusive programming for these students?

Youth Violence

Since the mid-1990s, a series of tragic school shootings has focused national attention on the issue of youth violence. On April 20, 1999, two teens killed 12 classmates and a teacher before turning the guns on themselves at Columbine High School in Littleton, Colorado. The Columbine tragedy, perhaps because it occurred in a middle-class neighborhood and so many were killed, became a standard for subsequent actions and attention to the issue of youth violence (U.S. Department of Health and Human Services [DHHS], 2001). Distressingly, a school shooting in March 2000, near Flint, Michigan, involved a 6-year-old boy who shot and killed a second-grade classmate (Rosenblatt, 2000) and as recently as Fall 2006, school shootings in Colorado, Wisconsin, and Pennsylvania prompted rapid federal responses ("Dealing with school violence," 2006). Despite these tragic events, the schools have been declared the safest environment in children's lives (DHHS, 2001; Donohue, Schiraldi, & Zeidenberg, 1998) and the rate of juvenile violent crime arrests has consistently declined since 1994 (Office of Juvenile Justice and Delinquency Prevention [OJJDP], 2006). However, public perception has been the opposite. As a result of this perception, more attention has been directed at determining what causes youth to become violent and what we can do about it. Although special education students were not implicated in school shootings, these students, especially those with EBD, may well be impacted by reactionary exclusionary and zero-tolerance policies adopted across the country. This section includes a discussion of the issue of youth violence and its relationship to special education, especially the education of youth with EBD.

Incidence and Nature of the Problem

Fortunately, in 2006 it was reported that the rate of juvenile violent crime arrests were at its lowest in a generation (OJJDP, 2006). The OJJDP (2006) reported a 65 percent decline in murders committed by juveniles from the mid-1990s to 2002, mostly due to a decrease in minority males killing minority males and a corresponding decrease in crimes committed with firearms. In 2003, 6 percent of high school students said they carried a weapon on school property in the past 30 days, down from 12 percent in 1993. Even so, the Children's Defense Fund (CDF; 2005) reported that each day in the United States 4,356 children are arrested, 181 for violent crimes. One in 12 murders in the United States involved a juvenile offender in 2002 and although arrest rates declined, the proportion of females arrested increased, especially for assault (OJJDP, 2006).

Furthermore, in 2003, school victimization rates for violent crimes (rape, sexual assault, robbery, aggravated assault) were estimated at 28 per 1,000 students (DeVoe, Peter, Noonan, Snyder, & Baum, 2005). In a national Youth Risk Behavior Survey (YRBS) in 2003, the Centers for Disease Control (CDC; 2004) found that nearly one in 10 high school students reported being threatened or injured with a weapon on school property during the preceding 12 months and 5.4 percent of 16,296 respondents reported failure to attend school due to safety concerns. The OJJDP (2006) also reported that gangs in urban areas are responsible for a disproportionate share of violent and nonviolent offenses, a continuing problem.

Despite relatively good news regarding the declining trend of violent acts committed by children and youth, children continue to be victims of violent acts by adults. It is estimated that 90 percent of homicide victims under age 12, and 75 percent of such victims who are 12–17 years old are killed by adults (Donohue et al., 1998). Two of the 2006 school shootings involved adults killing children ("Dealing with school violence," 2006). Additionally, each day 2,482 children in the United States are confirmed as abused or neglected (CDF, 2005). As early as 1993, the OJJDP began to call for a national commitment of public and private resources to reverse the disturbing trends in juvenile violence, juvenile victimization, and family disintegration in the United States (Wilson & Howell, 1993). This was 6 years before the Columbine massacre

Historical studies of school violence typically condemned inner-city/urban schools as the primary source for such tragedies (Smith & Smith, 2006). However, statistics show that violent acts occur across geographic and socioeconomic boundaries in today's schools (Vossekuil, Fein, Reddy, Borum, & Modzeleski, 2002). Likewise, males who have been responsible for more than 15 school shootings in the past decade (Kimmel & Mahler, 2003) may no longer be seen as the primary perpetrators. Girls are increasingly becoming part of the problem (Hudley, Wakefield, & Britsch, 2001; OJJDP, 2006).

Speculation about what causes young people to become violent more commonly targets environmental factors than intrinsic characteristics (Edelman, 1995; Kashani, Jones, Bumby, & Thomas, 1999; Knitzer et al., 1989; Patterson, 1983; Sugai & Horner, 2001; Walker et al., 2004). It is generally believed that children become violent primarily as a reaction to noxious economic and family factors and inadequate social policies. It is also believed that combinations of risk factors greatly increase the risk of negative outcomes for children. The factors contributing to youth violence are not greatly different from those contributing to emotional and behavioral disorders in youth. In terms of youth violence, Webber (1997a) arranged the most common causal factors into three categories:

1. Family factors, such as poverty, drug abuse, divorce, sexual and physical abuse, and unskilled parenting
2. Societal factors, such as unequal educational opportunity, media violence, and easy access to firearms
3. Individual factors, such as a difficult temperament, school failure, psychological disorders, and drug abuse

Enduring physical or emotional abuse is strongly correlated to later violent behavior (Salazar, Wingood, & DiClemente, 2004) with emotional abuse the better predictor of higher rates of aggression and hostility (Hamerman, Pope, & Czaja, 2002).

Additional family factors such as the level of parental bonding and involvement and parental criminality correlate with increased likelihood of violent behavior (Hawkins et al., 2000). Living in poverty and numerous related factors can also predict violent behavior (Hawkins et al., 2000). Children and youth living in poverty more often use drugs, witness violent crime in their neighborhood, are frequently around guns and other weapons, and experience less supervision from adults. Such direct exposure to violence is often predictive of later violent acts (Bolger & Patterson, 2003; Ozer & Weinstein, 2004), particularly for boys who have reported reacting with anger and a desire to retaliate after experiencing aggression (Foster, Kumpermic, & Price, 2004). Girls reactions to violence may put them at risk for EBD because they report greater levels of depression, anxiety, and posttraumatic stress after witnessing violence (Cummings, Pepler, & Moore, 1999; Sternberg, Lamb, & Guterman, 2006). Poverty may also result in poor nutrition and exposure to toxins that could negatively impact the ability to regulate one's own behavior. Diets lacking in B and C vitamins as well as magnesium or iron have been noted to trigger severe aggression as has exposure to high amounts of lead or other toxic materials common in the inner city and older homes (Hawkins et al., 2000).

As you learned in Chapter 10, school factors such as bullying and alienation seem to be related to increased acts of violence among youth (Kimmell & Mahler, 2003). Increased aggression might also be perpetuated by repeated failure and ineffective instruction, unclear expectations and consequences, singular punishment-oriented discipline models, failure to accommodate different learning needs, and lack of supervision (Mayer, 1995; Sugai & Horner, 1999). One study explored the relationship of special education status to student acts of aggression (Kaplan & Cornell, 2005). This research suggested that half of all threats of violence in schools stem from SPED students, the majority made by students with EBD. Seventy percent of these threats were deemed transient; yet given the disproportionate numbers of suspensions, expulsions, and arrests of students with EBD, we might assume that these students might benefit from violence prevention strategies.

Viewing the causes of youth violence from a multilevel perspective posits that prevention and treatment programs would also address multiple levels of the ecological context. Webber (1997a) presents a model for addressing youth violence based on the transactional–ecological framework conceptualized by Felner and Felner (1989). From this transactional–ecological perspective, youth violence is a function of: (1) unique individual characteristics, (2) the context in which the individual resides, and (3) the processes or interactions that account for developmental change. Thus, prevention and intervention strategies and programs must address individual risk factors, harmful contextual transactions, and societal contributors. Felner and Felner categorize treatment approaches as person-focused programs, transaction-focused programs, and environmentally focused programs. Given the myriad of violence prevention and intervention programs currently published (Dwyer et al., 1998; Fitzsimmons & Warger, 2000; Goldstein & Conoley, 1997; Lectenberger, 1999; Walker, 2000; Wilson & Lipsey, 2005), school personnel may need a framework for judging treatment efficacy. Table 12.1 organizes examples of violence prevention and intervention programs according to the transactional–ecological model.

Societal Responses

Societal responses to the Columbine massacre and subsequent school shootings initially ranged from recommendations to "crack down" (lockdowns, detector dogs, cops on campus, segregated educational facilities, uniforms, transparent backpacks, trying children as adults in criminal cases, suspension, expulsion) to calls for funding more counselors, mentors, recreational opportunities, and for programs for building psychological resilience (Cloud, 1999; Goldstein & Conoley, 1997; Lacayo, 1997; Morse, 2000). A 1999 White

TABLE 12.1 Youth Violence Programs Viewed in a Transactional–Ecological Framework

Person-Focused Programs

Assumption: The cause for violence lies solely within the individual. Treatment programs target behavior change and acquisition of knowledge.
Examples: Skill training, academic instruction, reinforcement systems, punishment, early childhood stimulation, parent shadowing, counseling, mentoring programs.

Transaction-Focused Programs

Assumption: Violence is a function of unique characteristics combined with unique environmental factors. Treatment targets specific relationships and interactions within the individual's immediate environment.
Examples: Functional behavioral assessment, antecedent manipulation, situation-specific skill training, support groups, parent involvement programs, transition programs, joint counseling, programs enhancing existing relationships.

Environmentally Focused Programs

Assumption: The cause of the violence lies solely outside the individual. Treatment aims to alleviate harmful environmental conditions.
Examples: Family preservation programs, school restructuring, flexible work and school scheduling, alternative schools, nutrition programs, health care and welfare reform, shared agency funding, community–school partnerships, gun control, media regulation.

Adapted from Webber, J. (1997a). Comprehending youth violence: A practicable perspective. *Remedial and Special Education, 18*(2), 94–104. Reprinted with permission of the publisher.

House strategy session resulted in recommendations to promote antiviolence education and program development alliances among various groups (i.e., media personnel; gun manufacturers; youth groups; federal, state, and local officials; and medical and police organizations) (Mollison, 1999). The Departments of Education, Justice, and Health and Human Services set aside several funding sources specifically for school violence prevention (Robelen, 1999).

Multiple national and state efforts began to develop and disseminate violence prevention and intervention programs. For example, in 2001, the U.S. Surgeon General outlined several youth violence prevention programs urging research and program evaluation to determine efficacy, calling on more citizens to become engaged in redressing the problem of youth violence. The U.S. Department of Education formed the Office of Safe and Drug-Free Schools (OSDFS) to facilitate violence prevention programs, influence program policy and legislative proposals, and to participate with other federal agencies to develop a research agenda for drug and violence prevention. Additionally, the Safe and Drug-Free Schools and Communities Advisory Committee, authorized by the NCLB Act, was established to provide advice regarding federal, state, and local programs designated to create safe and drug-free schools, and on issues related to crisis planning (Department of Education, 2006).

The Centers for Disease Control (2004) set a 2010 adolescent health objective to reduce the prevalence of physical fighting and carrying a weapon on school property. In 2006, in response to yet more school shootings, President George W. Bush called a White

House Summit on school violence. Summit participants discussed the need for better communication, more values education, better coordination with police, and community vigilance ("Dealing with school violence," 2006). Unfortunately, the summit failed to address proposed federal cuts to school safety funding and the continued easy access to guns in the United States.

Shortly after the Columbine incident, a safe schools guide titled *Early Warning, Timely Response: A Guide to Safe Schools* (Dwyer et al., 1998) was distributed by the U.S. Departments of Education and Justice, free of charge, to all schools in the country (Robelen, 1999). The recommendations in this document reflect the notion that youth violence is caused by a multitude of factors and should be addressed from an ecological perspective. Many of the recommendations correspond with what we believe to be best practices for students with EBD. Table 12.2 contains some of the recommendations discussed in the safe schools guide.

A second guide, *Safeguarding Our Children: An Action Guide*, was distributed a short time later (Center for Effective Collaboration and Practice (CECP), National Association of School Psychologists (NASP), 2000). A follow-up to the 1998 guide, this document recommended that communities develop a comprehensive team approach to prevention, involving educators, mental health professionals, law enforcement officials, parents, and students. A primary recommendation urged communities to provide immediate and intensive intervention for students who continue to experience significant emotional and behavior problems through coordinated, comprehensive, sustained, and family-focused services.

The public pressure to ensure safe schools and address youth violence was also evident in the hearings on the reauthorization of the IDEA in 1997 and 2004. In 1996, testimony was presented to Congress regarding the lack of parity in discipline procedures for

TABLE 12.2 ***A Summary of Recommendations from* Early Warning, Timely Response: A Guide to Safe Schools**

1. Emphasize positive relationships among students and staff and treat each other with respect.
2. Students with severe behavior problems or who are abused or neglected would benefit from sustained, multiple, coordinated interventions targeting family and child needs.
3. Students who are at risk for violence and aggression generally need a combination of several interventions, including effective academic instruction, character education, skill training, structured leisure time programs, therapeutic treatment, opportunities to share concerns, support from school to the world of work, and protection from psychological harm.
4. A full range of services and placements should be available for at-risk students and their families.
5. School personnel and family members would benefit from professional development and support services.
6. More students with severe behavior problems might benefit from functional behavioral assessment and special education services.
7. Expulsion, suspension, disciplinary alternative education programs, and other punitive measures have not been found to be singularly effective for violence prevention.
8. School personnel should identify problems, intervene early, and assess progress toward solutions, while sharing this information with families and the community at large.

Source: Dwyer et al., 1998.

students with and without disabilities (Conroy et al., 1999). On the one hand, school administrators, concerned with school safety, complained that they needed easier procedures to expel or suspend special education students who may present a threat to others. On the other hand, SPED advocates argued against any cessation of educational services to SPED students, particularly when the targeted behavior may be a manifestation of their disability, such as emotional/behavioral disorders. The IDEA 2004 provides a definition of "serious bodily injury" to assist schools in understanding when the level of risk warrants exclusion from school. This definition reads as follows:

> ". . . bodily injury which involves (1) a substantial risk of death; (2) extreme physical pain; (3) protracted and obvious disfigurement; or (4) protracted loss or impairment of the function of a bodily member, organ, or mental faculty" (ee 18 U.S.C. 1365).

While protecting SPED students' right to a free appropriate public education, these provisions also allow removal of students who bring dangerous weapons to school and/or possess illegal drugs. The IDEA 2004 requires school personnel to assess the disturbing behavior in relation to contextual variables (functional behavioral assessments), as discussed in Chapter 7, and to address troubling behavior with positive behavioral interventions (eg. PBS) (Conroy et al., 1999; Yell, 2006).

The contention surrounding the protective IDEA discipline provisions represents the variability of public responses to youth violence. Some advocate punishment, even for preschoolers (della Cava, 2005; Rimer, 2004); zero tolerance of even minor behavioral infractions (Skiba, 2004); and incarceration (Morse, 2000). Zero-tolerance policies, popular after the Columbine shootings, have resulted in increased rates of suspensions and expulsions for even something as minor as a second-grader swearing or a kindergartener bringing a toy ax with his firefighter Halloween costume ("Second grader suspended," 2004; Grant, 2006). Many experts dispute continued use of zero-tolerance policies in light of evidence to support various proactive violence prevention programs (Skiba, Rausch, & Ritter, 2004; Wilson & Lipsey, 2005). Some of these recommended programs are based on psychoeducational principles (Raywid & Oshiyama, 2000), cognitive theories (Kashani et al., 1999), and ecological approaches (Goldstein & Conoley, 1997; Van Acker & Talbott, 1999; Walker et al., 2004). The Positive Behavior Support (PBS) model that is discussed in the next section was developed partly in response to the IDEA discipline requirements and is often mentioned as a preferred school-based violence prevention model (Fitzsimmons & Warger, 2000; Sack, 2000; Van Acker & Talbott, 1999).

Implications for Schools

As you have learned, most current recommendations for school personnel relative to youth violence prevention are based in ecological theory and call for multilevel approaches. In Fall 2006 the National Consortium of School Violence Prevention Researchers and Practitioners (NCSVPP) published a position statement pertaining to school shootings. The statement delineated four key elements to keep children safe while at school:

1. *Balance:* A balanced approach with well-integrated programs that make sense and are effective and address physical safety, educational practices, and programs that support the social emotional and behavioral needs of students.

2. *Communication:* Maintaining close communication and trust with students and other community members to encourage reporting suspicious behaviors to school personnel and to look for violence indicators.
3. *Connectedness:* Students need to feel that they belong to a school community and are valued members of that community. Alienated students are at high risk for violent activities so school personnel need to build positive connections with these students.
4. *Support:* Students may experience stressors and need support from school and community personnel in the way of multilevel (universal, targeted, and intensive) strategies to address bullying, incivility, depression, and anxiety.

The NCSVPP (2006) also criticized the ready availability of guns to youth and adults with emotional problems. Finally, the position statement recommended that schools, with stakeholder groups, engage in comprehensive planning and coordination, data collection and analysis, and use of evidenced-based interventions to prevent violence and disruption. Wilson and Lipsey (2005) conducted a meta-analysis of effectiveness studies of school-based violence prevention programs, finding 219 research studies. They organized these programs into four broad categories: (1) universal programs (classwide behavioral strategies, cognitively oriented programs, social skills training, and counseling), (2) selected/indicated programs (person-specific behavioral, cognitive, social skills, counseling, and peer mediation), (3) comprehensive programs (multilevel programs within and outside of classrooms to include parents and administrators), and (4) special school/classes (SPED self-contained classes, alternative high schools, schools within a school).

The programs targeted preschool through adolescent students but were predominantly developed for elementary and middle school students. Generally these authors found that the universal (effect Size [ES] = .18), selected/indicated (ES = .29), and comprehensive programs (ES = .06) were successful in reducing fighting, name calling, intimidation, and other negative behaviors among high-risk students. However, they found no evidence that these programs would prevent something of great magnitude perpetrated by very disturbed youth. Studies involving special programs (ES = .06) did not find significant impact on disruptive and aggressive behavior. The panacea for eliminating youth violence has not yet been found, but promising practices seem to indicate a systems or ecological approach involving psychoeducational, cognitive, and behavioral components. These components need to be applied to all students in a comprehensive manner and include intensive, primarily positive, strategies for those students deemed to be at risk (e.g., recent rejection by someone close, multiple aggressive and disruptive behaviors, history of mental health treatment, dislike for popular students, expressions of a desire to kill others, cruelty to animals, fascination with and easy access to firearms; Morse, 2000).

Positive Behavioral Interventions and Supports

In response to mandates in the 1997 reauthorization of the IDEA and in an effort to address youth violence and antisocial behavior in schools, Sugai and Horner (1999) proposed that educators, families, and community agents adopt a systems approach to school discipline, especially for those students who are at risk. Based on what was known to be best practices for managing challenging behaviors, these authors developed a model for delivering and maintaining such practices in schools, the goal of which was to reduce the incidence and prevalence of antisocial behavior. Positive Behavioral Interventions and Supports (PBIS) or Positive Behavioral Supports (PBS), as the model came to be known, promotes the sustained use of effective school practices such as (1) functional assessment strategies; (2) instructional and curricular modifications and restructuring; (3) social and self-management instruction; (4) collaboration with parents, teachers, administrators, and community agencies; and (5) placement in prosocial, integrated, and inclusive settings for all students (Sugai & Horner, 1999). The practices are offered in the way of supports, or accommodations and adjustments, to the environment for the purpose of promoting successful student behavior and learning.

PBS emphasizes problem prevention using a three-tiered model of intervention across four different school-based systems (Horner & Sugai, 2000). The three-tiered model is based on the notion that most students in a school (about 80% of students) will respond appropriately to universal group interventions (teaching and promoting school rules and/or expectations and prompting compliance). However, students who are at risk for antisocial behavior (5–15% of all students) may need more directed and specialized group strategies to ensure appropriate behavior (e.g., social skills and self-management training). Finally, those students already immersed in an antisocial lifestyle (1–7% of the student body) will probably need intensive individually determined interventions (e.g., functionally based behavioral intervention plans). The students needing the most intensive interventions usually account for 50 percent of the discipline referrals in a school; they may also very likely have emotional and behavioral disorders. The four school systems targeted for implementation of the designated supports are (1) the schoolwide system, (2) classroom systems, (3) non-classroom systems (e.g., cafeteria, playground, hallways, bus), and (4) individual students.

Tier 1 of the PBS model is referred to as *primary prevention* and is applied to the entire student body. Schools are encouraged to establish, define, teach, and promote five or fewer schoolwide rules or expectations. School personnel, after choosing their expectations, behaviorally define them for all school settings. Figure 12.1 is an example of behaviorally defined schoolwide expectations for four settings.

At the beginning of each school year, teachers conduct lessons about schoolwide expectations. Once students have been taught the proper way to behave, teachers are to prompt appropriate behaviors before problems arise (called precorrection) and promote correct behavior through systematic reinforcement, components from a behavioral framework (Sugai, Horner, & Gresham, 2002). Schoolwide reinforcement systems may include "gotchas" for when students spontaneously self-correct behavior, "happening hornets" for students who are following a school rule, behavior report cards, and recognition assemblies (Netzel & Eber, 2003). Tokens are often turned in for school prize drawings, special club benefits, special trips, and so on.

Within classroom systems PBS strategies should include (1) clearly defined rules and routines, (2) direct instruction of appropriate behavior, (3) regular reinforcement of appropriate behavior, (4) consistent consequences for behavioral infractions, (5) curriculum matched to student interest (Clarke et al., 1995) and ability level (Mayer, 1995), (6) high rates of student academic success, (7) smooth transitions between activities, (8) teacher assistance (e.g., coaching and precorrection), (9) active supervision, and (10) coordination with the schoolwide management system (Lewis & Sugai, 1999). Many studies have been

	Be Safe	Be Respectful	Be Responsible
Classroom	a. Keep hands, feet, and objects to yourself b. Stay in your seat c. Wait patiently for your turn	a. Work quietly b. Listen when the teacher is talking c. Use kind words and actions	a. Follow directions the first time they are given b. Clean up after yourself c. Raise your hand for permission to speak
Hall	a. Keep hands, feet and objects to yourself b. Keep hands at your sides	a. Walk quietly b. Hold the door for others	a. Walk on the right side of the hall
Restroom	a. Keep feet on the floor b. Keep water in the sink c. Wash hands after use d. Put towels in the trash can	a. Knock on the stall door b. Give people privacy c. Use Level 1 or 2 voice	a. Flush toilet after use b. Clean up after yourself c. Return to the class quickly
Bus	a. Stay in your seat b. Face the front c. Keep hands, feet, and objects to yourself	a. Use Level 1 or 2 voice	a. Keep items in backpack

FIGURE 12.1 Positive Behavior Supports: Behaviorally Defined Schoolwide Expectations across Four Settings

conducted regarding the positive impact of such universal interventions in a variety of public schools settings; most suggest that about 80 percent of minor disruptive behavior can be quelled using PBS strategies (Gresham, 2002; Scott & Barrett, 2002; Sugai, Sprague, Horner, & Walker, 2000; Walker & Shinn, 2002).

Tier 2 or *secondary prevention* targets students considered "at risk" for antisocial behavior. These children are selected from the general population through two primary methods: systematic screening or analysis of office discipline referral (ODR) data (Sugai et al., 2000). Students who are not responding to Tier 1 interventions might additionally need direct instruction of social skills and self-management strategies or specific academic assistance and modifications (Walker & Shinn, 2002). For example, Anderson, Fisher, Marchant, Young, and Smith (2006) used social skills training, a "cool card" prompt, a self-recording form, and positive reinforcement to reduce inappropriate anger responses in two fourth-grade general education boys. After only 6 weeks, the "cool card" intervention was discontinued and both students maintained appropriate anger responses for the remainder of the school year. Literature regarding PBS suggests many of the more entrenched behaviors present in students not previously impacted by Tier 1 interventions will respond to Tier 2 strategies (Gresham, 2002; Scott & Barrett, 2002; Sugai et al., 2000; Walker & Shinn, 2002).

The PBS Tier 3 or *tertiary prevention* utilizes the functional behavior analysis process to provide individualized interventions for children who have not responded to interventions in Tiers 1 and 2 (Gresham, 2002; Scott & Barrett, 2002; Sugai et al., 2000; Walker & Shinn, 2002). As you learned in Chapter 7, FBAs are used to determine those variables that cue and/or reinforce inappropriate behavior in order that interventions can target modifications of those variables and instruction of new functional replacement skills. FBA-based behavioral interventions have been found to be successful when the assessment consisted of a standardized protocol for descriptive observational data and teacher interviews (Kamps, Wendland, & Culpepper, 2006). Also important to the FBA process are team collaboration and functional analysis to test hypotheses. Specific analysis of the influence of antecedents on behavior, known as structural analysis, has also lead to effective interventions with students in general education classrooms with serious problem behaviors (Sasso, Peck, & Garrison-Harrell, 1998; Scott & Barrett, 2004; Stichter, Hudson, & Sasso, 2005).

The PBS model is a proactive tool for preventing problem behavior in schools through instructional rather than singularly punitive strategies (Safran & Oswald, 2003). A schoolwide approach facilitates universal techniques for viewing and solving many of the precursors to violence, such as bullying and other forms of harassment, that occur in the public schools (Barton, 2006). Paramount to the PBS process is the establishment of a schoolwide PBS team and the use of systematic data collection to determine what problems are chronic within the school environments and the nature of those problems (Todd, Horner, Sugai, & Colvin, 1999). Data most often utilized includes office disciplinary (ODR) reports such as the types and number of office referrals and the location and time of infractions, suspension statistics, attendance, school arrests, and descriptions of referrals to special education (Skiba, Person, & Williams, 1997; Sugai et al., 2000; Turnbull et al., 2002). Table 12.3 lists the major components of a school-based PBS model.

TABLE 12.3 Major Components of a School-Based PBS Model

1. A schoolwide philosophy that seeks to improve relationships between students and school personnel and promote social and academic success
2. Quality staff development for administrators and teachers
3. A few positively stated, clearly defined rules or expectations
4. Expected student behaviors that are taught directly and reinforced regularly
5. Clearly defined problem behaviors and subsequent consequences
6. A team, including a school administrator, for behavior support planning and problem solving meeting often at regular intervals
7. Procedures for addressing emergency and dangerous situations
8. Regular staff feedback regarding problem behaviors
9. A budget for the PBS team to purchase reinforcers, curriculum, and staff development activities
10. All school staff involved in schoolwide and classwide interventions
11. Formal strategies for informing parents about expected student behavior
12. Regular strategies for involving parents and the community in school activities

Source: Lewis & Sugai (1999)

It is important to note that PBS has been criticized in respect to students with EBD. One criticism is that PBS is not oriented toward children with more severe emotional disorders, such as schizophrenia or bipolar disorder, who often have medication management issues as well as systemic needs (Vaughn, 2006). Vaughn (2006) also criticized PBS because of the lack of interface with wraparound services. However, Eber Sugai, Smith, and Scott (2002) discussed several recommendations for integrating PBS activities within a school-based wraparound program. Finally, numerous critics have expressed that the implementation of this process with children with EBD participating in the inclusive setting is impractical (Nelson et al., 1999; Scott et al., 2004). For example, the work of Scott and his colleagues (2004) found little agreement among collaborative team members regarding the function of a child's behavior and subsequent program components.

Additionally, the shift from a punishment model to a positive support model is difficult for most school personnel (Scott, 2002). Teachers and school administrators have many excuses for not wanting to directly address behavior and use prompts and reinforcement. Furthermore, frequent school personnel turnover requires that school districts commit to continuous improvement and training in order to sustain the model, sometimes a difficult request in the present academic accountability era. In spite of these criticisms and challenges, PBS has been found to be an effective model for reducing office referrals, promoting effective classroom instruction, and supporting students of varying abilities (Leedy, Bates, & Safran, 2004; Nelson, Martella, & Marchand-Martella, 2002; Safron & Oswald, 2003).

Although PBS has been relatively widely accepted and found to be effective, most school administrators remain singularly focused on academic achievement, as mandated in the NCLB Act, to the exclusion of children's social and emotional well-being. In fact many schools have eliminated much needed mental health services to children (Pavri, 2004). Eliminating counselors and counseling activities means that these activities must be provided by teachers who report they feel under-trained for this assignment. Pavri (2004) reports that teachers also indicated reduced time to provide direct instruction and positive supports such as social skills and self-management instruction due to increased emphasis on academic preparation resulting from the NCLB Act. With more attention and resources aimed at achieving higher academic standards, students with EBD and their teachers are rapidly being incorporated into general education programs, often without necessary effective supports and services.

Academic Interventions

Achieving at grade level as measured by standardized tests presents a particular challenge for students with EBD because most of them manifest substantial deficits in reading, reading comprehension, spelling, math, and written language (Cullinan, Evans, Epstein, & Ryser, 2003; Mattison, Hooper, & Glassberg, 2002; Nelson, Benner, Lane, & Smith, 2004; Reid, Gonzalez, Nordness, Trout, & Epstein, 2004; Trout, Nordness, Pierce, & Epstein, 2003). For example, Trout and colleagues (2003), in a review of 35 studies from 1961–2000, found that in 31 of the studies (91%) students with EBD tested below grade level or were found to be one or more years behind their peers in academic achievement. Furthermore, these deficits appear to remain stable over time or become more pronounced in older students (Anderson, Kutash, & Duchnowski, 2001). These authors found that children with EBD performed better than children with learning disabilities in both reading and mathematics in kindergarten and first grade. Yet, by fifth and sixth grade the reverse was true with students with learning disabilities (LDs) outperforming students with EBD. Another study explored longitudinal academic performance of students with EBD at ages 8–11, 12–14, and 15–18 (Mattison, et al., 2002). Academic lags were noted at each evaluation period, with 93 percent of primary school students with EBD, 97 percent of middle school students with EBD, and 94 percent of high school students with EBD demonstrating mathematics underachievement. Nelson and his colleagues (2004) confirmed these results with a comparison study of children and adolescents with EBD. Specifically, decreases were noted in mathematics at the secondary level. Reading and written language performance remained stable over time, yet still behind typical peers.

Directly related to academic skill deficits, perhaps even causing them, students with EBD also tend to manifest language deficits (Benner, Nelson, & Epstein, 2002; Nelson, Benner, Neill, & Stage, 2006). Many facets of language ability have been explored in relation to this population, with studies suggesting difficulty in expressive, receptive, and pragmatic ability as well as possible deficits in language processing (McDonough, 1989; Rinaldi, 2003; Rogers-Adkinson, 2003; Warr-Leeper, Wright, & Mack, 1993). Effective language skills are necessary for successful academic learning in all areas (Catts, Fey, Zhang, & Tomblin, 1999), so language deficits very likely predict academic deficits. For example, in a study using structural equation modeling, Nelson and colleagues (2006) found that language skills significantly influenced academic skills and academic fluency in a population of 126 students with EBD in grades K–12.

Approximately 60–80 percent of children with EBD manifest language deficits, often undiagnosed (Donahue, Hartas, & Cole, 1999; Nelson, Benner, & Cheney, 2005), and it appears that language delays increase over time, suggesting that linked maturational lags in language skills and socioemotional development create a compounding effect upon each other (Hill & Coufal, 2006; Nelson, Benner, & Rogers-Adkinson, 2003). The American Institute for Research (AIR; 2003) advocates language assessment as a part of the multidisciplinary evaluation for students with EBD. Yet, speech-language pathologists (SLPs) rarely participate in prereferral or initial assessment and evaluation activities (Hyter, Rogers-Adkinson, Self, Simmons, & Janz, 2001).

Furthermore, despite historical data confirming that students with EBD manifest below-average IQ and language and academic deficits (even when accounting for the low IQ), school-based interventions and IEP goals have tended to focus on behavioral and social competence, often to the exclusion of academic programming (Bos, Coleman, & Vaughn, 2002; Knitzer et al., 1990; Levy & Vaughn, 2002; Wehby, Symons, Canale, & Go, 1998), and usually to the exclusion of language development goals (Nelson et al., 2005). However, as a result of the increased focus on academic mastery for students with disabilities mandated in the NCLB Act and IDEA 2004, academic preparation of students with EBD is currently receiving more attention.

Academic Strategies for Students with EBD

The NCLB Act with IDEA 2004 requires that all students, including those with EBD, master academic content at grade level. Because schools stand to lose resources or be closed down when this does not occur, school administrators are searching for effective ways to boost academic performance of all SPED students on achievement measures, and are pressuring teachers to do more to meet annual yearly progress (AYP) goals. However, long before the federal requirements to increase academic test scores, advocates for students with EBD called for more attention to academic instruction for these students (Knitzer et al., 1990). Historical epidemiological studies found direct relationships between academic failure, particularly reading deficits, and EBD and antisocial behavior (McMichael, 1979; Rutter & Yule, 1970), and additional research confirmed correlations between chronic academic underachievement and negative outcomes (e.g., dropping out of school, arrests) for these students (Knitzer et al., 1990; Wagner, 1995). Research also showed that the longer we neglect academic instruction, the further students fall behind and the more at risk they are for more complex and challenging social and behavioral problems (Walker et al., 2004).

Reading Instruction. Because of the propensity to primarily focus on the social, emotional, and behavioral problems of students with EBD, relatively few studies have targeted academic instruction for these students. Of the studies available, reading instruction has received the most attention (Wehby, Lane, & Falk, 2005). Reading is an essential tool for mastery of content area knowledge, thus the inability to read most often predicts failure in school. In fact, research shows that first graders with the greatest reading deficits are unlikely to catch up with their peers and 90 percent will remain poor readers throughout their school careers (Torgesen, 1998). Others have targeted third grade as the pivotal year in terms of reading mastery (Levy & Vaughn, 2002).

The Reading First Initiative, a component of the NCLB Act, was included in an effort to address the dire consequences for children who do not learn to read early in their school careers, and also to reduce the need for special education services. Reading First requires that reading instruction validated by scientifically based research be provided to all students in primary grades. Scientifically based research has supported concentrating instruction on the following skills: (1) phonological awareness, (2) phonics, (3) fluency, (4) vocabulary, and (5) comprehension (Rivera, Al-Otaiba, & Koorland, 2006). Presumably, we would want to see these skills also taught to students with disabilities including EBD. Unfortunately, effective reading instruction for special education students, particularly those with EBD, has not been common practice (Moody, Vaughn, Hughes, & Fischer, 2000; Vaughn, Levy, Coleman, & Bos, 2002) and relatively few studies have been conducted with this population. Furthermore, several of the existing studies have been criticized in terms of sophistication, depth, and rigor (Mooney, Denny, & Gunter, 2004).

In a review of literature pertaining to reading interventions with elementary students with EBD, Coleman and Vaughn (2000) found only eight studies meeting their inclusion criteria and published between 1975 and 1998. Of these studies, three applied cross-age peer tutoring strategies, four studies applied a distinct instructional strategy, and one (Yell, 1992) compared three strategies (direct instruction, Language Master, and independent practice) on sight word acquisition. Because of the dearth of research in this area, Coleman and Vaughn also conducted a focus group activity with selected special education teachers to discuss effective reading strategies for students with EBD. In both the literature review and the focus group, cross-age peer tutoring was found to be an effective method for increasing reading skills and the motivation to read. Direct instruction of specific skills was also deemed effective by the teachers and supported in one study. The focus group identified two major problems relative to teaching academics and reading to students with EBD: (1) the variability of student responding due to emotional or behavioral issues and (2) the students' lack of motivation to read or complete tasks. Coleman and Vaughn wrote that the relative lack of research regarding reading instruction for students with EBD "is particularly disturbing in light of the push toward inclusion and the federal requirement for access to the general education curriculum" (p. 102).

A subsequent review of 44 observational studies targeting reading instruction with students having LD, EBD, or both disorders found that these students typically received less instruction than general education peers and failed to receive differentiated instruction (Vaughn, Levy, Coleman, & Bos, 2002). These authors also found that teachers used strategies such as whole group instruction and worksheets rather than the recommended scientifically based techniques, and appeared to attend more to behavior management than reading interventions.

In an extension of Coleman's (2000) review, Rivera and colleagues (2006) reviewed 11 studies conducted between 1975 and 2004 with primary grade students with EBD or at risk for EBD and found that all 11 studies reported successful literacy results. Six studies involved phonics, four provided phonemic awareness instruction, two targeted fluency training, and one included comprehension training. This review reported demonstrated efficacy for instructional strategies such as direct instruction, peer tutoring, time delay prompting (teacher waits for student response before providing cues), trial and error (student attempts response on own), and the use of differential reinforcement for reading and task behaviors. Rivera et al., also bemoaning the lack of robust and frequent research regarding reading and students with EBD, concluded that "students with EBD and students with reading and problem behaviors continue to be 'left behind'" (p. 336).

Nevertheless, several studies have produced promising results. In a study using intensive prereading intervention with young children at risk for emotional disturbance and reading problems, researchers found that those students receiving this prereading instruction improved in their phonological awareness, word reading, and rapid naming skills relative to those in a comparison group (Nelson, Benner, & Gonzalez, 2005). Trout and colleagues (2003) applied both a core reading program and supplementary word reading for kindergartners at risk for EBD and reading problems. Those students receiving the word-reading program increased their phonological awareness and word reading relative to their comparison peers. Wehby and colleagues (2005) applied a core reading program with direct phonological awareness training with four kindergarteners with EBD. Although all students improved reading performance (nonsense word and onset fluency measures), gains even with intensive early literacy instruction were moderate and variable.

Al-Otaiba and Fuchs (2002) delineated several characteristics of children like those in the Wehby study who fail to respond to early literacy instruction: (a) deficits in phonological memory and discrimination; (b) deficits in rapid letter naming; (c) intelligence, verbal IQ, and disability status; (d) attention deficits and behavioral problems; (e) orthographic processing; and (f) demographic variables such as age, native language, and parent characteristics. Nevertheless, it appears that young children with EBD respond positively to consistent, systematic reading instruction with supplementary strategies; although given their lower than average IQ, attention and behavioral problems, and emotional variability, more investigations of various instructional components are needed.

Mathematics Instruction. Students with EBD appear not to do any better in mathematics relative to their nondisabled peers than they do in reading. Knitzer and her colleagues (1990) estimated that only 30 percent of students with EBD perform at or above grade level and even after years of special education services their academic performance remains well below national averages in both reading and mathematics (Anderson et al., 2001). Nelson and colleagues (2004) found that 56 percent of students with EBD in their study (ages 5–12) scored below the norm on a mathematics achievement measure, as did 83 percent of adolescents with EBD (ages 13–18). Mathematics has been targeted, as has science, technology, and engineering (STEM disciplines), as essential for U.S. workforce development and for success in the global economy (Goals 2000: Education America Act, PL 103-227). Thus, public high schools are now requiring 4 years of mathematics for graduation, special academies and camps for math instruction have been developed, and early college credit is being offered for more complex mathematics courses (Barton, 2002; Hoffman, 2003). Unfortunately, students with EBD will probably struggle to successfully participate in such activities.

In a 1992 review of the literature on academic interventions and students with EBD, Ruhl and Berlinghoff found 12 studies published between 1976 and 1990 of which only three addressed mathematics instruction (basic facts and computation). A 2004 literature review of academic interventions with students with EBD found 30 studies, 1963–2004, of which 11 focused on mathematics instruction (Pierce, Reid, & Epstein, 2004). However, the number of different interventions reported in this group limited conclusions. A meta-analysis of mathematics interventions and students with disabilities resulted in 58 studies of which only one specifically targeted students with EBD and only four included them at all (Kroesbergen & Van Luit, 2003).

Hodge, Riccomini, Buford, and Herbst (2006) conducted a review of the literature specifically regarding mathematics instruction and students with EBD. They were able to locate 13 studies published between 1985 and 2005. Ten of these studies included student-directed interventions such as self-monitoring, rehearsal, mneumonics, and self-management. Three studies used teacher-directed instruction, peer tutoring, and computer-assisted instruction. Twelve of the 13 studies were single-subject designs. These studies measured math performance (basic facts and calculations) primarily with teacher-developed worksheets. Six studies were conducted in public elementary or middle schools, six in private or residential schools, and one in a summer program for students with EBD.

Three studies in this review found that self-monitoring during independent seatwork improved students' accuracy in basic math computations. One of these self-monitoring studies required students to record the number of math problems, the number completed, and the number completed correctly (Carr & Punzo, 1993). Another study simply required that students mark at 10-minute intervals if they were working on their math assignment

(Levendoski & Cartledge, 2000), and a third study required students to evaluate and record their math worksheet scores, set goals, and self-reinforce during 20-minute lessons (Lazarus, 1993). All three of these studies found improved math performance.

Seven of the studies used strategy instruction, which was introduced in Chapter 6, with students with EBD. One strategy was to memorize using a cover, copy, and compare (CCC) technique (e.g., Skinner, Bamberg, Smith, & Powell, 1991). Cade and Gunter (2002) used a musical mnemonic to improve multiplication facts and Scruggs, Mastropieri, and Tolfa-Veit (1986) applied test-taking strategies to improve scores on standardized measures of mathematics. Davis and Hajicek (1985) found enhanced performance with both learning strategies and self-talk.

One of the reviewed studies (Hodge et al., 2006) included direct instruction for difficult tasks and error analysis to determine the components of math problems that were difficult (Lee, Sugai, & Horner, 1999). Students received instruction on difficult tasks until they reached 85 percent mastery. The result was improved math skills and improved behavior. As with reading improvement, same-age peer tutoring was also found to improve math performance (Franca, Kerr, Reitz, & Lambert, 1990). The tutoring component consisted of problem presentation, instructions, error corrections, and social reinforcement. Ryan, Reid, and Epstein (2004) found similar results in a literature review of peer-mediated strategies and math performance of students with EBD.

Hodge et al. (2006) reported one study comparing computer-assisted instruction and pencil-and-paper drill and practice on math performance of students with EBD (Landeen & Adams, 1988). Pencil-and-paper practices were preferred by the students and resulted in faster learning, perhaps due to typing skill deficits. Finally, a mixed-method study (Bottge, Ruyeda, & Skivington, 2006) used enhanced anchored instruction (EAI) to increase math skills with 17 adolescents attending an alternative high school for at-risk students with challenging behaviors. The technique included multimedia-based and hands-on math problems. Students improved on problem-solving tests, but not on fraction computation or standardized math measures.

From the relatively few studies available, we can conclude that academic instruction for students with EBD is both important and challenging. We know generally what works to improve students' reading and math abilities. However, we do not know exactly what works for students with EBD different from students with learning disabilities and nondisabled peers. Peer tutoring, direct instruction, self-management, and behavioral techniques such as prompting and reinforcement strategies seem efficacious at this point, but we need further investigations to validate instructional practices for students with challenging emotional and behavioral characteristics (Mooney et al., 2004).

Response to Intervention (RTI). A relatively new model of academic intervention for all struggling learners parallels the concepts inherent in the Positive Behavioral Support model, namely (1) three tiers of increasing instructional intensity, (2) three tiers of students (not struggling, at risk for failure, failing), (3) emphasis on prevention, (4) schoolwide screening for problems, (4) general and special education involvement, and (5) systematic data-based decisions. The *Response to Intervention (RTI)* model is now entrenched in the NCLB Act and IDEA 2004 and supported by policy studies from the early 1990s (National Association of State Directors of Special Education [NASDSE], 2005). RTI has also been promoted as a way to identify specific learning disabilities and prevent failure for students with mild/moderate disabilities including those with EBD (Lembke & Stichter, 2006).

Response to Intervention Tier 1 or universal interventions provide an effective foundation of instruction and curriculum likely to result in the vast majority of students achieving at adequate levels (i.e., research-based curriculum and differentiated instruction). Teachers receive support and training at this level and schoolwide screening for reading difficulties occur three times a year with an intensive progress monitoring system such as the *Dynamic Indicators of Basic Early Literacy Skills* (DIBELS; Good & Kaminski, 2003). Teachers meet in grade-level teams to analyze the data and plan for whole class instructional goals and modifications (NASDSE, 2003). Children identified through the progress monitoring system as not responding to group instruction are targeted for Tier 2 interventions. Tier 2 interventions are provided as an addition to the core curriculum and are determined individually by school-based problem-solving teams. Strategies may include small group instruction, intensive instruction in specific reading or math components, and monthly progress assessments (Lembke & Stichter, 2006).

Students who do not respond to Tier 1 and 2 interventions are provided intensive individualized instructional interventions and programs such as Title I services, district remediation programs, or special education. Student progress is monitored weekly and adjusted based on individual needs. It is thought that only about 5 percent of students may need Tier 3 interventions, assuming that Tiers 1 and 2 are operating adequately (NASDSE, 2003). The RTI model promotes evidenced-based curriculum such as *Reading Mastery* (published by SRA) *Road to Code* (Blachman, Ball, Black, & Tangel, 2000), *Wilson Reading System* (Wilson, 1996), or other direct instruction programs (Forness et al., 1997) for Tier 2 and 3 students.

To explore the impact of widespread use of RTI with students with EBD, studies have focused, as mentioned previously, on structured and intense program models (Barton-Arwood, & Falik, 2005; Benner, in press; Pierce et al., 2004). For example, Pierce et al. (2004), in a meta analysis of teacher-mediated interventions, found that techniques such as a teacher planning strategy, structured academic tasks and modeling, and rehearsal and feedback improved reading and math performance for students with EBD. Benner (in press) explored the use of direct instruction to improve reading performance with 45 students with EBD applying the *Corrective Reading Decoding Program* (Englemann, Hanner, & Johnson, 2002). Results of this study indicated the children with EBD improved from low average to average performance on word attack skills as a result of intervention. Similar works confirm the impact of direct instruction models for improving decoding skills for this population (Barton-Atwood et al., 2005; Wehby, Falk, Barton-Arwood, Lane, & Cooley, 2003).

RTI as a method of identifying students with LD is controversial (Fletcher, Coulter, Reschly, & Vaughn, 2004), although, as a model for effective instruction, it appears to have promise for students at risk of or with EBD. "Screening all students and placing them in situations and curricula in which they can be successful increases their engagement in academics and their motivation for learning" (Lembke & Stichter, 2006, p. 8). Engaging students successfully in academic learning can also reduce problem behaviors. Concurrently applying a PBS and RTI model might offer the necessary support for students with EBD to successfully and consistently master general education curriculum in general

TABLE 12.4 Response to Intervention and Positive Behavioral Supports Tiers and Interventions

Tiers	RTI	PBS
Tier 1: Schoolwide applications. Approximately 80% of students should respond	• Researched-based curriculum • Differentiated instruction • Regular screening for achievement difficulties • Intensive benchmark progress monitoring • Grade-level teams (planning and referral to Tier 2) • Data-based decisions • Teacher support and training	• Set school-wide behavioral expectations across settings • Train and promote (reinforcement system) expectations • Instigate class-wide PBS strategies • Progress monitoring with ODR data • School PBS team (planning and referral) • Data-based decisions • Teacher support and training
Tier 2: At risk students not responding to Tier 1 strategies: Approximately 5–15% of students may be targeted for these interventions in addition to Tier 1 strategies	• Small group instruction • Intensive skill instruction • Additional research-based curriculum • Monthly progress assessment	• Social skills groups • Check-in/check-out with counselors • Mentors assigned • Regular progress monitoring
Tier 3: Students not responding to Tier 1 and 2 strategies (failing academically and/or displaying regular problem behavior)	• Individualized instruction and skill instruction • Title 1 or SPED programs • Intensive tutoring • Weekly progress monitoring and adjustment	• Functional behavioral assessment and analysis • Individual contracts and contingencies for replacement behaviors • Antecedent manipulation • Social skills and self-management skills • Additional services and supports as necessary • Daily/weekly monitoring of behavior

education settings. Table 12.4 provides a side-by-side list of RTI and PBS interventions by tier. Note that both models include regular progress monitoring, data based decisions, teams for problem-solving, and evidenced based strategies.

Inclusion

The practice of educating students with disabilities primarily in general education classrooms, called *inclusion,* is often controversial, particularly in regard to students with EBD (Cullinan, 2002). These students may become aggressive and noncompliant, disrupting learning for other students in the class and frustrating teachers who are often untrained to deal with them. Traditionally, students with EBD have been primarily taught in separate classrooms or settings the majority of the school day. In 2002, only 28.8 percent of students with EBD were educated in general education classrooms more than 79 percent of the school day (U.S. Department of Education, 26th Annual Report to Congress, 2006). This is compared to 47 percent of students with learning disabilities. This report found that in 2002, 23 percent of students with EBD spent 21–60 percent of their school day in separate classrooms; almost 31 percent spent more than 60 percent of their school day in a separate classroom, and 17.5 percent were educated in separate facilities (compared to 1% of students with learning disabilities).

However, with the federal mandates that *all* students meet academic standards and that teachers be highly qualified in the content they are teaching, a greater percentage of students with EBD are likely to be included in both general education classes and the state-mandated curriculum. Proponents of including SPED students in the general education curriculum maintain that special education has historically failed to provide quality IEPs for students with disabilities and a general education curriculum focus will finally force inspection of its appropriateness for diverse general education populations along with special education students (Pugach & Warger, 2001). Others worry that treating all students alike (i.e., placing them in the same curricula and accountability system) undermines "special" education by removing the option of creating individual plans based on individualized assessment (Lieberman, 2001; Webber, 2004). In fact, they fear that this move is a step to eliminating special education altogether. Most advocates want to preserve flexibility in special education for prescribing relevant curricula for each student and placing students where they will best learn it.

Inclusion and Students with EBD

The debate over inclusion into both general education classrooms and grade-level academic curriculum for students with EBD continues to be debated, especially when disruptive behavior is involved (Algozzine, Maheady, Sacca, O'Shea, & O'Shea, 1990; Braaten, Kauffman, Braaten, Polsgrove, & Nelson, 1988; Idol, 2006; Zigmond & Maglera, 2001; Zionts, 2004). For students with EBD, inclusion often involves reintroducing a student into classrooms from which he was removed because of extremely disturbing behavior and often because of failure to progress in the academic curriculum. Thus, the risk for rejection by teachers and students is high. For example, Idol (2006) found, in a program evaluation of eight schools regarding inclusion practices, that most of the staff had positive perceptions about inclusion programs unless it involved students with disruptive behavior. Inclusion may also present problems for students with EBD in regard to irrelevant curriculum and reduced access to mental health treatment (Coleman, Webber, & Algozzine, 1999; Long, 1994).

Curricular Issues and Inclusion. The issue of curriculum may be the most important consideration in the inclusion process. According to special education mandates, what a student is to learn is decided based on individualized assessment information and delineated in the form of an IEP (individualized education plan). General education curriculum, on the other hand, is based on state and national standards aimed at preparing all students to enter higher education institutions. If it is determined by an IEP team that a student with EBD needs to learn the college-bound curriculum, then placement in a general education classroom makes sense. However, for students who are several grade levels behind in the tool subjects (e.g., reading) and who display persistent disruptive behavior, inclusion into general education curriculum and classrooms may not make sense (Coleman et al., 1999). The pressure, however, on school personnel is to place all students in the standard curriculum, regardless of ability, because all students must be tested on that content, negatively impacting the school's standing if they fail to perform well. In 2003–2004, 13 percent of schools failed to make their annual yearly progress targets (AYP) due to low test scores of special education students (Olson & Huff, 2006).

Students with EBD who present with deficient social skills, low academic achievement, possible neurological deficits, low motivation to learn, and internalizing and externalizing disorders may better need to learn self-control skills, coping strategies, functional life skills, problem-solving skills, and various learning strategies (Brooks & Sabatino, 1996; Knitzer et al., 1990). If this is the case for a specific student, the problem with inclusion lies in convincing general education teachers who are accountable for all their students reaching academic targets to give up academic instruction time to teach such alternative curriculum and in training them to do so effectively. Given the federal mandates in the NCLB Act, it seems unlikely that this will occur.

For students who do need to learn the general education academic curriculum, research has been mixed as to where they might best learn it. Studies of students with mild disabilities in general education classrooms have shown improved academic performance (Higgens & Boone, 1992; Lipsky & Gartner, 1996; Maheady, Sacca, & Harper, 1988; Woodward & Brown, 2006). However, placement alone was not the independent variable in most of these studies, so it is difficult to determine whether the general education classroom or specific inclusive strategies positively affected learning (Coleman et al., 1999). On the other hand, some studies have not found significant impact on academic achievement for students with mild disabilities placed in general education classrooms (Bulgren, Schumaker, & Deshler, 1988, 1994). Unfortunately, few studies have targeted students with EBD specifically, so it is difficult to judge the efficacy of inclusion for this population (MacMillan et al., 1996).

Social Rejection and Mental Health Treatment. Sometimes, in addition to academic content instruction, students with EBD are placed into general education classrooms for the purpose of social skills development. Unfortunately, research has not supported the assumption that students with EBD learn better social skills from general education models nor that they are better accepted by teachers and peers when placed in general education classrooms (Coleman et al., 1999; MacMillan et al., 1996). Farmer and Hollowell (1994) did find that students with EBD made friends in general education classrooms; however, the friends tended to be peers who displayed aggressive and disruptive behavior. Additionally, students with EBD tend to be the least tolerated group of special education students by general education teachers (Coleman & Gilliam, 1983; Idol, 2006; Walker et al., 1995). Some think that wholesale inclusion of EBD students has actually resulted in more segregation for disciplinary purposes (Coleman et al., 1999). "Don't we have enough experience and knowledge about the nature of emotional disturbances to shatter the illusion that re-educating emotionally disturbed students is a simple process of restructuring the classroom by making reasonable accommodations?" (Long, 1994, p. 21).

Effective treatment of students with EBD most often includes recommendations for comprehensive and integrated services, not just academic and social instruction (Brooks &

Sabatino, 1996; Cullinan, 2002; Knitzer et al., 1990; Osher et al., 1994; Pfeiffer & Reddy, 1998). These services might include crisis intervention programs, intensive counseling, case management, substance abuse intervention, and a therapeutic milieu. Some argue that placement full time in a general education classroom may preclude these services, because of the singular emphasis on academic achievement (Coleman et al., 1999; Zionts, 2004). If students are pulled out for mental health services, instructional time will be lost, casting the student into a perpetual catching-up cycle.

Proponents of full inclusion for students with EBD point out that "eliminating inclusion in no way guarantees that curricular decisions for students with disabilities will be appropriate, that they will be accepted, or that mental health interventions will be part of their educational programs" (Coleman et al., 1999, p. 39). The assumption that special education teachers are better trained to teach relevant individualized curriculum and provide mental health services has not been substantiated (Knitzer et al., 1990). Relegating students to separate classrooms where they are simply controlled and not taught what they need to learn, as is too often the case, would most certainly not be in their best interest. Conversely, including students with their peers in classrooms where they learn would probably enhance their educational progress. Inclusion proponents believe that, if students with EBD would benefit from alternative curriculum and mental health treatment, then all students would probably benefit from such things. Thus, inclusion proponents recommend altering the way that public schools do business such that all students can be given what they need, when they need it, without maintaining a separate special education system.

Implications for Teachers. Despite the push, subsequent to the NCLB Act, to include SPED students in general education for most of their instruction, the percentage of students with EBD being educated primarily in general education classrooms has not substantially increased (U.S. Department of Education, 2006). This may be due to the fact that general education teachers are not trained in effective behavior management strategies or that inclusion programs have failed to target key considerations for such students. Cheney and Muscott (1997) recommend that teachers attend to the following components when establishing successful inclusion programs:

1. Develop a shared knowledge base about the nature and needs of students with emotional and behavioral disorders
2. Share responsibility for both academic and behavioral interventions
3. Implement PBS strategies
4. Arrange for therapeutic support services including crisis intervention
5. Provide academic rigor with differentiation toward individual academic needs

Idol (2006) recommends four collaborative teaching models for supporting special education students in general education classes. The main purpose for these models is to support classroom teachers through collaboration and partnerships.

1. *Consulting Teacher Model.* The special education teacher works directly with the classroom teacher to plan and evaluate instruction. Special education students receive this service indirectly (Idol, Nevin, & Paolucci-Whitcomb, 2000).

2. *Cooperative Teacher Model.* Special and general education teachers work together in co-teaching arrangements in the same classroom. Co-teaching can include: (a) *station teaching* (each teacher situated at a different learning station), (b) *parallel teaching* (one teacher teaches a small group while the other teaches the rest of the class), (c) *team teaching* (both teachers plan and teach one lesson in various formats), (d) *complementary teaching* (one teacher teaches content, the other teaches a lesson within the other about learning strategies, etc.), and (e) *teacher assistance teams* (problem-solving teams addressing specific student academic problems) (Smith, Polloway, Patton, & Dowdy, 2004; Vaughn, Schumm, & Arguelles, 1997; Walther-Thomas, Korinek, McLaughlin, & Williams, 2000; Webber, 2004). Important components of co-teaching include providing feedback to each other, sharing classroom management, planning daily together, and using cooperative learning techniques (Austin, 2001).
3. *Supportive Resource Programs.* Resource teachers provide specialized instruction for SPED students on a regular schedule and collaborate with general education teachers to construct IEPs. Attention is given to ensuring that resource instruction supports general education instruction and that transfer of student knowledge is facilitated. It is required under the NCLB Act and IDEA 2004 that special education teachers who are primarily responsible for teaching academic content be highly qualified to teach the designated subject matter. Thus, resource teachers responsible for multiple subjects may now opt for a cooperative teaching arrangement in lieu of having to demonstrate proficiency in various subjects.
4. *Instructional Assistants.* Paraprofessionals are provided to accompany special education students into general education classrooms for the purpose of prompting and promoting appropriate behavior, and to encourage students to stay on task and complete work (Idol, 2006). Teachers should attend to the possibility that accompanying paraprofessionals may embarrass and stigmatize individual students. This model may also promote students' overdependence on one-on-one assistance.

Frequently cited barriers to successful inclusion programming include (a) a lack of regularly scheduled planning and collaboration time and little administrative support (Austin, 2001); (b) failure to develop effective communication and cooperative skills (Harris, 1998); (c) incompatibility between teachers (Walther-Thomas et al., 2000); and (d) unclear expectations for various school personnel (Webber, 2004). Inclusion programs are not simple to develop and should be thoughtfully constructed. Remember that these students have already failed to progress in typically constructed general education classrooms. Unless instruction in those classrooms is modified and adequate supports provided, there is little reason to assume that these students will respond positively when reintroduced to these settings. If they respond negatively with inappropriate behavior, they may be relegated to a separate placement as punishment, undermining integration altogether. Table 12.5 lists some decision points that special educators might consider when developing inclusion programs for individual students. The order of the decisions may be construed differently, but all of these issues would best be addressed.

Public policies and federal mandates appear to be altering the structure of special education. Education plans are less often developed based on student need; more often plans reflect institutional attempts to meet AYP goals. Specially trained teachers are less often directly teaching special education students and more often acting as inclusion partners,

TABLE 12.5 Inclusion Decision Points

1. Decide what the student needs to learn.
2. Decide which instructional modifications might be necessary in order for the student to learn these things. Does someone need to be trained to provide the modifications?
3. Conceptualize the best instructional arrangement (e.g., inclusion model) for accommodating the student in the least restrictive environment where he can best learn the things that he needs to learn.
4. Decide if the student needs a behavior management plan. If yes, develop one based on functional assessment and positive behavioral supports.
5. Specify general and special educator roles.
6. List the types of administrative supports that might be necessary (e.g., schedule changes, personnel allocation, space utilization, materials acquisition). Assign someone to obtain these supports.
7. Decide if outside agency support is needed. If so, assign someone to acquire these services.
8. Decide how to best validate goals and objectives (i.e., formative assessment techniques).
9. Decide who will oversee the efficacy of the placement decision, provide necessary training, and communicate with the stakeholders.

Adapted from Webber, J. (1997). Responsible inclusion: Key components for success. In P. Zionts (Ed.), *Inclusion strategies for students with learning and behavior problems: Perspectives, experiences, and best practices* (pp. 27–56). Austin: Pro-Ed. Reprinted with permission of the publisher.

sometimes only indirectly dealing with their students. Special education students are more often pressured to respond to general education requirements and may be blamed if they do not conform. Students with EBD are especially at risk for such scorn. The effect of these policies and mandates on students with EBD have yet to be determined but under these circumstances, it is imperative that special educators work to protect their students with EBD and to continue to ensure them an appropriate education. Webber (1993) offered the following suggestions for taking care of students with EBD amid educational and social reform.

Caring for Students with EBD Amidst Educational Reform[1]

The first step in caring for students with EBD during this time of change is to accept the role of advocate. This means neither resisting change totally nor being passive in the face of ill-conceived recommendations. Instead, it means being guided by the needs of individual students. Advocates for children and youth with EBD will be pitted against some educators who may insist on "dumping" these students into hostile, inadequate situations or who may want to exclude these students from school altogether. The road has not and will not be easy or clear. The following list of suggested actions may act as an advocacy guide.

To advocate for children and youth with EBD it will be necessary to:

- Protect their right to the most effective treatment and education by expanding—not condensing—the range of choices available to these students regarding curriculum, interventions, and treatment strategies, services, and placements.
- Protect their right to an individualized team-decision-making process that first inspects a student's needs, prescribes curriculum and strategy adaptations, and only then addresses the best location to obtain an education.

- Resist the move to talk about all special education students needing a particular curriculum or strategy. Recognizing individual differences ensures the appropriateness of an education.
- Resist being bullied by zealots into losing sight of what is best for each student.
- Keep what has worked in special education and expand it to others who can benefit. Smaller student–teacher ratios, individualized planning and instruction, effective instructional strategies, relevant and instructional-level curricula, skill training, parent involvement, team decision making, and support services have been found to improve educational outcomes.
- Strengthen special education's empirical base (Kauffman, 1993) and use it to make decisions. Acting purely on emotion and choosing or resisting change only for the sake of doing so can do great damage to students.
- Question those practices that may not work, be willing to change them, and be accountable for replacing them with evidence-based strategies. Are our identification practices valid? Have we a clear definition for our population? Are we relying too heavily on a curriculum of control and questionable level systems and neglecting sound instruction? Are we using too many worksheets and giving too much free time? Have we created reinforcement junkies? Are we reluctant to let go of our students? Are we actively facilitating our students' integration into larger society? Conducting reviews of instructional practices and the quality of available services can promote continued improvement.
- Prepare students to succeed in general education. Assess the general education setting for necessary behaviors, directly teach those behaviors along with self-control techniques, use behavior management strategies that will transfer easily, train healthy thinking, provide positive behavioral and mental health support, and accomplish transition at a reasonable pace.
- Protect students with EBD in general education settings. General educators may have little understanding of their behavior and often become angry and frustrated. Trying to reintegrate students who have already failed in general education is more difficult than integrating students who have not previously been served by general education (e.g., those with multiple physical disabilities). Also, protect students from the undue frustration, anxiety, embarrassment, and anger that might result from large student–teacher ratios, fast-paced, irrelevant, and often frustrational curriculum, failing grades, and outright ridicule and/or rejection. Protect them also from harsher punishments that might be developed if other alternatives become unavailable.
- Commit to professional growth and development so as to be knowledgeable and assertive advocates.
- Promote the ownership of all children in school, the acceptance of people's humanity, the creation of supportive communities, the valuing of cooperation, and interdependence. These are noble notions and worthy of consistent attention.
- Work to ensure that a full range of mental health services is available to students with EBD and their families, preferably in or around the school. This means supporting the systems of care and OSEP agendas, promoting interagency collaboration and case management, and remaining focused on the needs of students and their families.

It seems wise to proceed carefully within this period of educational reform and to gauge the effects of change on the students for whom we are responsible. It might be necessary to actively resist some recommended changes. Instead, wisdom dictates preserving what is valid about special education—improving areas that have been neglected and expanding the range of educational and mental health services available to students with EBD. Change can be exciting and promising, particularly if it is well planned. Taking care of students with EBD means advocating, not abdicating; it means being responsible, reflective reformers.

Conclusions

This chapter has presented four topics (special issues) related to serving students with EBD in schools: youth violence, Positive Behavioral Supports, academic interventions, and inclusion. Youth violence is best explained from an ecological basis citing multilevel causes and interventions. The frequency of violent acts perpetrated by youth has declined, but instances of multiple killings in and around schools continue to cause great concern, as does the number of youth injured or killed by adults. In an effort to address aggressive and disruptive behavior in special education and schools in general, a model of Positive Behavioral Supports (PBS) was recommended in IDEA 2004 and elsewhere. PBS applies a three-tiered structure to address universal, setting-specific, and individual student problems. By supporting students with proactive effective instructional strategies and social skills instruction, the vast majority of inappropriate behaviors can be prevented and students spared punitive consequences.

Important to the PBS model and violence prevention is effective academic instruction. Reading and mathematics instructional strategies best used for students with EBD include peer mediation, direct instruction, learning strategy instruction, self-management, and behavioral techniques such as prompts and reinforcement. The Response to Intervention (RTI) framework, also a three-tiered model, relates to academic interventions provided at more intensive levels if students do not respond adequately on academic measures. For both PBS and RTI, ongoing progress monitoring is imperative. Finally, the issue of inclusion for students with EBD was addressed in light of the curricular, testing, and teacher qualification mandates of the NCLB Act and IDEA 2004. We must advocate for students with EBD who may be the most difficult to reintegrate into general education and protect them against possible negative outcomes. As Kauffman (1993) has so aptly stated, "In a world of rapidly changing social institutions and conventions, special education is being subjected to enormous pressures for change. Special education's future and the futures of the students who are its primary concern will largely be determined by responses to these pressures" (p. 6).

KEY POINTS

1. Youth violence continues to be a concern for all public schools. Alienated youth, lack of supervision, and the availability of guns are associated with multiple tragic school shootings.
2. Youth violence can be explained with an ecological perspective (e.g., multilevel causes and multilevel prevention and intervention programs).

3. The number of violent acts perpetrated by youth appears to be decreasing, although arrests for girls is on the rise.
4. One multilevel intervention model required in the 1997 reauthorization of IDEA and the IDEA 2004 is Positive Behavior Supports (PBS).
5. PBS is organized with three intervention tiers across four school-based systems: schoolwide, classwide, nonclassroom, and individual students. Constructing, teaching, and promoting expectations are cornerstones of this model.
6. NCLB and IDEA mandates require that special education students master standard academic content at grade level. The Reading First initiative in the NCLB Act requires that evidence-based reading practices be used with all children grades K–3.
7. More studies are needed to establish the best strategies for teaching academic content to students with EBD, although peer mediation, direct instruction, cognitive learning strategies, self-management, and prompts and reinforcement have been found to increase academic performance for these students.
8. Language assessment should be a critical component of the comprehensive assessment for students with EBD and language goals should be included on their IEPs.
9. Successful inclusion for students with EBD is especially challenging due to their behavioral difficulties and emotional variability. General education classes might offer more intensive academic instruction, peer support, and socially appropriate models. On the other hand, students may be subjected to teacher and peer rejection, academic failure, and too much pressure to perform.
10. Inclusion for students with EBD should be decided on an individual basis in keeping with the mandates of IDEA 2004. To date research is inconclusive about the relative social and academic benefits of different placements for students with EBD.
11. Teachers need to advocate for their students with EBD during this period of educational reform to guarantee their right to an appropriate education.

HOMEWORK QUESTIONS

1. Visit websites for the Office of Juvenile Justice and Delinquency Prevention and the Department of Health and Human Services and report about trends in youth violence and victimization. What changes have occurred in the past decade? Why do you think those changes have occurred?
2. List as many family, individual, and societal factors as possible thought to contribute to youth violence. Choose one factor and in no more than three paragraphs discuss what might be done to alleviate this factor.
3. Create a diagram showing the relationship of various levels of violence prevention and intervention strategies and programs for a school at-large. Describe why you would include what you did and what outcomes you hope to achieve.
4. Why does it make sense to discuss youth violence from an ecological perspective? Explain in-depth.
5. Relate the Positive Behavior Support model to an ecological perspective. What other theoretical perspective is found in this model? Explain in-depth.
6. Assume you are assigned to chair the schoolwide PBS team. Visit the PBIS website and download three items you will share with your team at the first meeting. Describe the

items and explain why you chose to include them. What would you think would be your first tasks as a team?

7. List and discuss various benefits and challenges related to the emphasis on academic achievement for students with EBD. Why do you think that the Department of Education would mandate that SPED students be able to achieve at similar levels to nondisabled peers?

8. List and discuss challenges inherent in raising academic performance of students with EBD.

9. Compare RTI with PBS and discuss methods for implementing both models simultaneously. Consider school structures, leadership, teacher time, interrelated goals, funding, community support, and assessment procedures.

10. List and discuss common barriers to successful inclusion for students with EBD in primary grades, intermediate grades, and secondary schools. Are the barriers different at the various grade levels? What might you suggest to address some of these barriers?

11. Choose one of the inclusion models discussed in this chapter. Discuss your role as a special or general education teacher. What activities might you conduct to ensure that this model is effective for included students with EBD?

12. Conduct a review of the literature on inclusion of students with disabilities. Include journal articles from 1997 to the present. What conclusions can you draw about the impact of various placements on SPED students and their abilities?

READINGS AND RESOURCES

Antisocial behavior in the school: Evidence-based practices, by Hill Walker, Elizabeth Ramsey, and Frank Gresham, Belmont, CA: Wadsworth, 2004, for a comprehensive view of child and youth violence and the best practice recommendations for dealing with it.

Early warning, timely response: A guide to safe schools, by K. Dwyer, D. Osher, and C. Warger, Washington, DC: U.S. Department of Education, 1998, for a comprehensive listing of what to look for and what to do to ensure safe schools.

Journal of Emotional and Behavioral Disorders, 8(2-3), *2000,* edited by Hill Walker and Mike Epstein, for two special journal issues devoted to school safety and substantiated practices for addressing youth violence that reflect the various models mentioned in this textbook.

Sexual and physical abuse among adolescents with behavioral disorders: Profiles and implications, by Darcy Miller, *Behavioral Disorders, 18,* 1993, 129–138, for results of a survey of adolescents with EBD who self-report their experiences with abuse.

School safety: A collaborative effort, *The ERIC Review, 7*(1), Spring 2000, entire issue, for an overview of the nature and extent of school violence; a description of steps that parents, school personnel, and communities can take to prevent it; and a list of resources for more in-depth information.

School violence intervention: A practical handbook, edited by A. P. Goldstein & J. C. Conoley, New York: Guilford Press, 1997, for a comprehensive view of the problem of school violence and a systems approach to dealing with it.

Journal of Emotional and Behavioral Disorders, 10(3), *2002,* edited by George Sugai and Robert Horner, for a special issue addressing Positive Behavior Supports and functional behavioral assessments in schools.

Removing roadblocks to effective behavior intervention in inclusive settings: Responding to typical objections by school personnel, by Terrance Scott, *Beyond Behavior, 12*(1), 2002, for responses to common arguments against the use of positive supports for behavior management purposes.

Teaching Exceptional Children, 37(1), *2004,* edited by Alec Peck and Stan Scarpati, for an issue containing articles about PBS and its application in inclusive settings.

Peer tutoring and students with emotional or behavioral disorders: A review of the literature, by Vicky Spencer, *Behavioral Disorders, 31*(2), 2006, for a review of the literature on the use of students with EBD as tutors and tutees.

The impact of NCLB and the reauthorization of IDEA on academic instruction of students with emotional or behavioral disorders, by Paul Mooney, R.

Kenton Denny, and Phil Gunter, *Behavioral Disorders, 29*(3), 2004, for an overview of the impact of these two laws regarding academic instruction and students with EBD.

Reading interventions for students with emotional/behavioral disorders, by Maggie Coleman and Sharon Vaughn, *Behavioral Disorders, 25*(2), 2000, for a review of studies specifically pertaining to reading instruction and students with EBD.

Behavioral Disorders, 31(3), 2006, for two literature reviews: one reviewing literature pertaining mathematics instruction for students with EBD (by Janie Hodge and colleagues) and one review of reading instruction studies for students with EBD in primary grades (by Mabel Rivera and colleagues).

Response to intervention: Policy considerations and implementation, by the National Association of State Directors of Special Education, Alexandria, VA: Author, 2005, for a brief description of RTI and related policies.

How we might achieve the radical reform of special education, by Jim Kauffman, *Exceptional Children, 60,* 1993, 6–16, for a thoughtful and thought-provoking response to pressures of proponents of full inclusion and other reform movements.

Inclusion of students with emotional and behavioral disorders (2nd ed.), edited by Paul Zionts, Austin, TX: Pro-Ed, 2004, for methods for planning and implementing inclusion with students with EBD.

Teaching students with special needs in inclusive settings (4th ed.), by Tom Smith, Ed Polloway, Jim Patton and Carol Dowdy, Boston: Allyn & Bacon, 2004, for an entire textbook of instructional practices and programs to promote successful inclusion.

TECHNICAL ASSISTANCE CENTERS AND WEBSITES

Center for Effective Collaboration and Practice (CECP) (*http://cecp.air.org/*)

Center for the Prevention of School Violence (*http://www.ncdjjdp.org/cpsv/*)

Centers for Mental Health in Schools Training and Technical Assistance (*http://www.promoteprevent.org/resources/technical_partners/*)

National Center for Conflict Resolution Education (NCCRE) (*http://www.nccre.org/*)

Center for Positive Behavioral Interventions and Supports (*http://www.pbis.org*) for information and resources pertaining to PBS.

U. S. Surgeon General's Office (*http://www.surgeongeneral.gov/*) for various reports on the health and well-being of children and youth.

Office of Juvenile Justice and Delinquency Prevention (*http://ojjdp.ncjrs.org/*), for reports on juvenile crimes and arrests.

U.S. Department of Health and Human Services (*http://www.hhs.gov/*), for information regarding youth and disabilities.

What Works Clearinghouse (*http://www.whatworks.ed.gov/*), for reviews of evidence-based school interventions.

No Child Left Behind Frequently Asked Questions page of the U.S. Department of Education (*http://www.ed.gov/nclb/landing.jhtml*), for updates regarding the NCLB Act and related policies.

IDEA 2004 News, Information, and Resources page of the U.S. Department of Education (*http://www.ed.gov/policy/speced/guid/idea/idea2004.html*), for updates regarding the IDEA and related policies.

Wrights Law resources on Response to Intervention (RTI) (*http://www.wrightslaw.com/info/rti.index.htm*)

National Mental Health Information Center, Center for Mental Health Services (*http://mentalhealth.samhsa.gov/cmhs/ChildrensCampaign/*), for information and resources pertaining to children's mental health.

ENDNOTE

1. This presentation was given by Jo Webber as a keynote address for the First General Session of the CCBD Forum on Inclusion, held in St. Louis, MO, October 1, 1993. It was published in L.M. Bullock & R. A. Gable (Eds.), *Monograph on inclusion: Ensuring appropriate services to children and youth with EBD-I.* Reston, VA: Council for Children with Behavioral Disorders. Adapted with permission of the author and the publisher.

REFERENCES

Abelsohn, D. (1983). Dealing with the abdication dynamic in the post-divorce family: A context for adolescent crisis. *Family Process, 22,* 359–383.

Abelson, R. P. (1986). Beliefs are like possessions. *Journal for the Theory of Social Behavior, 16,* 223–350.

Abikoff, H. (1985). Efficacy of cognitive training interventions in hyperactive children: A critical review. *Clinical Psychology Review, 5,* 479–512.

Abikoff, H., Gittelman, R., & Klein, D. F. (1980). Classroom observation code for hyperactive children: A replication study. *Journal of Consulting and Clinical Psychology, 48,* 555–565.

Abikoff, H., Gittelman-Klein, R., & Klein, D. F. (1977). Validation of a classroom observation code for hyperactive children. *Journal of Consulting and Clinical Psychology, 45,* 772–783.

Abrams, B. J. (1992). Values clarification for students with emotional disabilities. *Teaching Exceptional Children, 24*(3), 28–33.

Abramson, L. Y., Metalsky, G. I., & Alloy, L. B. (1989). Hopelessness depression: A theory-based subtype of depression. *Psychological Review, 96,* 358–372.

Abramson, L. Y., Seligman, M. E. P., & Teasdale, J. (1978). Learned helplessness in humans: Critique and reformulation. *Journal of Abnormal Psychology, 87,* 32–48.

Achenbach, T. M. (1974). *Developmental psychopathology.* New York: Ronald Press.

Achenbach, T. M. (1991). *Child behavior checklist.* Burlington, VT: Department of Psychiatry, University of Vermont.

Achenbach, T. M., & Edelbrock, C. S. (1978). The classification of child psychopathology: A review and analysis of empirical efforts. *Psychological Bulletin, 85,* 1275–1301.

Achenbach, T. M., & Edelbrock, C. S. (1979). The Child Behavior Profile: II. Boys aged 12–16 and girls aged 6–11 and 12–16. *Journal of Consulting and Clinical Psychology, 47,* 223–233.

Achenbach, T. M., & Edelbrock, C. S. (1981). Behavioral problems and competencies reported by parents of normal and disturbed children aged 4 through 16. *Monographs of the Society for Research in Child Development, 46* (Serial No. 188).

Achenbach, T. M., & Edelbrock, C. S. (1983). *Manual for the child behavior checklist.* Burlington, VT: University of Vermont Department of Psychiatry.

Achenbach, T. M., & Rescorla, L. A. (2001). *Manual for ASEBA School-Age Forms & Profiles.* Burlington: University of Vermont, Research Center for Children, Youth, & Families.

Adams, G. L., & Engelmann, S. (1996). *Research on direct instruction: 25 years beyond DISTAR.* Seattle, WA: Educational Achievement Systems.

Adelman, H. (1996). Restructuring education support services and integrating community resources: Beyond the full service school model. *School Psychology Review, 25,* 431–445.

Adler, P. A., & Adler, P. (1995). Dynamics of inclusion and exclusion in preadolescent cliques. *Social Psychology Quarterly, 58,* 145–162.

Adler, P. A., Kless, S. J., & Adler, P. (1992). Socialization to gender roles: Popularity among elementary school boys and girls. *Sociology of Education, 65,* 169–187.

Adrian, S. E. (1990). *The effects of a formal sexuality education program on the self-esteem of adolescents labeled emotionally disturbed.* Unpublished doctoral dissertation, The University of Texas at Austin.

Ager, C. L., & Cole, C. L. (1991). A review of cognitive-behavioral interventions for children and adolescents with behavioral disorders. *Behavioral Disorders, 16,* 276–287.

Aiello, B. (1976). Especially for special educators: A sense of our own history. *Exceptional Children, 42,* 244–252.

Al-Otaiba, S., & Fuchs, D. (2002). Characteristics of children who are unresponsive to early literacy intervention. *Remedial and Special Education, 23*(5), 300–316.

Albano, A.M., & Kendall, P.C. (2002). Cognitive behavioural therapy for children and adolescents with anxiety disorders: Clinical research advances. *International Review of Psychiatry, 14,* 129–134.

Alberto, P. A., & Troutman, A. C. (2006). *Applied behavior analysis for teachers* (7th ed.). Columbus, OH: Prentice Hall.

Alessi, N. E. (1986). *DSM-III diagnosis associated with childhood depressive disorders.* Paper presented at American Academy of Child Psychiatry, Los Angeles, CA.

Alessi, N. E., McManus, M., & Grapente, W. L. (1984). The characterization of depressive disorder in serious juvenile offenders. *Journal of Affective Disorders, 6,* 9–17.

Alexander, J. F., & Parsons, B. V. (1973). Short-term behavioral intervention with delinquent families: Impact on family process and recidivism. *Journal of Abnormal Psychology, 81,* 219–225.

Algozzine, B. (1977). The emotionally disturbed child: Disturbed or disturbing? *Journal of Abnormal Child Psychology, 5,* 205–211.

Algozzine, B., & Curran, T. J. (1979). Teachers' predictions of children's school success as a function of their behavioral tolerances. *Journal of Educational Research, 72,* 344–347.

Algozzine, B., Maheady, L., Sacca, K. D., O'Shea, L., & O'Shea, D. (1990). Sometimes patent medicine works: A reply to Braaten, Kauffman, Braaten, Polsgrove, & Nelson. *Exceptional Children, 56,* 552–557.

Algozzine, R., Serna, L., & Patton, J. R. (2001). *Childhood behavior disorders: Applied research and educational practices* (2nd ed.). Austin: Pro-Ed.

Allen, J. P., Philliber, S., Herrling, S., & Kupermine, G. P. (1997). Preventing teen pregnancy and academic failure: Experimental evaluation of developmentally based approach. *Child Development, 64,* 729–742.

Allen, R. (2003, March). The democratic aims of service learning. *Educational Leadership, 60*(6), 51–54.

Allen, S. J., & Graden, J. L. (2002). Best practices in collaborative problem solving for intervention design. In A. Thomas & J. Grimes (Eds.), *Best practices in school psychology IV* (pp. 565–582). Bethesda, MD: National Association of School Psychologists.

Allyon, T., Layman, D., & Kandel, H. J. (1975). A behavioral-educational alternative to drug control of hyperactive children. *Journal of Applied Behavior Analysis, 8,* 137–146.

Althen, G. (1998). *American ways—A guide for foreigners in the United States.* Yarmouth, ME: Intercultural Press.

American Association for Employment in Education (AAEE). (1999). *Educator supply and demand.* Columbus, OH: Author.

American Association of University Women Educational Foundation. (1992). *How schools short-change girls: A study of major findings on girls and education.* Washington, DC: Author.

American Educational Research Association, American Psychological Association, & National Council on Measurement in Education. (1999). *Standards for educational and psychological testing.* Washington, DC: American Educational Research Association.

American Institute of Research. (2002, April). Frequently asked questions. *Technical Assistance Partnership for Child and Family Mental Health.* Accessed September 30, 2002, at *www.air.org/tapartnership/advisors/education/faq/april02.htm.*

American Psychiatric Association. (2000). *Diagnostic and statistical manual of mental disorders—Trainer's revision* (4th ed., rev.). Washington, DC: Author.

American Psychiatric Foundation. (2006). *Typical or troubled? School mental health education grants.* Retrieved November 2, 2006, from http://www/psychfoundation.org/typical or troubled.cfm

Anderson, C. W. (1981a). Parent–child relationships: A context for reciprocal developmental influence. *The Counseling Psychologist, 4,* 35–44.

Anderson, C. W. (1981b). The handicapped child's effects on parent-child relations: A useful model for school psychologists. *School Psychology Review, 10,* 82–90.

Anderson, D. H., Fisher, A., Marchant, M., Young, K. R., & Smith, J. A. (2006). The cool card intervention: a positive support strategy for managing anger. *Beyond Behavior, 16*(1), 3–13.

Anderson, J. (1981). *Thinking, changing, rearranging.* Eugene, OR: Timberlane.

Anderson, J. A., Kutash, K., & Duchnowski, A. J. (2001). A comparison of the academic progress of students with E/BD and students with LD. *Journal of Emotional and Behavioral Disorders, 9,* 106–115.

Anderson, J. C., Williams, S., McGee, R. & Silva, P. A. (1987). DSMIII disorders in preadolescent children: Prevalence in a large sample from the general population. *Archives of General Psychiatry, 44,* 69–76.

Apter, A., Bernhout, E., & Tyano, S. (1984). Severe obsessive compulsive disorder in adolescence: A report of eight cases. *Journal of Adolescence, 7,* 349–358.

Apter, S. J. (1982). *Troubled children/troubled systems.* Elmsford, NY: Pergamon Press.

Apter, S. J., & Conoley, J. C. (1984). *Childhood behavior disorders and emotional disturbance.* Englewood Cliffs, NJ: Prentice Hall.

Archwamety, T., & Katsiyannis, A. (2000). Academic remediation, parole violations, and recidivism rates among delinquent youths, *Remedial and Special Education,* 21(3), 161–170.

Argulewicz, E. D., & Sanchez, D. (1983). The special education evaluation process as a moderator of false positives. *Exceptional Child, 49(5),* 452–454.

Asarnow, J. R., & Callan, J. W. (1985). Boys with peer adjustment problems: Social cognitive processes. *Journal of Consulting and Clinical Psychology, 53,* 80–87.

Asperger, H. (1991). "Autistic psychopathy" in childhood. In U. Frith (Ed. & Trans.), *Autism and Asperger syndrome* (pp. 37–92). Cambridge, UK: Cambridge University Press. (Original work published 1944)

Atkeson, B. M. & Forehand, R. (1984). Conduct disorders. In E. J. Mash & L. G. Terdal (Eds.), *Behavioral assessment of childhood disorders* (pp. 185–219). New York: Guilford.

Atkins, M. S., Frazier, S. L., & Abdul-Adil, J. (2003). Toward a new model for promoting urban children's mental health: Accessible, effective, and sustainable school-based mental health services. *School Psychology Review, 32,* 503–514.

Attention deficit disorder—Part I. (1995, April). *Harvard Mental Health Letter, 11*(10), 1–4.

Attention deficit disorder—Part II. (1995, May). *Harvard Mental Health Letter, 11*(11), 1–3.

Atwater, E. (1983). *Adolescence.* Englewood Cliffs, NJ: Prentice Hall.

Atwater, E. (1996). *Adolescence.* Upper Saddle River, NJ: Prentice-Hall.

Aust, P. H. (1984). Rational-emotive therapy in the school. *Social Work in Education, 6,* 106–117.

Austin, V. L. (2001). Teachers' beliefs about co-teaching. *Remedial and special Education, 22,* 245–255.

Baer, D. M. (1981). *How to plan for generalization.* Austin, TX: Pro-Ed.

Baer, D. M., Wolf, M. M., & Risley, T.R. (1968). Some current dimensions of applied behavior analysis. *Journal of Applied Behavior Analysis, 1,* 91–97.

Bagley, M. T., & Hess, K. K. (1984). *200 ways of using imagery in the classroom.* New York: Trillium Press.

Bailey, A., Le Couteur, A., Gottesman, I., Bolton, P., Simonoff, E., Yuzda, E., & Rutter, M. (1995). Autism as a strongly genetic disorder. *Psychological Medicine, 25,* 63–77.

Baker, J. A., Kamphaus, R. K., Horne, A., & Winsor, A. (2006). Evidence for a population-based service delivery model of behavior prevention and intervention. *School Psychology Review, 35,* 31–46.

Bandura, A. (1965a). Behavior modifications through modeling procedures. In L. Krasner & L. P. Ulman (Eds.), *Research in behavior modification* (pp. 310–340). New York: Holt, Rinehart & Winston.

Bandura, A. (1965b). Vicarious processes: A case of notrial learning. In L. Berkowitz (Ed.), *Advances in experimental social psychology* (Vol. 2). New York: Academic Press.

Bandura, A. (1968). Social learning interpretation of psychological dysfunctions. In P. London & D. Rosenhan (Eds.), *Foundations of abnormal psychology.* New York: Holt, Rinehart & Winston.

Bandura, A. (1977a). Self-efficacy: Toward a unifying theory of behavioral change. *Psychological Review, 84,* 191–215.

Bandura, A. (1977b). *Social learning theory.* Englewood Cliffs, NJ: Prentice Hall.

Bandura, A. (1978). The self system in reciprocal determinism. *American Psychologist,* 344–358.

Bandura, A. (1982). Self-efficacy mechanism in human agency. *American Psychologist, 37,* 122–147.

Bandura, A. (1986). *Social foundations of thought and action: A social cognitive theory.* Englewood Cliffs, NJ: Prentice Hall.

Bandura, A., Ross, D., & Ross, S. A. (1963). Vicarious reinforcement and imitative learning. *Journal of Abnormal and Social Psychology, 67,* 601–607.

Barbetta, P. (1990). GOALS: A group-oriented adapted levels systems for children with behavior disorders. *Academic Therapy, 25,* 645–656.

Barkley, R. A. (1984). Hyperactivity. In E. J. Mash, & L. G. Terdal (Eds.), *Behavioral assessment of childhood disorders* (3rd ed., pp. 127–184). New York: Guilford.

Barkley, R. A. (1990). *Attention-deficit hyperactivity disorder: A handbook for diagnosis and treatment.* New York: Guilford.

Barkley, R. A. (1998). *Attention-deficit hyperactivity disorder: A handbook for diagonosis and treatment* (2nd ed.). New York: Guilford Press.

Barkley, R. A., & Cunningham, C. E. (1979). The effects of Ritalin on the mother-child interactions of hyperactive children. *Archives of General Psychiatry, 36,* 201–208.

Barkley, R. A., Copeland, A. P., & Sivage, C. (1980). A self-control classroom for hyperactive children. *Journal of Autism and Developmental Disorders, 10*(1), 75–89.

Barlow, D. H., Craske, M. G., Cerny, J. A., & Klosko, J. S. (1989). Behavioral treatment of panic disorder. *Behavior Therapy, 20,* 261–282.

Barondes, S. H. (1998). Will genetics revolutionize psychiatry? *Harvard Mental Health Letter, 15*(5), 4–6.

Barrett, C. L., Hampe, I. E., & Miller, L. (1978). Research on psychotherapy with children. In S. L. Garfield & A. E. Bergin (Eds.), *Handbook of psychotherapy and behavior change* (2nd ed.) (pp. 411–436), New York: Wiley.

Barrett, P.M., Dadds, M.R., & Rapee, R.M. (1996). Family treatment of childhood anxiety: A controlled trial. *Journal of Consulting and Clinical Psychology, 64,* 333–342.

Barton, G. (2006, May). Ready-made lessons for busy teachers. *Times Educational Supplement,* p.29.

Barton, P. E. (2002). *The closing of the educational frontier.* Princeton, NJ: Educational Testing Service.

Barton-Arwood, S. M., Wehby, J. H., & Falk, K. B. (2005). Reading instruction for elementary-age students with EBD and students with LD. *Exceptional Children, 72*(1), 7–27.

Barton-Arwood, S. M., Wehby, J. H., Gunter, P. L., & Lane, K. L. (2003). Functional behavior assessment rating scales: Interrater reliability with students with emotional or behavioral disorders. *Behavior Disorders, 28*(4), 386–400

Baum, C. G., & Forehand, R. (1981). Long-term follow-up assessment of parent training by use of multiple outcome measures. *Behavior Theory, 12,* 643–652.

Baumrind, D. (1971). Current patterns of parental authority. *Developmental Psychology Monographs, 4,* 1.

Baumrind, D. (1977). Some thoughts about child-rearing. In S. Cohen & T. J. Comiskey (Eds.), *Child development: Contemporary perspectives.* Itasca, IL: F. E. Peacock.

Bauwens, J., & Hourcade, J. J. (1989). Hey, would you just listen. *Teaching Exceptional Children, 2*(4), 61.

Beck, A. T. (1964). Thinking and depression: II. Theory and therapy. *Archives of General Psychiatry, 10,* 561–571.

Beck, A. T. (1967). *Depression: Clinical, experimental and theoretical aspects.* New York: Harper & Row.

Beck, A. T. (1976). *Cognitive therapy and the emotional disorders.* New York: International Universities Press.

Beck, A. T., Rush, A. J., Shaw, B. F., & Emery, G. (1979). *Cognitive therapy of depression.* New York: Guilford Press.

Beck, A. T., Steer, R. A., Beck, J. S., & Newman, C. F. (1993). Hopelessness, depression, suicidal ideation, and clinical diagnosis of depression. *Suicide & Life-Threatening Behavior, 23*(2), 139–145.

Becvar, D. S., & Becvar, R. J. (1988). *Family therapy: A systemic integration.* Boston: Allyn & Bacon.

Beebe, C., & Mueller, F. (1993). Categorical offenses of juvenile delinquents and the relationship to achievement. *Journal of Correctional Education, 44,* 193–198.

Beilin, H. (1959). Teachers' and clinicians' attitudes toward the behavior problems of children: A reappraisal. *Child Development, 39,* 9–25.

Bellak, L., & Adelman, C. (1960). The children's apperception test (CAT). In A. I. Rabin & M. R. Haworth (Eds.), *Projective techniques with children.* New York: Grune & Stratton.

Bellak, L., & Bellak, S. S. (1949). *Children's apperception test.* Larchmont, NY: C.P.S., Inc.

Benard, B. (1991). *Fostering resiliency in kids: Protective factors in the family, school, and community.* Portland, OR: Northwest Regional Educational Laboratory.

Bender, L. (1954). Current research in childhood schizophrenia. *American Journal of Psychiatry, 110,* 855–856.

Bender, L. (1968). Childhood schizophrenia: A review. *International Journal of Psychiatry, 5,* 211.

Benner, G. J. (in press). The relative impact of remedial reading instruction on the basic reading skills of students with emotional disturbance and learning disabilities. *Journal of Direct Instruction.*

Benner, G. J., Nelson, J. R., & Epstein, M. H. (2002). The language skills of children with emotional and behavioral disorders; A review of the literature. *Journal of Emotional and Behavioral Disorders, 10,* 43–59.

Bentzen, F. A., & Petersen, W. (1962). Educational procedures with the brain-damaged child. In W. T. Daley (Ed.), *Speech and language therapy with the brain-damaged child.* Washington, DC: Catholic University Press.

Berk, L. E. (1999). *Infants, children and adolescents* (3rd ed.) Boston: Allyn & Bacon.

Berk, L.E. (2005). *Infants, children, and adolescents* (5th ed.). Boston: Allyn & Bacon.

Berkowitz, P. H., & Rothman, E. P. (1960). *The disturbed child: Recognition and psychoeducational therapy in the classroom.* New York: New York University Press.

Berna, J. M., & Hyman, I. A. (1993, April). *The trauma of divorce: A report of a study of the stressful life experiences of adolescents from divorced parents.* Paper presented at the annual meeting of the National Association of School Psychologists, Washington, DC.

Bernard, M., & Joyce, M. (1984). *Rational–emotive therapy with children and adolescents.* New York: John Wiley & Sons.

Berney, T., Kolvin, I., Bhate, S. R., Garside, R. F., Jeans, J., Kay, B., & Scarth, L. (1981). School phobia: A therapeutic trial with clomipramine and short-term outcome. *British Journal of Psychiatry, 138,* 110–118.

Bernstein, G. A., & Borchardt, C. M. (1991). Anxiety disorders of childhood and adolescence: A critical review. *Journal of American Academy of Children and Adolescent Psychiatry, 30,* 519–531.

Bernstein, G. A., Garfinkel, B. D., & Borchardt, C. M. (1990). Comparative studies of pharmacotherapy for school refusal. *Journal of American Academy of Child and Adolescent Psychiatry, 29,* 773–783.

Berreth, D., & Berman, S. (1997). The moral dimensions of schools. *Educational Leadership, 54*(8), 24–27.

Biederman, J., Rosenbaum, J. F., Hirshfield, D. R., Faraone, S. V., Bolduc, E. A., Gersten, M., Meminger, S. R., Kagan, J., Snidman, N., & Reznick, J. S. (1990). Psychiatric correlates of behavioral inhibition in young children of parents with and without psychiatric disorders. *Archives of General Psychology, 47,* 21–26.

Biglan, A. (1995). Translating what we know about the context of antisocial behavior into a lower prevalence of such behavior. *Journal of Applied Behavior Analysis, 28,* 479–492.

Bigler, E. D., Nielson, D., Wilde, E., Bartholomew, J., Brooks, M., & Bradford, L. W. (1999). Neuroimaging and genetic disorders. In S. Goldstein & C. R. Reynolds (Eds.), *Handbook of neurodevelopmental and genetic disorders in children* (pp. 61–83). New York: Guilford Press.

Billig, S. H. (2000). Research on K–12 school-based service-learning. *Phi Delta Kappan, 81*(9), 658–664.

Billingsley, B. (2005). *Cultivating and keeping committed special education teachers: What principals and district administrators can do.* Thousand Oaks, CA: Corwin Press.

Billingsley, B. S., Fall, A., & Williams, T O. (2006). Who is teaching students with Emotional and Behavioral disorders?: A profile and comparison to other special educators. *Behavioral Disorders, 31*(3), 252–264.

Biran, M., & Wilson, G. T. (1981). Treatment of phobic disorders using cognitive and exposure methods: A self-efficacy analysis. *Journal of Consulting and Clinical Psychology, 48,* 886–887.

Birmhauer, B., Waterman, G.S., Ryan, N., Cully, M., Balach, L., Ingram, J., et al. (1994). Fluoxetine for childhood anxiety disorders. *Journal of the American Academy of Child and Adolesent Psychiatry, 33,* 993–1000.

Blachman, B. A., Ball, E. W., Black, R., & Tangel, D. M. (2000). *Road to the code: a phonological awareness program for young children.* Baltimore: Brookes.

Blackham, G. J. (1967). *The deviant child in the classroom.* Belmont, CA: Wadsworth.

Blagg, N. R., & Yule, W. (1984). The behavioural treatment of school refusal—A comparative study. *Behaviour Research and Therapy, 22,* 119–127.

Blankenship, A. M., & Bullock, L. M. (Eds.) (1998). Kids of survival: Real-life lessons in resilience. *Reaching Today's Youth: The Community Circle of Caring Journal, 2*(3).

Blick, D. W., & Test, D. W. (1987). Effects of self-recording on high-school students' on-task behavior. *Learning Disability Quarterly, 10,* 203–213.

Boatman, B., Borkan, E. L., & Schetky, D. H. (1981). Treatment of child victims of incest. *American Journal of Family Therapy, 9,* 43–51.

Bodmer, W., & McKie, R. (1997). *The book of man: The human genome project and the quest to discover our genetic heritage.* New York: Oxford University Press.

Bolger, K., & Patterson, C. J. (2003). Sequelae of child maltreatment: Vulnerability and resilience. In S. Luthar (Ed.), *Resilience and vulnerability: Adaptation in the context of childhood adversities* (pp. 156–181). New York: Cambridge University Press.

Bolton, D., Collins, S., & Steinberg, D. (1983). The treatment of obsessive–compulsive disorder in adolescence: A report of fifteen cases. *British Journal of Psychiatry, 142,* 456–464.

Bolton, D., Eley, T.C., O'Connor, T.G., Perrin, S., Rabe-Hasketh, S., Rijsdijk, F., et al. (2006). Prevalence and genetic environmental influences on anxiety disorders in 6-year-old twins. *Psychological Medicine, 36,* 335–344.

Booher-Jennings, J. (2006). Rationing education in an era of accountability. *Phi Delta Kappa.* Retrieved November 3, 2006, from htt://www.pdkintl.org/kappan/k_v87/k0606boo.htm

Bornstein, P. H., & Quevillon, R. P. (1976). The effects of self-instructional package on over-active preschool boys. *Journal of Applied Behavior Analysis, 9*(2), 179–188.

Bos, C. S., Coleman, M., & Vaughn, S. (2002). Reading and students with EBD: What do we know and recommend? In K. L. Lane, F. M. Gresham, & T. E. O'Shaughnessy (Eds.), *Interventions for children with or at risk for emotional and behavioral disorders* (pp. 87–103). Boston: Allyn & Bacon.

Bottge, B., Rueda, E., & Skivington, M. (2006). Situating math instruction in rich problem-solving contexts: Effects on adolescents with challenging behaviors. *Behavioral Disorders, 31*(4), 394–407.

Bowen, R. C., Offord, D. R., & Boyle, M. H. (1990). The prevalence of overanxious disorder and separation anxiety disorder: Results from the Ontario Child Health Study. *Journal of American Child and Adolescent Psychiatry, 29,* 753–758.

Bower, E. M. (1961). *The education of emotionally handicapped children.* Sacramento, CA: California State Department of Education.

Bower, E. M. (1969). *Early identification of emotionally handicapped children in school* (2nd ed.). Springfield, IL: Thomas.

Bower, E. M. (1980). Slicing the mystique of prevention with Occam's razor. In N. J. Long, W. C. Morse, & R. G. Newman (Eds.), *Conflict in the classroom: The education of emotionally disturbed children* (4th ed.). Belmont, CA: Wadsworth.

Bower, E. M. (1982). Defining emotional disturbance: Public policy and research. *Psychology in the Schools, 19,* 55–60.

Bower, E. M., & Lambert, N. M. (1962). *A process for in-school screening of children with emotional handicaps.* Princeton, NJ: Educational Testing Service.

Braaten, S., Kauffman, J. M., Braaten, B., Polsgrove, L., & Nelson, C. M. (1988). The regular education initiative: Patent medicine for behavioral disorders. *Exceptional Children, 54,* 21–27.

Bradley, R., Henderson, K., & Monfore, D. A. (2004). A national perspective on children with emotional disorders, *Behavioral Disorders, 29*(3), 211–223.

Brendtro, L. K., & Van Bockern, S. (1994). Courage for the discouraged: A psychoeducational approach to troubled and troubling children. *Focus on Exceptional Children, 26*(8), 1–14.

Brendtro, L. K., Brokenleg, M., & Van Bockern, S. (1990). *Reclaiming youth at risk: Our hope for the future.* Bloomington, IN: National Education Service.

Brenner, G. J., Nelson, J. R., & Epstein, M. H. (2002). Language skills of children with EBD: A literature review. *Journal of Emotional & Behavioral Disorders, 10*(1), 43–59.

Brigham, F. J., Gustashaw, W. E., Wiley, A. L., & Brigham, M.S.P. (2004). Research in the wake of the No Child Left Behind Act: Why the controversies will continue and some suggestions for controversial research. *Behavioral Disorders, 29*(3), 300–310.

Brock, S. E., Sandoval, J., & Hart, S. (2006). Suicidal ideation and behaviors. In G. G. Bear & K. M. Minke (Eds.), *Children's needs III: Development, prevention, and intervention* (pp. 225–238). Bethesda, MD: National Association of School Psychologists.

Bronfenbrenner, U. (1979). *The ecology of human development: Experiements by nature and design.* Cambridge, MA: Harvard University Press.

Bronfenbrenner, U. (1989). Ecological systems theory. In R. Vasta (Ed.), *Annals of child development* (Vol. 6, pp. 187–251). Greenwich, CT: JAI Press.

Bronfenbrenner, U. (1993). The ecology of cognitive development: Research models and fugitive findings. In R. H. Wozniak & K. W. Fischer (Eds.), *Development in context* (pp. 3–44). Hillsdale, NJ: Lawrence Erlbaum.

Bronfenbrenner, U., & Evans, G. W., (2000). Developmental science in the 21st century: Emerging theoretical models, research designs, and empirical findings. *Social Development, 9,* 115–125.

Brooks, B. L., & Sabatino, D. A. (1996). *Personal perspectives on emotional disturbance/behavioral disorders.* Austin: Pro-Ed.

Brophy, J. E. (1977). *Child development and socialization.* Chicago: Science Research Associates.

Brophy, J., & Good, T. (1986). Teacher behavior and student achievement. In M. Wittrock (Ed.), *Handbook of research on teaching* (3rd ed.). New York: Macmillan.

Brosky, B.A., & Lally, S.J. (2004). Prevalence of trauma, PTSD, and dissociation in court-referred adolescents. *Journal of Interpersonal Violence, 19,* 801–814.

Broussard, C., & Northup, J. (1995). An approach to functional assessment and analysis of disruptive behavior in regular education classrooms. *School Psychology Quarterly, 10,* 151–164.

Brown, J., Montgomery, R., & Barclay, J. (1969). An example of psychologist management of teacher reinforcement procedures in the elementary classroom. *Psychology in the Schools, 6,* 336–340.

Brown, L. L., & Hammill, D. D. (1990). *Behavior Rating Profile-2: An ecological approach to behavior assessment.* Austin, TX: Pro-Ed.

Brown, L. M., & Gilligan, C. (1992). *Meeting at the crossroads: Women's psychology and girls' development.* Cambridge, MA: Harvard University Press.

Bruening, C. C., Wagner, W. G., & Johnson, J. T. (1997). Impact of rater knowledge on sexually abused and nonabused girls' scores on the Draw-A-Person: Screening procedure for emotional disturbance, *Journal of Personality Assessment, 68*(3), 665–677.

Brumbeck, R. A., Dietz-Schmidt, S., & Weinberg, W. A. (1977). Depression in children referred to an educational diagnosis center—Diagnosis, treatment and analysis of criteria and literature review. *Diseases of the Nervous System, 38,* 529–535.

Bulgren, J. A., Schumaker, J. B., & Deshler, D. D. (1988). Effectiveness of a concept teaching routine in enhancing the performance of LD students in secondary-level mainstream classes. *Learning Disability Quarterly, 11,* 3–17.

Bulgren, J. A., Schumaker, J. B., & Deshler, D. D. (1994). The effects of a recall enhancement routine on the test performance of secondary students with and without learning disabilities. *Learning Disabilities Research & Practice, 9*(1), 2–11.

Bullis, M., & Cheney, D. (1999). Vocational and transition interventions for adolescents and young adults with emotional or behavioral disorders. *Focus on Exceptional Children, 31*(7), 1–24.

Bullis, M., & Fredericks, H. D. (Eds.) (2002). *Providing effective vocational/transition services to adolescents with emotional and behavioral disorders.* Arden Hills, MN: Behavioral Institute for Children and Adolescents.

Bullis, M., Bull, B., Johnson, P., & Johnson, B. (1994). Identifying and assessing the community-based social behaviors of adolescents and young adults with emotional and behavioral disorders. *Journal of Emotional and Behavioral Disorders,* 2, 173–189.

Bullis, M., Yovanoff, P., Mueller, G., & Havel, E. (2002). Life on the "outs"—Examination of the facility-to-community transition of incarcerated youth. *Exceptional Children, 69,* 7–22.

Bullock, J. R. (1992, Winter). Children without friends. *Childhood Education,* 92–96.

Burrell, S., & Warboys, L. (2000, July). Special education and the juvenile justice system. *Juvenile Justice Bulletin.* Office of Juvenile Justice and Delinquency Prevention. Available at *http://www.ncjrs.gov/html/ojjdp/2000_6_5/contents.html*

Bush, J., & Bloomberg, M. R. (2006, August 13). How to help our students: Building on the 'No Child' law. *Washington Post.* Retrieved from August 14, 2006, *www.washingtonpost.com*

Bushman, B. J., & Huesmann, I. R. (2001). Effects of televised violence of aggression. In D. G. Singer & J. L. Singer (Eds.), *Handbook of children and the media* (pp. 223–254). Thousand Oaks, CA: Sage.

Buss, A. H., & Plomin, R. (1985). *Temperament: Early developing personality traits.* Hillsdale, NJ: Erlbaum.

Butcher, M. N., Williams, C. L., Graham, J. R., Archer, R. P., Tellegan, A., Ben-Porath, Y. S., et al. (1992). *Minnesota Multiphasic Personality Inventory—Adolescent: Manual for administration, scoring, and interpretation.* Minneapolis: University of Minnesota Press.

Butler, L., Miezitis, S., Friedman, R., & Cole, E. (1980). The effect of two school-based intervention programs on depressive symptoms in preadolescents. *American Educational Research Journal, 17,* 111–119.

Byne, W., Kemether, E., Jones, L., Haroutunian, V. & Davis, K. L. (1999). The neurochemistry of schizophrenia. In D. S. Charney, E. J. Nestler, & B. S. Bunney (Eds.), *Neurobiology of mental illness* (pp. 236–245). New York: Oxford University Press.

Cacioppo, J. T., von Hippel, W., & Ernst, J. M. (1997). Mapping cognitive structures and processes through verbal content: The thought-listing technique. *Journal of Consulting and Clinical Psychology, 65* (6), 928–949.

Cade, T., & Gunter, P. L. (2002). Teaching students with severe emotional or behavioral disorders to use a musical mnemonic technique to solve basic division calculations. *Behavioral Disorders, 27,* 208–214.

Cairns, R. B., & Cairns, B. D. (1994). *Lifelines and risks: Pathways of youth in our time.* New York: Harvester Wheatsheaf.

Camp, B. W., & Ray, R. S. (1984). Aggression. In A. W. Meyers & W. E. Craighead (Eds.), *Cognitive behavior therapy with children.* (pp. 315–348). New York: Plenum.

Campbell, S. B. (1973). Mother-child interaction in reflective, impulsive, and hyperactive children. *Developmental Psychology, 8,* 341–349.

Campbell, S. B. (1975). Mother-child interaction: A comparison of hyperactive, learning disabled, and normal boys. *American Journal of Orthopsychiatry, 45,* 51–56.

Campbell, S. B. (1986). Developmental issues. In R. Gittelman (Ed.), *Anxiety disorders of childhood* (pp. 24–57). New York: Guilford.

Campbell, S. G., & Ewing, L. J. (1990). Follow-up of hard-to-manage preschoolers: Adjustment at age 9 and predictors of continuing symptoms. *Journal of Child Psychology and Psychiatry, 31,* 871–889.

Canfield, J., & Hansen, M. V. (1995). *Chicken soup for the soul: 101 stories to open the heart and rekindle the spirit.* Deerfield Beech, FL: Health Communications, Inc.

Canfield, J., & Wells, H. C. (1994). *100 ways to enhance self-concept in the classroom: A handbook for teachers and parents* (2nd ed). Englewood Cliffs, NJ: Prentice Hall.

Cantwell, D. P. (1978). Hyperactivity and antisocial behavior. *Journal of the American Academy of Child Psychiatry, 17,* 252–262.

Cantwell, D. P. (1990). Depression across the early life span. In M. Lewis & S. M. Miller (Eds.), *Handbook of Developmental Psychopathology* (pp. 293–309). New York: Plenum Press.

Cantwell, D. P., & Satterfield, J. (1978). The prevalence of academic underachievement in hyperactive children. *Journal of Pediatric Psychology, 3,* 168–171.

Carlson, C. L., Lahey, B. B., & Neeper, R. (1984). Peer assessment of the social behavior of accepted, rejected, and neglected children. *Journal of Abnormal Child Psychology, 12,* 189–198.

Carlson, G. A., & Cantwell, D. P. (1986). Developmental issues in the classification of depression in children. In M. Rutter, C. E. Izard, & P. B. Read (Eds.), *Depression in young people: Developmental and clinical perspectives.* (pp. 399–434). New York: Guilford.

Carlson, N. (2004). *Physiological psychology* (8th ed.). Boston: Allyn & Bacon.

Carlson, P., & Stephens, T. (1986). Cultural bias and the identification of behaviorally disordered children. *Behavioral Disorders, 11,* 191–198.

Carpenter, R.L., & Apter, S.J. (1988). Research integration of cognitive-emotional interventions for behaviorally disordered children and youth. In M.C. Wang, M.C. Reynolds, & H.J. Walberg (Eds.), *Handbook of special education: Research and practice: Vol. 2. Mildly handicapped conditions* (pp. 155–169). New York: Pergamon.

Carr, E. G., & Durand, V. M. (1985a). Reducing behavior problems through functional communication training. *Journal of Applied Behavior Analysis, 18,* 111–126.

Carr, E. G., & Durand, V. M. (1985b). The social-communicative basis of severe behavior problems in children. In S. Reiss & R. Bootzin (Eds.), *Theoretical issues in behavior therapy* (pp. 219–254). New York: Academic Press.

Carr, S. C., & Punzo, R. P. (1993). The effects of self-monitoring of academic accuracy and productivity on the performance of students with behavioral disorders. *Behavioral Disorders, 18,* 241–250.

Carter, J., & Sugai, G. (1989). Survey on pre-referral practices: Responses from state departments of education. *Exceptional Children, 55,* 298–302.

Cartledge, G., Kea, C. D., & Ida, D. J. (2000). Anticipating differences—celebrating strengths: Providing culturally competent services for students with serious emotional disturbance. *Teaching Exceptional Children,* 32(3), 30–37.

Casey, R. J., & Berman, J. S. (1985). The outcome of psychotherapy with children. *Psychological Bulletin, 98,* 388–400.

Caspi, A. (1998). Personality development across the life course. In N. Eisenberg (Ed.), *Handbook of child psychology: Vol. 3. Social, emotional, and personality development* (5th ed., pp. 311–388). New York: John Wiley & Sons.

Catts, H. W., Fey, M. E., Zhang, X., & Tomblin, J. B. (1999). Language basis of reading and reading disabilities. *Scientific Studies of Reading, 3,* 331–361.

Cauffman, E., Scholle, S. H., Mulvey, E., & Kelleher, K. J. (2005). Predicting first time involvement in the juvenile justice system among emotionally disturbed youth receiving mental health services. *Psychological Services, 2*(1), 28–38.

Causeau, D. L., Luckasson, R., & Kroth, R. L. (1994). Special education services for girls with serious emotional disturbance: A case of gender bias? *Behavioral Disorders, 20*(1), 51–60.

Cavanagh, S. (2004, January 8). The testing dilemma. *Education Week: Quality Counts 2004,* pp. 53–56.

Cavazzana-Calvo, M., Hacein-Bey, S., de Saint Basile, G., Gross, F., Yvon, E., Nusbaum, P., et al. Gene therapy of human severe combined immunodeficiency (SCID)-X1 disease. *Science, 2000. 288*(5466): p. 669-72.

CEC pleased the IDEA regulations are released, urges department of education to act on missing pieces. (2006, August 7). Press Release. Retrieved August 8, 2006, from *http://www.cec.sped.org*

Center for Communication and Social Policy (Ed.), (1998). *National television violence study* (Vol. 2). Newbury Park, CA: Sage Publications.

Center for Effective Collaboration and Practice (CECP), & National Association of School Psychologists (NASP).

(2000). *Safeguarding our children: An action guide.* Washington D. C.: U.S. Department of Education Editorial Publication Center

Center for Mental Health in Schools (2006). *About The center for Mental health in schools,* retrieved February 9, 2007, from *http://smhp.psych.ucla.edu*

Center, D. B. (1989). *Curriculum and teaching strategies for students with behavior disorders.* Englewood Cliffs, NJ: Prentice Hall.

Center, D. B., & Callaway, J. M. (1999). Self-reported job stress and personality in teachers of students with emotional or behavioral disorders. *Behavioral Disorders, 25*(1), 22–40.

Centers for Disease Control (CDC). (2005, September). Mental health in the United States: Prevalence of medication therapy for attention-deficit/hyperactivity disorder. *Morbidity and Mortality Weekly Report.* Available at www.cdc.gov/mmwr/preview/mmwrhtml/

Centers for Disease Control and Prevention, (2004). *STD surveillance 2004.* Retrieved September 12, 2006, from *http://www.cdc.gov*

Centers for Disease Control and Prevention. (2005). *National youth risk behavior survey: 1991–2005.* Retrieved September 12, 2006, from *http://www.cdc.gov*

Centers for Disease Control and Prevention. (2006). *Healthy youth! Alcohol & drug use.* Available at http://www.cdc.gov/Healthy Youth/alcoholdrug/index.htm

Centers for Disease Control and Prevention. (CDC). (2000) *Adolescent and school health: Programmatic activities [on-line].* Available: http://www.cec.gov/nccdphp/dash/violence/programmatic.htm.

Centers for Disease Control. (2006). Violence-related behaviors among high school students—United States, 1991–2003. Retrieved November 18, 2006, from http://www.cdc.gov/

Chamberlain, S. (2005). Recognizing and responding to cultural differences in the education of culturally and linguistically diverse learners. *Intervention in School and Clinic, 40,* 195–211.

Chassin, L., Curran, P. J., Hussong, A. M., & Colder, C. R. (1996). The relation of parent alcoholism to adolescent substance use: A longitudinal follow-up study. *Journal of Abnormal Psychology, 105,* 70–80.

Cheney, D., & Muscott, H. S. (1996) Preventing school failure for students with emotional and behavioral disabilities through responsible inclusion. *Preventing School Failure, 40*(3), 109–116.

Cheney, D., Malloy, J., & Hagner, D. (1998). Finishing high school in many different ways: Project RENEW in Manchester, New Hampshire. *Effective School Practices, 17*(2), 43–52.

Cheney, L., & Morse, W. C. (1974). Psychodynamic interventions in emotional disturbance. In W. C. Rhodes & M. L. Tracy (Eds.), *A Study of child variance* (Vol. 2). Ann Arbor, MI: The University of Michigan Press.

Chess, S. (1967). The role of temperament in the child's development. *Acta Paedopsychiatrica, 34,* 91–103.

Children's Defense Fund (CDF). (2006). Cradle to Prison Pipeline Initiative. Retrieved September 29, 2006, from http://www.childrensdefense.org/

Children's Defense Fund. (2005). *Each day in America.* Retrieved November 4, 2006, from http://www.childrensdefense.ore/site/PageServer

Cicchetti, D., & Toth, S. L. (1998). The development of depression in children and adolescents. *American Psychologist, 53,* 221–241.

Cipiani, E. C., & Spooner, F. (1994). *Curricular and instruction approaches for persons with severe disabilities.* Boston: Allyn & Bacon.

Clarizio, H. F. (1985). Cognitive-behavioral treatment of childhood depression. *Psychology in the Schools, 22,* 308–322.

Clark, D. A. (1997). Twenty years of cognitive assessment: Current status and future directions. *Journal of Consulting and Clinical Psychology, 65* (6), 996–1000.

Clark, D. B., & Jacob, R. G. (1992). Anxiety disorders and alcoholism in adolescents: A preliminary report (Abstract). *Alcoholism, Clinical, and Experimental Research, 16,* 371.

Clark, D. B., Smith, M. G., Neighbors, B. D., Skerlec, L. M., & Randall, J. (1994). Anxiety disorders in adolescence: Characterisics, prevalence, and comorbidities. *Clinical Psychology Review, 14,* 113–137.

Clark, D. M., & Beck, A. T. (1988). Cognitive approaches. In C. G. Last & M. Hersen (Eds.), *Handbook of anxiety disorders* (pp. 362–385). New York: Pergamon.

Clark, L. A., & Watson, D. (1991). Tripartite model of anxiety and depression: Psychometric evidence and taxonomic implications. *Journal of Abnormal Psychology, 100,* 316–336.

Clarizio, H. F. (1985). Cognitive-behavioral treatment of childhood depression. *Psychology in the Schools, 22,* 308–322.

Clarke, G. N., DeBar, L. L., & Lewinsohn, P. M. (2003). Cognitive-behavioral group treatment for adolescent depression. In A. E. Kazdin & J. R. Weisz (Eds.), *Evidence-based psychotherapies for children and adolescents* (pp. 120–134). New York: Guilford Press.

Clarke, G. N., Hawkine, W., Murphy, M., Sheeber, L. B., Lewinsohn, P. M., & Seeley, J. R. (1995). Targeted prevention of unipolar depressive disorder in an at-risk sample of high school adolescents: A randomized trial of a group cognitive intervention. *Journal of the America Academy of Child and Adolescent Psychiatry, 34,* 312–332.

Clarke, H. B. (1998). *Transition to independence process: TIP operations manual.* Tampa: University of South Florida. Florida Mental Health Institute.

Clarke, H. B., & Clarke, R. T. (1996). Research on the wraparound process and individualized services for children with multi-system needs. *Journal of Child and Family Studies, 5,* 1–5.

Clarke, S., Dunlap, G., Foster-Johnson, L., Childs, K. E., Wilson, D., Shite, R., & Vera, A. (1995). Improving the conduct of students with behavioral disorders by incorporating student interests into curricular activities. *Behavioral Disorders, 20*(4), 221–237.

Cloud, J. (1999, May). What can the schools do? *Time, 153,* 38–40.

Cobb, N. (1995). *Adolescence.* Mountain View, CA: Mayfield Publishing.

Cocozza, J. J., & Skowyra, K. (2002). Youth with mental health disorders: Issues and emerging responses. *Juvenile Justice, 7*(1), 3–13.

Cohen, A. (1999, May 3). The curse of cliques. *Time,* pp. 44–45.

Cohen, E. C., Reinherz, H. Z., & Frost, A. K. (1994). Self-perceptions of unpopularity in adolescence: Locks to past and current adjustment. *Child and Adolescent Social Work Journal, 11,* 37–52.

Cole, C., Ferrara, V., Johnson, D., Jones, M., Schoenbaum, M., Tyler, R., Wallace, V., & Poulsen, M. (1989). *Today's challenge: Teaching strategies for working with young children prenatally exposed to drugs/alcohol.* Los Angeles: Los Angeles Unified School District.

Cole, D. A., & Turner, J. E. (1993). Models of cognitive mediation and moderation in child depression. *Journal of Abnormal Psychology, 102(2),* 271–281.

Coleman, M. C. (1996). *Emotional/behavior disorders: Theory and practice* (3rd Ed.). Boston: Allyn & Bacon.

Coleman, M. C., & Gilliam, J. E. (1983). Disturbing behaviors in the classroom: A survey of teacher attitudes. *Journal of Special Education, 17,* 121–129.

Coleman, M. C., & Gilliam, J. E. (1990). Preliminary findings: Differences between behavior disordered juvenile offenders and non-BD juvenile offenders. *Unpublished manuscript.* Austin, TX: The University of Texas.

Coleman, M. C., & Vaughn, S. (2000). Reading interventions for students with emotional/behavioral disorders, *Behavioral Disorders, 25*(2), 93–104.

Coleman, M. C., & Webber, J. (1988). Behavior problems? Try groups! *Academic Therapy, 23,* 265–274.

Coleman, M. C., Wheeler, L., & Webber, J. (1993). Research on interpersonal problem-solving training: A critical review. *Journal of Remedial and Special Education, 14,* 25–36.

Coleman, M., & Vaughn, S. (2000). Reading interventions for students with emotional/behavioral disorders. *Behavioral Disorders, 25*(2), 93–104.

Coleman, M., Webber, J., & Algozzine, B. (1999). Inclusion and students with emotional/behavioral disorders. *Special Services in the Schools, 15*(1/2), 25–47.

Coles, A. D. (2000, May 10). Educators welcome guidelines for diagnosing ADHD. *Education Week, 19*(35), 6.

Collins, F. (2006). *The language of God.* New York: Free Press/Simon & Schuster, Inc.

Commission on Violence and Youth. (1993). *Violence and youth.* Washington, DC: American Psychological Association.

Comstock, G. A., & Paik, H. (1994). The effects of television violence on antisocial behavior: A meta-analysis. *Communication Research, 21,* 269–277.

Conduct Problems Prevention Research Group. (2002). Evaluation of the first three years of the Fast Track Prevention Trial with children at high risk for adolescent conduct problems. *Journal of Abnormal Child Psychology, 30,* 19–35.

Conley, C. H. (1993). *Street gangs: Current knowledge and strategies.* Washington, DC: U.S. Department of Justice, National Institute of Justice.

Conners, C. K. (1970). Symptom patterns in hyperkinetic, neurotic, and normal children. *Child Development, 41,* 667–682.

Conoley, C. W., Conoley, J. C., McConnell, J. A., & Kimzey, C. E. (1983). The effect of the ABCs of rational emotive therapy and the empty-chair technique of gestalt therapy on anger reduction. *Psychotherapy: Theory, Research and Practice, 20,* 112–117.

Conoley, J. C., & Goldstein, A. P. (1997). The known, unknown, and future of violence reduction. In A. P. Goldstein & J. C. Conoley (Eds.), *School violence intervention: A practical handbook* (pp. 493–495). New York: The Guilford Press.

Conrad, D., & Hedin, D. (1991). School-based community service: What we know from research and theory, *Phi Delta Kappan, 72*(10), 743–749.

Conroy, M., Clark, D., Gable, R. A., & Fox, J. J. (1999). A look at IDEA 1997 discipline provisions: Implications for change in the roles and responsibilities of school personnel. *Preventing School Failure, 43*(2), 64–70.

Conroy, M., Fox, J. J., Bucklin, A., & Good, W. (1996). An analysis of the reliability and stability of the Motivation Assess Scale in assignment the challenging behaviors of persons with developmental disabilities. *Education and Training in Mental Retardation and Developmental Disabilities, 31,* 243–250.

Cook-Cottone, C., & Phelps, L. (2006). Adolescent eating disorders. In G. G. Bear & K. M. Minke (Eds.), *Children's needs III: Development, prevention, and intervention* (pp. 977–988). Bethesda, MD: National Association of School Psychologists.

Coontz, S. (1995). The American family and the nostalgia trap. *Phi Delta Kappan, 76,* K1–K20.

Costello, E. J., Gordon, P., Keeler, M. S., & Angold, A. (2001). Poverty, race/ethnicity, and psychiatric disorder:

a study of rural children. *American Journal of Public Health, 91*(1), 1494–1498

Council for Children with Behavioral Disorders: Executive Committee. (1987). Position paper on definition and identification of students with behavioral disorders. *Behavioral Disorders, 13,* 9–19.

Council for Exceptional Children (CEC). (2004). The new IDEA: CEC's summary of significant issues. Retrieved November 28, 2004, from *http://www.cec.sped.org/pp/IDEA-112304.pdf,*

Council for Exceptional Children (CEC). (2005). *NCLB Under Siege.* Retrieved September 20, 2005, from *http://www.cec.sped.org/*

Council for Exceptional Children. (1999, October). Advocacy in action: CEC calls for alternative programs for students who bring firearms to school. *CEC Today, 6* (3), 4.

Couvillon, M. A. (2003). Legal limits: Understanding restraint and time-out in schools: positive steps forward for Texas. *Beyond Behavior, 12*(3), 10–11.

Craighead, W. E., Meyers, A. W., & Wilcoxon-Craighead, L. W. (1985). A conceptual model for cognitive-behavioral therapy with children. *Journal of Abnormal Child Psychology, 13,* 331–342.

Crenshaw, T. M., Kavale, K. A., Forness, S. R., & Reeve, R. E. (1999). Attention deficit hyperactivity disorder and the efficacy of stimulant medication: A meta-analysis. In T. Scruggs & M. Mastropieri (Eds.), *Advances in learning and behavioral disabilities* (Vol. 13, pp. 135–165). Greenwich, CT: JAI Press.

Crockett, J. B., & Kauffman, J. M. (1998). Taking inclusion back to its roots. *Educational Leadership, 56*(2), 74–77.

Crooks, R. & Baur, K. (1983). *Our sexuality* (2nd ed.). Menlo Park, CA: Benjamin/Cummings Publishing.

Cross, L. H., & Billingsley, B. (1994). Testing a model of special educators' intent to stay in teaching. *Exceptional Children, 60,* 411–421.

Crothers, L. M., Field, J. E., & Kolbert, J. B. (2005). Navigating power, control, and being nice: Aggression in adolescent girls' friendships. *Journal of Counseling and Development, 83*(3), 349.

Crowe, R. R., Noyes, R., Pauls, D. L., & Slymen, D. (1983). A family study of panic disorder. *Archives of General Psychiatry, 40,* 1065–1069.

Cruickshank, W. M., Bentzen, F. A., Ratzeburg, F. H., & Tannhauser, M. T. (1961). *A teaching method for brain-injured and hyperactive children.* Syracuse: Syracuse University Press.

Cuban, L. (2004, March 17). The contentious "No Child" law: Who will fix it? And how? *Education Week,* pp. 72, 58–59.

Cullinan, D. (2002). *Students with emotional and behavioral disorders: An introduction for teachers and other helping professionals.* NJ: Upper Saddle River, Merrill/Prentice-Hall.

Cullinan, D. (2004). Classification and definition of emotional & behavioral disorders, In R.B. Rutherford, M. M. Quinn & S. R. Mathur (eds.), *Handbook of research in emotional and behavioral disorders (pp. 32–53).* New York: The Guilford Press.

Cullinan, D., & Epstein, M. H. (2001). Comorbidity among students with emotional disturbance. *Behavioral Disorders,* 26, 200–213.

Cullinan, D., & Sabornie, E. J. (2004). Characteristics of emotional disturbance in middle and high school students. *Journal of Emotional and Behavioral Disorders, 12*(3), 157–167.

Cullinan, D., Epstein, M.H., & Kaufman, J.M. (1984). Teachers' ratings of students' behaviors: What constitutes behavior disorder in school? *Behavioral Disorders, 10,* 9–19.

Cullinan, D., Evans, C., Epstein, M. H., & Ryser, G. (2003). Characteristics of emotional disturbance of elementary school students. *Behavioral Disorders, 28,* 94–110.

Cullinan, D., Osborne, S., & Epstein, M. H. (2004). Characteristics of emotional disturbance among female students. *Remedial and Special Education, 25*(5), 276–290.

Cummings, J. A. (1986). Projective drawings. In H. M. Knoff (Ed.), *The assessment of child and adolescent personality* (pp. 199–244). New York: Guilford Press.

Cummings, J.G., Pepler, D.J., & Moore, T.E. (1999). Behavior problems in children exposed to wife abuse: Gender differences. *Journal of Family Violence, 14,* 133–156.

Curran, D. K. (1987). *Adolescent suicidal behavior.* Washington: Hemisphere.

Cytryn, L., McKnew, D. H., Zahn-Waxler, C., & Gershon, E. S. (1986). Developmental issues in risk research: The offspring of effectively ill parents. In M. Rutter, C. E. Izard, & P. B. Read (Eds.), *Depression in young people: Developmental and clinical perspectives.* New York: Guilford.

D'Amico, R., & Blackorby, J. (1992). Trends in employment among out-of-school youth with disabilities. In M. Wagner, R. D'Amico, C. Marder, L. Newman, & J. Blackorby (Eds.), *What happens next? Trends in postschool outcomes of youth with disabilities* (pp. 4-1 to 4–47). Menlo Park, CA: SRI International.

Danielson, L. (2006, May 8). *Update from OSEP.* U.S. Office of Special Education Programs. Available at www.ndpc-sd.org/resources/docs/SEAForum2006/Danielson_L—Update_from_OSEP.pdf

Danino, G., Costello, E. J., & Angold, A. (1999). Assessing functional impairment and social adaptation for child mental health services research: A review of measures, *Mental Health Services Research, 1,* 93–108.

Davis, J. M., Sandoval, J., & Wilson, M. P. (1988). Strategies for the primary prevention of adolescent suicide. *School Psychology Review, 17,* 559–569.

Davis, R. W., & Hajicek, J. O. (1985). Effects of self-instructional training and strategy training on a mathematics task with severely behaviorally disordered students. *Behavioral Disorders, 10,* 275–282.

De La Paz, S. (1999). Teaching writing strategies and self-regulation procedures to middle school students with learning disabilities. *Focus on Exceptional Children, 31*(5), 1–16.

Dealing with school violence. (2006, October 27). *Minneapolis–St. Paul Star Tribune.com.* Retrieved October 27, 2006, from http://www.startribune.com/

Dean, R., & Woodcock, D. W. (2003). *Dean-Woodcock Neuropsychological Battery.* Itasca, IL: Riverside Corp.

deFur, S. H., & Patton, J. R. (1999). *Transition and school-based services: Interdisciplinary perspectives for enhancing the transition process.* Austin, TX: Pro-Ed.

Deiro, J. A. (2003, March). Do your students know you care? *Educational Leadership, 60*(6), 60–62.

Delaney, M. J., & Durand, M. V. (1986). *Motivation Assessment Scale.* Topeka, KS: Monaco & Associates.

Delis, D. C., Kaplan, E., & Kramer, J. H. (2001). *Delis-Kaplan Executive Function System: Examiner's manual.* San Antonio, TX: Psychological Corporation.

Della Cava, M. R. (2005, September 21). Out-of-line preschoolers increasingly face expulsion. *USA Today.* Retrieved September 27, 2005, from http://www.usatoday.com/printededition/news/20050921/1a_cover21.art.htm

Denham, S. A., & Almeida, M. C. (1987). Children's social problem-solving skills, behavioral adjustment and interventions: A meta-analysis evaluating theory and practice. *Journal of Applied Developmental Psychology, 8,* 391–409.

Department of Health and Human Services. (2001). *Report of the Surgeon General's Conference on Children's Mental Health: A national action agenda.* Washington, DC: Author.

Despert, J. L. (1965). *The emotionally disturbed child—Then and now.* New York: Robert Brunner.

DeStefano, L., & Wagner, M. (1992). Outcome assessment in special education: What lessons have we learned? In F. Rusch, L. DeStefano, J. Chadsey-Rusch, L. Phelps, & E. Szymanski (Eds.), *Transition from school to adult life* (pp. 173–207). Sycamore, IL: Sycamore Publishing.

DeVeaugh-Geiss, J., Moroz, G., Biederman, J., Cantwell, D., Fontaine, R., Greist, J.H., et al. (1992). Clomipramine hydrochloride in childhood and adolescent obsessive–compulsive disorder: A multicenter trial. *Journal of the American Academy of Child and Adolescent Psychiatry, 31,* 45–49.

Devers, R., Bradley-Johnson, S., & Johnson, C. M. (1994). The effect of token reinforcement on WISC-R performance for fifth through ninth grade American Indians. *Psychological Record, 44,* 441–449.

Devoe, J. F., Peter, K., Noonan, M., Snyder, T.D., & Baum, K. (2005). *Indicators of school crime and safety: 2005* (NCES 2006-001/MCJ 210697). U.S. Departments of Education and Justice. Washington, DC: Government Printing Office.

Devore, H. H., & Zionts, L. T. (2003). Standing up and speaking out: A new era in special education. *Beyond Behavior, 12*(2), 10–11.

Dixon, J. F., & Ahrens, A. H. (1992). Stress and attributional style as predictors of self-reported depression in children. *Cognitive Therapy and Research, 16(6),* 623–635.

Dodge, K. A. (1985). Attributional bias in aggressive children. In P. C. Kendall (Ed.), *Advances in cognitive-behavioral research and therapy* (Vol. 4, pp. 73–110). Orlando: Academic Press.

Donahue, M., Cole, D., & Hartas, D. (1999). Research on interactions among oral language and emotional/behavioral disorders. In D. Rogers-Adkinson & P. Griffith (Eds.), *Communication disorders and children with psychiatric and behavioral disorders* (pp. 69–97). San Diego: Singular.

Donnellan-Walsh, A., Gossage, L. D., LaVigna, G. W., Schuler, A., & Traphagen, J. D., (1976). *Teaching makes a difference: A guide for developing successful classes for autistic and other severely handicapped children.* Administrative manual. Sacramento, CA: California State Department of Education.

Donnelly, P., & Suter, K. (1994). *Juvenile gangs: It's not the Sharks and Jets anymore.* Austin, TX: Texas Juvenile Probation Commission.

Donnerstein, E., Slaby, R. G., & Eron, L. D. (1994). The mass media and youth aggression. In L. D. Eron, J. H. Gentry, & P. Schlegel (Eds.), *Reason to hope: A psychosocial perspective on violence and youth* (pp. 219–250). Washington, DC: American Psychological Association.

Donohue, E., Schiraldi, V., & Zeidenberg, J. (1998). *School house hype: The school shootings, and the real risks kids face in America.* San Francisco: Center on Juvenile and Criminal Justice. Retrieved November 4, 2006, from www.cjcj.org

"Don't blame students: Do special-ed programs produce lower test scores?" (2006, August 21). *Washington Post.* Retrieved August 22, 2006, from *www.washingtonpost.com.*

Doren, B., Bullis, M., & Benz, M. R. (1996). Predicting the arrest status of adolescents with disabilities in transition. *The Journal of Special Education, 29,* 363–380.

Doty, D. S. (2000). Public enragement or public engagement? *Education Week, 19*(25), 72, 47.

Douglas, V. I. & Peters, K. (1979). Toward a clearer definition of the attention deficit of hyperactive children. In G. Hale & M. Lewis (Eds.), *Attention and the development of cognitive skills.* New York: Plenum.

Draeger, S., Prior, M., & Sanson, A. (1986). Visual and auditory performance in hyperactive children: Competence or compliance. *Journal of Abnormal Child Psychology, 14,* 411–424.

Drakeford, W., & Staples, J. M. (2006). An examination of the influence of procedural, practical, and perceptual factors on bias in school disciplinary practices. *Teaching Exceptional Children, 38*(3), 29–38.

Dreikurs, R. (1948). *The challenge of parenthood.* New York: Duell, Sloan, & Pearch.

Drug Abuse Resistance Education (D.A.R.E.). (2006). About D.A.R.E. Retrieved February 16, 2007 from *http://www.dare.com/home/about dare.asp*

Dryden, W. (1998). *Developing self-acceptance.* New York: John Wiley & Sons.

Duchnowski, A.J., Kutash, K., & Friedman, R. M. (2002). Community-based interventions in a system of care and outcomes framework. In B. J. Burns & K. Hoagwood (Eds.), *Community treatment for youth: Evidence-based interventions for severe emotional and behavioral disorders* (pp. 16–37). New York: Oxford University Press.

Dunlap, G., Ferro, J., & Deperczel, M. (1994). Nonaversive behavioral intervention in the community. In E. C. Cipani & F. Spooner (Eds.), *Curricular and instructional approaches for persons with severe disabilities* (pp. 117–146). Boston: Allyn & Bacon.

DuPaul, G. J., Guevremont, D. C., & Barkley, R. A. (1992). Behavioral treatment of attention-deficit hyperactivity disorder in the classroom: The use of the attention training systems. *Behavior Modification, 16,* 204–225.

DuPaul, G. J., Power, T. J., Anastopoulos, A. D., & Reid, R. (1998). *ADHD Rating Scale—IV: Checklists, norms, and clinical interpretation.* New York: Guilford Press.

DuPaul, G. J., Stoner, G., & O'Reilly, M. J. (2002). Best practices in classroom interventions for attention problems. In A. Thomas & J. Grimes (Eds.), *Best practices in school psychology—IV* (pp. 1115–1127). Bethesda, MD: National Association of School Psychologists.

Durand, V. M., & Carr, E. G. (1985). Self-injurious behavior: Motivating conditions and guidelines for treatment. *School Psychology Review, 14*(2), 171–176.

Durant, W. (1939). *The life of Greece.* New York: Simon & Schuster.

Durant, W. (1961). *The story of philosophy: The lives and opinions of the great philosophers of the western world.* New York: Simon & Schuster.

Dweck, D. S. (1975). The role of expectations and attributions in the alteration of learned helplessness. *Journal of Personality and Social Psychology, 25,* 109–116.

Dwyer, K. P. (1999, Summer). Building safe and supportive schools for all children. *Family Matters,* 1–4.

Dwyer, K., Osher, D., & Warger, C. (1998). *Early warning, timely response: A guide to safe schools.* Washington DC: U.S. Department of Education.

Dwyer, K., Osher, D., & Warger, C. (2000). Warning signs of school violence, *ERIC Review, 7*(1), 16–17.

Earls, F., & Jung, K. (1987). Temperament and home environment characteristics as causal factors in early development of childhood psychopathology. *Journal of American Academy of Child and Adolescent Psychiatry, 26,* 491–498.

Eating Disorders—Part I. (1997, October). *Harvard Mental Health Letter, 14*(4), 1–5.

Eating Disorders—Part II. (1997, November). *Harvard Mental Health Letter, 14*(5), 1–5.

Eber, L. (1996). Restructuring schools through wraparound planning: The LADSE experience. In R. J. Illback & C. M. Nelson (Eds.), *School-based services for students with emotional and behavioral disorders* (pp. 139–154). Binghamton, NY: Haworth Press.

Eber, L., & Nelson, C. M. (1997). School-based wraparound planning: Integrating services for students with emotional and behavioral needs. *American Journal of Orthopsychiatry, 67*(3), 385–395.

Eber, L., Nelson, C. M., & Miles, P. (1997). School-based wraparound for students with emotional and behavioral challenges. *Exceptional Children, 63*(4), 539–555.

Eber, L., Sugai, G., Smith, C. R., & Scott, T. M. (2002). Wraparound and positive behavioral Interventions and supports in the schools. *Journal of Emotional and Behavioral Disorders,* 10(3), 171–180.

ED Review. (2006, June 28). ADA Anniversary. *ED Review.* Retrieved June 28, 2006, from *http://www.ed.gov/about/offices/list/osers/ada-event-2006.html*

Edelman, M. W. (1995, Spring). United we stand: A common vision. *Claiming Children, 1,* 6–12.

Egan, K., & Asher J. (June 6, 2005). Mental illness exacts heavy toll, beginning in youth [Press release]. Retrieved August 10, 2006, from *http://www.nimh.nih.gov/press/mentalhealthstats.cfm*

Eggelston, C. R. (1984). *Results of a national correctional/special education survey.* Paper presented at the Correctional/Special Education National Conference, Arlington, VA.

Elizalde-Utnick, G. (2002). Best practices in building partnerships with families. In A. Thomas, & J. Grimes (Eds.), *Best Practices in School Psychology IV* (pp. 413–429). Bethesda MD: National Association of School Psychologists.

Elkind, D. (1974). *Children and adolescents* (2nd ed.). New York: Oxford University Press.

Ellis, A. (1962). *Reason and emotion in psychotherapy.* New York: Lyle Stuart.

Ellis, A. (1973). *Humanistic psychotherapy: The rational-emotive approach.* New York: Julian.

Ellis, A. (1980). An overview of the clinical theory of rational-emotive therapy. In R. Grieger & R. Boyd (Eds.), *Rational-emotive therapy.* New York: Van Nostrand Reinhold.

Ellis, A. (2002). *Overcoming resistance: A rational emotive behavior therapy integrated approach* (2nd ed.). New York: Springer.

Emslie, G.J., Heiligenstein, J.H., Wagner, K.D., Hoog, S.L., Ernest, D.E., Brown, E., et al. (2002). Fluoxetine for acute treatment of depression in children and adolescents: A placebo-controlled, randomized clinical trial. *Journal of the American Academy of Child and Adolescent Psychiatry, 41,* 1205–1215.

Engelmann, S., Hanner, S., & Johnson, G. (2002). *Corrective reading.* Columbus, OH: SRA/McGraw-Hill.

Epstein, M. H., & Cullinan, D. (1998). *Scale for Assessing Emotional Disturbance: Examiner's manual.* Austin, TX: Pro-Ed.

Epstein, M. H., & Sharma, J. (1998). *Behavioral and Emotional Rating Scale: A strength-based approach to assessment.* Austin, TX: Pro-Ed.

Epstein, M. H., Cullinan, D., & Rosemier, R. A. (1983). Behavior problems of behaviorally disordered and normal adolescents. *Behavioral Disorders, 8,* 171–175.

Epstein, M. H., Cullinan, D., Ryser, G, & Pearson N. (2002). Development of a scale to assess emotional disturbance, *Behavioral Disorders,* 28(1), 5–22.

Epstein, M. H., Kinder, D., & Bursuck, B. (1989). The academic status of adolescents with behavioral disorders. *Behavioral Disorders, 14,* 157–165.

Epstein, M.H., Kutash, K., & Duchnowski, A. J. (2005). *Outcomes for children and youth with emotional and behavioral disorders and their families: Programs and evaluation best practices* (2nd ed.). Austin, TX: Pro-Ed.

ERIC/OSEP Special Project (1999, Winter). Positive behavioral support. *Research Connections in Special Education,* No. 4, 1–8.

Erickson, W. D. (1984), Sexual behavior disorders in adolescents. In S. Braaten, R. B. Rutherford, Jr., & C. A. Kardash (Eds.), *Programming for adolescents with behavioral disorders.* Reston, VA: Council for Children with Behavioral Disorders.

Erikson, E. H. (1968). *Identity: Youth and crisis.* New York: W. W. Norton & Co.

Esler, E. N., Godber, Y., & Christenson, S. L. (2002). Best practices in supporting home-school collaboration. In A. Thomas & J. Grimes (Eds.), *Best practices in school psychology IV* (pp. 389–411). Bethesda, MD: National Association of School Psychologists.

Etscheidt, S. (1991). Reducing aggressive behavior and improving self-control: A cognitive-behavioral training program for behaviorally disordered adolescents. *Behavioral Disorders, 16,* 107–115.

Evans, S. W., Dowling, C., & Brown, R. (in press). Psychosocial treatment of adolescents with attention deficit hyperactivity disorder. In K. McBurnett, L. Pfiffner, R. Schachar, G. R. Elliott, & J. Nigg (Eds.), *Attention deficit hyperactivity disorder.* New York: Marcel Dekker.

Exner, J. E., Jr. & Weiner, I. B. (1982). *The Rorschach, A Comprehensive System Volume 3: Assessment of Children and Adolescents.* New York: A Wiley-Interscience Publication, John Wiley & Sons, Inc.

Exner, J. E., Jr., & Weiner, I. B. (1994). *The Rorschach: A comprehensive system: Vol. 3. Assessment of children and adolescents* (2nd ed.). New York: Wiley.

Eysenck, H. J. (1965). The effects of psychotherapy. *Journal of Psychology, 1,* 97–118.

Eysenck, H. J. (Ed.). (1981). *A model for personality.* New York: Springer-Verlag.

Facomata, T., Roane, H., Hovanetz, A., Kettering, T., & Keeney, K. (2004). An evaluation of response cost in the treatment of inappropriate vocalizations maintained by automatic reinforcement. *Journal of Applied Behavior Analysis, 37,* 83–87.

Faedda, G.L., Baldessarini, R.J., Suppes, T., Tondo, L., Becker, I., & Lipschitz, D.S. (1995). Pediatric-onset bipolar disorder: A neglected clinical and public health problem. *Harvard Review of Psychiatry, 3,* 171–195.

Falk, G. D., Dunlap, G., & Kern, L. (1996). An analysis of self-evaluation and videotape feedback for improving the peer interactions of students with externalizing and internalizing behavioral problem. *Behavioral Disorders, 21*(4), 261–276.

Farmer, T. W., & Hollowell, J. H. (1994). Social networks in mainstream classrooms: Social affiliations and behavioral characteristics of students with EBD. *Journal of Emotional and Behavioral Disorders, 2*(3), 143–155, 163.

Fava, M., Copeland, P. M., Schweiger, U., & Herzog, D. B. (1989). Neurochemical abnormalities of anorexia nervosa and bulimia nervosa. *American Journal of Psychiatry, 146,* 963–971.

Federal Register. (1981, January 16). Washington, DC: U.S. Government Printing Office.

Feil, E. G., Walker, H. M., & Severson, H. H. (1995). The early screening project for young children with behavior problems. *Journal of Emotional and Behavioral Disorders,* 3(4), 194–202.

Feingold, B. F. (1975a). Hyperkinesis and learning disabilities linked to artificial food flavors and colors. *The American Journal of Nursing, 75,* 797–803.

Feingold, B. F. (1975b). *Why your child is hyperactive.* New York: Random House.

Felner, R. D., & Felner, T. Y. (1989). Primary prevention programs in the educational context: A transactional—ecological framework and analysis. In L. A. Bond & B. E. Compas (Eds.), *Primary prevention and promotion in the schools* (pp. 13–49). Newbury Park, CA: Sage Publications.

Fenichel, C. (1974). Carl Fenichel. In J. M. Kauffman & C. D. Lewis (Eds.), *Teaching children with behavior disorders: Personal perspectives.* Columbus, OH: Merrill.

Fergusson, D. M., & Lynskey, M. T. (1998). Conduct problems in childhood and psychosocial outcomes in young adulthood: A prospective study. *Journal of Emotional and Behavioral Disorders, 6,* 2–18.

Fergusson, D. M., & Lynskey, M. T. (1998). Conduct problems in childhood and psychosocial outcomes in young adulthood. A prospective study. *Journal of Emotional and Behavioral Disorders, 6*(1), 2–18.

Ferster, C. B. (1961). Positive reinforcement and behavioral deficits of autistic children. *Child Development, 32,* 437–456.

Fessler, M. A., Rosenberg, M. S., & Rosenberg, L. A. (1991). Concomitant learning disabilities and learning problems among students with behavioral/emotional disorders. *Behavioral Disorders, 16,* 97–106.

Fields, E., Farmer, E. M.Z., Apperson, J., Mustillo, S., & Simmers, D. (2006). Treatment and post-treatment effects of residential treatment using a re-education model. *Behavioral Disorders, 31*(3), 312–322.

Finn, K. V., Willert, H. J., & Marable, M. A. (2003). Substance use in schools. *Educational Leadership, 60*(6), 80–84.

Fish, M. C., & Mendola, L. R. (1986). The effect of self-instruction training on homework completion in an elementary special education class. *School Psychology Review, 15*(2), 268–276.

Fitzsimmons, M., & Warger, C. (2000). Schoolwide behavioral management systems. *ERIC Review, 7*(1), 23–27.

Flament, M. F., Whitaker, A., & Rapoport, J. L. (1988). Obsessive compulsive disorder in adolescence: An epidemiological study. *Journal of American Academy of Child and Adolescent Psychiatry, 27,* 764–771.

Flannery-Schroeder, E.C. (2004). Generalized anxiety disorder. In T. L. Morris & J. S. March (Eds.), *Anxiety disorders in children and adolescents* (2nd ed., pp. 125–140). New York: Guilford Press.

Fletcher, J. M., Coulter, W. A., Reschly, D. J., & Vaughn, S. (2004). Alternative approaches to the definition and identification of learning disabilities: some questions and answers. *Annals of Dyslexia, 54*(2), 304–331.

Flora, S. R. (2004). *The power of reinforcement.* Albany: State University of New York Press.

Foley, R. M., & Epstein, M. H. (1992). Correlates of the academic achievement of adolescents with behavioral disorders. *Behavioral Disorders, 18,* 9–17.

Ford, T., Goodman, R., & Meltzer, H. (2003). The British Child and Adolescent Mental Health Survey 1999: The prevalence of DSM-IV disorders. *Journal of the American Academy of Child and Adolescent Psychiatry, 42,* 1203–1211.

Forman, S. G., Bry, B. H., & Urga, P. (2006). Substance abuse. In G. G. Bear & K. M. Minke (Eds.), *Children's needs III: Development, prevention, and intervention* (pp. 1011–1023). Bethesda, MD: National Association of School Psychologists.

Forness, S. R. (1988a). Planning for the needs of children with serious emotional disturbance: The national special education and mental health coalition. *Behavioral Disorders, 13,* 127–132.

Forness, S. R. (1988b). School characteristics of children and adolescents with depression. In R. B. Rutherford, Jr., C. M. Nelson, & S. R. Forness (Eds.), *Issues of Severe Behavior Disorders in Children and Youth* (Vol. 10), 177–203. Boston: Little, Brown.

Forness, S. R. (2005). Personal reflections: Definition. In J. M. Kauffman, *Characteristics of emotional and behavioral disorders of children and youth* (pp. 23–25). Upper Saddle River, NJ: Merrill/Prentice-Hall.

Forness, S. R., & Kavale, K. A. (2000). Emotional or behavioral disorders: Background and current status of the E/BD terminology and definition. *Behavioral Disorders, 25*(3), 264–269.

Forness, S. R., & Kavale, K. A. (2001, Winter). Reflections on the future of prevention. *Preventing School Failure, 45,* 75–81.

Forness, S. R., & Knitzer, J. (1992). A new proposed definition and terminology to replace "serious emotional disturbance" in the Individuals with Disabilities Education Act. *School Psychology Review, 21,* 12–20.

Forness, S. R., Bennett, M. A., & Tose, B. A. (1983). Academic benefits in emotionally disturbed children revisited. *Journal of the American Academy of Child Psychiatry, 22,* 140–144.

Forness, S. R., Kavale, K. A., Blum, I. M., & Lloyd, J. W. (1997). Meta-analysis of what works in special education and related services. *Teaching Exceptional Children, 29*(6), 4–9.

Forness, S. R., Kavale, K. A., Sweeney, D. P., & Crenshaw, T. M. (1999). The future of research and practice in behavioral disorders: Psychopharmacology and its school implications. *Behavioral Disorders, 24*(4), 305–318.

Forness, S. R., Swanson, J. M., Cantwell, D. P., Guthrie, D., & Sena, R. (1992). Response to stimulant medication across six measures of school-related performance in children with ADHD and disruptive behavior, *Behavioral Disorders, 18,* 42–53.

Forness, S. R., Walker, H. M., & Kavale, K. A. (2003–2004, Winter). Psychiatric disorders and their treatment: A primer for school professionals. *Emotional and Behavioral Disorders in Youth, 4*(1), 3–6, 20–22.

Forsterling, F. (1980). Attributional aspects of cognitive behavior modification: a theoretical approach and suggestions for technique. *Cognitive Therapy and Research, 4,* 27–37.

Foster, J. D., Kupermic, G. P., & Price, A. W. (2004). Gender differences in posttraumatic stress and related symptoms among inner-city minority youth exposed to community violence. *Journal of Youth and Adolscence, 33*(1), 59–69.

Foster, S., Rollefson, J., Doksum, T., Noonan, D., & Robinson, G. (2005). *School Mental Health Services in the United States, 2002–2003* (DHHA Pub.No. (SMA) 05-4068). Rockville, MD: Center for Mental Health Services, Substance Abuse and Mental Health Services Administration.

Fournier, C. F. (1987). *Teacher perceptions of impact of hyperactivity on classroom situations and on ratings of intervention acceptability.* Unpublished doctoral dissertation: University of Texas.

Fox, J. J., & Conroy, M. A. (2000). Viewpoint: FBA for children and youth with emotional-behavioral disorders; Where we should go in the twenty-first century. *Preventing School Failure, 44*(4), 140–141.

Foxx, R. M. (1977). Attention training: The use of over-correction avoidance to increase the eye contact of autistic and retarded children. *Journal of Applied Behavior Analysis, 10,* 489–499.

Foxx, R. M., & Azrin, N. H. (1973). The elimination of autistic self-stimulatory behavior by over-correction. *Journal of Applied Behavior Analysis, 6,* 1–14.

Franca, V. M., Kerr, M. M., Reitz, A. L., & Lambert, D. (1990). Peer tutoring among behaviorally disordered students: Academic and social benefits to tutor and tutee. *Education and Treatment of Children, 13,* 109–128.

Francis, G., Last, C. G., & Strauss, C. C. (1987). Expression of separation anxiety disorder: The roles of age and gender. *Child Psychiatry and Human Development, 18,* 82–89.

Freud, S. (1957). Mourning and melancholia. In J. Strachey (Ed. and Trans.), *The standard edition of the complete psychological works of Sigmund Freud* (Vol. 14). London: Hogarth Press. (Original work published 1917).

Friedman, R. M., Kutash, K., & Duchnowski, A. J. (1996). The population of concern: Defining the issues. In B. Stroul (Ed.), *Children's mental health: Creating systems of care in a changing society* (pp. 69–96). Baltimore: Brookes.

Fuchs, D., & Fuchs, L. S. (1994). Inclusive schools movement and the radicalization of special education reform. *Exceptional Children, 60,* 294–309.

Fuchs, D., Fernstrom, P., Scott, S., Fuchs, L., & Vandermeer, L. (1994). Classroom ecological inventory: A process for mainstreaming. *Teaching Exceptional Children, 26,* 11–1.

Fujiki, M., Brinton, B., Morgan, M., & Hart, C. H. (1999). Withdrawn and sociable behavior of children with language impairment. *Language, Speech, and Hearing Services in the Schools, 30,* 183–195.

Gable, R. A., Quinn, M. M., Rutherford, R. B., Howell, K. W., & Hoffman, C. C. (2000). *Addressing student problem behavior—part III: Creating positive behavioral intervention plans and supports.* Washington, DC: CECP.

Gadow, K. D. (1983). Effects of stimulant drugs on academic performance in hyperactive and learning disabled children. *Journal of Learning Disabilities, 5,* 290–299.

Gadow, K. D. (1985). Relative efficacy of pharmacological, behavioral, and combination treatments for enhancing academic performance. *Clinical Psychology Review, 5,* 523–533.

Gadow, K. D. (1986a). *Children on medication, Vol. 1. Hyperactivity, learning disabilities, and mental retardation.* Austin, TX: Pro-Ed.

Gadow, K. D. (1986b). Fundamental concepts in pharmacotherapy: An overview. In K. D. Gadow (Ed.), *Children on medication: Epilepsy, emotional disturbance, and adolescent disorders* (pp. 1–19). San Diego: College-Hill.

Gagne, M. H., Lavoie, F., & Hebert, M. (2005). Victimization during childhood and revictimization in dating relationships in adolescent girls. *Child Abuse and Neglect, 29*(10), 1155–1172.

Gallagher, T. M. (1999). Interrelationships among children's language, behavior, and emotional problems. *Topics in Language Disorders, 19,* 1–15.

Garbarino, J. (1977). The human ecology of child maltreatment: A conceptual model for research. *Journal of Marriage and the Family, 39,* 721–736.

Garbarino, J., & Kostelny, K. (1997). Coping with the consequences of community violence. In A. P. Goldstein & J. C. Conoley (Eds.), *School violence intervention: A practical handbook* (pp. 366–387). New York: The Guilford Press.

Gardner, R., III. (1990). Life space interviewing: It can be effective, but don't. . . . *Behavioral Disorders, 15,* 111–119.

Gardner, R., Sainato, D. M., Cooper, J. O., Heron, T. E., Heward, W. L., Eshleman, J., et al. (1994). *Behavior analysis in education: Focus on measurably superior instruction.* Belmont, CA: Brooks/Cole.

Gardner, W. I., & Cole, C. L. (1988). Self-monitoring procedures. In E. S. Shapiro & T. R. Kratochwill (Eds.),

Behavioral assessment in schools: Conceptual foundations and practical applications (pp. 106–146). New York: The Guilford Press.

Garfinkel, P., & Garner, D. (1987). *The role of drug treatments for eating disorders.* New York: Brunner/Mazel.

Garner, D. M., & Bemis, K. M. (1982). A cognitive–behavioral approach to anorexia nervosa. *Cognitive Therapy and Research, 6,* 123–150.

Garnier, H. E., Stein, J. A., & Jacobs, J. K. (1997). The process of dropping out of high school: A 19-year perspective. *American Educational Research Journal, 34,* 395–419.

Garrett, B. (2003). *Brain and behavior.* Belmont, CA: Wadsworth/Thomson Learning.

Garrison, S. R. & Stolberg, A. L. (1983). Modification of anger in children by affective imagery training. *Journal of Abnormal Child Psychology, 11,* 115–130.

Gehring, J. (2004, August 11). To stem dropouts, urban districts switch strategies. *Education Week,* pp 1, 19.

Gehring, J. (2005, July 27). NCLB's mandates on delinquent youth get attention. *Education Week,* p. 3.

Gelso, C. J. (1992). *Counseling psychology.* Fort Worth, TX: Harcourt Brace Jovanovich College.

Genaux, M., Likins, M., & Morgan, D. (1993). *Teacher's desk reference: substance use prevention in special education,* (2nd ed.). Logan, UT: Utah State University.

George, N. L., George, M. P. Gersten, R., & Grosenick, J. R. (2004). To leave or to stay? An exploratory study of teachers of students with emotional and behavioral disorders. *Remedial and Special Education,* 16, 227–236.

Gerald, M., & Eyman, W. (1984). *Thinking straight and talking sense.* New York: Institute for Rational Living.

Gerber, M. M., & Solari, E. J. (2005). Teaching effort and the future of cognitive-behavioral interventions. *Behavioral Disorders, 30*(3), 289–299.

Gersten, R. Walker, H. M. & Darch, C. (1988). Relationship between teachers' effectiveness and their tolerance for handicapped students. *Exceptional Children, 54*(5), 433–438.

Gest, J. (2005, February 28). Governor enters No Child fray: Governor backs Neeley's challenge to law on testing. *Houston Chronicle.* Retrieved March 2, 2006, from *http://www.chron.com/cs/CDA/ssistory.mpl/metropolitan/3059865/*

Getty, L. A., & Summy, S. E. (2006). Language deficits in students with emotional and behavioral disorders: Practical applications for teachers, *Beyond Behavior, 15*(3), 15–22.

Gibson, J. (1991, Winter). Lesbian and gay youth. *News and Views.* Lincoln, NE: Child Guidance Center.

Gil, E. (1998). *Essentials of play therapy with abused children.* New York: Guilford Press.

Gilliam, J. E. (1995). *Gilliam Autism Rating Scale,* Austin, Tx: Pro-Ed.

Gilliam, J. E., & Scott, B. K. (1987). The behaviorally disordered offender. In C. M. Nelson, R. B. Rutherford, Jr., & B. I. Wolford, (Eds.), *Special education in the criminal justice system.* Columbus, OH: Merrill.

Gittelman, R., & Klein, D. F. (1984). Relationship between separation anxiety and panic and agoraphobic disorders. *Psychopathology, 17(Suppl. 1):* 56–65.

Gittelman-Klein, R., & Klein, D. F. (1971). Controlled imipramine treatment of school phobia. *Archives of General Psychiatry, 25,* 204–207.

Gittelman-Klein, R., & Klein, D. F. (1973). School phobia: diagnostic considerations in the light of imipramine effects. *Journal of Nervous Mental Disorders, 156,* 199–215.

Glasser, W. (1965). *Reality therapy: A new approach to psychiatry.* New York: Harper & Row.

Glasser, W. (1969). *Schools without failure.* New York: Harper & Row.

Glueck, S., & Glueck, E. (1968). *Delinquents and non-delinquents in perspective.* Cambridge, MA: Harvard University Press.

Goals 2000: Educate America Act of 1994, P.L. 103–227. 20 U.S.C. ξ 6301 et seq.

Golden, C. J. (1981). A standardized version of Luria's neuropsychological tests: A quantitative and qualitative approach to neuropsychological evaluation. In S. B. Filskov & T. J. Bell (Eds.), *Handbook of clinical neuropsychology.* New York: Wiley.

Golden, C. J. (1986). *Manual for the Luria-Nebraska neuropsychological battery: Children's revision.* Los Angeles: Western Psychological Services.

Golden, G. (1980). Nonstandard therapies in the developmental disabilities. *American Journal of Diseases of Children, 134,* 487–491.

Golden, J. M. (1981). Depression in middle and late childhood: Implications for intervention. *Child Welfare, 60,* 457–465.

Goldsmith, H. H., Buss, K. A., & Lemery, K. S. (1997). Toddler and childhood temperament: Expanded content, stronger genetic evidence, new evidence for the importance of the environment. *Developmental Psychology, 33,* 891–905.

Goldstein, A. P. (1988). *The Prepare Curriculum.* Champaign, IL: Research Press.

Goldstein, A. P., & Conoley, J. C. (Eds.). (1997). *School violence intervention: A practical handbook.* New York: The Guilford Press.

Goldstein, A. P., & Glick, B. (1987). *Aggression replacement training.* Champaign, IL: Research Press.

Goldstein, A. P., Sprafkin, R. P., Gershaw, N. J., & Klein, P. (1980). *Skillstreaming the adolescent.* Champaign, IL: Research Press.

Goldstein, S. (1999). Attention-deficit/hyperactivity disorder. In S. Goldstein & C. R. Reynolds (Eds.), *Handbook of neurodevelopmental and genetic disorders in children* (pp. 154–184). New York: Guilford Press.

Goldstein, S., & Goldstein, M. (1998). *Understanding and managing attention deficit hyperactivity disorder in children: A guide for practitioners* (2nd ed.). New York: Wiley.

Goldstein, S., & Reynolds, C. R. (1999). Introduction. In S. Goldstein & C. R. Reynolds (Eds.), *Handbook of neurodevelopmental and genetic disorders in children* (pp. 3–8). New York: Guilford Press.

Gonzalez, J. E., Nelson, J. R., Gutkin, T. B., Saunders, A., Galloway, A., & Shwery, C. S. (2004). Rational emotive therapy with children and adolescents: A meta-analysis, *Journal of Emotional and Behavioral Disorders, 12*(4), 222–235.

Good, R. H., & Kaminski, R. A. (2003). *Dynamic indicators of basic early literacy skills* (6th ed.) Longmont, CO: Sopris West Educational Services.

Good, T. L., & Brophy, J. E. (2002). *Looking in classrooms* (9th Ed.) Boston: Allyn & Bacon

Good, T. L., & Grouws, D. (1972). *Reaction of male and female teacher trainees to descriptions of elementary school pupils* (Tech. Rep. No. 62). Center for Research in Social Behavior, Columbus, MO: University of Missouri.

Goode, E. (2000, February 23). Psychiatric drug use is on the rise for preschoolers. *Austin-American Statesman*, pp. A-1, A-5.

Goodman, L. (1998). The Human Genome Project aims for 2003. *Genome Research, 8*, 997–999.

Gordon, S. (1983–84). The case for moral sex education. *Impact*, '83–'84, 2.

Gordon, T. (1974). *Teacher effectiveness training.* New York: Peter H. Wyden.

Gotlib, I. H., Lewisohn, P. M., Seeley, J. R., Rohde, P., & Redner, J. E. (1993). Negative cognitions and attributional style in depressed adolescents: An examination of stability and specificity. *Journal of Abnormal Psychology, 102(4)*, 607–615.

Graden, J. L., Casey, A., & Bonstrom, O. (1985). Implementing a prereferral intervention system: Part II. the data. *Exceptional Children, 51*, 487–496.

Grant, T. (2006, September 1). Back to school: Zero tolerance makes discipline more severe, involves the courts. *Pittsburgh Post-Gazette.com.* Retrieved September 1, 2006, from http://www.post-gazette.com/pg/pp/06243/717806.stm

Graubard, P. S. (1973). Children with behavioral disabilities. In L. Dunn (Ed.), *Exceptional children in the schools.* New York: Holt, Rinehart & Winston.

Graziano, A. M., DeGiovanni, I. S., & Garcia, K. A. (1979). Behavioral treatment of children's fears: A review. *Psychological Bulletin, 86*, 804–830.

Green, E. W. (2006, August 25). Taking measure of No Child Left Behind. *U.S. News World Reports* retrieved August 25, 2006, from *http://www.usnews.com/usnews/news/articles/060823/23nclb.htm*

Greenbaum, P. E., Dedrick, R. F., Freidman, R. M., Kutash, K., Brown, E. C., Lardieri, S. P., & Pugh, A. M. (1996). National Adolescent and Child Treatment Study (NACTS): Outcomes for children with serious emotional and behavioral disturbance. *Journal of Emotional and Behavioral Disorders, 4*, 130–146.

Greenberg, M. T., Kusché, C. & Mihalic, S.F. (1998). *Promoting alternative thinking strategies (PATHS): blueprints for violence prevention, book ten.* Boulder: Center for the Study and Prevention of Violence, Institute of Behavioral Science, University of Colorado.

Greenhill, L. L., Abikoff, H. G., Arnold, E., Cantwell, D. P., Conners, C. K., Elliott, G., Hectman, L., Hinshaw, S. P., Hoza, B., Jensen, P. S., March, J. S., Newcorn, J., Pelham, W. E., Severe, J. G., Swanson, J. M., Vitiello, B., & Wells, K. (1996). Medication treatment strategies in the MTA study: Relevance to clinicians and researchers. *Journal of the American Academy of Child and Adolescent Psychiatry, 34*, 1304–1313.

Gresham, F. M. (2005). Methodological issues in evaluating cognitive-behavioral treatments for students with behavioral disorders. *Behavioral Disorders, 30*(3), 213–225.

Gresham, F. M. (2002). Teaching social skills to high-risk children and youth: Preventative and remedial strategies. In M. R. Shinn, El. M. Walker, & G. Stoner (Eds.), *Interventions for academic and* behavior *problems II: Preventive and remedial approaches.* Bethesda, MD: National Association of School Psychologists.

Gresham, F. M. (2002). Best practices in social skills training. In A. Thomas & J. Grimes (Eds.), *Best practices in school psychology—IV* (pp. 1029–1040). Bethesda, MD: National Association of School Psychologists.

Gresham, F. M. (1998). Social skills training: Should we raze, remodel, or rebuild? *Behavioral Disorders, 24*(1), 19–25.

Gresham, F. M. (1985). Utility of cognitive-behavioral procedures for social skills training with children: a critical review. *Journal of Abnormal Child Psychology, 13*, 411–423.

Gresham, F. M., Lane, K. L., & Lambros, K. M. (2000). Comorbidity of conduct problems and ADHD: Identification of "fledgling psychopaths." *Journal of Emotional and Behavioral Disorders, 8*(2), 83–93.

Gresham, F. M., Watson, T. S., & Skinner, C. H. (2001). Functional behavioral assessment: Principles, procedures, and future directions. *School Psychology Review, 30*(2), 156–172.

Grosenick, J. K., George, N. L., George, M. P., & Lewis, T. J. (1991). Public school services for behaviorally disordered students: Program practices in the 1980s. *Behavioral Disorders, 16*, 87–96.

Grossman, D. C., Neckerman, H. J., Koepsell, T. D., Liu, P. Y., Asher, K. N., Beland, K., et al. (1997). Effectiveness of a violence prevention curriculum among children in elementary school. A randomized controlled trial. *Journal of the American Medical Association, 277,* 1605–1611.

Growing up gay. (1994, Jan. 6.) Los Angeles Times, *OC High Student News & Views.*

Guetzloe, E. (1988). Suicide and depression: Special education's responsibility. *Teaching Exceptional Children, 20,* 25–28.

Guetzloe, E. C. (1991). *Depression and suicide: Special education students at risk.* Reston, VA: Council for Exceptional Children.

Gunter, P. L., Hummel, J. H., & Venn, M. L. (1998). Are effective academic instructional practices used to teach students with behavior disorders? *Beyond Behavior, 9*(3), 5–11.

Gushee, M. (1984). *Student discipline policies.* Washington D.C.: Office of Educational Research and Improvement, U. S. Department of Education (ED 259–455).

Haaga, D. A. F., & Davison, G. C. (1991). Cognitive change methods. In F. H. Kanfer & A. P. Goldstein (Eds.), *Helping people change: A textbook of methods* (pp. 248–304), New York: Pergamon Press.

Hackett, L. (1990, April 8). Experts want sex education restructured. *Austin American-Stateman,* p. E12.

Hagborg, W. J. (1989). A study of persistent absenteeism of severely emotionally disturbed adolescents. *Behavioral Disorders, 15,* 50–56.

Hall, C. S. (1954). *A primer of Freudian psychology.* New York: William Collins Publishers.

Hall, C. S., & Lindzey, G. (1970). *Theories of personality* (2nd ed.). New York: Wiley.

Hall, M. (1991). Gadugi: A model of service-learning for Native American communities. *Phi Delta Kappan, 72*(10), 754–757.

Hallfors, D., Fallon, T., & Watson, K. (1998). An examination of psychotropic drug treatment for children with serious emotional disturbance. *Journal of Emotional and Behavioral Disorders, 6*(1), 56–64.

Halperin, J. M., Newcorn, J. H., Kopstein, I., McKay, K. E., Schwartz, S. T., Siever, L. J., & Sharma, V. (1997). Serotonin, aggression, and parental psychopathology in children with attention-deficit hyperactivity disorder. *Journal of the American Academy of Child and Adolescent Psychiatry, 36,* 1391–1398.

Halpern, F. (1960). The Rorschach test with children. In A. I. Rabin & M. R. Haworth (Eds.), *Projective techniques with children.* New York: Grune & Stratton.

Hamarman, S., Pope, K. H., & Czaja, S. J. (2002). Emotional abuse in children: Variations in legal definitions and rates across the United States. *Child Maltreatment, 7*(4), 303–311.

Hammen, C. (1988). Self-cognitions, stressful events, and the prediction of depression in children of depressed mothers. *Journal of Abnormal Child Psychology, 16(3),* 347–360.

Hammen, C. (1991). *Depression runs in families.* New York: Springer-Verlag.

Hammill, D. D. (1976). Defining "learning disabilities" for programmatic purposes. *Academic Therapy, 12,* 29–37.

Handwerk, M. L., & Marshall, R. M. (1998). Behavioral and emotional problems of students with learning disabilities, or both conditions, *Journal of Learning Disabilities, 31,* 327–338.

Hare, R. D. (1970). *Psychopathy: Theory and research.* New York: Wiley.

Haring, N. (1963). The emotionally disturbed. In S. Kirk & B. Weiner (Eds.), *Behavioral research on exceptional children.* Washington, DC: The Council for Exceptional Children.

Haring, N. G., & Phillips, E. L. (1962). *Educating emotionally disturbed children.* New York: McGraw-Hill.

Haring, N. G., Stern, G., & Cruickshank, W. (1958). *Attitudes of educators toward exceptional children.* New York: Syracuse University Press.

Harmin, M., Kirschenbaum, H., & Simon, S. (1973). *Clarifying values through subject matter.* Minneapolis, MN: Winston Press.

Harris, D. B. (1963). *Children's drawings as measures of intellectual maturity.* New York: Harcourt, Brace Jovanovich.

Harris, K. C. (1998). *Collaborative elementary teaching: A casebook for elementary special and general educators.* Austin, TX: Pro-Ed.

Harris, K. R. (1986). The effects of cognitive–behavior modification on private speech and task performance during problem solving among learning-disabled and normally achieving children. *Journal of Abnormal Child Psychology, 14*(1), 63–67.

Harris, K. R., & Graham, S. (1996). *Making the writing process work: Strategies for composition and self-regulation.* Cambridge, MA: Brookline.

Harris, K. R., & Schmidt, T. (1997). Learning self-regulation in the classroom. *ADHD Report, 5*(2), 1–6.

Harris, K. R., Friedlander, B. D., Saddler, B., Frizzelle, R., & Graham, S. (2005). Self-monitoring of attention versus self-monitoring of academic performance: Effects among students with ADHD in the general education classroom. *Journal of Special Education, 39*(3), 145–156.

Hart, S. L. (1991). Childhood depression: Implications and options for school counselors. *Elementary School Guidance & Counseling, 25*(4), 277–289.

Harter, S. (1985). *Manual for the Self-Perception Profile for Children.* Denver, CO: University of Denver.

Harter, S. (1999). *The construction of the self: A developmental perspective.* New York: Guilford Press.

Harvard Health Publications. (1995). Is cognitive therapy useful in treating substance abuse? *Harvard Mental Health Letter, 11*(12), 8.

Harvard Health Publications. (2005, April). Childhood and adolescent conduct disorder, *Harvard Mental Health Letter, 21*(10), 4–7.

Harvard Health Publications. (2006, April). Psychodynamic theory passes a test. *Harvard Mental Health Letter, 22*(10), 5.

Harvard Medical School. (2005, January). The treatment of attention deficit disorder: New evidence. *Harvard Mental Health Letter.* Cambridge, MA: Harvard Health Publications.

Harvard Medical School. (2005, July). The adolescent brain: Beyond raging hormones. *Harvard Mental Health Letter.* Cambridge, MA: Harvard Health Publications.

Hauser, S. T. (1972). Black and white identity formation: Aspects and perspectives. *Journal of Youth and Adolescence, 1,* 113–130.

Hawkins, J. D., & Catalono, R. F. (1988). *Preparing for the drug-free years* (2nd ed.). Seattle: Developmental Research and Programs.

Hawkins, J. D., Herrenkohl, D. P., Farrington, D. B., Catalano, R. F., Harachi, T. W., & Cothern, L. (2000, April). Predictors of youth violence. *Juvenile Justice Bulletin.* U.S. Department of Justice, Office of Justice Programs, Office of Juvenile Justice and Delinquency Prevention, Washington, DC.

Heavey, S. (2006, April 7). US FDA approves first skin patch for ADHD. *Reuters.* Available at *http://today.reuters.co.uk/misc*

Hebben, N. A., Whitman, R. D., Milberg, W. P., Andresko, M., & Galpin, R. (1981). Attention dysfunction in poor readers. *Journal of Learning Disabilities, 14,* 287–290.

Heckaman, K., Conroy, M., Fox, J., & Chait, A. (2000). Functional assessment-based intervention research on students with or at risk for emotional and behavioral disorders in school settings. *Behavioral Disorders, 25*(3), 195–203.

Henshaw, S. K. (1997). Teenager abortion and pregnancy statistics by state, 1992. *Family Planning Perspectives, 29,* 115–122.

Hester, P. P., & Kaiser, A. P. (1998). Early intervention for the prevention of conduct disorder: Research issues in early identification, implementation, and interpretation of treatment outcome. *Behavioral Disorders, 24*(1), 57–65.

Hetherington, E. M., & Kelly, J. (2003). *For better or worse: Divorce reconsidered.* New York: Norton.

Hetherington, E. M., & Stanley-Hagan, M. (2002). Parenting in divorced and remarried families. In M. H. Bornstein (Ed.), *Handbook of parenting: Vol. 3. Being and becoming a parent* (2nd ed., pp. 287–315). Mahwah, NJ: Erlbaum.

Hewett, F. (1965). Teaching speech to autistic children through operant conditioning. *American Journal of Orthopsychiatry, 35,* 927–36.

Hewett, F. M. (1974). Frank M. Hewett. In J. M. Kauffman & C. D. Lewis (Eds.), *Teaching children with behavior disorders: Personal perspectives.* Columbus, OH: Merrill.

Hewett, F. M., & Taylor, F. D. (1980). *The emotionally disturbed child in the classroom: The orchestration of success* (2nd ed.). Boston: Allyn & Bacon.

Higgens, J., Williams, R., & McLaughlin, T. F. (2001). The effects of a token economy employing instructional consequences for a third grade student with learning disabilities: A data-based case study. *Education and Treatment of Children, 24,* 99–106.

Higgens, K., & Boone, R. (1992). Hypermedia computer study guides for social studies: Adapting a Canadian history text. *Social Education, 56*(3), 154–159.

Hill, J. W., & Coufal, K. L. (2006). Emotional/Behavioral Disorders: A retrospective examination of social skills, linguistics, and student outcomes. *Communication Disorders Quarterly, 27*(1), 33–46.

Hill, S. M. (1989). *A study of the cognitive specificity hypothesis: Anger and depression in children and adolescents.* Unpublished doctoral dissertation, The University of Texas at Austin.

Hinshaw, S. P., & Anderson, C. A. (1996). Conduct and oppositional defiant disorders. In E. J. Mash & R. A. Barkley (Eds.), *Child psychopathology* (pp. 113–149). New York: Guilford Press.

Hiroto, D. S. (1974). Locus of control and learned helplessness. *Journal of Experimental Psychology, 102,* 187–193.

Hobbs, N. (1966). Helping disturbed children: Psychological and ecological strategies. *American Psychologist, 21,* 1105–1115.

Hobbs, N. (1974). Nicholas Hobbs. In J. M. Kauffman & C. D. Lewis (Eds.), *Teaching children and behavior disorders: Personal perspectives.* Columbus, OH: Merrill.

Hobbs, N. (1975a). *The futures of children: Categories, labels, and their consequences.* San Francisco: Jossey-Bass.

Hobbs, N. (1975b). *Issues in the classification of children.* San Francisco: Jossey-Bass.

Hobbs, N. (1982). *The troubled and troubling child.* San Francisco: Jossey-Bass.

Hoberman, H. M., & Clarke, G. N. (1993). Major depression in adults. In R. Ammerman & M. Hersen (Eds.), *Handbook of behavior therapy with children and adults: A developmental and longitudinal perspective. General psychology series, 171* (pp. 73–90). Boston: Allyn & Bacon.

Hoberman, H. M., & Lewisohn, P. M. (1985). The behavioral treatment of depression. In E. E. Beckham & W. R. Lever (Eds.), *Handbook of depression: Treatment, assessment and research* (pp. 39–81). Homewood, IL: Dorsey Press.

Hodapp, R. M., & Fidler, D. J. (1999). Special education and genetics: Connections for the 21st century. *Journal of Special Education, 33*(3), 130–137.

Hodge, J., Riccomini, P. J., Buford, R., & Herbst, M. H. (2006). A review of insructional interventions in mathematics for students with emotional and behavioral disorders. *Behavioral Disorders, 31*(3), 297–311.

Hodgman, C. H. (1985). Recent findings in adolescent depression and suicide. *Developmental and Behavioral Pediatrics, 6,* 162–169.

Hoff, K. E., Doepke, K., & Landau, S. (2002). Best practices in the assessment of children with attention deficit/hyperactivity disorder: Linking assessment to intervention. In A. Thomas & J. Grimes (Eds.), *Best practices in school psychology—IV* (pp. 1129–1150). Bethesda, MD: National Association of School Psychologists.

Hoffman, E. (1974). Treatment of deviance by the educational system: History. In W. C. Rhodes & S. Head (Eds.), *A study of child variance* (Vol. 3). Ann Arbor, MI: University of Michigan.

Hoffman, N. (July/August, 2003). College credit in high school: Increasing college attainment rates for underrepresented students. *Change,* pp. 43–47.

Hoffmann, N. G., Abrantes, A. M., & Anton, R. (2003–2004). Problems identified by the practical adolescent dual diagnostic interview (PADDI) in a juvenile detention center population. *Emotional and Behavioral Disorders in Youth, 4*(1), 9–12, 19.

Hollingsworth, H. (2006, August 17). "Feds threaten to withhold money from Missouri", *Associated Press Wire Service,* retrieved August 18, 2006, from *www.kansascity.com.*

Holt J. C. (1967). *How children learn.* New York: Pitman.

Hoover, J., & Juul, K. (1993). Bullying in Europe and the U.S. *Journal of Emotional and Behavioral Problems, 2*(1), 25–29.

Hornbeck, D. (2000). Service-learning and reform in the Philadelphia public schools. *Phi Delta Kappan, 81*(9), 665.

Horner, R. H., & Sugai, G. (2000). School-wide behavior support: An emerging initiative. *Journal of Positive Behavior Interventions, 2,* 231–232.

Horner, R., & Day, H. (1991). The effects for response efficiency on functionally equivalent competing behaviors. *Journal of Applied Behavior Analysis, 24,* 719–732.

Horney, Karen. (1937). *The neurotic personality of our time.* New York: W. W. Norton and Company, Inc.

Houlihan, D. D., & Jones, R. N. (1989). Treatment of a boy's school phobia within vivo systematic desensitization. *Professional School Psychology, 4,* 285–293.

Huang, L., Stroul, B., Friedman, R., Mrazek, P., Friesen, B., Pires, S., et al. (2005). Transforming mental health care for children and families. *The American Psychologist, 60*(6), 615–627.

Hubbard, D. D., & Adams, J. (2002). Best practices in facilitating meaningful family involvement in educational decision making. In A. Thomas, & J. Grimes (Eds.), *Best Practices in School Psychology IV* (pp. 377–387). Bethesda MD: National Association of School Psychologists.

Huberty, T.J., & Dick, A.C. (2006). In G.G. Bear & K.M. Minke (Eds.), *Children's needs III: Development, prevention, and intervention* (pp. 281–291). Bethesda, MD: National Association of School Psychologists.

Hudley, C., Wakefield, W. D., & Britsch, B. (2001). Multiple perceptions of children's aggression: Differences across neighborhood, age, gender, and perceiver. *Psychology in the Schools, 38*(1), 43–56.

Huesman, L. R., Eron, L. D., Lefkowitz, M. M., & Walder, L. O. (1984). Stability of aggression over time and generations. *Developmental Psychology, 20,* 1120–1134.

Huesmann, L. R., Moise-Titus, J., Podolski, C., & Eron, L. D. (2003). Longitudinal relations between children's exposure to TV violence and their aggressive and violent behavior in young adulthood: 1977–1992. *Developmental Psychology, 39,* 201–221.

Huff, C. R. (1992). *Juvenile justice and public policy: Toward a national agenda.* New York: Lexington Books.

Hughes, C. A., Ruhl, K. L., & Misra, A. (1989). Self-management with behaviorally disordered students in school settings: A promise unfulfilled? *Behavioral Disorders, 14,* 250–262.

Hughes, J. N. (1988). *Cognitive behavior therapy with children in schools.* New York: Pergamon Press.

Hutton, J. B., & Roberts, T. G. (2004). Social-Emotional Dimension Scale-Second Edition (SEDS-2). Austin, TX: PRO-ED.

Hyman, I., & Gasiewski, E. (1992). *Corporal punishment, psychological maltreatment and conduct disorders: A continuing American dilemma.* Paper presented at the 24th Annual Convention of the National Association of School Psychologists, Nashville, TN.

Hyman, I., Weiler, E., Perone, D., Romano, L., Britton, G., & Shanock, A. (1997). Victims and victimizers: The two faces of school violence. In A. P. Goldstein & J. C. Conoley (Eds.), *School violence intervention: A practical handbook* (pp. 426–459). New York: The Guilford Press.

Hyter, Y. D. (2003). Language intervention for children with emotional or behavioral disorders. *Behavioral Disorders, 29,* 65–76.

Hyter, Y. D., Rogers-Adkinson, D. L., Self, T. L., Simmons, B. F., & Janz, J. (2001). Pragmatic language intervention for children with language and emotional/behavioral disorders. *Communication Disorders Quarterly, 23*(1), 4–16.

Landeen, J. J., & Adams, D. A. (1988). Computer assisted drill and practice for behaviorally handicapped learners: Proceed with caution. *Education and Treatment of Children, 11,* 218–229.

Lane, K. L., Gresham, F. M., & O'Shaughnessy (2002). Serving students with or at-risk for emotional and behavioral disorders: Future challenges. *Education and Treatment of Children,* 25(4), 507–521.

Lane, K. L., Umbreit, J., & Beebe-Frankenberger, M. E. (1999). Functional assessment research on students with or at risk for EBD: 1990–present. *Journal of Positive Behavior Interventions, 1*(2), 101–111.

Lane, K. L., Wehby, J. H., Little, M. A., & Cooley, C. (2005). Academic, social and behavioral profiles of students with emotional and behavioral disorders educated in self-contained classrooms and self-contained schools: Part-I Are they more alike than different? *Behavioral Disorders 30*(4), 349–361.

Lang, P. (1967). Fear reduction and fear behavior. In J. Schlein (Ed.), *Research in psychotherapy.* Washington DC: American Psychological Association.

Larson, K. A., & Gerber, M. M. (1987). Effects of social metacognitive training for enhancing overt behavior in learning disabled and low achieving delinquents. *Exceptional Children, 54,* 201–211.

Lasser, J., & Tharinger, D. (2003). Visibility management in school and beyond: A qualitative study of gay, lesbian, bisexual youth. *Journal of Adolescence, 26,* 233–244.

Lasser, J., Tharinger, D., & Cloth, A. (2006). Gay, lesbian, and bisexual youth. In G. G. Bear & K. M. Minke (Eds.), *Children's needs III: Development, prevention, and intervention* (pp. 419–430). Bethesda, MD: National Association of School Psychologists.

Last, C. G., & Strauss, C. C. (1989). Panic disorder in children and adolescents. *Journal of Anxiety Disorders, 3,* 87–95.

Last, C. G., Francis, G., Hersen, M., Kazdin, A. E. & Strauss, C. C. (1987). Separation anxiety and school phobia: A comparison using DSM-III criteria. *American Journal of Psychiatry, 144,* 653–657.

Last, C. G., Hersen, M., Kazdin, A. E., Finkelstein, R., & Strauss, C. C. (1987). Comparison of DSM-III separation anxiety and overanxious disorders: Demographic characteristics and patterns of comorbidity. *Journal of American Academy of Child and Adolescent Psychiatry, 26,* 527–531.

Laurent, J., Landau, S., & Stark, K. (1993). Conditional probabilities in the diagnosis of depressive and anxiety disorders in children. *School Psychology Review, 22,* 98–114.

Lazarus, A. A. (1976). *Multimodal behavior therapy.* New York: Springer-Verlag.

Lazarus, B. D. (1993). Self-management and achievement of students with behavior disorders, *Psychology in the Schools, 30,* 67–74.

Leachman, G., & Victor, D. (2003, March). Student-led class meetings. *Educational Leadership, 60*(6), 64–68.

Lectenberger, D. (1999, Summer). Collaborative federal initiatives: Resources and technical assistance centers. *Family Matters,* pp. 5–6.

Ledingham, J. E., & Schwartzman, A. E. (1984). A 3-year follow-up of aggressive and withdrawn behavior in childhood: Preliminary findings. *Journal of Abnormal Child Psychology, 12,* 157–168.

Lee, J. (1993). *Facing the fire: Experiencing and expressing anger appropriately.* New York: Bantam Books.

Lee, Y. Y., Sugai, G., & Horner, R. H. (1999). Using an instructional inteventnion to reduce problem and off-task behaviors. *Journal of Positive Behavior Interventions, 1*(4), 195–204.

Leedy, A., Bates, P., & Safran, S. P. (2004). Bridging the research-to-practice gap: Improving hallway behavior using positive behavior supports. *Behavioral Disorders, 29*(2), 130–139.

Lefkowitz, M. M., & Tesiny, E. P. (1985). Depression in children: Prevalence and correlates. *Journal of Consulting and Clinical Psychology, 53,* 647–656.

Leichsenring, F., Rabung, S., & Leibing, E. (2004). The efficacy of short-term psychodynamic psychotherapy in specific psychiatric disorders: A meta-analysis. *Archives of General Psychiatry, 61*(12), 1208–1216.

Leitenberg, H., & Rosen, J. C. (1988). Cognitive–behavioral treatment of bulimia nervosa. In M. Hersen, R. M. Eisler, & P. M. Miller (Eds.), *Progress in Behavior Modification* (Vol. 23, pp. 11–35). Newbury Park, CA: Sage Publications.

Lembke, E. S., & Stichter, J. P. (2006). Utilizing a system of screening and progress monitoring within a three-tiered model of instruction: Implications for students with emotional and behavioral disorders. *Beyond Behavior, 15*(3), 10–15

Lemonick, M. D. (1997, September 29). The mood molecule. *Time,* pp. 74–82.

Leon, J. A., & Pepe, H. J. (1983). Self-instructional training: Cognitive behavior modification for remediating arithmetic deficits. *Exceptional Children, 50*(1), 54–60.

Leone, P. E. (1991). *Alcohol and other drugs: Use, abuse and disabilities,* ERIC/OSEP Special Project, ERIC Clearinghouse on Handicapped and Gifted Children. Reston, VA: The Council for Exceptional Children.

Leone, P. E., Greenberg, J. M., Trickett, E. J., & Spero, E. (1989). A study of the use of cigarettes, alcohol, and marijuana by students identified as "seriously emotionally disturbed." *Counterpoint, 9(3),* 6–7.

Lesse, S. (1974). Depression masked by acting out behavior patterns. *American Journal of Psychotherapy, 28,* 352–361.

Levendoski, L. S., & Cartledge, G. (2000). Self-monitoring for elementary school children with serious emotional disturbances: Classroom applications for increased academic responding. *Behavioral Disorders, 25,* 211–224.

Levendowski, L. S., & Cartledge, G. (2000). Self-monitoring for elementary school children with serious emotional disturbances: Classroom applications for increased academic responding. *Behavioral Disorders 25*(3), 211–224.

Levinson, E. M. (2002). Best practices in school-based vocational assessment. In A. Thomas & J. Grimes (Eds.), *Best practices in school psychology IV* (pp. 1579–1584). Bethesda, MD: National Association of School Psychologists.

Levitt, E. E. (1963). Psychotherapy with children: A further evaluation. *Behavior Research and Therapy, 60,* 326–329.

Levitt, E. E. (1971). Research on psychotherapy with children. In S. L. Garfield & A. E. Bergin (Eds.) *Handbook of psychotherapy and behavior change* (pp. 474–493), New York: Wiley.

Levy, F., Hay, D. A., McStephen, B., Wood, C., & Waldman, I. (1997). Attention-deficit hyperactivity disorder: A category or a continuum? Genetic analysis of a large-scale twin study. *Journal of the American Academy of Child and Adolescent Psychiatry, 36,* 737–744.

Levy, S., & Vaughn, S. (2002). An observational study of teachers' reading instruction on students with emotional and behavioral disorders. *Behavioral Disorders, 27*(3), 215–235.

Lewinsohn, P.M., Clarke, G.N., Seeley, J.R., & Rohde, P. (1994). Major depression in community adolescents: Age at onset, episode duration, and time to recurrence. *Journal of the American Academy of Child and Adolescent Psychiatry, 33,* 809–818.

Lewis, B. (1991). *The kids' guide to social action.* Minneapolis, MN: Free Spirit Publishing.

Lewis, D. O., Shanok, S. S., & Pincus, J. H. (1979). Juvenile male sexual assaulters. *American Journal of Psychiatry, 136,* 1191–1196.

Lewis, T. J., & Sugai, G. (1999). Effective behavior support: A systems approach to proactive schoolwide management. *Focus on Exceptional Children, 31*(6), 1–24.

Lewis, T. J., Chard, D., & Scott, T. M. (1994). Full inclusion and the education of children and youth with emotional and behavioral disorders. *Behavioral Disorders, 19,* 277–293.

Lewis, T. J., Scott, T. M., & Sugai, G. (1994). The Problem Behavior Questionnaire: A teacher-based instrument to develop functional hypotheses of problem behavior in general education classrooms. *Diagnostique, 19,* 103–115.

Lewisohn, P. M., & Arconad, M. (1981). Behavioral treatment of depression: A social learning approach. In J. F. Clarkin & H. I. Glazer (Eds.), *Depression: Behavioral and directive intervention strategies.* New York: Garland Press.

Lewisohn, P. M., & Gotlib, I. H. (1995). Behavioral theory and treatment of depression. In E. Beckham & W. Leber (Eds.), *Handbook of Depression* (2nd ed., pp. 352–375). New York: The Guilford Press.

Lewinsohn, P. M., Clarke, G. N., Seeley, J. R., & Rohde, P. (1994). Major depression in community adolescents: Age at onset, episode duration, and time to recurrence. *Journal of the American Academy of Child and Adolescent Psychiatry, 33,* 809–818.

Lieberman, L. M. (2001, January 17). The death of special education—Having the right to fail in regular education is no entitlement. *Education Week,* pp. 21, 23.

Lipman, E. L., Boyle, M. H., Dooley, M. D., & Offord, D. R. (2002). Child well-being in single-mother families. *Journal of the American Academy of Child and Adolescent Psychiatry,* 41, 75–82.

Lipsky, D. K., & Gartner, A. (1996). Questions most often asked: What research says about inclusion. *Impact on Instructional Improvement, 25*(1), 77–82.

Liu, R. X. (2004). The conditional effects of gender and delinquency on the relationship between emotional distress and suicidal ideation or attempt among youth. *Journal of Adolescent Research, 19*(6), 698–715.

Lloyd, J. (1980). Academic instruction and cognitive behavior modification: The need for attack strategy training. *Exceptional Education Quarterly, 1,* 53–63.

Lloyd, M. E., & Hilliard, A. M. (1989). Accuracy of self-recording as a function of repeated experience with different self-control contingencies. *Child & Family Behavior Therapy, 11(2),* 1–14.

Lochman, J. E., & Lampron, L. B. (1986). Situational social problem-solving skills and self-esteem of aggressive and nonaggressive boys. *Journal of Abnormal Child Psychology, 14,* 605–617.

Lochman, J. E., & Wells, K. C. (2003) Effectiveness of the Coping Power program and of classroom intervention with aggressive children: Outcomes at a 1-Year follow-up. *Behavior Therapy, 34*(4), 493–515.

Lochman, J. E., Whidby, J. M., & FitzGerald, D. P. Cognitive-behavioral assessment and treatment with aggressive children. In P. C. Kendall (Ed.) *Child and adolescent therapy: Cognitive-behavioral procedures* (2nd ed., pp. 31–87). New York: Guilford Press.

Lochman, J. E., White, K. J., & Wayland, K. K. (1990). Cognitive-behavioral assessment and treatment with aggressive children. In P. C. Kendall (Ed.), *Cognitive Behavioral Therapy with Children and Adolescents.* New York: Guilford.

Lock, J., & Steiner, H. (1999). Gay, lesbian, and bisexual youth risks for emotional, physical, and social problems: Results from a community-based survey. *Journal of the American Academy of Child and Adolescent Psychiatry, 38*(3), 297–304.

Locke, W. R., & Fuchs, L. S. (1995). Effects of peer-mediated reading instruction on the on-task behavior and social interaction of children with behavior disorders. *Journal of Emotional and Behavioral Disorders, 3,* 92–99.

Loehlin, J. C. (1992). *Genes and environment in personality development.* Newbury Park, CA: Sage Publications.

Loehlin, J. C., Willerman, L., & Horn, J. M. (1988). Human behavior genetics. *Annual Review of Psychology, 39,* 101–133.

Loney, J. P., Kramer, J., & Milich, R. (1981). The hyperkinetic child grows up: predictors of symptoms of delinquency and achievement at follow-up. In K. Gadow & J. Loney, (Eds.), *Psychosocial aspect of drug treatment for hyperactivity* (pp. 232–252). Boulder, CO: Westview Press.

Long, N. J. (1984). Teaching self-control and pro-social behavior by using therapeutic signs and sayings in classrooms for emotionally disturbed pupils. *The Pointer, 28*(4), 36–39.

Long, N. J. (1990). Comments on Ralph Gardner's "Life space interviewing: It can be effective, but don't. . .," *Behavioral Disorders, 15,* 119–125.

Long, N. J. (1994). Inclusion: Formula for failure? *Journal of Emotional and Behavioral Problems, 3*(3), 19–23.

Long, N. J., & Morse, W. C. (1996). *Conflict in the classroom: The education of at-risk and troubled students.* Austin: Pro-Ed.

Long, N. J., & Newman, R. G. (1965). Managing surface behavior of children in the school. In N. J. Long, W. C. Morse, & R. G. Newman (Eds.), *Conflict in the classroom: The education of emotionally disturbed children.* Belmont, CA: Wadsworth.

Long, N. J., Morse, W. C. & Newman, R. G. (1965). *Conflict in the classroom: The education of emotionally disturbed children.* Belmont, CA: Wadsworth.

Long, N. J., Wood, M.M., & Fecser, F. A. (2001). *Life space crisis intervention: Talking with students in conflict (2nd ed.).* Austin: Pro-Ed.

Louri, I. (1994). *Principles of local system development for children, adolescents, and their families.* Chicago: Kaleidoscope.

Luria, A. R. (1961). *The role of speech in the regulation of normal and abnormal behavior.* New York: Liveright Publishing.

Luthar, S. S., & Cushing, G. (1997). Substance use and personal adjustment among disadvantaged teenagers: A six-month prospective study. *Journal of Youth and Adolescence, 26,* 353–372.

Lynch, E. W. (1992). Developing cross-cultural competence. In E. W. Lynch & M. J. Hanson (Eds.), *Developing cross-cultural competence* (pp. 32–59). Baltimore, MD: Brookes.

Lynch, F., Mills, C., Daly, I., & Fitzpatrick, C. (2006). Challenging times: Prevalence of psychiatric disorders and suicidal behaviours in Irish adolescents. *Journal of Adolescence, 29,* 555–573.

Lyons, J. A. (1987). Posttraumatic stress disorder in children and adolescents: A review of the literature. *Development and Behavioral Pediatrics, 8,* 349–356.

Maag, J. W. (1999). Why they say no: Foundational precises and techniques for managing resistance. *Focus on Exceptional Children, 32*(1), 1–16.

Maag, J. W. (2001). Rewarded by punisment: Reflections on the disuse of positive reinforcement in schools. *Exceptional Children, 67*(2), 173–186.

Maag, J. W., & Behrens, J. T. (1989). Epidemiologic data on seriously emotionally disturbed and learning disabled adolescents: Reporting extreme depressive symptomatology. *Behavioral Disorders, 15,* 21–27.

Maag, J. W., & Katsiyannis, A. (1996). Counseling as a related service for students with emotional or behavioral disorders: Issues and recommendations, *Behavioral Disorders, 21*(4), 293–305.

Maag, J. W., & Swearer, S. M. (2005). Cognitive-behavioral interventions for depression: Review and implications for school personnel. *Behavioral Disorders, 30*(3), 259–276.

Maag, J. W., Rutherford, R. B., & DiGangi, S. A., (1992). Effects of self-monitoring and contingent reinforcement on on-task behavior and academic productivity of learning-disabled students: A social validation study. *Psychology in the Schools, 29,* 157–171.

Maag, J., & Katsiyannis, A. (1999). Teacher preparation in EBD: A national survey. *Behavioral Disorders, 24,* 189–196.

MacMillan, D. L., Gresham, F. M., & Forness, S. R. (1996). Full inclusion: An empirical perspective. *Behavioral Disorders, 21*(2), 145–159.

Mager, R. F. (1984). *Preparing instructional objectives.* Belmont, CA: Lake.

Mager, R. F. (1997). *Measuring instructional results* (3rd ed.). Atlanta, GA: CEP.

Maheady, L., Sacca, M. K., & Harper, G. F. (1988). Classwide peer tutoring with mildly handicapped high school students. *Exceptional Children, 55*(1), 52–59.

Mahler, M. S. (1952). On child psychosis and schizophrenia. *Psychoanalytic Studies of the Child, 7,* 286–305.

Mallon, G. (1992). Gay and no place to go: Assessing the needs of gay and lesbian adolescents in out-of-home care settings. *Child Welfare, LXXI,* 547–556.

Malmgren, K., Neel, R., & Edgar, E. (1998). Postschool status of youths with behavioral disorders. *Behavioral Disorders, 23,* 257–263.

Mandlawitz, M. (2006). *What every teacher should know about IDEA* 2004. Boston: Allyn & Bacon.

Manning, M. A., Bear, G. G., & Minke, K. M. (2006). Self-concept and self-esteem. In G. G. Bear & K. M. Minke (Eds.), *Children's needs III: Development, prevention, and intervention* (pp. 341–356). Bethesda, MD: National Association of School Psychologists.

Mansdorf, I. J., & Lukens, E. (1987). Cognitive–behavioral psychotherapy for separation anxious children exhibiting school phobia. *Journal of the American Academy of Child and Adolescent Psychiatry, 26,* 19–36.

March, J.S., Franklin, M.E., Leonard, H.L., & Foa, E.B. (2004). Obsessive–compulsive disorder. In T.L. Morris & J.S. March (Eds.), *Anxiety disorders in children and adolescents* (2nd ed., pp. 212–240). New York: Guilford Press.

Marchand-Martella, N. E., Slocum, T. A., & Martella, R. C. (Eds.). (2004). *Introduction to direct instruction.* Boston: Allyn & Bacon.

Marsh, D. T., & Fristand, M. A. (2002). *Handbook of serious emotional disturbance in children and adolescents.* New York: Wiley.

Marshall, E. (1996). The genome program's conscience. *Science, 274,* 488–491.

Mash, E. J., & Dozios, D. J. (1996). Child psychopathology: A developmental-systems perspective. In E. J. Mash & R. A. Barclay (Eds.), *Child psychopathology* (pp. 3–60). New York: The Guilford Press.

Maslow, A. H. (1967). A theory of metamotivation: The biological rooting of the value life. *Journal of Humanistic Psychology, 7,* 93–127.

Massman, P. J., Nussbaum, N. L., & Bigler, E. D. (1988). The mediating effect of age on the relationship between Child Behavior Checklist hyperactivity scores and neuropsychological test performance. *Journal of Abnormal Child Psychology, 16,* 89–95.

Masten, A. A., & Reed, M. J. (2002). Resilience in development. In C. R. Snyder & S. J. Lopez (Eds.), *Handbook of positive psychology* (pp. 74–88). New York: Oxford University Press.

Mastropieri, M. A., & Scruggs, T. E. (1994). *Effective instruction for special education* (2nd Ed.). Austin, TX: Pro-Ed.

Mastropieri, M., Jenkins, V., & Scruggs, T. (1985). Academic and intellectual characteristics of behavior disordered children and youth. In R. B. Rutherford, Jr. (Ed.), *Severe behavior disorders of children and youth.* (Vol. 8, pp. 86–104). Reston, VA: Council for Children with Behavioral Disorders.

Mattison, R. E., Hooper, S. R., & Glassber, L. A. (2002). Three-year course of learning disorders in special education students classified as behavior disorders. *Journal of the American Academy of Child and Adolescent Psychiatry, 41*(12), 1454–1461.

Mattison, R. E., Humphrey, J., Kales, S., Handford, H. A., Finkenbinder, R. L., & Hernit, R. C. (1986). Psychiatric background and diagnosis of children evaluated for special class placement. *Journal of the American Academy of Child Psychiatry, 25,* 514–520.

Mattison, R. E., Morales, J., & Bauer, M. A., (1992). Distinguishing characteristics of elementary school boys recommended for SED placement. *Behavioral Disorders, 17,* 107–114.

Mayer, G. R. (1995). Preventing antisocial behavior in the schools. *Journal of Applied Behavior Analysis, 28,* 467–478.

Mayer, M., Lochman, J., & Van Acker, R. (2005). Introduction to the special issue: Cognitive-behavioral interventions with students with EBD. *Behavioral Disorders, 30*(3), 197–212.

McArthur, D. S., & Roberts, D. E. (1982). *Roberts Apperception Test for Children.* Los Angeles: Western Psychological Services.

McCarney, S. B., & Leigh, J. E. (1990). *Behavior Evaluation Scale-2.* Austin, TX: Pro-Ed.

McConaughy, S. H., & Achenbach, T. M. (1994). *Manual for the Semistructured Clinical Interview for Children and Adolescents.* Burlington: University of Vermont Department of Psychiatry.

McConaughy, S. H., & Ritter, D. R. (2002). Best practices in multidimensional assessment of emotional or behavioral disorders. In A. Thomas & J. Grimes (Eds.), *Best practices in school psychology IV* (pp. 1303–1320). Bethesda, MD: National Association of School Psychologists.

McConnell, M. E. (1999). Self-monitoring, cueing, recording, and managing: Teaching students to manage their own behavior. *Teaching Exceptional Children, 32*(2), 14–21.

McDonough, K. M. (1989). Analysis of the expressive language characteristics of emotionally handicapped students in social interactions. *Behavioral Disorders, 14,* 127–139.

McDougal, D., & Brady, M. P. (1998). Initiating and fading self-management interventions to increase math fluency in general education classes. *Exceptional Children, 64,* 151–166.

McDowell, R. L. (1981). Adolescence. In G. Brown, R. L. McDowell, & J. Smith (Eds.), *Educating adolescents with behavior disorders.* Columbus, OH: Merrill.

McDowell, R. L., & Brown, G. B. (1978). The emotionally disturbed adolescent: Development of program alternatives in secondary education. *Focus on Exceptional Children, 10,* 1–15.

McGee, R., Feehan, M., Williams, S., Partridge, F., Silva, P. A., & Kelly, J. (1990). DSM-III disorders in a large sample of adolescents. *Journal of American Academy of Child and Adolescent Psychiatry, 29,* 611–619.

McGillivray, J. A., Cummins, R. A., & Prior, M. R. (1988). Cognitive behaviour modification of impulsive responding by hyperaggressive children in interpersonal problem situations. *Australia and New Zealand Journal of Development Disabilities, 14*(1), 55–70.

McGinnis, E., & Goldstein, A. P. (1984). *Skillstreaming the elementary school child.* Champaign, IL: Research Press.

McIntyre, T. (1993). Behaviorally disordered youth in correctional settings: Prevalence, programming, and teacher training. *Behavioral Disorders, 18,* 167–176.

McKnight, C. D., Compton, S. N., & March, J. S. (2004). Posttraumatic stress disorder. In T. L. Morris & J. S. March (Eds.), *Anxiety disorders in children and adolescents* (2nd ed., pp. 241–262). New York: Guilford Press.

McKnight, D. L., Nelson, R. O., Hayes, S. C., & Jarrett, R. B. (1984). Importance of treating individually assessed response classes in the amelioration of depression. *Behavior Therapy, 15,* 315–325.

McLaughlin, J. J., Leone, P. E., Warren, S. H., & Schofield, P. F. (1994). *Doing things differently; Issues and options for creating comprehensive school linked services for children and youth with emotional or behavioral disorders.* College Park, MD: University of Maryland in affiliation with Westat, Inc.

McLeer, S. V., Deblinger, E., Atkins, M. S., Foa, E. B., & Ralphe, D. L. (1988). Post-traumatic stress disorder in sexually abused children. *Journal of American Academy of Child and Adolescent Psychiatry, 27:* 650–654.

McMichael, P. (1979). The hen or the egg? Which comes first—antisocial emotional disorders or reading disability? *British Journal of Educational Psychology, 49,* 226–238.

McNally, R. J. (1993). Assessment of intrusive cognition in PTSD: Use of modified Stroop paradigm. *Journal of Traumatic Stress, 6,* 33–41.

McNeish, T. J., & Naglieri, J. A. (1993). Identification of individuals with serious emotional disturbance using the Draw-a-Person: Screening Procedure for Emotional Disturbance. *Journal of Special Education, 27,* 115–121.

McPherson, K. (1991). Project service leadership: School service projects in Washington State. *Phi Delta Kappan, 72*(10), 750–753.

Meadows, N., Neel, R. S., Parker, G., & Timo, K. (1991). A validation of social skills for students with behavioral disorders, *Behavioral Disorders, 16,* 200–210.

Medline Plus. *Depressed teens at higher risk for pregnancy, STDs.* National Library of Medicine and National Institutes of Health. Retrieved September 12, 2006, from http://www.nih.gov/medlineplus/news/fullstory_35746 .html

Medway, F. J., & Smith, R., C., Jr. (1978). An examination of contemporary elementary school affective education programs. *Psychology of the Schools,* 15, 260–269.

Meichenbaum, D. (1986). Cognitive–behavior modification. In F. H. Kanfer & A. P. Goldstein (Eds), Helping people change: A textbook of methods (3rd ed., pp. 346–380). Elmsford, NY: Pergamon Press.

Meichenbaum, D. H., & Goodman, J. (1971). Training impulsive children to talk to themselves: A means of developing self-control. *Journal of Abnormal Psychology, 77*(2), 115–126.

Meichenbaum, D., & Cameron, R. (1973). *Stress inoculation: A skills training approach to anxiety management,* unpublished manuscript, University of Waterloo, Ontario, Canada.

Meichenbaum, D., & Turk, D. (1976). The cognitive–behavioral management of anxiety, anger, and pain. In P. O. Davidson (Ed.), *The behavioral management of anxiety, depression, and pain* (pp. 1–34). New York: Brunner/Mazel.

Merrell, K. W. (2003). *Behavioral, social, and emotional assessment of children and adolescents.* Mahwah, NJ: Lawrence Erlbaum Associates, Inc.

Merydith, S. P. (1999). Psychodynamic approaches. In H. T. Prout & D. T. Brown (Eds.), *Counseling and psychotherapy with children and adolescents* (3rd ed., pp. 74–107). New York: Wiley.

Meyers, A. B., & Landau, S. (2002). Best practice in school-based sexuality education and pregnancy prevention. In A. Thomas & J. Grimes (Eds.), *Best practices in school psychology IV* (pp. 1523–1536). Bethesda, MD: National Association of School Psychologists.

Meyers, A. W., Cohen, R., & Schleser, R. (1989). A cognitive behavioral approach to education: Adopting a broad-based perspective. In J. N. Hughes & J. Hall (Eds.), Handbook of cognitive behavioral approaches in educational settings (pp. 62–84). New York: Guilford Press.

Mezzich, A., Tarter, K., Kirisci, L., Clark, D. B., Bukstein, O., & Martin, C. (1993). Subtypes of early age onset alcoholism. *Alcoholism: Clinical and Experimental Research, 17,* 767–770.

Milich, R. & Dodge, K. A. (1984). Social information processing in child psychiatric populations. *Journal of Abnormal Child Psychology, 91,* 183–198.

Miller, D. (1993). Sexual and physical abuse among adolescents with behavioral disorders: Profiles and implications. *Behavioral Disorders, 18,* 129–138.

Miller, D. (1994). Suicidal behavior of adolescents with behavior disorders and their peers without disabilities. *Behavioral Disorders, 20*(1), 61–68.

Miller, L. C. (1967). Louisville behavior checklist for males, 6–12 years of age. *Psychological Reports, 21,* 885–896.

Miller, L. C. (1980). Dimensions of adolescent psychopathology. *Journal of Abnormal Child Psychology, 8,* 161–173.

Miller, M. D., Brownell, M., & Smith, S. W. (1999). Factors that predict teachers staying in, leaving, or transferring from the special education classroom. *Exceptional Children, 65,* 201–218.

Miller, P. M. (1972). The use of visual imagery and muscle relaxation in the counterconditioning of a phobic child: A case study. *Journal of Nervous and Mental Disease, 154,* 457–460.

Miller, S. M., Birnbaum, A., & Durbin, D. (1990). Etiologic perspectives on depression in childhood. In M. Lewis &

S. M. Miller (Eds.), *Handbook of Developmental Psychopathology* (pp. 311–325). New York: Plenum Publishing.

Miller, S. P., & Hudson, P. (1994). Using structured parent groups to provide parental support. *Intervention in School and Clinic, 29,* 151–155.

Millon, T., Green, C. J., & Meagher, R. B. (1982). *Millon Adolescent Personality Inventory.* Minneapolis, MN: National Computer Systems.

Mills-Faraudo, T. S. (2006, August 23). For now, it appears special-ed students also must pass exam. Inside Bay Area, retrieved August 24, 2006, from *www.insidebayarea.com*

Mitchell, J., McCauley, E., Burke, P. M., & Moss, S. J. (1988). Phenomenology of depression in children and adolescents. *Journal of the American Academy of Child and Adolescent Psychiatry, 27,* 12–20.

Mollison, A. (1999, May 11). Leaders meet on youth violence. *Austin American-Statesman,* p. A4.

Montgomery, M. D. (1982). Educational services for emotionally disturbed children. In J. L. Paul & B. C. Epanchin (Eds.), *Emotional disturbance in children: Theories and methods for teachers.* Columbus, OH: Merrill.

Moody, S. W., Vaughn, S., Hughes, M. T., & Fischer, M. (2000). Reading instruction in the resource room: Set up for failure. *Exceptional Children, 66*(3), 305–316.

Mooney, P., & Gunter, P. L. (2004). The impact of NCLB and the Reauthorization of IDEA on academic instruction of students with emotional or behavioral disorders, *Behavioral Disorders, 29*(3), 237–246.

Mooney, P., Denny, R. K., & Gunter, P. L. (2004). The impact of NCLB and the reauthorization of IDEA on academic instruction of students with emotional or behavioral disorders. *Behavioral Disorders, 29,* 237–246.

Mooney, P., Epstein, M. H., Reid, R., & Nelson, J. R. (2003) Status of and treads in academic intervention research for students with emotional disturbance, *Remedial and Special Education, 24*(5), 273–287.

Moore, H. B., Presbury, J. H., Smith, L. W., & McKee, J. E. (1999). Person-centered approaches. In H. T. Prout & D. T. Brown (Eds.), *Counseling and psychotherapy with children and adolescents* (3rd ed., pp. 155–202). New York: Wiley.

Moore, R., Cartledge, G., & Heckaman, K. (1995). The effects of social skill instruction and self-monitoring on anger-control, reactions-to-losing, and reactions-to-winning behaviors of ninth-grade students with emotional and behavioral disorders. *Behavioral Disorders, 20,* 253–266.

Moran, D. J., & Malott, R. W. (2004). *Evidence-based educational methods.* New York: Elsevier

Moreau, D. L., Weissman, M., & Warner, V. (1989). Panic disorder in children of high risk for depression. *American Journal of Psychiatry, 146,* 1059–1060.

Morgan, D. P. (1993). *RESIST: A curriculum to prevent the use of alcohol, tobacco, and other drugs by students in special education.* Logan, UT: Utah State University.

Morgan, D. P., Likins, M., Friedman, S., & Genaux, M. (1994). *A preliminary investigation of the effectiveness of a substance use prevention program for students in special education programs.* Logan, UT: Utah State University.

Morris, R. J. (1991). Fear reduction methods. In F. H. Kanfer and A. P. Goldstein (Eds.), *Helping people change: A textbook of methods* (pp. 161–201). New York: Pergamon Press.

Morris, R. J., & Kratochwill, T. R. (1987). Dealing with fear and anxiety in the school setting: Behavioral approaches to treatment. *Special Services in the Schools, 3,* 53–68.

Morrison, G. M. & D'Incau, B. (1997). The web of zero-tolerance: Characteristics of students who are recommended for expulsion from school. *Education & Treatment of Children,* 20, 316–335.

Morse, J. (2000, April). Looking for trouble. *Time, 155*(16), 50–54.

Morse, W. C. (1969a). Preparing to teach the disturbed adolescent. In H. W. Harshman (Ed.), *Educating the emotionally disturbed: A book of readings.* New York: Thomas Y. Crowell.

Morse, W. C. (1969b). Training teachers in life space interviewing. In H. Dupont (Ed.), *Educating emotionally disturbed children: Readings.* New York: Holt, Rinehart & Winston.

Mowrer, D., & Conoley, D. (1987). Effect of peer administered consequences upon articulatory responses of speech defective children. *Journal of Communication Disorders, 20,* 319–326.

MTA Cooperative Group. (1999). Moderators and mediators of treatment response for children with attention-deficit/hyperactivity disorder. *Archives of General Psychiatry, 56,* 1088–1096.

Mufson, L., Weissman, M.M., Moreau, D., & Garfinkel, R. (1999). Efficacy of interpersonal psychotherapy for depressed adolescents. *Archives of General Psychiatry, 56,* 573–579.

Murphy, D. M. (1986). The prevalence of handicapping conditions among juvenile delinquents. *Remedial and Special Education, 7,* 70–71.

Murray, C. (2003). Risk factors, protective factors, vulnerability, and resilience: A framework for understanding and supporting the adult transitions of youth with high incidence disabilities. *Remedial and Special Education, 24*(1), 16–26.

Murray, C. A. (1976). *The link between learning disabilities and juvenile delinquency: Current theory and knowledge.* Washington, DC: U.S. Government Printing Office.

Murray, H. A. (1943). *Thematic Apperception Test manual.* Cambridge, MA: Harvard University Press.

Muscott, H. (2001, Spring). An introduction to service learning for students with emotional and behavioral disorders: Answers to frequently asked questions. *Beyond Behavior, 10*(3), 8–15.

Muse, N. J. (1990). *Depression and suicide in children and adolescents.* Austin, TX: Pro-Ed.

Myles, B. S., & Simpson, R. L. (1994). School violence to school safety: Reframing the issue for school psychologists. *School Psychology Review, 23,* 236–256.

Naglieri, J. A. (2002). Best practices in interventions for school psychologists: A cognitive approach to problem solving. In A. Thomas & J. Grimes (Eds.), *Best practices in school psychology IV* (pp. 1373–1392). Bethesda, MD: National Association of School Psychologists.

Naglieri, J. A., & Das, J. P. (1997). *Cognitive Assessment System.* Itasca, IL: Riverside.

Naglieri, J. A., & Pfeiffer, S. L. (1992). Performance of disruptive behavior disordered and normal samples on the Draw-A-Person: Screening Procedure for Emotional Disturbance. *Psychological Assessment, 4,* 156–159.

Naglieri, J. A., LeBuffe, P. A., & Pfeiffer, S. I. (1994). *Devereux Scales of Mental Disorders.* San Antonio: Psychological Corporation.

Naglieri, J. A., McNeish, T. J., & Bardos, A. N. (1991). *Draw A Person: Screening procedure for emotional disturbance.* Austin, TX: Pro-Ed.

Naierman, N. (1997). Reaching out to grieving students. *Educational Leadership, 55*(2), 62–65.

Nathan, J., & Kielsmeier, J. (1991). The sleeping giant of school reform. *Phi Delta Kappa, 72*(10), 739–742.

National Association of School Psychologists. (2002). Position statement of students with emotional and behavioral disorders. Retrieved August 2, 2005, from *http://www.nasponline.org/information/pospaper_sebd.html*

National Association of State Directors of Special Education. (2005). *Response to Intervention: Policy considerations and implementation.* Alexandria, VA: Author.

National Center for Education Statistics (2004). *Dropout rates in the United States: 2001.* Retrieved September 12, 2006 from *http://nces.ed.gov/pubsearch/pubsinfo.asp*

National Center for Educational Statistics (IES). (1999). *Digest of Educational Statistics Tables and Figures 1999.* Retrieved August 19, 2006, from http://nces.ed.gov/programs/digest/d99/lt6.asp

National Consortium of School Violence Prevention Researchers and Practitioners. (2006, November 2). *Fall 2006 school shootings position statement.* Retrieved November 6, 2006, from *www.ncsvprp.org*

National Institute of Mental Health. (February 8, 2005). *Antidepressant medications for children and adolescents: Information for parents and caregivers.* Available at http.www.nimh.nih/gov/healthinformation/antidepressant_child.cfm

National Institute on Drug Abuse. (1980). *Review of evidence on effects of marijuana use.* Washington, DC: U.S. Government Printing Office.

National Institute on Drug Abuse. (2001). *Some research-based drug abuse prevention programs.* Available at http://www.drugabuse.gov/

National Institutes of Health. (2001). *Blueprint for change: Research on child and adolescent mental health* (Report of the National Advisory Mental Health Council's Workgroup on child and adolescent mental health intervention development and deployment: Executive Summary and Recommendations) (NIH Pub. No. 01-4986). Washington, DC: Author.

National Mental Health and Special Education Coalition. (1989, April 4). *Statement to the House Committee on Select Education.*

National restraint death database. (2003). *Hartford Courant.* Retrieved February 2, 2003, from http://courant.ctnow.com/projects/restraint/data.stm.

National School Boards Association. (1992, July 15). Group urges new definition of emotional disorders: NSBA opposes any change that would dilute scarce resources. *NSBA Newsletter,* p. 2.

National Youth Violence Prevention Resource Center. (2006). *Teen facts: Youth gangs.* Retrieved September, 13, 2006, from http://www.safeyouth,org/scripts/teens/gangs.asp

Neel, R. S., & Cessna, K. K. (1993). Behavioral intent: Instructional content for students with behavior disorders. In K. K. Cessna (Ed.), *Instructionally differentiated programming: A needs-based approach for students with behavior disorders* (pp. 31–39). Denver, CO: Colorado Department of Education.

Neenan, M., & Dryden. W. (1999). *Rational emotive behavior therapy: Advances in theory and practice.* London: Whurr.

Neimark, E. D. (1975). Intellectual development during adolescence. In F. D. Horowitz (Ed.), *Review of child development research* (Vol. 4). Chicago: University of Chicago Press.

Nelson, C. M. (1983). Beyond the classroom: The teacher of behaviorally disordered pupils in a social system. In R. B. Rutherford, Jr. (Ed.), *Severe behavior disorders of children and youth.* Tempe, AZ: Arizona State University.

Nelson, C. M. (2005, July 11). Systems failure. Message posted to spedpro electronic mailing list. Retrieved July 12, 2005, from spedpro@list.mail.Virginia.edu.

Nelson, C. M., & Rutherford, R. B. (1989, September). *Impact of the Correctional Special Education Training (C/SET) Project on correctional special education.* Paper presented at CEC/CCBD National Topical Conference on Behavioral Disorders, Charlotte, NC.

Nelson, C. M., Rutherford, R. B., Jr., & Wolford, B. I. (1987). *Special education in the criminal justice system.* Columbus, OH: Merrill.

Nelson, C. M., Sugai, G., & Smith, C. R. (2005, Summer). Positive behavior support offered in juvenile corrections. *Counterpoint, 1,* 6–7

Nelson, J. R., Benner, G. J., & Cheney, D. (2005). An investigation of the language skills of students with emotional and behavioral disorders served in public school settings. *Journal of Special Education, 39,* 97–105.

Nelson, J. R., Benner, G. J., & Gonzales, J. (2005). An investigation of the effects of a prereading intervention on the early literacy skills of children at risk of emotional disturbance and reading problems. *Journal of Emotional and Behavioral Disorders, 13*(1), 3–12.

Nelson, J. R., Benner, G. J., Lane, K., & Smith, B. W. (2004). An investigation of the academic achievement of K–12 students with emotional and behavioral disorders in public school settings. *Exceptional Children, 71*(1), 59–74.

Nelson, J. R., Benner, G. J., Neill, S., & Stage, S. A. (2006). Interrelationaships among language skills, externalizing behavior, and academic fluency and their impact on the academic skills of students with ED. *Journal of Emotional and Behavioral Disorders, 14*(4), 209–216.

Nelson, J. R., Benner, G.J., & Rogers-Adkinson, D. L. (2003). An investigation of the characteristics of K–12 students with co-morbid emotional disturbance and significant language deficits served in public school settings. *Behavioral Disorders, 29*(1), 25–33.

Nelson, J. R., Martella, R., & Marchand-Martella, N. (2002). Maximizing student learning: The effects of a comprehensive school-based program for preventing problem behaviors. *Journal of Emotional and Behavioral Disorders 10*(3), 136–148.

Nelson, J. R., Roberts, M. L., Mathur, S. R., & Rutherford, R. B. (1999). Has public policy exceeded our knowledge base? A review of the functional behavioral assessment literature. *Behavioral Disorders, 24*(2), 169–179.

Nelson, J. R., Smith, D. J., Young, R. K., & Dodd, J. M. (1991). A review of self-management outcome research conducted with students who exhibit behavioral disorders. *Behavioral Disorders, 16,* 169–179.

Netzel, D. M., & Eber, L. (2003). Shifting from reactive to proactive discipline in an urban school district: A change of focus through PBIS implementation. *Journal of Positive Behavior Interventions, 5*(2), 71–79.

Newcomer, L. L., & Lewis, T. J. (2004). Functional behavioral assessment: An investigation of assessment reliability and effectiveness of function-based interventions. *Journal of Emotional and Behavioral Disorders, 12*(3), 168–181.

Newcomer, P. L. (1993). *Understanding and teaching emotionally disturbed children and adolescents* (2nd ed.). Austin, TX: Pro-Ed.

Newcomer, P. L., Barenbaum, E., & Pearson, N. (1995). Depression and anxiety in children and adolescents with learning disabilities, conduct disorders, and no disabilities. *Journal of Emotional and Behavioral Disorders, 3,* 27–40.

Newman, L. (1992). A place to call home: Residential arrangements of out-of-school youth with disabilities. In M. Wagner, R. D'Amico, C. Marder, L. Newman, & J. Blackorby (Eds.), *What happens next? Trends in postschool outcomes of youth with disabilities* (pp. 5-1 to 5-35). Menlo Park, CA: SRI International.

Nichols, P. (1996). *Clear thinking—clearing dark thought with new words and images: A program for teachers and counseling professionals.* Iowa City, IA: River Lights Publishers.

Nichols, P. (1997). Problem solving for personal power. *Reclaiming Children and Youth, 6*(2), 75–81.

Nichols, P., & Shaw, M. (1996). *Whispering shadows: A student work text.* Iowa City, IA: River Lights Publishers.

Nichols, P., & Steinberg, Z. (1996). Voices of courage. *Reclaiming Children and Youth, 5*(2), 64–67.

No Child Left Behind. (2006, August 3). Raising the achievement of students with disabilities: New ideas for IDEA. Retrieved August 4, 2006, from www.ed.gov

Nolen-Hoeksema, S., Girgus, J., & Seligman, M. E. P. (1986). Learned helplessness in children: A longitudinal study of depression, achievement, and explanatory style. *Journal of Personality and Social Psychology, 51,* 435–442.

Nottelmann, E. D., & Jensen, P. S. (1995). Comorbidity of disorders in children and adolescents: Developmental perspectives. *Advances in Clinical Child Psychology, 17,* 109–155.

Novaco, R. (1978). Anger and coping with stress. In J. Forety & D. Rathjen (Eds.), *Cognitive behavior therapy: Research and application.* New York: Plenum Press.

Nuechterlein, K. H. (1983). Signal detection in vigilance tasks and behavioral attitudes among offspring of schizophrenic mothers and among hyperactive children. *Journal of Abnormal Psychology, 92,* 4–28.

Nunez, C., & Collignon, K. (1997). Creating a community of learning for homeless children. *Educational Leadership, 55*(2), 56–61.

Nussbaum, N., & Bigler, E. (1990). *Identification and treatment of attention deficit disorder.* Austin, TX: Pro-Ed.

Obeidallah, D., Brennan, R. T., Brooks-Gunn, J., & Earls, F. (2004). Links between pubertal timing and neighborhood contexts: Implications for girls' violent behavior. *Journal of the American Academy of Child and Adolescent Psychiatry, 43*(12), 1460.

O'Farrell, T. J., Hedlund, M. A., & Cutter, H. S. (1986). Desensitization methods for school panic attacks. In

C. E. Schaefer, H. L. Millman, S. M. Sichel, & J. R. Zwilling (Eds.), *Advances in therapies for children* (pp. 90–93). San Francisco: Jossey-Bass.

Office of Juvenile Justice and Delinquency Prevention. (1994). *Juvenile crime, 1988–1992.* Washington, DC: Author.

Office of Juvenile Justice and Delinquency Prevention. (2006). *Juvenile offenders and victims: 2006 National Report.* Retrieved November 11, 2006, from *http://ojjdp.ncjrs.org/*

Ollendick, T. H. (1983). Reliability and validity of the revised Fear Survey Schedule for Children (FSSC-R). *Behaviour Research and Therapy, 21,* 685–692.

Ollendick, T. H., & Mayer, J. A. (1984). School phobia. In S. M. Turner (Ed.), *Behavioral theories and treatment of anxiety* (pp. 367–411). New York: Plenum Publishing.

Ollendick, T. H., Birmaher, B., & Mattis, S. G. (2004). Panic disorder. In T. L. Morris & J. S. March (Eds.), *Anxiety disorders in children and adolescents* (2nd ed., pp. 189–211). New York: Guilford Press.

Olson, L. (2004). Enveloping expectations: Federal law demands that schools teach the same content to children they wrote off a quarter-century ago. *Education Week: Quality Counts 2004, XXIII*(17), 8–20.

Olson, L., & Hoff, D. J. (2006, December 13). Framing the debate. *Education Week, 26*(15), 22–30.

Olweus, D. (1987). Bully/victim problems among school children. In J. P. Myklebust & R. Ommundsen (Eds.), *Psykolg-profesjonen mot ar 2000.* Oslo, Norway: Universitetsfor-laget.

Olweus, D. (1991). Bully/victim problems among school children: Basic facts and effects of a school-based intervention program. In D. Pepler & K. Rubin (Eds.), *The development and treatment of childhood aggression* (pp. 411–446). London: Lawrence Erlbaum.

Olweus, D. (2003, March). A profile of bullying at school. *Educational Leadership, 60*(6), 12–17.

O'Neill, R. E., Horner, R. H., Albin, R. W., Sprague, J. R., Storey, K., & Newton, J. S. (1997). *Functional assessment and program development for problem behavior: A practical handbook.* Pacific Grove: CA: Brooks/Cole Publishing.

Ortiz, A., & Maldonado, C. E. (1986). Recognizing learning disabilities in bilingual children: How to lessen inappropriate referrals of language minority students to special education. *Journal of Reading, Writing, and Learning Disabilities International, 2(1),* 43–56.

Ortiz, S. O. (2002). Best practices in nondiscriminatory assessment. In A. Thomas & J. Grimes (Eds.), *Best practices in school psychology IV* (pp. 1321–1336). Bethesda, MD: National Association of School Psychologists.

Ortiz, S. O., & Flanagan, D. P. (2002). Best practices in working with culturally diverse children and families. In A. Thomas & J. Grimes (Eds.), *Best practices in school psychology IV* (pp. 337–351). Bethesda, MD: National Association of School Psychologists.

O'Shaughnessy, T., Lane, K. L., Gresham, F. M., & Beebe-Frankenberger, M. (2002). Students with or at risk for learning and emotional-behavioral difficulties: an integrated system of prevention and intervention. In K. L. Lane, F. M. Gresham, & T. E. O'Shaughnessy (Eds.), *Interventions for children with or at risk for emotional and behavioral disorders* (pp. 3–17) Boston: Allyn & Bacon.

Osher, D., Cartledge, G., Oswald, D. Sugherland, K. S., Artiles, A. J., & Coutinho, M. (2004). Issues of cultural and linguistic competency in disproportionate representation. In R. B. Rutherford, M.M. Quinn, & S. R. Mathur (Eds.), *Handbook of research in emotional and behavioral disorders* (pp. 54–77) New York: Guilford Press.

Osher, D., Osher, T., & Smith, C. (1994). Toward a national perspective in emotional and behavioral disorders: A developmental agenda. *Beyond Behavior, 6*(1), 4–15.

Oster, G., & Gould, P. (1987). *Using drawings in assessment and therapy.* New York: Brunner/Mazel.

Overmier, J. B., & Seligman, M. E. P. (1967). Effects of inescapable shock upon subsequent escape and avoidance learning. *Journal of Comparative and Physiological Psychology, 63,* 23–33.

Ozer, E. J., & Weinstein, R. S. (2004). Urban adolescents' exposure to community violence: the role of support, school safety, and social constraints in a school-based sample of boys and girls. *Journal of Clinical Child and Adolescent Psychology, 33*(3), 463–47.

Papolos, D.F., & Papolos, J. (1999). *The bipolar child: The definitive and reassuring guide to childhood's most misunderstood disorder.* New York: Broadway Books.

Parish, T., Dyck, N., & Kappes, B. (1979). Stereotypes concerning normal and handicapped children. *The Journal of Psychology, 102,* 63–70.

Park, E. K., Pullis, M., Reilly, T., & Townsend, B. L. (1994). Cultural biases in the identification of students with behavioral disorders. In R. L. Peterson & S. Ishii-Jordan (Eds.), *Multicultural issues in the education of students with behavioral disorders.* Cambridge, MA: Brookline.

Parsons, B. V. & Alexander, J. F. (1973). Short-term family intervention: A therapy outcome study. *Journal of Consulting and Clinical Psychology, 41,* 195–201.

Patterson, G. R. (1976). The aggressive child: Victim and architect of a coercive system. In E. J. Mash, L. A. Hamerlynck, & L. C. Handy (Eds.), *Behavior modification and families.* New York: Brunner/Mazel.

Patterson, G. R. (1983). *Longitudinal investigation of antisocial boys and their families: Research* (Grant from the National Institute of Mental Health). Eugene, OR: Oregon Social Learning Center.

Patterson, G. R. (1988). Family process: Loops, levels, and linkages. In N. Bolger, A. Caspi, G. Downey, &

M. Moorehouse (Eds.), *Persons in context: Developmental processes* (pp. 114–151). New York: Cambridge University Press.

Patterson, G. R., & Cobb, J. A. (1973). Stimulus control for classes of noxious behavior. In J. S. Knutson (Ed.), *The control of aggression: Implications from basic research.* Chicago: Aldine.

Patterson, G. R., Chamberlain, P., & Reid, J. B. (1982). A comparative evaluation of a parent-training program. *Behavior Therapy, 13,* 638–650.

Patterson, G. R., Reid, J. B., & Dishion, T. J. (1992). *Antisocial boys (Vol. 4): A social interactional approach.* Eugene, OR: Castalia.

Patton, P. L. (1995). Rational behavior skills: A teaching sequence for students with emotional disabilities. *School Counselor, 43,* 133–141.

Pauls, D. L., & Leckman, J. F. (1986). The inheritance of Gilles de la Tourette's syndrome and associated behaviors: Evidence for autosomal dominant transmission. *New England Journal of Medicine, 315,* 993–997.

Pavri, S. (2004). General and special education teachers' preparation needs in providing social support: A needs assessment. *Teacher Education and Special Education, 27*(4), 433–443.

Pedlow, R., Sanson, A., Prior, M., & Oberklaid, F. (1993). Stability of maternally reported temperament from infancy to 8 years. *Developmental Psychology, 29,* 998–1007.

Pelham, W. E., Schnedler, R. W., Bologna, N. C., & Contreras, A. J. (1980). Behavioral and stimulant treatment of hyperactive children: A therapy study with methylphenidate probes in a within-subject design. *Journal of Applied Behavior Analysis, 13,* 221–236.

Pennington, B. F. (2002). *The development of psychopathology: Nature and nurture.* New York: Guilford Press.

Pennington, B. F., & Ozonoff, S. (1996). Executive functions and developmental psychopathology. *Journal of Child Psychology and Psychiatry, 37,* 51–87.

Pentz, M. A., Dwyer, J. H., MacKinnon, D. P., Flay, B. R., Hansen, W. B., Wang, E. U. I., & Johnson, C. A. (1989). A multicommunity trial for primary prevention of adolescent drug use. *Journal of the American Medical Association, 261,* 3259–3266.

Pescara-Kovach, L. A., & Alexander, K. (1994). The link between food ingested and problem behavior: Fact or fallacy? *Behavioral Disorders, 19,* 142–148.

Peterson, A. C., Compas, B. E., Brooks-Gunn, J., Stemmler, M., Ey, S., & Grant, K. E. (1993). Depression in adolescence. *American Psychologist, 48(2),* 155–168.

Peterson, C., Luborsky, L., & Seligman, M. E. P. (1983). Attributions and depressive mood shifts: A case study using the symptom-context method. *Journal of Abnormal Psychology, 92,* 96–103.

Peterson, D. R. (1961). Behavior problems of middle childhood. *Journal of Consulting Psychology, 25,* 205–209.

Pfeiffer, S. I., & Reddy, L. A. (1998). School-based mental health programs in the United States: Present status and a blueprint for the future. *School Psychology Review, 27*(1), 84–96.

Phelps, L., & Bajorek, E. (1991). Eating disorders of the adolescent: Current issues in etiology, assessment, and treatment. *School Psychology Review, 20,* 9–22.

Phelps, L., Cox, D., & Bajorek, E. (1992). School phobia and separation anxiety: Diagnostic and treatment comparisons. *Psychology in the Schools, 29,* 384–394.

Phi Delta Kappa. (1998, September). Addressing the issues surrounding school suspensions and expulsions. *Research Bulletin, 21,* 15–16. Bloomington, IN: Author.

Piaget, J. (1952). *The origins of intelligence in children.* New York: International Universities Press (original work published in 1936).

Piaget, J. (1972). Intellectual evolution from adolescence to adulthood. *Human Development, 15,* 1–12.

Pierce, C., Reid, R., & Epstein, M. H. (2004). Teacher-mediated interventions for children with EBD and their academic outcomes: A review. *Remedial and Special Education, 25,* 175–188.

Piers, E., & Harris, D. (1969). *The Piers-Harris Children's Self-concept Scale.* Nashville: Counselor Recordings and Tests.

Plomin, R. (1994). Nature, nurture, and social development. *Social Development, 3,* 37–53.

Poland, S., & Lieberman, R. (2002). Best practices in suicide prevention. In A. Thomas & J. Grimes (Eds.), *Best practices in school psychology IV,* (pp. 1151–1165). Bethesda, MD: National Association of School Psychologists.

Pope, H. G., Hudson, J. I., & Jonas, J. M. (1983). Bulimia treated with imipramine: A placebo-controlled, double blind study. *American Journal of Psychiatry, 140,* 554–558.

Portner, J. (2000a). Complex set of ills spurs rising teen suicide rate. *Education Week, 19*(31), 1, 22–31.

Portner, J. (2000b). Suicide: Many schools fall short on prevention. *Education Week, 19*(32), 1, 20–32.

Post, C. H. (1981). The link between learning disabilities and juvenile delinquency: Cause, effect, and "present solutions." *Juvenile and Family Court Journal, 32,* 58–68.

Power, T. J., DuPaul, G. J., Shapiro, E. S., & Parrish, J. M. (1995). Pediatric school psychology: The emergence of a subspecialty. *School Psychology Review, 24,* 244–257.

Poznanski, E. O., Cook, S. C., & Carroll, B. J. (1979). A depression rating scale for children. *Pediatrics, 64,* 442–450.

Premack, D. (1965). Reinforcement theory. In D. Levine (Ed.), *Nebraska Symposium on Motivation.* Lincoln: University of Nebraska Press.

Pressley, M. (2002). Effective beginning reading. *Journal of Literacy Research, 34,* 165–188.

Prout, H. T., & DeMartino, R. A. (1986). A meta-analysis of school-based studies of psychotherapy. *Journal of School Psychology, 24,* 285–292.

Pugach, M. C., & Warger, C. L. (2001). Curriculum matters: Raising expectations for students with disabilities. *Remedial and Special Education, 22*(4), 194–196.

Puig-Antich, J. (1982). Major depression and conduct disorder in prepuberty. *Journal of the American Academy of Child Psychiatry, 21,* 118–128.

Puig-Antich, J., & Weston, B. (1983). The diagnosis and treatment of major depressive disorder in childhood. *Annual Review of Medicine, 34,* 231–245.

Pumariega, A. J., & Winters, N. C. (2003). *The handbook of child and adolescent systems of care: The new community psychiatry.* San Francisco: Jossey-Bass

Pynoos, R. S., Frederick, C., & Nader, K. (1987). Life threat and post-traumatic stress in school-age children. *Archives of General Psychiatry, 44,* 1057–1063.

Quay, H. C. (1966). Personality patterns in pre-adolescent delinquent boys. *Educational and Psychological Measurement, 26,* 99–110.

Quay, H. C. (1972). Patterns of aggression, withdrawal and immaturity. In H. C. Quay & J. S. Werry (Eds.), *Psychopathological disorders of childhood.* New York: Wiley.

Quay, H. C. (1975). Classification in the treatment of delinquency and antisocial behavior. In N. Hobbs (Ed.), *Issues in the classification of children* (Vol. 1). San Francisco: Jossey-Bass.

Quay, H. C. (1977). Psychopathic behavior. In I. C. Uzgiris & F. Weizmann (Eds.), *The structuring of experience.* New York: Plenum.

Quay, H. C. (1986a). Classification. In H. C. Quay & J. S. Werry (Eds.). *Psychopathological disorders of childhood* (3rd ed.). New York: John Wiley & Sons.

Quay, H. C. (1986b). Conduct disorders. In H. C. Quay & J. S. Werry (Eds.) *Psychopathological disorders of childhood* (3rd ed., pp. 35–72). New York: John Wiley & Sons.

Quay, H. C., & Peterson, D. R. (1967). *Manual for the Behavior Problem Checklist.* Champaign, IL: Children's Research Center. Mimeographed.

Quay, H. C., & Peterson, D. R. (1987). *Manual for the Revised Behavior Problem Checklist.* Coral Gables, FL: Author.

Quay, H. C., Morse, W. C., & Cutler, R. L. (1966). Personality patterns of pupils in classrooms for the emotionally disturbed. *Exceptional Children, 32,* 297–301.

Quiggle, N. L., Garber, J., Panak, W. F., & Dodge, K. A. (1992). Social information processing in aggressive and depressed children. *Annual Progress in Child Psychiatry and Development,* 217–241.

Quijada, R.E., Montoya, C.M., Laserna, P.A., Toledo, A.P., Marco, E.M., & Rabadan, F.E. (2005). Depression prevalence in adolescents. *Actas Españolas de Psiquiatria, 33,* 298–302.

Quinn, M. M., Kavale, K. A., Mathur, S. R., Rutherford, R. B., & Forness, S. R. (1999). A meta-analysis of social skills interventions for students with emotional or behavioral disorders. *Journal of Emotional & Behavioral Disorders, 7*(1), 54–64.

Rachlin, H. (1984). Self-control. *Behaviorism, 2,* 94–107.

Rachman, S. (1971). *The effects of psychotherapy.* Oxford: Pergamon.

Raine, A., Brennan, P., & Mednick, S. A. (1997). Interaction between birth complications and early maternal rejection in predisposing individuals to adult violence: Specificity to serious, early-onset violence. *American Journal of Psychiatry, 154*(9), 1265–1271.

Ramirez, J. (2000). *Cognitive distortions in adolescents with substance-related disorders.* Unpublished doctoral dissertation. Austin, TX: The University of Texas.

Ramirez, S. Z. Feeney-Kettler K. A., Flores-Torres L. L., Kratochwill T. R., & Morris, R. J. (2006). Fears and anxiety disorders. In G. G. Bear & K. M. Minke (Eds.), *Children's needs III: Development, prevention, and intervention* (pp. 267–279). Bethesda, MD: National Association of School Psychologists.

Ramsey, M. (1994). Student depression: General treatment dynamics and symptom specific interventions. *School Counselor, 41,* 256–262.

Rapport, M. D. (1987). Attention deficit disorder with hyperactivity. In M. Hersen & V. B. Van Hasselt (Eds.), *Behavior therapy with children and adolescents* (pp. 325–361). New York: Wiley.

Rapport, M. D., Stoner, G., DuPaul, G. J., Birmingham, B. K., & Tucker, S. (1985). Methylphenidate in hyperactive children: Differential effects of dose on academic, learning, and social behavior. *Journal of Abnormal Child Psychology, 13,* 227–244.

Raths, I., Harmin, M., & Simon, S. (1978). *Values and teaching.* Columbus, OH: Charles E. Merrill.

Raywid, M. A., & Oshiyama, L. (2000). Musings in the wake of Columbine: What can schools do? *Phi Delta Kappan, 81*(6), 444–449.

Read, J. S. (1995, June/July). Ritalin: It's not the teacher's decision. *CEC Today, 2,* 14.

Realmuto, G. M. & Erickson, W. D. (1986). The management of sexual issues in adolescent treatment programs. *Adolescence, 21,* 347–356.

Reddy, L. A. (1999). Inclusion practices with special needs students: Theory, research, and application. *Special Services in the Schools, 15*(1/2), 3–24.

Reder, M. (2001). Dual diagnosis: Mental retardation and psychiatric disorders, In. M. L. Batshaw (Ed.), *Children with disabilities* (5th Ed., pp. 347–363). Baltimore: Paul H. Brookes.

Reder, M., & Borcherding, B. G. (1997). Dual diagnosis: Mental retardation and psychiatric disorders. In

M. L. Batshaw (Ed.), *Children with disabilities* (4th ed., pp. 405–424). Baltimore: Brookes.

Redl, F. (1959a). The concept of the life space interview. *American Journal of Orthopsychiatry, 29,* 1–18.

Redl, F. (1959b). The concept of a therapeutic milieu. *American Journal of Orthopsychiatry, 29,* 721–734.

Redl, F. (1965). The concept of the life space interview. In N. J. Long, W. C. Morse, & R. G. Newman (Eds.), *Conflict in the classroom: The education of emotionally disturbed children.* Belmont, CA: Wadsworth.

Redl, F. (1966). *When we deal with children.* New York: Free Press.

Redl, F., & Wineman, D. (1957). *The aggressive child.* New York: Free Press.

Reeve, R. E. (1990). ADHD: Facts and fallacies. *Intervention in School and Clinic, 26,* 70–77.

Reid, J. (1993). Prevention of conduct disorder before and after school entry: Relating interventions to developmental findings. *Development and Psycho-pathology, 5*(1/2) 243–262.

Reid, J. B., & Patterson, G. R. (1991). Early prevention and intervention with conduct problems: A social interactional model for the integration of research and practice. In G. Stoner, M. Shinn, & H. Walker (Eds.), *Interventions for achievement and behavior problems* (pp. 715–739). Silver Spring, MD: National Association of School Psychologists.

Reid, M. J., & Webster-Stratton, C. (2001). The incredible years parent, teacher, and child intervention: Targeting multiple areas of risk for a young child with pervasive conduct problems using a flexible, manualized, treatment program. *Journal of Cognitive and Behavior Practice, 8,* 377–386.

Reid, R. (1995). Assessment of ADHD with culturally different groups: The use of behavioral rating scales. *School Psychology Review, 24*(4), 536–560.

Reid, R. (1996). Self-monitoring for students with learning disabilities: The present, the prospects, the pitfalls. *Journal of Learning Disabilities, 29,* 317–331.

Reid, R. (1999). Attention deficit hyperactivity disorder: Effective methods for the classroom. *Focus on Exceptional Children, 32*(4), 1–20.

Reid, R., & Katsiyannis, A. (1995). Attention deficit-hyperactivity disorder and Section 504. *Remedial and Special Education, 16,* 44–52.

Reid, R., & Lienemann, T. O. (2006). Self-regulated strategy development for written expression with students with attention deficit/hyperactivity disorder. *Exceptional Children, 73*(10), 53–68.

Reid, R., Gonzalez, J. E., Nordness, P. D., Trout, A., & Epstein, M. H. (2004). A meta-analysis of the academic status of students with emotional/behavioral disturbance. *Journal of Special Education, 38,* 130–143.

Reid, R., Maag, J. W., & Vasa, S. F. (1994). Attention deficit-hyperactivity disorder as a disability category: A critique. *Exceptional Children, 60,* 198–214.

Reid, R., Schmidt, Harris, K. R., & Graham, S. (1997). Cognitive strategy instruction: Developing self-regulated learners. *Reclaiming Children and Youth, 6*(2), 97–102.

Reid, R., Trout, A., & Schartz, M. (2005). Self-regulation interventions for children with attention deficit hyperactivity disorder. *Exceptional Children, 71,* 361–377.

Reitan, R. M., & Wolfson, D. (1985). *The Halstead-Reitan neuropsychological battery: Theory and clinical interpretation.* Tucson, AZ: Neuropsychological Press.

Renshaw, P. D., & Asher, S. R. (1982). Social competence and peer status: The distinction between goals and strategies. In K. H. Rubin & H. S. Ross (Eds.), *Peer relationships and social skills in childhood* (pp. 375–395). New York: Springer-Verlag.

Repp, A., Felce, D., & Barton, L. (1991). The effects of initial interval size on the efficacy of DRO schedules of reinforcement. *Exceptional Children, 58,* 417–425.

Reschly, A. & Christenson, S. L. (2006). School completion. In G. G. Bear & K. M. Minke (Eds.), *Children's needs III: Development, prevention, and intervention* (pp. 103–113). Bethesda, MD: National Association of School Psychologists.

Reynolds, C. R., & Mayfield, J. W. (1999). Neuropsychological assessment in genetically linked neurodevelopmental disorders. In S. Goldstein & C. R. Reynolds (Eds.), *Handbook of neurodevelopmental and genetic disorders in children* (pp. 9–37). New York: Guilford Press.

Reynolds, C. R., & Richmond, B. O. (1985). *Revised Children's Manifest Anxiety Scale.* Los Angeles: Western Psychological Services.

Reynolds, C., & Kamphaus, R. (2004). *Behavior assessment system for children* (2nd Ed.). Circle Pines, MN: American Guidance Service.

Reynolds, L., & Kelley, M. L. (1997). The efficacy of a response cost-based treatment package for managing aggressive behavior in preschoolers. *Behavior Modification, 21,* (2), 216–230.

Reynolds, W. M. (1984). Depression in children and adolescents: Phenomenology, evaluation, and treatment. *School Psychology Review, 13,* 171–182.

Reynolds, W. M. (1987). *Reynolds Adolescent Depression Scale.* Odessa, FL: Psychological Assessment Resources.

Reynolds, W. M., & Coates, K. I. (1986). A comparison of cognitive-behavioral therapy and relaxation training for the treatment of depression in adolescents. *Journal of Consulting and Clinical Psychology, 54,* 1–8.

Rezmierski, V. (1984). Impulse control: Stages and interventions. *The Pointer, 28*(4), 13–19.

Rezmierski, V., and J. Kotre. (1972). A limited literature review of theory of the psychodynamic model, In

Rhodes, W., and M. Tracy (Eds.), A Study of Child Variance (Ann Arbor: University of Michigan), 181–258.

Rhode, G., Jenson, W. R., & Reavis, H. K. (1992). *The tough kid book: Practical classroom management strategies.* Longmont, CO: Sopris West.

Rhode, G., Morgan, D. P., & Young, K. R. (1983). Generalization and maintenance of treatment gains of behaviorally handicapped students from resource rooms to regular classrooms using self-evaluation procedures. *Journal of Applied Behavior Analysis, 16,* 171–188.

Rhodes, W. C. (1967). The disturbing child: A problem of ecological management. *Exceptional Children, 33,* 449–455.

Rhodes, W. C. (1970). A community participation analysis of emotional disturbance. *Exceptional Children, 36,* 306–314.

Rhodes, W. C., & Tracy, M. L. (Eds.) (1974). *A study of child variance* (3 vols.). Ann Arbor, MI: The University of Michigan Press.

Riddle, M. A., Scahill, L., & King, R. (1990). Obsessive compulsive disorder in children and adolescent: Phenomenology and family history. *Journal of American Academy of Child and Adolescent Psychiatry, 29,* 766–772.

Riley, C., & Paine, A. (2006, August 20). Scores point to problems in grad rates, special ed. *The Tennessean.* Retrieved August 21, 2006, from www.tennessean.com

Rimer, S. (2004, January 4). Unruly students facing arrest, not detention. *New York Times.* Retrieved January 6, 2004, from *http://www.nytimes.com*

Rimland, B. (1964). *Infantile autism.* New York: Meredith.

Rimm, D. C., & Masters, J. C. (1974). *Behavior therapy: Techniques and empirical findings.* New York: Academic Press.

Rinaldi, C. (2003). Language competence and social behavior of students with emotional or behavioral disorders. *Behavioral Disorders, 29*(1), 34–42.

Rivera, C. (1995, April 26). Violence against children at crisis level, report says. *Austin American-Statesman,* p. A-1.

Rivera, M. O., Al-Otaiba, S., & Koorland, M. A. (2006). Reading instruction for students with emotional and behavioral disorders and at risk of antisocial behaviors in primary grades: Review of literature. *Behavioral Disorders, 31*(3), 312–322.

Robbins, V. & Armstrong, B. J. (2005). The Bridges Project, In M. H. Epstein, K. Kutash, & A. J. Duchnowski (Eds), *Outcomes for children and youth with emotional and behavioral disorders and their families (2nd Ed.* pp. 355–374). Austin: PROED

Robelen, R. W. (1999, April 28). National policymakers trying range of measures to stem school violence. *Education Week, 18,* 19.

Robins, L. N. (1981). Epidemiological approaches to natural history research: Antisocial behaviors in children. *Journal of the American Academy of Child Psychiatry, 20,* 566–580.

Robins, L. N. (1991). Conduct disorder. *Journal of Child Psychology and Psychiatry, 32,* 193–214.

Rochlin, G. (1959). The loss complex. *Journal of American Psychoanalytic Association, 7,* 299–316.

Rock, E. E., Fessler, M. A., & Church, R. P. (1997). The concomitance of learning disabilities and emotional/behavioral disorders: A conceptual model. *Journal of Learning Disabilities, 30,* 245–263.

Rodriguez, E. (2002, March 24). Autopsy: Pressure killed student. *Austin American-Statesman,* p. 1.

Rodriguez, R. F. (1988). *Bilingual special education is appropriate for Mexican-American children with mildly handicapping conditions.* ERIC Clearing-house on Rural Education and Small Schools. ERIC Document Reproduction Service No. ED 293679.

Rogers, C. (1959). A theory of therapy, personality, and interpersonal relationships, as developed in the client-centered framework. In S. Kock (Ed.), *Psychology: A study of a science* (Vol. 3). New York: McGraw-Hill.

Rogers, C. R. (1969). *The freedom to learn: A view of what education might become.* Columbus, OH: Merrill.

Rogers, J. (1993, May). The inclusive revolution. *Phi Delta Kappa Research Bulletin,* pp. 1–6.

Rogers-Adkinson, D. L. (2003). Language processing in children with EBD. *Behavioral Disorders, 29*(1), 43–47.

Rogers-Adkinson, D. L., & Rinaldi, C. (in review). Language and behavioral competence in pre-school children.

Rogers-Adkinson, D., & Griffith, P. (Eds) (1999). *Communication disorders and children with psychiatric and behavioral disorders.* San Diego: Singular.

Rorschach, H. (1921). *Psychodiagnostics: A diagnostic test based on perception.* New York: Grune & Stratton.

Rortvedt, A., & Miltenberger, R. (1994). Analysis of a high probability instructional sequence and time-out in the treatment of child noncompliance. *Journal of Applied Behavior Analysis, 27,* 327–330.

Rose, J. (1984). Current use of corporal punishment in American public schools. *Journal of Educational Psychology, 76,* 427–441.

Rosenberg, M. S., Wilson, R., Maheady, L., & Sindelar, P. T. (1997). *Educating students with behavior disorders* (2nd ed.). Boston: Allyn & Bacon.

Rosenblatt, J. A., & Rosenblatt, A. (1999). Youth functional status and academic achievement in collaborative mental health and education programs: Two California care systems. *Journal of Emotional and Behavioral Disorders,* 7, 21–30.

Rosenblatt, J., Robertson, L., Bates, M., Wood, M., Furlong, M. J., & Sosna, T. (1998). Troubled or troubling? Characteristics of youth referred to a system of care without system-level referral constraints. *Journal of Emotional and Behavioral Disorders, 6*(1), 42–54.

Rosenblatt, R. (2000, March). The killing of Kayla. *Time, 155*(10), 26–29.

Rosenfeld, A. A., Nadelson, C. C., & Krieger, M. (1979). Fantasy and reality in patients' reports of incest. *Journal of Clinical Psychiatry, 40,* 159–164.

Rosenhan, D. L., & Seligman, M. E. P. (1989). *Abnormal psychology* (2nd Ed.). New York: W. W. Norton.

Rosenstock, H. A., & Vincent, K. R. (1979). Parental involvement as a prerequisite for successful adolescent therapy. *Journal of Clinical Psychiatry, 40,* 132–134.

Rosenthal, D. (1975). Heredity in criminality. *Criminal Justice and Behavior, 2,* 3–21.

Ross, D. M., & Ross, S. A. (1982). *Hyperactivity: Research, theory, and action.* New York: Wiley.

Rothbart, M. K., & Mauro, J. A. (1990). Questionnaire approaches to the study of infant temperament. In J. W. Fagen & J. Colombo (Eds.), *Individual differences in infancy: Reliability, stability and prediction* (pp. 411–429).

Rotter, J. (1966). Generalized expectancies for internal versus external control of reinforcement. *Psychological Monographs, 80*(1).

Rubin, K. H., & Mills, R. S. L. (1991). Conceptualizing developmental pathways to internalizing disorders in childhood. *Canadian Journal of Behavioural Science, 23,* 300–317.

Ruenzel, D. (1999). Pride and prejudice. *Education Week, 18*(31), 34–39.

Ruffolo, M. C., Sarri, R., & Goodkind, S. (2004). Study of delinquent, diverted, and high-risk adolescent girls: Implications for mental health intervention. *Social Work Research, 28*(4), 237.

Ruhl, K. L., & Berlinghoff, D. H. (1992). Research on improving behaviorally disordered students' academic performance: A review of the literature. *Behavioral Disorders, 17,* 178–190.

Ruhl, K. L., & Hughes, C. A. (1985). The nature and extent of aggression in special education settings serving behaviorally disordered students. *Behavioral Disorders, 10,* 95–104.

Ruhl, K. L., Hughes, C. A., & Camarata, S.M. (1992). Analysis of the expressive and receptive language characteristics of emotionally handicapped students served in public school settings. *Journal of Childhood Communication Disorders, 14,* 165–176.

Runnheim, V. A., Frankenberger, W. R., & Hazelkorn, M. N. (1996). Medicating students with emotional and behavioral disorders and ADHD: A state survey. *Behavioral Disorders, 21*(4), 306–314.

Russ, D. F. (1974). A review of learning and behavior theory as it relates to emotional disturbance in children. In W. Rhodes & M. L. Tracy (Eds.), *A study of child variance* (Vol. 1). Ann Arbor, MI: The University of Michigan Press.

Rutherford, R. B., & Polsgrove, L. J. (1981). Behavioral contracting with behaviorally disordered and delinquent children and youth: An analysis of the clinical and experimental literature. In R. B. Rutherford, A. G. Prieto, & J. E. McGlothlin (Eds.) *Severe behavior disorders of children and youth,* (Vol. 4). Reston, VA: Council for Exceptional Children.

Rutter, M. (1965). The influence of organic and emotional factors on the origins, nature and outcome of childhood psychosis. *Developmental Medicine and Child Neurology, 7,* 518–528.

Rutter, M. (1987). Psychosocial resilience and protective mechanisms. *American Journal of Orthopsychiatry, 57,* 316–331.

Rutter, M. (1991). Age changes in depressive disorders: Some developmental considerations. In J. Garber & K. A. Dodge (Eds.), *The development of emotion regulation and dysregulation* (pp. 273–300). New York: Cambridge University Press.

Rutter, M. L. (1997). Nature-nurture integration: The example of antisocial behavior. *American Psychologist, 52,* 390–398.

Rutter, M., & Yule, W. (1970). Reading retardation and antisocial behaviour: the nature of the association. In M. Rutter, J. Tizard, & K. Whitmore (Eds.), *Education, health, and behaviour* (pp. 240–255). London: Longman.

Rutter, M., Izard, C. E., & Read, P. B. (1986). *Depression in young people: Developmental and clinical perspectives.* New York: Guilford.

Ryan, A. L., Halsey, H. N., & Matthews, W. J. (2003). Using functional assessment to promote desirable students behavior in schools, *Teaching Exceptional Children 35*(5), 8–15.

Ryan, J. AB., Reid, R., & Epstein, M. H. (2004). Peer-mediated intervention studies on academic achievement for students with EBD: A review. *Remedial and Special Education, 25,* 330–341.

Ryan, J. B., & Peterson, R. L. (2004). Physical restraint in school. *Behavioral Disorders, 29*(2), 154–168.

Ryan, L., Ehrlich, S., & Finnegan, L. (1987). Cocaine abuse in pregnancy: Effects in the fetus and newborn. *Neurotoxicology and Teratology, 9,* 295–299.

Ryan, N. D. (1992). The pharmacologic treatment of child and adolescent depression. *Psychiatric Clinics of North America, 15(1),* 29–39.

Ryan, N. D. (2003). The pharmacological treatment of child and adolescent bipolar disorder. In B. Geller & M. P. DelBello (Eds.), *Bipolar disorder in childhood and early adolescence* (pp. 255–271). New York: Guilford Press.

Ryan, N. D., Bhatara, V. S., & Perel, J. M. (1999). Mood stabilizers in children and adolescents. *Journal of the American Academy of Child and Adolescent Psychiatry, 38,* 529–536.

Sack, J. (2000, February 9). Study shows early intervention can avert sp. ed. needs. *Education Week*, 26.

Sack, J. L. (1999, March 17). Department issues IDEA regulations: Rules offer some discipline flexibility, *Education Week*, 1, 40.

Safer, D. J., & Heaton, R. C. (1982). Characteristics, school patterns, and behavioral outcomes of seriously disruptive junior high school students. In D. J. Safer (Ed.), *School programs for disruptive adolescents*. Baltimore: University park Press.

Safran, S. P., & Oswald, K. (2003). Positive behavior supports: Can schools reshape disciplinary practices? *Exceptional Children, 69*, 361–373.

Salazar, L. F., Wingood, G. M., & DiClemente, R. J. (2004). The role of social support in the psychological well-being of African-American girls who experience dating violence victimization. *Violence and Victims, 19*(2), 171–187.

Salovey, P., & Singer, J. A. (1991). Cognitive behavior modification. In F. H. Kanfer & A. P. Goldstein (Eds.), *Helping people change: A textbook of methods*. New York: Pergamon Press.

Saluja, G., Iachan, R., Scheidt, P.C., Overpeck, M.D., Sun, W., & Giedd, J.N. (2004). Prevalence of and risk factors for depressive symptoms among young adolescents. *Archives of Pediatric Adolescent Medicine, 158*, 760–765.

Salvia, J., & Ysseldyke, J. (1995). *Assessment in special and remedial education* (6th ed.). Boston: Houghton Miflin.

Samuels, C. A. (2006, March 15). Study: States including special education students in tests. *Education Week*, p. 11.

Sarampote, C. S., Efron, L. A., Robb, A. S., Pearl, P. L., & Stein, M. A. (2002). Can stimulant rebound mimic pediatric bipolar disorder? *Journal of Child and Adolescent Psychopharmacology, 12*(1), 63–67.

Sasso, G. M., Conroy, M. A., Peck-Stichter, J., & Fox, J. J. (2001). Slowing down the bandwagon: The misapplication of functional assessment for students with emotional or behavioral disorders. *Behavioral Disorders, 26*, 282–296.

Sasso, G. M., Melloy, K. J., & Kavale, K. A. (1990). Generalization, maintenance, and behavioral covariation associated with social skills training through structured learning. *Behavioral Disorders, 16*, 9–22.

Sasso, G. M., Peck, J., & Garrison-Harrell, L. (1998). Social interaction setting events: Experimental analysis of contextual variables. *Behavioral Disorders, 24*, 34–43.

Satterfield, J. H., Hoppe, C. M., & Schell, A. M. (1982). A prospective study of delinquency in 110 adolescent boys with attention deficit disorder and 88 normal adolescent boys. *American Journal of Psychiatry, 139*, 797–798.

Sattler, J. M. (2002). *Assessment of children: Behavioral and clinical applications* (4th ed.). La Mesa, CA: Author.

Sattler, J. R., & Hoge, R. D. (2006) *Assessment of children: Behavioral, social, and clinical foundations* (5th ed.). San Diego: Sattler.

Saxe, L., Cross, T., & Silverman, N. (1988). Children's mental health. The gap between what we know and what we do. *American Psychologist, 43*(10), 800–807.

Scarr, S. (1997). Behavior-genetic and socialization theories of intelligence: Truce and reconciliation. In R. J. Sternberg & E. L. Grigorenko (Eds.), *Intelligence, heredity, and environment* (pp. 3–41). New York: Cambridge University Press.

Scheuermann, B., & Webber, J. (1996). Best practices in developing level systems. In L. M. Bullock & R. A. Gable (Eds.), *Best practices for managing adolescents with emotional/behavioral disorders within the school environment* (pp. 21–30). Council for Children with Behavioral Disorders Mini-Library Series on Emotional/Behavioral Disorders. Reston, VA: Council for Exceptional Children.

Scheuermann, B., & Webber, J. (2002). *Autism: Teaching DOES make a difference*. Belmont, CA: Wadsworth

Scheuermann, B., Webber, J., Partin, M., & Knies, W. C. (1994). Level systems and the law: Are they compatible? *Behavioral Disorders, 19*, 205–220.

Schickedanz, J. A., Schickedanz, D. I, Forsyth, P. D., & Forsyth, C. A. (1998). *Understanding children and adolecents* (3rd ed.). Boston: Allyn & Bacon.

Schloss, P. J., & Smith, M. A. (1987). Guidelines for ethical use of manual restraint in public school settings for behaviorally disordered students. *Behavioral Disorders, 12*, 207–213.

Schloss, P. J., Schloss, C., & Harris, L. (1984). A multiple baseline analysis of an interpersonal skills training program for depressed youth. *Behavioral Disorders, 9*, 182–188.

Schlosser, L., & Algozzine, B. (1979). The disturbing child: He or she? *The Alberta Journal of Educational Research, 25*, 30–36.

Schmid, R., & Slade, D. (1981). Adolescent programs. In R. Algozzine, R. Schmid, & C. D. Mercer (Eds.), *Childhood behavior disorders: Applied research and educational practice*. Rockville, MD: Aspen.

Schultz, B. K., & Cobb, H. (2005). Behavioral consultation for adolescents with ADHD: Lessons learned in the challenging horizons program. *Emotional and Behavioral Disorders in Youth, 5*(4), 91–99.

Scott, T. M., (2002). Removing roadblocks to effective behavior intervention in inclusive settings: Responding to typical objections by school personnel. *Beyond Behavior, 12*(1), 4–8.

Scott, T. M., & Barrett, S. B. (2004). Using staff and student time engaged in disciplinary procedures to evaluate the impact of school-wide PBS. *Journal of Positive Behavior Interventions, 6*, 21–27.

Scott, T. M., & Nelson, C. M. (1999). Functional behavioral assessment: Implications for training and staff development. *Behavioral Disorders, 24*(3), 249–252.

Scott, T. M., & Nelson, C. M. (1999). Universal school discipline strategies: Facilitating positive learning environments. *Effective School Practices, 17*(4), 54–64.

Scott, T. M., Bucalos, A., Liaupsin, C., Nelson, C.M., Jolivette, K., & DeShea, L. (2004). Using functional behavior assessment in general education settings: Making a case for effectiveness and efficiency. *Behavioral Disorders, 29*(2), 189–201.

Scott, T. M., Liaupsin, P., Nelson, C. M., & McIntyre, J. (2005). Team based functional behavioral assessment as a proactive public school process: A descriptive analysis of current barriers. *Journal of Behavioral Education, 14*(1), 57–71.

Scott, T. M., Mucalso, A., Nelson, C. M., Liaupsin, C., Julivette, K., & Deshea, L. (2004). Using functional assessment in general education settings: Making a case for effectiveness and efficiency. *Behavioral Disorders, 29*(2), 189–201.

Scruggs, T. E., Mastropieri, M. A., & Tolfa-Veit, D. (1986). The effects of coaching on standardized test performance of learning disabled and behaviorally disordered students. *Remedial and special Education, 7,* 37–41.

Second-grader suspended for swearing. (2004, February 4). *CNN.com.* Retrieved February 6, 2004, from *http://www.cnn.com/2004/EDUCATION02/04/swearing suspension ap/index.html*

Seery, B. (1990). *Generalized and specific sources of job satisfaction related to attrition and retention of teachers of behavior disordered and severely emotionally disturbed students in Georgia.* Unpublished doctoral dissertation, Georgia State University, Atlanta.

Segal, Z. V., & Shaw, B. F. (1988). Cognitive assessment: Issues and methods. In K. S. Dobson (Ed.), *Handbook of cognitive—behavioral therapies* (pp. 39–81). New York: The Guilford Press.

Seligman, M. E. (1975). *Helplessness: On depression, development, and death.* San Francisco: Freeman.

Seligman, M. E., Peterson, C., Kaslow, N. J., Tanenbaum, R. L., Alloy, L. B., & Abramson, L. Y. (1984). Attributional style and depressive symptoms among children. *Journal of Abnormal Psychology, 93,* 235–238.

Seligman, M.E., Walker, E. F., & Rosenhan, D. L. (2001). *Abnormal psychology* (4th ed.). New York: Norton.

Sellstrom, E. A. (1989). *Schematic processing and self-reference in childhood depression.* Unpublished doctoral dissertation. The University of Texas at Austin.

Semrud-Clikeman, M., & Hynd, G. W. (1991). Review of issues and measures in childhood depression. *School Psychology International, 12,* 275–298.

Severson, H. H., & Walker, H. M. (2002). Pro-active approaches for identifying children at risk for sociobehavioral problems. In K. L. Lane, F. M. Gresham, & T. E. O'Shaughnessy (Eds.), *Interventions for students with or at-risk for emotional and behavioral disorders* (pp. 33–53). Boston: Allyn & Bacon.

Shapiro, E. S., DuPaul, G. J., Bradley, K. L., & Bailey, L. T. (1996). A school-based consultation program for service delivery to middle school students with attention-deficit/hyperactivity disorder. *Journal of Emotional and Behavioral Disorders, 4*(2), 73–81.

Shelly, L. (1985). American crime: An international anomaly? *Comparative Social Research, 8,* 81–95.

Shinn, M. R. (2002). Best practices in using curriculum-based measurement in a problem-solving model. In A. Thomas & J. Grimes (Eds.), *Best practices in school psychology IV* (pp. 671–697). Bethesda, MD: National Association of School Psychologists.

Shumaker, J. G., Deshler, D. D., Bulgren, J. A., Davis, B., Lenz, B. K., & Grossen, B. (2002). Access of adolescents with disabilities to general education curriculum: Myth or reality? *Focus on Exceptional Children, 35*(3), 1–16.

Shure, M. B. (1992). *ICPS I Can Problem Solve: An interpersonal cognitive problem-solving program for children.* Champaign, IL: Research Press.

Shure, M. B., & Spivack, G. (1982). Interpersonal problem-solving in young children: A cognitive approach to prevention. *American Journal of Community Psychology, 10,* 341–356.

Siegel, J. M., & Platt, J. J. (1976). Emotional and social real-life problem-solving thinking in adolescent and adult psychiatric patients. *Journal of Clinical Psychology, 32,* 230–232.

Siennick, S. E., Findling, R. L., & Guelzow, B. T. (2005). Conduct disorder/aggression. *Emotional and Behavioral Disorders in Youth, 5*(2), 35–37, 44.

Sigel, I. (1960). The application of projective techniques in research with children. In A. I. Ragin & M. R. Haworth (Eds.), *Projective techniques with children.* New York: Grune & Stratton.

Silver, L. B. (1987). *Attention deficit disorders. Booklet for parents.* Summit, NJ: CIBA.

Silverman, W. K., & Kurtines, W. M. (2001). Anxiety disorders. In J. N. Hughes, A. M. LaGreca, & J. C. Conoley (Eds.), *Handbook of psychological services for children and adolescents* (pp. 225–244). New York: Oxford University Press.

Simon, D. J., & Johnston, J. C. (1987). Working with families: The missing link in behavior disorder interventions. In R. B. Rutherford, Jr., C. M. Nelson, & S. R. Forness (Eds.), *Severe behavior disorders of children and youth.* Boston: Little, Brown.

Simon, S., Howe, I., & Kirschenbaum, H. (1972). *Values clarification: A handbook of practical strategies for teachers and students.* New York: Hart Publishing Co.

Simpson, G., Cohen, R., Pastor, P., & Reuben, C. (2005, January–June). *U.S. children 4–17 years of age who received services for emotional or behavioral difficulties: Preliminary data from the 2005 national health interview survey, National Center for Health Statistics.* Available at http.www.cdc.gov/nchs/products/pubs/pubd/hestats/children2005/children2005.htm

Sinacola, R. S., & Peters-Strickland, T. S. (2006). *Basic psychopharmacology for counselors and therapists.* Boston, MA: Allyn & Bacon.

Skiba, R. (2004). Zero tolerance: The assumptions and the facts. *Indiana Youth Services Education Policy Briefs, 2*(1), 1–7.

Skiba, R. J., Peterson, R. L., & Williams, T. (1997). Office referrals and suspension: Disciplinary intervention in middle schools. *Education and Treatment of Children, 20*(3), 1–21.

Skiba, R., Rausch, M. K., & Ritter, S. (2004). "Discipline is always teaching": Effective alternatives to zero tolerance in Indiana's schools. *Indiana Youth Services Education Policy Briefs, 2*(3), 1–11.

Skinner, B. F. (1953). *Science and human behavior.* New York: Macmillan.

Skinner, C. H., Bamberg, H. W., Smith, E. S., & Powell, S. S. (1993). Cognitive cover, copy and compare: Subvocal responding to increase rates of accurate division responding. *Remedial and Special Education, 14,* 49–56.

Slaby, R. G., Roedell, W. C., Arezzo, D., & Hendrix, K. (1995). *Early violence prevention.* Washington, DC: National Association for the Education of Young Children.

Smith, C. R., Wood, F. H., & Grimes, J. (1988). Issues in the identification and placement of behaviorally disordered students. In M. C. Wang, M. C. Reynolds, & H. J. Walberg (Eds), *Handbook of special education: Research and practice* (Vol. 2, pp. 95–123). Oxford: Pergamon.

Smith, D. J., Young, K. R., Nelson, J. R., & West, R. P. (1992). The effect of a self-management procedure on the classroom and academic behavior of students with mild handicaps. *School Psychology Review, 21,* 59–72.

Smith, D. J., Young, K. R., West, R. P., Morgan, D. P., & Rhode, G. (1988). Reducing the disruptive behavior of junior high school students: A classroom self-management procedure. *Behavioral Disorders, 13,* 231–239.

Smith, D. L., & Smith, B. J. (2006). Perceptions of violence: The views of teachers who left urban schools. *High School Journal, 89*(3), 34–42.

Smith, M. D. (1988). Statement supporting the ASA resolution on the use of aversives. *The Advocate, 20(4),* 10–11.

Smith, S. W., & Farrell, D. T. (1993). Level system use in special education: Classroom intervention with prima facie appeal. *Behavioral Disorders, 18,* 251–264.

Smith, S. W., Lochman, J. E., & Daunic, A. P. (2005). Managing aggression using cognitive-behavioral interventions: State of the practice and future directions. *Behavioral Disorders, 30*(3), 227–240.

Smith, S. W., Siegel, E. M., O'Connor, A. M., & Thomas, S. B. (1994). Effects of cognitive-behavioral training on angry behavior and aggression of three elementary-aged students. *Behavioral Disorders, 19,* 126–135.

Smith, T. E. C., Polloway, E., Patton, J. R., & Dowdy, C. A. (2004). *Teaching students with special needs in inclusive settings* (4th ed.). Boston: Allyn & Bacon.

Snider, V. (1987). Use of self-monitoring of attention with LD students: Research and application. *Learning Disability Quarterly, 10,* 139–151.

Snider, V. E., Busch, T., & Arrowood, L. (2003). Teacher knowledge of stimulant medication and ADHD. *Remedial and Special Education, 24*(1), 46–56.

Society of Clinical Child and Adolescent Psychology & The Network on Youth Mental Health. (2006, July 19). *Evidence-based treatment for children and adolescents.* Retrieved July 19, 2006, from *www.effectivechildtherapy.com*

Solyom, I., Beck, P., Solyom, C., & Hugel, R. (1974). Some etiological factors in phobic neurosis. *Canadian Psychiatry Association Journal, 19,* 69–78.

Sommers-Flanagan, J., & Sommers-Flanagan, R. (1996). Efficacy of antidepressant medication with depressed youth: What psychologists should know. *Professional Psychology: Research and Practice, 27,* 145–153.

Special education works! (1999). *CEC Today, 6*(2), 1, 5, 15.

Spielberger, C. (1973). *Manual for the State—Trait Anxiety Inventory for Children.* Palo Alto, CA: Consulting Psychologists Press.

Spivack, G., & Shure, M. B. (1974). *Social adjustment of young children.* San Francisco: Jossey-Bass.

Spivak, G., Platt, J. J., & Shure, M. B. (1976). *The problem-solving approach to adjustment.* San Francisco: Jossey-Bass.

Sprague, J. R., Sugai, G., Horner, R., & Walker, H. M. (1999). Using office discipline referral data to evaluate school-wide discipline and violence prevention interventions. *Oregon School Study Council Bulletin, 42*(2), 1–18.

Sprague, J., & Walker, H. (2000). Early identification and intervention for youth with antisocial and violent behavior. *Exceptional Children, 66*(3), 367–379.

Stark, K. D., Humphrey, L. L., Crook, K., & Lewis, K. (1990). Perceived family environments of depressed and anxious children: Child's and maternal figure's perspectives. *Journal of Abnormal Child Psychology, 18,* 527–547.

Stark, K. D., Humphrey, L. L., Laurent, J. L., Livingston, R., & Christopher, J. C. (1993). Cognitive, behavioral, and family factors in the differentiation of depressive and anxiety disorders during childhood. *Journal of Consulting and Clinical Child Psychology, 61,* 878–886.

Stark, K. D., Rouse, L. W., & Livingston, R. (1991). Treatment of depression during childhood and adolescence: Cognitive-behavioral procedures for the individual and family. In P. C. Kendall (Ed.), *Child and adolescent therapy: Cognitive-behavioral procedures.* (pp. 165–206). New York: Guilford.

Stark, K. D., Sander, J. B., Yancy, M. G., Bronik, M. D., & Hoke, J. A. (2000). Treatment of depression in childhood and adolescence: Cognitive-behavioral procedures for the individual and family. In P.C. Kendall (Ed.), *Child and adolescent therapy: Cognitive-behavioral procedures* (pp. 173–234). New York: Guilford Press.

Stark, K. D., Swearer, S., Delaune, M., Knox, L., & Winter, J. (1995). Depressive disorders. In R. T. Ammerman & M. Hersen (Eds.), *Handbook of child behavior therapy in the psychiatric setting* (pp. 269–300). New York: Wiley.

Stephens, R. D. (1997). National trends in school violence: Statistics and prevention strategies. In A. P. Goldstein & J. C. Conoley (Eds.), *School violence intervention: A practical handbook* (pp. 72–90). New York: The Guilford Press.

Sternberg, K., Lamb, M. E., & Guterman, E. (2006). Effects of early and later family violence on children's behavior problems and depression: A longitudinal, multi-informant perspective. *Child Abuse and Neglect, 30*(3), 283–306.

Stevens-Long, J. (1973). The effects of behavioral context on some aspects of adult disciplinary practice and affect. *Child Development, 44,* 476–484.

Stichter, J. P., Hudson, S., & Sasso, G. S. (2005). The use of structural analysis to identify setting events in applied settings for students with emotional/behavioral disorders. *Behavioral Disorders, 30*(4), 403–420.

Still, G. F. (1902). The Coulstonian lectures on some abnormal physical conditions in children. *Lancet, 1,* 1163–1168.

Stoiber, K. C., & McIntyre, H. (2006). Adolescent pregnancy and parenting. In G. G., Bear & K. M. Minke (Eds.), *Children's needs III: Development, prevention, and intervention* (pp. 705–719). Bethesda, MD: National Association of School Psychologists.

Stokes, T. F., & Baer, D. M. (1977). An implicit technology of generalization. *Journal of Applied Behavior Analysis, 10,* 349–368.

Strain, P. S., Young, C. C., & Horowitz, J. (1981). Generalized behavior change during oppositional child training: An examination of child and family demographic variables. *Behavior Modification, 5,* 15–26.

Strauss, A. A., & Lehtinen, L. E. (1947). *Psychopathology and education of the brain-injured child.* New York: Grune & Stratton.

Strauss, C. C. (1987). Anxiety. In M. Hersen & V. B. Van Hasselt (Eds.) *Behavior therapy with children and adolescents.* (pp. 109–136). New York: Wiley.

Strauss, C. C. (1988). Behavioral assessment and treatment of over-anxious disorder in children and adolescents. *Behavioral Modifications, 12,* 234–251.

Strauss, C. C., Lease, C. A., Last, C. G., & Francis, G. (1988). Overanxious disorder: An examination of developmental differences. *Journal of Abnormal Child Psychology, 16,* 433.

Stroul, B. A. (1993, September). *Systems of care for children and adolescents with severe emotional disturbances: What are the results?* Washington, DC: Child and Adolescent Service System Program (CASSP). Technical Assistance Center, Center for Child Health and Mental Health Policy, and Georgetown University Child Development Center. (ERIC Document Reproduction Service No. ED 364 025.)

Stroul, B. A., & Friedman, R. M. (1986). *A system of care for severely emotionally disturbed children and youth.* Washington, DC: Georgetown University Child Development Center, CASSP Technical Assistance Center.

Sue, S. (1988). Sociocultural issues in the assessment and classroom teaching of language minority students. *Cross-cultural Special Education Series* (Vol. 3). Sacramento, CA: California State Department of Education.

Sugai, G. (1992). Educational assessment of the culturally diverse and behavior disordered student: An examination of critical effect. In A. A. Ortiz & B. A. Ramirez (Eds.), *Schools and the culturally diverse exceptional student: Promising practices and future directions* (pp. 63–75). Reston, VA: Council for Exceptional Children.

Sugai, G., & Horner, R. H. (1999). Discipline and behavioral support: Practices, pitfalls, and promises. *Effective School Practices, 17*(4), 10–22.

Sugai, G., & Horner, R. H. (2001). Introduction to the special series on positive behavior support in schools. *Journal of Emotional and Behavioral Disorders, 10*(1), 130–135.

Sugai, G., & Horner, R. H. (2002). Introduction to the special series on positive behavior support in schools. *Journal of Emotional and Behavioral Disorders, 10*(3), 130–135.

Sugai, G., Horner, R. H., & Gresham, E. M. (2002). Behaviorally effective school environments. In M. R. Shinn, H. M. Walker, & G. Stoner (Eds.), *Interventions for academic and behavior problems II: Preventive and remedial approaches* (pp. 315–350). Bethesda, MD: National Association of School Psychologists.

Sugai, G., Horner, R. H., & Sprague, J. R. (1999). Functional-assessment-based behavior support planning: Research to practice to research. *Behavioral Disorders, 24*(3), 253–257.

Sugai, G., Horner, R. H., Dunlap, G., Hieneman, M., Lewis, T. J., Nelson, C. M., et al. (1999). *Applying positive behavioral support and functional behavioral assessment in schools.* Eugene, OR: OSEP Center on Positive Behavioral Interventions and Support.

Sugai, G., Sprague, I. R., Horner, R. H., & Walker, H. M. (2000). Preventing school violence: The use of office discipline referrals to assess and monitor school-wide discipline interventions. *Journal of Emotional and Behavioral Disorders, 8,* 94–101.

Suicide—Part I. (1996, November). *Harvard Mental Health Letter, 13*(5), 1–4.

Suicide—Part II. (1996, December). *Harvard Mental Health Letter, 13*(6), 1–5.

Sutherland, K. S., Denny, R. K., & Gunter, P. L. (2005). Teachers of students with emotional and behavioral disorders reported professional development needs: Differences between fully licensed and emergency-licensed teachers. *Preventing School Failure, 49*(2), 41–46.

Swedo, S. E., Leonard, H. L., & Rapoport, J. L. (1992). Childhood-onset obsessive compulsive disorder. *Psychiatric Clinics of North America, 15,* 767–775.

Sweeney, D. P., Forness, S. R., Kavale, K. A., & Levitt, J. G. (1997). An update on psychopharmacologic medication: What teachers, clinicians, and parents need to know. *Intervention in School and Clinic, 33,* 4–21, 25.

Symons, F., McDonald, L., & Wehby, J. (1998). Functional assessment and teacher collected data. *Education and Treatment of Children, 21,* 135–159.

TADS Team. (2004). Fluoxetine, cognitive-behavioral therapy, and their combination for adolescents with depression: Treatment for Adolescents with Depression Study (TADS) randomized, controlled trial. *Journal of the American Medical Association, 292,* 807–820.

Tahmisian, J. A., & McReynolds, W. T. (1971). Use of parents as behavioral engineers in the treatment of a school phobic girl. *Journal of Counseling Psychology, 18,* 225–228.

Talan, J. (1997, August 31). Anti-depressant studies tend to ignore children. *Austin-American Statesman,* p. A1.

Tankersley, M., & Landrum, T. J. (1997). Comorbidity of emotional and behavioral disorders. In J. W. Lloyd, El J. Kameenui, & D. Chard (Eds), *Issues in educating students with disabilities* (pp. 153–173). Mahwah, NJ: Erlbaum.

Tanner, L. (2000, May 2). Diagnostic rules issued for attention disorder. *Austin-American Statesman,* pp. A-1, A-9.

Tarver, S. G. (1998). Myths and truths about direct instruction. *Effective School Practices, 17,* 18–22.

Taylor, C. (1999, May). Digital dungeons, *Time,* p. 50.

Taylor, R. L. (1997). *Assessment of exceptional students: Educational and psychological procedures* (4th Ed.). Boston: Allyn & Bacon.

Taylor, R., Smiley, L., & Ziegler, E. (1983). The effects of labels and assigned attributes on teacher perceptions of academic and social behavior. *Education and Training of the Mentally Retarded, 18,* 45–51.

Teglasi, H. (2006). Temperament. In G. G. Bear & K. M. Minke (Eds.), *Children's needs III: Development, prevention, and intervention* (pp. 391–403). Bethesda, MD: National Association of School Psychologists.

Tems, C. L., Stewart, S. M., Skinner, J. R., Hughs, C. W., & Emslie, G. (1993). Cognitive distortions in depressed children and adolescents: Are they state dependent or traitlike? *Journal of Clinical Psychology, 22(3),* 316–326.

Tenenbaum, I. M. (2000). Building a framework for service-learning: The South Carolina experience. *Phi Delta Kappan, 81*(9), 666–669.

Terr, L. C. (1981). Psychic trauma in children: Observations following the Chowchilla school-bus kidnapping. *American Journal of Psychiatry, 138,* 14–19.

Texas Juvenile Probation Commission. (2005). *The state of juvenile probation activity in Texas, calendar year 2003.* Austin, TX: Author.

Tharinger, D., Wilkinson, A., & Lasser, J. (2006). Sexual interest and expression. In G. G., Bear & K. M. Minke (Eds.), *Children's needs III: Development, prevention, and intervention* (pp. 405–417). Bethesda, MD: National Association of School Psychologists.

Thomas, A., & Chess, S. (1977). *Temperament and development.* New York: Brunner/Mazel.

Thomas, A., Chess, S., & Birch, H. (1969). *Temperament and behavior disorders in children.* New York: New York University Press.

Thompson, J. M., & Sones, R. A. (1973). *Education Apperception Test.* Los Angeles: Western Psychological Services.

Thorndike, E. L. (1932). *The fundamentals of learning.* New York: Teacher's College.

Thurlow, M. L., & Ysseldyke, J. E. (1980). *Factors influential on the psychoeducational decisions reached by teams of educators* (Research Report No. 25). Minneapolis: University of Minnesota Institute for Research on Learning Disabilities.

Tievsky, D. L. (1988). Homosexual clients and homophobic social workers. *Journal of Independent Social Work, 2,* 51–62.

Tobin, T. J., & Sugai, G. M. (1999). Discipline problems, placements, and outcomes for students with serious emotional disturbance. *Behavioral Disorders, 24,* 109–121.

Todd, A. W., Horner, R. H., Sugai, G., & Colvin, G. (1999). Individualizing school-wide discipline for students with chronic problem behaviors: A team approach. *Effective School Practices, 17,* 72–82.

Toffalo, D. A. D., & Pederson, J. A. (2005). The effect of a psychiatric diagnosis on school psychologists' special education eligibility decisions regarding emotional disturbance. *Journal of Emotional and Behavioral Disorders, 13*(1), 53–60.

Torgersen, S. (1983). Genetic factors in anxiety disorders. *Archives of General Psychiatry, 40,* 1085–1089.

Torgeson, J. K., (1998, Spring/Summer). Catch them before they fall. *American Educator,* 32–41.

Toth, M. K. (1990). *Understanding and treating conduct disorders.* Austin, TX: Pro-Ed.

Towns, P. (1981). *Educating disturbed adolescents: Theory and practice.* New York: Grune & Stratton.

Tramontana, M. G. (1980). Critical review of research on psychotherapy outcome with adolescents: 1967–1977. *Psychological Bulletin, 88,* 429–450.

Trevor, W. (1975 March). *Teacher discrimination and self-fulfilling prophecies.* Paper presented at the annual meeting of the American Educational Research Association.

Trout, A. L., Epstein, M. H., Mickelson, W. T., Nelson, J. R., & Lewis, L. M. (2003). Effects of a reading intervention for kindergarten students at risk of emotional disturbance and reading deficits. *Behavioral Disorders, 28,* 313–326.

Trout, A. L., Nordness, P. D., Pierce, C. D., & Epstein, M. H. (2003). Research on the academic status of students with emotional and behavioral disorders: A review of the literature from 1961–2000. *Journal of Emotional and Behavioral Disorders, 11,* 198–210.

Tucker, D. M. (1988). Neuropsychological mechanisms of affective self-regulation. In M. Kinsbourne (Ed.), *Cerebral hemisphere function in depression.* Washington, DC: American Psychiatric Press.

Turnbull, A., Edmunson, H., Griggs, P., Wickham, D., Sailor, W., Freeman, R., et al. (2002). A blueprint for schoolwide positive behavior support: Implementation of three components. *Teaching Exceptional Children, 68*(3), 377–402.

Turner, S. M., Beidel, D. C., & Costello, A. (1987). Psychopathology in the offspring of anxiety disorders patients. *Journal of Consulting and Clinical Psychology, 55,* 229–235.

U. S. Census Bureau. (2003). *Statistical abstract of the United States* (123rd ed.). Washington, DC: U. S. Government Printing Office.

U.S. Department of Education. (2006). Office of Safe and Drug Free Schools Home page. Retrieved November 17, 2006, from http://www.ed.gov/about/offices/list/osdfs/programs .html

U.S. Department of Education. (2006). *Twenty-sixth annual report to Congress on the implementation of the Individuals with Disabilities Act.* Washington, DC: Author.

U.S. Department of Education (2003). *Twenty-fifth annual report to Congress on the implementation of the Individuals with Disabilities Act,* Washington, DC: Author

U.S. Department of Education (2001). *Twenty-third annual report to Congress on the implementation of the Individuals with Disabilities Act,* Washington, DC: Author

U.S. Department of Education (1998). *Twentieth annual report to Congress on the implementation of the Individuals with Disabilities Act,* Washington, DC: Author

U.S. Department of Education. (1997). *Digest of education statistics 1997.* Washington, DC: U.S. Government Printing Office.

U.S. Department of Education. (2000). *Twenty-second annual report to Congress on the implementation of the Individuals with Disabilities Education Act.* Washington, DC: Author.

U.S. Dept. of Health and Human Services (2006). *National youth risk behavior survey: 1991-2005, Trends in the prevalence of sexual behaviors.* Retrieved September 12, 2006 from *http://www.cdc.gov/yrbss*

U.S. Department of Health and Human Services. (2001). *Youth violence: A report of the Surgeon General.* Washington, DC: Author.

U. S. Department of Health and Human Services (DHHS) (2001). Report of the surgeon general's conference on children's mental health: a national action agenda. Washington D. C.: author

U.S. Department of Health and Human Services (1999). *Health United States 1997–1998 and injury chartbook.* Washington, DC: U.S. Bureau of the Census.

U. S. Department of Health and Human Services. (1999). *Report of the Surgeon General's Conference on Children's Mental Health: A national action agenda.* Washington, DC: Author

U.S. Department of Health and Human Services. (1997). *National survey results on drug use from the Monitoring the Future Study, 1975–1995: Vol. 1. Secondary School Students.* Washington, DC: U.S. Government Printing Office.

Unruh, D., & Bullis, M. (2005). Female and male juvenile offenders with disabilities: Differences in the barriers to their transition to the community. *Behavioral Disorders, 30*(2), 105–117.

Urbain, E. S., & Kendall, P. C. (1980). Review of social–cognitive problem-solving with children. *Psychological Bulletin, 88,* 105–143.

Vaac, N. A., & Kirst, N. (1977). Emotionally disturbed children and regular classroom teachers. *Elementary School Journal, 77,* 309–317.

Vail, K. (2005, March). The medicated child. *American School Board Journal.* Available at http://www.asbj .com/specialreports/0305Special Reports?Sl.html

Van Acker, R., & Talbott, E. (1999). The school context and risk for aggression: Implications for school-based prevention and intervention efforts. *Preventing School Failure, 44*(1), 12–20.

VanDenBerg, J. E., & Grealish, E. M. (1996). Individualized services and supports through the wrap-around process:

Philosophy and procedures. *Journal of Child and Family Studies, 5*(1), 7–21.

Vaughn, B. J. (2006). The wave of SWPBS: Who is left behind? *Research and Practice for Persons with Severe Disabilities, 31*(1), 66–69.

Vaughn, S. R., Ridley, C. A., & Bullock, D. D. (1984). Interpersonal problem-solving skills training with aggressive young children. *Journal of Applied Developmental Psychology, 5,* 213–223.

Vaughn, S., Levy, S., Coleman, M., & Bos, C. S. (2002). Reading instruction for students with LD and EBD: A synthesis of observation studies. *Journal of Special Education, 36,* 2–13.

Vaughn, S., Schumm, J. S., & Arguelles, M. E. (1997). The ABCDEs of co-teaching. *Teaching Exceptional Children, 30*(2), 4–10.

Velez, C. N., Johnson, J., & Cohen, P. (1989). A longitudinal analysis of selected risk factors for childhood psychopathology. *Journal of American Academy of Child and Adolescent Psychiatry, 28,* 861–864.

Vernon, A. (1989a). *Thinking, feeling, behaving: An emotional education curriculum for children. Grades 1–6.* Champaign, IL: Research Press.

Vernon, A. (1989b). *Thinking, feeling, behaving: An emotional education curriculum for adolescents. Grades 7–12.* Champaign, IL: Research Press.

Vernon, A. (1998a). *The Passport Program: A journey through emotional, social, cognitive and self-development. Grades 1–5.* Champaign, IL: Research Press.

Vernon, A. (1998b). *The Passport Program: A journey through emotional, social, cognitive and self-development. Grades 6–8.* Champaign, IL: Research Press.

Vernon, A. (1998c). *The Passport Program: A journey through emotional, social, cognitive and self-development. Grades 9–12.* Champaign, IL: Research Press.

Viadero, D. (1999, March 17). A direct challenge. *Education Week,* 41–43.

Vincent, J. P., Williams, B. J., Harris, G. E., & Duval, G. C. (1981). Classroom observations of hyperactive children: A multiple validation study. In K. D. Gadow & J. Looney (Eds.), *Psychological aspects of drug treatment for hyperactivity* (pp. 207–248). Boulder, CO: Westview Press.

Violence and Mental Health–Part I. (2000, January). *Harvard Mental Health Letter, 16*(7), 1–4.

Vitiello, B., Behar, D., Wolfson, S., & McLeer, S. V. (1990). Case study: Diagnosis of panic disorder in prepubertal children. *Journal of American Academy of Child and Adolescent Psychiatry, 29,* 782–784.

Voltz, D. L. Sims, M. J., & Nelson, B. (2005). M2ECCA: A framework for inclusion in the context of standards-based reform. *Exceptional Children, 37*(5), 14–19.

Von Korff, M. R., Eaton, W. W., & Keyl, P. M. (1985). The epidemiology of panic attacks and panic disorder: Results of three community surveys. *American Journal of Epidemiology, 122,* 970–981.

Vossekuil, B., Fein, R., Reddy, M., Borum, R., & Modzeleski, W. (2002). *The final report and findings of the safe school initiative: Implications for the prevention of school attacks in the United States.* U.S. Department of Education, Office of Elementary and Secondary Education, Safe and Drug-Free Schools Program and U.S. Secret service, National Threat Assessment Center, Washington, DC.

Vygotsky, L. S. (1962). *Thought and language.* New York: Wiley. (originally published 1934)

Vygotsky, L. S. (1978). *Mind in society: The development of higher psychological processes.* Cambridge, MA: Harvard University Press.

Waas, G. A. (2006). Peer relationships. In G. G. Bear & K. M. Minke (Eds.). *Children's Needs III: Development, Prevention, and Intervention* (325–340). Bethesda, MD: National Association of School Psychologists.

Wagner, M. (1991a, September). *Drop outs with disabilities: What do we know? What can we do?* Menlo Park: SRI International.

Wagner, M. (1991b). *The benefits associated with secondary vocational education for young people with disabilities.* Menlo Park, CA: SRI International.

Wagner, M. Kutash, K., Duchnowski, A. J., Epstein, M. H., & Sumi, W. C. (2005). The children and youth we serve: A national picture of the characteristics of students with emotional disturbances receiving special education. *Journal of Emotional and Behavioral Disorders, 13,* 79–96.

Wagner, M. M. (1995). Outcomes for youths with serious emotional disturbance in secondary school and early adulthood. *The Future of Children,* 5, 90–111

Wagner, M. Newman, L., Cameto, R., Levine, P., & Marder, C. (2003). *Going to school: Instructional contexts, programs, and participation of secondary school students with disabilities.* Menlo Park, CA: SRI International.

Wagner, M., Blackorby, J., Cameto, R., & Newman, L. (1993). *What makes a difference? Influences on postschool outcomes of youth with disabilities.* Menlo Park, CA: SRI International.

Wagner, M., D'Amico, R. Marder, C., Newman, L., & Blackorby, J. (1992). *What happens next? Trends in post school outcomes of youth with disabilities. The second comprehensive report from the National Longitudinal Transition Study of Special Education Students.* Menlo Park, CA: SRI International.

Wagner, M., Friend, M., Bursuck, W. D., Kutash, K., Duchnowski, A. J., Sumi, W. C., et al. (2006). Educating students with emotional disturbances: A national perspective on school programs and services. *Journal of Emotional and Behavioral Disorders, 14*(1), 12–30.

Wagner, M., Kutash, K., Duchnowski, A. J., & Epstein, M. H. (2005). The Special Education Elementary Longitudinal Study (SEELS) and the National Lognitudinal Transition Study-2 (NLTS2): Study designs and implications for students with emotional disturbance. *Journal of Emotional and Behavioral Disorders, 13,* 25–41.

Wahler, R. G. (1976). Deviant child behavior within the family: Developmental speculations and behavior change strategies. In H. Leintenberg (Ed.), *Handbook of behavior modification and behavior therapy.* Englewood Cliffs, NJ: Prentice Hall.

Walker, D. (2000). School violence prevention. *ERIC Review, 7*(1), 18–21.

Walker, H. M. (1979). *The acting out child: coping with classroom disruption.* Boston: Allyn & Bacon.

Walker, H. M. (1993). Anti-social behavior in school. *Journal of Emotional and Behavioral Problems, 2*(1), 20–23.

Walker, H. M., & Rankin, R. (1980). *Assessment for Integration into Mainstream Settings (AIMS).* Eugene, OR: Social Behavior Survival Project, Center on Human Development.

Walker, H. M., & Severson, H. H. (1992). *Systematic Screening for Behavior Disorders (SSBD): User's guide and technical manual.* Longmont, CO: Sopris West.

Walker, H. M., & Shinn, M. R. (2002). Structuring school-based interventions to achieve integrated primary, secondary, and tertiary prevention goals for safe and effective schools. In M. R. Shinn, H. M. Walker, & G. Stoner (Eds.), *Interventions for academic and* behavior *problems II: Preventive and remedial approaches* (pp. 1–26). Bethesda, MD: National Association of School Psychologists.

Walker, H. M., Colvin, G., & Ramsey, E. (1995). *Anti-social behavior in school: Strategies for practitioners.* Pacific Grove, CA: Brooks-Cole.

Walker, H. M., Horner, R. H., Sugai, G., Bullis, M., Sprague, J. R., Bricker, D., & Kaufman, M. J. (1996). Integrated approaches to preventing anti-social behavior patterns among school-age children and youth. *Journal of Emotional and Behavioral Disorders, 4,* 194–209.

Walker, H. M., McConnell, S., Holmes, D., Todis, B., Walker, J., & Golden, N. (1983). *The Walker Social Skills Curriculum: The ACCEPTS Program.* Austin, TX: Pro-Ed.

Walker, H. M., Ramsey, E., & Gresham, F. M. (2004). *Antisocial behavior in school: Eveidence-based practices* (2nd ed.). Belmont, CA: Wadsworth

Walker, H. M., Severson, H. H., & Feil, E. G. (1995). *Early screening project: A proven child-find process.* Longmont, CO: Sopris West.

Walker, H. M., Severson, H. H., Nicholson, F., Kehle, T., Jenson, W. R., & Clark, E. (1994). Replication of the systematic screening for behavior disorders (SSBD) procedure for the identification of at-risk children. *Journal of Emotional and Behavioral Disorders, 2*(2), 66–77.

Walker, H. M., Severson, H., Stiller, B., Williams, G., Haring, N., Shinn, M., & Todis, B. (1988). Systematic screening of pupils in the elementary age range at risk for behavior disorders: Development and trial testing of a multiple gating model. *Remedial and Special Education, 9(3),* 8–14.

Walker, H. M., Todis, B., Holmes, D., & Horton, G. (1988). *The ACCESS program.* Austin, TX: Pro-Ed.

Walker, H. M., Zeller, R. W., Close, D. W., Webber, J., & Gresham, F. (1999). The present unwrapped: Change and challenge in the field of behavioral disorders. *Behavioral Disorders, 24*(4), 293–304.

Walker, H.M., Ramsey, E., & Gresham, F.M. (2004). *Antisocial behavior in school: Evidence-based practices* (2nd ed.). Belmont, CA: Wadsworth.

Wallace, M., & Iwata, B. (1999). Effects of session duration on functional analysis outcomes. *Journal of Applied Behavior Analysis, 32,* 175–183.

Wallace, M., & Knight, D. (2003). An evaluation of a brief functional analysis format within a vocational setting. *Journal of Applied Behavior Analysis, 36,* 125–128.

Wallack, L., & Corbett, K. (1990). Illicit drug, tobacco, and alcohol use among youth: *Trends and promising approaches in prevention. Youth and drugs: Society's mixed messages* (pp. 5–29). (OSAP Monograph No. 6). Washington, DC: U.S. Department of Health and Human Services. (DHHS Publication No. ADM 90-90-1689).

Walther-Thomas, C., Korinek, L., McLaughlin, V. L., & Williams, B. T. (2000). *Collaboration for inclusive education.* Boston: Allyn & Bacon.

Warr-Leeper, G., Wright, N. A., & Mack, A. (1994). Language disabilities of antisocial boys in residential treatment. *Behavior Disorders, 19,* 159–169.

Warren, J. (1990, June 24). Zinc helps anorexics, study shows. Knight-Ridder News Service. *Austin American Statesman,* D4.

Watson, J. B., & Raynor, R. (1920). Conditioned emotional reactions. *Journal of Experimental Psychology, 3,* 1–14.

Watson, T. S., & Steege, M. W. (2003). *Conducting school-based functional behavioral assessments.* New York: Guilford Press.

Webber, J. (1993, August). President's message. *Council for Children with Behavioral Disorders Newsletter, 2,* 4.

Webber, J. (1994). Psychological immunization: Resisting depression, neurosis, and physical illness in a strenuous profession. *Preventing School Failure, 38*(4), 21–26.

Webber, J. (1997a). Comprehending youth violence: A practicable perspective. *Remedial and Special Education, 18*(2), 94–104.

Webber, J. (1997b). Mind-sets for a happier life. *Reclaiming Children and Youth, 6*(2), 109–113.

Webber, J. (1998). Responsible inclusion: Key components for success. In P. Zionts (Ed.), *Inclusion of students with emotional and behavioral disorders.* Austin, TX: ProEd.

Webber, J. (2004). Responsible inclusion In P. Zionts (Ed.), *Inclusion strategies for students with learning and behavior problems: Perspectives, experiences, and best practices* (2nd ed., pp. 27–56). Austin, TX: Pro-Ed.

Webber, J., & Coleman, M. (1988). Using rational-emotive therapy to prevent classroom problems. *Teaching Exceptional Children, 21* (1), 32–35.

Webber, J., & Scheuermann, B. (1991). Managing behavior problems: Accentuate the positive. . .eliminate the negative! *Teaching Exceptional Children, 24,* 13–19.

Webber, J., & Scheuermann, B. (1997). A challenging future: Current barriers and recommended action for our field. *Behavioral Disorders, 22*(3), 167–178.

Webber, J., Anderson, T., & Otey, L. (1991). Teacher mindsets for surviving in BD classrooms. *Intervention in School and Clinic, 26*(5), 288–292.

Webber, J., Scheuermann, B., McCall, C., & Coleman, M. (1993). Research on self-monitoring as a behavior management technique in special education classrooms: A descriptive review. *Remedial and Special Education, 14,* 38–56.

Webster-Stratton, C., & Herbert, M. (Eds.). (1994). *Troubled families–problem children.* New York: John Wiley & Sons.

Wechsler, D. (2004). *Wechsler Intelligence Scale for Children—Fourth Edition.* San Antonio, TX: Psychological Corporation.

Weckerly, J. (2002). Pediatric bipolar mood disorder. *Developmental and Behavioral Pediatrics, 23*(1), 42–56.

Wehby, J. H., Falk, K. B., Barton-Arwood, S., Lane, K. L., & Cooley, C. (2003). The impact of comprehensive reading instruction on the academic and social behavior of students with emotional and behavioral disorders. *Journal of Emotional and Behavioral Disorders, 11,* 553–557.

Wehby, J. H., Lane, K. L., & Falk, K. B. (2005). An inclusive approach to improving early literacy skills of students with emotional and behavioral disorders. *Behavioral Disorders, 30*(2), 135–154.

Wehby, J. H., Symons, F. J., Canale, J. A., & Go, F. J. (1998). Teaching practices in classrooms for students with emotional and behavioral disorders: Discrepancies between recommendations and observations. *Behavioral Disorders, 24,* 51–56.

Wehlage, G., Rutter, R., Smith, G., Lesko, N., & Fernandez, R. (1989). *Reducing the risk: Schools as communities of support.* Philadelphia: Falmer Press.

Weiner, B. (Ed.). (1974). *Achievement motivation and attribution theory.* Morristown, NJ: General Learning Press.

Weiss, B., Harris, V., & Catron, T. (2003). Efficacy of the RECAP intervention program for children with concurrent internalizing and externalizing problems. *Journal of Consulting and Clinical Psychology, 27*(2), 364–374.

Weiss, G. & Hechtman, L. T. (1986). *Hyperactive children grown up: Empirical findings and theoretical considerations.* New York: Guilford Press.

Weissberg, R. P., Resnik, H. Payton, J., & O'Brien, M. U. (2003, March). Evaluating social and emotional learning programs. *Educational Leadership, 60*(6), 46–50.

Weissman, M. M., Gammon, G. D., John, K., Merikangas, K. R., Warner, V., Prusoff, B. A., & Sholomskas, D. (1987). Children of depressed parents. *Archives of General Psychiatry, 44,* 847–853.

Weissman, M. M., Leckman, J. F., Merikangas, K. R., Gammon, G. D., & Prusoff, B. A. (1984). Depression and anxiety disorders in parents and children. *Archives of General Psychiatry, 41,* 845–852.

Welch, M. (1994). Ecological assessment: A collaborative approach to planning instructional interventions. *Intervention in School and Clinic, 29,* 160–164.

Weller, E. B., Weller, R. A., & Fristad, M. A. (1995). Bipolar disorder in children: Misdiagnosis, underdiagnosis, and future directions. *American Academy of Child and Adolescent Psychiaty, 34*(6), 709–714.

Wells, K. C., Forehand, R. & Griest, D. L. (1980). Generality of treatment effects from treated to untreated behaviors resulting from a parent training program. *Journal of Clinical Child Psychology, 9,* 217–219.

Werner, E. E., & Smith, R. S. (2001). *Journeys from childhood to midlife: Risk, resilience, and recovery.* Ithaca, NY: Cornell University Press

Werner, E., & Smith, R. (1982). *Vulnerable but invincible: A longitudinal study of resilient children and youth.* New York: McGraw-Hill.

Werry, J., & Quay, H. C. (1971). The prevalence of behavior symptoms in younger elementary school children. *American Journal of Orthopsychiatry, 41,* 136–143.

West, J. F. (1990). *Analysis of classroom and instructional demands.* Austin, TX: Institute for Learning and Development.

Whalen, C. K., Henker, B., Collins, B. E., McAulliffe, S., & Vaux, A. (1979). Peer interaction in a structured communication task: Comparisons of normal and hyperactive boys and of methylphenidate (Ritalin) effects. *Child Development, 50,* 388–401.

Wickman, E. K. (1928). *Children's behavior and teachers' attitudes.* New York: Commonwealth Fund.

Wiggington, E. (1986). *Sometimes a shining moment: The Foxfire experience.* Garden City, NY: Doubleday & Co.

Wilens, T. E. (1999). *Straight talk about psychiatric medications for kids.* New York: Guilford Press.

Will, M. (1984). *OSERS programming for the transition of youth with disabilities: Bridges from school to working life.* Washington, DC: U.S. Department of Education.

Wilson, B. (1996). *Wilson reading system.* Millsbury, MA: Wilson Language Training

Wilson, J. P., Smith, W. K., & Johnson, S. K. (1985). A comparative analysis of PTSD among various survivor groups. In C. R. Figley (Ed.), *Trauma and Its Wake* (pp. 142–172). New York: Brunner/Mazel.

Wilson, J., & Howell, J. (1993). *A comprehensive strategy for serious, violent, and choronic juvenile offenders.* Washington, DC: U. S. Department of Justice, Office of Juvenile Justice and Delinquency Prevention.

Wilson, S. J., & Lipsey, M. W. (2005). *The effectiveness of school-based violence prevention programs for reducing disruptive and aggressive behavior.* Nashville, TN: Center for Evaluation Research and Methodology, Institute for Public Policy Studies, Vanderbilt University.

Winokur, G., Clayton, P. J., & Reich, J. (1984). *Manic depressive illness.* St. Louis, MO: Mosby.

Wirt, R. D., Lachar, D., Seat, P. D., & Broen, W. E., Jr. (2001). *Personality Inventory for Children—Second Edition.* Los Angeles: Western Psychological Services.

Witte, R. (2002). Best practices in transition to post-secondary work. In A. Thomas & J. Grimes (Eds.), *Best practices in school psychology IV* (pp. 1585–1597). Bethesda, MD: National Association of School Psychologists.

Wolford, B. I. (2000). Youth education in the juvenile justice system. *Corrections Today, 62,* 128–130.

Wood, F. H., Cheney, C. O., Cline, D. H., Sampson, K., Smith, C. R., & Guetzloe, E. C. (1991). *Conduct disorders and social maladjustments: Policies, politics, and programming.* Reston, VA: Council for Exceptional Children.

Wood, M., & Long, N. (1991). *Life space intervention: Talking with children and youth in crisis.* Austin, TX: Pro-Ed.

Woodcock, R. W., McGrew, K. S., & Mather, N. (2001). *The Woodcock-Johnson III Tests of Cognitive Abilities.* Itasca, IL: Riverside.

Woodruff, D. W., Osher, D., Hoffman, C. C., Gruner, A., King, M. A., Snow, S. T., et al. (1998). The role of education in a system of care: Effectively serving children with emotional or behavioral disorders (*Systems of Care: Promising Practices in Children's Mental Health, 1998 Series, Volume III*). Washington, DC: Center for Effective Collaboration and Practice, American Institutes for Research.

Woodward, J., & Brown, C. (2006). Meeting the curricular needs of academically low-achieving students in middle grade mathematics. *Journal of Special Education, 40*(3), 151–159.

Wright, J. H., & Beck, A. T. (1983). Cognitive therapy of depression: Theory and practice. *Hospital and Community Psychiatry, 34,* 1119–1127.

Yasutake, D., Bryan, T., & Dohrn, E. (1996). The effects of combining peer tutoring and attribution training on students' perceived self-competence. *Remedial and Special Education, 17*(2), 83–91.

Yee, L. Y. (1988). Asian children, *Teaching Exceptional Children 20(4),* 49–50.

Yell, M. (1994). Time-out and students with behavior disorders: A legal analysis. *Education and Treatment of Children, 17*(3), 293–301.

Yell, M. (1998). *The law and special education.* Upper Saddle River, NJ: Merrill/Prentice Hall.

Yell, M. L. (1992). A comparison of three instructional approaches on task attention, interfering behaviors, and achievement of students with emotional and behavioral disorders. Unpublished doctoral dissertation. *Dissertations Abstracts International 53*(09), 3174. (University Microfilms No. 9236987.)

Yell, M. L. (2006). *The law and special education* (2nd ed.). Columbus, OH: Merrill/Prentice-Hall

Yell, M. L., & Shriner, J. G. (1997). The IDEA amendments of 1997: Implications for special and general education teachers, administrators, and teacher trainers. *Focus on Exceptional Children, 30*(1), 1–18.

Youniss, J., McLeellan, J. A., & Strouse, D. (1994). "We're popular, but we're not snobs": Adolescents describe their crowds. In R. Montemayor, G. R. Adams, & T. P. Gullotta (Eds.), *Personal relationships during adolescence* (pp. 101–122). Thousand Oaks, CA: Sage Publications.

Ysseldyke, J. E., & Christenson, S. L. (1987). *The Instructional Environment Scale.* Austin, TX: Pro-Ed.

Ysseldyke, J. E., Algozzine, B., & Thurlow, M. (1992). *Critical issues in special education* (2nd ed.) Boston: Houghton Mifflin.

Zabel, M. (1986). Timeout use with behaviorally disordered students. *Behavioral Disorders, 12,* 15–21.

Zabel, R. H., & Nigro, F. A. (1999). Juvenile offenders with behavioral disorders, learning disabilities, and no disabilities: Self-reports of personal, family, and school characteristics. *Behavioral Disorders, 25*(1), 22–40.

Zabel, R. H., & Zabel, K. (2001). Revisiting burnout among special education teachers: Do age, experience, and preparation still matter? *Teacher Education and Special Education, 24,* 128–139.

Zabin, L. S., Hirsch, M. B., Streett, R., Emerson, M. R., Smith, M., Hardy, J. B., & King, T. M. (1988). The Baltimore pregnancy prevention program for urban teenagers: I. How did it work? *Family Planning Perspectives, 20,* 182–187.

Zametkin, A. J. (1995). Attention-deficit disorder: Born to be hyperactive? *Journal of the American Medical Association, 273,* 1871–1874.

Zaragosa, N., Vaughn, S., & McIntosh, R. (1991). Social skills intervention and children with behavior problems: A review. *Behavioral Disorders 16,* 260–275.

Zewekas, S. H., Vitiello, B., & Norquist, G. S. (2006). Recent trends in stimulant medication use among U.S. children. *American Journal of Psychiatry, 163,* 586–593.

Zigmond, N., & Magiera, K. (2002). Co-teaching. *Current Practice Alerts, 6,* 1–4.

Zimmerman, J. (1999). Columbine and the cult of high school sports. *Education Week, 18*(38), 32.

Zins, J. E., & Erchul, W. P. (2002). Best practices in school consultation. In A. Thomas & J. Grimes (Eds.), *Best practices in school psychology IV* (pp. 625–643). Bethesda, MD: National Association of School Psychologists.

Zionts, P. (1996). *Teaching disturbed and disturbing students* (2nd ed.). Austin, TX: Pro-Ed.

Zionts, P. (1998). Rational Emotive Behavior Therapy: A classroom mental health curriculum. *Beyond Behavior, 9*(1), 4–11.

Zionts, P. (2004). Inclusion: Chasing the impossible dream? Maybe. In P. Zionts (Ed.), *Inclusion strategies for students with learning and behavior problems: Perspectives, experiences, and best practices* (2nd ed., pp. 3–26). Austin, TX: Pro-Ed.

INDEX

S